Office for
National Statistics

D0808127

Social Trends

No. 39
2009 edition

Editor: Matthew Hughes

Assistant editors: Jenny Church
Linda Zealey

Office for National Statistics

ISBN 978-0-230-22050-8
ISSN 0306–7742

A National Statistics publication

National Statistics are produced to high professional standards as set out in the Code of Practice for Official Statistics. They are produced free from political influence.

Not all of the statistics contained in this publication are National Statistics because it is a compilation from various data sources.

About us

The Office for National Statistics

The Office for National Statistics (ONS) is the executive office of the UK Statistics Authority, a non-ministerial department which reports directly to Parliament. ONS is the UK government's single largest statistical producer. It compiles information about the UK's society and economy which provides evidence for policy and decision-making and in the allocation of resources.

The Director of ONS is also the National Statistician.

Palgrave Macmillan

This publication first published 2009 by Palgrave Macmillan, Houndmills, Basingstoke, Hampshire RG21 6XS and 175 Fifth Avenue, New York, NY 10010, USA
Companies and representatives throughout the world.

Palgrave Macmillan is the global academic imprint of the Palgrave Macmillan division of St. Martin's Press, LLC and of Palgrave Macmillan Ltd. Macmillan® is a registered trademark in the United States, United Kingdom and other countries. Palgrave is a registered trademark in the European Union and other countries.

A catalogue record for this book is available from the British Library.

10   9   8   7   6   5   4   3   2   1
18 17 16 15 14 13 12 11 10 09

Contacts

Editorial

For information about the content of this publication, contact the Editor
Tel: 01633 455931
Email: social.trends@ons.gsi.gov.uk

Other customer and media enquiries
ONS Customer Contact Centre
Tel: 0845 601 3034
International: +44 (0)845 601 3034
Minicom: 01633 812399
Email: info@statistics.gsi.gov.uk
Fax: 01633 652747
Post: Room 1015, Government Buildings, Cardiff Road, Newport, South Wales NP10 8XG
www.statistics.gov.uk

Publication orders

To obtain a print copy of this publication, contact Palgrave Macmillan
Tel: 01256 302611
www.palgrave.com/ons

Copyright and reproduction

Printing

This book is printed on paper suitable for recycling and made from fully managed and sustained forest sources. Logging, pulping and manufacturing processes are expected to conform to the environmental regulations of the country of origin.

Printed and bound in Great Britain by Hobbs the Printer Ltd, Totton, Southampton

Typeset by Academic + Technical Typesetting, Bristol

Contents

List of figures and tables

The 'last appeared' and the 'previous number' columns refer to the Social Trends (ST) edition and location in which the same or similar chart or table last appeared. The 'type' column provides information on the status of the statistics included in this edition; National Statistics (NS) or Non-National Statistics (Non-NS). Page number refers to the page on which the table or chart can be found in Social Trends 39.

Hover and click over tables and graphs on the online pdf of Social Trends and you can download them in Microsoft Excel. It's as simple as that.

www.statistics.gov.uk/socialtrends39

Contributors and acknowledgements

The Editor would like to thank colleagues in contributing Departments and other organisations for their generous support and helpful comments, without which this edition of *Social Trends* would not have been possible.

Authors:	Jenny Church
	Tania Corbin
	Anna Donabie
	Joanne Evans
	Cathy Glass
	Steve Howell
	Ian Macrory
	Chris Randall
	David Sweet
Production manager:	Steve Howell
Production team:	Andrew Barnard
	Victoria Chenery
	Angela Collin
	Claire Collins
	Julie Crowley
	Marc Evans
	Tony James
	Andrew White
Lead reviewer:	Paul Allin
Design:	ONS Design
Typesetting:	Academic + Technical
Publishing management:	Mark Bristow
Index:	ONS Library and Information
Maps:	Jeremy Brocklehurst
	Nick Richardson

Introduction

Croeso (welcome) to the 39th edition of *Social Trends*, one of the flagship publications from the Office for National Statistics (ONS). *Social Trends* provides an up to date and comprehensive description of society, drawing on statistics from a wide range of government departments and other organisations to show how society is changing, as well as some of the factors which may be driving these trends.

Social Trends is aimed at a wide audience: policy makers in the public and private sectors, service providers, people in local government, journalists and other commentators, academics and students, schools, and the general public.

What's new?

In response to user feedback, this edition of *Social Trends* has undergone several changes. The Overview section has again been used, to highlight at a glance some of the key and emerging trends in today's society. This year's theme, 'households, families and children' has been supported by an article to help explain the definitions, terminology, and different levels of analysis relating to households, families and children. We are also committed to publishing high professional standard statistics and have revisited the list of figures and tables to include information on the status of the statistics included in this edition; National Statistics or Non-National Statistics. You may also have noticed that the insert colour for this edition of *Social Trends* is blue, replacing the red used in previous editions. This style change brings *Social Trends* in line with other ONS 'social' publications. Your views on these changes and continued suggestions on how *Social Trends* could be improved are welcomed. Please write to the Editor at the address shown below with your comments.

New material, definitions and terms

Each year, to preserve topicality around one-third of data used in *Social Trends* is new. The remainder, where possible have been carried forward from previous editions and updated.

Due to variations in coverage and definitions, some care may be needed when comparing data from more than one source. Anyone seeking to understand the figures and tables in detail will find it helpful to read the Appendix and Symbols and conventions pages towards the end of the book. A list of further reading and websites is also provided.

Availability on electronic media

Social Trends 39 is available electronically on the National Statistics website, www.statistics.gov.uk/socialtrends. The full report is available as an interactive PDF file where excel spreadsheets containing the data used in the publication can be accessed and downloaded by clicking on the relevant chart or table.

Contact

Matthew Hughes

Editor: Social Trends
Office for National Statistics
Room: 1.024
Government Buildings
Cardiff Road
Newport
Gwent
NP10 8XG

Email: social.trends@ons.gov.uk

In this year's edition...

- **Threefold increase in the population aged 90 and over in Great Britain.**
  The number of people aged 90 and over in Great Britain increased from around 125,000 in 1971 to around 417,000 in 2007.

- **Rise in early years education.**
  Between 1970/71 and 2007/08 the proportion of three and four-year-olds enrolled in schools in the UK tripled from 21 per cent to 64 per cent.

- **Employment rates are lowest for lone mothers with a child aged under five.**
  In Q2 2008, 35 per cent of lone mothers in the UK with a child aged under five were working, compared with 63 per cent for those with a partner.

- **More than three-fifths of children immunised against measles, mumps and rubella.**
  In 2006/07, 86 per cent of children in the UK were immunised against measles, mumps and rubella.

- **Grandparents are a common source of child care for working mothers.**
  In 2006, 40 per cent of children with working mothers in Great Britain relied on informal child care: the most common source was the child's grandparents.

- **High incidence of personal crime among young people.**
  In 2006, more than one-quarter of young people aged under 26 in England and Wales were victims of personal crime in the previous 12 months.

- **Fall in residential property transactions.**
  The number of residential property transactions per month in the UK halved between January and November 2008, from 104,000 to 52,000.

- **Rise in energy generation from renewable sources.**
  The proportion of electricity generated from renewable sources accounted for around 5 per cent of all electricity generated in the UK in 2007.

- **Record pump prices for premium unleaded petrol and diesel.**
  The average prices of premium unleaded petrol and diesel in the UK reached a peak in July 2008, at 119.6 pence per litre and 133.0 pence per litre respectively.

- **Increase in holiday trips taken in Europe.**
  Between 2003 and 2007, holiday trips by UK residents to Latvia increased from 4,000 to around 50,000.

Overview

Social Trends provides a unique overview of the state of the nation. In this year's edition there are updated statistics on population changes, labour market participation, key health indicators, travel patterns and environmental behaviour. In addition to these staple items, we also examine changing aspects of households, families and children, the theme of this year's *Social Trends*.

Chapter 1: Population shows that demographic patterns in the UK continue to change. In 2007, there were 61.0 million people resident in the UK. Falls in birth rates and decreases in mortality have resulted in the UK population being skewed towards the older age groups. Population projections indicate that by 2031 there will be more than 1.1 million people aged 90 and over in Great Britain. Population growth can also be attributed to changes in the pattern of people entering and leaving the UK. In 2007, net migration was 237,000, slightly below the record 244,000 in 2004. Of the UK nationals moving abroad in 2007, almost one-third were destined for Australia or New Zealand, with Spain and France also continuing to be a popular destination (24 per cent each).

As the UK population continues to grow there are notable changes in family and household types. Chapter 2: Households and families highlights the growing trend in one person households and lone parent families. In Q2 (April–June) 2008 these household types accounted for almost one-quarter of the proportion of the population living in private households in Great Britain. We also learn that adult children in the UK are living with their parents for longer and getting married later in life. Changing attitudes are affecting the age at which women give birth. In 2007, the average age for women giving birth in England and Wales was 29.3 years, compared with 26.6 years in 1971. Despite these changes in society more than one-half (56 per cent) of adults surveyed in 2006 agreed that marriage is still the best kind of relationship.

Chapter 3: Education and training highlights the major expansion in early years education and the different strategies available across the countries of the UK. The focus on pre-school education has undoubtedly helped to build a foundation for future learning and in 2006/07, we learn of increased numbers of young people in the UK continuing in full-time education beyond school leaving age. In this year, there were around 3.6 million further education students, more than twice the number than in 1970/71. In addition to following these traditional education routes, there has been an increase in job-related training and in the award of vocational qualifications.

Chapter 4: Labour market indicates that although the gap in employment rates between men and women was the smallest on record in Q2 2008, rates differ by household composition and the presence of dependent children. We learn that almost three-quarters of married or cohabiting mothers were in employment compared with more than one-half of lone parent mothers. The opportunity to work flexible hours may have contributed to women balancing home and work responsibilities. We also learn that people aged 50 and over and people born overseas have become an increasing feature of the labour market. The employment rate of older people increased from 33 per cent in Q2 1997 to 39 per cent in Q2 2008, while employment levels for non-UK born workers increased from 2.0 million to 3.7 million over the same period.

As well as differences in employment rates by household type, Chapter 5: Income and wealth indicates that the composition of income also varies between the different types of households. Wages and salaries formed 81 per cent of gross income in 2006/07 for couple households without dependent children in the UK under state pension age (65 for men and 60 for women). Social security benefits, excluding state pension, were more important to lone parent households, at 50 per cent of gross income. In addition, children were at greater risk of living in a low income family if they were living in a lone parent family. However, household net wealth has more than doubled in real terms over the last 20 years to 2007, and in 2006/07 we learn that households with two adults and no dependent children, where one or both were over state pension age, were most likely of all household types to have savings in excess of £20,000.

The increase in household wealth is reflected in Chapter 6: Expenditure where the volume of expenditure by UK households has almost tripled over the last 36 years. A result of this expenditure has been an increase in household ownership of consumer durables. Modern technology is a key feature of everyday life. In 2007, 78 per cent of UK households owned a mobile phone and 61 per cent had an Internet connection. We also examine the changes in expenditure patterns in 2008 as the economic downturn began. The amount of lending in the UK secured on dwellings fell to £4.4 billion by the third quarter of 2008, and bankruptcies in England and Wales rose sharply between 2003 and 2007.

Chapter 7: Health indicates that healthy lifestyles and improved diets have contributed to lower death rates for circulatory diseases among males and females in the UK. Over the past 33 years there has been a substantial decline in the proportion of adults in Great Britain who smoke cigarettes.

Despite these falls there are an increasing number of children and adults in England who are overweight or obese. We examine the link between affordability and access to a healthy diet. In England in 2007 the higher the level of weekly household income the more likely men and women are to meet the recommendation to eat five or more portions of fruit and vegetables per day.

Changes in demographic patterns and household structures undoubtedly have an influence on social security benefit expenditure. Chapter 8: Social protection shows that £74.9 billion (60 per cent of benefit expenditure in Great Britain) in 2007/08 was directed at people above state pension age. In this year, 2.9 million people in Great Britain were in receipt of disability living allowance and 1.5 million received attendance allowance. The main support given to sick and disabled people is care provided through the National Health Service (NHS). According to the British Social Attitudes Survey in 2007, around one-quarter (24 per cent) of adults aged 18 and over in Great Britain thought that staffing levels of nurses in NHS hospitals were in need of a lot of improvement. Charities offer another source of social protection in the UK. The total number of calls and letters received by Childline increased by 53 per cent between 1997/98 and 2007/08, and the number of boys using this service more than doubled over this period.

Chapter 9: Crime and justice reports that the most recorded crime in England and Wales in 2007/08 was theft and handling stolen goods, with particularly high incidence rates of personal theft among young people. According to the 2006/07 British Crime Survey (BCS) 5 per cent of young people aged between 16 and 24 had their mobile phone stolen in the last 12 months. Of those offenders found guilty of, or cautioned for, theft and handling stolen goods in England and Wales in 2007, the most common sentence given was a community sentence (38 per cent). According to the BCS, overall confidence in the police in England and Wales increased between 2006/07 and 2007/08, and 83 per cent of respondents believed local police would treat them with respect if they had contact with them.

Changes in family and household structure combined with recent economic pressures have impacted on housebuilding and the housing market. In Chapter 10: Housing, we examine the first percentage decrease in the number of housebuilding completions in the UK in more than five years. In the 11 months to November 2008 there were 870,000 residential property transactions in the UK, a large decrease from the 1.5 million recorded during the same period in 2007. We also learn that of all household types in England in 2006/07,

lone parents with dependent children spent the highest proportion (24 per cent) of their monthly income on mortgage repayments.

Chapter 11: Environment reveals that climate change is a key environmental concern of the European Union (EU-27) population. Individuals are taking measures to become more environmentally-friendly, although attitudes differ by household type. In 2007, couple households with dependent children in England were more likely to do one or two things that are environmentally-friendly than lone parent households with dependent children, 40 per cent and 36 per cent respectively. Recyclable material collected from households in England has increased rapidly over the last decade, possibly as a result of more recycling schemes and collections being introduced. Despite increased awareness of environmental issues, nearly one-quarter (24 per cent) of adults aged 16 and over in England in 2007 left their television on stand-by overnight.

In Chapter 12: Transport, we learn that in November 2008 the UK was the 12th most expensive country in the EU-27 in which to buy a litre of premium unleaded petrol. Despite this, the proportion of households with two cars in Great Britain increased more than fourfold between 1971 and 2007, to 27 per cent. We also find that government targets to improve road safety have contributed to the UK having one of the lowest road death rates among EU-27 member states in 2006, at 5.4 per 100,000 population. International travel and in particular the demand for air travel continued to rise. In 2007, 189 million passengers were carried between the UK and abroad, with 2009 projections suggesting that passenger numbers could reach 464 million by 2030.

Finally, Chapter 13: Lifestyles and social participation examines the growing popularity of holiday trips by UK residents to the EU member states that joined in 2004. Between 2003 and 2007 holiday trips to Latvia by UK residents increased by 1,164 per cent. Traditional leisure activities also remain popular: watching TV remained the most common activity undertaken in free time by men and women in England in 2006/07. In the same period theatre performances were the most common type of art event attended by all types of households, apart from lone parent households, for whom carnival and street events were more popular. The use of social networking sites on the Internet has become a popular way of communicating with family and friends. In 2007, nearly one-half (49 per cent) of people aged eight to 17 in the UK who use the Internet had a page or profile on a social networking site, compared with 15 per cent of parents with children in this age group.

Households, families and children

The underlying theme of *Social Trends 39* is households, families and children, and this introduction aims to provide an insight into how these three topics overlap. As illustrated by the contents of this edition, there are many national and official statistics produced relating to households, families and children. Sometimes it can be difficult to digest the volume of information available, in part because of the different ways in which households, families and children can be analysed. The first part of this introduction explains the different levels of analysis to help provide a better understanding of families in the UK.

Many topics, such as social security and benefits, naturally relate to households and families rather than to individuals. Household and family statistics also provide a greater understanding of kinship, social participation and economic dependence. The final part of this section explores some aspects of households, families and children based on the content of this edition of *Social Trends*.

The difference between households and families

Definitions of households and families have changed over time and are often the subject of debate. Nevertheless, existing definitions make clear the distinction between a household and a family. Figure A.1 provides a summary of different household types, illustrating that not all households are family households.

A household may contain unrelated people who are financially or socially independent, but a family is defined as a couple (with or without children) or a lone parent with children. For

the purpose of government statistics, a family unit is almost identical to a benefit unit, although family units may include non-dependent children (children who are over 18 or aged 16 to 18 and not in full-time education).

In 2007 the UK population was 61 million (see Table 1.1 in this edition of *Social Trends*), but not all of this population live in households, with approximately 1 per cent living in non-households (mainly communal establishments). The remaining 99 per cent live in either family or non-family households. Table A.2 gives estimates of the household population in 1998 and 2008 based on the same categories shown in Figure A.1 (the household population is also shown in Table 2.3 in the Households and families chapter in this edition). Family households may include one family, more than one family or a family living with non-family members. The largest group of non-family households are one person households.

Families and children

There are three main types of family: a married couple, a cohabiting couple or a lone parent family. A family may also be a civil partnered or same-sex cohabiting couple (Figure 2.15 shows the number of registered civil partnerships in the UK since 2005). Importantly, families may also be classified according to whether they contain children. A family may have: no children, dependent children, or non-dependent (adult) children only. Dependent children are those aged under 16 or those aged 16 to 18 and in full-time education.

Families with no children tend to be newly formed couples or couples whose children have either moved away from home or formed their own family. Once a child forms their own family (through partnership or having children) they are no longer included in their parent's family, even if they live in the same household.

A common explanation for differences between family statistics is whether they look at all families or only families with children. The type of child is also important: many people use the term 'child' as shorthand for 'dependent child', so statistics on children often include only families with dependent children. It is important to remember that families may contain adult children, also known as non-dependent children. Different definitions are required for different purposes: for example, adult children are counted as separate benefit units from their parents (Table 2.8 shows the number of adult children living with their parents and Figure 2.9 indicates their reasons for staying at home).

The majority of dependent children in the UK live in families, but statistics on dependent children can still be confusing. For

Figure A.1

Household types

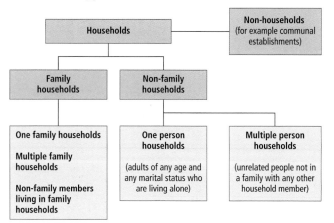

Table A.2

The household[1] population

United Kingdom

	1998[2]		2008[2]	
	People in households (millions)	People in households (percentages)	People in households (millions)	People in households (percentages)
People in family households	49.0	85	50.8	84
Family members[3] in one family households	47.6	82	48.7	80
Family members[3] in multiple family households	0.8	1	1.2	2
Non-family members[4] in family households	0.6	1	0.8	1
People in non-family households	8.7	15	9.8	16
People in one person households	6.7	12	7.5	12
People in multiple person households	1.9	3	2.3	4
All people in households	57.7	100	60.5	100

1 See Appendix, Part 2: Households.
2 Data are at Q2 (April–June) each year and are not seasonally adjusted. See Appendix, Part 4: Labour Force Survey.
3 Family members are nuclear family members (according to the ONS definition of a family). See Appendix, Part 2: Families.
4 Non-family members may still be related to other household members (for example, aunts and uncles).

Source: Labour Force Survey, Office for National Statistics

example, some statistics show the proportion of lone parent families with dependent children, while others show the proportion of dependent children living in lone parent families. To illustrate this point, Figure A.3 shows that although lone

Figure A.3

Proportion of all families and dependent children[1] in families: by family type, 2008[2]

United Kingdom

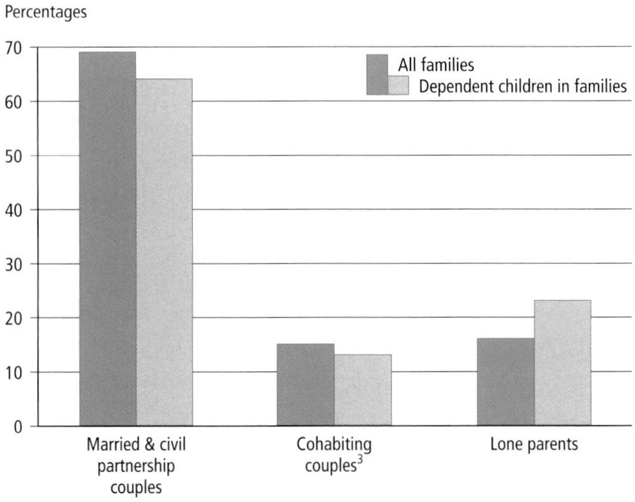

Percentages

1 Children aged under 16 and those aged 16 to 18 who have never married and are in full-time education. See Appendix, Part 2: Families.
2 Data are at Q2 (April–June) and are not seasonally adjusted. See Appendix, Part 4: Labour Force Survey.
3 Includes same-sex couples.

Source: Labour Force Survey, Office for National Statistics

parent families accounted for 16 per cent of all families in the UK in Q2 2008, 23 per cent of dependent children lived in lone parent families.

The main reason for this difference is the inclusion of couple families with no children in the overall family proportions (used to calculate the 16 per cent). A second difference is that the number of families includes families with adult (non-dependent) children only. As illustrated by Figure A.4 overleaf, a more appropriate comparison might use the proportion of families with dependent children that are lone parents rather than overall family proportions. The comparison in Figure A.4 shows that the proportion of dependent children in lone parent families (23 per cent) is actually slightly lower than the proportion of families with dependent children that are lone parents (25 per cent).

Family transitions

Aside from estimates of households and families at a given point in time, another consideration is the stability of household and family forms. One aspect of this is family transitions, or the flow of people between different family types over time. For example, the proportion of married couples may remain the same from one year to the next, even if there are large changes in the number of marriages and divorces. Marriage and divorce are two types of family transition (for more information see Chapter 2: Households and families in the Partnerships section). The birth of a child

Figure A.4

Proportion of families with dependent children[1] and proportion of dependent children in families: by type, 2008[2]

United Kingdom

Percentages

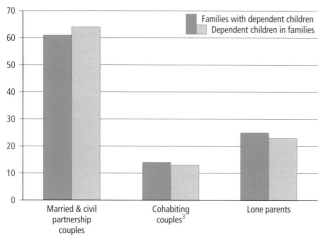

Legend: Families with dependent children / Dependent children in families

(Categories: Married & civil partnership couples; Cohabiting couples[3]; Lone parents)

1 Children aged under 16 and those aged 16 to 18 who have never married and are in full-time education. See Appendix, Part 2: Families.
2 Data are at Q2 (April–June) and are not seasonally adjusted. See Appendix, Part 4: Labour Force Survey.
3 Includes same-sex couples.

Source: Labour Force Survey, Office for National Statistics

is another event that may cause a family transition (a change in family type). This depends on the family for which the birth occurs. A couple without children will become a couple with dependent children. Female adults living alone will become lone mothers and therefore be defined as a family from the moment they register their child's birth.

Some family transitions are easier to measure than others. As cohabitations are not registered or formally dissolved, it is very difficult to measure the flow of people into and out of cohabiting families. The same could be said for other household types such as one person households. One particular issue is that changes in the estimates of different household and family types will not only occur because of partnership formation and dissolution, or births to parents, but also because of migration, death and children leaving (or returning) home. Any attempt to reconcile movements of people between household and family types will be confounded by these issues. These issues are in addition to any misreporting of families by survey respondents. It is worth remembering that different individuals will respond to questions about families and relationships in different ways. For example, parents may report that their adult children still live at home, while the children believe that they are living independently.

Aspects of households, families and children

There are many aspects of society that vary according to household or family type. *Social Trends* gives an insight into these aspects and how they change over time. The remainder of this overview introduces some key aspects of households, families and children that appear in *Social Trends* (see the individual chapters for more information).

Since the 1960s there have been several long-term trends that have affected UK families (see Chapter 2: Households and families). The most significant of these include rises in the numbers of people cohabiting and living alone, and a fall in marriage rates. Fertility rates fell after reaching a peak in the 1960s and stabilised in the 1980s (although they have recently begun to rise). Additionally, there was an increase in divorce rates in the 1970s, after which divorce rates have remained broadly stable (and have fallen in the last few years). There is much debate in academic research about the reasons for these social changes: many factors are likely to be involved, but two of the most commonly cited are the rise of individualism and changes in the roles of the sexes.

Families, employment and income

The economic activity of women in the UK has increased over the last ten years (Table 4.2) and the median gender pay gap in Great Britain has decreased since 1975 (Figure 5.10). Nevertheless, broad social changes have not affected all people equally. For example, the gender pay gap is much larger at older ages and employment rates vary by family type and age. Young lone mothers in the UK have the lowest employment rate (Table 4.6), and lone parents (male and female) with dependent children are more likely to be unemployed than couples with dependent children (Table 4.17). Despite this, women with dependent children over 10 years old are no less likely to be in work than women who have no dependent children (Table 4.3). In some cases, caution should be exercised when generalising about differences between the sexes. Table 4.17 shows that although men and women have similar levels of unemployment overall, in some families men are more likely to be unemployed than women. In Q2 2008, unemployment rates for 16 to 24-year-old married or cohabiting fathers (20 per cent) were slightly higher than for equivalent mothers (14 per cent).

There is an obvious link between employment and income, but income is also affected by savings and benefits. This is particularly true for lone parents with one or more dependent children. Compared with other households in the UK, a smaller proportion of lone parent household income is from wages and salaries, and a larger proportion is from benefits (Table 5.7). For families with dependent children, 89 per cent of lone parents receive one or more income-related benefit compared with 56 per cent of couples (Table 8.19). Both family types are equally likely to be claiming child benefit, but lone parents in Great Britain are more likely to have persistent low incomes (Table 5.19). Another factor affecting income is household savings (excluding pension rights and property). In 2006/07 lone parent households with one or more dependent children in the UK were more likely than couple households with one or more dependent children to have no savings, 53 per cent and 28 per cent respectively (Table 5.21).

Children in families

Parents with young children often require child care to enable them to work and working mothers in Great Britain were more likely to rely on informal child care than formal child care (Table 8.20). More than one-quarter of working mothers used formal child care, regardless of family type, and a similar proportion of working mothers in each family type used informal care provided by grandparents (31 per cent for lone parents and 32 per cent for couples). Lone parent working mothers were more likely than those in couples to use other types of informal care, such as ex-partners or non-resident parents, and older siblings or other relatives.

Children enter the education system at different ages, but in the long-run there has been an increase in early years education. The proportion of children at school in the UK aged under five has risen from 21 per cent in 1970/71 to more than 60 per cent in 2007/08 (Figure 3.1). The majority of dependent children are in education, which means that leaving the education system is usually synonymous with becoming non-dependent (children aged 16 to 18 are only defined as dependent if they are in full-time education). Eventually, most non-dependent children will leave home, but the number of these (adult) children living with their parents has increased over the last six years, particularly for those aged 20 to 24 (Table 2.8). The most common reason given for this is because they cannot afford to buy or rent, (Figure 2.9 and Table 10.17).

Living arrangements

There are variations in the proportion of households living in different types of dwelling (Table 10.6). For example, compared with other household types in Great Britain, couples are more likely to live in houses or bungalows, whereas one person households are more likely to live in a flat or maisonette. Lone parents are more likely than other household types to live in a

terraced house, and in England they are also more likely to be accepted as homeless (Figure 10.9), or to report poor living conditions (compared with all households with children, Table 10.12).

Overall satisfaction with the area lived in is strongly related to household type (Table 10.14). For example, couple households with no dependent children are more likely than other household types to be satisfied with the area where they live.

Other aspects of families

Another important activity that concerns many UK households is the provision of informal care. When informal care is provided from within the same household, the carer is most likely to be a partner (Figure 8.8). However, it is important to remember that over 60 per cent of informal care is provided by a non-household member, most often by a parent. Families are not just a source of care, but also a source of help: 40 per cent of men aged 55 and over reported receiving help with shopping or work around the house and garden from a partner and 23 per cent from a child or child-in-law (Table 8.18). The equivalent figures for women were 29 per cent and 36 per cent respectively.

There are many other aspects of households and families discussed in this edition of *Social Trends*, and the above is just a flavour of the information available. Other items relating to families and households include:

- the qualifications of couples and lone parents by family type (Table 3.19)

- work and workless households by regions and countries of the UK (Table 4.4)

- household expenditure by selected household types (Table 6.5 and Table 6.6)

- attitudes towards extra spending on social benefits by household type (Table 8.2)

- attitudes towards the environment by household type (Table 11.2)

Conclusion

One aim of this overview is to help explain the definitions and terminology relating to households, families and children. The text, tables and charts provide an explanation of the different types of analysis. This helps to make the statistics more accessible and help to build a more comprehensive understanding of households, families and children in the UK.

Increasing understanding is not only helpful for interpreting the information in Chapter 2: Households and families, but also the rest of the chapters in this edition. There are very few aspects of society that do not touch upon households, families and children, and these three themes provide one way to explore the wealth of information in this edition of *Social Trends*.

Looking to the future, the Office for National Statistics (ONS) continuously aims to improve data, methods and statistical reporting on households, families and children. Work is under way to develop knowledge of family transitions and link analysis of families with other topics in demography. Other

project work aims to develop knowledge of non-resident parents using the Omnibus survey. In addition, ONS continues to focus on preparations for the 2011 Census, which should provide more detailed information on families than any previous census.

ONS welcomes any questions, comments or contributions relating to this section or the content of this edition of *Social Trends*. For questions relating specifically to families, please contact: ben.wilson@ons.gov.uk. For all other questions, please email: social.trends@ons.gov.uk.

Chapter 1

Population

- In 2007, there were 61.0 million people resident in the UK, an increase of almost 400,000 (0.6 per cent) on 2006, equivalent to an average increase of around 1,000 people a day. (Table 1.1)

- More boys than girls have been born each year in the UK since 1922. Out of the 772,200 live births in 2007 around 396,700 (51 per cent) were male and 375,500 were female. (Page 2)

- The proportion of the UK population aged under 16 dropped below the proportion over state pension age for the first time in 2007. (Table 1.2)

- In 1971 there were around 96,000 women and 29,000 men aged 90 and over in Great Britain. By 2007 these numbers had increased more than threefold to 311,000 women and 106,000 men. (Figure 1.3)

- Around 173,000 people left the UK for work-related reasons in 2007, compared with 139,000 in 1997. (Table 1.11)

- In 2007 there were 160,980 applications for British citizenship, a rise of 8 per cent on 2006. (Page 10)

The number of births and deaths in each area and the number of people entering, leaving and moving around the country all affect the size, age and sex structure, and geography of the population. Changes in demographic patterns influence social structures, and have implications for public policy in a wide range of areas such as the provision of education, transport and health services. Demographic patterns also influence commercial decisions, such as the development of new products and the location of retail outlets and other business premises.

Population profile

In 2007 there were 61.0 million people resident in the UK (Table 1.1), an increase of almost 400,000 (0.6 per cent) on 2006 and equivalent to an average increase of around 1,000 people a day. Since 1971 the population has increased by 5.0 million. The populations of England, Wales and Northern Ireland have all increased steadily over the period, by 4.7 million in England, 240,000 in Wales and 220,000 in Northern Ireland. In Scotland, the population slightly declined between the late 1970s and the late 1980s and then remained broadly stable until 2003, since when the population has risen slightly each year. Between 2001 and 2007 the average annual population growth in the UK was 0.5 per cent, compared with 0.3 per cent between 1991 and 2001, and 0.2 per cent between 1981 and 1991.

The recent rate of population growth varied within the UK. In 2006/07 Northern Ireland experienced the fastest growth, at around 1.0 per cent, taking the population to 1.8 million. The population of England grew by 0.6 per cent to around 51.1 million. In Scotland and Wales the populations grew slightly more slowly, at 0.5 per cent, to reach 5.1 million and 3.0 million respectively in 2007.

The UK population is projected to increase by around 10.1 million people between 2007 and 2031. Average annual growth is expected to be around 0.7 per cent in England, 0.5 per cent in Northern Ireland, 0.4 per cent in Wales and 0.2 per cent in Scotland. The 2006-based population projections suggest that the UK population could exceed 65 million by 2017 and 70 million by 2028. Based on these projections the population will still be rising in 2081, the end of the projection period, when the population is expected to exceed 85 million.

The age structure of the population reflects trends in births, deaths and migration: how many people there are within the population depends on how many babies are born, how long they live and how many people enter and leave the country (see the International migration section later in this chapter).

More boys than girls have been born each year in the UK since 1922, the first year these figures were available. Out of the 772,200 live births in 2007 around 396,700 (51 per cent) were male and 375,500 were female. However, because of higher mortality rates for males at all ages and also some higher adult migration for males, there are slightly more females than males in the overall population. In 2007 there were more than 31 million females compared with fewer than 30 million males resident in the UK (Table 1.2).

Women begin to outnumber men when in their early 30s, and the difference is most pronounced in the oldest age groups. In 2007 the numbers of men and women aged between 35 and 64 were roughly equal: 49 per cent were men and 51 per cent women. However, 61 per cent of the population aged 75 and over was female. This reflects the higher life expectancy of women and also higher young adult male mortality during World War Two.

Table 1.1

Population[1] of the United Kingdom

Millions

	1971	1981	1991	2001	2007	2011	2021	2031
United Kingdom	55.9	56.4	57.4	59.1	61.0	62.8	67.2	71.1
England	46.4	46.8	47.9	49.5	51.1	52.7	56.8	60.4
Wales	2.7	2.8	2.9	2.9	3.0	3.0	3.2	3.3
Scotland	5.2	5.2	5.1	5.1	5.1	5.2	5.3	5.4
Northern Ireland	1.5	1.5	1.6	1.7	1.8	1.8	1.9	2.0

1 Mid-year estimates for 1971 to 2007; 2006-based projections for 2011 to 2031. See Appendix, Part 1: Population estimates and projections.

Source: Office for National Statistics; Government Actuary's Department; General Register Office for Scotland; Northern Ireland Statistics and Research Agency

Table 1.2

Population:[1] by sex and age

United Kingdom   Thousands

	Under 16	16–24	25–34	35–44	45–54	55–64	65–74	75 and over	All ages
Males									
1971	7,318	3,730	3,530	3,271	3,354	3,123	1,999	842	27,167
1981	6,439	4,114	4,036	3,409	3,121	2,967	2,264	1,063	27,412
1991	5,976	3,800	4,432	3,950	3,287	2,835	2,272	1,358	27,909
2001	6,077	3,284	4,215	4,382	3,856	3,090	2,308	1,621	28,832
2007	5,895	3,788	3,936	4,578	3,941	3,546	2,398	1,835	29,916
2011	5,961	3,846	4,235	4,314	4,292	3,592	2,636	2,018	30,893
2016	6,187	3,647	4,707	4,043	4,487	3,642	3,052	2,324	32,088
2021	6,485	3,490	4,784	4,318	4,217	4,045	3,153	2,761	33,253
2026	6,557	3,670	4,553	4,787	3,957	4,238	3,230	3,322	34,313
Females									
1971	6,938	3,626	3,441	3,241	3,482	3,465	2,765	1,802	28,761
1981	6,104	3,966	3,975	3,365	3,148	3,240	2,931	2,218	28,946
1991	5,709	3,691	4,466	3,968	3,296	2,971	2,795	2,634	29,530
2001	5,786	3,220	4,260	4,465	3,920	3,186	2,640	2,805	30,281
2007	5,615	3,580	3,924	4,670	4,039	3,686	2,660	2,887	31,059
2011	5,682	3,613	4,200	4,375	4,413	3,744	2,883	2,958	31,868
2016	5,909	3,420	4,572	4,092	4,620	3,796	3,323	3,156	32,887
2021	6,202	3,272	4,591	4,321	4,323	4,242	3,438	3,549	33,938
2026	6,271	3,453	4,368	4,691	4,048	4,448	3,512	4,155	34,946

1 Mid-year estimates for 1971 to 2007; 2006-based projections for 2011 to 2026. See Appendix, Part 1: Population estimates and projections.

Source: Office for National Statistics; Government Actuary's Department; General Register Office for Scotland; Northern Ireland Statistics and Research Agency

The UK population is ageing as a result of past changes in fertility and mortality rates. Over the past 150 years there have been falls in both the death and birth rates. The fall in death rates has resulted in increased chances of survival into later life and therefore in increases in the size of successive generations. Decreases in mortality during the second half of the 20th century, combined with fertility below replacement level (see the Replacement level fertility text box on page 10) since 1973, have resulted in today's population being skewed towards the older age groups. In 2007, for the first time ever, the proportion of the population aged under 16 dropped below the proportion over state pension age (men aged 65 and women aged 60). This is partly due to the number of women born in the post World War Two 'baby boom' who reached state pension age in 2007.

The population of the UK is expected to continue ageing over the next few decades. This is mostly due to the effect of large numbers of people from the 1960s 'baby boom' reaching

retirement age, combined with smaller numbers of people replacing them in the working population and fertility at below replacement levels.

The 'oldest old' are the fastest growing sub-group of the population. This term is used to identify the oldest extreme of the population. In the past 'oldest old' was commonly used to represent those aged 85 and over in Great Britain. As the chance of survival to the age of 85 increases, the age of 90 is becoming a popular threshold for identifying the 'oldest old'. In 1971 there were around 96,000 women (0.3 per cent of the female population) and 29,000 men (0.1 per cent of the male population) aged 90 and over in Great Britain (Figure 1.3 overleaf). By 2007 these numbers had increased more than threefold to 311,000 women (1 per cent of the female population) and 106,000 men (0.4 per cent of the male population). Population projections indicate that in 2008 there will be a slight drop in the number of people aged 90 and over, this is because of relatively lower fertility during the First World

Figure 1.3

Population aged 90 years and over: by sex[1]

Great Britain

Thousands

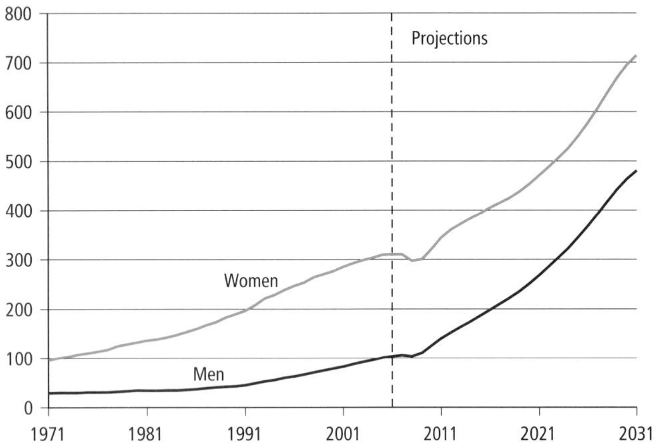

(Line chart showing population aged 90 years and over, by sex, for Great Britain, 1971 to 2031. Y-axis in thousands from 0 to 800. The Women line rises from about 100 in 1971 to a projected 715 in 2031. The Men line rises from about 30 in 1971 to a projected 480 in 2031. A vertical dashed line around 2007 marks the start of "Projections".)

1 Mid-year estimates for 1971 to 2007 and 2006-based projections for 2008 to 2031. See Appendix, Part 1: Population estimates and projections.

Source: Office for National Statistics

Figure 1.4

Proportion[1] who consider their identity to be British, English, Scottish or Welsh: by ethnic group,[2] 2007[3]

Great Britain

Percentages

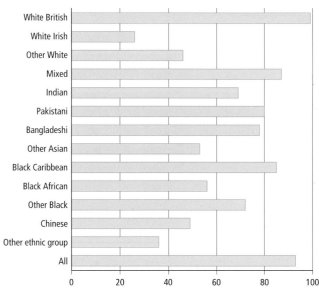

(Horizontal bar chart showing percentages for ethnic groups: White British ~98, White Irish ~26, Other White ~46, Mixed ~87, Indian ~70, Pakistani ~80, Bangladeshi ~78, Other Asian ~53, Black Caribbean ~85, Black African ~56, Other Black ~72, Chinese ~49, Other ethnic group ~36, All ~93. X-axis from 0 to 100.)

1 People aged 16 and over.
2 See Appendix, Part 1: Classification of ethnic groups.
3 Data are at January to December. See Appendix, Part 4: Annual Population Survey.

Source: Annual Population Survey, Office for National Statistics

War. However, this drop is likely to be only temporary. Projections suggest that the 'oldest old' will continue to grow both in number and as a proportion of the population. By 2031 there may be as many as 715,000 women (2.1 per cent of the female population) and 480,000 men (1.4 per cent of the male population) aged 90 and over. The rise in the numbers of the 'oldest old' is mainly a result of increased survival between the ages of 80 and 100 because of improvements in medical technology and treatment, hygiene and sanitation, housing and living standards and nutrition over the last century (see Chapter 7: Health and Chapter 10: Housing).

One consequence of the ageing population is growth in the number of centenarians. In England and Wales, it is projected that 3 per cent of men and 4 per cent of women who were aged 85 in 2001 will live to be 100 years old. Long-term projections suggest that 22 per cent of males and 27 per cent of females born in 2001 will reach 100 and that of those who reach 85 in 2086, about one-third will survive to 100. In comparison, males and females born in 1901 had less than a 1 per cent chance of reaching 100 years of age.

In 2007 the majority of people in many non-White ethnic groups living in Great Britain described their national identity as British, English, Scottish or Welsh (Figure 1.4). This included almost nine in ten (87 per cent) people from the Mixed group, 85 per cent of people from the Black Caribbean group, and eight in ten from the Pakistani and the Bangladeshi groups (80 per cent and 78 per cent respectively). Less than one-half of people in the Chinese group (49 per cent) and around one-quarter (26 per cent) of people in the White Irish group

identified themselves as being either British, English, Scottish or Welsh.

Only one-third (34 per cent) of people from the White British group described themselves as British. White British were much more likely to describe themselves as English, Welsh or Scottish. Non-White groups were more likely than White groups to identify themselves as British. Only around 7 per cent of people in the Indian group and 6 per cent of people in the Bangladeshi and the Black African groups described themselves as English, Scottish or Welsh.

Despite changing demographic trends across the UK as a whole, the populations of England, Wales, Scotland and Northern Ireland as proportions of the UK population varied little between 1971 and 2007. In 2007 England represented approximately 84 per cent of the UK population (around 51 million), Scotland 8 per cent (more than 5 million), Wales 5 per cent (almost 3 million) and Northern Ireland 3 per cent (almost 2 million). Projections suggest the proportions will be broadly similar in 2031.

The South East had the largest population of all regions and countries in the UK (Table 1.5), with 8.3 million residents (around 14 per cent of the UK population) in 2007, closely

Table 1.5

Population: by region, 2007[1]

	Area (sq km)	Population density (sq km)	Population (thousands)		
			Males	Females	All people
United Kingdom	242,495	251	29,916	31,059	60,975
England	130,279	392	25,114	25,978	51,092
North East	8,573	299	1,254	1,311	2,564
North West	14,106	487	3,366	3,498	6,864
Yorkshire and the Humber	15,408	336	2,550	2,627	5,177
East Midlands	15,607	282	2,173	2,227	4,400
West Midlands	12,998	414	2,648	2,734	5,382
East	19,109	296	2,778	2,883	5,661
London	1,572	4,807	3,738	3,819	7,557
South East	19,069	436	4,071	4,237	8,309
South West	23,837	217	2,536	2,642	5,178
Wales	20,733	144	1,454	1,526	2,980
Scotland	77,907	66	2,486	2,659	5,144
Northern Ireland	13,576	130	862	897	1,759

1 Mid-2007 population estimates. See Appendix, Part 1: Population estimates and projections.

Source: Office for National Statistics; General Register Office for Scotland; Northern Ireland Statistics and Research Agency

followed by London, with around 7.6 million residents (12 per cent). When combined, London and the South East are home to more than one-quarter (26 per cent) of the UK population and almost one-third (31 per cent) of the population of England. In 2007 the region with the highest proportion of people over state pension age was the South West, with 22 per cent of its population aged 60/65 and over. The South West also had the lowest proportion of young people with only 18 per cent of its population aged under 16. London had the lowest proportion of people over state pension age with around 14 per cent aged 60/65 and over. The West Midlands had the highest proportion of young people with around 19 per cent aged under 16.

The population density of the four constituent countries of the UK varies considerably. England was the most densely populated country in the UK in 2007, with 392 people per square kilometre (sq km), while Scotland was the least densely populated, with 66 people per sq km. London had 4,807 people per sq km, around double the population density of Belfast, at 2,441, and Cardiff at 2,293, and almost three times that of Edinburgh, which had 1,775 people per sq km. The London Borough of Kensington and Chelsea had the highest population density of local authorities within the UK, with 14,728 people per sq km, while in the Scottish

Highlands there were as few as eight people per sq km (Map 1.6 overleaf).

Boundary and area classification changes make it difficult to trace regional population densities over time. Nonetheless, it is clear that London had the highest concentration of people in both 1901 and 2007, and this was also true in 1801 when London was part of the county of Middlesex. In 1901 Belfast County Borough was the second most densely populated region in the UK, with 5,228 people per sq km. In Scotland, Lanark was the most densely populated region in 1901, with 588 people per sq km and, in Wales, Glamorganshire, which included Cardiff, was the most densely populated region with 410 people per sq km.

Population change

As noted earlier, the rate of population change over time depends upon two interrelated factors; the natural change, that is the difference between births and deaths, and the net effect of people migrating to and from the country. Table 1.7 overleaf shows that between 1951 and 2001 natural increase was the most important factor in population growth in the UK. In the 1960s and 1970s more people left the UK than arrived but this net outflow was compensated for by high positive

Map 1.6

Population density:[1] by area,[2] 2007

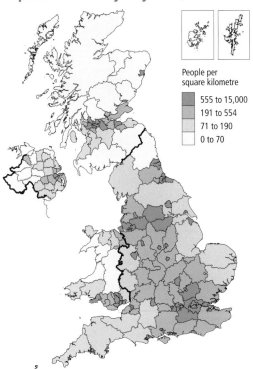

People per
square kilometre

555 to 15,000
191 to 554
71 to 190
0 to 70

1 Mid-2007 population estimates. See Appendix, Part 1: Population
   estimates and projections.
2 Counties, unitary authorities, Inner and Outer London in England,
   unitary authorities in Wales, council areas in Scotland and district
   council areas in Northern Ireland.

*Source: Office for National Statistics; General Register Office for Scotland;
Northern Ireland Statistics and Research Agency*

natural change, and so the population continued to grow. The influence of natural change decreased in the 1970s, with lower numbers of live births than in previous decades, but then increased again in the 1980s and 1990s influenced by falling numbers of deaths. During the 1980s the flow of migrants into the UK changed to a net inflow, reversing the trend of the two previous decades. As both factors continued into the 1990s the impact of migration on population change became increasingly influential. Between 1951 and 1961, natural change accounted for 98 per cent of the UK's population growth. Between 2001 and 2007 this had fallen to 38 per cent. Projections suggest that population growth for the rest of this decade is likely to remain attributable to both natural change and net migration in roughly equal measure. However, over the period 2011–2021 natural change is expected to become more important in influencing population change, accounting for around 57 per cent of the increase in population. Some of this increase may be attributed to the birth of children to migrant mothers, meaning that migration could have a more important influence on population change than indicated by the summary figures in Table 1.7.

The age structure of the female population naturally affects trends in births. For example, the number of births rose during the late 1980s as women born during the 'baby boom' of the 1960s reached their late 20s and early 30s, the peak reproductive years. Similarly, the decrease in the number of births during the 1990s is partly a result of the smaller number of women born in the 1970s reaching their 20s. In 2001 the

Table 1.7

Population change[1]

United Kingdom

Thousands

	Population at start of period	Annual averages				
		Live births	Deaths	Net natural change	Net migration and other[2]	Overall change
1951–1961	50,287	839	593	246	6	252
1961–1971	52,807	962	638	324	-12	312
1971–1981	55,928	736	666	69	-27	42
1981–1991	56,357	757	655	103	5	108
1991–2001	57,439	731	631	100	68	167
2001–2007	59,113	710	591	119	191	310
2007–2011	60,975	784	563	221	225	447
2011–2021	62,761	802	551	252	191	443

1 Mid-year estimates for 1951–1961 to 2001–2007; 2006-based projections for 2007–2011 and 2011–2021. The start population for 2007–2011 is the
   mid-year estimate for 2007. See Appendix, Part 1: Population estimates and projections.
2 The annual average for 'net migration and other' for 2007–2011 includes an adjustment to reconcile the transition from estimates to projected
   population data. See Appendix, Part 1: International migration estimates.

Source: Office for National Statistics; General Register Office for Scotland; Northern Ireland Statistics and Research Agency

Figure 1.8

Births[1,2] and deaths[1]

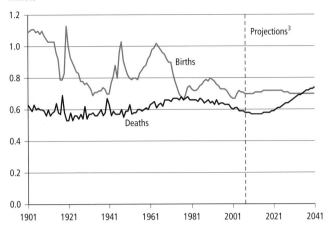

United Kingdom
Millions

1 Data for 1901 to 1921 exclude Ireland which was constitutionally part of the UK during this period.
2 Data from 1981 exclude the non-residents of Northern Ireland.
3 2006-based projections for 2007 to 2041.

Source: Office for National Statistics; Government Actuary's Department; General Register Office for Scotland; Northern Ireland Statistics and Research Agency

Babies' names

The popularity of particular names for babies changes over time and across the UK, although there are some steady favourites. In 2007, Jack was the number one name for baby boys born in England and Wales for the 13th consecutive year, while Grace, which only joined the top five in 2006, was the most popular name for baby girls.

For baby girls born in 2007 in England and Wales, Ruby moved up two places to become the second most popular name, and was the most popular for girls born in Wales. Olivia dropped from the number one position in England and Wales to third place. The second most popular name for baby boys born in England and Wales was Thomas, although Dylan was the second most popular after Jack for boys born in Wales.

Jack was also the most popular name for baby boys born in Northern Ireland in 2007. Katie, which ranked 18th for baby girls in England and Wales and fourth in Scotland, was the most popular name for baby girls. In Scotland, Jack fell one place in the rankings to number two and Lewis (16th in England and Wales, 21st in Northern Ireland) moved up one place to become the most popular name for baby boys. Sophie, the most popular name for baby girls in Scotland, ranked sixth in England and Wales and third in Northern Ireland.

number of UK births (669,100) was at the lowest level since 1977 (656,900) but has since increased steadily. In 2007 there were around 772,200 live births in the UK (Figure 1.8), an increase of more than 15 per cent (103,100 births) compared with 2001 and of 3 per cent (23,600 births) compared with 2006. There were around 655,400 live births to residents in England in 2007, 34,400 in Wales, 57,800 in Scotland and 24,500 in Northern Ireland. Further information on births and fertility can be found in Chapter 2: Households and families.

There have been fewer deaths than births in the UK every year since 1901, with the exception of 1976 when there were around 680,800 deaths and 675,500 births. Current demographic patterns mean that births are likely to exceed deaths for the foreseeable future.

Although there was considerable population growth in the last century, the number of deaths remained fairly stable, fluctuating between 570,000 and 680,000 per year in the second half of the century. There were 574,700 deaths in 2007, compared with 572,200 in 2006. In 2007 there were around 470,700 deaths in England, 32,100 in Wales, 56,000 in Scotland and 14,600 in Northern Ireland. Projections suggest that the number of deaths is not likely to exceed 600,000 until the late 2020s when the people born in the early to middle part of the 20th century reach advanced ages. The number of deaths could exceed 700,000 deaths per year by the late 2030s.

Although the number of deaths each year over the last century remained relatively constant, this is in the context of an increasing population, so death rates have fallen considerably. Improving standards of living, the changing occupational structure and developments in both medical technology and practice help to explain the decline in mortality rates. Between 1976 and 2007, death rates fell by more than 22 per cent, from 12.1 per 1,000 people in 1976 to 9.4 in 2007. Infant mortality rates have seen a marked decrease over the last 30 years, falling by two-thirds from 14.5 per 1,000 live births in 1976 to 4.8 per 1,000 live births in 2007.

Natural change in the population, that is the difference between births and deaths, varies across the country. Natural increase occurs when the number of births exceeds the number of deaths. Figure 1.9 overleaf shows the rate of natural change in all regions of the UK in 2006 compared with 1981. There was an increase in the rate of natural change over this period in all regions and countries of the UK except Scotland and Northern Ireland, where the rate of natural change fell from 1.1 per 1,000 population in 1981 to 0.1 per 1,000 population in 2006 and from 7.1 per 1,000 population in 1981 to 5.0 per 1,000 in 2006 respectively. In spite of this fall, Northern Ireland had the second highest rate of natural change in the UK in 2006. In 1981 the South West was the only region to experience negative natural change. Although this region

Figure 1.9

Net natural change in population:[1] by region

United Kingdom

Rates per 1,000 population

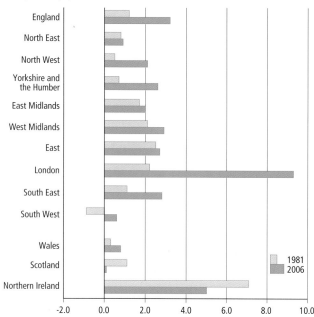

1 The difference between birth and death rates. Figures based on the usual area of residence of the mother/deceased.

Source: Office for National Statistics; General Register Office for Scotland; Northern Ireland Statistics and Research Agency

Figure 1.10

Net migration from north to south[1]

United Kingdom

Thousands

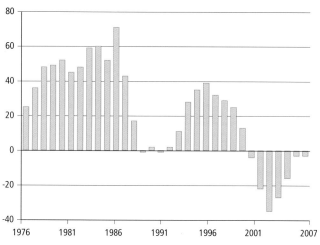

1 The south comprises the Government Office Regions of London, South East, South West, East of England and East Midlands; the north is the remainder of the UK. See Appendix, Part 1: Internal migration estimates.

Source: National Health Service Central Register; General Register Office for Scotland; Northern Ireland Statistics and Research Agency

experienced natural increase in 2006, it had the lowest rate of natural change in England at just 0.6 per 1,000 population. The region with the highest rate of natural gain was London, where the rate increased more than fourfold from 2.2 (a net increase of around 14,800 people) in 1981 to 9.3 (a net increase of around 70,700 people) in 2006.

Internal migration

A 2004 study by the University of Sheffield looked at different statistical, social, cultural and economic factors to define what constitutes the north and south of the UK. Their conclusions placed the dividing line along a diagonal from just above Gloucester in the south to just below Grimsby in the north. This dividing line is approximated in Figure 1.10 using Government Office Region boundaries. During the 20th century there was a movement of population from the north of England, Scotland and Wales, where the coal, shipbuilding and steel industries were in decline, to the Midlands and the South East, where many light industries and service industries are based. This movement peaked in 1986, when there was a net gain to the south of around 71,000 people (Figure 1.10). So far the 21st century has seen a reversal of this trend, with a net gain to the north every year since 2001 and the south recording a loss of as many as 35,000 people in 2003.

In 2007 the south recorded a net loss of around 2,500 people moving to other parts of the UK. As in 2006 the region recording the largest net outflow was London, with a net loss of around 83,000 people, around 4,000 more than in 2006. All other regions in the south experienced a net gain. Three regions in the north recorded a net outflow. They were the West Midlands (8,000), the North West (7,000) and Yorkshire and the Humber (4,000). The South West recorded the largest net inflow of around 29,000. The South East experienced the most movement overall, with an inflow of more than 220,000 people and an outflow of around 198,000.

International migration

The pattern of people entering and leaving the UK has changed over the last century. In the early part of the 20th century, more people left than entered the UK. The balance has gradually shifted and, since the early 1990s, net migration into the UK has been an increasingly important factor in population growth (see Appendix, Part 1: International migration estimates).

In 2007 the inflow of people arriving to live in the UK for at least one year was estimated at 577,000 (Table 1.11), of whom 87 per cent were non-British citizens. The outflow was around 340,000 and just over one-half of these emigrants were British citizens. Net migration in 2007 was 237,000, which was 7,000 lower than the record of 244,000 estimated for 2004 but 46,000 higher than in 2006. This increase was

Table 1.11

International migration: by main reason

United Kingdom   Thousands

	1997			2007		
	Inflow	Outflow	Balance	Inflow	Outflow	Balance
Definite job	63	88	-25	172	100	72
Looking for work	41	51	-9	71	73	-2
Accompany/join[1]	74	62	12	85	43	42
Formal study	87	15	72	149	15	134
No reason stated	15	29	-14	35	60	-25
Other	46	35	11	65	49	16
All reasons	327	279	48	577	340	237

1 Includes partners, family members and friends.

Source: Office for National Statistics

the result of a fall in emigration rather than an increase in immigration.

There are various reasons why people choose to move from one country to another. In 2007 the majority of people cited work-related reasons for moving to the UK, with around 243,000 people coming either to start work or to look for work, compared with around 104,000 people in 1997. Around

173,000 people left the UK for work-related reasons in 2007, compared with 139,000 in 1997. There was an increase of 71 per cent in the number of people moving to the UK for formal study, from 87,000 in 1997 to 149,000 in 2007. The number of people leaving the UK to study abroad remained the same, at around 15,000 people in 1997 and 2007.

Almost one-third (32 per cent) of UK nationals moving abroad in 2007 were destined for Australia or New Zealand. Around one-quarter (24 per cent) were heading to Spain and one-quarter (24 per cent) to France. The USA was the fourth most popular destination (8 per cent). Within the European Union (EU), Spain had the highest recorded number of resident UK nationals in 2007, although data were not available for Bulgaria, Cyprus, Estonia, France, Greece and Malta (Table 1.12). The table shows that there were more Irish nationals resident in the UK in 2005 (around 369,700) than nationals from any other EU state, followed by people from Poland (around 110,000), France (100,300) and Germany (100,300). People from these four countries constituted nearly three-fifths (58 per cent) of the total number of EU nationals living in the UK. In comparison, 97,300 UK nationals lived in the Republic of Ireland and 105,000 lived in Germany in 2007, while Poland was home to 600 UK nationals.

Nationals of the European Economic Area (EEA) – all 27 EU member states plus Iceland, Liechtenstein and Norway – have

Table 1.12

UK nationals living in other EU states and EU nationals living in the UK

Thousands

	UK nationals living in other EU states 2007	EU nationals living in the UK 2005		UK nationals living in other EU states 2007[1]	EU nationals living in the UK 2005
Ireland	97.3	369.7	Greece	..	13.5
Poland	0.6	110.0	Belgium	26.2	12.2
France	..	100.3	Bulgaria	..	12.2
Germany	105.0	100.3	Cyprus	..	10.5
Italy	24.7	88.4	Finland	2.9	9.7
Portugal	19.8	84.6	Czech Republic	2.9	6.7
Spain	322.8	60.9	Malta	..	5.6
Netherlands	40.3	45.5	Hungary	1.9	5.2
Lithuania	0.1	26.1	Latvia	0.3	4.4
Sweden	15.1	25.7	Estonia	..	3.6
Slovakia	0.7	24.3	Luxembourg	4.9	0.6
Austria	7.8	19.8	Slovenia	0.2	-
Romania	0.3	17.6			
Denmark	13.2	16.5	All	687.0	1,173.9

1 Data for Belgium are at 2003.

Source: Eurostat

Figure 1.13

Grants of British citizenship:[1] by basis of grant

United Kingdom

Thousands

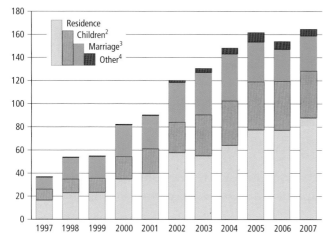

1 Data from November 2001 include grants of British citizenship in the Channel Islands and Isle of Man. See Appendix, Part 1: International migration estimates.
2 Children aged under 18.
3 Includes civil partnerships from 5 December 2005.
4 Includes British Overseas Territories citizens from Gibraltar registered as British citizens under section 5 of the *British Nationality Act 1981*.

Source: Home Office

the right to reside in the UK provided they are able to support themselves financially. Nearly all other overseas nationals wishing to live permanently in the UK require Home Office acceptance for settlement and many people with this status go on to apply for full citizenship.

The number of applications received for British citizenship was 160,980 in 2007, a rise of 8 per cent compared with 2006, when 149,695 applications were submitted. During 2007, 164,635 British citizenships were granted, a 7 per cent increase on 2006. A total of 15,630 applications for British citizenship were refused in 2007, withdrawn or the applicant was found to be British anyway, a similar number to the previous year (around 15,310).

The most frequent basis on which British citizenship was granted in 2007 continued to be residence, at 53 per cent of total citizenships (87,785) (Figure 1.13). Children accounted for one-quarter (40,535) of all British citizenships granted in 2007. The number of grants to people on the basis of marriage to a British citizen was 30,425 (18 per cent). This number rose compared with 2006 but was still considerably below the record 40,405 granted on the basis of marriage in 2004.

In 2007 people from countries in Africa constituted almost one-third (31 per cent) of all grants of British citizenship (51,255 grants). The number of grants made to Europeans from outside the EEA fell by more than one-quarter to 14,515 over the year, following Bulgaria and Romania becoming part

of the EEA when they joined the EU in January 2007. In 2006 British citizenship was granted to around 625 people originally from Bulgaria and to around 600 people originally from Romania.

International perspective

In 2007 the world population was estimated to be more than 6.6 billion. Nearly two-thirds (3.9 billion) of the global population lived in Asia. Africa was the youngest continent, with 41 per cent of its population aged under 15 and only 3 per cent aged 65 and over. Europe was the oldest continent, with around 16 per cent of its population aged under 15 and 16 per cent aged 65 and over. The total fertility rate (TFR – see text box below) varies widely within and between the continents of the world. In Africa it was 5.0 children per woman on average in 2007, partly reflecting the high rates of infant mortality; for every 1,000 live births, 86 babies will not survive infancy. However in Europe and North America the average TFR remains below replacement level (see Replacement level fertility text box below), at 1.5 and 2.0 children per woman respectively.

The Group of Eight (G8) are the world's eight largest industrial market economies, whose finance ministers meet several times a year to discuss major economic and political issues. Estimates and projections for the period 2005 to 2010 suggest that none of the countries in the G8 are projected to have a TFR at replacement level or above. Japan has the lowest estimated TFR of the G8 during this period, at 1.27 children per woman, and the USA has the highest, at 2.05 children per woman (Table 1.14). The Russian Federation is the only one of the G8 countries to

Total fertility rate

The total fertility rate (TFR) is the average number of children per woman a group of women would have if they experienced the age specific fertility rates of a particular year for their entire childbearing years. Changes in the number of births result in part from changes in the population age structure. Therefore the TFR is commonly used to analyse fertility because it standardises for the changing age structure of the population.

Replacement level fertility

Replacement level fertility is the level of fertility needed for a population to replace itself in size in the long term, in the absence of migration. In developed countries this is usually valued at 2.1 children per woman. It is slightly higher than two children per woman to take account of infant mortality and the fact that more boys are born than girls.

Table 1.14

Demographic indicators: G8 comparison, 2005

	Population (millions)	Population density (sq km)	Infant mortality rate[1,2]	Total fertility rate[2]	Life expectancy at birth (years)[2]	
					Males	Females
Canada	32.3	3	4.8	1.53	78.3	82.9
France	61.0	111	4.2	1.89	77.1	84.1
Germany	82.7	232	4.3	1.36	76.5	82.1
Italy	58.6	195	5.0	1.38	77.5	83.5
Japan	127.9	338	3.2	1.27	79.0	86.1
Russian Federation	144.0	8	16.6	1.34	59.0	72.6
United Kingdom	60.2	248	4.8	1.82	77.2	81.6
USA	299.9	31	6.3	2.05	75.6	80.8
World	6,514.8	48	49.4	2.55	65.0	69.5

1 Per 1,000 live births.
2 Data are estimates and projections for the period 2005–2010.

Source: United Nations

have had a TFR above replacement level during the last three decades and projections suggest that, although seven of the G8 countries will see a gradual increase in the TFR, it is unlikely any will achieve a TFR above 2.10 in the next few decades. The USA is the only country in the G8 where a slight fall is expected.

Estimates and projections for the period 2005 to 2010 show that Japan has one of the lowest rates of infant mortality in the world, at just 3.2 infant deaths per 1,000 live births. The Russian Federation has the highest rate in the G8 (16.6), more

than five times the rate in Japan. The infant mortality rate in the USA is almost double that of Japan and is the second highest of the G8 countries. Estimates and projections for the period 2005 to 2010 suggest that Sierra Leone has the highest rate of infant mortality (160.3) and Singapore has the lowest rate at 3.0 infant deaths per 1,000 live births, below that of any of the G8 countries.

Table 1.15 compares the demographic indicators of the UK with those of seven other countries that sit on the Greenwich

Table 1.15

Demographic indicators: countries on the Greenwich meridian line, 2005

	Population (millions)	Population density (sq km)	Infant mortality rate[1,2]	Total fertility rate[2]	Life expectancy at birth (years)[2]	
					Males	Females
United Kingdom	60.2	248	4.8	1.82	77.2	81.6
France	61.0	111	4.2	1.89	77.1	84.1
Spain	43.4	86	4.2	1.41	77.7	84.2
Algeria	32.9	14	31.1	2.38	70.9	73.7
Mali	11.6	9	128.5	6.52	52.1	56.6
Burkina Faso	13.9	51	104.4	6.00	50.7	53.8
Togo	6.2	110	88.6	4.80	56.7	60.1
Ghana	22.5	94	56.6	3.84	59.6	60.5

1 Per 1,000 live births.
2 Data are estimates and projections for the period 2005–2010.

Source: United Nations

meridian line. This is an imaginary line, known as zero longitude, which runs from the North Pole to the South Pole and from which all other lines of longitude are measured. The prime meridian line and the opposite, 180th, meridian line (the international date line) encircle the globe, dividing it into the eastern and western hemispheres.

This table illustrates the vast differences between demographic indicators worldwide. At least for this set of countries, the highest rates of infant mortality and fertility and lowest life expectancies are found in countries near the equator. For example, United Nations' estimates and projections for the period 2005 to 2010 show that Mali has an infant mortality rate more than 26 times higher than the UK (128.5 deaths per 1,000 live births compared with 4.8). In Burkina Faso life expectancy at birth is 50.7 years for males and 53.8 for females, and the median average age of the population is just 16.7 years. In comparison, life expectancy at birth in Spain is 77.7 for males and 84.2 for females, and the median average age is 40.7 years. Only an estimated 2.5 per cent of the population in Burkina Faso are aged 65 and over whereas around 46.3 per cent are estimated to be aged 14 and under. In Spain, estimates suggest that 17.9 per cent of the population are aged 65 and over and 14.4 per cent are aged 14 and under. Mali, Burkina Faso, Togo and Ghana all have life expectancies below the global average of 65.0 for males and 69.5 for females.

Longer female life expectancy contributes to the higher proportion of females than males in many countries, even though there are generally more boys than girls at birth. Research shows that for every 100 conceptions of female embryos, there are approximately 120 male conceptions. However, the male embryo is more vulnerable than the female embryo, and there are around 105 live male births for every 100 live female births. The ratio of females to males becomes

Figure 1.16

Number of women per 100 men: EU comparison, 2007

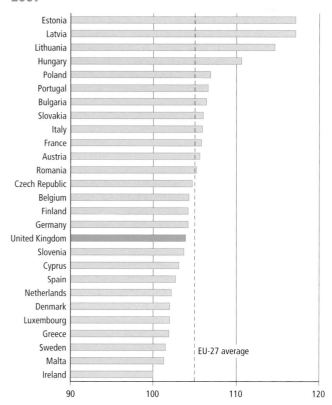

Source: Eurostat

greater with age; in the European Union in 2007, none of the member states had more males than females in their overall population (Figure 1.16). Ireland was the only member state with parity between the sexes. At 103.9 females per 100 males, the UK was just below the EU average (104.9 females per 100 males). Latvia and Estonia had the highest ratios in the EU, at 117.1 females per 100 males. For more information on life expectancy see Chapter 7: Health.

Chapter 2

Households and families

- There were 25.0 million households in Great Britain in Q2 2008, a 4 per cent increase on Q2 2001 when there were 23.9 million. (Table 2.1)

- In Q2 2008 around 10 million dependent children in the UK lived with two parents, the most common family arrangement. Of these the majority (8.3 million) lived with married parents. (Table 2.4)

- In Q2 2008, 1.8 million men in the UK aged 20 to 34 lived with their parents, compared with 1.1 million women in the same age group. (Table 2.8)

- There were around 237,000 marriages in England and Wales in 2006, the lowest number recorded since 1895. (Figure 2.10)

- The majority of people who married in the UK in 2006 did so for the first time: around 71 per cent of men and 72 per cent of women. (Table 2.11)

- In 2007 the average age for women giving birth in England and Wales was 29.3 years, compared with 28.3 years in 1997 and 26.6 years in 1971. (Figure 2.18)

DATA

Download data by clicking the online pdf

www.statistics.gov.uk/ socialtrends39

People live in different types of households and families during their lifetime. Most begin life in the parental home, and later they may set up home alone, or with other non-related adults, or by starting a family. Families are started when people form partnerships or marry, and when they have children. Understanding the distribution of the population by household and family type is important for many different organisations in the public and private sectors, including policy makers dealing with issues such as health, housing and benefits. Issues such as unemployment and poverty can often be better understood by looking at the characteristics of households and families, rather than simply defining them as the number of people out of work or earning less than a certain income threshold. Information about households and families also shows how society is changing. Cohabiting couples, lone parent families and people living alone have all increased, while the proportion of households with three or more people has decreased, reflecting changes over time and between generations in attitudes to marriage, divorce and childbearing.

Household composition

A household may consist of a single person living alone or a group of people who live and eat together, whether related or not. The definition of a family is a married or cohabiting couple with or without children, or a lone parent with one or more children. A household can consist of more than one family, or a family and other non-related adults. People who live in non-private residences are not covered in this chapter. For further information on the definitions of households and families, see Appendix, Part 2: Households, and Families, and the article, Households, families and children, in the Overview section.

In Q2 (April to June) 2008 there were 25.0 million households in Great Britain (Table 2.1), a 2 per cent increase on 2007 (24.4 million). The trend towards more one person households and lone parent families means that the number of households has grown faster than the population. Between 1971 and Q2 2008 the British household population grew by around 10 per cent. Over the same period the number of households increased by around 34 per cent. This is reflected in the fall in average household size from 2.9 people per household in 1971 to 2.4 people per household in 2001, since when it has remained stable.

In Q2 2008 the proportion of households in Great Britain comprising couple families with children had fallen by 16 percentage points since 1971, to 27 per cent, and was lower than the proportion of couple families with no children in Q2 2008 (29 per cent) (Table 2.2). There was also a fall in the

Table 2.1

Households:[1] by size

Great Britain
Percentages

	1971	1981	1991	2001[2]	2008[2]
One person	18	22	27	29	29
Two people	32	32	34	35	35
Three people	19	17	16	16	16
Four people	17	18	16	14	13
Five people	8	7	5	5	5
Six or more people	6	4	2	2	2
All households (=100%) (millions)	18.6	20.2	22.4	23.9	25.0
Average household size (number of people)	2.9	2.7	2.5	2.4	2.4

1 See Appendix, Part 2: Households, Families, and Multi-sourced tables.
2 Data are at Q2 (April–June) each year and are not seasonally adjusted. See Appendix, Part 4: Labour Force Survey.

Source: Census, Labour Force Survey, Office for National Statistics

Reference persons

Though the majority of households contain one family, some households contain multiple families, while others do not contain a family at all (for example, where the household consists of one person or of non-related adults). This chapter mainly refers to data based on the household reference person although some data are based on the family reference person. The UK Census 2001 defined household reference person and family reference person as follows:

Household reference person (HRP)

A person living alone is the HRP. If the household contains one family the HRP is the same as the family reference person (FRP, see below). If there is more than one family in the household, the HRP is chosen from the FRPs using the same criteria as for choosing the FRP. If there is no family, the HRP is chosen from the individuals living in the household using the same criteria. See also Appendix, Part 7: Household reference person.

Family reference person (FRP)

In a couple family the FRP is chosen from the two people in the couple on the basis of their economic activity in priority order of full-time job, part-time job, unemployed, retired, other. If both have the same economic activity, the FRP is defined as the elder of the two, or if they are the same age, the first member of the couple listed on the census form. In a lone parent family the FRP is the lone parent.

Table 2.2

Households:[1] by type of household and family

Great Britain   Percentages

	1971	1981	1991	2001[2]	2008[2]
One person households					
Under state pension age[3]	6	8	11	14	15
Over state pension age[3]	12	14	16	15	15
One family households					
Couple[4]					
No children	27	26	28	29	29
1–2 dependent children[5,6]	26	25	20	19	18
3 or more dependent children[5,6]	9	6	5	4	3
Non-dependent children only	8	8	8	6	6
Lone parent[4]					
Dependent children[5,6]	3	5	6	7	7
Non-dependent children only	4	4	4	3	3
Two or more unrelated adults	4	5	3	3	3
Multi-family households	1	1	1	1	1
All households					
(=100%) (millions)	18.6	20.2	22.4	23.9	25.0

1 See Appendix, Part 2: Households, Families, and Multi-sourced tables.
2 Data are at Q2 (April–June) each year and are not seasonally adjusted.
  See Appendix, Part 4: Labour Force Survey.
3 State pension age is currently 65 for men and 60 for women.
4 These households may contain individuals who are not family
  members. Couples include a small number of same-sex couples and
  civil partners.
5 Children aged under 16 and those aged 16 to 18 who have never
  married and are in full-time education. May also include some
  non-dependent children.
6 These families may also contain non-dependent children.

Source: Census, Labour Force Survey, Office for National Statistics

proportion of large family households. Between 1971 and Q2 2008 the proportion of households consisting of a couple family and three or more dependent children fell from 9 per cent to 3 per cent. Over the same period, the proportion of one person households where the person was under state pension age (65 for men and 60 for women) more than doubled from 6 per cent to 15 per cent. The proportion of one person households where the person was over state pension age increased by 3 percentage points from 1971 to Q2 2001 and has remained stable since.

Between Q2 2001 and Q2 2008 the proportion of lone parent households with dependent children in Great Britain remained stable, at 7 per cent, although this is more than double the proportion in 1971. However, the proportion of lone parent households with non-dependent children fell slightly between 1971 and Q2 2001 to 3 per cent and has remained stable since.

There were 59.2 million people resident in Great Britain in 2007 (see Chapter 1: Population, Table 1.1) and, of these, 58.4 million lived in private households. The remaining 0.8 million, around 1 per cent of the population, lived in one of a range of communal establishments, for example, prison inmates, long-term residents in hospitals and care homes, and live-in staff in hotels. See Appendix, Part 4: Labour Force Survey.

In Q2 2008 the number of people living in one family households in Great Britain (47.8 million) represented around 81 per cent of the population living in private households, compared with 85 per cent (45.4 million people) in 1971 (Table 2.3). One-quarter (25 per cent) of people in households in Q2 2008 were couples without children, compared with around one-fifth (19 per cent) in 1971. In 1971 people living in couple families with dependent children accounted for more than one-half (52 per cent) of all people living in private households compared with around one-third (36 per cent) in Q2 2008. The proportion of people living alone doubled between 1971 and Q2 2001, to 12 per cent, and remained the same in Q2 2008.

Between 1971 and Q2 2008 the proportion of lone parent households increased almost threefold to 11 per cent.

Table 2.3

People in households:[1] by type of household and family

Great Britain   Percentages

	1971	1981	1991	2001[2]	2008[2]
One person households	6	8	11	12	12
One family households					
Couple					
No children	19	20	23	25	25
Dependent children[3]	52	47	41	38	36
Non-dependent children only	10	10	11	9	9
Lone parent[4]	4	6	10	11	11
Other households[5]	9	9	4	5	6
All people in private households					
(=100%) (millions)	53.4	53.9	54.1	56.7	58.8

1 See Appendix, Part 2: Households, Families, and Multi-sourced tables.
2 Data are at Q2 (April–June) each year and are not seasonally adjusted.
  See Appendix, Part 4: Labour Force Survey.
3 Children aged under 16 and those aged 16 to 18 who have never
  married and are in full-time education. May also include some
  non-dependent children.
4 Includes those with dependent children only, non-dependent children
  only and those with both dependent and non-dependent children.
5 Includes same-sex couples and civil partners.

Source: Census, Labour Force Survey, Office for National Statistics

Table 2.4

Dependent children:[1] by family type[2]

United Kingdom   Millions

	1997	2001	2005	2008
Married couple	9.57	9.00	8.57	8.32
Cohabiting couple	1.00	1.34	1.46	1.66
Female lone parent	2.51	2.66	2.75	2.81
Male lone parent	0.23	0.24	0.25	0.24

1 Children aged under 16 and those aged 16 to 18 who have never
  married and are in full-time education. See Appendix, Part 2: Families.
2 Data are at Q2 (April–June) each year and are not seasonally adjusted.
  See Appendix, Part 4: Labour Force Survey.

Source: Labour Force Survey, Office for National Statistics

Households headed by lone mothers were considerably more common than those headed by lone fathers; around nine in ten children living in lone parent families lived with their mothers in the UK in Q2 2008 (Table 2.4).

In Q2 2008 there were more than 13 million dependent children living with at least one parent in the UK. The majority (77 per cent) of dependent children lived with two parents in Q2 2008. The proportion of dependent children living with two parents fell during the 1970s, 1980s and early 1990s, from 92 per cent in 1972, to 88 per cent in 1981 and 83 per cent in 1992. This proportion continued to fall during the 1990s so that by Q2 2001, 78 per cent of dependent children lived with two parents, a figure that has remained broadly stable since. The traditional family structure of a married mother and father with a child or children remains the most common family type. More than 8 million (64 per cent) dependent children lived with married parents in the UK in Q2 2008. However, between Q2 1997 and Q2 2008 the proportion of children living with cohabiting couples increased from 8 per cent to 13 per cent. The proportion of children living with lone mothers also increased, from 19 per cent in Q2 1997 to 22 per cent in Q2 2008, while the proportion living with just their father remained stable, at around 2 per cent.

The pattern of dependent children in households varies considerably across ethnic groups in the UK (Table 2.5). In Q2 2008 very few dependent children in the Chinese ethnic group lived in families headed by cohabiting parents, compared with 14 per cent of dependent children from a White background and 13 per cent from a Mixed background. Asian or Asian British children were more likely than children of other ethnic groups to live in families headed by married parents (87 per cent lived in married couple families). Apart from Chinese children, they were also least likely to live in cohabiting couple families. Nearly one-half (48 per cent) of Black or

Table 2.5

Dependent children:[1] by family type and ethnic group,[2] 2008[3]

United Kingdom   Percentages

	Married couple[4]	Cohabiting couple[5]	Lone parent
White	63	14	23
Mixed	48	13	39
Asian or Asian British	87	1	13
Black or Black British	46	6	48
Chinese	79	*	21
Other ethnic group	72	4	24
Total	64	13	23

1 Children aged under 16 and those aged 16 to 18 who have never
  married and are in full-time education.
2 See Appendix, Part 1: Classification of ethnic groups.
3 Data are at Q2 (April–June) and are not seasonally adjusted.
  See Appendix, Part 4: Labour Force Survey.
4 Includes civil partnerships.
5 Includes same-sex couples.

Source: Labour Force Survey, Office for National Statistics

Black British children lived in a lone parent family with 6 per cent living in a cohabiting couple family and 46 per cent in a married couple family.

According to General Household Survey figures, more than four in ten (42 per cent) women of working age in Great Britain had dependent children living with them in 2007 (Table 2.6). This proportion varies according to marital status. More than one-half of married working-age women (53 per cent) and 44 per cent of cohabiting working-age women had at least one dependent child living with them, compared with almost two-thirds (65 per cent) of separated working-age women, 37 per cent of divorced working-age women, and less than one-fifth (18 per cent) of single working-age women. In 2007 single working-age women were the most likely to have no children living with them (81 per cent) compared with around one-third (31 per cent) of married working-age women.

The presence of a partner in the household has a considerable impact on the mother's employment status. According to the Labour Force Survey, more than seven in ten (72 per cent) married or cohabiting mothers with dependent children were working in Q2 2008. The comparable figure for lone mothers with dependent children was more than one-half (56 per cent). For further information on mothers and work, see Chapter 4: Labour Market, Table 4.6.

More people are living alone than ever before and Table 2.2 shows that in Q2 2008 one person households accounted for

Table 2.6

Whether women[1] have children in the household: by marital status, 2007

Great Britain   Percentages

	Dependent children[2]	Non-dependent children only	No children
Married[3]	53	16	31
Non-married			
Cohabiting	44	4	52
Single	18	-	81
Widowed	15	35	51
Divorced	37	23	41
Separated	65	9	26
All working-age women	42	11	47

1 Women aged 16 to 59.
2 These households may contain non-dependent children.
3 Living with spouse. Includes people in a legally recognised civil partnership.

Source: General Household Survey (Longitudinal), Office for National Statistics

three in ten (30 per cent) households in Great Britain. In 2007 a larger proportion of men between the ages of 16 and 44 lived alone than women in the same age group: 17 per cent of men compared with 10 per cent of women (Figure 2.7). The difference between men and women is partly because, following the breakdown of a relationship where children are involved, men are much more likely than women to leave the family home

and live alone. However, for those aged 65 and over, and particularly among those aged 75 and over, women are much more likely than men to live alone. In 1998, 29 per cent of men and 59 per cent of women aged 75 and over lived alone, compared with 35 per cent of men and 61 per cent of women in 2007. The higher proportion of women living alone in the oldest age group reflects the higher numbers of women than men in the population at these ages (see Chapter 1: Population, Table 1.2). In part these differences reflect the lower life expectancy of males compared with females.

In Q2 2008 around 2.8 million men and women between the ages of 20 and 34 in the UK lived with one or both of their parents (Table 2.8 overleaf). Men of this age group were much more likely than women to remain in the family home; 1.8 million (29 per cent) men and 1.1 million (18 per cent) women aged 20 to 34 lived with their parents in Q2 2008 compared with 27 per cent of men and 15 per cent of women in these age groups in Q2 2001. More than one-half of men aged 20 to 24 (52 per cent) lived with their parents in Q2 2008, a similar proportion (55 per cent) as in Q2 2001. In both Q2 2001 and Q2 2008 around one-quarter (24 per cent) of men aged 25 to 29 and one in ten men (10 per cent) aged 30 to 34 lived in the parental home. These figures were considerably lower for women. In Q2 2001, 35 per cent of women aged 20 to 24 lived with their parents; in Q2 2008 this had risen to 37 per cent. The proportion of women in their late 20s living in the family home rose slightly from 11 per cent to 12 per cent during this period and the proportion of women in their early 30s rose 1 percentage point to 4 per cent.

Figure 2.7

People living alone: by sex and age[1]

Great Britain
Percentages

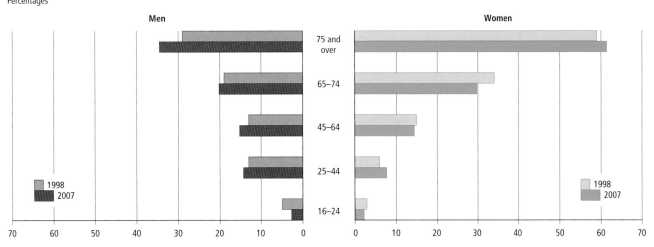

1 Data for 2007 are weighted to compensate for nonresponse and to match known population distributions. See Appendix, Part 2: General Household Survey.

Source: General Household Survey (Longitudinal), Office for National Statistics

Table 2.8

Adults living with their parents:[1] by age and sex[2]

United Kingdom
Thousands

	2001	2002	2003	2004	2005	2006	2007	2008
Men								
20–24	949	996	969	1,054	1,079	1,103	1,085	1,086
25–29	454	390	416	434	432	438	445	486
30–34	208	213	216	203	194	185	178	180
Women								
20–24	624	638	641	675	685	733	747	745
25–29	220	193	184	201	211	210	232	245
30–34	75	68	84	89	66	64	63	70

1 Includes stepchildren. Does not include foster children or children-in-law.
2 Data are at Q2 (April–June) each year and are not seasonally adjusted. See Appendix, Part 4: Labour Force Survey.

Source: Labour Force Survey, Office for National Statistics

Leaving home is a way of establishing independence and is an important step in the transition to adulthood. However, young adults are tending to stay in the parental home longer than their parents did. A narrowing of the generational gap has led to changing relationships between parents and children, which can make it easier for adult children (non-dependent) to remain in the parental home. Additionally, there has been a large increase in the numbers of students in higher education. In 2006/07 there were more than four times the number of higher education students than in 1970/71 (see Chapter 3:

Figure 2.9

Young adults' reasons[1] for living at parents' home: EU comparison, 2007

Percentages

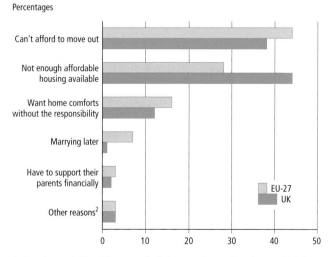

1 People aged 15 to 30 were asked the question, 'What do you think is the main reason that young adults live in their parents' homes longer than they used to?'
2 Includes those who answered 'don't know' or did not answer.

Source: Eurobarometer

Education). The introduction of university fees in 1997 resulted in some students continuing to live in the family home while studying, or moving away and then returning home afterwards for financial reasons.

The majority of people aged 15 to 30 across the rest of the European Union member states (EU-27) are strongly influenced by financial issues when deciding to remain in the parental home. In 2007 more than four in ten (44 per cent) EU-27 adults in this age group believed that the costs of moving out were prohibitive while more than one-quarter (28 per cent) felt that there was a lack of affordable housing (Figure 2.9). More than one in six (16 per cent) agreed that young adults wanted the comforts of home without the responsibilities. In the UK around four in ten (38 per cent) young adults believed that young adults couldn't afford to move out and that there was a lack of affordable housing (44 per cent). Only 1 per cent of people aged 15 to 30 in the UK believed that they stayed at home longer because they were marrying later than young adults in the past, compared with 7 per cent of their counterparts across the EU-27.

Partnerships

The *Marriage Act 1836* and the *Registration Act 1836* came into force in 1837 in England and Wales, providing the statutory basis for regulating and recording marriages. Records show that 118,000 marriages were registered in 1838, the first full year of civil registration. The annual number of marriages generally rose until the 1940s, apart from peaks and troughs around the two world wars (Figure 2.10). The number of marriages fluctuated during the 1950s but rose annually from 1959 to 1968 and peaked in 1972, at around 426,000.

Figure 2.10

Marriages[1,2]

England & Wales

Thousands

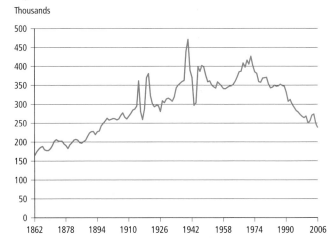

1 Includes first marriages and remarriages.
2 Data do not include marriages of UK residents taking place abroad but include non-UK residents who marry in the UK.

Source: Office for National Statistics; General Register Office for Scotland; Northern Ireland Statistics and Research Agency

The pattern of forming partnerships in the UK has changed since then, with a falling trend in the number of people marrying and an increase in the number of people cohabiting. In 2006 there were around 237,000 marriages in England and Wales, the lowest number recorded since 1895 (228,200 marriages).

There were around 29,900 marriages in Scotland in 2007, a similar figure to 2006, but a fall of 3 per cent compared with 2005. In Northern Ireland there were around 8,700 marriages in 2007, an increase of 5 per cent on 2006.

Overall there were around 278,000 marriages in the UK in 2006. UK figures include foreign citizens who came to the UK to get married but do not include UK residents who travelled abroad to marry. Research suggests that since 2002 there may be between 20,000 and 40,000 marriages of UK residents that are not recorded in the UK each year.

The majority of people who married in the UK in 2006 did so for the first time: around 71 per cent of men and 72 per cent of women (Table 2.11). This proportion remained stable between 1996 and 2006, fluctuating between 70 and 71 per cent for men and 70 and 72 per cent for women. Around one-quarter of men (27 per cent) and women (25 per cent) who married in 2006 had been married and divorced at least once before. In 2006, the proportion of people remarrying who were widowed was 2 per cent, a figure that has remained stable over the last ten years.

Table 2.11

People marrying: by sex and previous marital status

United Kingdom   Thousands

	1996	2000	2004	2005	2006
Men					
Single[1]	222	214	221	202	195
Divorced	87	85	85	79	74
Widowed	9	7	7	7	6
Women					
Single[1]	222	216	224	206	199
Divorced	88	83	83	75	70
Widowed	8	7	7	6	6

1 Single men and single women are those who had not been married before.

Source: Office for National Statistics; General Register Office for Scotland; Northern Ireland Statistics and Research Agency

First marriages (first for both partners) in England and Wales peaked in 1940, at 91 per cent of all marriages. This proportion has since fallen, with first marriages accounting for 58 per cent of all marriages in 1996 and 61 per cent in 2006. Following the *Divorce Reform Act 1969*, remarriages (for one or both parties) in England and Wales rose by about one-third between 1971 and 1972 to around 120,000 and then levelled off. In 2006 around four in ten marriages were remarriages for one or both parties.

People in the UK are generally getting married later in life than a decade ago. In 1996 more than one-half (52 per cent) of people who got married in the UK were aged between 16 and 29 (Figure 2.12 overleaf). In 2006 this proportion had fallen to 38 per cent. The largest fall was among men and women aged between 20 and 24. In 1996 this age group accounted for 19 per cent of people getting married compared with 11 per cent in 2006. The proportion of people getting married at the age of 30 and over increased, most noticeably for people aged between 35 and 39. More than one in six people who got married in 1996 (16 per cent) were in this age group compared with nearly one-quarter (24 per cent) in 2006.

The average age at first marriage rose between 1996 and 2006. For men it was 29.3 in 1996 and 31.8 in 2006. For women it rose from 27.2 to 29.7. For men who had been married and divorced at least once before, the average age at remarriage rose from 41.7 in 1996 to 46.0 in 2006. For women who had been married and divorced at least once before the equivalent ages were 38.6 and 43.1. This trend towards delayed marriage is not new. In 1966 the average age at first

Figure 2.12

Age distribution of marriages[1]

United Kingdom

Percentages

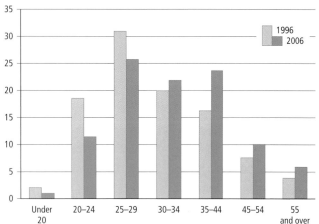

1 Includes first marriages and remarriages.

Source: Office for National Statistics; General Register Office for Scotland; Northern Ireland Statistics and Research Agency

Figure 2.13

Divorce: by duration of marriage

United Kingdom

Thousands

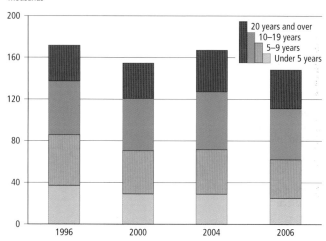

Source: Office for National Statistics; General Register Office for Scotland; Northern Ireland Statistics and Research Agency

marriage was 24.9 for men and 22.5 for women. At remarriage it was 39.3 for men and 36.2 for women.

Divorces granted in the UK peaked in 1993, at slightly more than 180,000. In 2007 the number of divorces granted in the UK was close to 144,000. This was the third consecutive fall in the number of UK divorces and the lowest number of divorces since 1977. In England and Wales there were around 129,000 divorces in 2007, a fall of 3 per cent on 2006. This is the lowest number since 1979 when there were around 127,000 divorces. The number of divorces in Scotland also decreased, falling from around 13,000 in 2006 to slightly less than 13,000 in 2007. In Northern Ireland the number of divorces increased between 2006 and 2007 by 14 per cent to around 2,900.

In 2006 around 25,000 divorces in the UK were granted to couples who had been married for fewer than five years, a fall of 32 per cent compared with 1996 (Figure 2.13). Around one in four divorces granted in 2006 were to couples who had been married for 15 years or more. The average duration of marriage for divorces granted in England and Wales in 2005 was 11.6 years compared with 9.9 years in 1996.

More than one-half (51 per cent) of couples divorcing in England and Wales in 2007 had at least one child aged under 16. Of those children under 16 who were involved in divorce, 20 per cent were under five years old and 63 per cent were under eleven. Around one-third (34 per cent) of divorces in 2007 did not involve children of any age.

Attitudes towards marriage and family life have changed over time and many people now have different attitudes from their parents. According to the 2006 British Social Attitudes Survey, two-thirds (66 per cent) of people in Great Britain think that there is little social difference between being married and living together. However, more than one-half (56 per cent) of adults surveyed in 2006 agreed that marriage is still the best kind of relationship, a fall of 3 percentage points since the 2000 survey (Table 2.14). Almost three in ten (29 per cent) people in Great Britain felt that married couples make better parents than unmarried ones, similar to 2000 when 28 per cent agreed with this statement. When asked if they agree that marriage is financially more secure than cohabitation, almost one-half (49 per cent) of respondents agreed in 2000. By 2006 this proportion had risen to almost two-thirds (64 per cent). This increase may partly be the result of a government-funded campaign in 2004 to raise awareness that cohabiting couples do not have the same legal rights as people who are married. In spite of this campaign, less than one-fifth (19 per cent) of cohabiting couples questioned in 2006 had sought advice about their legal position and an even lower proportion (15 per cent) of cohabiting couples who owned their accommodation had a written agreement about their share in the ownership.

The *Civil Partnership Act 2004* enables same-sex couples aged 16 and over to obtain legal recognition of their partnership (see Appendix, Part 2: Civil partnership). The Act came into force in the UK on 5 December 2005 and by 31 December almost 2,000 couples had registered their partnership

Table 2.14

Attitudes to marriage[1]

Great Britain   Percentages

	Agreed with statement 2000	Agreed with statement 2006
Married couples make better parents than unmarried ones	28	29
Even though it might not work out for some people, marriage is still the best kind of relationship	59	56
Marriage gives couples more financial security than living together	49	64
There is no point getting married – it's only a piece of paper	9	9

1 Adults aged 18 and over were asked if they agreed with the above statements. Excludes those who responded 'don't know' or did not answer.

Source: British Social Attitudes Survey, National Centre for Social Research

(Figure 2.15). In 2007 around 8,700 civil partnerships were formed in the UK, a fall of 46 per cent from 2006. The fall is because of the artificially high 2006 figure, this being the first full year that existing same-sex couples who wished to register a partnership were legally allowed to do so.

The majority (87 per cent) of civil partnerships formed in the UK in 2007 were in England, followed by Scotland (8 per cent), Wales (3 per cent) and Northern Ireland (1 per cent). The

corresponding proportions of the resident adult populations in the constituent countries were 84 per cent, 9 per cent, 5 per cent and 3 per cent (for further information see Chapter 1: Population, Table 1.1).

In 2007 male civil partnerships accounted for 55 per cent of all UK civil partnerships compared with 60 per cent in 2006. More men than women registered partnerships in England (56 per cent) and Northern Ireland (54 per cent) in 2007. In Wales there were more female civil partnerships (56 per cent) and in Scotland slightly more female partnerships (51 per cent).

To dissolve a civil partnership a couple must have been in a registered partnership for at least 12 months. There were 42 civil partnership dissolutions granted in the UK in 2007, of which 14 were to male couples and 28 were to female couples.

Partnership trends show a marked increase in the number of people cohabiting. In 2006 almost one-quarter (24 per cent) of unmarried men aged between 16 and 59 were cohabiting in Great Britain compared with 11 per cent in 1986. One-quarter (25 per cent) of unmarried women in the same age group were cohabiting in Great Britain in 2006 compared with 13 per cent in 1986.

For the generation of people born between 1966 and 1970, the proportion of men and women who were cohabiting at ages 15 to 19 was almost 1 per cent. For those born between 1976 and 1980, this figure rose to almost 2 per cent (Figure 2.16). The proportion of adults cohabiting in their early

Figure 2.15

Civil partnerships:[1] by sex, 2005 to 2007

United Kingdom

Number of partnerships

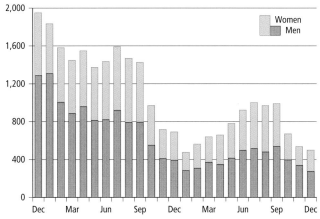

1 Data do not include civil partnerships of UK residents taking place abroad but will include non-UK residents who form a partnership in the UK. See Appendix, Part 2: Civil partnership.

Source: Office for National Statistics; General Register Office for Scotland; Northern Ireland Statistics and Research Agency

Figure 2.16

Proportion of individuals cohabiting: by year of birth and age at survey, 2006

Great Britain

Percentages

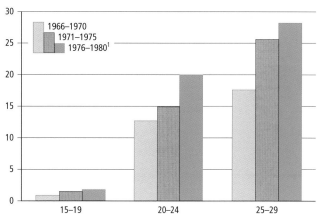

1 Data are not yet complete for age 25 to 29 where individuals were born between 1976 and 1980.

Source: General Household Survey (Longitudinal), Office for National Statistics

20s has also risen for younger generations. For those born between 1966 and 1970, the proportion cohabiting between the ages of 20 and 24 was 13 per cent compared with 20 per cent for those born between 1976 and 1980. The most pronounced shift in cohabitation patterns can be seen by comparing adults born between 1966 and 1970 with those born between 1971 and 1975 in terms of the proportions who were cohabiting between the ages of 25 and 29. At these ages, almost 18 per cent of people born between 1966 and 1970 were cohabiting, compared with around one-quarter (26 per cent) of those born between 1971 and 1975.

Women's experiences of family events have changed over time, reflecting the trends of delayed marriage and motherhood and increasing levels of cohabitation. Just 1 per cent of women aged between 55 and 59 in 2001–03 had cohabited before the age of 25 compared with 21 per cent of those aged between 25 and 29 in 2001–03 (Figure 2.17). Conversely, three-quarters (75 per cent) of women aged between 55 and 59 in 2001–03 had been married before the age of 25 compared with around one-quarter (24 per cent) of women aged between 25 and 29. More than one-half (51 per cent) of women aged between 55 and 59 in 2001–03 had become a mother before the age of 25. For women aged between 25 and 29 in 2001–03 it was less than one-third (30 per cent). The proportion of women experiencing marriage breakdown before they reached the age of 25 has more than doubled for younger generations, rising from 6 per cent for women in their late 50s in 2001–03 to 13 per cent for women in their late 20s.

Family formation

Changing attitudes to family size, marriage and cohabitation, and increasing female participation in education and the labour market have all affected the age at which women give birth. The average age of mothers at childbirth in England and Wales fell from 28.7 years for women born in 1920 to a low of 26.0 years for women born in the mid-1940s, alongside a slight decrease in the average age of marriage. The average age at childbirth has risen steadily since then and is projected to be around 29 years for women born in the early 1980s onwards.

In 2007 the average age for women giving birth in England and Wales was 29.3 years, compared with 28.3 in 1997 and 26.6 years in 1971 (Figure 2.18). The average age of women in England and Wales at the birth of their first child was 27.5 in 2007, compared with 26.1 years in 1997 and 23.7 years in 1971. Unmarried women tend to give birth at younger ages than married women; the average age of unmarried mothers at childbirth was 27.1 years in 2007 compared with 31.5 years for married mothers.

The conception rate for females in England and Wales rose for the fifth consecutive year between 2005 and 2006 to 78 conceptions per 1,000 women. It is estimated there were 870,000 conceptions to women resident in England and Wales in 2006, 78 per cent of which led to a maternity. Around 26 per cent of conceptions were to women aged 25 to 29 in 2006, compared with almost 31 per cent in 1996. In both 1996 and 2006 around one-quarter (24 per cent) of conceptions

Figure 2.17

Experience of family events by women when aged 25: by age[1] in 2001–03[2]

Great Britain

Percentages

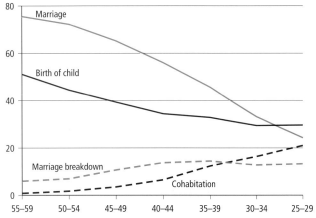

1 Age at time of interview.
2 Combined years: 2001, 2002 and 2003.

Source: General Household Survey (Longitudinal), Office for National Statistics

Figure 2.18

Average age of mother:[1] by birth order[2]

England & Wales

Mean age (years)

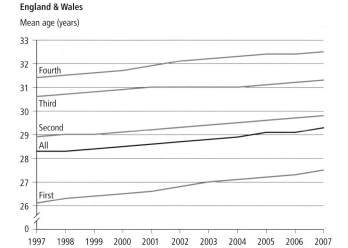

1 Standardised for the age-distribution of the population. This measure is more appropriate for use when analysing trends or making comparisons between different geographies.
2 See Appendix, Part 2: True birth order.

Source: Office for National Statistics

Table 2.19

Teenage conceptions:[1] by age at conception and outcome, 2006

England & Wales[2]

	Conceptions (numbers)	Leading to abortions (percentages)	Rates per 1,000 females[3]		
			All conceptions	Leading to maternities	Leading to abortions
Under 14	295	63	0.9	0.3	0.6
14	1,764	65	5.2	1.8	3.4
15	5,767	58	16.8	7.1	9.7
All aged under 16	7,826	60	7.8	3.1	4.7
16	13,107	49	38.6	19.8	18.8
17	20,835	44	61.3	34.3	27.0
All aged under 18	41,768	48	40.9	21.1	19.8
18	28,494	39	82.1	50.0	32.1
19	32,858	36	95.7	61.3	34.3
All aged under 20	103,120	42	60.2	35.0	25.2

1 See Appendix, Part 2: Conceptions.
2 Residents only.
3 Rates for females aged under 14, under 16, under 18 and under 20 are based on the population of females aged 13, 13 to 15, 15 to 17 and 15 to 19 respectively.

Source: Office for National Statistics

were to women aged between 30 and 34 but the proportion to women in their late 30s rose from 9 per cent in 1996 to 13 per cent in 2006. Overall, 56 per cent of conceptions in 2006 were outside marriage compared with almost one-half (49 per cent) in 1996.

There were around 103,000 conceptions to females aged under 20 in England and Wales in 2006 (Table 2.19) compared with almost 95,000 in 1996. Of the conceptions to females aged under 20 in 2006, 59 per cent were to women aged 18 and 19, 33 per cent were to women aged 16 and 17, and 8 per cent were to girls under 16. The likelihood that conceptions among teenage girls will lead to abortion decreases with age; in 2006, six in ten (60 per cent) conceptions to girls aged under 16 led to an abortion, compared with less than one-half for women aged 16 and 17 and less than four in ten for 18 and 19-year-olds.

In 2007 there were around 21,100 multiple births in England and Wales. The multiple maternity rate was 15.3 per 1,000 maternities, compared with 14.5 per 1,000 in 1997 and 9.9 per 1,000 in 1975 (Figure 2.20). There were 10,300 sets of twins and 140 sets of triplets or higher born in England and Wales in 2007.

The Human Fertilisation and Embryology Authority (HFEA) estimates that around one in seven couples in the UK

experience difficulty conceiving and, although around 95 per cent of women who are trying to get pregnant conceive within two years, a minority will not. The National Institute for Clinical Excellence (NICE) defines infertility as failing to get pregnant after two years of regular unprotected sex and suggests that eligible couples should be offered up to three

Figure 2.20

Maternities with multiple births[1]

England & Wales

Rates per 1,000 maternities

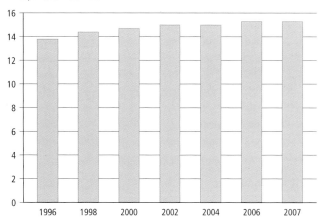

1 Data include maternities where live births and/or stillbirths occurred.

Source: Office for National Statistics

cycles of in vitro fertilisation (IVF) treatment on the National Health Service.

The risk of multiple births is around ten times higher with IVF than through natural conception; around one in four IVF pregnancies result in the birth of twins. Multiple maternities carry risks associated with premature birth and low birth weight, as well as longer term health risks for surviving children. For example, the risk of death before birth or within the first week of life is more than four times greater for twins than for single births and almost seven times greater for triplets.

Sometimes families come under pressure and for a variety of reasons children cannot live with their parents. Children may need temporary care while parents overcome an illness or sort out problems that adversely affect the family. Children may have problems and need help to get through a difficult period in their lives. In some instances children are neglected or abused and need to get away from their family. There were 59,500 children being looked after in England at 31 March 2008 (excluding children looked after in a series of short-term placements) compared with 60,000 in 2007 and 61,200 in 2004 (Table 2.21). Fostering is one way of providing a family life for children who cannot live with their own parents and the majority (71 per cent) of looked after children were in foster placements. Around 42 per cent of looked after children were

in foster care provided by a council and around one in ten (11 per cent) were cared for by a relative or friend. In some cases care was provided outside the child's local council area.

The figures in Table 2.21 are a snapshot at two points in time and the number of children passing into and out of care is different from the number in care at a given point. In the year ending March 2008, 23,000 children started to be looked after in England and 17,300 of these were placed in foster care. Around 24,100 children ceased to be looked after in the same year; 12,600 children left foster care and altogether 3,100 children were placed for adoption. Of those children placed for adoption, 14 per cent were placed for adoption with their current foster carer. A pilot scheme announced by the Government in 2008 (the *Staying Put* pilots) will give young people in some regions of England the opportunity to stay on in their foster families after the age of 18, until they feel ready to move on to independent living. This may have an affect on the future number of children looked after, fostered and adopted.

There were 4,630 children looked after in Wales at 31 March 2008 (excluding children looked after in a series of short-term placements). As in England, the majority (75 per cent) were in foster care. During the year ending 31 March 2008, 1,450 children started to be looked after and 1,430 children ceased being looked after in Wales.

Some children cannot live with their parents and need a permanent family to care for them. The *Adoption and Children Act 2002* was fully implemented at the end of December 2005. This modernised the legal framework for adoption in England

Table 2.21

Looked after children in foster placements[1]

England		Percentages
	2004	2008
Foster placements	*67*	*71*
Foster placement inside council boundary		
With relative or friend	*9*	*8*
With other foster carer		
Provided by council	*34*	*33*
Arranged through agency	*2*	*5*
Foster placements outside council boundary		
With relative or friend	*3*	*3*
With other foster carer		
Provided by council	*8*	*9*
Arranged through agency	*10*	*13*
All looked after children[2]		
(=100%) (thousands)	*61.2*	*59.5*

1 At 31 March each year.
2 Figures exclude children looked after under an agreed series of short-term placements.

Source: Department for Children, Schools and Families

Figure 2.22

Adoptions: by age of child[1]

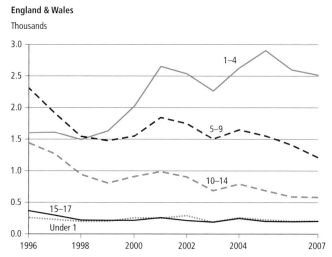

England & Wales
Thousands

1 By age of child at entry of adoption order in the Adopted Children Register. Data for 2001, 2006 and 2007 include cases where the child was older than 17 years.

Source: Office for National Statistics

and Wales, allowing for adoption orders to be made in favour of civil partners, same-sex couples and unmarried couples, as well as single people and married couples.

Approximately 4,700 children were entered in the Adopted Children Register in England and Wales following court orders in 2007, the lowest number since 1998. This included a considerable number of adoptions by relatives and step-parents as well as adoptions of children in foster care. Around 55 per cent of all children adopted in 2007 were aged between one and four years old (Figure 2.22) compared with 53 per cent in 2006 and 31 per cent in 1997. More than one-quarter (26 per cent) of children adopted in 2007 were aged between five and nine, compared with 28 per cent in 2006 and 36 per cent in 1997. Only 4 per cent of adoptions in 2007 involved children aged between 15 and 17, a figure that has remained stable since 2000. Longer-term trends show that there were almost 21,500 adoptions in England and Wales in 1971, at least four times more than in 2007. The number of adoptions fell rapidly during the 1970s and then continued to fall steadily during the 1980s and 1990s.

2

Education and training

- The proportion of three and four-year-olds enrolled in all schools in the UK tripled from 21 per cent in 1970/71 to 64 per cent in 2007/08. (Figure 3.1)

- The most common reason for exclusion from school in England in 2006/07 was persistent disruptive behaviour, which accounted for 31 per cent of all permanent exclusions. (Table 3.5)

- In 2007, 59 per cent of parents in England whose child was in Year one or two were always confident helping with homework compared with 17 per cent of parents whose child was in Years ten to 12. (Figure 3.6)

- In 2007/08, 16 per cent of pupils in maintained nursery and primary schools in the UK were eligible for free school meals, and 13 per cent took them. (Table 3.7)

- Around 673,000 National Vocational Qualifications and Scottish Vocational Qualifications were awarded in the UK in 2006/07 compared with around 153,000 in 1991/92. (Page 40)

- Married or cohabiting parents in the UK in Q2 2008 were more likely to be educated to degree level or higher than lone parents, 23 per cent compared with 11 per cent. (Table 3.19)

DATA

Download data by clicking the online pdf

www.statistics.gov.uk/ socialtrends39

Young people are generally spending more years in formal education. Early learning and participation in pre-school education builds a foundation for future learning and is taken up by a considerable number of pre-school age children. Most young people in the UK continue in full-time education beyond school-leaving age and supplement qualifications and skills attained at school with those from further and higher education. Apart from formal education, other training opportunities are increasingly helping to equip people with the skills required by a modern labour market and to keep these skills current.

Early years education

Since records began more than 35 years ago, data for the UK show a major expansion in early years education provided for young children in all settings. The proportion of three and four-year-olds enrolled in all schools in the UK rose from 21 per cent in 1970/71 to 64 per cent in 2007/08, although this is slightly down from a peak of 65 per cent in 2003/04 (Figure 3.1). This increase in participation partly reflects the growth in the number of places available – in 1970/71 there were 723 state nursery schools compared with 3,273 in 2007/08.

Although some form of free pre-school education is available across all the countries of the UK, it is delivered under different strategies. In September 2008, the Early Years Foundation

Figure 3.1

Children under five[1] in schools

United Kingdom
Percentages

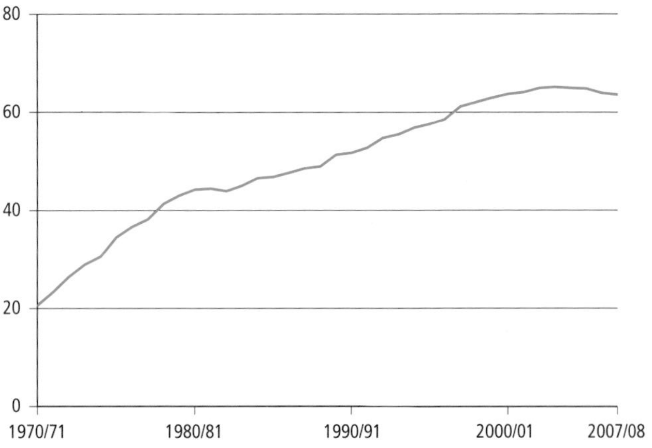

1 Pupils aged three and four at 31 December each year as a proportion of all three and four-year-olds, with the exception of Scotland where reference dates differ over the period. See Appendix, Part 3: Stages of education.

Source: Department for Children, Schools and Families; Welsh Assembly Government; Scottish Government; Northern Ireland Department of Education

Stage (EYFS) was introduced in England for children aged under five replacing the foundation stage profile, and aims to develop young children's learning in six broad areas: personal, social and emotional development; communication, language and literacy; problem solving, reasoning and numeracy; knowledge and understanding of the world; physical development; and creative development. All three and four-year-olds in England are entitled to a free part-time education place for 12.5 hours per week (for 38 weeks of the year). From 2010, this will be extended to 15 hours per week. In Wales all children are entitled to a free part-time (10 hours per week) education place from the term following their third birthday. From September 2008 the Foundation Phase became statutory for three to four-year-olds and by 2011/12 will be extended to three to seven-year-olds. In Scotland, the Curriculum Framework for children aged three to five provides guidelines for early years learning although this has been under review since 2004. A new Curriculum for Excellence is due for implementation from 2009. The delivery of early years education in Northern Ireland also aims to develop young children's learning and a new early years strategy is due for implementation from 2010.

The pattern of participation in pre-compulsory education varies by region. In January 2008, a higher proportion of children aged three and four were enrolled with private and voluntary providers in the south of England than in other parts of the UK, 57 per cent in the South West and 54 per cent in the South East, compared with between 15 and 48 per cent elsewhere. However, twice the proportion of three and four-year-olds attended maintained nursery and primary schools in Wales (85 per cent) and the North East (81 per cent) compared with the South East and the South West (42 per cent each). In Northern Ireland 56 per cent of three and four-year-olds attended maintained nursery and primary schools, and in Scotland 70 per cent of children in this age group were enrolled in early years education in schools (this figure includes independent and special schools). It is worth noting that in England and Scotland, any child attending more than one provider may have been counted twice so it is difficult to make exact comparisons between the regions of the UK.

In 2007, the Childcare and Early Years Survey of Parents asked parents in England their views on, and experiences of, various aspects of child care and early years provision. The survey showed that an estimated 3.3 million families in England had used informal child care (provided by siblings, grandparents, other family members and friends) at some point in the last 12 months (see Chapter 8: Social Protection, Table 8.20) compared with 2.8 million families who had used formal child care or early years provision.

The survey also explored take-up of child care for economic reasons (so that parents could work, look for a job or study) and for reasons related to the children's educational development. A higher proportion of parents used some form of child care in the week prior to interview for economic reasons only (36 per cent) than for reasons connected with their child's educational development only (25 per cent). The proportion using child care for economic reasons has not changed since 2004. However, the proportion using child care for educational reasons has declined slightly, from 27 per cent in 2004 to 25 per cent in 2007.

When comparing very young children with those of a later pre-school age the same survey showed that 46 per cent of children aged under three in a child care setting in 2007 were receiving care for economic reasons only and 13 per cent for educational reasons only (Figure 3.2). While for three or four-year-old children, the opposite was true – 17 per cent were receiving child care for economic reasons only and 43 per cent solely for educational purposes.

The 2007 Growing up in Scotland survey asked parents of children aged 10 months and 34 months for their reasons for using child care. Across both cohorts the most common response cited was 'so that I can work' (69 per cent).

Figure 3.2

Reasons given by parents for using child care:[1] by age of child, 2007

England

Percentages

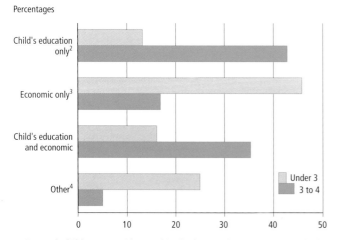

1 For each child care provider used in the last week, parents were asked to give their reasons for doing so. They were shown a list of options and could pick more than one reason.
2 This response was 'for my child's educational development'.
3 These data are combined responses by parents relating to their work, and/or study.
4 Includes responses associated with parents being able to look after the home/other children, go shopping or attend appointments, and responses associated with children spending time at provider for the child's enjoyment and leisure.

Source: Childcare and Early Years Survey of Parents, Department for Children, Schools and Families

Respondents could provide more than one answer and 23 per cent gave their child's educational development as a reason. There were some differences between the two age groups with parents of the older children more likely to say that they used child care so that their children could take part in leisure activities (17 per cent compared with 5 per cent) and for educational development (38 per cent compared with 12 per cent).

Compulsory education

In 2007/08, there were 33,661 schools in the UK (a fall of 1,054 since 2000/01), attended by 9.7 million pupils (Table 3.3 overleaf). The majority (87 per cent) were public sector mainstream schools. The peak year for pupil numbers in the UK reflects the birth rate (see Chapter 1: Population) and was in 1976/77 when 11.3 million pupils attended 38,612 schools.

In 2007/08, 92 per cent of pupils attended one of the 29,250 public sector schools (not including special schools and pupil referral units (PRUs)) in the UK while 6 per cent attended one of the 2,527 non-maintained mainstream schools and 1 per cent of pupils attended one of the 1,378 special schools. These proportions have remained at similar levels since the 1970s. There were also 506 PRUs with 17,000 pupils in England and Wales. PRUs provide suitable alternative education on a temporary basis for pupils who have been excluded from mainstream schools and children with medical problems. PRUs may also provide education for pregnant schoolgirls and school-aged mothers, school-phobics, and pupils awaiting placement in a maintained school.

Around two-thirds (67 per cent) of the 4,209 state-funded secondary schools in the UK in 2007/08 were specialist schools, all of which were in England. Any maintained secondary school in England can apply to be designated as a specialist school in one of ten specialisms: arts, business and enterprise, engineering, humanities, languages, mathematics and computing, music, science, sports, and technology. Schools can also combine any two specialisms. Specialist schools receive extra funding to establish curriculum centres of excellence and although they focus on one or two chosen specialisms, these schools must still meet National Curriculum requirements and deliver a broad and balanced education to all pupils (see Appendix, Part 3: The National Curriculum).

In January 1990, around 20 per cent of maintained primary schools in England had classes of 31 or more pupils taught by one teacher. By January 1998 this peaked at 29 per cent. However, by January 2008 this proportion had fallen to 11 per cent. This drop, particularly at Key Stage 1 (pupils aged five to seven), was driven by the *School Standards and*

Table 3.3

Schools: by type of school[1]

United Kingdom

Numbers

	1990/91	2000/01	2005/06	2006/07	2007/08
Public sector mainstream schools[2]					
Nursery	1,364	3,228	3,349	3,326	3,273
Primary	24,135	22,902	22,156	21,968	21,768
State-funded secondary[3]	4,797	4,352	4,244	4,232	4,209
of which, specialist schools[4]	.	523	2,381	2,611	2,799
of which, admissions policy[5]					
Comprehensive	3,696	3,443	3,424	3,398	3,304
Selective	222	231	233	233	233
Modern	171	145	115	113	172
City technology colleges	7	15	11	10	5
Academies	.	.	27	46	83
Not applicable	701	518	434	432	412
All public sector mainstream schools	30,296	30,482	29,749	29,526	29,250
Non-maintained schools	2,501	2,397	2,455	2,486	2,527
Special schools[6]	1,830	1,498	1,416	1,391	1,378
Pupil referral units	.	338	481	489	506
All schools	34,627	34,715	34,101	33,892	33,661

1 See Appendix, Part 3: Main categories of educational establishments.
2 Excludes special schools and pupil referral units (PRUs).
3 From 1993/94 excludes sixth-form colleges in England and Wales, which were reclassified as further education colleges on 1 April 1993.
4 Numbers of specialist schools in England, operational from September of each academic year shown.
5 See Appendix, Part 3: School admissions policy.
6 For children with special educational needs. Includes maintained (the majority) and non-maintained sectors.

Source: Department for Children, Schools and Families; Welsh Assembly Government; Scottish Government; Northern Ireland Department of Education

Framework Act 1998, which aimed to reduce Key Stage 1 class sizes in maintained schools to no more than 30 pupils by 2001/02. In 2007/08, at Key Stage 1, the proportion of classes of 31 or more pupils in Wales, Scotland and Northern Ireland were 3 per cent, 1 per cent and 3 per cent respectively.

Overall, the average class size in Great Britain in 2007/08 was 25 pupils for Key Stage 1 and 27 pupils for Key Stage 2 (seven to 11-year-olds). Average class size in secondary schools in England was 21 pupils and in Wales, 20 pupils, despite secondary schools usually having more pupils than primary schools. This smaller average class size is in part because students choose different subjects in preparation for formal exams taken towards the end of their compulsory secondary schooling.

Parents have the right to express a preference for a maintained school at all stages of their child's education. If their choice is not met, parents in England and Wales may appeal against the decision to a panel made up of representatives that are

independent of the school's governing body and the local education authority. Not all appeals are heard by an appeal panel, as parents may be offered places that become available either at the school they have appealed for, or at another suitable school, before their appeal can be heard. As parents may lodge multiple appeals, they may withdraw other appeals if an earlier one has been successful.

In 2006/07, there were 26,440 appeals against non-admission to primary schools in England and of the 17,380 that went to the appeal panel, 32 per cent were decided in the parents' favour. In the same year 53,570 appeals were lodged against non-admission to secondary schools and of the 39,230 that went to the appeal panel, 35 per cent were decided in the parents' favour.

Some pupils have special educational needs (SEN), that is, they have significantly greater difficulty in learning than other children of the same age, or have a disability that makes it difficult for them to use normal educational facilities. When a school identifies a child with SEN it must try to meet the child's needs, in line with the provisions in the SEN Code of Practice. If the initial attempts do not meet the child's needs then an education authority or board may determine the education required for the child with SEN, draw up a formal statement of needs, and the action it intends to take to meet them. In Scotland, local authorities' responsibilities towards children with additional support needs are set out in the *Additional Support for Learning Act 2004*, which also introduced a statutory document called a co-ordinated support plan (CSP). These plans are aimed at pupils whose support needs are complex and require support from a range of sources.

In 2007/08, 261,800 pupils (2.7 per cent) in the UK had statements of SEN or CSP; 223,600 (2.8 per cent of pupils) in England, 14,900 (3.1 per cent) in Wales, 10,300 (1.2 per cent) in Scotland and 13,000 (3.9 per cent) in Northern Ireland. Figure 3.4 shows the types of special educational need among pupils with statements of SEN in England. In January 2008, the

Figure 3.4

Pupils with statements of special educational needs (SEN):[1] by type of need, 2008[2]

England
Percentages

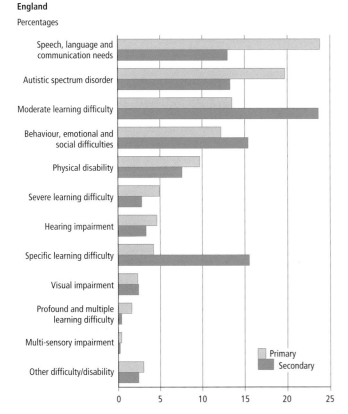

1 As a proportion of all children with statements of SEN in maintained primary and secondary schools, respectively. See Appendix, Part 3: Special educational needs (SEN) data.
2 Data are at January.

Source: Department for Children, Schools and Families

most prevalent need of pupils in primary schools was extra help with speech, language and communication (24 per cent) followed by particular need because of autistic spectrum disorder (20 per cent). The most prevalent type of need among secondary school pupils was help with moderate learning difficulty (24 per cent). Children with moderate learning difficulty find it harder than their peers to acquire basic literacy and numeracy skills and to understand concepts. They may also have low levels of concentration and under-developed social skills. The next most prevalent types of need among secondary school pupils were help with specific learning difficulty (16 per cent) and behavioural, emotional and social difficulties (15 per cent). Children with a specific learning difficulty have particular trouble learning to read, write, spell or manipulate numbers, so their performance in these areas is not as good as their performance in other areas. The types of need in Wales were very similar to England with the most common need at primary level in 2008 being for extra help with speech, language and communication (24 per cent) and at secondary level, help with moderate learning difficulty (28 per cent).

In 2006/07, there were 8,680 permanent exclusions of pupils from primary, secondary and special schools in England; that is they were excluded from the school and their name removed from the school register. These pupils would then be educated at another school or through some other form of provision, for example PRUs (see page 29). The number of permanent exclusions in 2006/07 was 7 per cent lower than 2005/06 and 31 per cent lower than 1996/97, when there were 12,668 permanent exclusions. The number of permanent exclusions of boys (6,850) in 2006/07 outnumbered girls (1,790) by almost four to one. It is important to note that these data are the number of exclusions, not the number of pupils excluded, as some pupils were excluded more than once. In the same year there were also 425,600 fixed period exclusions, which is when the pupil is excluded from school for a period but remains on the register.

The most common reason for exclusion from school in England in 2006/07 was persistent disruptive behaviour, which accounted for 31 per cent of all permanent exclusions and 23 per cent of all fixed period exclusions (Table 3.5 overleaf). Although comprising a smaller proportion of the total number of exclusions, 11 per cent of permanent exclusions and 4 per cent of fixed period exclusions in the same year were for physical assault against an adult. However, verbal abuse/ threatening behaviour against an adult was the second highest proportion for fixed period exclusions (21 per cent). Racist abuse, bullying, and sexual misconduct were the least common reasons for both permanent and fixed period exclusion in England.

Table 3.5

Permanent and fixed period exclusions from schools:[1] by reason, 2006/07

England

Percentages[2]

	Permanent exclusions	Fixed period exclusions
Persistent disruptive behaviour	31	23
Physical assault against a pupil	16	19
Physical assault against an adult	11	4
Verbal abuse/threatening behaviour against an adult	10	21
Drug or alcohol related	5	2
Verbal abuse/threatening behaviour against a pupil	4	4
Theft	2	2
Damage	2	3
Sexual misconduct	2	1
Bullying[3]	1	2
Racist abuse	-	1
Other	15	19
All exclusions (=100%) (thousands)	8.7	425.6

1 Maintained primary, state-funded secondary and all special schools. Includes middle schools as deemed.
2 The number of exclusions by reason expressed as a percentage of the total number of exclusions.
3 Includes both verbal and physical abuse when directed at one child or group of children.

Source: Department for Children, Schools and Families

In Wales in 2006/07, there were 291 permanent exclusions although this figure is not comparable with previous years because of different approaches taken to exclusion between local authorities.

In 2006/07, there were 44,794 exclusions from local authority schools in Scotland, an increase of 4 per cent from 2005/06. Nearly all (44,546) of these were temporary. The most common reason for exclusion was general or persistent disobedience (32 per cent) followed by verbal abuse towards members of staff (26 per cent). There were also 45 permanent expulsions in Northern Ireland in 2006/07 and a further 4,981 fixed period suspensions of pupils. The most common reason for expulsion was verbal abuse towards staff and for suspension it was persistent infringement of school rules.

An area of research interest is the involvement of parents and carers in their children's education. In 2007, a report by the Department for Children, Schools and Families showed that around one-half (51 per cent) of parents in England said that they felt very involved in their child's school life. This proportion

had increased from 29 per cent in 2001 and 38 per cent in 2004.

In the same survey, parents were asked to rate how important it was to help their child with homework. The rating was on a five-point scale, between 'not at all important' and 'extremely important'. Nearly three-quarters (73 per cent) of respondents in 2007 said it was extremely important to help their child with homework. Parents were less likely to think this the older their child gets, as the proportion of parents rating it as 'extremely important' to help their child with homework decreased gradually the higher the school year. For example, 84 per cent of parents whose child was in Year one or two (aged five to seven) felt that helping with homework was 'extremely important', compared with 61 per cent of those whose child was in Years ten to 12 (aged 14 to 16). Reflecting this pattern are data on parents' confidence in helping their children with their homework. Figure 3.6 shows that 59 per cent of parents whose child was in Year one or two said they were 'always confident' helping with homework compared with 17 per cent of parents whose child was in Years ten to 12. Confidence was considerably lower (less than 20 per cent) for parents with a child in Year seven or above (aged 11 and over).

Parents of children (across all year groups) who were 'never confident' or only confident some of the time with their child's homework were asked why they did not feel very confident. The two main reasons cited overall were because of 'different

Figure 3.6

How confident parents feel helping their children with homework:[1] by school year of child,[2] 2007

England

Percentages

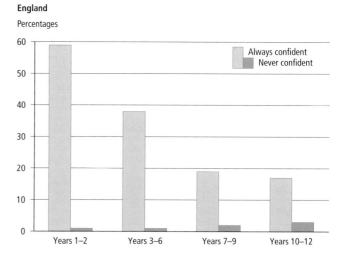

1 Parents were asked the question 'How confident do you (or if their child never had homework, would you) feel helping your child with their homework?' and were provided with the following options: Always confident; most of the time; some of the time; never confident.
2 See Appendix, Part 3: Stages of education.

Source: Parental Involvement in Children's Education, Department for Children, Schools and Families

teaching methods these days' (39 per cent) and because they 'don't understand the work their child does' (38 per cent).

The 2008 Northern Ireland Omnibus Survey reported that 52 per cent of parents felt very involved in their child's school life and 83 per cent felt that it was very important to help their child with homework. Thirty six per cent of parents reported that they were always confident in helping their children with homework, with a similar proportion feeling confident most of the time.

In the UK some families do not have to pay for school meals if they fulfil certain criteria, which include the parents being in receipt of some social welfare benefits, see Chapter 8: Social protection. Children who receive income support or income-based jobseeker's allowance in their own right also qualify.

In education research datasets there is often a measure of pupils' free school meal (FSM) eligibility, and FSM status is often used as an indicator of low household income,

deprivation and social class. In 2007/08, 16 per cent of pupils in maintained nursery and primary schools in the UK were eligible for free school meals and 13 per cent took them (Table 3.7). For state-funded secondary level pupils, the equivalent rates were 13 per cent and 10 per cent respectively. However, there were variations in eligibility rates across the regions of England and countries of the UK. The highest FSM eligibility rates were for pupils in London, where nearly one-quarter (24 per cent) of nursery and primary level pupils and more than one-fifth (22 per cent) of secondary level pupils were eligible. For both levels of education, FSM eligibility was lowest in the South East. There were variations in academic attainment between those eligible for free school meals and those who were not. In 2007/08, 40 per cent of all pupils in England who were eligible for free school meals achieved five or more GCSE grades A* to C (see Appendix, Part 3: Qualifications) compared with 67 per cent of those who were not. For more information see the Educational attainment section later in this chapter.

Table 3.7

Eligibility and uptake of free school meals: by region, 2007/08

Percentages

	Maintained nursery and primary schools[1,2]		Maintained secondary schools[2,3]	
	Eligible for free school meals	Taking free school meals[4]	Eligible for free school meals	Taking free school meals[4]
United Kingdom	15.8	13.2	13.3	9.8
England	15.5	13.0	13.1	9.9
North East	19.6	16.8	15.5	10.8
North West	18.2	15.4	16.4	12.4
Yorkshire and the Humber	15.4	12.7	14.0	9.9
East Midlands	11.9	9.9	9.8	7.3
West Midlands	18.0	15.2	15.3	11.7
East	10.7	8.9	8.5	6.6
London	24.3	20.7	22.5	17.6
South East	9.4	7.7	7.8	5.9
South West	10.5	8.7	8.4	6.2
Wales	16.1	14.2	14.2	11.0
Scotland	16.9	13.7	12.7	7.1
Northern Ireland	17.9	14.6	17.0	12.9

1 Data for Northern Ireland include reception pupils and pupils in preparatory departments of grammar schools. Data for Scotland exclude nursery schools.
2 Includes middle schools as deemed.
3 State-funded schools in England (including city technology colleges and academies).
4 Data shown for Wales are calculated as the proportion of day pupils present on the school census day, therefore the proportion taking free school meals may exceed the proportion known to be eligible. Data for England, Scotland, Northern Ireland and the UK, are proportions of the numbers of pupils on the school roll.

Source: Department for Children, Schools and Families; Welsh Assembly Government; Scottish Government; Northern Ireland Department of Education

Post-compulsory education

In 2005, the Longitudinal Study of Young People in England, asked pupils in Year 10 'When you're 16 and have finished Year 11, what do you want to do next?' Overall, 84 per cent of pupils in this year group stated that they had intentions to stay on in further education. Subsequently, 72 per cent of these pupils actually stayed on (Table 3.8). Those with parents in higher professional occupations were most likely to say that they intended to stay on in full-time education, at 94 per cent, and to actually stay on in full-time education (86 per cent). This group was closely followed by pupils with parents in lower professional occupations, 89 per cent intended to stay on and 81 per cent actually stayed on. Those least likely to want to continue in full-time education were those whose parents were in lower supervisory, or routine occupations, at 77 and 75 per cent respectively, with 63 and 62 per cent staying on in full-time education. Pupils with parents in intermediate and lower supervisory occupations had the highest difference between intending to stay on and actually staying on with the exception of 'Other', which mostly comprised parents who were long-term unemployed, pupils for whom there were no parental data, and those whose parents' occupations could not be coded. This group, along with pupils with parents in routine occupations, had the lowest actual staying on rates (62 per cent).

Table 3.8

Intentions of pupils aged 14 or 15 to remain in full-time education at age 16, and outcomes: by socio-economic classification[1] of parent, 2005[2]

England		Percentages
	Intention[2] to remain in education	Actually[3] remained in education
Higher professional	94	86
Lower professional	89	81
Intermediate	85	71
Lower supervisory	77	63
Routine	75	62
Other[4]	84	62
All	84	72

1 See Appendix, Part 3: National Statistics Socio-economic Classification (NS-SEC).
2 Pupils in Year 10 in 2005 were asked 'When you're 16 and have finished Year 11, what do you want to do next?'
3 The proportion of those aged 16 who had finished Year 11 and who were in full-time education in 2007.
4 Mostly long-term unemployed, but also includes cases with no parental data or where data cannot be coded.

Source: Longitudinal Study of Young People in England, Department for Children, Schools and Families

Table 3.9

Students in further and higher education:[1] by type of course and sex

United Kingdom								Thousands
	Men				Women			
	1970/71	1980/81	1990/91	2006/07	1970/71	1980/81	1990/91	2006/07
Further education								
Full-time	116	154	219	515	95	196	261	531
Part-time	891	697	768	1,027	630	624	986	1,567
All further education	1,007	851	986	1,542	725	820	1,247	2,098
Higher education								
Undergraduate								
Full-time	241	277	345	563	173	196	319	706
Part-time	127	176	148	267	19	71	106	451
Postgraduate								
Full-time	33	41	50	120	10	21	34	124
Part-time	15	32	46	143	3	13	33	181
All higher education[2]	416	526	588	1,094	205	301	491	1,463

1 Home and overseas students attending further education or higher education institutions. See Appendix, Part 3: Stages of education.
2 Figures for 2006/07 include a small number of higher education students for whom details are not available by level.

Source: Department for Children, Schools and Families; Department for Innovation, Universities and Skills; Welsh Assembly Government; Scottish Government; Northern Ireland Department for Employment and Learning

According to administrative data 63 per cent (1.3 million) of 16 to 18-year-olds in England were in some form of full-time post-compulsory education at the end of 2007, an increase of 2 percentage points since 2006. There have been changes in the proportions of men and women of this age group in post-compulsory education in recent years. In 1985, when the series began, a larger proportion of young women than young men were in post-compulsory education in England (34 per cent compared with 30 per cent). Since then the gap between the sexes has widened and the proportions fluctuated slightly in the late 1990s and early 2000s before increasing to 67 per cent of women aged 16 to 18 and 59 per cent of 16 to 18-year-old men in post-compulsory education in 2007.

There were around 3.6 million further education students in the UK in 2006/07, more than twice the number in 1970/71 (Table 3.9), although it should be noted there have been changes to data coverage and methodologies over time (see Appendix, Part 3: Stages of education). This total comprised 2.1 million female further education students, nearly three times as many as in 1970/71, and around 1.5 million male students, over 50 per cent more. Over the period, the proportion of further education students who were women increased from 42 per cent in 1970/71 to 58 per cent in 2006/07 while the proportion of men fell from 58 per cent to 42 per cent, a complete reversal of the proportions. More women than men were taking part-time further education courses in 2006/07 compared with 1970/71, with the proportions also in reversal. In 1970/71, 59 per cent of people taking part-time courses were men. In 2006/07, this had dropped to 40 per cent.

There have also been substantial increases in the number of students in higher education in the UK, studying in both further and higher education institutions (see Appendix, Part 3: Stages of education). In 2006/07, there were close to 2.6 million students in higher education compared with 621,000 in 1970/71. The proportion of female higher education students increased from 33 per cent to 57 per cent over the 36-year period, and there has been a higher proportion of female than male higher education students each year since 1995/96. There were around seven times as many female higher education students in 2006/07 as in 1970/71, 1.5 million compared with 205,000 and more than twice as many male students, 1.1 million compared with 416,000.

When higher education institution student numbers are broken down by subject choice the data reveal that the most popular subject for men was business and administrative studies, studied by 159,300 men (16 per cent of male higher education students) followed by engineering and technology studied by 118,200 men (12 per cent) (Table 3.10). For women, the highest

Table 3.10

Students in higher education:[1] by subject[2] and sex, 2006/07

United Kingdom			Percentages
	Men	Women	All
Business and administrative studies	15.8	11.2	13.1
Subjects allied to medicine	5.5	18.2	12.7
Education	5.4	12.0	9.2
Social studies	7.5	9.3	8.5
Biological sciences	5.9	7.7	7.0
Creative arts and design	6.2	7.2	6.8
Engineering and technology	11.7	1.7	5.9
Languages	4.5	7.0	5.9
Computer science	8.3	1.7	4.5
Historical and philosophical studies	4.6	4.2	4.4
Law	3.7	4.0	3.8
Physical sciences	4.8	2.6	3.6
Medicine and dentistry	2.6	2.7	2.7
Architecture, building and planning	4.1	1.4	2.6
Mass communications and documentation	2.0	2.1	2.0
Mathematical sciences	2.1	0.9	1.4
Agriculture and related subjects	0.6	0.7	0.7
Veterinary science	0.1	0.3	0.2
Combined	4.5	5.3	5.0
All subject areas (=100%) (thousands)	1,010	1,352	2,363

1 Full-time and part-time, undergraduate and postgraduate, and home and overseas students in higher education institutions only. See Appendix, Part 3: Stages of education.
2 Subject data are classified using the Joint Academic Coding System. See Appendix, Part 3: Joint Academic Coding System.

Source: Higher Education Statistics Agency

number, 245,700 (18 per cent of female higher education students) were studying subjects allied to medicine, followed by 162,200 (12 per cent) studying education. The least popular subjects for both sexes were veterinary science, with 4,900 students, and agricultural and related subjects, with 16,100 students.

The number of higher education students in the UK from European Union (EU-25) member states rose from 106,200 to 112,300 between 2005/06 and 2006/07, an increase of 6 per cent. The largest proportional increase was for students whose domicile was Poland, who accounted for 4,300 EU-domiciled students in the UK in 2005/06 and 6,800 in 2006/07, a rise of 57 per cent, overtaking both Spain and Italy in terms of the number of students studying in the UK. The second largest proportional increase was for Cyprus-domiciled

Table 3.11

People working towards a qualification:[1] by age, 2008[2]

United Kingdom   Percentages

	Degree or equivalent and higher	Higher education[3]	GCE A level or equivalent	GCSE or equivalent	Other qualifications	All studying
16–19	15	22	74	67	13	35
20–24	45	20	9	6	12	21
25–29	13	12	3	5	17	11
30–39	13	22	5	9	25	14
40–49	10	17	6	9	21	12
50–59/64	4	7	2	5	12	6
All aged 16–59/64[4] (=100%) (millions)	2.0	0.5	1.4	0.9	1.7	6.5

1 For those working towards more than one qualification, the highest is recorded. See Appendix, Part 3: Qualifications. Excludes those who did not answer and those who did not state the qualification they were working towards.
2 Data are at Q2 (April–June) and are not seasonally adjusted. See Appendix, Part 4: Labour Force Survey.
3 Below degree level but including National Vocational Qualification (NVQ) level 4.
4 Men aged 16 to 64 and women aged 16 to 59.

Source: Labour Force Survey, Office for National Statistics

students, at 21 per cent, with the number of students increasing from 7,200 to 8,700. Conversely, the largest proportional decrease over the period was for students of Greek nationality, from 17,700 to 16,000, a fall of 9 per cent. The decrease in students domiciled in Greece meant that the EU member state with the highest number of students studying in the UK in 2006/07 was Ireland, with 16,300 students. There were also 239,200 higher education students in the UK from non-EU countries in 2006/07, an increase of 7 per cent since 2005/06. The largest number of these students (49,600) were China-domiciled, although in the 12 months to 2006/07 this number decreased by 2 per cent. The next most common domicile was for those students from India (23,800), which represented an increase of 24 per cent over the same period.

Not everyone working towards a qualification beyond the age of 16 have worked their way continuously through the various levels of education. More than 2.8 million (44 per cent) people of working age (16 to 64 for men and 16 to 59 for women) studying towards a qualification in the UK in Q2 2008 were aged 25 and over (Table 3.11). Around 1.2 million (19 per cent) were aged 40 and over. The age distribution varied according to the qualification being studied. Working-age adults aged 25 and over comprised 27 per cent of those studying towards a GCSE or equivalent and 17 per cent of those studying towards a GCE A level or equivalent. The proportion for this age group rose to 58 per cent of working-age people taking higher education qualifications

below degree level (such as a Higher National Diploma, Higher National Certificate or a National Vocational Qualification/ Scottish Vocational Qualification), and 41 per cent of those studying at degree level or higher.

Adult training and learning

Learning in working life is often necessary because of the need to develop skills to keep up with the pace of change within the labour market. There are also various education and training options available to young people who decide not to continue in full-time education, including a number of government-supported training initiatives. In England and Wales, Work-Based Learning for Young People aims to ensure that all young people aged 16 to 24 have access to post-compulsory education or training. Included in this initiative are apprenticeships, which provide structured learning that combines work-based training with off-the-job learning. Apprenticeships offer training to National Vocational Qualification (NVQ) level 2 (see Appendix, Part 3: Qualifications). Advanced apprenticeships offer training to NVQ level 3, and aim to develop technical, supervisory and craft-level skills. In 2007/08, 112,600 learners aged 16 and over funded by the Learning and Skills Council (LSC) in England completed an apprenticeship, a slight increase (1 per cent) since 2006/07.

The need for job-related training in the labour market is not only confined to young people, although they were more likely than older age groups to receive this. The Labour Force Survey

Figure 3.12

Employees receiving job-related training:[1] by age and sex, 2008[2]

United Kingdom

Percentages

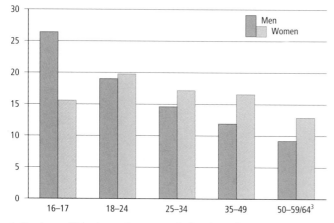

1 Employees (those in employment excluding the self-employed, unpaid family workers and those on government programmes) who received job-related training in the four weeks prior to interview.
2 Data are at Q2 (April–June) and are not seasonally adjusted. See Appendix, Part 4: Labour Force Survey.
3 Men aged 50 to 64 and women aged 50 to 59.

Source: Labour Force Survey, Office for National Statistics

includes questions regarding employment training and found that in Q2 2008, 26 per cent of male employees aged 16 and 17 and 16 per cent of female employees in this age group received job-related training in the four weeks prior to interview (Figure 3.12). For employees aged 18 to 24, the proportions were 19 per cent and 20 per cent respectively. This compares with 9 per cent of men aged 50 to 64 and 13 per cent of women aged 50 to 59. Overall 15 per cent of employees of working age in the UK had received job-related training in the four weeks prior to interview. In general greater proportions of women (16 per cent) than men (13 per cent) received job-related training.

Over the 12 months to 2007/08, the number of adults aged 19 and over in LSC-funded further education (including further education, work-based learning and other adult learning) in England fell from 3.2 million to 3.1 million. Learners in this age group comprise three-quarters (75 per cent) of all those in LSC-funded further education. Skills for Life is the Government strategy to improve adult literacy and numeracy skills in England. In 2007/08, almost 1.2 million learners were enrolled on LSC-funded Skills for Life programmes, a 3 per cent increase on 2006/07.

The modern working environment demands skills such as computer literacy, as well as communication, problem solving and customer handling skills. The National Employers Skills Survey in 2007 looked at the extent of skills deficiencies among employees in England, as reported by employers. This found a minority (15 per cent) of employers were affected by skills gaps and most employees were considered fully proficient; only 6 per cent of employees were considered by employers to have skills gaps.

Employers were asked to define what skills they felt needed improving in jobs where staff were not fully proficient. They thought that around one-half (51 per cent) of employees identified as having a skills gap lacked adequate technical and practical skills and 41 per cent lacked both oral communication and customer handling skills (Figure 3.13). Employers were asked what they thought were the causes of these skills gaps (they could provide more than one answer). From their responses the majority (68 per cent) of skill gaps were caused by lack of experience while 28 per cent were because staff lacked motivation. Other reasons given by employers were a failure to train and develop staff (20 per cent of skills gaps), staff not being good at keeping up with change (19 per cent), recruitment problems (15 per cent) and a high staff turnover (15 per cent).

In 2006, employers were asked in the Workforce Training in England Survey their reasons for providing their staff with

Figure 3.13

Skills characteristics of skills gaps,[1] 2007

England

Percentages

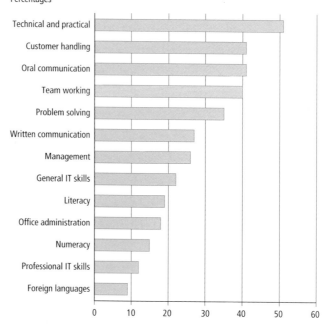

1 Employers who had experienced skills gaps were asked to define what skills they felt needed improving for an occupation where staff were considered not fully proficient. Percentages do not sum to 100 per cent as employers could give more than one answer. See Appendix, Part 3: National Employers Skills Survey.

Source: Learning and Skills Council

training. The main reasons cited were concerned with business improvement – almost one-half (49 per cent) of employers said they provided training to increase productivity and improve staff performance, and nearly one-quarter (23 per cent) said training improved the quality of their goods and services. However, more than one-quarter (26 per cent) said they provided training because of legislative requirements.

A similar survey in Scotland, the Scottish Employers Skills Survey, found that in 2006, 57 per cent of employees who were identified by employers as having a skills gap lacked adequate planning and organising skills, and 56 per cent lacked customer handling skills. More than one-half (51 per cent) of these employees were identified as having gaps in problem solving skills and the same proportion in team working skills.

Educational attainment

Assessment at Key Stages in England is an essential component of the National Curriculum (see Appendix, Part 3: The National Curriculum). Assessment is done through both teacher assessment and tests which measure pupils' attainment against the levels set by the National Curriculum. Wales, Scotland and Northern Ireland each have their own guidelines for assessing the curriculum.

Between 1998 and 2008, although the proportion of girls reaching the required standard in Key Stage 1 (teacher assessment), in England was generally higher than that for boys, there were improvements in the performance of both sexes (Table 3.14). At Key Stage 1, the proportion of boys who reached the required standard in reading by teacher assessment increased by 4 percentage points over the period to 80 per cent and for writing, there was an increase of 2 percentage points to 75 per cent. For girls, the proportions also increased between 1998 and 2008 by 3 percentage points for reading (to 88 per cent) and 2 percentage points for writing (to 86 per cent).

In tests at Key Stages 2 and 3 there were also some differences in the performance of boys when compared with girls. In 1998, 57 per cent of boys reached or exceeded the expected standard in English tests at Key Stage 2, compared with 73 per cent of girls. Boys and girls performed about the same in both mathematics (59 per cent of boys compared with 58 per cent of girls) and science (70 per cent compared with 69 per cent). By 2008, boys continued to perform less well than girls in English tests (76 per cent compared with 85 per cent). Science rates had risen to 87 per cent for boys and 89 per cent for girls, and for mathematics had risen to 79 per cent for boys compared with 78 per cent for girls. There is a similar picture for Key Stage 3 in all three assessed subjects,

Table 3.14

Pupils reaching or exceeding expected standards:[1] by Key Stage and sex

England				Percentages
	1998		2008	
	Boys	Girls	Boys	Girls
Key Stage 1[2]				
English				
Reading	76	85	80	88
Writing	73	84	75	86
Mathematics	83	87	88	91
Science	85	87	87	90
Key Stage 2[3]				
English	57	73	76	85
Mathematics	59	58	79	78
Science	70	69	87	89
Key Stage 3[4]				
English	56	73	66	80
Mathematics	60	59	76	77
Science	57	55	72	71

1 See Appendix, Part 3: The National Curriculum.
2 Pupils achieving level 2 or above through teacher assessment at Key Stage 1.
3 Pupils achieving level 4 or above through tests at Key Stage 2.
4 Pupils achieving level 5 or above through tests at Key Stage 3.

Source: Department for Children, Schools and Families

although the proportions who achieved the expected standard in tests at this stage was generally lower than at Key Stage 2.

There is a difference in overall performance between boys and girls at GCSE level. In 2006/07, 66 per cent of girls in the UK in their last year of compulsory education achieved five or more GCSEs at grades A* to C or equivalent, compared with 57 per cent of boys. This was an increase for both sexes since 1996/97, when the figures were 41 per cent and 51 per cent respectively. Overall, 61 per cent of pupils achieved five or more GCSEs at grades A* to C or equivalent in 2006/07 compared with 46 per cent in 1996/97.

The GCSE attainment levels of pupils from all ethnic groups have improved in recent years. However, differences in educational attainment exist between ethnic groups. According to data from the Longitudinal Study of Young People in England and the Youth Cohort Study (YCS), those from the Other Asian group (which includes Chinese pupils) and the Indian group were the most likely of all ethnic groups in England to achieve five or more GCSE grades A* to C or equivalent in 2006, at 77 per cent and 72 per cent respectively

Figure 3.15

Attainment of five or more GCSE grades A* to C or equivalent:[1] by ethnic group[2]

England

Percentages

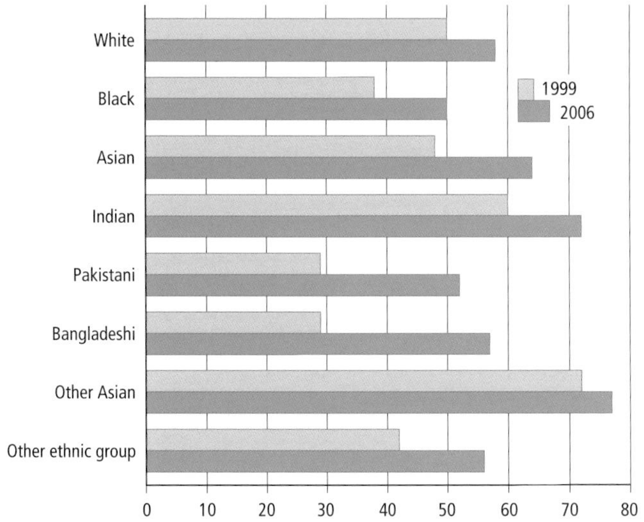

(chart: horizontal bar chart showing attainment by ethnic group for 1999 and 2006: White, Black, Asian, Indian, Pakistani, Bangladeshi, Other Asian, Other ethnic group; x-axis 0 to 80)

1   Includes General National Vocational Qualifications (GNVQ) achieved in
    Year 11. See Appendix, Part 3: Qualifications.
2   Pupils from each ethnic group achieving these grades, as a proportion
    of all pupils within that group, in their last year of compulsory
    education. See Appendix, Part 1: Classification of ethnic groups, and
    Part 3: Stages of education.

_Source: Longitudinal Study of Young People in England, and Youth Cohort
Study, from the Department for Children, Schools and Families_

(Figure 3.15). Pupils from the Pakistani and Bangladeshi ethnic groups were least likely of the Asian ethnic groups to achieve this, at 52 per cent and 57 per cent respectively. However, these two groups showed the largest improvement in attainment between 1999 and 2006 with the proportions of pupils achieving five or more GCSEs at these grades increasing by 28 percentage points for Bangladeshis and 22 percentage points for Pakistanis. This increase has brought the attainment of pupils from Bangladeshi and Pakistani backgrounds to similar levels of both White (58 per cent) and Black (50 per cent) pupils, whose increase was less marked over the same period (8 percentage points for White pupils and 11 percentage points for Black pupils).

The GCSE attainment of pupils can also vary according to the socio-economic status of parents (see Appendix, Part 3: National Statistics Socio-economic Classification (NS-SEC)). In England, 81 per cent of pupils whose parents were in higher professional occupations achieved five or more GCSE grades A* to C or equivalent in 2006. The proportion of pupils whose parents were in routine occupations achieving the same level was far lower, at 42 per cent. However, this represented an increase of 16 percentage points since 1999 for this group, compared with an increase of 6 percentage points for pupils

Figure 3.16

Academic attainment: by truancy,[1] 2006

England

Percentages

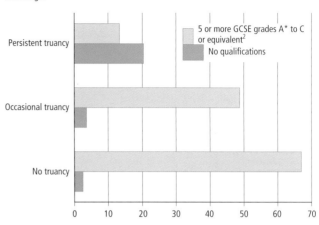

1   Truancy in Year 11. See Appendix, Part 3: Stages of education.
2   Includes General National Vocational Qualifications (GNVQ) achieved in
    Year 11. See Appendix, Part 3: Qualifications.

_Source: Longitudinal Study of Young People in England, and Youth Cohort
Study, from the Department for Children, Schools and Families_

with parents in higher professional occupations. The educational attainment of parents can also influence the attainment of their children; 83 per cent of young people with at least one parent qualified to degree level achieved five or more GCSE grades A* to C, as did 67 per cent with at least one parent whose highest qualification was a GCE A level. This compared with 46 per cent of young people with parents whose highest qualification was below GCE A level (this figure includes a small number of cases where highest qualification of parent was not known).

Absence from school through truancy is strongly associated with poor educational attainment. In 2006, persistent truants in Year 11 were around five times less likely than those who did not truant to gain five or more GCSEs grades A* to C, 13 per cent compared with 67 per cent (Figure 3.16). One-fifth (20 per cent) of pupils who were persistent truants gained no qualifications in 2006 compared with 3 per cent who did not truant.

GCE A level examinations are usually taken after two years post-GCSE study in a school sixth form, sixth-form college or further education college by those who stay in education full time beyond the age of 16. The proportion of young people aged 17 at the start of the academic year in the UK who gained two or more GCE A levels (or equivalent) by the end of the academic year increased from 19 per cent in 1990/91 to 37 per cent in 2005/06. In 2006/07 this figure rose sharply to 45 per cent although this is because the figure for England included a wider range of qualifications equivalent to GCE A level than the previous time series. Although this

Figure 3.17

Achievement of two or more GCE A levels[1] or equivalent: by sex[2]

United Kingdom

Percentages

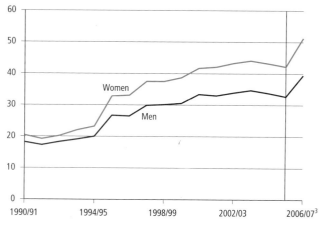

1 See Appendix, Part 3: Qualifications.
2 Young people aged 17 at the start of the academic year as a proportion of the 17-year-old population.
3 Figures for England cover achievements in all level 3 qualifications approved under Section 96 of the *Learning and Skills Act (2000)*, therefore UK aggregates are not comparable with previous years.

Source: Department for Children, Schools and Families; Welsh Assembly Government; Scottish Government; Northern Ireland Department of Education

change produces a step in the trend, it does not change the picture when comparing attainment of young men and women. The proportion of young women in the UK who achieved two or more GCE A levels or equivalent increased from 20 per cent in 1990/91 to 42 per cent in 2005/06 and 51 per cent in 2006/07 (Figure 3.17). For young men, the proportion increased from 18 per cent to 33 per cent in 2005/06 and 40 per cent in 2006/07. Thus the performance gap between the sexes at this level increased from 2 percentage points in 1990/91 to 9 percentage points in 2005/06 and 12 percentage points in 2006/07.

In 2006/07 there were around 319,300 first degrees obtained by UK and overseas domiciled students at higher education institutions in the UK, including 291,400 classified degrees and 27,900 unclassified degrees (certain qualifications obtained at first degree level are not subject to classification, for example medical degrees). Of those classified first degrees, 13 per cent were graded first class and similar proportions of men (13 per cent) and women (12 per cent) achieved this level. A higher proportion of women than men achieved upper second class, 51 per cent compared with 44 per cent, while similar proportions of women and men achieved lower second class qualifications, at 31 per cent and 33 per cent respectively. A third class (or pass) qualification was achieved by 8 per cent of all first degree students.

An alternative, and increasingly additional, type of qualification to the more traditional academic qualifications are National Vocational Qualifications (NVQs) and Scottish Vocational Qualifications (SVQs), which are qualifications aimed at a particular occupation or group of occupations (see Appendix, Part 3: Qualifications). There has been an increase in the take-up of these qualifications since they were introduced in 1987, shown by the numbers awarded. In 2006/07, around 673,000 NVQs and SVQs were awarded in the UK compared with around 153,000 awarded in 1991/92. The majority (62 per cent) of NVQs and SVQs were at level 2 (equivalent to five GCSEs at grades A* to C) in 2006/07. Awards at this level have nearly doubled since 2001/02, from 231,000 to 415,000 (Figure 3.18). A further 25 per cent of awards were at level 3 (equivalent to two GCE A levels) and 5 per cent were at levels 4 and 5 (equivalent to first or higher degrees).

In 2006/07, 23 per cent of all NVQs and SVQs awarded in the UK were in health, public services and care, with 33 per cent of all level 3 NVQs and SVQs awarded in this sector subject area. The next most common sector subject areas were retail and commercial enterprise (20 per cent of all awards) and business, administration and law (16 per cent).

There are differences in the subjects studied by men and women in order to gain NVQ/SVQ qualifications. In 2006/07, 133,000 NVQ/SVQ awards in health, public services and care were made to women compared with 24,000 to men; in engineering and manufacturing technologies 82,000 awards were to men and 9,000 to women and in construction,

Figure 3.18

NVQ/SVQs awarded:[1] by level of qualification

United Kingdom

Thousands

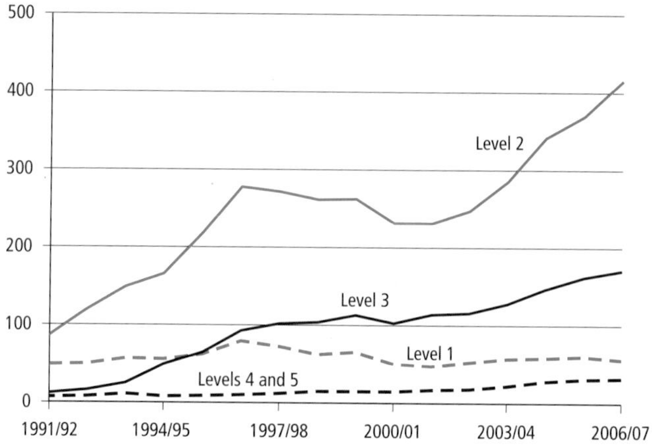

1 National Vocational Qualifications (NVQs) and Scottish Vocational Qualifications (SVQs). Data for 2000/01 are NVQ awards only. See Appendix, Part 3: Qualifications.

Source: Department for Children, Schools and Families

Table 3.19

Highest level of qualification: by marital status and presence of dependent children,[1] 2008[2]

United Kingdom   Percentages

	Degree or equivalent and higher	Higher education[3]	GCE A level or equivalent	GCSE grades A* to C or equivalent	Other qualifications	No qualifications
Mothers with dependent children	19	11	17	29	12	12
Married/cohabiting mothers	22	11	17	28	12	10
Lone mothers	10	9	17	32	14	18
Women without dependent children	19	10	14	20	14	22
Fathers with dependent children	23	9	25	19	15	10
Married/cohabiting fathers	23	9	25	19	15	10
Lone fathers	13	7	25	27	14	14
Men without dependent children	21	8	28	14	14	15
All parents with dependent children	21	10	20	24	14	11
Married/cohabiting parents	23	10	21	23	14	10
Lone parents	11	9	18	32	14	17
All people without dependent children	20	9	21	17	14	19

1 Children aged under 16 and those aged 16 to 18 who have never married and are in full-time education.
2 Data are at Q2 (April–June) and are not seasonally adjusted. People of working age (men aged 16 to 64 and women aged 16 to 59) or those in employment with qualifications. See Appendix, Part 4: Labour Force Survey.
3 Below degree level but including National Vocational Qualification (NVQ) level 4. See Appendix, Part 3: Qualifications.

Source: Labour Force Survey, Office for National Statistics

planning and the built environment 74,000 awards were made to men while less than 1,000 were made to women, see Chapter 4: Labour market, Table 4.9 for different occupational patterns between men and women.

The Labour Force Survey (LFS) provides statistical data on the highest qualifications that people hold. People of working-age (men aged 16 to 64 and women aged 16 to 59) in the UK are more likely to be educated to at least degree level than to be without formal qualifications. Figures for Q2 2008 show that 20 per cent of people held degrees or equivalent and higher compared with around 13 per cent of people with no qualifications. Differences emerge when attainment is analysed by sex and age, essentially reflecting differences between cohorts passing through a changing education and training scene. Among working-age women, those aged 50 and over (22 per cent in Q2 2008) were more likely than women in other age groups to hold no qualifications, followed by 16 to 19-year-olds (18 per cent). Among working-age men, 18 per cent aged 50 and over, and 19 per cent aged 16 to 19 held no qualifications; both higher proportions than men in other working-age groups. The high figures for 16 to 19-year-olds are largely accounted for by the fact that the majority of those who are 16 in Q2 will not have had their Year 11 examination results and therefore will not yet have the first set of qualifications counted in the LFS. When 16-year-olds are not

included in the calculation, the figure for the proportions who held no qualifications fell to 9 per cent for 17 to 19-year-old men and 7 per cent for women of the same age range.

An overall picture of the educational qualifications of adults within families in the UK in Q2 2008 is provided in Table 3.19. Parents who were married or cohabiting in Q2 2008 were more likely than lone parents to be educated to at least degree level or equivalent and higher (23 per cent compared with 11 per cent). Although lone parents (17 per cent) were also more likely than married or cohabiting parents (10 per cent) to have no qualifications, adults without dependent children were the most likely to be without qualifications (19 per cent). There were smaller differences between men and women than between married or cohabiting parents and lone parents in the proportions with a highest qualification of degree level or higher. More than one-fifth of married or cohabiting fathers (23 per cent) and mothers (22 per cent) were qualified to degree level or higher compared with 13 per cent of lone fathers and 10 per cent of lone mothers.

Educational resources

There are more female teachers than male teachers in all public sector schools in the UK. In the early to mid-1980s women accounted for around 60 per cent of teaching staff across

Figure 3.20

Full-time teachers:[1] by sex and type of school

United Kingdom
Thousands

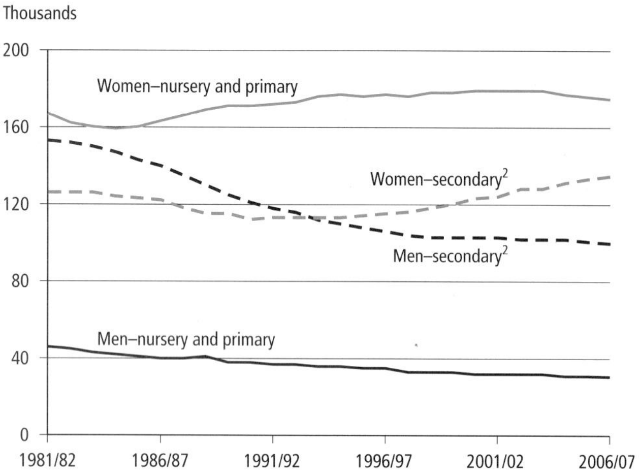

1 Qualified teachers in public sector mainstream schools.
2 From 1993/94 data exclude sixth-form colleges in England and Wales, which were reclassified as further education colleges on 1 April 1993.

Source: Department for Children, Schools and Families; Scottish Government; Northern Ireland Department of Education

nursery, primary and secondary schools. This increased to around 70 per cent in the late 1990s and remained at that level in 2006/07. Examining these data by school type there is a smaller difference between the sexes at secondary level than at nursery and primary level (Figure 3.20). Men accounted for around 55 per cent of teaching staff in secondary schools in the early 1980s. However, the proportion of male teachers in secondary schools gradually decreased from the 1980s to around 43 per cent in 2006/07, with female teachers accounting for 57 per cent of secondary staff. Female teachers accounted for between 78 and 82 per cent of teaching staff in nursery and primary schools in the 1980s and by 2006/07 had increased to 85 per cent.

The number of part-time teaching staff in nursery and primary schools in England rose by around 86 per cent from 14,800 in 1997 to 27,600 in 2008. In nursery and primary schools the proportion of teaching staff who worked part time increased over the period from 8 per cent to 14 per cent, while in secondary schools the proportion increased, although to a lesser extent, from 7 per cent to 10 per cent. As nursery and primary school teaching staff are more likely to be female than male, this may reflect that women are generally more likely than men to work part time (see Chapter 4: Labour market, Table 4.9).

Over the period 1997 to 2008, the pupil to teacher ratio in maintained nursery schools in England dropped from 18.9 pupils per teacher to 16.5, a fall of 13 per cent. Across maintained primary schools in England the ratio also dropped from 23.4 pupils per teacher to 21.6 in the same time period –

a fall of 8 per cent. In secondary schools there was a shallower fall, from 16.7 pupils per teacher in 1997 to 16.1 in 2008.

The number of support staff in maintained schools in England increased by 6 per cent from 239,600 to 253,900 between 2007 and 2008. These comprise teaching assistants, technicians and other support staff, but exclude administrative staff. Primary schools had the highest number, 141,000 (56 per cent of all support staff), followed by secondary schools with 81,100 (32 per cent). Special schools and pupil referral units accounted for 28,600 support staff, around 11 per cent of the total, with nursery schools employing the lowest number of support staff, at 3,200 (1 per cent).

Public expenditure on education in the UK as a proportion of gross domestic product (GDP), using the Classification of the

Table 3.21

Expenditure on education[1] as a percentage of GDP: EU comparison,[2] 2005

Percentages

	Primary and secondary education[3]	Higher education	All levels[4]
Denmark	4.5	1.7	7.4
Sweden	4.2	1.6	6.4
United Kingdom	4.6	1.3	6.2
Belgium	4.1	1.2	6.0
France	4.0	1.3	6.0
Finland	3.9	1.7	6.0
Poland	3.7	1.6	5.9
Portugal	3.8	1.4	5.7
Hungary	3.4	1.1	5.6
Austria	3.7	1.3	5.5
Germany	3.4	1.1	5.1
Netherlands	3.4	1.3	5.0
Italy	3.3	0.9	4.7
Ireland	3.4	1.2	4.6
Czech Republic	3.0	1.0	4.6
Spain	2.9	1.1	4.6
Slovakia	2.9	0.9	4.4
Greece	2.7	1.5	4.2
Luxembourg[5]	3.7	..	..

1 Public and private direct expenditure on institutions and public subsidies to students, for example for tuition fees and living costs.
2 Data for remaining EU-27 countries not available from source.
3 Includes post-secondary non-higher education.
4 Includes expenditure for early childhood education and other miscellaneous expenditure.
5 Public expenditure only.

Source: Organisation for Economic Co-operation and Development

Functions of Government (see Appendix, Part 3: Classification of the Functions of Government (COFOG)), fluctuated between 4.4 per cent in 1998/99 and 1999/2000 and 5.4 per cent in 2005/06 and 2007/08. As these data are for state-funded institutions only they differ from the European Union (EU) figures below, which also include private expenditure.

Total public and private education spending in the UK was relatively high compared with many EU member states. Of the 19 EU member states for which data were available on education expenditure as a proportion of GDP, Denmark was highest, at 7.4 per cent for all levels of education in 2005 (Table 3.21). Sweden was second, at 6.4 per cent, closely followed by the UK, at 6.2 per cent. The countries with the smallest spend per head on education as a proportion of GDP were Greece, at 4.2 per cent and Slovakia, slightly higher at 4.4 per cent. For primary, secondary and post-secondary non-higher education (for example further education colleges), the UK had the highest spend as a proportion of GDP in the EU, at 4.6 per cent.

3

Chapter 4

Labour market

- In the second quarter of 2008 (Q2 2008), 16.0 million men and 13.6 million women were in employment in the UK. (Table 4.2)

- Lone mothers in the UK with a child aged under five were less likely to be working than those who had a partner, 35 per cent compared with 63 per cent in Q2 2008. (Table 4.3)

- The gap in employment rates between working-age men and women in the UK was the smallest gap on record in Q2 2008, at 8 percentage points. In the period Q2 1992 to 2007 it varied between 9 and 11 percentage points. (Figure 4.5)

- In Q2 2008 almost one-fifth (18 per cent) of full-time employees in the UK usually worked more than 48 hours a week. (Table 4.12)

- The unemployment rate for working-age lone parents in the UK in Q2 2008 (12 per cent) was higher than the rate for married or cohabiting parents (3 per cent). (Table 4.17)

- In 2007, 1.041 million working days in the UK were lost because of labour disputes, only the third time since 1990 that days lost reached one million. (Figure 4.21)

DATA

Download data by clicking the online pdf

www.statistics.gov.uk/ socialtrends39

Although many people spend a large proportion of their lives in the labour force (see Glossary on page 61), this proportion is falling. Young people remain longer in education (see Chapter 3: Education and training) and older people spend more years in retirement as life expectancy rises (see Chapter 7: Health). Nevertheless, the labour force has grown as the population has increased. In Q2 2008 (see the Labour Force Survey (LFS) text box below), there were 31.2 million people in the UK labour force, approaching two in three (64 per cent) of the total adult population aged 16 and over of 49.1 million. The composition of the labour force has been changing: employment in service industries has been increasing while employment in manufacturing continues to fall. In recent years there has also been an increase in the number of non-UK born workers in the UK. There are differences in the employment patterns of men and women over their working lives, and between those who are unemployed and economically inactive.

Labour market profile

The labour market comprises three main groups: the employed, the unemployed (who together make up the economically active) and the economically inactive (see Glossary). This latter group consists of those people who are out of work, but who do not satisfy all of the International Labour Organisation criteria for unemployment because they either are not seeking work or are unavailable to start work. In the UK, those over state pension age (65 for men and 60 for women) make up the largest proportion of this group.

The number of people who are economically active is primarily determined by the size of the population: both these measures have increased since Labour Force Survey (LFS) records began in 1971. For example, the number of economically active people aged 16 and over in the UK increased by 5.6 million from 25.6 million in Q2 1971 to 31.2 million in Q2 2008, while the number of people aged 16 and over increased by 8.5 million

Labour Force Survey (LFS)

The LFS is the largest regular household survey in the UK and much of the labour market data published in this chapter are measured by the LFS. Calendar quarter 2 (Q2) data from the LFS refers to the months April to June in a given year. The earliest year for which LFS data are available is 1971 but only for limited time series. Where time series data are quoted in this chapter the earliest comparable year that is available is usually used. For more information on the LFS, including differences between calendar and seasonal quarters, see Appendix, Part 4: Labour Force Survey.

Figure 4.1

Economic activity and inactivity rates[1]

United Kingdom
Percentages

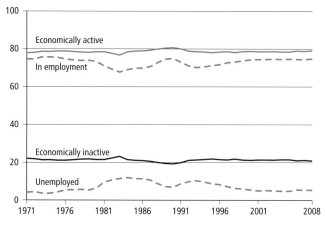

1 Data are at Q2 each year and are seasonally adjusted. Rates are expressed as a proportion of men aged 16 to 64 and women aged 16 to 59 with the exception of unemployment rates, which are expressed as a proportion of people aged 16 and over. See Appendix, Part 4: Labour Force Survey.

Source: Labour Force Survey, Office for National Statistics

from 40.6 million to 49.1 million. Among those of working age (see Glossary) the number of economically active people in the UK increased by 5.0 million from 24.8 million to 29.9 million over the period Q2 1971 to Q2 2008, while population levels for those of this age also increased by a similar amount. As a result the working-age economic activity rate has remained relatively stable, at 78 per cent in 1971 and 79 per cent in 2008, dipping slightly in 1983 at a time of economic downturn (77 per cent) and peaking in 1990 (81 per cent) (Figure 4.1).

As those in employment make up the majority of those who are economically active, the working-age employment rate between Q2 1971 and Q2 2008 followed a similar trend to the economic activity rate, but with more marked fluctuations according to the economic cycle. The proportion of the working-age population in the UK who were in employment (the employment rate) decreased from 76 per cent in the mid-1970s to a low of 68 per cent in Q2 1983. Since then employment rates have generally risen and, although there was a fall following the recession in the early 1990s, the employment rate in Q2 2008 was 75 per cent, the same as in Q2 1971. The unemployment rate (the proportion of the economically active who are unemployed) also reflects fluctuations associated with the economic cycle (see Figure 4.15).

People of working age who are economically inactive are neither in employment nor looking for work, but are a potential source of labour supply at some time in the future.

Table 4.2

Economic activity:[1] by employment status[2] and sex

United Kingdom   Millions

	1998			2008		
	Men	Women	All	Men	Women	All
Economically active						
In employment						
Full-time employees	11.0	6.2	17.3	11.7	7.3	19.1
Part-time employees	1.0	4.9	5.8	1.4	5.1	6.4
Self-employed	2.5	0.9	3.4	2.8	1.1	3.8
Others in employment[3]	0.1	0.1	0.3	0.1	0.1	0.2
All in employment	14.6	12.1	26.7	16.0	13.6	29.6
Unemployed	1.1	0.7	1.8	1.0	0.7	1.7
All economically active	15.6	12.9	28.5	16.9	14.3	31.2
Economically inactive	6.3	10.9	17.2	6.9	10.9	17.8
of which, working age[4]	2.9	4.8	7.7	3.2	4.7	7.9

1 Data are at Q2 each year and are seasonally adjusted. People aged 16 and over. See Appendix, Part 4: Labour Force Survey.
2 The Labour Force Survey asks people to classify themselves as either full time or part time, based on their own perceptions.
3 Those on government-supported training and employment programmes, and unpaid family workers.
4 Men aged 16 to 64 and women aged 16 to 59.

Source: Labour Force Survey, Office for National Statistics

In recent years there has been a growing policy focus on reducing economic inactivity, as well as unemployment, as a means of boosting economic performance. Nevertheless working-age economic inactivity rates have been relatively stable, ranging from 22 per cent in Q2 1971 to 21 per cent in Q2 2008 with a peak of 23 per cent in 1983 and a low of 19 per cent in 1990 (see also Figure 4.18).

In Q2 2008, 29.6 million people were in employment in the UK (Table 4.2). Comparing the labour market in Q2 2008 with ten years earlier, the number of people in employment has risen by 2.8 million. More people, especially women, are working, the total population aged 16 and over has also increased (by 3.4 million), and slightly fewer people are unemployed. The number of employees in full-time employment rose from 17.3 million in Q2 1998 to 19.1 million in Q2 2008. Of these, 11.7 million were men (an increase of 6 per cent since 1998) and 7.3 million were women (an increase of 18 per cent). The number of employees in part-time employment also increased from 5.8 million in Q2 1998 to 6.4 million in Q2 2008. Of these, 1.4 million were men (a 41 per cent increase on 1998) and 5.1 million were women (an increase of 4 per cent). Of the 3.8 million people who were self-employed in Q2 2008, the majority (73 per cent) were men, the same proportion as in 1998, when 3.4 million people

in the UK were self-employed. Over the last ten years the number of unemployed people in the UK fell from 1.8 million in Q2 1998 to 1.7 million in Q2 2008.

One of the themes in this chapter is the increased participation of women in the labour market. However, the presence of a dependent child in the family continues to have a major effect on the economic activity of women of working age (Table 4.3 overleaf). For both lone mothers and those with a partner, employment rates are lowest when they have a child aged under five. However, lone mothers with a child under five were less likely to be working than those who had a partner, 35 per cent compared with 63 per cent in Q2 2008. This differential decreases as the age of the youngest child increases, so that for mothers whose youngest dependent child is aged 16 to 18, 76 per cent of lone mothers worked in 2008, only 6 percentage points lower than for mothers with a partner (82 per cent). For women without dependent children a higher proportion of those who were married or cohabiting were working (76 per cent) than those who were not married or cohabiting (68 per cent).

Table 4.2 showed the increase in employment in the UK between 1998 and 2008 and one of the outcomes of this has been an increase in the number of working households

Table 4.3

Economic activity status of women:[1] by marital status and age of youngest dependent child, 2008

United Kingdom

Percentages

	Age of youngest dependent child				No dependent children[3]	All women
	Under 5	5–10	11–15	16–18[2]		
Not married/cohabiting[4]						
In employment	35	59	70	76	68	63
Unemployed	7	8	6	6	7	8
Economically inactive	58	34	24	17	27	31
All (=100%) (millions)	0.6	0.5	0.4	0.2	3.1	4.8
Married/cohabiting						
In employment	63	75	81	82	76	74
Unemployed	3	2	1	1	4	3
Economically inactive	34	23	18	17	21	23
All (=100%) (millions)	2.3	1.5	1.2	0.5	7.0	12.5

1 Data are at Q2 and are not seasonally adjusted. Aged 16 to 59. See Appendix, Part 4: Labour Force Survey.
2 Children aged 16 to 18 who have never been married and are in full-time education.
3 Includes women without dependent children and those with non-dependent children only.
4 Includes single, widowed, separated or divorced.

Source: Labour Force Survey, Office for National Statistics

(see Glossary). In Q2 2008, there were 11.1 million working households, compared with 10.0 million in Q2 1998. However, because there was also an increase in the total number of working-age households over the period, the proportion of all working-age households that were working households remained relatively stable over the period, at between 55 and 58 per cent. The converse of a working household is a workless household (see Glossary). In Q2 2008, there were 3.1 million workless households in the UK, representing 16 per cent of total working-age households, a slight decrease from 3.2 million ten years earlier.

Lone parents with dependent children were more likely than working-age people in any other household type to be living in a workless household (35 per cent). It is worth noting that because lone parent households will usually contain only one person of working age, the economic activity status of these households will usually be either workless or working and will be far less likely to contain both working and workless members. Table 4.4 shows the variations in the proportions of people in working and workless working-age households across the regions of England and countries of the UK in Q2 2008. The South West and the South East of England had the highest proportions of people in working households, both at 60 per cent. Scotland had a rate of 59 per cent, Wales had 52 per cent and Northern Ireland had the lowest proportion of

people living in working households (45 per cent). The highest proportions of people living in workless households were in Inner London (19 per cent) and the North East (16 per cent).

Data from the 2007 Annual Population Survey (see Appendix, Part 4: Annual Population Survey) household datasets shows the variations in the proportion of workless households in local areas within the countries and regions of Great Britain in 2007. This shows that there can be more variation within regions and countries than there is between them. For example, some of the highest proportions of workless households were in local authorities in the North West of England – Barrow-in-Furness (28 per cent), Liverpool (27 per cent), and Knowsley (27 per cent). However Trafford, also in the North West, had a relatively low proportion of workless households (11 per cent). The local authority with the highest overall proportion of workless households in Great Britain was Glasgow City in Scotland (29 per cent), followed by Barrow-in-Furness. In Wales the highest rate was in Merthyr Tydfil (26 per cent).

Employment

Although Figure 4.1 showed stability in the overall employment rate between 1971 and 2008, trends for men and women converged over the period (Figure 4.5). The employment rate of working-age men fell from 92 per cent in Q2 1971 to 79 per cent in Q2 2008, while the rate for

Table 4.4

People[1] in working-age households:[2] by region and household economic status, 2008[3]

United Kingdom   Percentages

	Working households	Households containing both working and workless members	Workless households
United Kingdom	55.5	33.0	11.5
England	55.7	32.9	11.4
North East	51.6	32.3	16.1
North West	54.2	32.0	13.8
Yorkshire and the Humber	56.1	31.3	12.6
East Midlands	56.8	33.5	9.7
West Midlands	52.7	34.2	13.1
East	58.8	32.2	9.0
London	49.3	37.0	13.7
Inner London	49.5	32.0	18.5
Outer London	49.1	40.5	10.4
South East	60.2	32.1	7.6
South West	60.3	30.3	9.5
Wales	52.5	35.0	12.5
Scotland	59.3	29.2	11.6
Northern Ireland	45.3	43.1	11.6

1 Men aged 16 to 64 and women aged 16 to 59 where economic activity status was known.
2 A working-age household is a household that includes at least one person of working age.
3 Data are at Q2 and are not seasonally adjusted. See Appendix, Part 4: Labour Force Survey.

Source: Labour Force Survey, Office for National Statistics

working-age women rose from 56 per cent to 70 per cent over the same period.

This convergence largely took place in the 1970s and 1980s. Between Q2 1971 and Q2 1993 the gap in employment rates between men and women fell from 35 percentage points to 10 percentage points as the rate for men fell to 75 per cent and the rate for women rose to 65 per cent. Since then, the trend towards convergence has slowed. The gap in employment rates between men and women was between 9 and 11 percentage points in the period Q2 1992 to 2007. However, in Q2 2008 it was 8 percentage points – the smallest gap on record.

For both sexes there were fluctuations in employment rates between 1971 and 2008 around these general trends. For example, following the recession in the early 1990s employment rates for both sexes fell. For men, the rate fell to 75 per cent in 1993, the lowest since LFS records began in

Figure 4.5

Employment rates:[1] by sex

United Kingdom
Percentages

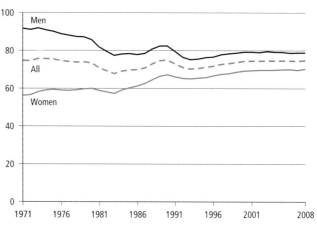

1 Data are at Q2 each year and are seasonally adjusted. Men aged 16 to 64 and women aged 16 to 59. See Appendix, Part 4: Labour Force Survey.

Source: Labour Force Survey, Office for National Statistics

1971. In the late 1990s employment rates for both working-age men and women increased and since the turn of the century they have been steady at around 79 per cent for men and 70 per cent for women.

Table 4.3 showed the overall economic activity status of working-age women in the UK according to whether they had dependent children. Table 4.6 overleaf focuses on employment rates and shows the variation in employment rates of working-age men and women who are parents with dependent children, compared with those without dependent children. Note that this latter group includes parents with non-dependent children and people who do not have children. The Q2 2008 figures show there are clear differences in employment rates between parents and people without dependent children, between mothers and fathers, and between couple parents and lone parents. Working-age mothers in the UK with dependent children were less likely to be in employment than working-age women without dependent children (68 per cent compared with 73 per cent). For men the opposite was true. Working-age fathers with dependent children were more likely to be in employment than working-age men without dependent children (90 per cent compared with 74 per cent). This pattern was true of all age groups with the exception of 50 to 59-year-old women and was most marked in the 16 to 24 age group.

Fathers have higher employment rates than mothers across all age groups, 90 per cent overall compared with 68 per cent in Q2 2008. Couple parents have higher employment rates than lone parents, 81 per cent compared with 56 per cent. Lone

Table 4.6

Employment rates for working-age people[1] with and without dependent children:[2] by age and sex, 2008[3]

United Kingdom

Percentages

	16–24	25–34	35–49	50–59/64	All
Women with dependent children	34	61	74	74	68
Married/cohabiting mothers	41	65	76	76	72
Lone mothers	25	49	65	65	56
Women without dependent children	59	89	83	70	73
Men with dependent children	68	90	92	85	90
Married/cohabiting fathers	69	91	93	85	91
Lone fathers	57	44	67	66	64
Men without dependent children	56	88	84	71	74
All parents with dependent children	42	72	82	81	78
Married/cohabiting parents	51	76	85	82	81
Lone parents	26	48	66	66	56
All people without dependent children	58	88	83	71	73

1 Men aged 16 to 64 and women aged 16 to 59. Excludes people with unknown employment status.
2 Children aged under 16 and those aged 16 to 18 who have never been married and are in full-time education.
3 Data are at Q2 and are not seasonally adjusted. See Appendix, Part 4: Labour Force Survey.

Source: Labour Force Survey, Office for National Statistics

fathers have higher employment rates than lone mothers, 64 per cent compared with 56 per cent.

Although employment rates for lone parents have generally increased in recent years, from 46 per cent in Q2 1998 to 57 per cent in Q2 2007, there was a slight fall to 56 per cent in the 12 months to Q2 2008. In comparison the employment rate for married or cohabiting mothers was 72 per cent in Q2 2008, up by 3 percentage points from 1998.

In recent years the employment rate of people aged 50 and over has increased, from 33 per cent in Q2 1997 to 39 per cent in Q2 2008 (Figure 4.7). The employment rates for both men and women in this age group increased. The proportion of men aged 50 and over in employment rose from 41 per cent to 46 per cent between 1997 and 2008, while the employment rate for women aged 50 and over rose from 26 per cent to 32 per cent. The main increases occurred among those approaching state pension age (65 for men and 60 for women). For example, between Q2 1997 and Q2 2008 the employment rate among men aged 60 to 64 increased by 11 percentage points to 58 per cent and for women aged 55 to 59 the rate went up by 13 percentage points to 64 per cent. This compares with an overall increase of 2 percentage points among those aged 65 and over. For information on the contribution of earnings to pensioners' incomes see Chapter 5: Income and wealth.

Employment rates differ across the UK. The Annual Population Survey (see Appendix, Part 4: Annual Population Survey) showed that in 2007 employment rates were highest in Scotland (76 per cent), followed by England (74 per cent), Wales (71 per cent) and Northern Ireland (70 per cent). The

Figure 4.7

Employment rates[1] of people aged 50 and over[2]

United Kingdom

Percentages

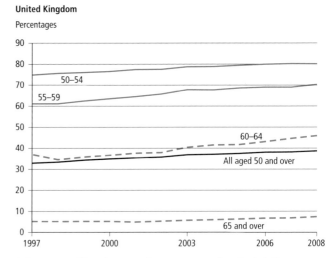

1 Data are at Q2 each year and are not seasonally adjusted. The percentage of the age bands shown that are in employment. See Appendix, Part 4: Labour Force Survey.
2 State pension age is currently 60 for women and 65 for men.

Source: Labour Force Survey, Office for National Statistics

English region with the highest working-age employment rate was the South East (78 per cent) and the lowest was London (70 per cent). These data are at an individual level and differ from those working household data presented in Table 4.4, which measure the combined labour market status of households.

Differences in employment rates in local areas within regions of England or countries of Great Britain were greater than the differences between regions and countries. The greatest contrast between employment rates in local authorities in 2007 was in London. This region contains the London Borough of Tower Hamlets, which has the lowest working-age employment rate in Great Britain (57 per cent), and the City of London, with the highest working-age employment rate (89 per cent) although the estimate for the City of London is based on a small number of respondents. Excluding the City of London, the difference between the highest and lowest working-age employment rates in London was 25 percentage points, with the London Borough of Bromley having the highest working-age employment rate (82 per cent).

Wales had the narrowest spread of working-age employment rates, with 14 percentage points between Monmouthshire (77 per cent) and Ceredigion (63 per cent). This was closely followed by the North East of England, with 15 percentage points between Derwentside (81 per cent) and Easington (66 per cent). The local authority with the highest employment rate in Great Britain outside London was Test Valley, Hampshire, with a rate of 88 per cent.

People living in the UK who were born overseas are an increasing feature of the labour market – in Q2 2008 there were 3.7 million non-UK born workers in the UK, up from 2.0 million in Q2 1997. The significant expansion to the European Union (EU) in 2004 is the most recognisable factor in this trend because it can be clearly defined in time. In May 2004, ten states joined the existing 15 member states to create an EU-25. However, as two of the accession countries, Cyprus and Malta, already had close links with the UK, having only gained independence from the UK in 1960 and 1964 respectively, for the purpose of the analysis below a group of eight accession countries (A8) is used (see Appendix, Part 4: Accession to the European Union (EU)). Also, in these analyses the UK is shown separately from the EU-15 and a notional EU-14 group has been created for the existing countries apart from the UK.

Although the highest Q2 2008 working-age employment rates of the non-UK born workforce were for those born in South Africa (86 per cent), Australia and New Zealand combined (84 per cent) and the A8 countries (84 per cent), the largest

Figure 4.8

Employment rates:[1] by country of birth

United Kingdom
Percentages

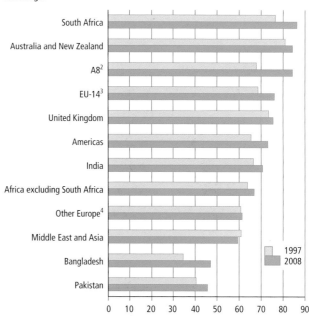

1 Data are Q2 each year and are not seasonally adjusted. Men aged 16 to 64 and women aged 16 to 59. Data excludes those who did not state their country of birth. See Appendix, Part 4: Labour Force Survey, and Employment status by country of birth.
2 Czech Republic, Estonia, Hungary, Latvia, Lithuania, Poland, Slovakia and Slovenia. See Appendix, Part 4: Accession to the European Union (EU).
3 The EU-15 states excluding the United Kingdom.
4 European countries not in the European Union, plus Cyprus, Malta, Bulgaria and Romania.

Source: Labour Force Survey, Office for National Statistics

increase between 1997 and 2008 has been for those born in the A8 countries. In Q2 1997 the working-age employment rate for those born in the A8 was 68 per cent, by Q2 2008 it had increased to 84 per cent (Figure 4.8). This increase placed the A8 employment rate 9 percentage points higher than the equivalent rate for the UK working-age population. The lowest rates were for people born in Pakistan and Bangladesh, although these rates also increased over the same period.

The employment rate of the UK born working-age population in Q2 1997 was higher than the rate for the non-UK born population overall (73 per cent and 63 per cent respectively). However, the increase in the rates among those born in the A8 countries, together with the increase in the employment rates for people born in other countries such as Pakistan and Bangladesh, meant that by Q2 2008 the gap in employment rates between those born in the UK (75 per cent) and those born overseas (69 per cent) had closed to 6 percentage points.

When interpreting LFS results, users should bear in mind that the survey is not designed to cover everyone who is present in the UK. For example people living in communal establishments,

Table 4.9

All in employment: by sex, type of employment[1] and occupation, 2008[2]

United Kingdom

Percentages

	Men			Women		
	Full time	Part time	All (=100%) (millions)	Full time	Part time	All (=100%) (millions)
Managers and senior officials	96	4	3.0	81	19	1.6
Professional	91	9	2.2	72	28	1.6
Associate professional and technical	91	9	2.1	68	32	2.2
Administrative and secretarial	85	15	0.7	58	42	2.6
Skilled trades	95	5	3.0	57	43	0.2
Personal service	81	19	0.4	53	47	2.0
Sales and customer service	60	40	0.7	35	65	1.5
Process, plant and machine operatives	92	8	1.8	75	25	0.3
Elementary	74	26	1.9	31	69	1.5
All occupations	89	11	15.8	58	42	13.5

1 The Labour Force Survey asks people to classify themselves as either full time or part time, based on their own perceptions. Data exclude those whose type of employment, or occupation, was not known. See Appendix, Part 4: Standard Occupational Classification 2000 (SOC2000).
2 Data are at Q2 and are not seasonally adjusted. People aged 16 and over. See Appendix, Part 4: Labour Force Survey.

Source: Labour Force Survey, Office for National Statistics

apart from those living in National Health Service (NHS) accommodation and students living in halls of residence who have a UK-resident parent, are not surveyed in the LFS and thus not included in LFS household population estimates. Another factor to consider is that until December 2007, to be included in the LFS, a respondent had to be resident in the UK for at least six months. This restriction was removed at the end of 2007. See Appendix, Part 4: Employment status by country of birth.

Patterns of employment

In Q2 2008, 16 per cent of people in employment in the UK were managers or senior officials – the largest of nine occupational groups – followed by 15 per cent who were employed in the group of associate professional and technical occupations, such as nurses, financial advisers and IT technicians (see Appendix, Part 4: Standard Occupational Classification 2000 (SOC2000)). Process, plant and machine operatives were the least common occupation overall (7 per cent of people in employment) followed by sales and customer service (8 per cent).

Men and women follow a different pattern of occupations. In Q2 2008 men were most likely to be employed as managers or senior officials, or in skilled trades (each 19 per cent), whereas women were most likely to be employed in administrative or secretarial occupations (19 per cent). Occupations least likely to be performed by men were those classified as personal service, for example, hairdressers and child care assistants (3 per cent).

For women the least likely occupation to be followed were skilled trades, and process, plant and machine operatives (each 2 per cent).

Table 4.9 provides data on whether people in employment in different occupations work full or part time (in the Labour Force Survey (LFS) people are asked to classify themselves as either full time or part time, based on their own perceptions). People in employment as managers or senior officials were most likely to work full time for both men (96 per cent) and women (81 per cent) while the occupations most likely to be followed on a part-time basis among men were sales and customer service (40 per cent) and, among women, elementary occupations such as catering assistants, bar staff and shelf fillers (69 per cent).

In Q2 2008 the White Irish group had the highest proportion of people in employment working in managerial and senior official occupations (21 per cent), exceeding the proportion of those from the White British (16 per cent) and Other Asian (16 per cent) groups (Figure 4.10). The groups with the lowest proportions employed in these occupations were the Black African (8 per cent), followed by Black Caribbean and Other Black groups (10 per cent each). Those from the Other Black group (6 per cent) and the White Irish group (7 per cent) had the lowest proportions of people in employment working in elementary occupations whereas the highest proportions were Black Africans (19 per cent) and Other Whites (18 per cent). See Appendix, Part 1: Classification of ethnic groups.

Figure 4.10

Managers and senior officials in employment:[1] by ethnic group, 2008[2]

United Kingdom
Percentages

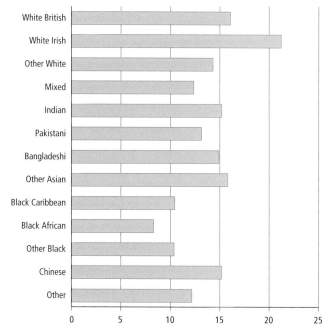

1 As a proportion of all in employment in each ethnic group. People aged 16 and over. See Appendix, Part 1: Classification of ethnic groups.
2 Data are at Q2 and are not seasonally adjusted. See Appendix, Part 4: Labour Force Survey, and Standard Occupational Classification 2000 (SOC2000).

Source: Labour Force Survey, Office for National Statistics

A different pattern emerges from the distribution of employment by ethnicity across industries (See Appendix, Part 4: Standard Industrial Classification 2003) rather than by occupation. In Q2 2008, the ethnic groups with the highest proportion of people in employment working in the finance and business services sector were Chinese (27 per cent), Black Africans (24 per cent), followed by Other Black and Indians (both at 23 per cent). Other White had the highest proportion of people working in the manufacturing sector at 14 per cent, followed by White British at 12 per cent. Bangladeshis had the highest proportion of people in employment working in the distribution, hotels and restaurant sector at 44 per cent, followed by Other Black at 36 per cent and Chinese at 32 per cent. The ethnic group with the lowest proportion in this sector were White Irish at 11 per cent.

During the last 30 years the UK economy has experienced a structural change with a decline in the manufacturing sector and an increase in service industries (Figure 4.11). Jobs in the service industries increased by 52 per cent, from 14.9 million in June 1978 (when the series began) to 22.6 million in June 2008, while those in manufacturing have fallen by

58 per cent from 6.9 million to 2.9 million. Virtually all the increase in women's labour market participation has been through taking up jobs in the service sector. In 1978 there were fewer jobs done by women (10.3 million) than by men (14.0 million). However, by 2008 the number of jobs done by women and men were both around 13.6 million. Note that these data are based on jobs rather than people – one person may have more than one job, and jobs may vary in the number of hours of work they involve.

The largest increase in both male and female employee jobs has been in financial and business services, which accounted for about one in ten employee jobs in 1978 compared with one in five employee jobs in 2008.

Another important distinction in the analysis of employment is between private and public sector employment (for example central government, local government and public corporations). The public sector employment series, which uses both LFS employment estimates for the whole economy and the public sector employment estimates, showed that in Q2 2008, 5.8 million people worked in the public sector, which accounted for 19.5 per cent of all people in employment in the UK. The most recent peak for public sector employment, using Q2 data, was in 2005 when 5.9 million people worked in the public sector accounting for 20.3 per cent of those in employment.

As Table 4.2 showed, there were 19.1 million full-time and 6.4 million part-time employees in the UK in Q2 2008. However, to distinguish only between full-time and part-time

Figure 4.11

Employee jobs:[1] by sex and industry

United Kingdom
Millions

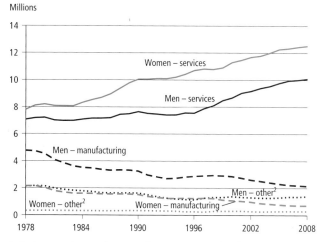

1 Data are at June each year and are not seasonally adjusted.
2 Includes agriculture, construction, energy and water. See Appendix, Part 4: Standard Industrial Classification 2003.

Source: Short-Term Employment Surveys, Office for National Statistics

Table 4.12

Employees who usually worked more than 48 hours a week:[1] by sex and occupation, 2008[2]

United Kingdom   Percentages

	Men	Women	All employees
Managers and senior officials	34	19	29
Professional	25	25	25
Associate professional and technical	18	8	13
Administrative and secretarial	7	2	4
Skilled trades	19	6	18
Personal service	13	6	8
Sales and customer service	12	4	7
Process, plant and machine operatives	26	8	24
Elementary	16	6	13
All occupations	22	10	18

1 Full-time employees aged 16 and over. Time rounded to the nearest hour respondents worked on their main job. Includes regular paid and unpaid overtime. Excludes employees who did not state their usual hours and those whose occupation was not known.
2 Data are at Q2 and are not seasonally adjusted. See Appendix, Part 4: Labour Force Survey, and Standard Occupational Classification 2000 (SOC2000).

Source: Labour Force Survey, Office for National Statistics

masks a wide range of usual working hours. The 1998 Working Time Regulations implemented the EU Working Time Directive on working time in the UK. The regulations apply to full-time, part-time and temporary workers and provide for a maximum working week of 48 hours (on average over a 17-week period), although individual workers can choose to work longer hours. In Q2 2008 almost one-fifth (18 per cent) of full-time employees in the UK usually worked more than 48 hours a week (Table 4.12). A higher proportion of male employees (22 per cent) than female (10 per cent) usually worked these longer hours, reflecting the different patterns of occupations between the sexes. The occupational group most likely to work more than 48 hours a week were managers and senior officials (29 per cent), whereas those who worked in administrative and secretarial jobs were least likely (4 per cent). Although men were more likely than women to usually work more than 48 hours in most occupational groups, the exception were those working in professional occupations – in Q2 2008 the same proportion of professional women as professional men usually worked these longer hours (25 per cent).

The opportunity to work flexible hours can help people to balance home and work responsibilities. Legislation in the UK provides parents and carers (under certain criteria) with the right to request a flexible work pattern. More than one-fifth of

full-time employees and more than one-quarter of part-time employees had some form of flexible working arrangement in Q2 2008 (Table 4.13). The most common form for full-time employees of both sexes was flexible working hours. This was also the most common arrangement among men who worked part time and second most common for women, with term-time working the most popular option for part-time female employees.

In 2007 the Third Work-Life Balance Employer Survey asked employers about various aspects of work-life balance. While more than nine in ten employers agreed with the statement 'People work best when they can balance their work and other aspects of their lives', one in three agreed with the statement 'It is not the employer's responsibility to help people balance their work with other aspects of their lives'.

The same survey also created an overall measure of employers' attitudes towards work-life balance by assigning scores to their responses to the various questions. These scores represented

Table 4.13

Employees with flexible working patterns:[1] by sex and type of employment,[2] 2008[3]

United Kingdom   Percentages

	Men	Women	All employees
Full-time employees			
Flexible working hours	10.4	14.7	12.0
Annualised working hours[4]	4.5	4.9	4.6
Four and a half day week	1.2	0.8	1.1
Term-time working	1.3	6.2	3.2
Nine day fortnight	0.5	0.4	0.4
Any flexible working pattern[5]	18.3	27.7	21.9
Part-time employees			
Flexible working hours	7.7	10.0	9.5
Annualised working hours[4]	3.1	4.6	4.3
Term-time working	4.1	11.5	9.9
Job sharing	1.2	3.1	2.7
Any flexible working pattern[5]	18.1	30.1	27.6

1 Percentages are based on totals that exclude people who did not state whether or not they had a flexible working arrangement. Respondents could give more than one answer. People aged 16 and over.
2 The Labour Force Survey asks people to classify themselves as either full time or part time, based on their own perceptions.
3 Data are at Q2 and are not seasonally adjusted. See Appendix, Part 4: Labour Force Survey.
4 The number of hours an employee has to work are calculated over a full year allowing for longer hours to be worked over certain periods of the year and shorter hours at others.
5 Includes other categories of flexible working not separately identified.

Source: Labour Force Survey, Office for National Statistics

negative and positive attitudes to work-life balance. This research suggested that overall attitudes towards work-life balance were strongly associated with the number of existing flexible working practices that were available in the workplace. Employers at workplaces with a high number of flexible working practices tended to be more positive about work-life balance than those with few policies or none at all. More than six in ten (63 per cent) employers with five or six flexible working practices available were positive about work-life balance overall compared with 13 per cent that operated no flexible working practices. The association may indicate that employers with positive attitudes towards work-life balance seek to bring in more flexible working practices. Conversely, it may also indicate that by putting in place flexible working practices, employers become aware of potential benefits and are therefore more positive about work-life balance.

In 2007 the British Social Attitudes Survey asked those adults who were in paid work their main reason for working. The most common reason cited for working, mentioned by one-half of respondents, was for money to pay for basic essentials such as food, rent or mortgage and this was cited by a greater proportion of men (57 per cent) than women (42 per cent) (Table 4.14). However, more than twice the proportion of women (17 per cent) than men (8 per cent) said their main reason for working was to either earn money of

their own, or to earn money to buy extras that were considered by respondents not to be basic essentials. A higher proportion of women cited enjoyment of work as the main reason (19 per cent) compared with men (13 per cent).

The reasons for working also varied by age. For example, while similar proportions of those aged 18 to 24 and those aged 55 to 64 said their main reason for working was to pay for basic essentials (around 45 per cent), a higher proportion of the younger age group compared with the older group said they worked mainly to either earn money of their own, or to earn money to buy extras (21 per cent compared with 11 per cent). Those aged 55 to 64 were more likely than those aged 18 to 24 to say enjoyment was their main reason (22 per cent compared with 7 per cent).

Dissatisfaction with working hours is one reason why an employed person might look for another job. In the LFS, respondents who say they are looking for another job are asked their reasons for doing so. In Q2 2008, 6 per cent of both male and female full-time employees in the UK were looking for a new job. Unsatisfactory pay in their current job was the trigger for 30 per cent of men and 24 per cent of women. Another trigger was job insecurity, with 13 per cent of male employees and 16 per cent of females looking for a new job because they thought that their present job might come to an end. Other reasons included unsatisfactory journey to work (8 per cent of employees looking for a new job) and wanting to work shorter hours (6 per cent).

Table 4.14

Main reason for working:[1] by sex, 2007

Great Britain			Percentages
	Men	Women	All
Need money for basic essentials such as food, rent or mortgage	57	42	50
I enjoy working	13	19	16
Working is the normal thing to do	12	9	11
To follow my career	7	8	7
To earn money of my own	5	9	7
To earn money to buy extras	3	8	6
For the company of other people	1	2	1
For a change from my children or housework	-	1	1
Other	2	2	2

1 Respondents aged 18 and over who were in paid work were shown a card of statements and asked 'Which ones best describe your own reasons for working at present?' Respondents who mentioned more than one reason were then asked 'And which one of these would you say is your main reason for working?' Excludes those who responded 'don't know' or did not answer.

Source: British Social Attitudes Survey, National Centre for Social Research

Unemployment

The unemployment rate (see Glossary) fluctuates through the economic cycle. During periods of economic growth the number of jobs generally grows and unemployment falls, although any mismatches between the skill needs of the new jobs and the skills of those available for work may slow this process. Conversely, as the economy slows and particularly if it goes into recession, so unemployment tends to rise, though a rise in unemployment tends to lag behind an economic slowdown. The unemployment rate in Q2 2008 was 5.4 per cent (equivalent to around 1.7 million people aged 16 and over). Since 1971, when Labour Force Survey (LFS) records began, total unemployment peaked in 1984 and 1993 (Figure 4.15 overleaf).

Unemployment for men peaked in Q2 1983, at a rate of 12.2 per cent, equivalent to 1.9 million unemployed men. The unemployment peak for women was in Q2 1984 when the rate was 11.8 per cent, equivalent to 1.3 million unemployed women. The recession in the early 1990s had a much greater effect on unemployment among men than women, and the

Figure 4.15

Unemployment rates:[1] by sex

United Kingdom

Percentages

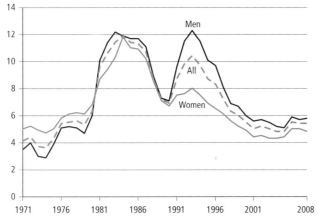

1 Data are at Q2 each year and are seasonally adjusted. People aged 16 and over. See Appendix, Part 4: Labour Force Survey.

Source: Labour Force Survey, Office for National Statistics

unemployment rate for men peaked at 12.3 per cent in 1993, the highest rate since the series began. The female unemployment rate also peaked in 1993, but at a lower rate of 8.0 per cent. In Q2 2008 unemployment rates were 5.8 per cent for men and 4.8 per cent for women.

In 2007 the average unemployment rate in the European Union (EU-27) was 7.1 per cent, ranging from 3.2 per cent in the Netherlands to 11.1 per cent in Slovakia, which replaced Poland as the member state with the highest unemployment rate in the EU-27. The UK had the 11th lowest overall unemployment rate of the EU-27 (5.3 per cent). The lowest unemployment rates tend to be recorded by the newer member states. For example, six of the nine states that had an overall unemployment rate above the EU-27 average were from the original EU-15, before the expansions of the EU in 2004 and 2007.

The LFS asks unemployed respondents who have worked within the last eight years about their last job. This information can be used to calculate unemployment rates according to a person's previous occupation (see Appendix, Part 4: Standard Occupational Classification 2000 (SOC2000)). In Q2 2008 unemployment rates were highest among those who previously worked in the elementary occupations (9.1 per cent) and lowest among those who previously worked in professional occupations (1.3 per cent) (Figure 4.16). Similarly, the questions provide data on the previous industry in which unemployed respondents had worked (see Appendix, Part 4: Standard Industrial Classification 2003). In Q2 2008 unemployment rates were highest for those who had previously worked in the distribution, hotel and restaurant industry (5.7 per cent) and

Figure 4.16

Unemployment rates:[1] by previous occupation, 2008[2]

United Kingdom

Percentages

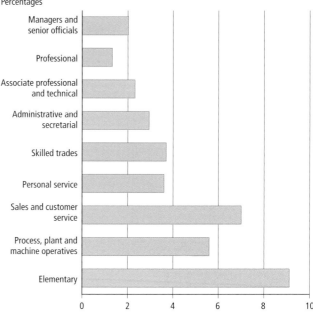

1 As a proportion of all persons in employment in the relevant occupation plus those unemployed who last worked in that occupation.
2 Data are at Q2 and are not seasonally adjusted. People aged 16 and over. See Appendix, Part 4: Labour Force Survey, and Standard Occupational Classification 2000 (SOC2000).

Source: Labour Force Survey, Office for National Statistics

lowest for those whose last job was in either public administration, education and health, or agriculture and fishing (each 2.2 per cent).

The unemployment rate in the UK is higher for young people at the beginning of their working life than for people who are nearing state pension age. In Q2 2008 the unemployment rate was 28.2 per cent for 16 to 17-year-old men and 23.6 per cent for young women of this age. In contrast, the lowest unemployment rates in Q2 2008 were among men and women aged 50 and over, at 3.4 per cent for men and 2.2 per cent for women. However, higher proportions of men and women of this age were economically inactive, in other words not working but not looking for work.

Younger people are less likely than older people to be unemployed for a long period. In Q2 2008, one in five (19.9 per cent) of unemployed 18 to 24-year-olds had been unemployed for more than 12 months, compared with two in five (39.5 per cent) of those aged 50 and over. Since 1992, across all age groups, unemployed men were more likely than unemployed women to be out of work for more than 12 months (29 per cent and 18 per cent respectively in Q2 2008).

Table 4.17

Unemployment rates for working-age people[1] with and without dependent children:[2] by age and sex, 2008[3]

United Kingdom   Percentages

	16–24	25–34	35–49	50–59/64	All
Women with dependent children	21	6	3	3	5
Married/cohabiting mothers	14	5	2	2	3
Lone mothers	31	13	8	8	11
Women without dependent children	11	3	3	2	5
Men with dependent children	20	5	3	3	4
Married/cohabiting fathers	20	5	2	3	3
Lone fathers	*	34	15	6	16
Men without dependent children	15	5	5	4	7
All parents with dependent children	20	6	3	3	4
Married/cohabiting parents	17	5	2	2	3
Lone parents	31	14	9	8	12
All people without dependent children	13	4	4	3	6

1 Men aged 16 to 64 and women aged 16 to 59. Excludes people with unknown economic status.
2 Children aged under 16 and those aged 16 to 18 who have never been married and are in full-time education.
3 Data are at Q2 and are not seasonally adjusted. See Appendix, Part 4: Labour Force Survey.

Source: Labour Force Survey, Office for National Statistics

Unemployment rates are also available from the LFS for parents with dependent children. In Q2 2008 the unemployment rate in the UK for working-age lone parents (12 per cent) was higher than the rate for married or cohabiting parents (3 per cent), and the rate was higher for lone fathers (16 per cent) than lone mothers (11 per cent) (Table 4.17). The rate for younger married and cohabiting parents was markedly higher than the rates for older parents – 17 per cent of economically active married and cohabiting parents aged between 16 and 24 with dependent children were unemployed compared with 2 per cent of equivalent parents aged 35 and over. Overall unemployment rates were the same for married or cohabiting mothers and fathers (3 per cent), but slightly higher for 16 to 24-year-old married or cohabiting fathers (20 per cent) than for equivalent mothers (14 per cent).

It is worth remembering that the unemployment rate is expressed as a proportion of the economically active population. This means that those who are economically inactive are not included in either the numerator or the denominator and therefore the unemployment rate should not be interpreted as the total proportion of a group who are not working. For example, although the unemployment rate was higher for lone fathers than lone mothers in Q2 2008, a higher proportion of lone mothers than lone fathers were economically inactive (37 per cent compared with 24 per cent).

Economic inactivity

Economically inactive people (those who are not in, or looking for, employment, see Glossary), especially those of working age, could move into the labour market at some time in the future and as such are a potential source of labour market supply.

The overall economic inactivity rate (the proportion of the working-age population who are economically inactive) was stable at around 21 and 22 per cent throughout the 1970s, but this masked the convergence of economic inactivity rates for men and women, as rates for women fell while those for men rose (Figure 4.18 overleaf). The overall rate dipped in the 1980s to 19 per cent in Q2 1990, driven by a sharp fall in economic inactivity rates for women between 1983 and 1990, while the rate for men remained stable. Throughout the 1990s and into the next decade the overall rate returned to the levels experienced in the 1970s and was 21 per cent in Q2 2008.

Although the number of economically inactive working-age people in the UK has risen by 0.8 million over the period Q2 1971 to Q2 2008, this increase was caused by the rising trend in economically inactive working-age men, which increased by 2.4 million to 3.2 million. In contrast the number of economically inactive working-age women fell by 1.5 million to 4.7 million. As a result, the economic inactivity rate among working-age men rose from 5 per cent in Q2 1971 to

Figure 4.18

Economic inactivity rates:[1] by sex

United Kingdom

Percentages

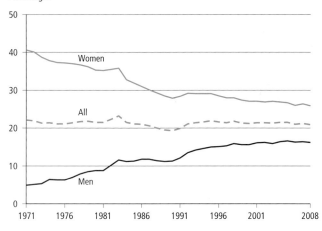

1 Data are at Q2 each year and are seasonally adjusted. Men aged 16 to 64 and women aged 16 to 59. See Appendix, Part 4: Labour Force Survey.

Source: Labour Force Survey, Office for National Statistics

Figure 4.19

Economic inactivity rates: by sex and highest qualification,[1] 2008[2]

United Kingdom

Percentages

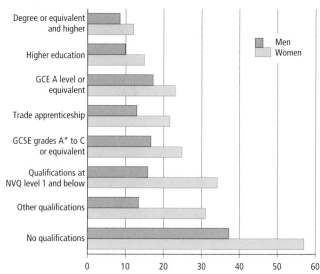

1 Excludes those who did not state their highest qualification. See Appendix, Part 3: Qualifications.
2 Data are at Q2 and are not seasonally adjusted. Men aged 16 to 64 and women aged 16 to 59. See Appendix, Part 4: Labour Force Survey.

Source: Labour Force Survey, Office for National Statistics

16 per cent in Q2 2008. Over the same period, although the inactivity rate for working-age women remained higher than that for men, it fell from 41 per cent to 26 per cent.

Economic inactivity rates of working-age people vary considerably in relation to their highest educational qualification. In Q2 2008, 47 per cent of working-age people with no qualifications in the UK were economically inactive, compared with 10 per cent of those with at least a degree or equivalent. In the same quarter, 37 per cent of working-age men with no qualifications were economically inactive, compared with 17 per cent of those whose highest qualification was a GCSE grade A* to C or equivalent, and 8 per cent of those with at least a degree or equivalent (Figure 4.19). The same pattern was evident among women, although those with no qualifications (57 per cent) were more likely to be inactive than their male counterparts. Among graduates the difference in activity rates between men and women was much smaller. For example, there was a gap in the economic inactivity rate of 20 percentage points between men and women with no qualifications compared with 4 percentage points between those with a degree or higher qualification.

The Annual Population Survey (see Appendix, Part 4: Annual Population Survey) showed that in 2007 the local authority with the highest inactivity rate in Great Britain was the London Borough of Tower Hamlets (36 per cent) while the lowest rate (9 per cent) was in Purbeck in the South West region of England. Differences in economic inactivity rates in local areas within the regions and countries of Great Britain are greater

than differences between the regions and countries. In 2007 the East Midlands region had the greatest difference between the highest and lowest working-age inactivity rates, with 22 percentage points separating Nottingham (31 per cent) and Kettering (10 per cent). The narrowest spread of working-age inactivity rates in Great Britain was in Yorkshire and the Humber, with 10 percentage points between Scarborough (28 per cent) and Harrogate (17 per cent).

Broadly speaking, people of working-age who are economically inactive can be divided into those who want a job and those who do not, on the basis of questions along these lines in the Labour Force Survey. While this is not an exact reflection of whether people will move into economic activity in the near future, it does give some indication of the potential labour force within this group. In Q2 2008, 7.9 million working-age people in the UK were economically inactive and an estimated 2.2 million of these wanted a job. Three in ten of those who wanted a job were economically inactive because of long-tem sickness or disability (30 per cent), and around a further three in ten were looking after the family or home (28 per cent).

Long-term sickness or disability was the main reason for economic inactivity among working-age men in the UK (34 per cent) in Q2 2008, although this proportion has fallen

Table 4.20

Reasons for economic inactivity: by sex and age, 2008[1]

United Kingdom   Percentages

	16–24	25–34	35–49	50–59/64	All aged 16–59/64
Men					
Long-term sick or disabled	5	40	62	49	34
Looking after family or home	1	9	16	6	6
Student	82	27	4	-	33
Retired	0	0	1	33	13
Other	10	17	12	9	11
All men (=100%) (millions)[2]	1.2	0.3	0.5	1.3	3.3
Women					
Long-term sick or disabled	3	8	24	41	19
Looking after family or home	23	72	61	27	45
Student	66	10	4	1	22
Retired	0	0	-	14	3
Other	8	8	8	14	9
All women (=100%) (millions)[2]	1.3	0.9	1.4	1.1	4.7

1 Data are at Q2 and are not seasonally adjusted. See Appendix, Part 4: Labour Force Survey.
2 Includes discouraged workers and those who are temporarily sick.

Source: Labour Force Survey, Office for National Statistics

from a peak in Q2 1998 (42 per cent). Among working-age women, looking after the family or home was the most common reason for inactivity; 45 per cent gave this as their main reason for not seeking work. This proportion has also fallen from 55 per cent in Q2 1993, when the series began. Reasons for economic inactivity vary by age. Table 4.20 shows that in Q2 2008 for both men and women aged 16 to 24 being a student was the main reason for economic inactivity, 82 per cent and 66 per cent respectively. Long-term sickness or disability was the main reason for economic inactivity among working-age men aged 25 and over, and particularly for those aged 35 to 49 (62 per cent). Looking after the family or home was the most common reason for inactivity among women aged 25 to 34 (72 per cent) and for those aged 35 to 49 (61 per cent). For those approaching state pension ages, men were more likely than women to be economically inactive because of retirement – 33 per cent of men aged 50 to 64 were retired compared with 14 per cent of women aged 50 to 59.

Industrial relations at work

In 2007, 1.041 million working days in the UK were lost from 142 recorded stoppages associated with labour disputes (see Appendix, Part 4: Labour disputes), only the third time

since 1990 that the number of working days lost reached one million (Figure 4.21).

This total was considerably higher than that of 2006 (754,500) and also higher than the average number of working days lost

Figure 4.21

Labour disputes:[1] working days lost

United Kingdom

Millions

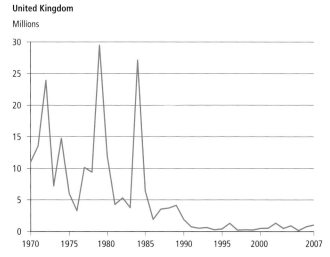

1 See Appendix, Part 4: Labour disputes.

Source: Office for National Statistics

per year in the 1990s (660,000). However, it is considerably lower than the average for both the 1980s (7.2 million) and the 1970s (12.9 million) when single disputes accounted for large proportions of the total working days lost.

In 2007, 66 per cent of all working days lost resulted from disputes over pay, which also accounted for 50 per cent of all stoppages. Disputes concerning hours worked accounted for 30 per cent of days lost and 25 per cent of all stoppages. Redundancy issues accounted for 2 per cent of days lost and 11 per cent of all stoppages.

Disputes in the workplace are sometimes taken to employment tribunals, which are judicial bodies aiming to resolve disputes over employment rights between employers and employees in Great Britain. They have powers to determine more than 70 different types of complaint, including unfair dismissal, payment-related complaints and discrimination. A claim taken to an employment tribunal can cover more than one type of complaint. In 2006/07, 132,600 claims covering a total 238,500 complaints were registered with employment tribunals. The most common nature of claim was for unfair dismissal, which accounted for 19 per cent of all complaints.

Once a year, in Q4 (October–December), the Labour Force Survey asks questions on trade union membership of all those in employment excluding those on training programmes and unpaid family workers. This section concentrates on employees since they have less direct control over many aspects of their working lives than the self-employed.

The proportion of employees in the UK who were members of a trade union, known as trade union density, fell from 32.4 per cent in 1995 to 28.0 per cent in 2007. During this period the rate for male membership fell from 35.0 to 26.4 per cent whereas for female employees, union density was fairly stable, between 28.4 and 29.7 per cent, and in 2007 was 29.6 per cent.

Trade union density varies considerably between those employed in the private and the public sectors. Around one in

Figure 4.22

Trade union membership of employees:[1] by sector and sex

United Kingdom
Percentages

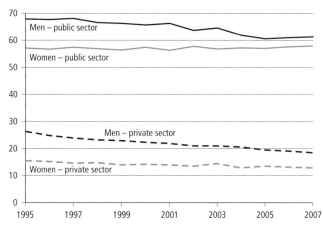

1 Union membership (including staff associations) as a proportion of all employees. Excludes members of the armed forces. Data are at Q4 each year and are not seasonally adjusted. People aged 16 and over. See Appendix, Part 4: Labour Force Survey.

Source: Labour Force Survey, Office for National Statistics; Department for Business, Enterprise and Regulatory Reform

six (16.1 per cent) private sector employees in the UK were union members in 2007, down 5.3 percentage points from 1995. This compares with almost three in five (59.0 per cent) public sector employees in the UK, down 2.3 percentage points since 1995. Public sector employees accounted for 58.6 per cent of all employee union members in the UK in 2007, and private sector employees accounted for 41.4 per cent.

In both the private sector and, to a lesser extent, the public sector, union density was higher for men than for women. In the private sector in 2007 union density for men was 18.5 per cent, compared with 12.8 per cent for women (Figure 4.22). In the public sector male union density was 61.3 per cent compared with 57.8 per cent for women.

Glossary

Economically active (or the **labour force**) – those aged 16 and over who are **in employment** or are **unemployed**.

Economic activity rate – the proportion of the population, for example in a given age group, who are **economically active**.

In employment – a measure, obtained from household surveys and censuses, of those aged 16 and over who are **employees**, **self-employed**, people doing unpaid work for a family-run business, and participants in government-supported employment and training programmes.

Employment rate – the proportion of any given population group who are **in employment**. The main presentation of employment rates is the proportion of the population of **working age** who are in employment.

Employees (Labour Force Survey measure) – a measure, obtained from household surveys, of people aged 16 and over who regard themselves as paid employees. People with two or more jobs are counted only once.

Self-employed – a measure, obtained from household surveys, of people aged 16 and over who regard themselves as self-employed, that is, who in their main employment work on their own account, whether or not they have employees.

Unemployment – a measure, based on International Labour Organisation guidelines and used in the Labour Force Survey, which counts as unemployed those aged 16 and over who are without a job, are available to start work in the next two weeks, who have been seeking a job in the last four weeks or are out of work and waiting to start a job already obtained in the next two weeks.

Unemployment rate – the proportion of the **economically active** who are **unemployed**. The main presentation of unemployment rates is the proportion of the economically active population aged 16 and over who are unemployed.

Economically inactive – those aged 16 and over who are neither **in employment** nor **unemployment**. For example, those looking after a home, retirees, or those unable to work because of long-term sickness or disability.

Economic inactivity rate – the proportion of a given population group who are **economically inactive**. The main presentation of economic inactivity rates is the proportion of the population of **working age** who are economically inactive.

Working age – men aged 16 to 64 and women aged 16 to 59.

Working-age household – a household that includes at least one person of **working age**.

Working household – a household that includes at least one person of **working age** and where all the people of working age are **in employment**.

Workless household – a household that includes at least one person of **working age** where no one aged 16 and over is **in employment**.

4

4

Chapter 5

Income and wealth

- Between 2006 and 2007, growth in real household disposable income per head in the UK at 0.1 per cent was far lower than growth in economic activity overall, as measured by GDP per head (3.0 per cent). (Figure 5.1)

- Average household net wealth per head in the UK more than doubled in real terms between 1987 and 2007, to reach an average of £113,000 per head. (Figure 5.4)

- Wages and salaries formed 81 per cent of the gross income of couple households under state pension age without dependent children in the UK in 2006/07, compared with 38 per cent for lone parent households. (Table 5.7)

- In April 2008 median hourly earnings of full-time employees in the financial intermediation sector in the UK, at £16.47, were more than twice those of employees in the hotel and restaurant sector, at £7.00. (Table 5.11)

- The proportion of children living in households with income below 60 per cent of median disposable income in the UK fell from a peak of 26 per cent in 1998/99 and 1999/2000 to 22 per cent in 2006/07. (Figure 5.18)

- Around one-quarter of households in the UK had no savings in 2006/07. Households with two adults and no dependent children, where one or both were over state pension age, were most likely to have savings of £20,000 or more. (Table 5.21)

Download data by
clicking the online pdf

www.statistics.gov.uk/
socialtrends39

People's income plays an important role in their economic and social well-being, because it determines how much they have to spend on goods and services, to save or invest, or to be able to borrow. All of this contributes to their standard of living. Generally income is analysed at the level of either the family or the household, because these are the units across which income and outgoings are considered to be pooled, so that the income of the family or household can be regarded as representative of the standard of living of each person living in it. However, for some purposes, for example analysis of earnings from employment, income is analysed for individuals.

Overview

Household income depends on the level of activity within the economy as a whole each year – the national income – and on the way in which national income is distributed. The UK National Accounts, and in particular gross domestic product (GDP) in total and per head, are often used as summary measurements of economic well-being. Although for some years and for an increasing number of public policy needs there is an acknowledgement that 'there is more to life than GDP' (a phrase drawing on a speech by Robert Kennedy in 1968), GDP continues to be used as a proxy measure for societal as well as purely economic well-being.

GDP measures the overall level of economic activity in a country. The total income generated is distributed between individuals, in the form of wages and salaries, between companies and other organisations in, for example, the form of profits retained for investment, and government, in the form of taxes on production. If GDP per head is growing in real terms (after adjustment to remove inflation), this means the economy is expanding beyond what is attributable to changes in the size of the population. GDP per head in the UK more than doubled in real terms between 1971 and 2007 (Figure 5.1). Over this period there were times when the economy contracted, for example in the mid-1970s at the time of the international oil crisis, and again during periods of world economic recession in the early 1980s and early 1990s. The UK economy has grown each year since 1992, and between 2006 and 2007 GDP per head grew by 3.0 per cent.

There are a number of countries that have much higher rates of growth in GDP than the UK or indeed other countries in the developed world. For example, the World Bank estimates that China's total GDP grew by 11.6 per cent in 2006, and in India it grew by 9.7 per cent.

Comparing GDP per head across the countries of the EU in 2007 shows that Luxembourg had the highest level of economic activity (Table 5.2). This is partly because of the

Figure 5.1

Real household disposable income per head[1] and gross domestic product per head[2]

United Kingdom

Index numbers (1971=100)

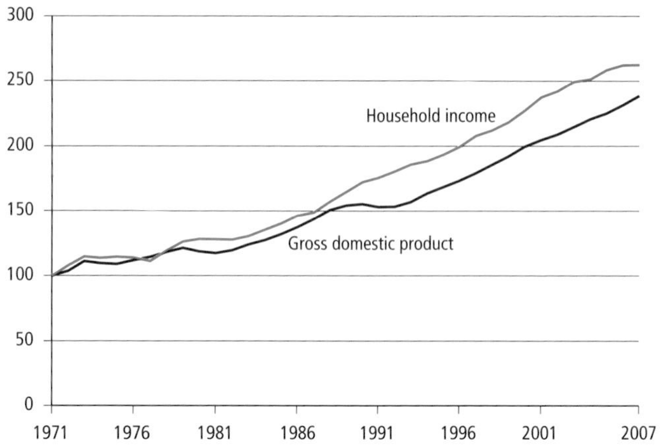

1 Adjusted to real terms using the expenditure deflator for the household sector. See Appendix, Part 5: Household income data sources.
2 Adjusted to real terms using the GDP deflator.

Source: Office for National Statistics

importance of the financial sector within Luxembourg's economy, but also because of the large share of cross-border workers in total employment. While contributing to GDP, cross-border workers are not included in the resident population used to calculate GDP per head. Luxembourg GDP per head was 85 per cent higher than Ireland, which had the second highest GDP per head. All of the EU-15 countries who were members before 2004 had GDP per head higher than the 12 member states that joined the EU in 2004 and 2007, with the exception of Portugal, where GDP per head was lower than in Cyprus, Slovenia, the Czech Republic or Malta (see Appendix, Part 4: Accession to the European Union (EU)). Romania and Bulgaria, the newest member states, both had GDP per head less than one-half of the average for the 27 member states. UK GDP per head was 17 per cent higher than the EU-27 average. These figures have been converted to a common basis making adjustments for the relative purchasing power of national currencies (see Appendix, Part 5: Purchasing power parities).

The gap between Luxembourg and the EU-27 average grew between 1997 and 2007: in 1997, its GDP per head was 115 per cent above the EU-27 average compared with 177 per cent in 2007. In general, there has been some convergence of the GDP per head of member states towards the EU-27 average, particularly for the 12 new member states, of which five had GDP per head less than one-half the EU-27 average in 1997 compared with two in 2007. However, the most dramatic increase in GDP per head was in Ireland, where it rose from 15 per cent above the EU-27 average in 1997 to

Table 5.2

Gross domestic product[1] per head: EU-27 comparison

Index EU-27 =100

	1997	2001	2007
Luxembourg	215	235	277
Ireland	115	133	150
Netherlands	127	134	133
Austria	132	125	127
Sweden	124	122	126
Denmark	133	128	123
Belgium	126	124	119
United Kingdom	118	120	117
Finland	111	116	117
Germany	125	117	113
France	115	116	111
Spain	94	98	107
Italy	119	118	101
Greece	85	87	97
Cyprus	86	91	93
Slovenia	77	80	91
Czech Republic	73	70	81
Malta	81	78	77
Portugal	76	77	75
Estonia	42	46	71
Slovakia	51	52	69
Hungary	52	59	63
Lithuania	38	42	60
Latvia	35	39	58
Poland	47	48	54
Romania	..	28	41
Bulgaria	26	29	38

1 Gross domestic product per inhabitant at current market prices compiled on the basis of the European System of Accounts 1995, expressed in purchasing power standards, an artificial currency unit that eliminates price level differences between countries. See Appendix, Part 5: Purchasing power parities.

Source: Eurostat

50 per cent above average in 2007, and from being tenth highest (equal with France) to second. The UK has remained more or less in the same place in the ranking, being ninth in 1997 and eighth in 2001 and 2007.

If a country's economy is growing then there is more 'cake' available for distribution across the population, which itself may be increasing in size. Household disposable income per head represents the average amount of this cake that, in theory, each person has available to spend or save. This measure is commonly used to summarise people's economic well-being, rather than the economic well-being of the country as a whole. However, it is important to note that this is simply a calculation dividing total household disposable income by the number of people in the population. It does not take into account how income is actually distributed – see Figure 5.3. Household disposable income comprises income derived directly from economic activity in the form of wages and salaries and self-employment income, as well as transfers such as social security benefits. It is then subject to a number of deductions such as income tax, council tax (domestic rates in Northern Ireland), and contributions towards pensions and national insurance.

Household disposable income per head in the UK, adjusted for inflation, increased by more than 160 per cent between 1971 and 2007 (Figure 5.1). During the 1970s and early 1980s growth fluctuated, and in some years there were small year on year falls, such as between 1973 and 1974, 1975 and 1976, 1976 and 1977, 1980 and 1981, and 1981 and 1982. Since 1982 there has been growth each year. Over the period 1971 to 2007 as a whole, growth in household disposable income per head averaged 2.7 per cent per year compared with that in GDP per head of 2.4 per cent. However, there were years when this pattern was reversed, most recently between 2006 and 2007 when the growth in real household disposable income per head was considerably lower than that in GDP per head (0.1 per cent compared with 3.0 per cent), and much lower than the average annual growth rate of 2.7 per cent between 1971 and 2007.

Real household disposable income per head measures how people's incomes have been changing on average. However, income is not evenly distributed across the population, and people at different points in the income distribution may experience different levels of income growth. This is demonstrated in Figure 5.3 overleaf, which shows how incomes have changed at the 90th and 10th percentiles of the distribution, and at the median (see the Analysing income distribution text box overleaf for an explanation of these terms). During the 1980s there was little change in income in real terms (that is adjusted to remove the effects of inflation) at the bottom of the distribution, while income at the top of the distribution showed strong growth in real terms. The early 1990s were a period of economic downturn, when there was little real growth in incomes anywhere in the distribution. Between 1995/96 and 2005/06, income at all three points in the distribution grew by similar amounts in real terms, with median income increasing by one-quarter. However, between 2005/06 and 2006/07, although income rose slightly at the 90th percentile and at the median (by 0.8 and 0.5 per cent

5

Figure 5.3

Distribution of real[1] household disposable income[2]

United Kingdom/Great Britain[3]

£ per week at 2006/07 prices

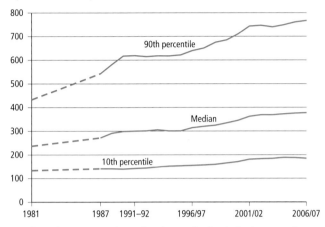

1 Adjusted to 2006/07 prices using the retail prices index less council tax/domestic rates.
2 Equivalised household disposable income before deduction of housing costs, using OECD equivalisation scale. See Appendix, Part 5: Households Below Average Income (HBAI), and Equivalisation scales for variations in source and definition on which the time series is based.
3 Data for 1994/95 to 1997/98 are for Great Britain only.

Source: Households Below Average Income, Department for Work and Pensions

Analysing income distribution

Equivalisation – in analysing the distribution of income, household disposable income is usually adjusted to take account of the size and composition of the household. This recognises that, for example, to achieve the same standard of living a household of five requires a higher income than a single person. This process is known as equivalisation (see Appendix, Part 5: Equivalisation scales).

Quintile and decile groups – the main method of analysing income distribution used in this chapter is to rank units (households, individuals or adults) by a given income measure, and then to divide the ranked units into groups of equal size. Groups containing 20 per cent of units are referred to as 'quintile groups' or 'fifths'. Thus the 'bottom quintile group' of income is the 20 per cent of units with the lowest incomes. Similarly, groups containing 10 per cent of units are referred to as 'decile groups' or 'tenths'.

Percentiles – an alternative method is to present the income level above or below which a certain proportion of units fall. Thus the 90th percentile is the income level above which 10 per cent of units fall when ranked by a given income measure – this is also known as the **top decile point**. The **median** is then the midpoint of the distribution above and below which 50 per cent of units fall.

respectively), there was a small fall of 1.6 per cent at the 10th percentile.

The income distribution and the extent of inequality have changed considerably over the last three decades. In Figure 5.3 the closer the percentiles are to the median line, the greater the equality within the distribution. Inequality grew throughout the 1980s. During the first half of the 1990s, the income distribution appeared to be broadly stable, though at a much higher level of income inequality than in 1981. The Gini coefficient, a widely used measure of inequality (see Appendix, Part 5: Gini coefficient) fluctuated only slightly between 1994/95 and 2006/07, though there is evidence of a marginal increase in inequality over the period. There was no change in the Gini coefficient between 2005/06 and 2006/07.

Researchers at the Institute for Fiscal Studies (IFS) have investigated possible explanations for the changes in inequality observed between 1979 and 2006/07. Changes to the labour market appear to have played an important role. In particular, inequality rose during the 1980s when the incomes of the higher paid grew much more rapidly than those of the lower paid or of households where no one was working. Growth in self-employment income and in unemployment were also found to be associated with periods of increased inequality. It appears that demographic factors such as the growth in one person households made a relatively unimportant contribution compared with labour market changes. However, the research found that changes in the tax and benefit system had an impact. The tax system became less progressive in the 1980s as the higher rates of income tax were cut. Had these higher rates stayed in place, inequality would have grown less quickly, though what effect the higher rates would have had on underlying income distribution is uncertain. Because most benefits were increased only in line with price inflation during the 1980s and 1990s, the income of most of those dependent on benefits also fell further behind that of the working population, leading to increased inequality. The impact of substantial spending on tax credits since the late 1990s has been to mitigate inequality.

Figure 5.3 indicates that the main cause for the increase in inequality has been the much higher than average growth in income at the top of the distribution. The IFS researchers explored the trends at the top of the income distribution in some depth. They concluded that since 1996/97, people in the top 10 per cent of the income distribution have indeed experienced faster growth in disposable incomes than the rest of the population. The top 1 per cent experienced still faster growth and the top 0.1 per cent the fastest growth of all. However, this exceptional growth in income was mostly confined to the late 1990s up to 2000/01. Between 2000/01 and 2003/04 there was a slow-down in income growth across most of the income distribution, with the slow-down being particularly pronounced at the top of the distribution where high-income individuals reported low or negative growth. As will be seen in Figure 5.4, net wealth per head also fell in real terms during this period as stock market values fell. There is more information about the distribution of income in the section on Income distribution later in this chapter.

Income represents a flow of resources over a specified period of time received either in cash or in kind – for example, earnings or the use of a company car. Wealth on the other hand describes the ownership of assets valued at a particular point in time. Thus although the terms 'wealthy' and 'high income' are often used interchangeably, they are quite distinct concepts. People's ownership of wealth, such as savings, a house or pension rights, is another important aspect of their economic well-being, in that wealth may provide financial security as well as in some cases providing a current income flow (for example, interest on savings).

The UK National Accounts indicate that the wealth owned by the household sector (net of liabilities) totalled £7,523 billion in 2007, or an average of £113,000 per head. Household net wealth per head in the UK increased nearly two-and-one-half times in real terms between 1987 and 2007 (Figure 5.4), but there has not been steady growth over the period. Two of the main components of household net wealth are residential housing (less the value of the loans outstanding on their purchase) and stocks and shares, and so the trends reflect both

the state of the housing market (see Chapter 10: Housing) and that of the stock market. There is more information on household wealth in the section on Wealth later in this chapter.

As with income, it is not only the overall level of wealth that is of interest but how it is actually distributed between individuals. Estimates of wealth distribution produced by HM Revenue and Customs indicate that wealth is very much less evenly distributed than income. In 2003, the latest year for which data are available, one-half of the population in the UK owned 7 per cent of total wealth and this proportion has scarcely changed since 1991. Conversely, the wealthiest 1 per cent of the population owned 21 per cent of total wealth in 2003, having risen from 17 per cent in 1991. Updates to these statistics have been delayed while problems with the data and methodology are addressed.

Income is important to people's overall well-being in terms of the access that it provides to goods and services. People's satisfaction with their income depends on their material needs and expectations, and the extent to which the income available to them enables these to be met. It is therefore possible that individuals with the same income but different needs, real or perceived, may differ in how they feel about the adequacy of their income. The same may be true of those who are faced with different prices for the same level and quality of goods or services, for example housing, or with different levels of debt. Table 5.5 explores trends in people's perception of economic hardship or lack of it. The proportion of respondents in Great Britain who said that they were 'living comfortably' rose from 24 per cent in 1986 to a peak of 44 per cent in 2003, but fell to 41 per cent in 2006 and showed a further sharp fall to

Figure 5.4

Real household net wealth per head[1]

United Kingdom

Index numbers (1987=100)

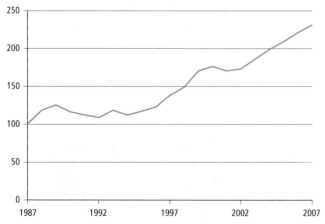

1 Adjusted to real terms using the expenditure deflator for the household sector. See Appendix, Part 5: Household income data sources.

Source: Office for National Statistics

Table 5.5

People's perceptions of the adequacy of their household's income[1]

Great Britain   Percentages

	1986	1994	2003	2005	2006	2007
Living comfortably	24	29	44	40	41	36
Coping	50	49	43	44	45	45
Finding it difficult to manage	18	15	10	12	10	14
Finding it very difficult to manage	8	6	3	4	4	4
Other answer	-	-	-	-	-	-

1 Respondents aged 18 and over were asked, 'Which of these phrases would you say comes closest to your feelings about your household's income these days?' and shown the first four options given in the table above. Excludes those who responded 'don't know' or did not answer.

Source: British Social Attitudes Survey, National Centre for Social Research

36 per cent in 2007. In contrast the proportion finding it difficult or very difficult to manage fell from 26 per cent in 1986 to 14 per cent in 2006, but then rose to 19 per cent in 2007. This is consistent with the slow-down in growth of real household disposable income per head in 2007 shown in Figure 5.1.

Composition of income

Alongside strong growth in household disposable income per head seen in Figure 5.1 there has been considerable stability in income composition since 1992. In 2007, 50 per cent of total household income in the UK was derived from wages and salaries, with social benefits the next largest source of income, at 18 per cent of the total (Figure 5.6), compared with 50 per cent and 20 per cent respectively in 1992. Income from investments (net property income) fell from 16 to 14 per cent over the period, having reached a low of 12 per cent in 2002 and 2003. Self-employment income, including income from rentals, rose from 11 to 13 per cent of the total.

The data in Figures 5.1, 5.4 and 5.6 are derived from the UK National Accounts, whereas Figure 5.3, Table 5.5 and the tables and charts in most of the remainder of this chapter are derived from surveys of households or surveys of businesses. There are a number of definitional differences between these two types of data source. Appendix, Part 5: Household income data sources describes the main differences between

household income as defined in the National Accounts and as defined in most survey sources.

The composition of income varies between different types of households according to factors such as age, geographic location, family composition and ethnicity. Wages and salaries are the largest component of gross (before any deductions) household income in the UK averaged over all households (Table 5.7). However, for households without dependent children, where both adults were under state pension age (65 for men and 60 for women), wages and salaries formed 81 per cent of gross income in 2006/07, compared with 38 per cent for lone parent households. Conversely, social security benefits (other than the state retirement pension) formed 50 per cent of the income of lone parent households compared with 2 per cent of that of two adult households with no children (where both adults were under state pension age) and 8 per cent of that of all households. Self-employment income was most important to households with two adults and one or more dependent children, at 13 per cent of gross income. Investment income formed 2 per cent of income for all households, but 6 per cent for households without children with one or both adults over state pension age.

Households over state pension age had a very different income composition profile compared with those of working age. The state retirement pension (basic state pension plus additional state pension), together with any associated payments of pension credit, was the largest source of income for one adult households without dependent children over state pension age, at 45 per cent of gross income, followed by private pensions (including occupational pensions) at 27 per cent. For two adult households with at least one adult over state pension age and without dependent children, these two types of pension income formed very similar proportions of gross income, at 29 per cent and 32 per cent respectively. Wages and salaries were also important to the incomes of two adult households with at least one adult over state pension age, at 19 per cent, though were negligible to one adult households over state pension age, at 4 per cent of gross income.

Figure 5.8 overleaf illustrates trends between 1994/95 and 2006/07 in the income from these various sources received by pensioner families (pensioner couples where one or both are over state pension age, or single people over state pension age – see Appendix, Part 5: Pensioners' income). Benefits, including the state retirement pension and pension credit, were the most important component in their gross (pre-tax) income throughout this period, and grew by 26 per cent in real terms. Nearly all pensioner families (95 per cent) received the state retirement pension in 2006/07. However, between

Figure 5.6

Composition of total household income, 2007

United Kingdom

Percentages

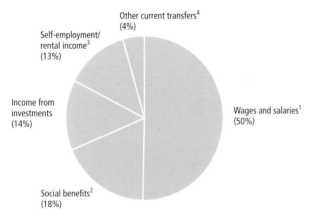

Total household income: £1,243 billion

1 Excludes employers' social contributions.
2 Comprises pensions and benefits.
3 Includes self-employment income for sole-traders.
4 Mostly other government grants, but includes transfers from abroad and non-profit making bodies.

Source: Office for National Statistics

Table 5.7

Sources of gross household income: by household type, 2006/07

United Kingdom   Percentages

	Wages and salaries	Self-employed income	Investments	State retirement pension[1]	Other pensions	Other social security benefits[2]	Other sources	All income
Households without dependent children[3]								
One adult, over state pension age	4	1	6	45	27	16	2	100
One adult, under state pension age	74	9	2	-	3	10	2	100
Two adults, one or both over state pension age	19	5	6	29	32	7	2	100
Two adults, both under state pension age	81	9	2	-	3	2	2	100
Households with dependent children[3,4]								
One adult, with one or more dependent children	38	2	-	-	1	50	9	100
Two adults, with one or more dependent children	75	13	1	-	-	9	1	100
Other households[5]	74	10	1	2	3	5	4	100
All households	65	9	2	6	7	8	2	100

1 Includes any payment of pension credit.
2 Includes disability benefits and tax credits.
3 Aged under 16, or aged 16 to 19 and not married or in a civil partnership and living with their parents and in full-time non-advanced education or in unwaged government training.
4 Includes adults both under and over state pension age.
5 Includes households with three or more adults both under and over state pension age, with or without dependent children.

Source: Family Resources Survey, Department for Work and Pensions

2005/06 and 2006/07 reported benefit income fell by an average of £5 per week. Administrative data on the payments of benefits by the Department for Work and Pensions suggests that the change may not be as large as this. However, at least part of the reason is that two one-off payments made to qualifying pensioners in 2005/06 to help with council tax and living expenses were not repeated in 2006/07.

The vast majority of pensioner families had some private income in addition to benefits (94 per cent of pensioner couples and 81 per cent of single pensioners in 2006/07) and these sources of income grew faster than benefits between 1994/95 and 2006/07. The average contribution of personal pensions (pensions provided through a contract between the individual and a pension provider) to pensioners' incomes more than quadrupled over this period making personal pensions the faster growing source of pensioner income. However, it is still only a small minority of pensioners who receive them – 13 per cent in 2006/07 – with recently retired pensioner families more likely to receive them than older pensioners, reflecting the relatively recent expansion in the numbers contributing to personal pensions. Also, the average amount

received only increased by 23 per cent, from £79 to £97 per week. (Note that personal pensions are shown separately from occupational pensions in Figure 5.8 whereas in Table 5.7 the two were combined). Average receipts of investment income fell in real terms between 2000/01 and 2002/03, reflecting the fall in stock market values over this period. They then recovered, and in 2006/07 overtook their 2000/01 level. More information on investments may be found in the Wealth section at the end of this chapter. Information on pensions and benefit receipts of older people may be found in Chapter 8: Social protection.

Pensioner incomes have grown faster than average earnings across the economy as a whole since 1994/95. The gross income of pensioner families rose by 39 per cent in real terms between 1994/95 and 2006/07 compared with an increase of about 17 per cent in real average earnings. Note, however, that change in average income does not simply reflect changes experienced by individual pensioners; it also reflects changes in the composition of the group, for example as new retirees with greater entitlement to occupation and personal pensions join the group, and as the ratio of couple pensioner families to

Figure 5.8

Pensioners'[1] gross income: by source

Great Britain/United Kingdom[2]

£ per week at 2006/07 prices[3]

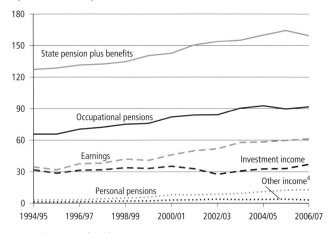

1 Pensioner couples where one or more are over state pension age, or single pensioners over state pension age (65 for men and 60 for women).
2 Geographic coverage changed from Great Britain to United Kingdom in 2002/03.
3 Adjusted to 2006/07 prices using the retail prices index less council tax/domestic rates.
4 Includes benefits from Friendly Societies, income from dependent children, and, from November 2000, free TV licences for those aged 75 and over.

Source: Pensioners' Income Series, Department for Work and Pensions

singles increases as mortality rates decline (see Chapter 1: Population).

Earnings

Income from employment in the form of wages and salaries is the most important component of income overall (Figure 5.6). The average earnings index (AEI), a monthly measure of the pay of a representative sample of all employees across all sectors of the economy in Great Britain, is one of the indicators used to judge the state of the economy. If the index rises rapidly, this may indicate that the labour market does not have enough employees with the right skills to meet the level of demand within the economy. In addition, a rapid rise may indicate that wage settlements are higher than the rate of economic growth can sustain and thus create inflationary pressures. A fall in the index may be a reflection of reduced demand within the economy and may be a warning that GDP is about to fall and unemployment is about to increase. The relationship between the AEI and price inflation in the UK, measured by the retail prices index (RPI, see Appendix, Part 6: Retail prices index) is also important. If earnings rise faster than prices, this means that employees' pay is increasing faster than the prices they have to pay for goods and services and that all things being equal, their purchasing power will rise and they will be 'better off'.

During the two decades from 1971, the AEI and RPI showed broadly similar patterns of change, with the RPI generally showing slower growth (Figure 5.9). For example, the peak in earnings growth over this period occurred in February 1975 when it reached an annual rate of 32 per cent. The peak in the RPI occurred in August that year at 27 per cent. During most of the 1990s and from 2000 until late in 2006, the AEI continued to outpace the RPI. This was made possible mainly through increases in productivity, enabling employers to pay higher wages while not increasing their prices to the same extent to finance their wage bill. Between June 2006 and June 2008, the AEI and RPI were at very similar levels with the AEI growth averaging 4.0 per cent and the RPI growth slightly higher, at 4.1 per cent. However, during summer 2008 earnings growth was again lower than growth in prices, with the annual rate of growth in the AEI at 3.4 per cent in August 2008 compared with growth in the RPI of 4.8 per cent.

Legislation in the 1970s established the principle of equal pay for work that can be established to be of equal value to that done by a member of the opposite sex, employed by the same employer, under common terms and conditions of employment. The impact of this legislation, together with other factors such as the opening up of more highly paid work to women, has been to narrow the difference between the earnings of men and women, though it has not yet been eliminated. The gender pay gap is determined by calculating women's average pay as a percentage of men's, and deducting this from 100 per cent. Based on average hourly earnings of

Figure 5.9

Average earnings index and retail prices index[1]

United Kingdom/Great Britain[2]

Percentage change over 12 months

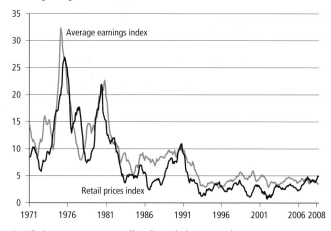

1 Whole economy, seasonally adjusted, three-month average.
2 Data for the retail prices index are for United Kingdom and the average earnings index data are for Great Britain. See Appendix, Part 6: Retail prices index.

Source: Office for National Statistics

full-time employees from their main job, the gap fell from 28.7 per cent in the UK in 1975 to 12.0 per cent in 2006. It has fallen for all ages over this period. However, in Great Britain in 1975 the gap appeared as people entered the adult job market at 18, generally increased to around the age of 40, before levelling off and then slightly falling for those in their late 50s (Figure 5.10). In contrast, some 30 years later in 2006 the gender pay gap was not evident until the age of 34. Until this age it fluctuated around equality. It then increased before levelling off around the age of 46 and then fell again for those in their late 50s. This shift may partly be a consequence of women having children later in life in 2006 compared with 1975 (see Chapter 2: Households and families, Figure 2.18).

On average part-time employees receive lower hourly earnings than full-time employees, and the difference between the hourly earnings of men and women working part time is smaller than that for full-time workers. In April 2008 part-time women's median hourly earnings excluding overtime in the UK, at £7.51, were slightly higher than those of men (£7.26). This is partly because a higher proportion of women than men work part time throughout their careers (see Chapter 4: Labour Market, Table 4.2).

Wage rates vary considerably between industrial sectors (see Appendix, Part 4: Standard Industrial Classification 2003). Agriculture has traditionally been a relatively low-paid sector in the UK, and this is still the case, with median hourly earnings of full-time employees of £7.67 (excluding overtime) in April 2008 (Table 5.11 overleaf). However, the hotel and restaurant sector

Figure 5.10

Median gender pay gap[1] of full-time employees: by age

Great Britain

Percentages

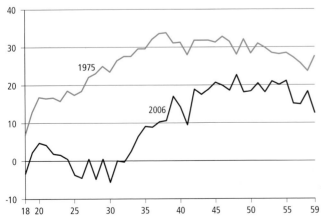

1 The gender pay gap is determined by calculating women's average pay as a percentage of men's, and deducting this from 100 per cent.

Source: New Earnings Survey/Annual Survey of Hours and Earnings panel datasets, Office for National Statistics

Annual Survey of Hours and Earnings

The source of much of the data in this section is the Annual Survey of Hours and Earnings (ASHE), which replaced the New Earnings Survey (NES) in 2004 (see Appendix, Part 5: Earnings surveys for a summary of the differences between the two). In Figure 5.10 and Table 5.11 a series has been used that applies ASHE methodology to NES data for years prior to 2004. ASHE includes supplementary information that was not available in the NES (for example, on employees in businesses outside the PAYE system). Data for 2004 onwards include the supplementary information and so care should be taken in comparing these with estimates for 2003 and earlier. For 2006 and 2007 ASHE results, the Office for National Statistics (ONS) has also introduced a small number of methodological changes. These include changes to the sample design as well as the introduction of an automatic occupation coding tool. Again, care should be taken when comparing these estimates with those for 2005 and earlier, as the changes introduce a small discontinuity in the series.

was the lowest paid industry in each year between 1997 and 2008, with hourly earnings averaging £7.00 in 2007. At the other end of the scale, median hourly earnings of full-time employees in the financial intermediation sector were more than twice those of employees in the hotel and restaurant sector, at £16.47. Averaged over all industries and services, hourly earnings increased by 52 per cent between 1997 and 2008, but the increase was highest in mining and quarrying, at 71 per cent and lowest in education, at 33 per cent. However, these data are affected by changes over time in the mix of lower and higher paid workers within a sector, as well as discontinuities in the annual survey of hours and earnings (ASHE, see text box above) and so do not necessarily indicate changes in wage rates for particular employees or jobs.

If earnings are calculated on a weekly rather than an hourly basis, the mining and quarrying sector recorded the highest median earnings in April 2008, at £648 per week. This was £35 per week more than the second highest – the electricity, gas and water supply sector at £613 – and financial intermediation was the third highest, at £597 per week. The weekly earnings for the mining and quarrying sector and also the electricity, gas and water supply sector are boosted by longer paid hours worked by these employees than those worked in the financial intermediation sector.

Earnings also vary by occupation. In April 2008 those in the highest paid jobs in the UK were directors and chief executives of large organisations, with median gross pay for full-time

Table 5.11

Median hourly earnings:[1] by industry[2]

United Kingdom

£ per hour

	1997	2001	2006	2007	2008
Financial intermediation	10.50	12.65	14.54	15.44	16.47
Mining and quarrying	8.86	10.20	13.99	13.19	15.20
Electricity, gas and water supply	9.76	11.00	13.18	13.53	14.71
Education	10.94	11.65	13.95	14.14	14.58
Public administration and defence, and compulsory social security	9.63	10.62	12.47	12.77	13.38
Real estate, renting and business activities	8.51	10.51	12.32	12.60	13.03
Health and social work	7.60	9.11	11.10	11.55	11.95
Construction	7.19	8.68	11.04	11.37	11.74
Manufacturing	7.56	8.88	10.68	10.93	11.50
Transport, storage and communication	7.29	8.59	10.31	10.76	11.20
Other community, social and personal service activities	6.76	8.11	9.87	10.19	10.54
Wholesale and retail trade, and repair of motor vehicles, motorcycles and personal and household goods	6.21	7.34	8.63	8.85	9.15
Agriculture, hunting and forestry	4.95	5.90	7.23	7.50	7.67
Hotels and restaurants	4.62	5.49	6.52	6.81	7.00
All industries and services	7.83	9.21	11.03	11.36	11.87

1 Full-time employees on adult rates, excluding overtime, whose pay for the survey period was unaffected by absence. There is a discontinuity in results between 2001 and 2006. See Annual Survey of Hours and Earnings text box.
2 See Appendix, Part 4: Standard Industrial Classification 2003.

Source: Annual Survey of Hours and Earnings, Office for National Statistics

employees of £1,878 per week, followed by senior officials in central government at £1,276 per week. These high earners contrast with leisure and theme park attendants who, with median gross earnings of £227 per week were the lowest paid of all full-time employees.

From October 2007 there were three rates for the national minimum wage: one for those aged between 16 and 17 (£3.40 per hour, increased to £3.53 from 1 October 2008), one for those aged between 18 and 21 (£4.60 per hour, increased to £4.77 from October 2008) and one for those aged 22 and over (£5.52 per hour, increased to £5.73 from October 2008). Young people are more likely to be in jobs paid below the national minimum wage. In April 2008, 3.9 per cent of jobs in the UK held by those aged 16 to 17 were paid below the relevant rate, compared with 2.6 per cent of those held by people aged 18 to 21, and 0.9 per cent of those held by people aged 22 and over. Part-time jobs were more likely than full-time jobs to pay less than the minimum wage. However, it is important to note that these estimates do not measure non-compliance with the national minimum wage legislation as the ASHE does not indicate whether jobs are exempt from the

legislation, such as apprentices or new trainees. The increased likelihood of young people being in jobs paid below the minimum wage is likely to be at least in part because they are more likely to be in a job that is exempt.

Taxes

People's incomes are subject to a number of deductions over which they have little or no control. The main ones are income tax and social contributions. Social contributions, in the form of national insurance contributions, are paid according to an individual's earnings rather than their total income, and for employees, payments are made both by the individual and their employer. In 2008/09 employees with earnings less than £105 per week in the UK paid no contributions, and neither did their employers. Employees paid Class 1 contributions equal to 11 per cent of their earnings between £105 and £770 per week, and an additional 1 per cent on earnings above £770 per week. According to the UK National Accounts, in 2007 around 12 per cent of total gross household income was paid out in employees' national insurance contributions, compared with 17 per cent paid out in income tax.

Under the UK income tax system, every individual is entitled to a personal allowance and those with an annual income below this do not pay any income tax. For 2008/09, the personal allowance was set at £6,035 for those aged under 65, with further allowances for people aged 65 and over. The income tax regime on earnings for 2008/09 includes two different rates of tax. Taxable income of up to £34,800 (that is, after the deduction of allowances and any other tax relief to which the individual may be entitled) is charged at 20 per cent. Taxable income above £34,800 is charged at 40 per cent. Special rates apply to income from savings and dividends.

HM Revenue and Customs estimated that in 2008/09 there will have been around 31.0 million taxpayers in the UK (Table 5.12), 0.9 million fewer than in 2007/08. Given the progressive nature of the income tax system, the amount of tax payable increases as income increases, both as a proportion of income and in cash terms. The average rate of income tax for taxpayers with taxable incomes between the personal annual allowance of £6,035 and £7,499 was 1.9 per cent compared with average rates in excess of 30.0 per cent for taxpayers with incomes of £100,000 and over.

Table 5.12

Income tax payable: by annual income,[1] 2008/09[2]

United Kingdom

	Number of taxpayers (thousands)	Total tax liability after tax reductions[3] (£ million)	Average rate of tax (percentages)	Average amount of tax (£)
£6,035–£7,499	1,440	184	1.9	128
£7,500–£9,999	2,900	1,270	5.0	439
£10,000–£14,999	6,390	6,690	8.4	1,050
£15,000–£19,999	4,930	10,000	11.7	2,030
£20,000–£29,999	6,910	23,700	14.0	3,430
£30,000–£49,999	5,810	34,900	15.8	6,000
£50,000–£99,999	2,010	30,700	23.3	15,300
£100,000–£199,999	470	19,000	30.1	40,500
£200,000–£499,999	143	14,000	33.8	97,800
£500,000–£999,999	26	6,330	35.4	242,000
£1,000,000 and over	11	8,390	35.9	776,000
All incomes	31,000	155,000	17.9	5,000

1 Total income of the individual for income tax purposes including earned and investment income. Figures relate to taxpayers only.
2 Based on projections in line with the March 2008 Budget and subsequent changes (May 2008) to the income tax personal allowance and basic rate limit.
3 In this context tax reductions refer to allowances given at a fixed rate, for example the married couple's allowance.

Source: HM Revenue and Customs

Figure 5.13

Indirect taxes[1] as a percentage of disposable income: by income grouping[2] of household, 2006/07

United Kingdom
Percentages

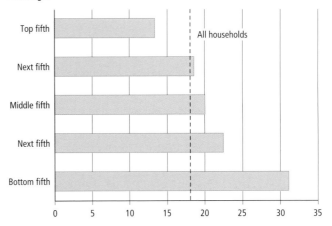

1 Includes intermediate taxes, which are those taxes paid by industry and commerce (for example duty on derv) and assumed to be passed on to consumers in the prices of the goods and services they buy.
2 Equivalised disposable income has been used to rank the households into quintile groups. See Appendix, Part 5: Equivalisation scales.

Source: Office for National Statistics

In addition to direct taxes such as income tax, households pay indirect taxes through their expenditure. Indirect taxes include value added tax (VAT), customs duties and excise duties, and are included in the prices of consumer goods and services. These taxes are specific to particular commodities. For example, in 2006/07 and 2007/08 VAT was payable on most consumer goods and services at 17.5 per cent of their value, though not on most foods, books and newspapers, and children's clothing and footwear; and was payable at a reduced rate of 5 per cent on some items such as heating and lighting for household use. However, the standard rate of VAT was reduced to 15 per cent from December 2008. Customs and excise duties paid on goods such as alcohol and tobacco products tend to vary by the volume rather than value of goods purchased.

On average, households paid 18 per cent of their disposable income in indirect taxes in 2006/07 (Figure 5.13). High income households are more likely to devote a larger proportion of their income to investments or repaying loans, which do not attract indirect taxes. Low income households may be funding their expenditure through taking out loans or drawing down savings, resources that are not included in disposable income. Also, the expenditure of low income households is directed more at items that attract indirect taxes such as tobacco and fuel. As a result, the proportion of disposable income paid in indirect taxes tends to be higher for those on low incomes than for those on high incomes. In 2006/07 households in the top quintile or top 'fifth' of the income distribution (see Analysing income distribution text box) paid 13 per cent of their disposable income in indirect taxes, compared with 31 per cent paid by those in the bottom 'fifth' of the distribution.

Income distribution

The various components of income vary in importance for different household types, and levels of earnings vary between individuals. Taken together, this results in an uneven distribution of total income between households. The inequality is reduced to some extent by the deduction of taxes and social contributions and their redistribution to households in the form of social security benefits. For this reason, the analysis of income distribution is usually based on household disposable income. In the analysis of Households Below Average Income (HBAI) carried out by the Department for Work and Pensions (DWP), on which most of the tables and figures in this and the next section are based, payments of income tax, council tax (domestic rates in Northern Ireland) and employee national insurance contributions are deducted from gross income, including social security benefits, to obtain disposable income. For more details see Appendix, Part 5: Households Below Average Income (HBAI).

In the HBAI analysis, disposable income is presented both before and after the deduction of housing costs. It can be argued that the costs of housing at a given time may or may not reflect the true value of the housing that different households actually enjoy. For example, the housing costs of someone renting a property from a private landlord may be much higher than those for someone renting a local authority property of similar quality, for which the rent may be set without reference to a market rent. Equally, a retired person living in a property that they own outright may enjoy the same level of housing as their younger neighbour in an identical property owned with a mortgage, although their housing costs will be very different. Estimates are presented on both bases to take into account variations in housing costs that do not correspond to comparable variations in the quality of housing. Neither is given pre-eminence over the other.

Figure 5.03 showed how the UK income distribution has evolved over the last three decades. The picture of the income distribution in 2006/07, summarised in Figure 5.14, shows considerable inequality. Each bar represents the number of people (children as well as adults) who were living in households with equivalised weekly household disposable income in a particular £10 band (see Analysing income distribution text box for definition of equivalisation). There is a

Figure 5.14

Distribution of weekly household disposable income,[1] 2006/07

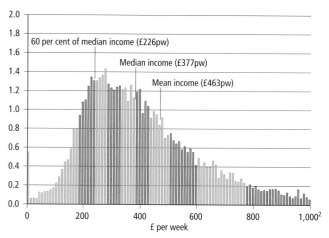

United Kingdom

Millions of individuals

1 Equivalised household disposable income before deduction of housing costs (in £10 bands), using OECD equivalisation scale. The £10 bands are grouped into decile groups in alternating colours. See Appendix, Part 5: Households Below Average Income (HBAI), and Equivalisation scales.
2 There were also an additional 2.7 million individuals with income above £1,000 per week.

Source: Households Below Average Income, Department for Work and Pensions

greater concentration of people at the lower levels of weekly income, with nearly two-thirds of individuals living in households with below average (mean) income. The long tail at the upper end of the distribution is in fact considerably longer than shown: there were an estimated additional 2.7 million individuals living in households with disposable income greater than £1,000 per week who are not shown on the chart, but who are included in the calculation of mean and median income. The highest bar represents 1.4 million people in households with incomes of between £270 and £280 per week. The substantial numbers of individuals living in households with relatively high incomes skews the distribution in Figure 5.14, and produces the large difference between the overall mean income of £463 per week and the median of £377 per week. For some households, disposable income before deduction of housing costs may be negative over the survey period, for example if they record a loss from self-employment. Any negative incomes are set to zero in the HBAI analysis.

The Gini coefficient is a commonly used summary measure of the extent of income inequality. It is usually expressed as a percentage, with 0 representing complete equality (all persons receiving exactly the same income) and 100 representing complete inequality (one person within a population receiving all the income, others receiving nothing) – see Appendix, Part 5: Gini coefficient. Gini coefficients calculated for EU-27 member states for 2006 indicate that there was greatest equality in the income distribution within Bulgaria, Denmark, Slovenia and Sweden, all with values of 24 (Figure 5.15). Countries where income inequality was greatest were Latvia (39) and Portugal (38). The Gini coefficient for the UK of 32 was above the EU-27 average of 30, indicating that UK households experience a higher degree of income inequality than the average within the EU-27. (Note that because of differences in the income concepts and methods used in the EU Survey of Income and Living Conditions, this estimate for the UK will not necessarily be comparable with estimates derived from UK sources).

People in households headed by someone from the White ethnic group were fairly evenly spread within the distribution of disposable income in 2006/07, with a very slight tendency to be towards the higher end of the distribution (Table 5.16). However, people in households from most other ethnic groups

Figure 5.15

Income inequality:[1] EU-27 comparison, 2006

Percentages

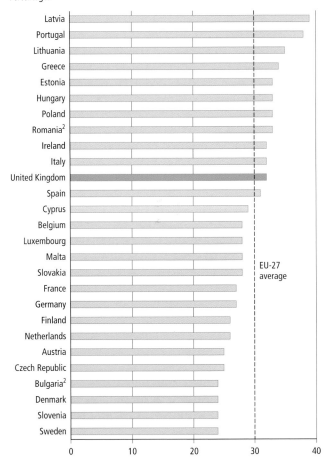

1 As measured by the Gini coefficient, which can take values between 0 and 100, with 0 representing complete equality and 100 representing complete inequality. See Appendix, Part 5: Gini coefficient.
2 Source of data is Household Budget Survey.

Source: EU Survey of Income and Living Standards, Eurostat

Table 5.16

Distribution of equivalised disposable income:[1] by ethnic group[2] of head of household, 2006/07

United Kingdom						Percentages
	Bottom fifth	Next fifth	Middle fifth	Next fifth	Top fifth	All
White	19	20	20	21	21	100
Mixed	27	18	17	15	23	100
Asian or Asian British	37	20	16	13	13	100
Indian	23	17	21	17	21	100
Pakistani/Bangladeshi	54	26	9	7	4	100
Black or Black British	31	22	20	15	12	100
Black Caribbean	27	23	19	19	13	100
African/Other Black	35	22	21	11	10	100
Chinese or Other ethnic group	27	21	14	16	22	100
All households	20	20	20	20	20	100

1 Equivalised household disposable income before deduction of housing costs has been used to rank individuals into quintile groups. See Appendix, Part 5: Households Below Average Income (HBAI), and Equivalisation scales.
2 See Appendix, Part 1: Classification of ethnic groups.

Source: Households Below Average Income, Department for Work and Pensions

tended to be concentrated towards the lower end of the distribution. This pattern was particularly marked for the Pakistani/Bangladeshi groups, with more than one-half of the individuals in these families living in households in the bottom 20 per cent of the income distribution.

Ethnicity is one of a variety of factors that are associated with an individual's position in the income distribution. For example, other groups with greater than average risks of being in the bottom 20 per cent of the income distribution in 2006/07 were people in lone parent families and in workless families where one or more adults were unemployed. Couples without dependent children had a greater than average likelihood of being in the top 20 per cent of the distribution.

Low income

It is possible to define people as poor if they are in the bottom quintile or decile group of the income distribution (see Analysing income distribution text box), but such a definition is not generally used because it would mean that 20 per cent or 10 per cent of the population would always be defined as poor. Other approaches generally involve fixing a threshold in monetary terms, below which a household is considered to be 'poor'. This threshold may be calculated in a variety of ways.

In countries at a very low level of development it may be useful to cost the bare essentials to maintain human life and use this as the yardstick against which to measure low income. This approach has led to the definition of 'a dollar a day' as the threshold for poverty in developing countries. However, this 'basic needs' measure is of limited usefulness for a developed country such as the UK.

The approach generally used in more developed countries is to fix a low income threshold in terms of a fraction of the median income of the population. This threshold may then be fixed in real terms for a number of years, or it may be calculated in respect of the income distribution for each successive year. The Government's Opportunity for All (OfA) indicators use both approaches. The proportions of people living in households with incomes below various fractions of contemporary median income are monitored, and are referred to as those with relative low income. The proportions with incomes below various fractions of median income in 1998/99 (the reference year for which the threshold was set), are also monitored. A third OfA indicator measures the number of people with persistent low income, defined as being in a low income household in three out of the last four years. In addition, the Government has announced that to monitor progress against its target of halving the number of children in low income households by 2010 compared with 1998/99 and eradicating child poverty by 2020, there will be another measure that combines material deprivation (not being able to afford to buy essential goods and services) and relative low income for families with children.

The low income threshold generally adopted in the UK, and used in the remainder of this section, is 60 per cent of contemporary equivalised median household disposable income before the deduction of housing costs, see Appendix, Part 5: Equivalisation scales. In 2006/07 this represented an income of £226 per week.

In 1987, 18 per cent of the UK population were living in low income households (Figure 5.17). This proportion peaked at 22 per cent of the population in 1990–91 and 1991–92. The trend was then generally downwards during the 1990s and early 2000s, to reach 17 per cent in 2004/05, though in 2005/06 and 2006/07 it was estimated to have risen slightly to 18 per cent of the population or 10.7 million people. This pattern is also reflected in the proportion of people with incomes less than 50 per cent of the median. Note that between 1994/95 and 1997/98 these figures exclude Northern Ireland, but this is estimated to have a minimal impact on the trends.

Figure 5.17

Proportion of people whose income is below various percentages of median household disposable income[1]

United Kingdom/Great Britain[2]

Percentages

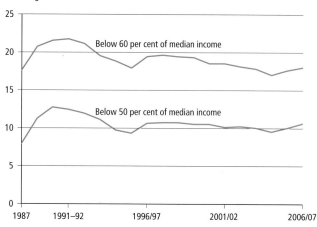

1 Contemporary household disposable income before deduction of housing costs, using OECD equivalisation scale. See Appendix, Part 5: Households Below Average Income (HBAI), and Equivalisation scales, for variations in source and definition on which the time series is based.
2 Data for 1994/95 to 1997/98 are for Great Britain only.

Source: Households Below Average Income, Department for Work and Pensions

Although the overall risk of living in a low income household fell by 4 percentage points between 1990–91 and 2006/07 from 22 per cent to 18 per cent, different groups within the population experienced varying changes in risks. People of working age were at less risk of living in a low income household than either pensioners or children, and this risk varied little between 1990–91 and 2005/06. Taking this period as a whole, the biggest reductions in risk have been experienced by pensioners. The proportion living in a low income household fell from 37 per cent in 1990–91 to 21 per cent in 2004/05 and 2005/06, though it then rose slightly to 23 per cent in 2006/07. The proportion of children living in low income households also fell over this period, from 27 per cent in 1990–91 to 21 per cent in 2004/05, the same risk as for pensioners, but rose slightly to 22 per cent in 2005/06 and 2006/07 (2.9 million children in 2006/07).

In 2006/07 children were at greater than average risk of living in a low income family if they were living in a workless family, if they were living in a lone parent family, or if they were living in a family where the head of the household came from an ethnic minority group. This was particularly the case for those headed by someone from the Pakistani or Bangladeshi groups, where the majority of children were in low income households. The size of the family is also a risk factor. Around one-third of children in larger families, those with three children or more,

Figure 5.18

Proportion of children living in households below 60 per cent of median household disposable income:[1] by number of children in family

United Kingdom/Great Britain[2]

Percentages

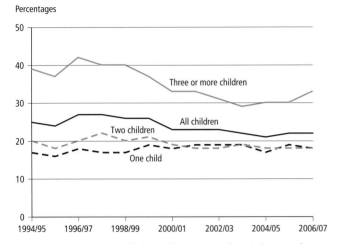

1 Contemporary household disposable income before deduction of housing costs, using OECD equivalisation scale. See Appendix, Part 5: Households Below Average Income (HBAI), and Equivalisation scales, for variations in source and definition on which the time series is based.
2 Data for 1994/95 to 1997/98 are for Great Britain only.

Source: Households Below Average Income, Department for Work and Pensions

were living in households with below 60 per cent of median income (before deduction of housing costs) in 2006/07, compared with less than one-fifth of those living in families with one or two children (Figure 5.18). The proportion of children living in larger families with low income fell from a peak of 42 per cent in 1996/97 to level off at around 29 and 30 per cent in 2003/04 to 2005/06. It is the reduction in risk of low income among children living in larger families that accounts for the majority of the reduction in child poverty overall, since there is only a small decline in the risk of low income among children living in families with one or two children.

Research carried out by the Institute of Social and Economic Research for DWP using pooled data from five years (1999/2000 to 2003/04) of the Family Resources Survey (FRS) enabled analysis of children living in large families with four or more children. These families made up less than 5 per cent of all families but contained more than 20 per cent of children living in households below 60 per cent of median income (before deduction of housing costs). The research showed that there were two main reasons for poverty among large families. First, both the mothers and fathers of large families were less likely to be in work than parents with one or two children, and if they were in work they tended to have lower earnings. Secondly, they found that benefits and tax credits did not fully

compensate large families for the extra cost of children, so they tended to be worse off than families with fewer children but otherwise in similar circumstances.

The DWP's HBAI analysis provides an annual cross-sectional snapshot of the distribution of income based on the FRS. The British Household Panel Survey complements this by providing longitudinal information about how the incomes of a fixed sample of individuals in Great Britain change from year to year. This makes it possible to track how people move in and out of low income over time, and to identify the factors associated with such movements.

For some people, such as students and those unemployed for a brief period, the experience of low income may be a relatively transient one, but for others it may be more permanent. The definition of the Government's OfA indicator for persistent low income is 'at least three years out of four below thresholds of 60 or 70 per cent of median income'. Between 1991–94 and 2002–05, the proportion of individuals experiencing persistent low income, based on the threshold of below 60 per cent of median disposable income, fell from 12 per cent to 9 per cent (Table 5.19). However, the proportion of lone parent families experiencing persistent low income has shown a much steeper decline, from 40 per cent during 1991–94 to 19 per cent during 2002–05. The proportion of single pensioners experiencing persistent low income rose from 21 per cent in 1991–94 to 23 per cent in 1996–99, but has since fallen to

Table 5.19

Persistent low income: by family type[1]

Great Britain   Percentages

	3 out of 4 years below 60 per cent of median income[2]			
	1991–94	1996–99	2001–04	2002–05
Pensioner couple	13	17	14	13
Single pensioner	21	23	19	18
Couple with children	13	11	9	8
Couple without children	3	3	4	5
Single with children	40	27	22	19
Single without children	6	7	7	6
All individuals	12	11	10	9

1 Families are classified according to their type in the first year of the relevant period.
2 Contemporary household disposable income before housing costs, using McClements equivalisation scale. See Appendix, Part 5: Households Below Average Income (HBAI), and Equivalisation scales.

Source: Department for Work and Pensions from the British Household Panel Survey, Institute for Social and Economic Research

5

18 per cent in 2002–05. Pensioner couples experiencing persistent low income showed the same trend over time, but the proportions were consistently lower than for single pensioners. Single people and couples without dependent children experienced very low risks of persistent low income.

Wealth

Wealth can be held in the form of financial assets, such as savings accounts or shares, which provide a flow of current income, or pension rights, which provide entitlement to a future income flow. These types of asset form financial wealth. Ownership of non-financial wealth may provide financial security even if it does not provide a current income flow; a house or a work of art, for example, could be sold to provide income if necessary. In this section the term 'wealth' includes both financial and non-financial assets. There is a further distinction sometimes made between marketable and non-marketable wealth. Marketable wealth comprises assets that can be sold and their value realised, whereas non-marketable wealth comprises mainly pension rights that often cannot be cashed in. Wealth may be accumulated either by acquiring new assets through saving or by inheritance, or by existing assets increasing in value.

Aggregate data on the wealth of the household sector compiled in the UK National Accounts indicate that of total assets of around £9,062 billion in 2007, 45 per cent were held in the form of residential buildings (Table 5.20). Even when account is taken of the loans outstanding on the purchase of housing, this form of wealth grew strongly at an average of 5.2 per cent per year between 1991 and 2006. This reflected the buoyant state of the housing market over the period, as well as the continued growth in the number of owner-occupied dwellings. However, between 2006 and 2007 the value of residential buildings less loans secured on dwellings grew by only 1.3 per cent in real terms (see Chapter 10: Housing).

The second most important element of household wealth is financial assets held in life assurance and pension funds, amounting to £2,226 billion in 2007. This element of household wealth grew strongly in real terms during the 1990s, as a result of increases in the contributions paid into occupational pension schemes as well as increased take-up of personal pensions. It fell by 11 per cent in real terms between

Table 5.20

Composition of the net wealth[1] of the household sector

United Kingdom

£ billion at 2007 prices[2]

	1991	2001	2004	2005	2006	2007
Non-financial assets						
Residential buildings	1,881	2,694	3,902	3,881	4,035	4,077
Other	553	625	825	825	845	839
Financial assets						
Life assurance and pension funds	1,015	1,992	1,986	2,247	2,304	2,226
Securities and shares	425	799	697	749	716	674
Currency and deposits	634	870	1,049	1,089	1,109	1,103
Other assets	107	118	128	126	149	144
Total assets	4,614	7,098	8,587	8,917	9,157	9,062
Financial liabilities						
Loans secured on dwellings	527	751	1,067	1,092	1,142	1,147
Other loans	140	202	259	264	267	255
Other liabilities	75	79	108	107	137	138
Total liabilities	741	1,031	1,435	1,462	1,546	1,539
Total net wealth	3,873	6,067	7,152	7,455	7,612	7,524

1 At end of each year. See Appendix, Part 5: Net wealth of the household sector.
2 Adjusted to 2007 prices using the expenditure deflator for the household sector. See Appendix, Part 5: Household income data sources.

Source: Office for National Statistics

Table 5.21

Household savings: by household type and amount, 2006/07

United Kingdom

Percentages

	No savings	Less than £1,500	£1,500 but less than £10,000	£10,000 but less than £20,000	£20,000 or more	All households
Households without dependent children[1]						
One adult, over state pension age	20	23	28	12	17	100
One adult, under state pension age	31	28	23	7	11	100
Two adults, one or both over state pension age	13	16	24	14	33	100
Two adults, both under state pension age	19	23	28	12	18	100
Households with dependent children[1,2]						
One adult, with one or more dependent children	53	35	9	1	2	100
Two adults, with one or more dependent children	28	26	24	8	13	100
Other households[3]	22	23	27	11	16	100
All households	24	24	25	10	17	100

1 Aged under 16, or aged 16 to 19 and not married or in a civil partnership and living with their parents and in full-time non-advanced education or in unwaged government training.
2 Includes adults both under and over state pension age.
3 Includes households with three or more adults both under and over state pension age, with or without dependent children.

Source: Family Resources Survey, Department for Work and Pensions

2001 and 2002, reflecting the fall in stock market values over this period, but recovered to reach its 2001 level in 2004. It grew strongly between 2004 and 2006, but then fell again in real terms between 2006 and 2007.

The assets that people probably most closely identify with savings are securities and shares, and currency and deposits, being the most easily accessible forms of financial assets. These formed around one-fifth of total assets of the household sector in 2007. Data from the FRS based on individuals' estimates of their savings indicated that around one-quarter of households in the UK had no savings at all in 2006/07 (Table 5.21). Savings patterns vary with household composition. Households with two adults and no dependent children, where one or both were over state pension age were the most likely to have substantial savings – one-third of such households had savings of £20,000 or more. This reflects life cycle effects, since older people may have been able to build up savings during their working lives and some may have received a lump sum pension on their retirement. Earlier in the life cycle the majority of lone parent households had no savings (53 per cent), as did more than one-quarter (28 per cent) of couple households with dependent children.

The term 'financial exclusion' is sometimes used to describe people who do not use formal financial services at all. Data from the FRS indicate that in 2006/07, 6 per cent of

individuals did not have any kind of direct payment account (defined as any that can accept automatic credit transfers). This proportion was the same for individuals living in households with an income below 60 per cent of the median (before deduction of housing costs), also at 6 per cent.

Occupational, personal and stakeholder pensions are important determinants of where older people appear in the income distribution, and so the extent to which people of working age are making provision for their retirement is of considerable policy interest. In 2005/06 the Family Resources Survey (FRS) found that 56 per cent of all adult employees of working age in the UK had some non-state pension provision, compared with 34 per cent of the self-employed and only 3 per cent of other adults of working age (including the unemployed, those looking after the family/home and those who were sick or disabled). Among employees, the most common form of provision was an occupational pension only, for which 45 per cent had provision. However, among the self-employed, 2 per cent had occupational pension provision only compared with 32 per cent with a personal or stakeholder pension.

For around one-half of adults under state pension age who responded to the 2006/07 Wealth and Assets Survey (experimental statistics) in Great Britain, having a pension

Table 5.22

Attitudes to saving for retirement among adults under state pension age,[1] 2006/07[2]

Great Britain
Percentages

	Agree[3]	Neither agree nor disagree	Disagree[3]	Total[4]
I would rather have a good standard of living today than save for retirement	39	26	33	100
Having a pension is the best way to save for retirement	49	20	27	100
Investing in property is the best way to save for retirement	60	21	15	100

1 People aged 16 and over and under state pension age (65 for men and 60 for women) and not yet retired. Excludes persons aged 16 to 19 and in full-time education, in the family unit and living in the household.
2 Enumeration period: July 2006 to June 2007.
3 Includes those who strongly agreed/disagreed and those who tended to agree/disagree.
4 Includes a small proportion who said 'Don't know' or did not express an opinion for each statement.

Source: Wealth and Assets Survey (Experimental statistics), Office for National Statistics

was seen as the best way to save for retirement (Table 5.22). A higher proportion (three-fifths) felt that investing in property was the best way to do so, though the survey found that only 8 per cent owned any real estate other than the family home. However, two-fifths felt that they would rather have a good standard of living today than save for retirement, and only one-third of respondents disagreed with this statement. This feeling of 'living for today' was stronger among those with no current pension scheme, of whom nearly one-half agreed with the statement.

Chapter 6

Expenditure

- Total household expenditure in the UK increased by more than two-and-one-half times between 1971 and 2007. (Figure 6.1)

- In 2007, the volume of household expenditure by UK tourists abroad, at £32.3 billion, was more than eight times greater than in 1971. (Table 6.3)

- Average weekly household expenditure in the UK for couples with dependent children was £657.70 in 2007, compared with £389.90 for lone parents with dependent children. (Table 6.5)

- Between 1997/98 and 2007, household ownership of mobile phones increased from 20 per cent of UK households to 78 per cent. (Figure 6.7)

- Net lending secured on dwellings in the UK reached the most recent peak of £31.0 billion in the last quarter of 2006, before falling to £4.4 billion by the third quarter of 2008. (Figure 6.8)

- Despite total household debt in the UK increasing more than threefold between 1987 and 2007, it remained around 90 per cent of annual household disposable income as disposable income also increased. (Figure 6.9)

Patterns of spending can be used as a measure of societal well-being and a way of assessing living standards and quality of life. Expenditure does not necessarily equate with income. For example, households may spend more than their income over a period by using credit facilities or withdrawing from their savings. Alternatively, they may spend less than their income and save some for the future. Some households have a low level of expenditure irrespective of income, for example, those who own their home outright, as paying rent or a mortgage is usually the largest item of household expenditure. Expenditure patterns also vary over time according to the make up of the household, and provide an insight into changing consumer preferences.

Household and family expenditure

There has been an upward trend in the volume of household expenditure in the UK over the last 36 years. In 2007 the volume of UK domestic household expenditure was 2.7 times greater than in 1971 (Figure 6.1). The volume of spending closely followed the growth pattern in gross domestic product and household income (see Chapter 5: Income and wealth,

Figure 6.1

Volume of domestic household expenditure[1]

United Kingdom

Index numbers (1971=100)

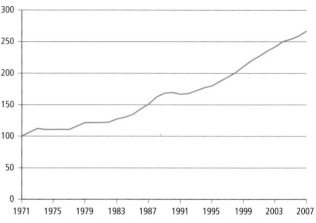

1 Chained volume measure. See Appendix, Part 6: Household expenditure.

Source: Office for National Statistics

Table 6.2

Household expenditure: by purpose[1]

United Kingdom   Percentages

	1971	1981	1991	2001	2007
Food and non-alcoholic drinks	21	17	12	9	9
Alcoholic drinks and tobacco	7	6	5	4	4
Clothing and footwear	9	7	6	6	6
Housing, water and fuel[2]	15	17	18	18	20
Household goods and services	7	7	6	6	6
Health	1	1	1	2	2
Transport	12	15	15	15	14
Communication[2]	1	2	2	2	2
Recreation and culture	9	9	10	12	12
Education	1	1	1	1	1
Restaurants and hotels[2]	10	11	12	11	11
Miscellaneous goods and services[3]	7	7	11	11	11
Total domestic household expenditure	100	100	100	98	98
of which goods	65	61	53	49	47
of which services	35	40	47	49	51
UK tourist expenditure abroad	1	2	3	4	4
less Foreign tourist expenditure	2	2	2	2	2
All household expenditure[4] (=100%) (£ billions)	34	147	358	632	838

1 According to the Classification of Individual Consumption by Purpose (COICOP). See Appendix, Part 6: Household expenditure.
2 Housing, water and fuel excludes mortgage interest payments and council tax (domestic rates in Northern Ireland). Communication includes mobile phone equipment and services. Restaurants and hotels includes purchases of alcoholic drinks in pubs, restaurants and hotels.
3 Includes personal care, social protection, insurance and financial services.
4 Includes expenditure by UK households in the UK and abroad.

Source: Office for National Statistics

Figure 5.1) and increased every year between 1971 and 2007, with the exceptions of 1974, 1975, 1977, 1980, 1981 and 1991. These years all correspond to periods of economic recession in the UK.

Total household expenditure in the UK was £838 billion in 2007 (Table 6.2). The proportion of household expenditure on food and non-alcoholic drinks in 2007 (9 per cent) was less than one-half of the proportion spent in 1971 (21 per cent). However, the volume of expenditure on food and non-alcoholic drinks increased by one-and-one-half times between 1971 and 2007 (see Table 6.3) despite the fall as a proportion of total household expenditure. On average, expenditure on housing (excluding mortgage interest payments and council tax/domestic rates in Northern Ireland), water and fuel accounted for 20 per cent of total expenditure in 2007 compared with 15 per cent in 1971. Of this 20 per cent, almost three-quarters was spent on mortgages and rentals. There was a steady increase in the proportion of expenditure on mortgages between 1971 (4.5 per cent) and 2007 (10.5 per cent) as a

greater number of people opted to buy their homes rather than rent (see Chapter 10: Housing, Figure 10.4). Transport was the second largest expenditure category in 2007, accounting for 14 per cent of total household expenditure. Transport includes the purchase of vehicles, the running costs of personal vehicles (such as fuel and maintenance costs) and the cost of using public transport. The proportion of household income spent on transport has remained fairly stable since 1981.

Historically, households spent more on household goods than on services. In 1971 almost two-thirds (65 per cent) of expenditure was on goods. Since then the proportion of household expenditure on goods has gradually decreased while spending on services has gradually increased. From 1998 a higher proportion of total expenditure has been devoted to services compared with goods. Between 1971 and 2007 the volume of consumption of goods almost tripled, while consumption of services grew by less than two-and-one-half times (Table 6.3). This is because the price of services have increased faster than

Table 6.3

Volume of household expenditure: by purpose[1]

United Kingdom   Index numbers (1971=100)

	1971	1981	1991	2001	2007	£ billions (current prices) 2007
Food and non-alcoholic drinks	100	105	117	137	158	77
Alcoholic drinks and tobacco	100	99	92	88	91	30
Clothing and footwear	100	120	187	344	516	48
Housing, water and fuel[2]	100	117	139	152	161	169
Household goods and services	100	117	160	262	305	47
Health	100	125	182	188	220	13
Transport	100	128	181	246	273	120
Communication[2]	100	190	307	790	1,031	18
Recreation and culture	100	158	279	545	841	102
Education	100	160	199	255	233	12
Restaurants and hotels[2]	100	126	167	193	214	96
Miscellaneous goods and services[3]	100	121	231	282	311	93
Total domestic household expenditure	100	121	165	220	258	825
of which goods	100	117	156	227	290	397
of which services	100	128	180	218	236	428
UK tourist expenditure abroad	100	193	298	668	807	32
less Foreign tourist expenditure	100	152	187	210	250	19
All household expenditure[4]	100	121	167	227	267	838

1 Chained volume measure. According to the Classification of Individual Consumption by Purpose (COICOP). See Appendix, Part 6: Household expenditure.
2 Housing, water and fuel excludes mortgage interest payments and council tax (domestic rates in Northern Ireland). Communication includes mobile phone equipment and services. Restaurants and hotels includes purchases of alcoholic drinks in pubs, restaurants and hotels.
3 Includes personal care, social protection, insurance and financial services.
4 Includes expenditure by UK households in the UK and abroad.

Source: Office for National Statistics

Analysing household expenditure

Estimates of household expenditure are presented in two distinct and complementary ways. The first approach analyses the proportions of expenditure that households allocate to different goods and services, relative to the total value of expenditure in each year (Table 6.2). The second method highlights changes in levels of expenditure over time and is measured using volume indices (Figure 6.1 and Table 6.3). Volume indices remove the effect of price changes, which differ depending on the category of expenditure, and are useful for analysing time trends in consumption.

the prices of goods, meaning services have gradually made up a greater proportion of total household expenditure. Slower growth in the price of goods allowed an increasing volume of goods to be purchased for the same proportion of total expenditure. Conversely, although an increasing proportion of expenditure has been spent on services, the overall increase in the price of those services means that the volume of consumption of services increased more slowly.

There were considerable variations in the volume of expenditure on goods and services in the UK between 1971 and 2007. The largest category of household expenditure in 2007 was housing, water and fuel, at £169.5 billion. However, the largest increase in volume of expenditure since 1971 was in communication, including mobile phone equipment and services, which increased more than ten times. The volume of expenditure on recreation and culture rose more than eight times between 1971 and 2007. Transport was the second highest category of household expenditure in 2007, at £119.8 billion, and households spent 2.7 times more on transport in 2007 compared with 1971. The largest element within this expenditure category was the running costs associated with owning a vehicle (see Chapter 12: Transport, Figure 12.12).

The volume of expenditure by UK tourists abroad almost tripled between 1971 and 1991, making this one of the three largest growing categories of household expenditure over that period, along with communication, and recreation and culture. This pattern continued: by 2007 volume of expenditure by UK tourists abroad (£32.3 billion) was more than eight times that in 1971. These statistics reflect great changes in UK society: more spending on leisure time activities, including international travel, and more communication especially by mobile phone and the Internet.

Total household expenditure varies across the regions of the UK (Figure 6.4). In 2007, expenditure per head in Scotland was almost the same as the UK average, at £194.70 and

Figure 6.4

Household expenditure[1] per head: by region, 2007

United Kingdom
£ per week

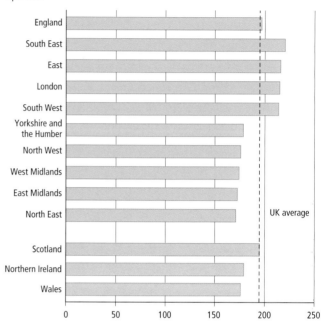

1 See Appendix, Part 6: Expenditure and Food Survey.

Source: Expenditure and Food Survey, Office for National Statistics

£194.80 per week respectively, whereas expenditure per head in England (£196.50) was 1 per cent higher than the UK average. In Northern Ireland (£179.10) it was 8 per cent lower than the UK average and in Wales (£175.80) 10 per cent lower.

Regional differences in household gross income per head followed similar patterns to those of household expenditure. In 2007 gross income per head in England was 2 per cent higher than the UK average of £279.80 per week, whereas in Scotland, Northern Ireland and Wales gross income per head was less than the UK average, by 2 per cent, 18 per cent and 13 per cent respectively. In the same year households in the South East spent 13 per cent more than the UK average, whereas households in the North East spent 12 per cent less than the UK average.

Household expenditure patterns vary according to the size and composition of the household (Table 6.5). In 2007, couples with dependent children spent on average £107.10 per week (19 per cent) more than couples without dependent children. Lone parents with dependent children spent £267.80 per week (41 per cent) less than couples with dependent children. Lone parents however, spent more on food and non-alcoholic drinks, clothing and footwear and housing, fuel and power, than adults living alone. Lone parents had the lowest expenditure of all household types on transport. Lone mothers in the UK with

Table 6.5

Household expenditure:[1] by selected working household types, 2007

United Kingdom   £ per week

	One adult[2]		Two adults[2,3]		
	With dependent children	No dependent children	With dependent children	No dependent children	All households
Food and non-alcoholic drink	41.70	25.20	66.90	49.10	48.10
Alcoholic drinks, tobacco and narcotics	8.50	7.10	12.00	14.30	11.20
Clothing and footwear	26.10	11.60	33.40	24.50	22.00
Housing (net),[4] fuel and power	68.20	49.60	57.00	56.70	51.80
Household goods and services	22.70	23.90	41.20	37.20	30.70
Health	2.60	3.40	6.70	7.70	5.70
Transport	36.20	48.30	91.90	78.30	61.70
Communication[5]	13.10	9.10	15.30	13.20	11.90
Recreation and culture	49.50	35.30	80.60	68.80	57.40
Education	2.40	4.20	15.60	3.30	6.80
Restaurants and hotels[6]	28.60	27.80	48.70	49.50	37.20
Miscellaneous goods and services	35.00	24.70	54.60	41.00	35.30
Other expenditure items	55.20	81.80	133.80	107.00	79.30
All household expenditure	389.90	351.90	657.70	550.60	459.20

1 See Appendix, Part 6: Expenditure and Food Survey. Expenditure rounded to the nearest 10 pence.
2 Men aged 16 to 64 and women aged 16 to 59.
3 Includes same-sex couples.
4 Excludes mortgage interest payments and council tax (domestic rates in Northern Ireland). These are included in 'Other expenditure items'.
5 Includes mobile phone equipment and services.
6 Includes purchases of alcoholic drinks in pubs, restaurants and hotels.

Source: Expenditure and Food Survey, Office for National Statistics

a child aged under five were less likely to be working than mothers who had a partner in Q2 2008 (see Chapter 4: Labour market, Table 4.3).

Pensioner households (pensioner couples where one or both are of state pension age or over – 65 for men and 60 for women – or single people of state pension age or over) can be divided into those who are reliant on the state retirement pension as their primary source of income and those who have another primary source of income (see Chapter 5: Income and wealth, Figure 5.8). Table 6.6 overleaf shows the amount spent per week by pensioners in the UK on various categories of items in 2007. Pensioner couple households who had a main income other than the state pension spent £119.50 (50 per cent) more per week than those who relied on the state retirement pension as their primary source of income. The categories with the greatest absolute difference in expenditure between these two groups of households were recreation and culture, and transport, where pensioner couples who did not rely on the state pension spent on average £30.20 (102 per cent) and £20.10 (80 per cent) more than those

pensioners who did rely on the state pension as their primary income. There was, however, only a small difference in the total expenditure between the single pensioner households who did and did not rely on the state pension as their primary source of income. Those who did not rely on the state pension in 2007 spent on average £20.00 (12 per cent) more per week than those who did rely on the state pension. Additionally there were no substantial differences between the patterns of expenditure of these two groups of households.

The ownership of goods and the use of services reflect household income (or access to credit) and expenditure. The volume of expenditure on 'household goods and services' increased more than threefold between 1971 and 2007. One consequence of this has been an increase in household ownership of consumer durables. Ownership of such items is often used as an indicator of living standards. Figure 6.7 overleaf shows ownership of some of the more recently available consumer durables. Over the last decade household ownership of mobile phones rose from 20 per cent of UK households in 1997/98 to 78 per cent in 2007, whereas

6

Table 6.6

Household expenditure:[1] by pensioner[2] household type, 2007

United Kingdom

£ per week

	Pensioner one adult[2]		Pensioner two adults[2,3]		All pensioner households
	State pension[4]	Other pension[5]	State pension[4]	Other pension[5]	
Food and non-alcoholic drink	24.30	25.90	45.10	49.40	37.40
Alcoholic drinks, tobacco and narcotics	3.50	4.60	6.70	9.50	6.90
Clothing and footwear	5.00	6.40	9.00	12.10	9.70
Housing (net),[6] fuel and power	30.90	34.10	32.50	39.10	36.50
Household goods and services	16.60	15.80	13.50	25.00	20.50
Health	1.60	4.90	2.30	8.30	5.60
Transport	13.20	13.90	25.10	45.20	27.80
Communication[7]	4.70	5.50	6.00	8.00	7.10
Recreation and culture	24.00	22.70	29.60	59.80	38.30
Education	0.00	1.20	0.00	0.60	0.70
Restaurants and hotels[8]	6.70	9.70	14.30	25.60	16.80
Miscellaneous goods and services	13.40	15.50	17.00	30.20	22.20
Other expenditure items	21.00	24.40	36.10	43.70	33.80
All household expenditure	164.70	184.70	237.10	356.60	263.10

1 See Appendix, Part 6: Expenditure and Food Survey. Expenditure rounded to the nearest 10 pence.
2 State pension age is currently 65 for men and 60 for women.
3 Includes same-sex couples.
4 State pension as their primary source of income.
5 Includes occupational retirement pensions, investments and annuities.
6 Excludes mortgage interest payments and council tax (domestic rates in Northern Ireland). These are included in 'Other expenditure items'.
7 Includes mobile phone equipment and services.
8 Includes purchases of alcoholic drinks in pubs, restaurants and hotels.

Source: Expenditure and Food Survey, Office for National Statistics

Figure 6.7

Household ownership of selected consumer durables

United Kingdom
Percentages

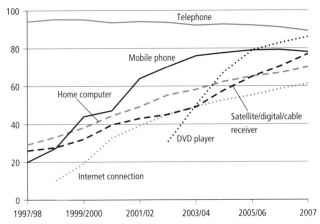

Source: Expenditure and Food Survey, Family Expenditure Survey, Office for National Statistics

ownership of landline telephones fell from 94 per cent to 89 per cent during the same period. As ownership of home computers increased (from 29 per cent to 70 per cent) so has the proportion of households that have an Internet connection (from less than 10 per cent to 61 per cent). Separating households into income quintile groups reveals how ownership of these items increases as household income increases (see Chapter 5: Income and wealth, Analysing income distribution text box on page 66). In the lowest income quintile group, 35 per cent of households owned home computers and 25 per cent had an Internet connection in the home in 2007, compared with 95 per cent and 92 per cent respectively in the highest income group. Ownership of DVD players increased rapidly between 2002/03 and 2005/06 from 31 per cent to 79 per cent and by 2007 reached 86 per cent.

Credit

Total net lending to individuals by banks, building societies and other lenders is a measure of the value of new loans less

Figure 6.8

Net[1] lending to individuals[2]

United Kingdom

£ billion per quarter at 2007 prices[3]

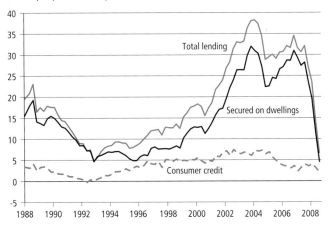

1 New loans less repayments on existing loans.
2 Data are seasonally adjusted. Lending secured on dwellings and consumer credit. Also includes lending to housing associations.
3 Adjusted to 2007 prices using the retail prices index. See Appendix, Part 6: Retail prices index.

Source: Bank of England

repayments over a given period. It is made up of lending secured on dwellings and consumer credit (for example, lending on credit cards, overdrafts and non-secured loans). Total net lending to individuals fell in the late 1980s to reach a low of £4.8 billion in the last quarter of 1992 (at 2007 prices) (Figure 6.8). This corresponds with the recession of the early 1990s. Although levels of consumer credit gradually increased from 1992, the majority of total net lending was secured against dwellings. The amount of lending secured on dwellings increased sharply from 2000 to a peak of £32.0 billion in the last quarter of 2003. The amount of lending secured on dwellings fell in 2004 but started to increase again in 2005, to reach £31.0 billion in the last quarter of 2006. The amount of secured lending then decreased sharply from the last quarter of 2007 and was £4.4 billion by the third quarter of 2008 as the economic downturn began.

Consumer credit increased to a high in 2004 of around £7 billion per quarter (at 2007 prices). This level of consumer credit led to increasing levels of individual insolvency (see Figure 6.10) and debt write-off. As this trend became apparent, lenders reduced consumer credit lending (and therefore borrowers reduced borrowing) with the result that in 2006 lending averaged £3.5 billion per quarter. Consumer credit remained roughly flat throughout 2006 to 2007 before falling to £2.1 billion in the third quarter of 2008.

The amount of outstanding household debt in the UK increased more than threefold between 1987 and 2007.

Figure 6.9

Household debt[1] as a proportion of household income

United Kingdom

Percentages

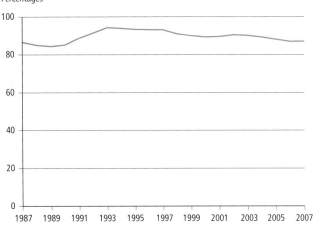

1 Includes secured and unsecured debt.

Source: Office for National Statistics

However, household disposable income also increased and this reduced the impact of the outstanding debt. Total household debt (both secured and unsecured) as a proportion of annual total household disposable income was relatively steady over the period 1987 to 2007 (Figure 6.9). It rose from 84.4 per cent in 1989 to 94.4 per cent in 1993, before falling to 87.1 per cent in 2007. Although there was a 331 per cent increase in the total amount of debt between 1987 and 2007, there was also a 330 per cent increase in the amount of household disposable income over the same period, leaving the debt ratio almost the same in 2007 as in 1987.

As the level of household borrowing increased over time, so has the total outstanding amount owed by individuals. This was accompanied by an increase in the number of individual insolvencies as debtors found themselves unable to keep up with repayments. Some of the main statutory insolvency instruments available to individuals in financial difficulties are bankruptcy and individual voluntary arrangements (IVAs). An individual may be declared bankrupt when the court concludes that there is no likelihood of the debt being repaid. However, in some circumstances the court will encourage the setting up of an IVA, where the debtor formally agrees to pay part, or all, of the debts over a period of time. The number of bankruptcies and IVAs in England and Wales remained generally stable from 1995 until 2002, when they started to increase (Figure 6.10 overleaf). Bankruptcies were the first to increase, from 2003, closely followed by an increase in the number of IVAs from 2004. The total number of insolvencies in England and Wales reached a peak of 106,650 individuals in

Figure 6.10

Individual insolvencies

England & Wales
Thousands

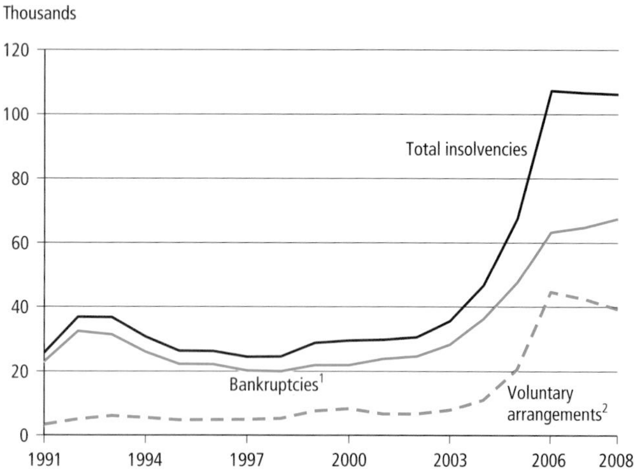

1 Individuals declared bankrupt by a court.
2 Individuals who make a voluntary agreement with their creditors. Includes Deeds of Arrangement, which enable debtors to come to an agreement with their creditors.

Source: Insolvency Service

2007. Subsequently there was a slight decrease in the number of new insolvencies although numbers remained high, at 106,540 in 2008.

Homeowners have better access to credit than those who are not because they have collateral in the form of housing equity. Borrowing by withdrawing housing equity can be a significant supplement to household income. Figure 6.11 shows new

Figure 6.11

Housing equity withdrawal[1] as a proportion of post-tax income

United Kingdom
Percentages

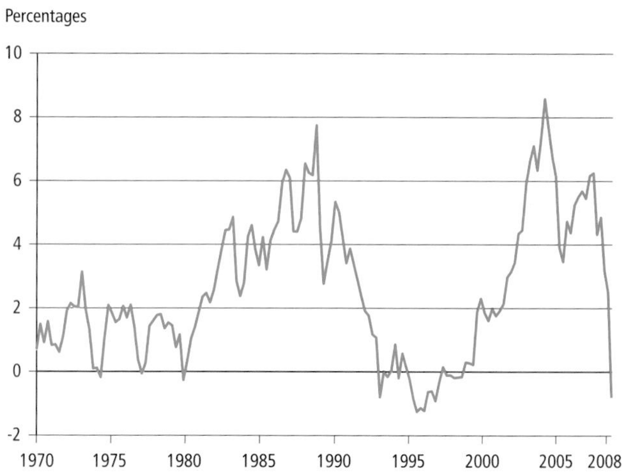

1 New borrowing secured on dwellings that is not invested in house purchases or home improvements.

Source: Bank of England

borrowing secured on dwellings in the UK that is not invested in house purchases or home improvements. Housing equity withdrawal increased in the late 1980s to reach a peak of an additional 8 per cent of post-tax income. This was followed by a decrease along with other forms of borrowing in the early 1990s. In 1993 and between 1995 and 1998 housing equity withdrawal was often negative, indicating that repayments were greater than new lending during these periods. New equity withdrawal increased sharply from 2001 to 2003 reaching a similar level to the 1980s as house prices increased rapidly. There was a fall during 2004 followed by an increase between 2005 and 2007. After this increase housing equity withdrawal fell once again as the increase in house prices slowed down. Housing equity withdrawal was negative in the second and third quarters of 2008.

People have different perceptions of their ability to manage their finances. In 2006, 90 per cent of all families (see Appendix, Part 2: Families) with children in Great Britain thought they were managing financially 'very well', 'quite well' or 'all right' (Table 6.12). However, around 9 per cent of all families with children thought they either were managing 'not very well', with 'some financial difficulties' or in 'deep financial trouble'. Lone parents were more likely to have financial difficulties than couple households; 81 per cent of lone parents stated that they were managing financially compared with 94 per cent of couple households. Another factor associated with how well families with children managed their finances

Table 6.12

Ability of families[1] to manage financially, 2006[2]

Great Britain
Percentages

	Very well	Quite well	Get by all right	Not very well	Some financial difficulties	Deep financial trouble
Family type						
Couple	24	38	32	3	4	1
Lone parent	8	25	48	6	10	3
Age of youngest child						
0–4 years	17	33	39	4	5	1
5–10 years	18	36	36	3	6	1
11–15 years	24	35	32	3	5	1
16–18 years	30	34	28	4	4	1
All families	20	34	36	3	5	1

1 Families with children.
2 Respondents were asked 'Would you describe your family as managing your finances?' and shown the above options. Excludes those who responded 'don't know'.

Source: Families and Children Study, Department for Work and Pensions

was the age of the youngest child. A greater proportion of families said that they were coping 'very well' as the age of their youngest child increased. Working parents often have to pay for child care for pre-school children, and for out-of-school clubs for older children. According to the Daycare Trust, the average cost of placing a child aged under two in a nursery full time in England was £159 per week in 2007, and the cost of placing a child aged two and over in a nursery full time was £149 per week. Therefore, as the age of the youngest child increases, the associated costs of formal child care decreases. Similarly, as the youngest child reaches compulsory school age parents are more likely to be in paid employment, which in turn increases household income thus allowing families more opportunity to cope financially (see Chapter 4: Labour market, Table 4.3).

Transactions

The volume of retail sales reflects the trends in overall consumer expenditure and, to a certain extent, the level of consumer confidence at any time. The retail sales index is a monthly measure of the turnover of retail businesses in Great Britain and is used as a key economic indicator. The volume of retail sales is highly seasonal. The non-seasonally adjusted index shows how the volume of sales varies considerably over the course of the year and how sales increase sharply in the run-up to Christmas (Figure 6.13). There is also a smaller but consistent increase in the summer months, corresponding with holiday spending. However, between 1998 and 2008 there was steady growth in the volume of retail sales underlying these seasonal factors.

Figure 6.13

Volume of retail sales[1]

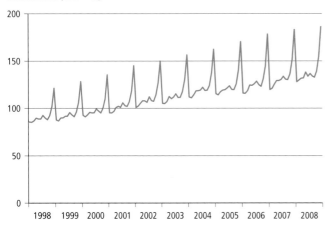

Great Britain

Index numbers (2000=100)

1 See Appendix, Part 6: Retail sales index.

Source: Office for National Statistics

Figure 6.14

Non-cash transactions:[1] by method of payment

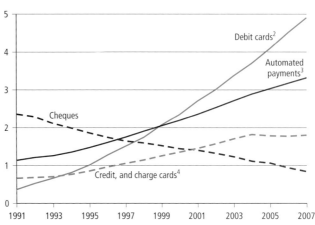

United Kingdom

Billions

1 Figures are for payments made by individuals. Cheque encashments and cash withdrawals from cash machines and branch counters using credit, charge and debit cards are not included. Based on data supplied by UK card issuers.
2 Includes all Visa Debit, Maestro and Solo cards.
3 Direct Debits, standing orders, remote Internet and telephone banking payments.
4 Visa, MasterCard, travel/entertainment cards and store cards.

Source: The Payments Council

The availability and use of non-cash methods of payment have changed over time. Since 1991 there has been a rapid decline in cheque payments in the UK, and less than one-half the number of cheques were written in 2007 compared with 1991 (Figure 6.14). The average value of a cheque payment has risen over this period to just under £1,000 in 2007, partly because businesses are the main users of cheques (by value). The average value of a personal cheque payment was just over £200. Many large retailers ceased to accept personal cheques as a form of payment from around 2007 onwards. There was a fourteenfold increase in the value of payments by debit card between 1991 and 2007, while the value of automated payments (which include Direct Debits and standing orders) increased nearly threefold over the period. The value of payments by credit card and store card slowly increased between 1991 and 2003, and then stabilised. As the Internet has become more accessible to households (see Figure 6.7), it has also been increasingly used to pay bills and transfer funds between accounts; Internet payments are included in automated transactions. The number of adults in the UK using Internet banking increased from fewer than 3.5 million in 2000 to more than 21 million (or 53 per cent of adults aged 16 and over with Internet access) in 2007.

More than nine in ten adults aged 16 and over in Great Britain held at least one plastic card in 2007 (Table 6.15 overleaf). Automated teller machine (ATM) cards were the most

Table 6.15

Plastic card holders:[1] by age, 2007

Great Britain

Percentages

	16–24	25–34	35–44	45–54	55–64	65 and over
Credit, and charge cards[2]	22	67	74	72	76	69
Debit card	77	91	90	88	90	84
Store card	6	24	24	21	23	25
Cheque guarantee card[3]	51	81	85	82	86	82
ATM card[4]	92	96	94	92	92	87
Any plastic card	92	97	96	94	94	91

1 Percentage of all adults in age group holding each type of card.
2 Includes people aged 16 and 17 who are ineligible for credit, and charge cards.
3 Includes multi-functional and stand-alone cheque guarantee cards.
4 Cards used in cash machines for cash withdrawals and other bank services. Includes single function automated teller machine (ATM) cards and multi-function debit cards, but excludes credit, and charge cards, most of which can be used to access cash machines.

Source: The Payments Council

Figure 6.16

Retail prices index[1] and consumer prices index[2]

United Kingdom

Percentage change over 12 months

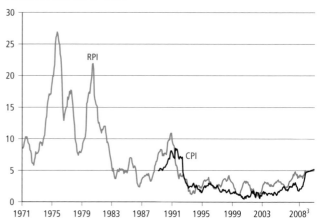

1 See Appendix, Part 6: Retail prices index.
2 Data for years prior to 1996 are estimates. See Appendix, Part 6: Consumer prices index.
3 Data for 2008 are up to and including September.

Source: Office for National Statistics

commonly held cards for all age groups, closely followed by debit cards. The pattern of ownership of plastic cards was broadly similar across all age groups among people aged 25 and over. However, young people aged 16 to 24 were a lot less likely than the other age groups to have a store card; 6 per cent of 16 to 24-year-olds held a store card compared with 21 per cent or more of those in older age groups. Younger people were also less likely to have a credit or charge card; 22 per cent held one, compared with at least 67 per cent of those in older age groups. More than three-quarters (77 per cent) of 16 to 24-year-olds owned a debit card, although this was also a lower proportion than for the other age groups.

The proportion of people aged 16 and over in Great Britain owning store cards fell by 14.5 percentage points between 2001 and 2007. A possible reason for the decline is that interest rates are less favourable than for most credit cards and since 2007 'wealth warnings' have been introduced on cards that carry an interest rate greater than 25 per cent.

Prices

The way individuals and families choose to spend their income is affected by the prices of goods and services. The retail prices index (RPI) measures the average monthly change in the prices of a variety of goods and services purchased. It was introduced in 1947 and is the longest standing measure of inflation in the UK. The RPI is measured using a 'basket of goods and services' which typically reflect the goods and services people spend their money on.

The consumer prices index (CPI, previously called the UK harmonised index of consumer prices) is the main measure of inflation used by the Government's monetary policy framework and for international comparison. There are some differences between the RPI and CPI in terms of the items and population covered by these indices. For example, council tax (domestic rates in Northern Ireland) and owner-occupier housing costs (including mortgage interest payments, house depreciation and buildings insurance) are excluded from the CPI. The CPI covers spending by all private households, foreign visitors to the UK and residents in institutions, whereas the RPI covers spending by private households only and excludes the spending of the highest income households and pensioner households that are mainly dependent on state pensions.

Since 1993 the RPI and CPI have remained relatively stable (Figure 6.16). At the beginning of 2008 the CPI started to increase and was 5.2 per cent in September 2008, 3.2 percentage points above the Government's inflation target of 2.0 per cent. In the same month, however, the RPI was unusually lower than the CPI, at 5.0 per cent and even though this RPI figure was higher than in September 2007 (3.9 per cent) it was still very much lower than it was in the 1970s, when the RPI exceeded 26 per cent.

While the overall rate of inflation has been low over the last 15 years, the prices for some categories of goods and services have increased more than others. Education recorded the largest rate of price increase (13.7 per cent) between 2006

Figure 6.17

Percentage change[1] in consumer prices index: by purpose of expenditure, 2007

United Kingdom
Percentage change over 12 months

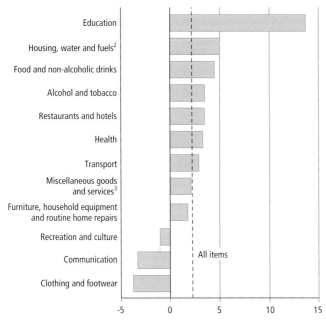

1 Percentage change between 2006 and 2007. See Appendix, Part 6: Consumer prices index.
2 Excludes mortgage interest payments.
3 Includes personal care, personal effects (for example jewellery and watches), social protection, insurance and financial services.

Source: Office for National Statistics

and 2007 (Figure 6.17). This category also recorded the largest rate of increase between 2002 and 2007 (44.0 per cent). Between 2006 and 2007 the second largest rate of price increase was for housing, water and fuels, at 5.0 per cent. Prices in this category also increased substantially over the five years to 2007, by 28.9 per cent, along with transport (17.4 per cent) and restaurants and hotels (17.1 per cent). Prices of food and non-alcoholic drinks rose by 4.5 per cent between 2006 and 2007. From September 2007 to September 2008 food and non-alcoholic drinks was the category with the greatest rate of increase in price (11.4 per cent), followed by education (10.8 per cent) and transport (7.7 per cent).

The prices of items in some categories fell in the five years from 2002 to 2007. Proportionately clothing and footwear decreased the most in price, by 19.7 per cent. Communication, and recreation and culture also fell in price by 5.6 per cent and 5.4 per cent respectively. Between 2006 and 2007 clothing and footwear, communication, and recreation and culture continued to fall in price, by 3.8 per cent, 3.3 per cent and 1.0 per cent respectively, pulling down the overall CPI to an increase of 2.4 per cent in 2007.

The extent to which price change contributes towards the overall level of price inflation depends not just on the size of the price change but also on the importance of items, or groups of items, within total household expenditure. For example, while the price index of education increased by 13.7 per cent between 2006 and 2007 the proportion of disposable income that households spent on average on education was small (1 per cent). By comparison the price index for food and non-alcoholic drinks increased by 4.5 per cent between 2006 and 2007 but accounts for a larger proportion (9 per cent) of average household expenditure. As a result, the price change for education had a less dramatic effect on overall inflation than the price change for food and non-alcoholic drinks.

People's perceptions of the rate of inflation can be different to the actual rate. Generally price increases have more of an impact on people's perceptions of inflation than prices that do not change or fall. Price increases reduce the amount of income available for other purchases and people are more affected by price increases on frequently bought or essential items, for example, food and drink, and petrol, so tend to notice these more. Conversely, there is a tendency to overlook the fall in the prices of items such as clothing and footwear. Moreover, items that are purchased annually or less frequently, such as washing machines or cars, tend to go unnoticed. This is partly because they are not part of regular weekly or monthly household expenditure and also because it can be difficult to gauge how prices have changed over a longer period of time. In the case of large purchases like washing machines, and technology items like computers that are bought infrequently, the quality and specification of the item is likely to have changed since the last purchase, so like-for-like comparisons become more difficult to make.

In February 2008 the Bank of England conducted a survey to find out which factors influence people's perceptions of the causes of current inflation. The survey asked 'What are the major factors influencing inflation?' Respondents were shown a list of potential factors to choose from and could choose more than one. The main factor influencing inflation for most respondents (67 per cent) was household energy (Figure 6.18 overleaf). This was closely followed by transport (including petrol), listed by 63 per cent of respondents. More than one-half (53 per cent) listed food and drink, 39 per cent listed housing and even though Figure 6.17 showed that average prices for clothing and footwear fell between 2006 and 2007, 29 per cent of respondents in the Bank of England survey agreed that clothing and footwear had a major influence on current inflation. In addition to their own purchasing experiences, 25 per cent of people stated that they

6

Figure 6.18

People's perceptions of factors influencing current inflation,[1] 2008

United Kingdom

Percentages

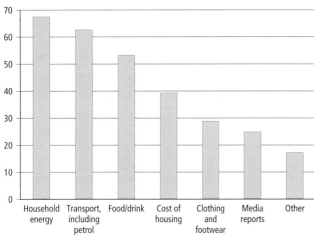

1 Respondents were asked 'What are the major factors influencing inflation?' and presented with a list of options. Data are the proportion who strongly agreed that each factor was a cause.

Source: Bank of England

Table 6.19

Cost of selected items

United Kingdom   Pence[1]

	1971	1981	1991	2001	2007
White fish fillets, per kg	58	245	629	866	1044
500g back bacon[2]	37	142	235	343	386
Eggs (large), per dozen	26	78	118	172	214
250g cheddar cheese	13	58	86	128	145
1 pint pasteurised milk[3]	5	19	32	36	37
800g white sliced bread	10	37	53	51	90
New potatoes,[4] loose per kg	13	31	34	87	83
Mushrooms, loose per kg	60	211	290	262	259
Tomatoes, loose per kg	35	95	147	125	151
Apples (dessert), per kg	22	55	120	116	132
Bananas, per kg	18	64	119	106	87
Packet of 20 cigarettes (filter tip)[5]	27	97	186	412	502
Pint of beer[6]	15	65	137	203	262
Whiskey (per nip)	..	..	95	148	187
Litre of unleaded petrol	..	..	45	76	94

1 The average price in pence sterling in the corresponding calendar year.
2 In 1971 and 1981 the price is for unsmoked. In 1991 the price is an average of vacuum and not vacuum-packed.
3 Delivered milk included from 1996.
4 In season new potatoes prior to 1993.
5 Change from standard to king size in 1991.
6 Bottled until 1981 and draught lager after.

Source: Office for National Statistics

thought reports by the media had a major influence on inflation levels.

The items included in the 'basket of goods and services' used to determine both the CPI and RPI are subject to change over time as they are updated to reflect the changing spending patterns of consumers. Examples of items that were added to the basket of goods and services in 2007 were olive oil, mobile phone downloads and satellite navigation equipment. Items that were removed from the basket included vegetable oil, children's wellington boots and VHS video recorders. However, several items like bread, milk and eggs have been in the basket for many years and so it is possible to track the price changes of these items over time. A pint of milk, for example, went up more than sevenfold between 1971 and 2007, from 5 pence to 37 pence (average price in each year). A dozen eggs went up eightfold, from 26 pence to £2.14 and a kilogram of white fish fillets went up eighteenfold, from 58 pence to £10.44 (Table 6.19). A packet of 20 filter tipped cigarettes went up more than two-and-one-half times since 1991, partly because of increased duties levied on tobacco products. The price of unleaded petrol also more than doubled between 1991 and 2007 (see Chapter 12: Transport, Figure 12.14). Both the world market price and, to a lesser extent, the increase in indirect

Table 6.20

Percentage change[1] in consumer prices:[2] EU comparison, 2007

Percentage change over 12 months

Latvia	10.1	United Kingdom	2.3
Hungary	7.9	Austria	2.2
Bulgaria	7.6	Cyprus	2.2
Estonia	6.7	Italy	2.0
Lithuania	5.8	Slovakia	1.9
Romania	4.9	Belgium	1.8
Slovenia	3.8	Denmark	1.7
Czech Republic	3.0	Sweden	1.7
Greece	3.0	Finland	1.6
Ireland	2.9	France	1.6
Spain	2.8	Netherlands	1.6
Luxembourg	2.7	Malta	0.7
Poland	2.6		
Portugal	2.4	EU-27 average	2.4
Germany	2.3		

1 Percentage change between 2006 and 2007.
2 See Appendix, Part 6: Consumer prices index.

Source: Office for National Statistics; Eurostat

taxes such as fuel duties and value added tax (VAT) influenced the price of petrol. There are some items, however, that have fallen in price, for example, bananas were 27 per cent cheaper in 2007 than in 1991.

The CPI methodology is harmonised across the European Union (EU-27) and therefore the CPI can be used to compare inflation in the UK with other EU-27 member states. In 2007 the UK had the same rate of inflation as Germany, and this was slightly lower than the average inflation rate across the EU-27, 2.3 per cent compared with 2.4 per cent (Table 6.20). The inflation rates across the EU ranged from 0.7 per cent in Malta to 10.1 per cent in Latvia. The countries with the highest rates of inflation tended to be countries that had recently joined the EU, with the exception of Cyprus, Malta and Slovakia.

6

6

Chapter 7

Health

- In 2006/07, 86 per cent of children in the UK were immunised against measles, mumps and rubella (MMR) by their second birthday. The peak was 90 per cent in 1991/92. (Figure 7.6)

- In 1974 in Great Britain, 51 per cent of all men aged 16 and over and 41 per cent of women were smokers. By 2007, this had fallen to 22 per cent of men and 20 per cent of women. (Figure 7.10)

- The number of alcohol-related deaths in the UK more than doubled since 1991 to reach 8,724 in 2007, although the peak was in 2006, at 8,758 deaths. (Page 102)

- The number of anti-depressant prescriptions dispensed in England was nearly four times higher in 2007 than in 1991, rising from nine million to 34 million. (Figure 7.14)

- An increasing proportion of children in England were classified as either overweight or obese in 2007, 31 per cent of boys aged two to 15 and 30 per cent of girls. (Figure 7.16)

- In the UK the most common sexually transmitted infection in both sexes in 2007 was chlamydia, at 204.7 diagnosed cases per 100,000 men and 198.1 per 100,000 women. (Figure 7.20)

DATA

Download data by clicking the online pdf

www.statistics.gov.uk/ socialtrends39

Patterns of health and ill health in the UK change from generation to generation. Over the last century, improvements in nutrition and sanitation, advances in medical science and technology, and the development of widely available health services have led to notable improvements in health and longevity. Many of the current most common causes of morbidity and premature mortality are linked to a range of individual behaviours such as diet, physical activity levels, smoking and drinking. Current government health strategies place a strong emphasis on reducing ill health through promoting healthy lifestyles.

Key health indicators

Life expectancy is a widely used summary indicator of the state of the nation's health. There have been large improvements in expectancy of life at birth over the last century for both males and females. In 1901 males born in the UK could expect to live to 45 years, and females 49 years (Figure 7.1). By 2006 life expectancy at birth had risen to 77 years for males and 82 years for females. Female life expectancy has been consistently higher than that for males since the start of the 20th century. The disparity was at its greatest in 1969 and 1970, when females could expect to live around six years longer than males born in the same year. Since then the gap has steadily narrowed and this trend is projected to continue until 2014, when the difference is expected to level off at 3.5 years. Life expectancy at birth is projected to continue to rise for both sexes, to reach more than 81 years for males and more than 84 years for females by 2021.

Despite long-term improvements in life expectancy at birth, it was not until the late 1970s that life expectancy for adults in the UK showed continuous improvement. Between 1971 and 2006 life expectancy for men aged 65 increased by nearly five years, compared with an increase of around two years between 1901 and 1971. The improvement in life expectancy was less in women, between 1971 and 2006 life expectancy for women aged 65 increased by nearly four years, compared with an increase of nearly five years between 1901 and 1971.

In 2004 life expectancy at birth in the UK of 76.8 years for males was higher than the latest European Union (EU-27) average of 75.2 years. Sweden had the highest male life expectancy at birth, at 78.4 years. For females, the UK life expectancy of 81.0 years was slightly below the EU-27 average of 81.5. France and Italy had the highest life expectancy at birth for females, at 83.8 years.

Despite its use as a general indicator of the population's health, life expectancy does not take into account quality of life and whether it is lived in good health, with disability or dependency. Summary health measures such as healthy life expectancy and disability-free life expectancy focus on the population's health-related quality of life. In the UK between 2004 and 2006, the healthy life expectancy of males was 68.2 years at birth and 12.8 years at age 65. For females, the equivalent figures were 70.4 years and 14.5 years respectively (Table 7.2).

Disability-free life expectancy, defined as the expected number of years lived free from a limiting chronic illness, is calculated using life expectancy and self-reported limiting chronic illness

Figure 7.1

Expectation of life[1] at birth: by sex

United Kingdom

Years

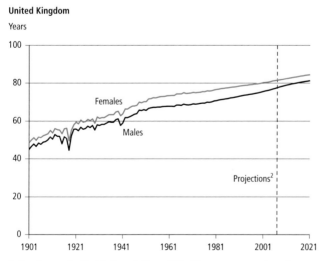

1 See Appendix, Part 7: Expectation of life. The average number of years a new-born baby would survive if he or she experienced age-specific mortality rates for that time period throughout his or her life.
2 2006-based projections for 2007 to 2021.

Source: Office for National Statistics

Table 7.2

Life expectancy, healthy life expectancy and disability-free life expectancy:[1] by sex, 2004–06

United Kingdom
Years

	Males		Females	
	At birth	At age 65	At birth	At age 65
Life expectancy	76.9	16.9	81.3	19.7
Healthy life expectancy	68.2	12.8	70.4	14.5
Years spent in poor health	8.7	4.1	10.9	5.2
Disability-free life expectancy	62.4	10.1	63.9	10.6
Years spent with disability	14.5	6.8	17.4	9.1

1 See Appendix, Part 7: Expectation of life, and Healthy life expectancy and disability-free life expectancy.

Source: Office for National Statistics

data drawn from surveys. The conditions taken into account include arthritis, back pain, heart disease and mental disorders. There are similar patterns for males and females in terms of the number of years they could expect to live free from limiting chronic illness or disability. In the UK between 2004 and 2006, on average males could expect to live 62.4 years free from a limiting chronic illness or disability, and 10.1 years at age 65. For females the equivalent figures were 63.9 years at birth, and 10.6 years at age 65.

Of countries within the UK, England had the highest life expectancy and disability-free life expectancy at birth, for both males, at 77.2 years and 62.8 years respectively, and females, at 81.5 years and 64.1 years respectively. The lowest life expectancy was in Scotland, at 74.6 years for males and 79.6 years for females. The lowest disability-free life expectancy for males was in Wales, at 59.8 years and for females in Northern Ireland, at 60.7 years.

Between 1971 and 2005, circulatory diseases were the most common cause of death among both males and females in the UK. Circulatory diseases include cardiovascular disease (CVD), a generic term covering diseases of the heart or blood vessels. The major types of CVD are angina and heart attack, known as coronary heart diseases, and stroke. These diseases have also shown the greatest decline among the main diseases that cause death, particularly among males. In 1971 the age-standardised death rates (see Appendix, Part 7: Standardised rates) for circulatory diseases were 6,936 per million males and 4,285 per

million females (Figure 7.3). By 2007 these had fallen to 2,349 per million males, and 1,486 per million females. Circulatory disease has remained the most common cause of death among males. However, in 2006 the death rate for circulatory disease in females was lower than for cancers for the first time, a trend that has continued in 2007.

CVD are associated with risk factors such as smoking, sedentary lifestyles, heavy alcohol consumption and diets that contain high levels of cholesterol, saturated fat and salt, and low levels of fresh fruit and vegetables. In 2006 the prevalence of CVD for men aged 35 and over in England generally increased as equivalised household income decreased (see Appendix, Part 5: Equivalisation scales). Prevalence of CVD was 17 per cent for men of this age in the highest income quintile group (see Chapter 5: Income and wealth, Analysing income distribution text box on page 66), compared with between 20 per cent and 21 per cent for those in the two lowest quintile groups, though the lowest prevalence was in the second highest quintile group (Figure 7.4 overleaf). For women there was no strong association between CVD and income. The prevalence of CVD was highest for women in the highest income group, at 20 per cent, and slightly lower in the lowest two quintile groups, between 18 per cent and 19 per cent. It was lowest for women in the middle income group, at 15 per cent.

In the Scottish Health Survey the association between CVD and income was apparent in both sexes. The latest data for 2003 showed that the prevalence of CVD among adults aged 16 and

Figure 7.3

Mortality:[1] by sex and leading cause groups

United Kingdom[2]

Rates per million population

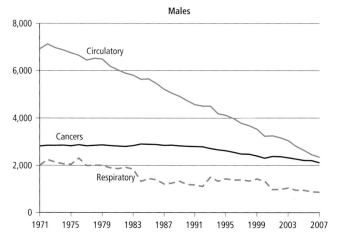

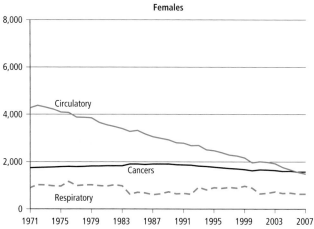

1 Data are for all ages and have been age-standardised using the European standard population. See Appendix, Part 7: Standardised rates, International Classification of Diseases, and European standard population.
2 Data for 2000 are for England and Wales only.

Source: Office for National Statistics

Figure 7.4

Prevalence of cardiovascular disease: by income group[1] and sex,[2] 2006

England
Percentages

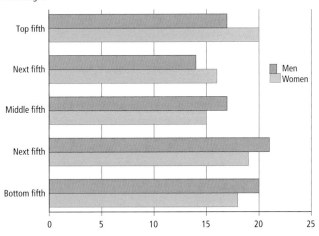

1 Equivalised household income has been used to rank the households into five groups of equal size. The bottom fifth, or bottom quintile group, is then the 20 per cent of households with the lowest incomes. See Appendix, Part 7: Household income group.
2 Adults aged 35 and over.

Source: The NHS Information Centre for health and social care

over increased as the household income decreased. For men in the highest income quintile group the prevalence of CVD was 11 per cent, compared with 20 per cent for men in the lowest income group. For women in the highest income quintile group the prevalence of CVD was also 11 per cent, compared with 18 per cent for those in the lowest income group.

Cancers were the second most common cause of death in males during the period 1971 to 2007. Death rates from cancer peaked in 1984 for males, at 2,899 per million, and by 2007 had fallen to 2,111 per million males. Death rates from cancer are typically lower in females than in males, and peaked in 1989 at 1,905 per million females, since when they have gradually fallen to 1,567 per million females in 2007. These variations in mortality trends partly reflect differences in the type of cancers males and females are likely to experience, the risk factors associated with developing them and the relative survival rates for different cancers. The incidence and mortality rates for the most common forms of cancer are examined in the Cancer section later in this chapter.

Infant mortality (defined as deaths in the first year of life) in the UK has decreased since 1930 and is one of the main factors contributing to increases in life expectancy. In England and Wales infant mortality fell from 60.0 deaths per 1,000 live births in 1930 to 4.8 per 1,000 in 2007. In Scotland there was a similar trend, with 83.0 deaths per 1,000 live births in 1930 and 4.7 per 1,000 in 2007. In Northern Ireland, infant mortality

rates increased from 67.8 per 1,000 live births in 1930 to 85.9 per 1,000 live births in 1940, but have steadily fallen since, to 4.9 per 1,000 live births in 2007.

Analysis of infant mortality in England and Wales in 2005 indicated differences both between ethnic groups and within the Asian and Black populations (see Appendix, Part 1: Classification of ethnic groups). Infant mortality rates were lowest for babies born into the Bangladeshi population, at 4.2 deaths per 1,000 live births, and highest for babies born into the Caribbean population, at 9.8 per 1,000 live births. However, the infant mortality rate in the Pakistani population was more than double the rate in the Bangladeshi population at 9.6 deaths per 1,000 live births, while the infant mortality rate in the African population was one-third lower than the Caribbean population, at 6.0 deaths per 1,000 live births.

Although infant mortality rates have declined overall, there remain inequalities between different socio-economic groups in England and Wales, see Appendix, Part 3: National Statistics Socio-economic Classification (NS-SEC). In 2007 the infant mortality rate in England and Wales for babies born inside marriage to fathers who worked in large employers and higher managerial occupations was 2.7 per 1,000 live births (Table 7.5). This was less than one-half the infant mortality rate of babies born inside marriage to fathers who worked in routine occupations, at 6.3 deaths per 1,000 live births, and

Table 7.5

Infant mortality:[1] by socio-economic classification,[2] 2007

England & Wales   Rates per 1,000 live births[3]

	Inside marriage	Outside marriage[4]
Large employers and higher managerial	2.7	3.3
Higher professional	3.1	3.9
Lower managerial and professional	3.3	3.5
Intermediate occupations	4.5	3.9
Small employers and own account workers	3.9	4.0
Lower supervisory and technical	3.8	4.1
Semi-routine occupations	6.0	6.0
Routine occupations	6.3	5.5
All	4.2	5.0

1 Deaths within one year of birth.
2 Based on father's occupation at death registration of the child. See Appendix, Part 3: National Statistics Socio-economic Classification (NS-SEC).
3 Figures for live births are a 10 per cent sample coded for father's occupation.
4 Jointly registered by both parents.

Source: Office for National Statistics

Figure 7.6

Completed primary immunisation courses[1] at two years of age

United Kingdom[2]
Percentages

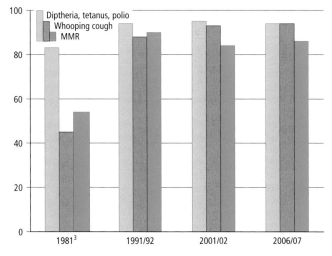

1 Primary immunisation courses are the first immunisations given to babies at two, three and four months.
2 England and Wales data are based on actual numbers of immunisations; Northern Ireland data are based on populations by calendar year; Scotland data are based on all children reaching a specified age who were alive and registered on the Scottish Immunisation Recall System at the end of the reporting period.
3 Data are not available for Scotland.

Source: The NHS Information Centre for health and social care; Welsh Assembly Government; NHS in Scotland; Communicable Disease Surveillance Centre, Northern Ireland

semi-routine occupations, at 6.0 per 1,000. There is a similar, but slightly less pronounced, pattern for babies born outside marriage.

In 1981, 83 per cent of children were immunised against diphtheria, tetanus and polio by the age of two (Figure 7.6). In 2000/01 this had risen to 95 per cent before falling slightly to 94 per cent in 2006/07. The largest increase in immunisation was against whooping cough, which increased from 45 per cent in 1981 to 94 per cent in 2006/07. In 1981 more than one-half (54 per cent) of children were immunised against measles, mumps and rubella (MMR) by their second birthday. This increased to 90 per cent in the early 1990s. However, concerns over the safety of the MMR vaccine led to a fall in the proportion of children immunised against MMR. In 2001/02, 84 per cent of children had received this vaccine by their second birthday. Vaccinations then increased slightly to 86 per cent in 2006/07, but were still below the peak rate of 90 per cent in 1991/92.

There are differences in immunisation levels between the four constituent countries of the UK. In 2006/07 England had the lowest immunisation rates for children by their second birthday while Scotland and Northern Ireland had the highest rates. In

England 93 per cent of children had been vaccinated against diphtheria, tetanus and polio, and whooping cough, compared with 98 per cent in Scotland and Northern Ireland and 97 per cent in Wales. Similarly, 85 per cent of children in England had been vaccinated against MMR compared with 92 per cent in Scotland.

Cancer

Around one-third of the population develop cancer at some time in their lives. Trends in lung cancer incidence are strongly linked to those for cigarette smoking, which is by far the greatest single risk factor for the disease. Lung cancer incidence has fallen in men since the mid-1990s, mainly as a result of the decline in cigarette smoking, see the Alcohol, smoking and drugs misuse section later in this chapter. In 1996 there were 20,000 incidences of lung cancer for men in England (Figure 7.7 overleaf). By 2006 this had fallen 11 per cent to 18,000. Lung cancer incidence among women is far lower (13,000 incidences in 2006), largely as a consequence of a historically lower incidence of smoking among women. Over the last decade, lung cancer incidence for both men and women in Northern Ireland has remained fairly steady; there were 887 new cases in 2006.

The incidence of prostate cancer among men in England has risen 51 per cent in the last decade, from around 20,000 incidences in 1996 to 30,000 in 2006. In 1998 prostate cancer overtook lung cancer as the most commonly diagnosed cancer among men. Uterus cancer cases among women have risen considerably over the last ten years, by 42 per cent between 1996 and 2006, but the number of incidences remains relatively low, at 5,600 cases in 2006. In Northern Ireland, the incidence of prostate cancer among men has risen 78 per cent in the last decade, from around 460 incidences in 1996 to 818 in 2006; in 2000 prostate cancer overtook lung cancer as the most commonly diagnosed cancer among men in Northern Ireland, probably the result of increased Prostate Specific Antigen testing.

Breast cancer has been the most commonly diagnosed form of cancer among women in England over the last decade. In 1996 there were 31,000 cases: by 2006 this had risen 21 per cent to 38,000. The increase in the number of breast cancer incidences has been partly explained by increases and improvements in breast cancer screening services (see Appendix, Part 7: Breast cancer and cervical cancer screening programmes). Between 1996 and 2006, breast cancer was also the most commonly diagnosed form of cancer among women in Northern Ireland. Over that period, incidence of breast cancer rose by 15 per cent from 850 to 977 cases.

7

Figure 7.7

Incidence of major cancers:[1] by sex

England

Thousands

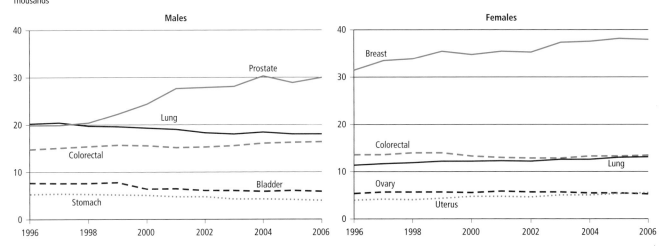

1 Cancers are coded to the International Classification of Diseases, Tenth Revision (ICD-10). See Appendix, Part 7: International Classification of Diseases.

Source: Office for National Statistics

To understand trends in the outcomes of cancer incidences, it is important to take into account the changing age distribution of the population and thus to compare age-standardised mortality rates (see Appendix, Part 7: Standardised rates). Between 1995 and 2004 age-standardised mortality rates for lung cancer in men and breast cancer in women have generally fallen (Figure 7.8). Lung cancer mortality rates for men showed the largest decrease during the period, down 26 per cent from

76 per 100,000 population to 56 per 100,000. The lung cancer mortality rate for women remained at around 30 per 100,000 population. Breast cancer mortality rates for women decreased by 22 per cent from 37 per 100,000 population in 1995 to 29 per 100,000 in 2004. Mortality rates for colorectal cancer also went down for both sexes. For men it fell from 29 per 100,000 population in 1995 to 24 per 100,000 in 2004 while for women it fell from 19 per 100,000 population to 15 per 100,000.

Figure 7.8

Mortality rates of major cancers:[1] by sex

United Kingdom

Rates per 100,000 population

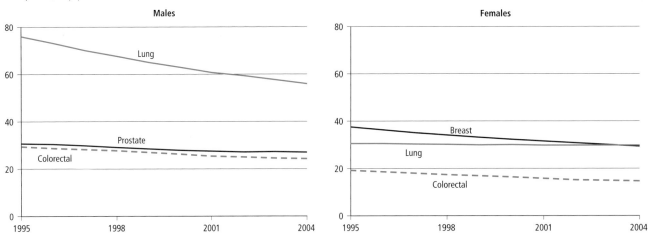

1 Data are for all ages and have been age-standardised using the European standard population. See Appendix, Part 7: Standardised rates, International Classification of Diseases, and European standard population.

Source: Office for National Statistics

Figure 7.9

Breast cancer and cervical cancer screening[1]

United Kingdom
Percentages

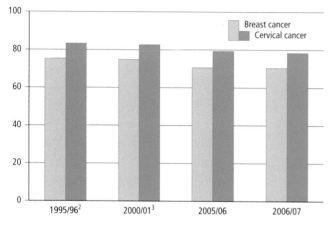

1 As a proportion of the target population screened which varies among the countries of the UK. See Appendix, Part 7: Breast cancer and cervical cancer screening programmes.
2 Cervical screening data for England are 1996/97, Scotland data are 1997/98.
3 Cervical screening data for Northern Ireland are 1999/2000.

Source: Department of Health; Information Services Division, NHS in Scotland; Breast Test Wales; Cervical Screening Wales; Quality Assurance Reference Centre (Northern Ireland)

Figure 7.10

Prevalence of adult[1] cigarette smoking:[2] by sex

Great Britain
Percentages

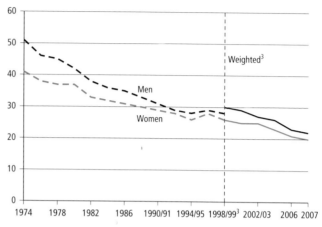

1 People aged 16 and over.
2 Between 1974 and 2000/01 the surveys were run every two years. See Appendix, Part 2: General Household Survey. From 1988 onwards data are for financial years.
3 From 1998/99 data are weighted to compensate for nonresponse and to match known population distributions. Weighted and unweighted data for 1998/99 are shown for comparison.

Source: General Household Survey (Longitudinal), Office for National Statistics

Although the number of people attending screening services has increased, the target population has also increased and the proportion screened tended to fall between 1995/96 and 2006/07 (Figure 7.9). In 1995/96, three-quarters (75 per cent) of the target population in the UK were screened for breast cancer. In 2006/07 this had fallen to 71 per cent. Scotland was the only UK country to show an increase, from 69 per cent in 1995/96 to 76 per cent in 2006/07.

The proportion of women screened for cervical cancer in the UK fell from 83 per cent in 1995/96 to 79 per cent in 2006/07. The largest fall was in Scotland, a 10 percentage point drop from 87 per cent in 1995/96 to 77 per cent in 2006/07. Northern Ireland has the lowest proportion of women screened for cervical cancer in the UK. However, Northern Ireland was the only country of the UK to show an increase in screening, from 66 per cent in 1995/96 to 73 per cent in 2006/07.

Alcohol, smoking and drugs misuse

Since 1974 there has been a substantial decline in the proportion of adults aged 16 and over in Great Britain who smoke cigarettes (Figure 7.10). Smoking is related to a range of health problems, including lung cancer, bronchitis, emphysema and heart disease. In 1974 more than one-half (51 per cent) of men aged 16 and over and more than two-fifths (41 per cent)

of women were smokers. By 2007 these proportions had more than halved in Great Britain, to 22 per cent of men and 20 per cent of women. In Northern Ireland, 23 per cent of both men and women aged 16 and over were smokers in 2007/08.

In 2007, 67 per cent of households in Great Britain with children aged under 16 living at home, and 61 per cent of those in Northern Ireland, did not allow smoking in the home. Those in managerial and professional occupations (see Appendix, Part 3: National Statistics Socio-economic Classification (NS-SEC)) in Great Britain were most likely (72 per cent) of all occupational groups to prohibit smoking in the home, while those in routine and manual occupations were most likely to allow smoking either in some rooms or at some times, or to allow smoking anywhere in the home. These survey data also suggest that the majority of people do not allow smoking in their homes because of the dangers of second-hand smoking on non-smokers. In homes where smoking is not allowed, on average 67 per cent of people in Great Britain and 61 per cent in Northern Ireland believe 'second-hand smoke' increases the likelihood of non-smokers contracting certain medical conditions such as respiratory diseases and pneumonia.

Excessive alcohol consumption can lead to an increased likelihood of developing health problems such as cancer and

Table 7.11

Adults drinking more than the recommended guidelines:[1,2] by sex and socio-economic classification,[3] 2007

Great Britain   Percentages

	Managerial and professional	Intermediate	Routine and manual	Total[4]
Men				
More than 4 units and up to 8 units	45	40	37	41
More than 8 units	27	23	22	24
Women				
More than 3 units and up to 6 units	40	35	26	34
More than 6 units	17	17	12	15

1 On at least one day in the previous week.
2 Department of Health advice is that men should not regularly drink more than 3 to 4 units of alcohol per day, and women should not drink more than 2 to 3 units per day. Harmful drinking is considered to be twice the recommended daily amount. See Appendix, Part 7: Alcohol consumption.
3 See Appendix, Part 3: National Statistics Socio-economic Classification (NS-SEC).
4 See Appendix, Part 7: Household reference person. Where the household reference person was a full-time student, had an inadequately described occupation, had never worked or was long-term unemployed these are not shown as separate categories, but are included in the total.

Source: General Household Survey (Longitudinal), Office for National Statistics

cirrhosis of the liver. The Department of Health advises that consumption of three to four units of alcohol per day for men and two to three units per day for women should not lead to significant health risks.

In Great Britain in 2007, 65 per cent of all men and 49 per cent of all women reported that they had exceeded the recommended level of daily alcohol consumption on at least one day in the week prior to interview (Table 7.11). Men in managerial and professional occupations were more likely than men in other occupations to have exceeded the recommended level on at least one day in the previous week, at 45 per cent, and 27 per cent drank more than double the recommended daily units at least once in the previous week. Women in managerial and professional occupations were also more likely than those in other occupational groups to exceed recommended levels (57 per cent). Women in routine and manual occupations were the least likely to exceed drinking recommendations (38 per cent).

In 1998 more than one-half (52 per cent) of young men aged 16 to 24 reported that they drank more than four units of alcohol on at least one day in the previous week, falling to

more than two-fifths (44 per cent) in 2007. The proportion of young men who drank more than eight units on at least one day in the previous week fell from a peak of 39 per cent in 1998 to 32 per cent in 2007. The proportion of young women who reported drinking more than three units fell from 42 per cent in 1998 to 40 per cent in 2007, while the proportion of young women who drank more than double the recommended three units was 24 per cent in 1998 and 2007, although it peaked at 28 per cent in 2002.

The rate of alcohol consumption among children and young people aged 11 to 16 in Great Britain fell between 2002 and 2006. Males aged 15 to 16 in Wales were most likely among all 11 to 16-year-olds in Great Britain to drink alcohol in the previous week, with 42 per cent reporting having done so. However, this group also showed the largest decline in drinking among all 11 to 16-year-olds, down 15 percentage points from 2002. Among females, those aged 15 to 16 in both England and Wales were most likely to drink among 11 to 16-year-olds in Great Britain, at 38 per cent. Girls aged 11 to 12 in Scotland were least likely among 11 to 16-year-olds in Great Britain to drink alcohol, at 3 per cent.

The number of alcohol-related deaths in the UK more than doubled between 1991 and 2007, from 4,144 to 8,724. The 2007 figure is slightly below the peak of 8,758 in 2006. Death rates from alcohol-related causes are much higher for males than females (Figure 7.12). In 2007 males accounted for 66 per cent of all alcohol-related deaths, with a death rate of 18.1 per 100,000 males, more than twice the rate of 8.7 per 100,000 for females. Alcohol-related death rates among males increased in all age groups between 1991 and 2007. In 2007 male rates were highest among those aged 55 to 74, at 44.3 per 100,000. There were similar patterns by age among females with the highest death rate in 2007 also being among those aged 55 to 74, at 20.8 per 100,000.

There are large variations in alcohol-related death rates between the four countries of the UK. In 2006 Scotland had the highest rates for both men and women in all age groups between the ages of 15 and 74. The rates in Scotland were 18.6 per 100,000 males, and 7.6 per 100,000 females for people aged between 15 and 44. The rates rose to 90.2 per 100,000 males and 37.6 per 100,000 females for people aged 65 to 74. England had the lowest all-ages rates for men and women, 16.2 per 100,000 males and 8.2 per 100,000 females.

The number of deaths in England and Wales related to drug misuse increased by 38 per cent from 1,312 deaths in 1997 to 1,805 in 2001. The number then fell to 1,604 in 2007. Death from drug misuse continued to be much higher in men: 1,287

7

Figure 7.12

Death rates[1] from alcohol-related causes:[2] by sex

United Kingdom
Rates per 100,000 population

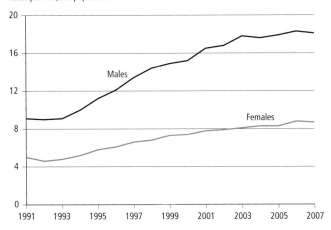

1 Age-standardised to the European standard population. Rates from 2001 are not directly comparable with those for earlier years because of the change from ICD-9 to ICD-10. See Appendix, Part 7: Standardised rates, International Classification of Diseases, and European standard population.
2 See Appendix, Part 7: Alcohol-related causes of death.

Source: Office for National Statistics

deaths in 2007 compared with 317 for women (Figure 7.13). Mortality rates for deaths relating to drug misuse increased in England and Wales in the last 15 years, rising from 22.1 per 100,000 males in 1993 to 48.5 per 100,000 males in 2007. This is a fall from the peak of 55.6 per 100,000 males in 2001. For females the rates were much lower, rising from 8.6 per

Figure 7.13

Deaths related to drug misuse:[1] by sex

England & Wales
Thousands

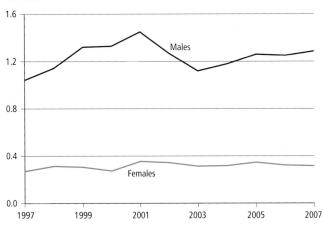

1 Deaths where the underlying cause was poisoning, drug abuse or drug dependence, and where any of the substances controlled under the *Misuse of Drugs Act 1971* were involved. See Appendix, Part 7: Death related to drug misuse.

Source: Office for National Statistics

100,000 females in 1993 to a peak of 13.0 per 100,000 in 2001, before falling to 11.5 in 2007. The number of drug-related deaths in Scotland increased by 73 per cent between 1996 and 2006, from 244 deaths to 421. As in England and Wales men accounted for around 80 per cent of deaths from drug misuse in Scotland.

Since 2005 the largest number of deaths from drug misuse in England and Wales has been in the 30 to 39 age group for both sexes: 498 men and 98 women in 2007. Between 1996 and 2007 the most common underlying cause of drug-related death in men was mental and behavioural disorders, accounting for 41 per cent (552 deaths) in 2007. For women the most common underlying cause was accidental poisoning, accounting for 39 per cent of drug-related deaths (124 deaths).

In England there was a 42 per cent increase in the number of National Health Service (NHS) hospital admissions for drug poisoning in the last decade, from 7,057 in 1996/97 to 10,047 in 2006/07. The most common age group admitted were those aged between 16 and 24, accounting for nearly 27 per cent (2,674) of admissions for drug poisoning in 2006/07.

Mental health

There is growing awareness of mental health problems, which can take a variety of forms such as anxiety, depression, Alzheimer's disease, and eating disorders. In the UK many people with mental health problems seek advice from a qualified health professional, in most cases their general practitioner (GP). Treatment will typically be provided through counselling, prescription of an anti-depressant drug, or a combination of these. For counselling, women aged 16 and over in England are more likely than men to use NHS secondary mental health care (out-patient or community services, or a day hospital). In 2005–06, 632,000 women in England received NHS secondary mental health care, compared with 510,000 men. There has been a large increase in the number of NHS prescription items for anti-depressant drugs in England since 1991 (Figure 7.14 overleaf). There were 34 million anti-depressant prescription items dispensed in 2007, nearly four times more than in 1991 when nine million were dispensed.

There were similar large increases in the number of prescription drugs dispensed in Scotland and Northern Ireland. In the decade from 1992/93, the number of anti-depressant prescription items dispensed in Scotland rose from around one million to more than three million in 2002/03. In Northern Ireland the number of anti-depressant prescriptions dispensed was five times higher in 2007 than in 1991, 1.5 million compared with 0.3 million. Anti-depressant prescription items

Figure 7.14

Number of prescription items for anti-depressant drugs[1]

England

Millions

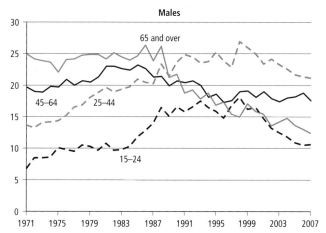

1 Dispensed in the community. See Appendix, Part 7: Prescription Cost Analysis System. Anti-depressants are defined as those drugs within the British National Formulary (BNF) section 4.3, anti-depressant drugs.

Source: Department of Health

dispensed in Wales rose by nearly 16 per cent between 2005 and 2007, from 2.4 million to 2.7 million.

Mental health problems can ultimately lead people to commit suicide. Trends in suicide rates have varied by age group and sex in the UK since 1971. In each age group, males generally had a higher suicide rate than females (Figure 7.15). Between 1971 and 1988, men aged 65 and over had the highest suicide

rates of males in the UK, of the four age groups shown, peaking at 26.3 per 100,000 men in 1986. Women aged 65 and over generally had the highest suicide rates for females between 1971 and 1999; although the rate for this age group was only slightly higher than that for women aged 45 to 64. This younger group had the highest suicide rate for women recorded in the period since 1971, with a rate of 17.1 per 100,000 women in 1979. The suicide rate for men aged 65 and over has declined since the late 1980s. In 2007 the rate was 12.3 per 100,000 men, less than one-half the 1986 peak. The rates for all women aged 45 and over have also declined. In 2007 the rate for women aged 65 and over was 4.7 per 100,000 women, around four times less than the peak of 16.5 per 100,000 in 1980. The rate for women aged 45 to 64 fell from a peak of 17.1 per 100,000 in 1979 to 6.5 per 100,000 in 2007.

In contrast, suicide rates among younger men generally increased over the decades since 1971, in particular for those aged 25 to 44. The suicide rate for this age group almost doubled from 13.6 per 100,000 men in 1971 to a peak of 26.9 per 100,000 in 1998; since then it has declined, but remained the highest of all age groups and of both sexes, at 21.1 per 100,000 men in 2007. The lowest suicide rates for both sexes in 2007 were among 15 to 24-year-olds, at 10.6 per 100,000 males and 2.6 per 100,000 females.

Suicide rates by sex and marital status in England and Wales show a clear difference between men and women. In 2004 the suicide rate for men aged 25 and over in England and Wales

Figure 7.15

Suicide rates:[1] by sex and age

United Kingdom

Rates per 100,000 population

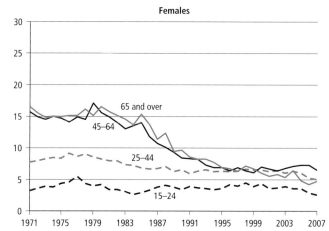

1 Includes deaths with a verdict of undetermined intent (open verdicts). Rates from 2001 are coded to ICD-10. See Appendix, Part 7: International Classification of Diseases. Rates have been age-standardised using the European standard population. See Appendix, Part 7: Standardised rates, and European standard population.

Source: Office for National Statistics; General Register Office for Scotland; Northern Ireland Statistics and Research Agency

was 19 per 100,000 men, three times higher than for women aged 25 and over, at 6 per 100,000 women. Single and divorced men had higher rates of suicide than married men. Three-year averages show that between 2002 and 2004 rates of suicide for single and divorced men were 31 per 100,000 men for each group. Single and divorced women also showed the highest suicide rate of all women, an average of 11 per 100,000 women for each group in the same period.

The most common method of committing suicide among men in England was by hanging, strangulation and suffocation. In 2007 more than one-half (53 per cent) of all male suicides were by this method. For women the most common method was by drug-related poisoning (36 per cent).

Health-related behaviour

Obesity is linked to heart disease, diabetes and premature death. The body mass index (BMI) is a common measure for assessing an individual's weight relative to their height (calculated as weight (kilograms) divided by height (metres) squared). A BMI score of 30 or more is the usual definition of obesity (see Appendix, Part 7: Body mass index).

In recent years the proportion of the adult population in England who are obese has increased. Between 1997 and 2007 the proportion of men aged 16 and over who were classified as obese increased from 17 per cent to 24 per cent, while among women the proportion rose from 20 per cent to 24 per cent. In addition, a further 41 per cent of men and 32 per cent of women were classified as overweight (those with a BMI score of 25 or more, but less than 30) in 2007. Overall, 65 per cent of men and 56 per cent of women were classified as either overweight or obese in 2007 (Figure 7.16).

An increasing proportion of children are also overweight or obese. Between 1997 and 2007, the number of boys in England aged two to 15 who were classified as overweight or obese increased from 26 per cent to 31 per cent, and peaked in 2005 at 34 per cent. There was nearly a 10 percentage point increase in the proportion of girls classified as overweight or obese between 1997 and 2004, from 26 per cent to 35 per cent, although the proportion had fallen to 30 per cent in 2007.

There is considerable scientific, media, policy and public interest in the high levels of children and young people who are overweight or obese. Children who are obese are more likely than any other children to suffer from health problems, including the risk of cardiovascular illness, a high incidence of premature atherosclerosis, and insulin resistance. Regular physical activity is promoted as a way of helping to reduce the

Figure 7.16

Proportion of adults and children[1] who are overweight or obese:[2] by sex

England

Percentages

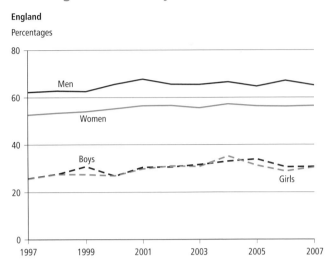

1 Adults aged 16 years and over, children aged 2 to 15 years.
2 Using the body mass index (BMI) for people aged 16 and over and the 1990 UK National BMI percentile classification for those aged 2 to 15. See Appendix, Part 7: Body mass index.

Source: The NHS Information Centre for health and social care

proportion of children who are overweight or obese and so bring health benefits. The Chief Medical Officer for England recommends that children and young people should achieve a minimum of 60 minutes of at least moderate intensity activity every day.

In England, boys and girls aged 11 to 15 in the lowest household income quintile group (see Chapter 5: Income and wealth, Analysing income distribution text box on page 66) are less likely than those in the highest quintile group to participate in sport and exercise (Table 7.17 overleaf). In 2006, 35 per cent of boys in the lowest income group did no sports or exercise in the week prior to interview, compared with 22 per cent in the highest quintile group. Girls in the lowest income group were twice as likely as girls in the highest quintile group to do no sports or exercise, 48 per cent compared with 24 per cent. In the highest quintile group, 31 per cent of boys participated in sport or exercise on five or more days, compared with 26 per cent of boys in the lowest group. However, among boys and girls who do participate in sport or exercise, children in the lowest income group are more likely to do so on five or more days, rather than on one to four days. (See Chapter 13: Lifestyles and social participation, Figure 13.14).

This pattern is repeated for boys aged between two and ten. In 2006, 43 per cent of boys in each of the lowest two income quintile groups in England participated in no sport or exercise in the week prior to interview, compared with 28 per cent in

Table 7.17

Children's participation in sports and exercise:[1] by income group[2] and sex, 2006

England   Percentages

	Bottom fifth	Next fifth	Middle fifth	Next fifth	Top fifth
Boys					
None	35	34	22	20	22
1–2 days	23	25	27	29	25
3–4 days	16	20	23	18	22
5 or more days	26	20	28	33	31
Girls					
None	48	42	38	34	24
1–2 days	26	33	31	31	39
3–4 days	11	15	18	18	22
5 or more days	16	10	13	17	14

1 Children aged 11 to 15. Levels of participation in sports and exercise are given in terms of how many days a child had been active in the week prior to interview and no assumptions were made on the intensity of that activity. Interviews were carried out throughout 2006.

2 Equivalised household income has been used to rank the households into five groups of equal size. The bottom fifth, or bottom quintile group, is then the 20 per cent of households with the lowest incomes. See Appendix, Part 7: Household income group.

Source: The NHS Information Centre for health and social care

Figure 7.18

Proportion of people meeting physical activity recommendations:[1] by sex and age, 2006

England

Percentages

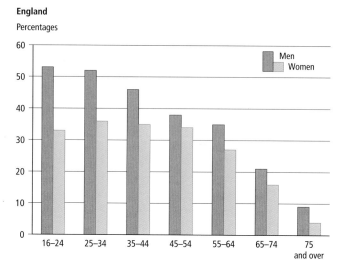

1 Guidelines for England currently recommend that adults should do at least 30 minutes of moderately intensive physical activity on five or more days per week.

Source: The NHS Information Centre for health and social care

each of the highest two groups. However, 23 per cent of boys of this age group in the lowest income group participated in sport on five or more days in the week prior to interview, compared with 19 per cent in the highest group. Girls in the lowest income quintile group were least likely of any quintile group to participate in sports and exercise, and were also least likely to have participated in five or more days of sport and exercise in the week prior to interview.

The Chief Medical Officer for England's guidelines recommend that adults should do at least 30 minutes of moderate intensity physical activity on five or more days per week. Adults who are physically active have a 20 to 30 per cent reduced risk of premature death and up to a 50 per cent reduced risk of developing major chronic diseases. In 2006, 40 per cent of men, compared with 28 per cent of women, met these physical activity guidelines, with a consistently higher proportion of men than women in all age groups meeting them. Over one-half (53 per cent) of men aged 16 to 24 in England met the physical activity recommendations, compared with 33 per cent of women (Figure 7.18). The proportion of men achieving the recommended level of physical activity declined with age, while the proportion of women doing so was generally stable for those aged between 16 and 54, after which it also declined with age.

Physical activity recommendations elsewhere in the UK are similar to those for England, based on at least 30 minutes of moderate intensity physical activity on five or more days per week. Men in Scotland and in England were more likely than men in the rest of the UK to meet physical activity recommendations, with 40 per cent doing so, while men in Northern Ireland were least likely, 33 per cent. The proportion of women meeting the recommendations ranged from 29 per cent in Scotland, to 25 per cent in Wales. (See Chapter 13: Lifestyles and social participation, Figure 13.13 for reasons why adults do not participate in sports).

In 2006 men in the highest fifth of the household income distribution in England were more likely than men in the lowest fifth to have high physical activity levels, 42 per cent compared with 35 per cent. Nearly one-half (44 per cent) of all women in the lowest fifth of the income distribution had low levels of activity compared with one-third (33 per cent) of those in the highest fifth.

As well as exercise, diet has an important influence on obesity and thus on health. Diets that are high in fat and low in fresh fruit and vegetables can contribute to a person being overweight or obese. According to the Food Standards Agency, a healthy diet contains plenty of fruit and vegetables (the Department of Health recommends five 80 grams portions per day), plenty of starchy foods such as wholegrain bread, pasta and rice, some protein-rich foods such as meat, fish, eggs and lentils, and some dairy foods. It should also be low in fat

Figure 7.19

Consumption of five or more portions of fruit and vegetables per day: by income group and sex,[1] 2007

England

Percentages

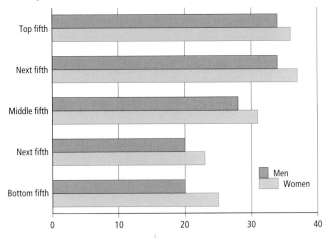

1 Equivalised household income has been used to rank the households into five groups of equal size. The bottom fifth, or bottom quintile group, is then the 20 per cent of households with the lowest incomes. See Appendix, Part 7: Household income group.

Source: The NHS Information Centre for health and social care

(especially saturated fat), salt and sugar. Access to a healthy diet is partly linked to affordability. In general, the higher the level of weekly household income, the more likely men and women are to meet the recommendation to eat five or more portions of fruit and vegetables per day (Figure 7.19). In England in 2007, 34 per cent of men and 36 per cent of women living in households in the top income quintile group consumed five or more portions of fruit and vegetables per day, compared with 20 per cent of men and 25 per cent of women in the bottom quintile group. Women in the top quintile group were almost twice as likely to do so as men in the bottom group, 36 per cent compared with 20 per cent. There was a similar pattern in Scotland. The latest data for 2003 show women in the highest income quintile group were twice as likely to consume five or more portions as women in the lowest group, 32 per cent compared to 16 per cent. For men in Scotland, 28 per cent in the highest quintile group ate five or more portions per day, compared with 16 per cent in the lowest quintile group.

Between 2005 and 2007, people in England consumed more grams of fruit and vegetables per person per week than people in the rest of the UK. On average 1,320 grams of fruit and 1,176 grams of vegetables were consumed per person per week in England compared with 1,076 grams of fruit and 876 grams of vegetables in Northern Ireland. People in Northern Ireland consumed more meat per person per week

(256 grams) than those in the rest of the UK, while people in Wales consumed more sugars and preserves (130 grams) and alcoholic drinks (873 millilitres). Scotland consumed the least amount of fats and oils per person per week (172 grams), but consumed the most soft drinks and confectionary, 2,117 millilitres and 142 grams respectively.

Sexual health

Over the past decade there has been an increase in the diagnosis of sexually transmitted infections (STI). At greatest risk are people who have multiple sexual partners and people who have unprotected sex.

For men and women in Great Britain, having multiple (more than one) sexual partners in the previous year were most common among those aged 16 to 24 in 2007/08. In this age group 33 per cent of men and 23 per cent of women reported having multiple partners. In comparison, 19 per cent of men and 8 per cent of women aged 25 to 29 reported having more than one sexual partner. The figures decrease with age with 7 per cent of men and 4 per cent of women aged 40 to 44 reporting having multiple partners in the previous year. In 2007/08 only 1 per cent of married or cohabiting men and women reported having had more than one sexual partner in the previous year, compared with 31 per cent of single men and 21 per cent of single women.

The most common sexually transmitted infection diagnosed in genito-urinary medical clinics in the UK in 2007 for both men and women was chlamydia, with 204.7 diagnosed cases per 100,000 men and 198.1 per 100,000 women (Figure 7.20 overleaf). This represents the largest increase in new diagnoses of STIs since 2000, when there were 103.9 cases of chlamydia per 100,000 men and 127.6 per 100,000 women. Genital warts were the second most commonly diagnosed sexually transmitted infection in both sexes in 2007, with 159.1 cases per 100,000 men and 137.9 cases per 100,000 women, compared with 131.2 per 100,000 men and 111.6 per 100,000 women in 2000.

Rates of chlamydia, genital warts, herpes and syphilis increased between 2000 and 2007. However, there was a decline in diagnosed cases of gonorrhoea for both men and women. Diagnoses for men were 53.1 per 100,000 men in 2000 and 43.6 per 100,000 in 2007, and for women were 21.7 per 100,000 women in 2000 falling to 18.7 per 100,000 in 2007. The least common STI diagnosed in 2007 was syphilis, as it has been since 2000. There were 8.1 diagnoses per 100,000 men in 2007, and 0.9 per 100,000 women, representing less than 2 per cent and considerably less than 1 per cent respectively of selected STIs diagnosed in 2007.

7

Figure 7.20

New diagnoses[1] of selected sexually transmitted infections: by sex,[2] 2007

United Kingdom

Rates per 100,000 population

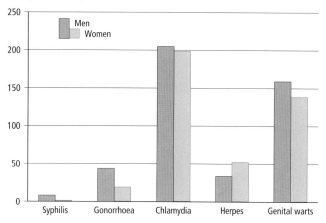

1 Cases seen at genito-urinary medical clinics.
2 Rates are calculated using resident population.

Source: Health Protection Agency; Information Services Division, NHS Services Scotland; The Communicable Disease Surveillance Centre Wales; The Communicable Disease Surveillance Centre Northern Ireland

STIs, including HIV, remain one of the most important causes of illness from infectious disease among young people aged 16 to 24. Since 1998, diagnosis rates of almost all STIs among young people attending genito-urinary medical clinics have risen in the UK. Since 2000, genital chlamydia infection has been the most commonly diagnosed STI. In 2007 diagnoses of chlamydia among young people were 1,102 per 100,000 population, having more than doubled from 447 per 100,000 in 1998. Rates of genital wart diagnoses in 16 to 24-year-olds also rose over the same period but at a lower rate, from 573 per 100,000 population to 682 per 100,000. Young people aged 16 to 24 were the age group most at risk of being diagnosed with an STI (other than HIV), representing 12 per cent of the total population but accounting for nearly one-half of all STIs diagnosed in genito-urinary medical clinics across the UK in 2007.

Among adults aged between 16 and 44-years-old, those in the 25 to 44 age group had consistently lower rates of diagnosis of chlamydia and genital warts than 16 to 24-year-olds. In 1998, of all chlamydia cases diagnosed among 16 to 44-year-olds, around two-fifths (40 per cent) were in the 25 to 44 age group; in 2007 this had decreased to around one-third (32 per cent). Diagnoses of genital warts in 25 to 44-year-olds remained stable, at around 44 per cent of the total notifications in 16 to 44-year-olds in the last decade.

By the end of 2007 an estimated 77,000 people were living with HIV in the UK. In 2007 around 7,800 new HIV cases were diagnosed. The annual rate of newly diagnosed cases almost

doubled between 1985 and 2007, from 66.5 diagnoses per million population to 126.8 per million (Figure 7.21), although this has fallen from a peak of 148.0 per million population in 2004. Increases in diagnoses may reflect greater certainty of diagnosis through more testing and improved diagnostic methods, as well as indicating increased unsafe sexual behaviour among young people. The numbers of those living with HIV will continue to rise as life expectancy of HIV sufferers increases. This is mainly because of developments in in-patient care for HIV. However it does mean that the cohort of those living with HIV will continue to rise.

Deaths of HIV-infected individuals showed a large increase between 1985 and 1995, from 3.3 per million population to 36.7 per million. The rate of deaths of HIV-infected individuals then fell sharply, to 15.7 deaths per million in 1997 and has continued to fall to 8.1 per million in 2007.

The number of older HIV-infected adults aged 55 and over accessing care at an NHS site in the UK increased from 821 in 1998 to 4,714 in 2007. Men who have sex with men are the majority of those aged 55 and over accessing care, accounting for 64 per cent in 1998 and 54 per cent in 2007. The number of older adults accessing care who acquired HIV heterosexually increased in the last decade, forming 28 per cent of the overall number of adults aged 55 and over accessing care in 1998 and 41 per cent in 2007.

Figure 7.21

New diagnoses of HIV and deaths of HIV-infected individuals[1]

United Kingdom[2,3]

Rates per million population

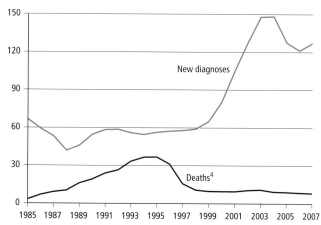

1 Reports to the end of June 2008. See Appendix, Part 7: New HIV diagnoses database.
2 Excludes new diagnoses of deaths in the Channel Islands or the Isle of Man.
3 UK total includes deaths among HIV-infected individuals where the place of death is not known.
4 Includes all deaths among HIV-infected individuals, regardless of whether the death was HIV or AIDS-related or not.

Source: Health Protection Agency; Office for National Statistics

Chapter 8

Social protection

- In 2006/07 local authorities in England spent £20.1 billion on personal social services, more than double the £9.3 billion spent in 1996/97. More than two-fifths (43 per cent) was directed at older people. (Figure 8.3)

- The proportion of service users in England receiving high intensity home care increased from 12 per cent in 1993 to 52 per cent in 2007. (Figure 8.6)

- Between 1996/97 and 2006/07 discharges from a hospital in the UK following an emergency admission, where the stay was less than one day, increased by 161 per cent. (Page 118)

- In 2006, 40 per cent of children with working mothers in Great Britain relied on informal child care: the most common source was the child's grandparents. (Page 122)

- The number of boys counselled by Childline in the UK doubled from 24,115 in 1997/98 to 58,311 in 2007/08, increasing from 21 per cent of all contacts to 33 per cent. (Figure 8.21)

- In 2007 more than 81,000 children were being looked after by local authorities in the UK, an increase of 18 per cent since 1997. (Table 8.22)

Social protection describes the help given to those in need or at risk of hardship. It provides a safety net to protect the vulnerable in society who are unable to make provision for themselves for a minimum decent standard of living, such as those affected by illness, low income, adverse family circumstances and age-related problems. Central government, local authorities and private bodies such as voluntary organisations (the 'third sector') all provide this sort of help and support. Social protection policies reduce poverty and wealth gaps through means-tested benefits, payments such as tax credits to low earners and assistance with child care. Other assistance is provided through direct cash payments such as social security benefits or pensions, payments in kind such as free prescriptions, and the provision of services such as the National Health Service (NHS). Unpaid care, such as that provided by family members, also plays a key part.

Expenditure

The Department for Work and Pensions (DWP) in Great Britain and the Department for Social Development in Northern Ireland are responsible for managing social security benefits, for example, the state retirement pension, disability allowances, income support and pension credit. After allowing for inflation, social security benefit expenditure in the UK doubled from £69 billion in 1979/80 to £141 billion in 2007/08 (Figure 8.1). Spending on social security benefits is influenced by the economic cycle, demographic changes and government policies. After falling between 1986/87 and 1989/90, there

Figure 8.1

Social security benefit expenditure[1] in real terms[2]

United Kingdom
£ billion at 2007/08 prices

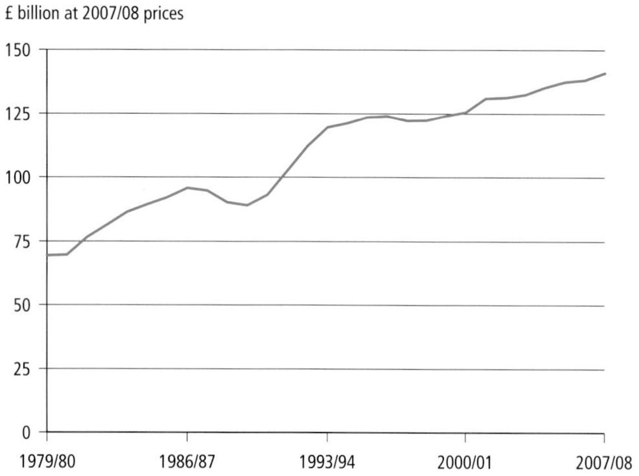

1 See Appendix, Part 8: Expenditure on social protection benefits.
2 Adjusted to 2007/08 prices using the GDP market prices deflator (third quarter 2008).

Source: Department for Work and Pensions; HM Revenue and Customs; Veterans Agency; Department for Social Development, Northern Ireland

was a rapid increase in spending on social security benefits, rising to £120 billion in 1993/94 reflecting increases in the number of people who were unemployed or economically inactive during the economic recession in the early 1990s (see Glossary in Chapter 4: Labour market, page 61). From 1994/95 to 2007/08 the increase in social protection expenditure was steadier, except between 2000/01 and 2001/02 when expenditure rose by £5.5 billion. This was because it was the first full year of working and child tax credits, having been introduced part way through 1999. Child tax credit is available to families with children, working tax credit is available to those on low or moderate incomes and can be claimed in addition to child tax credit. This rate of increase did not continue and although expenditure has continued to rise it has done so at a more gradual pace.

Of the £141 billion UK benefit expenditure in 2007/08, £126 billion was managed by the DWP in Great Britain. Most of this, £74.9 billion (60 per cent of the Great Britain total), was for people of state pension age (age 65 and over for men and 60 and over for women), £32.9 billion (26 per cent) was directed at people of working age, £15.8 billion (13 per cent) was directed at those with disabilities and £1.7 billion (1 per cent) was for children. Expenditure directed at children comprises benefits provided to adults with responsibility for children. These include income support, disability allowances, housing benefit and council tax benefit, but exclude child benefit payments.

Child benefit payments across the UK are administered and paid by HM Revenue and Customs (HMRC) and totalled £10.6 billion in the UK in 2007/08. HMRC has also provided financial assistance since 1999/2000 in the form of tax credits. Expenditure on tax credits reached £20 billion in 2007/08, paid to around 5.7 million families. Furthermore the Veterans Agency paid £1 billion in war pensions in the UK.

In Northern Ireland, the Department for Social Development spent nearly £4.2 billion in 2007/08 on pensions and income-related pension credit, contributory and disability benefits, job seeker's allowance and income support, and social fund payments such as winter fuel payments. Of the £4.2 billion, £446 million (10 per cent) was spent on housing benefits and assistance with domestic rates. Around one-half (49 per cent) of the remaining £3.7 billion was directed at those over state pension age, 26 per cent was directed at those of working age and 25 per cent was directed at those with disabilities and carers.

The British Social Attitudes Survey includes questions on attitudes towards various aspects of welfare expenditure. In 2007, one-third (33 per cent) of adults aged 18 and over in

Table 8.2

Attitudes towards extra spending on social benefits:[1] by household type[2]

Great Britain   Percentages

	Agree		Neither agree nor disagree		Disagree	
	1996	2007	1996	2007	1996	2007
One adult	48	40	29	30	23	30
One adult with children	52	39	27	40	21	22
Two adults	44	36	28	28	27	36
Two adults with children	39	24	30	38	31	38
Three or more adults	44	29	29	36	27	35
Three or more adults with children	44	30	34	44	22	26
All households	44	33	29	34	27	34

1 Respondents aged 18 and over were asked 'Please tick a box to show how much you agree or disagree that the Government should spend more
  money on welfare benefits for the poor, even if it leads to higher taxes.' Excludes those who responded 'don't know' or did not answer.
2 Data shown are household composition and not relationships within a household. Children are those aged under 18.

Source: British Social Attitudes Survey, National Centre for Social Research

Great Britain thought that the government should spend more money on welfare benefits for the poor, even if this led to higher taxes, compared with nearly one-half (44 per cent) in 1996 (Table 8.2). This may, in part, be a reflection of the fact that expenditure on social security payments increased by nearly 14 per cent, allowing for inflation, between 1996/97 and 2007/08 (see Figure 8.1). The decline in the proportion of people favouring higher government expenditure on welfare benefits is common to all household types, although one adult households (40 per cent) and one adult households with children (39 per cent) are still most likely to agree with the statement. One adult households with children also remain the group least likely to disagree, at 21 per cent in 1996 and 22 per cent in 2007. Two adult households with children were the least likely to agree with the statement in both 1996 (39 per cent) and 2007 (24 per cent).

In 2006/07 local authorities in England spent £20.1 billion on personal social services, more than double the £9.3 billion spent in 1996/97. This includes expenditure on home help and home care, looked after children, children on child protection registers and foster care provided by local authorities (see Table 8.22). Nearly £8.7 billion was spent on older people (those aged 65 and over) (Figure 8.3). This remains the largest category, at 43 per cent of the total spend, although this share has fallen from 49 per cent in 1996/97. Spending on children and families, at £5 billion, accounted for 25 per cent of total personal social services expenditure, an increase from £2.1 billion in 1996/97. Combined spending on adults aged under 65 with learning difficulties, physical disabilities or

mental health needs was £5.8 billion (29 per cent of expenditure) up from £2.3 billion (25 per cent of expenditure) in 1996/97.

Information about expenditure on social protection within the European Union (EU-27) is collated by Eurostat as part of the

Figure 8.3

Local authority personal social services expenditure:[1] by recipient group

England

£ billion

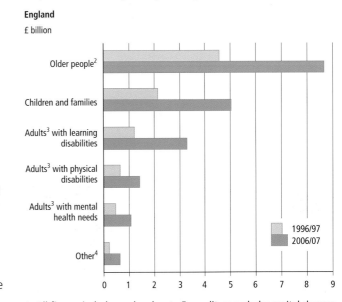

1 All figures include overhead costs. Expenditure excludes capital charges,
  income from joint arrangements and other income.
2 Aged 65 and over, includes people of this age group with learning
  disabilities, physical disabilities and mental health needs.
3 Adults aged under 65.
4 Includes expenditure on asylum seekers and overall service strategy.

Source: The NHS Information Centre for health and social care

8

European System of integrated Social Protection Statistics (ESSPROS). ESSPROS defines social protection as encompassing all interventions from public or private bodies intended to relieve households and individuals of the burden of a defined set of risks or needs. The list of risks or needs that may give rise to social protection is fixed by convention. These are categorised as sickness and health care, disability, old age, survivors, family and/or children, unemployment, housing and social exclusion not elsewhere classified, such as legal aid assistance.

Total UK expenditure on social protection as defined by ESSPROS in 2006/07 was estimated at £345 billion. This was equivalent to 26 per cent of gross domestic product (GDP) at market prices or around £5,800 per person. However, social protection is not spread evenly over the whole population. Expenditure on benefits for old age and 'survivors' (defined as those whose entitlement derives from their relationship to a deceased person, for example, widows, widowers and orphans) accounted for £153 billion (44 per cent) of the UK total (Figure 8.4). Spending on sickness, health care and disability accounted for £142 billion (41 per cent), while families and children accounted for £21 billion (6 per cent). In real terms (after allowing for inflation) there was a 33 per cent rise in total social protection expenditure between 1996/97 and 2006/07. Expenditure on sickness, health care and disability increased by 59 per cent over the period and spending on benefits for old age and survivors increased by 34 per cent. The latter category

includes payments for disability and income support, as old people and survivors were the main recipients of these benefits, accounting for £13.2 billion (8.6 per cent) of expenditure on them. These figures do not include expenditure on tax credits, which increased from £1 billion in 1999/2000 to £20 billion in 2007/08. Other expenditure on families and children decreased by 10 per cent to £21 billion, although it remained more than that on housing, unemployment and other expenditure, which includes, for example, provision of legal aid. Spending on unemployment declined by 35 per cent over the period, from £12.6 billion to £8.2 billion. There were only small year on year fluctuations around this decline with the exception of 2001/02 when spending on unemployment increased by £2 billion to £10.7 billion, before falling again to £8.4 billion the following year.

To allow meaningful comparisons to be made across the EU-27, levels of expenditure are adjusted to take account of differences in prices for goods and services within each country. The adjustments are made using 'purchasing power parities' (PPPs) (see Appendix, Part 5: Purchasing power parities). In 2005, UK spending on social protection was equivalent to purchasing power standard (PPS) 7,100 per head, above the EU-27 average of PPS 6,100 per head (Figure 8.5). In 1996 both the UK and EU-15 average expenditure was PPS 4,900 per head. UK expenditure increased by 47 per cent between 1996 and 2005, slightly higher than the EU-15 average increase of 42 per cent. Luxembourg spent the most per head in both 1996 (PPS 7,200 per head) and 2005 (PPS 12,950 per head), an increase of 79 per cent. However, a large proportion of benefits in Luxembourg are paid to people who are or have been working there but live outside the country, primarily on health care, pensions and family allowances, which inflates the per head of country population figure. Portugal had the lowest spend per head of the EU-15 countries in 1996 at PPS 2,300 per head and was still the lowest in 2005 despite having increased by 84 per cent to PPS 4,300 per head. The countries that joined the EU in January 2007, Bulgaria and Romania, recorded the lowest expenditure of all EU-27 countries in 2005 at PPS 1,300 and PPS 1,100 respectively.

The Organisation for Economic Co-operation and Development (OECD) compared social expenditure data in 2005 for countries across the world. UK gross public social expenditure as a proportion of GDP at factor cost was 24.1 per cent compared with 20.1 per cent for Japan, 19.1 per cent for Australia, 17.1 per cent for the USA and 7.8 per cent for Mexico. According to this measure, UK expenditure was above the OECD average of 23.2 per cent, but below the proportion of expenditure in, for example, Sweden (35.0 per cent),

Figure 8.4

Expenditure on social protection benefits[1] in real terms:[2] by function

United Kingdom

£ billion at 2006/07 prices

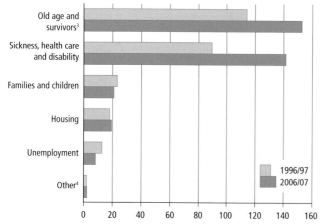

1 See Appendix, Part 8: Expenditure on social protection benefits.
2 Adjusted to 2006/07 prices using the GDP market prices deflator.
3 Survivors are those whose entitlement derives from their relationship to
    a deceased person (for example, widows, widowers and orphans).
4 Includes expenditure on legal aid and local authority social services.

Source: Office for National Statistics

Figure 8.5

Expenditure[1] on social protection per head: EU-27 comparison, 2005

PPS thousand per head

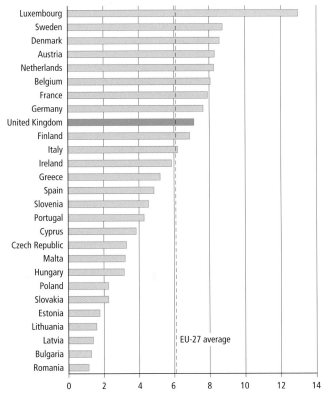

1 Before deduction of tax, where applicable. Tax credits are generally excluded. Figures are purchasing power standard (PPS) per inhabitant. Includes administrative and other expenditure incurred by social protection schemes. See Appendix, Part 5: Purchasing power parities.

Source: Eurostat

France (33.8 per cent), Denmark (32.4 per cent) and Norway, Poland and Spain (24.4 per cent each).

Carers and caring

The *Community Care Reforms Act* was introduced in 1993 to help people who need care to continue to live in their own homes as independently as possible. Home care is defined as services that assist the client (the person who needs the care) to function as independently as possible and/or continue living in their own home. Such services may involve routine household tasks within or outside the home, personal care of the client, or respite care to support the client's regular carers.

Local authority home care services are provided to those with physical disabilities (including frailty associated with ageing), dementia, mental health problems and learning difficulties. Services in the form of regular visits were provided to around 335,000 households or 347,000 service users in England in 2007, down 3 per cent from 2006. In recent years there has been a decline in the number of people receiving care services

but an increase in the intensity of care provided. Of all households receiving care, the proportion that received high intensity home care (six or more visits per week and more than five hours per week) increased steadily from 12 per cent in 1993 to 52 per cent in 2007 (Figure 8.6). This reflects a focus by councils with social services responsibilities on increasing the number and intensity of home care visits. As part of this change councils are providing equipment and modifications such as hand rails and chair lifts to clients. These reduce the need for low intensity care (a single visit of two hours or less per week) by enabling clients to carry out tasks independently for which they would have previously required some form of assistance. The proportion of households receiving low intensity care decreased from 37 per cent in 1993 to 11 per cent in 2007. A further 29 per cent of households received between two and nine visits per week of up to five hours per visit in 2007.

These visits to households represented 3.9 million contact hours provided or purchased by local authorities during the survey week in September 2007, a 4 per cent increase from 2006. The average number of contact hours per household in 2007 was 11.6, which was double the figure in 1998, at 5.8 hours. There has also been a change in the way local authority home care services are sourced. In 1998 the majority (58 per cent) of home help contact hours were directly provided by local authorities in England; this proportion more than halved to 22 per cent in 2007. Instead, the number of hours of care purchased by local authorities from the

Figure 8.6

Home help and home care: by intensity[1] of care provided

England

Percentages

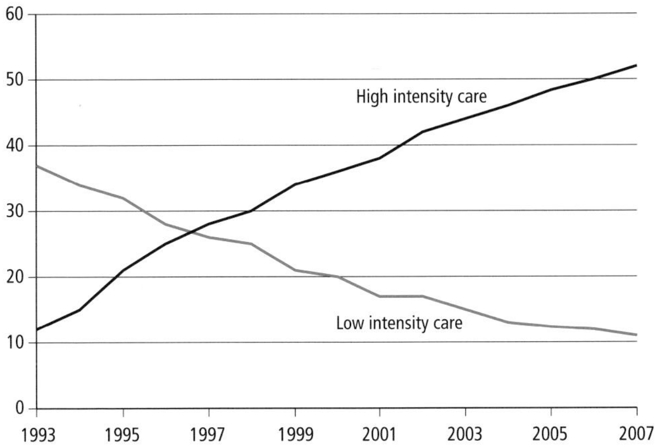

1 Low intensity care is a single visit of two hours or less per week. High intensity care is six or more visits and more than five hours per week. Survey week in September each year.

Source: The NHS Information Centre for health and social care

Table 8.7

New contacts with councils:[1] by source of referral

England

Thousands

	2000/01	2001/02	2002/03	2003/04	2004/05	2005/06	2006/07
Self-referral	263	241	214	554	536	592	586
Secondary health	503	499	527	486	493	495	487
Family/friend/neighbour	253	257	251	280	265	281	277
Primary health/Community health	240	259	259	243	260	264	274
Internal[2]	220	201	200	140	133	134	135
Other departments of own local authority or other local authority	34	34	32	40	45	47	40
Local authority housing department or housing association	28	26	26	31	32	34	37
Legal agency	17	17	21	32	30	30	34
Not known	127	81	75	77	49	46	52
Other	95	111	110	113	116	117	117
All contacts	1,779	1,727	1,715	1,996	1,960	2,041	2,040

1 Councils with social services responsibilities.
2 Council's own social services department.

Source: The NHS Information Centre for health and social care

independent sector (both private and voluntary) increased threefold over the decade, from 1.2 million in 1998 to 3.0 million in 2007, and has become the main source of local authority care provision increasing from 46 per cent in 1998 to 78 per cent in 2007.

Councils and local authorities provide a range of services from in-home care to equipment, depending on the circumstances and requirements of those being assessed. In 2006/07 an estimated two million adults in England were referred to councils with social services responsibilities for the first time, a 15 per cent increase from 2000/01 (Table 8.7). Around one million of these contacts resulted in further assessment or the commissioning of ongoing services, which include home care, day care, meals, equipment and direct payments. These payments are in lieu of social care services. They provide individuals and couples with greater choice and control over their lives and allow them to make their own decisions about how their care is delivered. Self-referrals accounted for 29 per cent of all contacts. Referrals to councils from secondary health providers such as hospitals, accounted for 24 per cent of contacts and referrals from families, friends and neighbours accounted for 14 per cent. Referrals from primary health providers, for example, general practitioners (GPs) (see Appendix, Part 8: General practitioners) or community health centres, accounted for 13 per cent of contacts. Community-based services such as places at day care centres were provided

to around 1.5 million clients during 2006/07, an increase of 2 per cent from 2005/06 and accounted for 86 per cent of all clients receiving services from local authorities in England. Of the 1.5 million clients, 39 per cent of clients received home care, 33 per cent received professional support (for example, occupational therapy), 32 per cent received equipment and adaptations and 16 per cent received day care as a service following assessment.

Informal carers are adults or children who provide any regular service or help to someone who is sick, disabled or elderly, but not in a paid capacity. In 2006/07 around two-thirds (65 per cent) of informal carers in the UK provided care to someone living outside the carer's household. Family members are the main recipients of informal care from both household and non-household members (Figure 8.8). There is little difference between the sexes in the relationship between the carer and the person being cared for. The largest group cared for by both males and females were parents who were non-household members (34 per cent and 38 per cent respectively). Within the household the largest recipients of care for both men (21 per cent) and women (14 per cent) were partners, spouses or cohabitees. Care provided to non-family members accounted for 11 per cent of male carers' activity and 13 per cent of female carers' activity.

Many carers balance their caring responsibilities with work to support themselves. Those in full-time employment made up

Figure 8.8

Informal carers: by sex and relationship to person being cared for, 2006/07

United Kingdom

Percentages

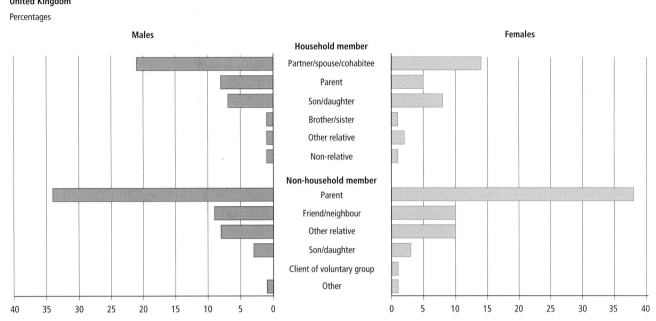

Source: Family Resources Survey, Department for Work and Pensions

the largest group (31 per cent) of carers, regardless of whether care was provided inside or outside the household, followed by those in retirement (23 per cent), part-time employees (15 per cent) or those who were economically inactive (14 per cent).

A study by the University of Leeds on behalf of Carers UK, the organisation that acts as the 'voice' of unpaid carers, looked at the services and support available to informal, or unpaid, carers of working-age in Great Britain. In 2006/07 one-quarter (25 per cent) of such carers across Great Britain used domiciliary services or home care and around one-fifth used respite care (22 per cent) and day centres (20 per cent) (Table 8.9). Carers in Scotland were most likely (28 per cent) of all working-age carers in Great Britain to use respite services. However, nearly two-thirds (60 per cent) of carers identified at least one service that they were not currently using but would like to. Nearly one-quarter (24 per cent) of carers identified carer services such as carer breaks as a service they would like, but did not currently use. Respite care was identified by 23 per cent as a service they would like to use, while sitting services were identified by 22 per cent. Welsh carers were the most likely to want carer services and sitting services (32 per cent for both). Carers in both Wales and Scotland (where many lived in rural areas) were less likely (6 per cent and 8 per cent respectively) to use community transport than carers in England (11 per cent). More than one-third (35 per cent) of carers in England and around three in ten carers in Scotland

Table 8.9

Types of services[1] informal carers currently use and would like to use, 2006/07

Great Britain   Percentages

	Currently use	Would like to use
Domiciliary/home care	25	17
Respite care	22	23
Day centre	20	12
Community mental health services	13	9
Specialist/nursing care/palliative care	11	8
Carers' services[2]	10	24
Sitting services	10	22
Community transport	10	15
Residential care	4	7
Other	11	12
None	33	18

1 All informal carers of working age (men aged 16 to 64 and women aged 16 to 59) were asked 'Do you or the person you care for currently use any of the following services?' and 'What other type of services would you like to have available?' Percentages do not sum to 100 per cent as respondents could give more than one answer.
2 For example, carer breaks.

Source: Carers Employment and Services, report No 4; Carers UK; University of Leeds

8

(30 per cent) and Wales (28 per cent) said that they and the person they were supporting were not using any formal services.

Carers were asked about factors that limited their use of the services available to them. The most common reasons given were that services were not flexible enough (47 per cent), that the person cared for did not want to use services (44 per cent) and that the services were not sufficiently sensitive to individual needs (43 per cent). More than one-third (37 per cent) of carers did not know what services were available locally and a similar proportion (34 per cent) thought that the services available were too expensive. Around one-fifth (18 per cent) of carers in Great Britain did not identify any services that they would like to use.

Sick and disabled people

Sick and disabled people, depending upon the nature and severity of their condition, are entitled to a number of financial benefits. Disability living allowance (DLA) is a benefit for people who are disabled, have personal care needs, mobility needs, or both, and who are aged under 65. Attendance allowance (AA) is paid to people who are ill or disabled after their 65th birthday and because of the extent or severity of their physical or mental condition, need someone to help with their personal care. In 2007/08 there were 4.5 million people in receipt of DLA and/or AA in Great Britain, compared with 4.1 million in 2004/05. This increase reflects changes in entitlement conditions for benefits, demographic changes and increased take-up.

In 2007/08, 2.9 million people in Great Britain were in receipt of DLA and 1.5 million received AA (Table 8.10). Both these figures have increased steadily since 2004/05, by around 9 per cent over the period. Payment for these benefits can be for a range of conditions. For recipients of DLA, arthritis is the most common ailment with 18 per cent of all claimants suffering from this condition. The next most common conditions are 'other mental health causes' (16 per cent), learning difficulties (10 per cent), back ailments and muscle, bone and joint disease (both 8 per cent). The most common condition for claimants of AA was also arthritis at 32 per cent followed by frailty (14 per cent), heart disease (9 per cent), 'other mental health causes' (8 per cent) and stroke-related illness (7 per cent). Much of the difference in the most common conditions for which the benefits are paid may be because AA is paid to those above retirement age.

Incapacity benefit (IB) and severe disablement allowance (SDA) are benefits for people of working age who are unable to work because of illness and/or disability, which can be claimed in

Table 8.10

Recipients of selected benefits for sick and disabled people[1]

Great Britain | | | | Thousands

	2004/05	2005/06	2006/07	2007/08
Incapacity and other benefits (working-age recipients)[2]	2,800	2,747	2,704	2,660
Incapacity benefit only	818	777	737	696
Severe disability allowance	296	283	271	259
Incapacity benefit and disability living allowance	526	532	535	537
Incapacity benefit and income support/pension credit	645	625	614	600
Incapacity benefit, income support/pension credit and disability living allowance	467	480	496	513
Income support/pension credit only	840	824	828	804
Attendance allowance/ disability living allowance[3,4]	4,124	4,246	4,365	4,488
Attendance allowance	1,411	1,461	1,504	1,542
Disability living allowance	2,713	2,786	2,861	2,946

1 See Appendix, Part 8: Expenditure on social protection benefits. At February each year.
2 Includes other benefit combinations not listed here. Men aged 16 to 64 and women aged 16 to 59.
3 Individuals receiving both attendance allowance and disability living allowance are counted twice.
4 Includes those in receipt of an allowance but excludes those where payment is currently suspended (for example, because of a stay in hospital).

Source: Work and Pensions Longitudinal Study, Department for Work and Pensions

addition to other benefits. The total number of people receiving IB or SDA or those benefits they replaced, such as sickness benefit and invalidity benefit, fell slightly between 2004/05 and 2007/08 from 2.8 million claimants to 2.7 million. This resulted mainly from a fall in recipients of IB and IB plus some other benefits. This was partially offset by an increase in recipients of IB plus other benefits including DLA: recipients of both IB and DLA increased by 11,000 to 537,000 between 2004/05 and 2007/08 and those claiming IB, DLA and income support/pension credit increased by 46,000 to 513,000 over the same period. These increases reflect an increase of 233,000 in take-up of DLA over the same period. Income support and pension credit are means-tested benefits payable to people of working age (income support) and those above working age (pension credit) on low incomes, and may be paid on top of other benefits or income. Between 2004/05 and 2007/08 there was a decline of 36,000 (4 per cent) in the number of sick or disabled people claiming only income support or pension credit.

The main support given to sick and disabled people is care provided through the National Health Service (NHS). In 2007 NHS secondary care services, that is hospitals and community health services, employed more than 1.2 million full-time equivalent staff in the UK. There was an almost even split between medical staff, such as nurses, midwives, health visitors, and dental staff (600,000) and non-medical staff, such as therapists, administrative support, management and infrastructure support (619,000). A further 278,000 people were employed in personal social services such as home carers, residential care staff, social workers and administrative support. The number of full-time equivalent staff throughout health and personal social services remained broadly the same in 2006 and 2007 across the UK. There were small decreases in the number of direct care staff in England and Scotland and small increases in Northern Ireland and Wales.

An in-patient is a person who is admitted to a hospital ward for assessment or treatment, whereas an out-patient is a person attending a hospital clinic or accident and emergency department. In the UK between 1993/94 and 2006/07 the number of 'finished consultant episodes' (those where the patient completed a period of care under one consultant, which included an in-patient stay) classified as 'acute' almost

doubled to reach 14.3 million, while the number of 'acute in-patient episodes' per bed per year more than doubled from 53.4 to 115.6 (Table 8.11). This increase is supported by the reduction in the mean length of stay from 5.4 days to 4.0 days over the same period and reflects the policy that patients spend less time recuperating from operations in hospital. The number of finished consultant episodes for the mentally ill has fallen in recent years and in 2006/07 was 31 per cent lower than in 1993/94. The number of in-patient episodes per bed per year for the mentally ill generally increased between 1993/94 and 2006/07, from 4.8 to 6.1. Over the same period the number of in-patient episodes per bed for people with learning disabilities doubled from 2.8 to 5.9.

Around 14 million people each year visited accident and emergency (A&E) departments in UK hospitals between 1987/88 and 2002/03. Between 2002/03 and 2005/06 this increased to 19 million and has since remained at this level. Major A&E departments are able to assess and treat people with serious injuries and illness, around 13 million people attend each year with these sorts of conditions. There are also other services that can provide timely care for patients without an appointment, dealing with minor injuries and illness. NHS walk-in centres can provide advice, assessment and treatment for minor ailments and injuries such as cuts, bruises, minor infections, strains and skin complaints, while minor injury units

Table 8.11

NHS in-patient activity for sick and disabled people[1]

United Kingdom

	1993/94	2003/04	2004/05	2005/06	2006/07
Acute[2]					
Finished consultant episodes (thousands)	7,519	12,885	13,217	13,959	14,350
In-patient episodes per available bed (numbers)	53.4	99.0	101.8	108.7	115.6
Mean duration of stay (days)	5.4	4.9	4.6	4.3	4.0
Mentally ill					
Finished consultant episodes (thousands)	294	238	232	211	203
In-patient episodes per available bed (numbers)	4.8	6.2	6.2	5.9	6.1
Mean duration of stay[3] (days)	76.9	49.3	52.3	55.6	55.2
People with learning disabilities					
Finished consultant episodes (thousands)	61	34	31	27	26
In-patient episodes per available bed (numbers)	2.8	5.4	5.7	5.5	5.9
Mean duration of stay[3] (days)	317.1	42.7	64.8	70.0	48.5

1 See Appendix, Part 8: In-patient activity.
2 General patients on wards, excluding elderly, maternity and neonatal cots in maternity units.
3 Scotland data unavailable from 2003/04 onwards.

Source: The NHS Information Centre for health and social care; Welsh Assembly Government; NHS in Scotland; Department of Health, Social Services and Public Safety, Northern Ireland

Figure 8.12

Hospital discharges[1] following emergency admission from A&E[2] departments: by length of stay[3]

Great Britain[4]

Millions

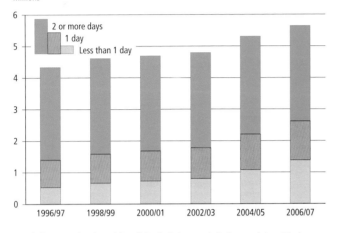

1 Discharge episodes with valid admission and discharge dates. Discharge episodes are counted rather than admission episodes as length of stay can only be determined on discharge.
2 Accident and emergency.
3 See Appendix, Part 8: Length of stay.
4 Scotland data are based on calendar years.

Source: The NHS Information Centre for health and social care; Welsh Assembly Government; NHS in Scotland

can provide assessment and treatment for people with minor injuries such as strains and sprains. A visit to an A&E department may result in an emergency admission to hospital. Between 1996/97 and 2006/07 discharges from emergency admissions to hospital increased from 4.3 million to 5.6 million (Figure 8.12). Discharges following emergency admission to hospital, where the stay was less than one day, increased by 161 per cent over the ten-year period, from 0.5 million in 1996/97 to 1.4 million in 2006/07. Stays of one day also increased, by 43 per cent since 1996/97, from 0.9 million to 1.2 million, while longer stays of two or more days remained stable at around 3 million. During the same period there was an increase in emergency admissions for children and young people aged under 20, from 853,000 in 1996/97 to 989,000 in 2006/07, an increase of 16 per cent even though the population of this age group decreased by 1 per cent over this period (see Chapter 1: Population). Admissions of those aged 20 and over increased by 34 per cent, from 3.5 million in 1996/97 to 4.7 million, in 2006/07 while the population of the over-20s in Great Britain increased by 4.3 per cent.

The statistics on emergency admissions to hospital show that in an emergency situation, people are more likely to use A&E as their first point of contact with a hospital rather than being referred by their general practitioner (GP). In 2006/07,

57 per cent of emergency admissions in England and Wales of people aged 0–19 were through the A&E department of the health care provider, compared with 50 per cent of emergency admissions in 1996/97. Emergency admissions for adults aged 20 and over showed a similar trend, from 46 per cent through the A&E department in 1996/97 to 65 per cent in 2006/07. Emergency admissions from GPs decreased for both the 0–19 and over-20s age groups, from 34 per cent and 37 per cent respectively in 1996/97 to 25 per cent and 21 per cent in 2006/07.

The British Social Attitudes Survey includes questions on attitudes towards various aspects of NHS care and provides insights into the general public's views on these services. In 2007 there was a marked difference between satisfaction levels with GPs and with hospital services, with higher levels of satisfaction with GP services than with hospital services. More than one-half (57 per cent) of adults in Great Britain aged 18 and over thought that their ability to choose which GP to see was either satisfactory or very good (Table 8.13). Furthermore nearly three-quarters (70 per cent) thought the quality of medical treatment delivered by GPs was either satisfactory or very good. In comparison, one-half (50 per cent) believed the quality of nursing care and the quality of medical treatment in hospitals were satisfactory or very good. When asked about the staffing levels in hospitals, two-thirds thought the staffing level of nurses (66 per cent) and the staffing level of doctors (65 per cent) were in need of some or a lot of improvement.

The number of NHS dentists in Great Britain increased by 4 per cent from 23,735 in 2006 to 24,608 in 2007. Within Great Britain, Wales recorded the largest increase (8.5 per cent), followed by Scotland (4.4 per cent) and England (3.1 per cent). There were 4.2 NHS dentists per 10,000 people in Great Britain in 2007. Again there were differences between countries: in England the figure was 4.2 per 10,000, Wales 3.8 and Scotland 5.7 (see Appendix, Part 8: Dentists). Within England there were further regional differences, ranging from 4.9 dentists per 10,000 people in the South East to 3.9 dentists per 10,000 people in the West Midlands. The number of people who have been seen by an NHS dentist in the 24 months to March 2008 was 32 million, 53 per cent of the population. This includes scheduled check-ups, subsequent and emergency treatment.

The General Household Survey included a question on the main reason for not receiving a dental examination or treatment in 2007. The most common reason given was that respondents were unable to find an NHS dentist willing to accept them as a patient, accounting for one-half of all responses (Table 8.14). Waiting for an appointment or treatment was the second

8

Table 8.13

Satisfaction with NHS GPs and hospitals, 2007[1]

Great Britain   Percentages

	In need of a lot of improvement	In need of some improvement	Satisfactory	Very good
GP services				
Being able to choose which GP to see	12	31	46	11
Quality of medical treatment by GPs	6	23	50	20
Hospital services				
Staffing level of nurses in hospitals	24	42	29	4
Staffing level of doctors in hospitals	22	43	31	4
Quality of nursing care in hospitals	15	36	40	10
Quality of medical treatment in hospitals	16	34	39	11

1 Respondents aged 18 and over were asked 'From what you know or have heard, please tick a box for each of the items to show whether you think the National Health Service in your area is, on the whole, satisfactory or in need of improvement.' Excludes those who responded 'don't know' or did not answer.

Source: British Social Attitudes Survey, National Centre for Social Research

most common reason for not having received treatment in the 12 months prior to interview and accounted for 14 per cent of replies. The third most common reason given (12 per cent) was that respondents could not afford treatment, although the survey did not record whether or not they are registered with an NHS dentist or how expensive the treatment would have been privately or through the NHS. The availability of NHS dentists was the most common reason given by respondents

Table 8.14

Main reason for not receiving dental examination or treatment,[1] 2007[2]

Great Britain   Percentages

Can't find NHS dentist willing to take me on as a patient	51.0
Waiting list	13.6
Could not afford to (too expensive)	11.6
Fear of dentists/hospitals/examination/treatment	3.0
Didn't know any good dentist	1.9
Wanted to wait and see if problem got better on its own	1.5
Too far to travel/no means of transportation	1.1
Could not take time because of work, care for children or for others	0.6
Other reasons	15.7

1 Respondents aged 16 and over who said they had not received dental treatment since the last interview were asked 'What was the main reason for not receiving the dental examination or treatment (the most recent time)?'
2 See Appendix, Part 2: General Household Survey.

Source: General Household Survey (Longitudinal), Office for National Statistics

whatever their socio-economic classification. However, it varied from 47 per cent for those in the managerial and professional occupations to 60 per cent for those in the lower supervisory and technical occupations.

Older people

In the UK much of central government expenditure on social protection for older people is through payment of the state retirement pension (basic state pension plus additional state pension). Nearly everyone of state pension age (currently age 65 for men and 60 for women) receives this pension, whatever the level of their other income. Some also receive income-related state benefits, such as council tax benefit or pension credit. As well as the state pension, people can also make their own provision for retirement through an occupational, personal or stakeholder pension (see Chapter 5: Income and wealth, Figure 5.8). In 2006/07, 54 per cent of single male pensioners in the UK had an occupational pension in addition to the state pension, compared with 24 per cent of single female pensioners and 58 per cent of pensioner couples (Table 8.15 overleaf). Almost one-quarter (23 per cent) of single women received a state pension plus other pension (that was not an occupational or personal pension) which could be a widow's pension, annuity pension, trust pension or trade union pension. In previous years those receiving a widow's pension were included in the 'Occupational but not personal pension' category. The proportions of pensioners who received a personal pension as well as the state pension were much lower than those who received an occupational pension, 7 per cent

8

Table 8.15

Pension receipt: by type of pensioner unit,[1] 2006/07

United Kingdom

Percentages

	Pensioner couples	Single male pensioners	Single female pensioners	All pensioners
State retirement pension[2]/minimum income guarantee/pension credit only	19	34	44	33
Plus				
Occupational, but not personal pension[3]	58	54	24	42
Personal, but not occupational pension[3]	10	7	4	7
Both occupational and personal pension[3]	9	1	1	4
Other, no occupational or personal pension[4]	1	2	23	11
Other combinations, no retirement pension/minimum income guarantee/ pension credit	1	1	1	1
None	1	1	2	1
All people	100	100	100	100

1 Pensioner benefit units. See Appendix, Part 8: Benefit units.
2 Includes receipt of other contributory benefits. See Appendix, Part 8: Pension schemes.
3 Occupational and personal pensions include survivor's benefits.
4 Includes widows, trade union, annuity and trust pensions.

Source: Family Resources Survey, Department for Work and Pensions

of single male pensioners and 4 per cent of single female pensioners. The lower proportions for women may be in part because women traditionally had lower employment rates than men (see Chapter 4: Labour market, Figure 4.5). Women were also less likely to have been self-employed, an employment status where personal pension is the main source of pension provision.

The basic state pension in the UK at April 2008 was £90.70 per week, provided that a claimant's own national insurance (NI) contributions were sufficient. Women who have not worked or have not made sufficient NI contributions of their own can claim a pension of £54.35 per week based on criteria, such as their husband's NI contributions. There is also a range of state benefits available for older people in the UK, including a winter fuel payment of £250 for households aged between 60 and 79, or £400 if aged 80 and over, and pension credit.

Pension credit is a means-tested benefit comprising guarantee credit and savings credit. Guarantee credit is for people aged 60 and over living in the UK. It ensured a minimum income of £124.05 a week for single pensioners and £189.35 for pensioner couples in 2008/09. The savings credit element is for those saving towards retirement whether single or living with a partner where either partner is aged 65 and over. The maximum savings credit payable in 2008/09 was £19.71 per week for single people or £26.13 for people with a partner.

Pension credit has an overall take-up rate of between 59 per cent and 67 per cent. The guarantee credit element has the highest take-up rate of between 72 per cent and 82 per cent while savings credit has a lower take-up rate of between 42 per cent and 49 per cent measured by caseload. These take-up figures are for the latest year available, 2006/07, and relate to Great Britain only.

Single pensioners are more likely than pensioner couples to receive some kind of income-related benefit. In 2006/07, 40 per cent of single male pensioners and 45 per cent of single female pensioners in the UK received income-related benefits, compared with 20 per cent of pensioner couples (Table 8.16). Among single pensioners, a greater proportion of women than men received income support, minimum income guarantee or pension credit (30 per cent compared with 23 per cent) because they were less likely to receive a state retirement pension. For pensioner couples the proportion was lower, at 12 per cent. Compared with 2005/06, these proportions remained steady, with single female pensioners and pensioner couples both showing a 1 per cent decrease in 2006/07 while single male pensioners increased by 1 per cent. Around one-quarter of pensioners received disability-related benefits, whether single (23 per cent of males and 24 per cent of females) or in a couple (25 per cent).

In the UK there are an increasing number of elderly people (see Chapter 1: Population). One of the most common health issues

Table 8.16

Receipt of selected social security benefits among pensioners: by type of benefit unit,[1] 2006/07

United Kingdom   Percentages

	Single male pensioners	Single female pensioners	Pensioner couples
Income-related			
Council tax benefit	34	39	17
Income support/minimum income guarantee/ pension credit	23	30	12
Housing benefit	25	24	7
Any income-related benefit[2]	40	45	20
Non-income-related[3]			
Incapacity or disablement benefits[4]	23	24	25
Any non-income-related benefits[2]	100	100	100
Any benefit[2]	100	100	100

1 Pensioner benefit units. See Appendix, Part 8: Benefit units.
2 Includes benefits not listed here. Components do not sum to the total as each benefit unit may receive more than one benefit.
3 Includes state retirement pension.
4 Includes incapacity benefit, disability living allowance (care and mobility components), severe disablement allowance, industrial injuries disability benefit, war disablement pension and attendance allowance.

Source: Family Resources Survey, Department for Work and Pensions

that affect the elderly is dementia. The Alzheimer's Society has reported that one in six people aged 80 and over, and one in 14 of those aged 65 and over has a form of dementia. Dementia is a progressive condition used to describe a collection of symptoms, including a decline in memory, reasoning and communication skills, and a gradual loss of skills needed to carry out daily activities. The disease affects people both under and over 65 years of age but is more common in people aged over 65. Those who develop the illness before the age of 65 are often described as having early onset Alzheimer's disease, and people aged over 65 are described as having late onset Alzheimer's disease. The Alzheimer's Society estimated that in 2007 there were 684,000 people with dementia in the UK. This represents one person in every 88 (1.1 per cent) of the UK population. The majority (63 per cent) live in private households in the community, the rest live in some form of institutional care setting.

The Alzheimer's Society estimated that the cost of care provided to support people aged 65 and over with late onset dementia in 2005/06 was £17.03 billion (Figure 8.17).

Figure 8.17

People aged 65 and over with late onset dementia: by service costs of care, 2005/06

United Kingdom
Percentages

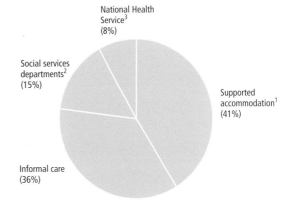

Total service costs: £17.03 billion

1 Includes elderly and mentally infirm (EMI) residential homes.
2 Includes the provision of day care centres and home care.
3 Includes doctors, community health care and hospital stays.

Source: Dementia UK report, Alzheimer's Society

Supported accommodation, which includes elderly and mentally infirm (EMI) residential homes providing necessary personal care, meals and help with every day living, accounted for more than two-fifths (41 per cent) of the cost, and informal care (see also Figure 8.8) accounted for more than one-third (36 per cent) of the total cost. Social services department costs include the provision of day care centres and home care. NHS costs include doctors, community health care and hospital stays, which tend to be longer for dementia sufferers.

The 2006 English Longitudinal Study of Ageing (ELSA) asked questions about whether respondents experienced difficulty carrying out various daily tasks. The survey report classifies respondents to four age bands; 55–64, 65–74, 75–84 and 85 and over. The proportions of those reporting difficulty in carrying out tasks were higher for those in the older age groups, those aged 75 and over. The most common difficulties reported were with dressing or washing (18 per cent of men and 20 per cent of women who reported difficulties) and with shopping or doing work around the house or garden (15 per cent of men and 22 per cent of women).

ELSA also collected information about the sources of help with daily tasks that are available to older people. Informal sources, which include family, neighbours and friends, provided the highest proportions of support reported by both men (64 per cent) and women (71 per cent) aged 55 and over in England in 2006 (Table 8.18 overleaf). Of those who reported receiving help with shopping or work around the house and

8

Table 8.18

Sources of help reported with shopping or work around the house and garden: by sex and age, 2006

England

Percentages[1]

	55–64	65–74	75–84	85 and over	All aged 55 and over
Men who reported help from					
All informal sources[2]	62	64	68	65	64
Spouse or partner	47	46	40	14	40
Any child or child-in-law[3]	19	18	23	42	23
Other relatives	1	3	7	5	4
Formal source[4]	1	5	5	17	5
None of these[5]	37	30	24	16	29
Women who reported help from					
All informal sources[2]	79	70	67	69	71
Spouse or partner	50	41	16	6	29
Any child or child-in-law[3]	34	27	36	48	36
Other relatives	5	3	11	10	7
Formal source[4]	4	9	18	30	15
None of these[5]	17	20	16	7	15

1 Percentages may sum to more than 100 per cent because people can receive help from multiple sources.
2 Includes family, neighbours and friends.
3 Respondents are left to interpret who to include here, but theoretically can include adopted, step and foster children.
4 Includes statutory/voluntary services/paid help.
5 Includes help from a small number of other sources which are not shown separately as it was not known if the care was informal or formal.

Source: The English Longitudinal Study of Ageing, The Institute for Fiscal Studies

garden, the largest source of help for men was from a spouse or partner (40 per cent), except for men aged 85 and over for whom the most important source of help was a child or child-in-law. A child or child-in-law was also the most important source of help for women aged 55 and over (36 per cent) although for those aged 55 to 74 the proportion receiving help from a spouse or partner was higher. This is partly because women live longer than men (see Chapter 1: Population) so many older women do not have this source of help available. Formal sources of help increased with age for both men and women, with 17 per cent of men and 30 per cent of women aged 85 and over reporting this source of help.

Families and children

The Government provides a number of social security benefits targeted at families with children in the UK. They include income-related benefits paid to low income families, such as housing benefit, council tax benefit and income support; and non-income-related benefits, such as child benefit and incapacity or disablement benefits. In 2006/07, 89 per cent of

lone parents with dependent children in the UK and 56 per cent of couples with dependent children received income-related benefits (Table 8.19). Among lone parents with dependent children, 71 per cent received working families tax credit or income support compared with 17 per cent of couples with dependent children. This may reflect the employment status of lone parent mothers, who head the majority of lone parent families and are less likely to be employed than mothers with a partner (see also Chapter 2: Households and families). According to the Department for Work and Pensions 2006 Families and Children Study (FACS 2006) 42 per cent of lone parent mothers did not work compared with 27 per cent of mothers in couple families. Neither parent worked in 5 per cent of couple families (see Chapter 4: Labour Market, Table 4.17 for further details on unemployment rates).

Child care can be provided informally by grandparents and other relatives, older siblings, partners, ex-partners and friends. In 2006, two-fifths (40 per cent) of all families in Great Britain where the mother was in work, relied on informal child care. Grandparents were the most common source, for both couples and lone parents (32 per cent and 31 per cent respectively)

Table 8.19

Receipt of selected social security benefits among families: by type of benefit unit,[1] 2006/07

United Kingdom   Percentages

	Lone parent with dependent children[2]	Couple with dependent children[2]
Income-related		
Council tax benefit	47	7
Housing benefit	45	6
Working families tax credit, income support or pension credit	71	17
Jobseeker's allowance	1	2
Any income-related benefit	89	56
Non-income-related		
Child benefit	96	96
Incapacity or disablement benefits[3]	9	7
Any non-income-related benefit	97	96
Any benefit or tax credit[4]	98	97

1 Families under state pension age. See Appendix, Part 8: Benefit units.
2 Children aged under 16, or aged 16 to 19 and not married or in a civil partnership and living with their parents and in full-time non-advanced education or in unwaged government training.
3 Incapacity benefit, disability living allowance (care and mobility components), severe disablement allowance, industrial injuries disability benefit, war disablement pension, attendance allowance and disabled persons tax credit.
4 Includes all benefits not listed here. Components do not sum to the total as each benefit unit may receive more than one benefit.

Source: Family Resources Survey, Department for Work and Pensions

(Table 8.20 overleaf). Other relatives or older siblings provided child care for 8 per cent of couples and 15 per cent of lone parents. Lone parents (14 per cent) were more likely to rely on ex-partners for child care than couples (1 per cent). As children get older, the use of formal child care decreases. In 2006 more than one-half (54 per cent) of children under five whose mothers worked were looked after under formal child care arrangements. This fell to one-third (33 per cent) for children of primary school age (aged five to ten), and decreased further to around one in 20 (6 per cent) when they reached secondary education age. Around six in ten (59 per cent) of children aged between five and ten with working mothers in Great Britain received some form of child care in 2006. Use of informal child care decreased more slowly with age than use of formal child care, with around one-half (51 per cent) of children under ten, and around one-quarter (26 per cent) of children between ages 11 and 16 receiving this form of child care.

Parental perceptions of the affordability of local child care provision varied between lone parents and couples. In the FACS 2006 nearly one-third (31 per cent) of lone parents in Great Britain described their local child care provisions as 'not at all affordable' compared with more than one-fifth (22 per cent) of couples. A further 34 per cent of lone parents found the provisions 'fairly affordable' compared with 45 per cent of couples. Couples where both worked 16 hours or more per week were more likely than those where either partner worked between one and 15 hours per week to consider local child care to be 'fairly affordable' – 48 per cent compared with 42 per cent. The age of the child may also affect parental perceptions of affordability; almost one-half (49 per cent) of parents with a child aged under five believed that child care was 'fairly affordable' compared with three in ten (30 per cent) of those with a child aged 16 and older, despite child care generally being more expensive for younger children.

The FACS 2006 showed that of families where the mother worked, those with young children were most likely of all families with children to receive financial help from relatives. Of families where the youngest child was aged under five, 43 per cent reported that they received financial help from their families. Families where the youngest child was aged 16 to 18 were least likely to receive financial help from their families (20 per cent). This help took the form of money gifts or loans, or financial contributions towards bills, clothing, holidays or other items. Lone parents working up to 15 hours per week were the most likely of all types of family to receive financial help from relatives (55 per cent). Lone parent families were more likely than couples to receive financial help from their family; 51 per cent received such help compared with 30 per cent of couples. The largest source of help for both groups was relatives buying clothes for the parent or children; 31 per cent of lone parents and 16 per cent of couples received such help.

Asked whether money runs out before the end of the month/week, nearly twice the proportion of couples (38 per cent) reported in the FACS 2006 that they 'never' run out of money compared with lone parents (21 per cent). Additionally lone parents were three times more likely than couples 'always' to run out of money, 18 per cent compared with 6 per cent, and lone parents working up to 15 hours per week were twice as likely 'always' to run out of money as those working 16 or more hours per week (25 per cent and 12 per cent respectively). There was a similar pattern among couples; 13 per cent of couples where both worked up to 15 hours per week 'always' ran out of money compared with 7 per cent of couples where one worked 16 or more hours per week, and 5 per cent where both worked 16 or more hours per week.

8

Table 8.20

Child care arrangements for children with working mothers: by family characteristics, 2006

Great Britain

Percentages[1]

	Child care not required	Formal child care[2]	Informal child care				
			Ex partner/ non-resident parent	Grand-parent	Older sibling/ other relative	Other informal[3]	Total informal
Family type							
Lone parent	47	28	14	31	15	11	46
Couple	39	27	1	32	8	7	39
Family type working status							
Lone parent: 1 to 15 hours	54	14	9	20	11	21	37
Lone parent: 16 hours and above	38	29	15	33	15	10	47
Couple – both: 16 hours and above	43	31	2	34	8	8	40
Couple – one only: 16 hours and above	57	17	0	28	9	8	35
Age of child							
0 to 4	21	54	4	42	9	8	49
5 to 10	34	33	6	39	12	12	51
11 to 16	71	6	3	18	8	5	26

1 Percentages do not sum to 100 per cent as respondents could give more than one answer.
2 Includes nurseries/crèches, nursery schools, playgroups, registered childminders, after school clubs/breakfast clubs, and holiday play schemes.
3 A friend, neighbour or babysitter, who came to the home.

Source: Families and Children Study, Department for Work and Pensions

Voluntary organisations and charities play a role in providing help to children who have problems. Children call or write to Childline about a wide range of problems. Since it was launched in 1986, Childline has counselled more than two million children and young people, including finding refuges for children in danger on the streets. In 2007/08 counselling was provided to more than 176,000 children and young people in the UK, around two-thirds of whom were girls (Figure 8.21). However, the number of boys using the service has more than doubled over the last ten years, from 24,115 calls and letters in 1997/98 (21 per cent of all contacts) to 58,311 in 2007/08 (33 per cent of contacts). This was largely a result of the National Society for the Prevention of Cruelty to Children running advertising campaigns specifically targeted at boys and promoting the service through the Internet and young people's social networking sites, as well as through popular magazines and in schools. The most common reported problem by both girls and boys was bullying, accounting for 18 per cent of all calls. The next most common were family tensions (including divorce and separation) and physical abuse, at 13 per cent and 10 per cent respectively. The total number of calls and letters received increased by 53 per cent between 1997/98 and 2007/08, but the pattern of concerns remained broadly the same.

In cases where parents have difficulty in looking after their children, local authorities can take them into care (see Chapter 2: Households and families, Table 2.21). These children are usually described as being 'looked after'. In 2007 more than

Figure 8.21

Childline calls and letters: by sex

United Kingdom
Thousands

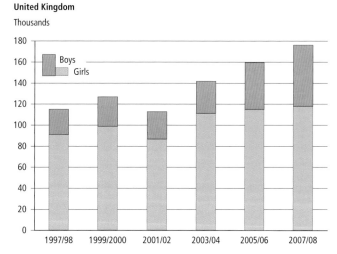

Source: National Society for the Prevention of Cruelty to Children

Table 8.22

Children looked after by local authorities:[1,2] by type of accommodation

United Kingdom   Thousands

	1997	1998	1999	2000	2001	2002	2003	2004	2005	2006	2007
Foster placements	40.1	42.1	43.5	44.9	45.2	46.4	48.6	49.3	49.6	50.5	51.1
Children's homes	9.9	9.6	9.8	10.3	10.1	10.1	10.2	10.4	10.1	9.8	9.8
With parents	11.9	12.2	12.5	12.8	12.5	12.4	12.3	12.1	12.0	12.0	12.2
Placed for adoption[3]	2.5	2.5	3.1	3.8	4.4	4.6	4.1	3.9	3.8	3.4	3.1
Other accommodation[4]	4.1	3.3	3.4	3.7	3.5	3.6	3.7	4.1	4.4	4.7	4.9
All looked after children	68.5	69.9	72.3	75.3	75.8	77.3	78.8	79.7	80.0	80.2	81.1

1 At 31 March.
2 See Appendix, Part 8: Children looked after by local authorities.
3 England and Wales for 1997 to 1999, Great Britain from 2000 onwards. Not collected for Northern Ireland.
4 Includes living independently, living in a family care unit, living under the care of an NHS trust or living in young offender establishments.

Source: Department for Children, Schools and Families; Welsh Assembly Government; Scottish Government; Department of Health, Social Services and Public Safety, Northern Ireland

81,000 children were being looked after by local authorities in the UK (Table 8.22), an increase of 18 per cent since 1997. The largest increase of all types of local authority care was in foster placements (27 per cent). The next largest increases were for children placed for adoption (24 per cent) and children placed in other accommodation (20 per cent), which includes living independently, living in a family care unit, in care of a NHS trust or living in a young offender establishment. Over the same period children looked after by local authorities in children's homes and with parents each fell by 2 percentage points as a proportion of all children looked after, although there was a small increase in the actual numbers being cared for by parents. In 2007 foster placements accounted for the majority (63 per cent) of children in local authority care, up from 59 per cent in 1997. However, there were regional differences in local authority care of children across the UK in 2007. While fostering was most common in Wales (76 per cent), England (70 per cent) and Northern Ireland (58 per cent), in Scotland it was the second most common form of provision (29 per cent) behind 'with parents' (43 per cent).

8

Chapter 9

Crime and justice

- In 2007/08 the crime most commonly recorded by police in England and Wales (36 per cent) and Scotland (33 per cent) was theft and handling stolen goods. In Northern Ireland it was criminal damage (28 per cent). (Table 9.1)

- Between 2006/07 and 2007/08 there was a 10 per cent decrease in the incidence of crime measured by the British Crime Survey (BCS) in England and Wales, from 11.3 million to 10.1 million crimes. (Figure 9.2)

- Violent crime, which comprises assault with or without injury, wounding and robbery, accounted for one-fifth (2.2 million incidents) of all BCS crime in England and Wales in 2007/08. (Table 9.3)

- In 2006, 26 per cent of ten to 25-year-olds in England and Wales were victims of personal crime in the last 12 months, including robbery, personal theft and assault (either with or without injury). (Table 9.4)

- In 2007/08 there were 17,300 crimes reported to the police in England and Wales in which a firearm was used, a 6 per cent decrease from 2006/07. (Figure 9.7)

- Of offenders aged 18 and over leaving prison or starting a community sentence in England and Wales in the first quarter of 2006, 39 per cent reoffended within one year, the lowest reoffending rate since the series began. (Page 136)

Crime can affect anyone, regardless of whether or not they have been a victim. In addition to suffering or loss resulting directly from crime, people may be affected by their perceptions of changing crime levels and their fear of crime may affect the way they live their daily lives. Dealing with crime and associated problems is an ever-present concern for society and the Government. There are two main sources of crime statistics: police-recorded crime and household population surveys of crime (see Measures of crime text box).

Crime levels

This chapter discusses both the incidence and prevalence of crime (see Appendix, Part 9: Prevalence rates and incidence rates). The incidence of crime, defined as the number of crimes that have taken place, is analysed in this section. The prevalence of crime, or the proportion of people who were victims, is covered in the Offences and victims section later in the chapter.

Following the introduction of the National Crime Recording Standard (NCRS) in England and Wales in 2002 (see Appendix, Part 9: National Crime Recording Standard) there was an overall increase in the number of crimes recorded by the police that year, with less serious crimes, including criminal damage, minor theft and assault without injury, increasing the most. The introduction of the Scottish Crime Recording Standard (SCRS) in April 2004 resulted in similar increases in the number of less serious crimes recorded by the police in Scotland.

In 2007/08 around 5.5 million crimes were recorded by the police across the UK (Table 9.1). Nearly three-quarters (72 per cent) of recorded crimes in England and Wales were property crimes; these include theft and handling stolen goods, burglary, criminal damage, and fraud and forgery. Violence against the person accounted for around one-fifth (19 per cent) of all recorded crime in England and Wales, the same proportion as in 2006/07.

Measures of crime

There are two main measures of the extent of crime in the UK: surveys of the public, and crime recorded by the police. The British Crime Survey (BCS) interviews adults aged 16 and over who are living in private households in England and Wales. The Scottish Crime and Victimisation Survey (SCVS) and the Northern Ireland Crime Survey (NICS) interview adults aged 16 and over in Scotland and Northern Ireland respectively. In some ways the BCS, the SCVS and the NICS give a better measure of many types of crime than police-recorded crime statistics. These surveys show the large number of offences that are not reported to the police and also give a more reliable picture of trends, as they are not affected by changes in levels of reporting to the police or by variations in police recording practice (see Appendix, Part 9: Types of offence in England and Wales, in Scotland, and in Northern Ireland).

Recorded crime data cover offences reported to and recorded by the police. The National Crime Recording Standard (NCRS), introduced in England and Wales in 2002 and the Scottish Crime Recording Standard (SCRS), introduced in 2004, were implemented with the aim of taking a more victim-centred approach and providing consistency between police forces (see Appendix, Part 9: National Crime Recording Standard).

Police-recorded crime and survey-measured crime have different coverage. Unlike crime data recorded by the police, surveys are generally restricted to crimes against adults living in private households and their property and do not include some types of crime (for example, fraud, murder and victimless crimes such as drug use, where there is not a direct victim).

See also Appendix, Part 9: Availability and comparability of data from constituent countries.

Table 9.1

Crimes recorded by the police: by type of offence,[1] 2007/08

United Kingdom			Percentages
	England & Wales	Scotland	Northern Ireland
Theft and handling stolen goods	36	33	23
Theft from vehicles	9	4	3
Theft of vehicles	3	3	3
Criminal damage	21	31	28
Violence against the person[2]	19	3	27
Burglary	12	7	11
Drugs offences	5	11	3
Fraud and forgery	3	2	3
Robbery	2	1	1
Sexual offences	1	1	2
Other offences[3]	1	12	3
All notifiable offences (=100%) (thousands)	4,951	386	108

1 See Appendix, Part 9: Types of offence in England and Wales, in Scotland, and in Northern Ireland, and Availability and comparability of data from constituent countries.
2 Data for Scotland are serious assaults only. Those for England and Wales and Northern Ireland are all assaults including those that cause no physical injury.
3 Northern Ireland includes 'offences against the state'. Scotland excludes 'offending while on bail'.

Source: Home Office; Scottish Government; Police Service of Northern Ireland

The definition of crime in Northern Ireland is broadly comparable with that used in England and Wales. In 2007/08 the police in Northern Ireland recorded 108,000 crimes, nearly two-thirds (65 per cent) of which were property crimes. More than one-quarter (27 per cent) of recorded crime in Northern Ireland involved violence against the person, again showing little change from 2006/07.

In Scotland the term 'crime' is reserved for the more serious offences, broadly equivalent to 'indictable' and 'triable-either-way' offences in England and Wales, while less serious crimes are called 'offences' (see Appendix, Part 9: Availability and comparability of data from constituent countries). In 2007/08, 386,000 crimes were recorded by the police in Scotland. The most common recorded crime in Scotland was theft and handling stolen goods (33 per cent), followed by criminal damage (31 per cent), unchanged from 2006/07.

The number of crimes recorded by the police tends to be lower than that reported by household surveys, largely because survey respondents identify a large number of offences that have not been reported to the police. Based on the 2007/08 British Crime Survey (BCS), 42 per cent of incidents of BCS comparable crime in England and Wales, that is crimes where BCS data can be directly compared with police statistics (see Appendix, Part 9: Comparable crimes), were reported to the police, or became known to the police by some other means. Victims gave a variety of reasons for not reporting crime to the police, with the most common being that they felt the crime was too trivial, there was no loss or that in their view the police would not, or could not, do anything about it.

The incidence of crime estimated by the BCS in England and Wales rose steadily throughout the 1980s and early 1990s and peaked in 1995, at 19.4 million offences. There was then a steady decline and the level remained relatively stable between 2004/05 and 2006/07. However, between 2006/07 and 2007/08 there was a 10 per cent decrease in the incidence of BCS crime, from 11.3 million to 10.1 million crimes and the level of crime in 2007/08 was almost one-half the level in the peak year of 1995 (Figure 9.2). The Northern Ireland Crime Survey (NICS) estimated that 199,000 crimes were committed against adults living in private households in the 12 months prior to interview in 2007/08. This was an increase from 195,000 crimes identified in 2006/07, but still much lower than the 295,000 identified in the 2003/04 NICS. Because there was no Scottish Crime and Victimisation Survey (SCVS) in 2007, the most recent available data for Scotland are for 2005/06. The survey estimated that around 1.1 million crimes were committed against adults in private households in the 12 months prior to interview in 2005/06, an increase from

Figure 9.2

British Crime Survey offences[1]

England & Wales
Millions

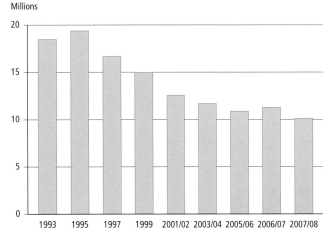

1 Until 2000, respondents were asked to recall their experience of crime in the previous calendar year. From 2001/02 onwards the British Crime Survey became a continuous survey and the recall period was changed to the 12 months prior to interview.

Source: British Crime Survey, Home Office

900,000 in 2003/04. The incidence of SCVS crime in 2005/06 was at the same level it was in 1992.

Of the 10.1 million crimes reported by the BCS in England and Wales in 2007/08, almost two-thirds (6.4 million) were household crimes and more than one-third (3.7 million) were personal crimes (Table 9.3 overleaf). There was an overall reduction in the incidence of both types of crime reported in 2007/08. The most common crime reported, accounting for more than one-quarter of all BCS crime, was vandalism, with an estimated 2.7 million incidents experienced in the 12 months prior to interview. This was the most commonly experienced household crime each year since 2001/02, but during the 1990s vehicle theft was the most common, ranging from 3.5 million to 4.4 million crimes. Violent crime, which comprises assault with or without injury, wounding and robbery, accounted for one-fifth (2.2 million incidents) of all BCS crime reported in 2007/08.

Offences and victims

The likelihood of being a victim of crime varies according to where you live. The highest levels of household crime in England and Wales according to the 2007/08 British Crime Survey (BCS), including theft of, or from, vehicles, bicycle theft, household theft, burglary, and vandalism, were experienced by those living in Yorkshire and the Humber where one-fifth (20 per cent) of households reported being a victim once or more in the 12 months prior to interview. The North East

9

Table 9.3

Incidents of crime: by type of offence[1]

England & Wales

Millions

	1981	1991	1995	2001/02	2005/06	2006/07	2007/08
Household crime							
Vandalism	2.7	2.8	3.4	2.6	2.7	2.9	2.7
All vehicle-related theft[2]	1.8	3.8	4.4	2.5	1.7	1.7	1.5
Burglary	0.7	1.4	1.8	1.0	0.7	0.7	0.7
Bicycle theft	0.2	0.6	0.7	0.4	0.4	0.5	0.4
Other household theft[3]	1.5	1.9	2.3	1.4	1.2	1.2	1.1
All household crime	6.9	10.4	12.4	7.9	6.8	7.1	6.4
Personal crime							
Theft from the person	0.4	0.4	0.7	0.6	0.6	0.6	0.6
Other thefts of personal property	1.6	1.7	2.1	1.4	1.2	1.1	1.0
All BCS violence	2.1	2.6	4.2	2.7	2.3	2.5	2.2
Assault with minor injury	0.6	0.8	1.4	0.7	0.6	0.6	0.5
Assault with no injury	0.8	1.0	1.6	1.0	0.9	1.0	0.9
Wounding	0.5	0.6	0.9	0.6	0.5	0.6	0.5
Robbery	0.2	0.2	0.3	0.4	0.3	0.3	0.3
All personal crime	4.1	4.7	6.9	4.7	4.1	4.2	3.7
All crimes reported to BCS	11.0	15.1	19.4	12.6	10.9	11.3	10.1

1 Until 2000 respondents were asked to recall their experience of crime in the previous calendar year. From 2001/02 onwards the British Crime Survey (BCS) became a continuous survey and the recall period was changed to the 12 months prior to interview.
2 Includes theft of, or from, a vehicle, as well as attempts.
3 Includes thefts and attempted thefts from domestic garages, outhouses and sheds, not directly linked to the dwelling, as well as thefts from both inside and outside a dwelling.

Source: British Crime Survey, Home Office

(19 per cent) and the North West (18 per cent) had the next highest incidence of household crime. The lowest incidence was reported by those living in the South West (14 per cent). There are also differences in the characteristics of those households more at risk and this varies by the type of crime. For example, households with no security measures were more than ten times as likely than average to be victims of burglary according to the 2007/08 BCS, and households headed by someone aged 16 to 24 were three times more likely than average to be burgled.

The highest rate of personal crime, including assault, sexual offences, robbery, theft from the person and other personal theft, was experienced by those living in London, with 8 per cent having been victims in the 12 months prior to interview. The areas with the lowest risk of personal crime were Wales and the South West, at 5 per cent each. Risk of personal crime also varied according to the characteristics of the victim. Men and women aged 16 to 24 were more likely to have experienced a violent offence than those in any other age group. The risk for young men was more than double that for

young women (13 per cent compared with 6 per cent) and although the difference declined with age, men of all ages were more likely than women to have experienced a violent offence. The risk of being a victim of violence had decreased to less than 1 per cent by the age of 55 for women and age 65 for men.

The incidence of personal crime continues to be high among young people aged under 26. The 2006 Offending, Crime and Justice Survey (OCJS) reported that 12 per cent of ten to 25-year-olds had experienced at least one incident of personal theft in England and Wales in the 12 months prior to interview (Table 9.4). More than one-quarter (26 per cent) were victims of some kind of personal crime over the same period, including robbery, personal theft and assault (either with or without injury). Young males were more likely than young females to be victims of a personal crime within the last 12 months (31 per cent compared with 21 per cent). The difference was most pronounced among ten to 15-year-olds; nearly two-fifths (38 per cent) of boys of this age group were victims compared with around one-fifth (22 per cent) of girls.

Table 9.4

Young people who were victims of personal crime:[1] by age and sex, 2006

England & Wales   Percentages

	Males			Females			All aged 10–25
	10–15	16–25	All	10–15	16–25	All	
Any personal thefts	17	11	13	8	11	10	12
Robbery	2	3	2	1	1	1	2
Theft from the person	7	5	5	3	5	4	5
Other personal thefts	11	6	8	5	7	6	7
Any assault	28	18	22	15	11	12	17
Assault (no injury)	21	10	14	11	7	8	11
Assault (with injury)	14	11	12	7	5	6	9
Any personal crime	38	27	31	22	20	21	26

1 In the 12 months prior to interview.

Source: Offending, Crime and Justice Survey, Home Office

According to the 2006 OCJS, the most common type of personal crime among ten to 25-year-olds was assault, at 17 per cent, with 11 per cent of young people being victims of assault without injury and 9 per cent victims of assault with injury. Males aged ten to 25 had the highest victimisation rates for these crimes, at 14 per cent and 12 per cent respectively, around double the rates for females (8 per cent and 6 per cent respectively). While the definition of personal victimisation in the survey is broadly consistent with the BCS, the questions are adjusted to make them suitable for the younger respondents, and are asked in a different context, so it is not possible to draw direct comparisons between the OCJS and BCS measures of victimisation.

The 2006/07 BCS showed that in England and Wales, 2 per cent of individual mobile phone owners had their mobile stolen in the last 12 months, the same proportion as in 2005/06. Mobile phone theft varied by age of the victim with children aged 12 to 15 and young adults aged 16 to 24 being the most likely to experience mobile phone theft in the last 12 months, around 5 per cent of each group of owners (Figure 9.5). Around 2 per cent of adults aged between 25 and 44 had their mobile stolen in the last 12 months. The 2006/07 BCS asked adults aged 16 and over who had personally experienced a theft (therefore excluding other household members and children) about the circumstances of the theft. Nearly one-quarter (24 per cent) reported that the theft had taken place while the victim was on public transport or in another public place, such as a shop or hospital. A further 22 per cent had their phone stolen from a bar, pub or club.

The 2007/08 BCS asked victims of violent incidents (including wounding, assault with minor injury, assault with no injury and robbery) whether they believed the offender to have been under the influence of alcohol or drugs (except in incidents where the victim perceived the offender to be under school-leaving age or could not describe the offender). More than two-fifths (45 per cent) of victims of violent offences believed the offender to be under the influence of alcohol.

Figure 9.5

Mobile phone owners experiencing theft:[1] by age, 2006/07

England & Wales

Percentages

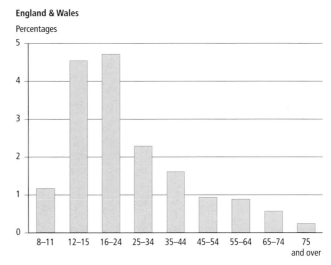

1 Based on the number of people who experienced theft of at least one mobile phone in the last 12 months. Does not reflect the number of phones stolen.

Source: British Crime Survey, Home Office

Violence committed by a stranger was the most common type of incident in which victims believed the offender was under the influence of alcohol (58 per cent) followed by violent incidents committed by an acquaintance (48 per cent) (Table 9.6). The most common type of offence was assault with minor injury, with around three-fifths (61 per cent) of victims seeing alcohol as a contributing factor. It is harder for victims to identify whether the perpetrator of their violent incident was under the influence of drugs but this too was most commonly identified in incidents of assault with minor injury (24 per cent).

The introduction of The Licensing Act 2003 in November 2005 abolished set licensing hours in England and Wales with the aim of passing responsibility for licensing from the magistrates' courts to local authorities. Although this led to some concerns about introducing a '24-hour drinking culture', the aim was to reduce the problems of heavy drinking and disorder associated with a standard closing time and, over the longer term, encourage a more relaxed drinking culture. The Home Office evaluation of the impact of the Act on crime and disorder found that there was little evidence to support concerns about increased violence. Comparing the 12 months before and after implementation, a survey of 30 police forces showed falls in the number of recorded incidents involving violence, criminal

Table 9.6

Proportion of violent incidents where the offender was perceived to be under the influence of alcohol or drugs,[1,2] 2007/08

England & Wales				Percentages
	Alcohol		Drugs	
	Yes	No	Yes	No
Type of violence				
Domestic	37	61	12	82
Mugging	17	63	13	58
Stranger	58	28	14	47
Acquaintance	48	46	28	51
Type of offence				
Wounding	48	42	15	60
Robbery	19	63	14	58
Assault with minor injury	61	32	24	49
Assault with no injury	44	47	20	56
All violence	45	45	19	56

1 Percentages do not sum to 100 per cent as victims could answer 'don't know'.
2 Question not asked if offenders were perceived to be of school age.

Source: British Crime Survey, Home Office

damage and harassment (1 per cent) and in serious violent crimes (5 per cent). However, the timing of these incidents changed with a small rise in the number of incidents between 6 pm and 6 am and a 25 per cent increase in the number of offences committed between 3 am and 6 am. In addition, the BCS Night Time Economy Module shows that there was no significant change following the introduction of the Act in the proportion of people who said they felt unsafe in town centres at night, or who had witnessed drunken anti-social behaviour in town centres.

The 2007/08 BCS estimated that there were nearly 2.2 million violent incidents against adults in England and Wales, a decrease of 12 per cent since 2006/07 (see Table 9.3). Weapons were used in nearly one-quarter (24 per cent) of all violent incidents, the same proportion as in 2006/07. This proportion has remained stable over the last decade. Weapons were most commonly used in offences of robbery, wounding, and assault with no injury, with around one-quarter of these incidents each involving the use of some kind of weapon (23 per cent, 26 per cent and 27 per cent respectively).

Hitting implements (including sticks and clubs) and knives were the most common weapons used in violent incidents reported in the 2007/08 BCS (used in 7 per cent and 6 per cent of incidents respectively). A knife was used in 15 per cent of robberies and 8 per cent of woundings. Nearly one-half (49 per cent) of victims of violent incidents in 2007/08 sustained a physical injury.

In 2007/08 around one-fifth (19 per cent) of police-recorded serious offences in England and Wales, including attempted murder, wounding with intent to do grievous bodily harm (GBH), wounding or inflicting GBH (without intent) and robbery (of business or personal property) involved a knife or sharp instrument.

In 2007/08 there were 17,343 crimes reported to the police in England and Wales in which a firearm was used, a 6 per cent decrease from 18,481 offences in 2006/07. The number of offences involving a firearm increased every year from 1998/99 (13,874 offences) to peak in 2002/03 and 2003/04 at around 24,000 offences. The number of firearm offences then began to decline and the decrease in 2007/08 was the fourth consecutive fall since 2003/04. Air weapons were reported to have been used in 7,478 offences in 2007/08, a decrease from 8,836 in 2006/07 (Figure 9.7), and accounted for more than two-fifths (43 per cent) of all firearm offences. However, offences involving a firearm excluding air weapons increased by 2 per cent between 2006/07 and 2007/08; from 9,645 to 9,865 offences. Handguns were the most common type of

Figure 9.7

Crimes[1] reported to the police in which a firearm had been used

England & Wales
Thousands

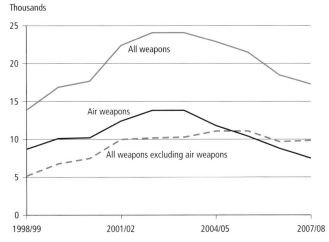

1 Changes in counting offences were made in April 1998 and the National Crime Recording Standard was implemented in April 2002. See Appendix, Part 9: National Crime Recording Standard.

Source: Home Office

non-air weapon used, and were involved in more than two-fifths (42 per cent) of all non-air weapon firearm offences in 2007/08.

Firearms are defined as having been involved in an incident if they have been discharged (fired), used as a blunt instrument against a person, or used as a threat. In 2007/08 more than nine in ten (92 per cent) air weapons involved in incidents were fired compared with around three-quarters (73 per cent) of imitation firearms, around one-half (53 per cent) of rifles, unidentified and 'other' weapons, and more than one-third (37 per cent) of shotguns. Handguns were the least likely to be fired with only 10 per cent of handguns involved in incidents being fired. However, handguns that were fired were the most likely firearm to result in a fatal or serious injury (36 per cent) compared with 1 per cent as a result of discharged air weapons.

In Scotland in 2007/08 there were 1,125 firearm offences recorded by the police. More than one-half (576) involved air weapons (including air guns, air pistols, air rifles and BB guns). The proportion of crimes involving a firearm has decreased by 11 per cent since 2006/07 and those involving air weapons has decreased by 17 per cent.

In Northern Ireland there were 544 crimes reported to the police in 2007/08 in which a firearm was used, a 9 per cent decrease compared with 2006/07. Between 2005/06 and 2006/07 there was a 35 per cent decrease. While crimes involving firearms excluding air weapons decreased by

12 per cent, those involving air weapons decreased by 2 per cent between 2006/07 and 2007/08.

The risk of being a victim of homicide (which includes the offences of murder, manslaughter and infanticide) continues to be low in England and Wales. In 2007/08 there were 763 offences recorded, a 3 per cent increase on the number recorded in 2006/07 and a rate of 14.1 per million population. Homicide figures are based on the year they are recorded by the police and not the year they occur so trend data should be treated with caution (see Appendix, Part 9: Homicides). However, over the last ten years the homicide rate has remained relatively stable, between 13 and 15 per million population, apart from an increase in 2002/03 to 18 per million population. This increase resulted from 172 homicides attributed to Harold Shipman which, although took place over a number of years, were recorded in 2002/03 following Dame Janet Smith's inquiry.

Males are more at risk of homicide than females; around three-quarters (73 per cent) of all homicide victims were male in 2007/08. The risk was highest for men aged 16 to 20, at 45 per million population (Figure 9.8). This is a change from 2006/07 where men aged 21 to 29 had the highest risk of homicide, at 42 per million population compared with 29 per million for those aged 16 to 20. For females the highest risk of homicide in 2007/08 was for infants under one year old, at 30 per million population. The homicide rate for males was higher than that for females at all ages apart from those aged 70 and over when the rate was slightly lower.

Figure 9.8

Offences recorded as homicide:[1] by sex and age of victim, 2007/08

England & Wales
Rates per million population

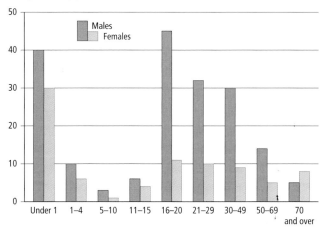

1 Offences currently recorded as homicide as at 4 November 2008. Figures are subject to revision as cases are dealt with by the police or courts, or as further information comes to light. See Appendix, Part 9: Homicides.

Source: Home Office

In 2007/08 more than one-third (35 per cent) of all homicide victims were apparently killed by sharp instruments. This was the most common method of killing for both male and female victims with 212 and 58 offences respectively. For males the second most common method was 'hitting and kicking, etc.' (140 offences) but for females it was strangulation, including asphyxiation (41 offences).

In Scotland there were 114 offences currently recorded as homicide in 2007/08, a rate of 22 per million population. Around four-fifths (79 per cent) of the victims were male. People aged 16 to 30 were at the highest risk, with a rate of 38 homicides per million population overall, and men were again particularly at risk, at 64 per million population in this age group. However, as in England and Wales, the number of homicides in Scotland was very small and these offences accounted for 0.1 per cent of all violent crime (which includes homicide, attempted murder, sexual assault, abduction, serious assault, minor assault and robbery).

In Northern Ireland there were 24 offences currently recorded as homicide in 2006/07, a rate of 14 per million population, the same as for England and Wales. Most of the victims (19) were men and the homicide rate was highest among men aged 30 to 49 years old with 11 of the male victims in this age group.

Perceptions of crime

The 2007/08 BCS reported that despite a decrease in the incidence of crime in England and Wales, almost two-thirds (65 per cent) of people perceived there to be more crime (either 'a lot more' or 'a little more') than two years ago in the country as a whole. This perception was unchanged since 2006/07 (Table 9.9). More than one-third (35 per cent) of respondents perceived that crime had increased a lot in the country as a whole. People were more positive about their local area, with 39 per cent perceiving there was either a little or a lot more crime than two years ago. The proportion of people perceiving more crime in the country as a whole has remained fairly stable since 2003/04, but the proportion perceiving more crime in their local area has decreased from 54 per cent in 2002/03.

The Northern Ireland Crime Survey (NICS) showed that the proportions of people in Northern Ireland perceiving more crime in the country as a whole and in their local area were similar to those for England and Wales in 2007/08. However, both these proportions had decreased compared with 2006/07, from 73 per cent to 65 per cent for the whole country and from 44 per cent to 39 per cent for crime in the local area.

Respondents to these crime surveys were asked how likely they thought they were to be victims of particular crimes in the

Table 9.9

Perceptions of changing crime levels[1]

England & Wales		Percentages
	Whole country	Local area[2]
2001/02	65	51
2002/03	72	54
2003/04	65	48
2004/05	61	42
2005/06	63	42
2006/07	65	41
2007/08	65	39

1 British Crime Survey (BCS) respondents were asked if they thought there was more or less crime than two years ago and given the following options; 'A lot more', 'a little more', 'about the same', 'a little less' or 'a lot less'. Data are the proportion of people who answered 'a lot more' or 'a little more'.
2 Question only asked of respondents who had lived in their area for three years or more.

Source: British Crime Survey, Home Office

12 months following their interview. According to the 2007/08 BCS, 14 per cent of people in England and Wales thought they were likely (either 'very likely' or 'fairly likely') to be victims of burglary or violent crime and 23 per cent of car owners thought they were likely to be victims of vehicle crime. However, in the same year the actual incidence of these crimes reported to the BCS was much lower. Around 6 per cent of households reported being a victim of vehicle related theft or damage in the previous 12 months, 2 per cent reported being victims of burglary, and 3 per cent of adults had experienced violent crime in the last 12 months. Apart from men aged 16 to 24, the crime both men and women thought they were most likely to experience was vehicle crime (Figure 9.10). Men aged 16 to 24, however, perceived they were more likely to be victims of violent crime. When analysed by marital status, respondents who were separated were the most likely to think they would be a victim of vehicle crime (31 per cent) within the next 12 months, while one-fifth (20 per cent) of single people thought they were likely to be a victim of violent crime. However, people who were widowed were the least likely of all marital status groups to think that they would be a victim of vehicle crime, burglary or violent crime within the next 12 months.

In 2007/08 both men and women in Northern Ireland felt they were more likely to be victims of vehicle crime than any other crime within the next 12 months. This was true for all ages although the perception was most prevalent among men aged 55 to 64 (28 per cent) and among women aged 25 to 34 (25 per cent). One-fifth (21 per cent) of young men aged 16 to

Figure 9.10

Perceived likelihood of being a victim of crime:[1,2] by sex and age, 2007/08

England & Wales

Percentages

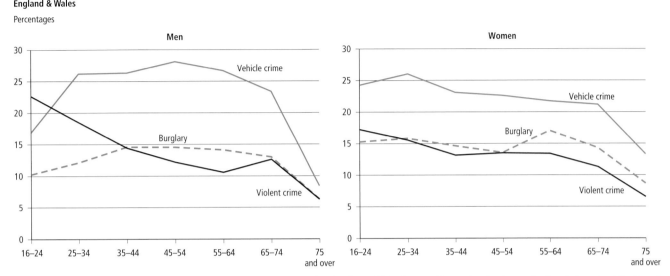

1 Those who answered they were 'fairly' or 'very likely' to be victims of each crime within the next 12 months. See Appendix, Part 9: Perceived likelihood of being a victim of crime.
2 All respondents were asked, irrespective of whether or not they had been a victim of crime in the previous 12 months.

Source: British Crime Survey, Home Office

24 felt they were likely to be victims of violent crime within the next 12 months.

Offenders

In 2007, 1.41 million offenders were sentenced for indictable and summary offences in England and Wales (see Appendix, Part 9: Types of offence in England and Wales), compared with 1.42 million in 2006. Most of the offenders were male and of these 7 per cent were aged under 18. In 2007 the peak age for men being found guilty of, or cautioned for, one or more indictable offence was 17, with 6 per cent of men of this age being found guilty or cautioned, compared with 1 per cent of women of the same age (Figure 9.11). For females the peak age for being found guilty of, or cautioned for, an indictable offence was 15 (2 per cent). As young men and women entered their 20s the proportion of offenders started to decline but this happened at a younger age for women than for men. Less than 1 per cent of women at each age over the age of 20 were found guilty of, or cautioned for, an indictable offence in 2007 but for men the proportions did not decline to less than 1 per cent until the age of 45.

In Northern Ireland 7,600 offenders were found guilty of, or cautioned for, indictable offences in 2006. Of these, 88 per cent were male. Young men aged 19 and 20 were the most likely to be offenders with nearly 4 per cent of all men in this age group being found guilty of, or cautioned for, an indictable offence.

The proportion of women who were offenders was less than one-half of 1 per cent for all age groups.

Theft and handling stolen goods accounted for 179,000 offences in England and Wales in 2007 and was the most common indictable offence for both men and women to be

Figure 9.11

Offenders[1] as a proportion of the population: by sex and age,[2] 2007

England & Wales

Percentages

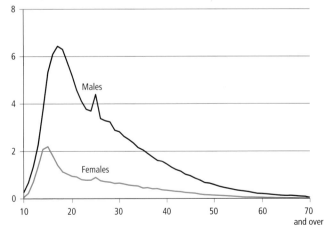

1 People found guilty of, or cautioned for, indictable offences in 2007.
2 Age 25 includes those offenders for whom age is not known.

Source: Office for Criminal Justice Reform, Ministry of Justice

found guilty of, or cautioned for; 30 per cent of male offences and 51 per cent of female offences (Figure 9.12). The next most common offences for men were drugs offences and violence against the person, with 78,000 and 77,000 offences respectively, 19 per cent each. The proportion of men found guilty of, or cautioned for, drugs offences in 2007 was double that of women (9 per cent). For women, the next most common offences, with 17,000 each, were violence against the person and other offences (17 per cent each).

In Northern Ireland, the most common indictable offence for men to be found guilty of, or cautioned for in 2006, was violence against the person, accounting for 2,000 offences (30 per cent), followed by theft and handling stolen goods (20 per cent). For women, the most common offence to be found guilty of, or cautioned for (370 offences) was theft and handling stolen goods, accounting for two-fifths (40 per cent) of all offences.

Of the 518,000 offenders found guilty of, or cautioned for, indictable offences in England and Wales in 2007, three-fifths (60 per cent) were sentenced. The type of sentence given depends on the offence committed and other factors that may be applied on a case-by-case basis (see Appendix, Part 9: Sentences and orders). The most common sentence for indictable offences in 2007 was a community sentence

Figure 9.12

Offenders found guilty of, or cautioned for, indictable offences:[1] by sex and type of offence, 2007

England & Wales
Thousands

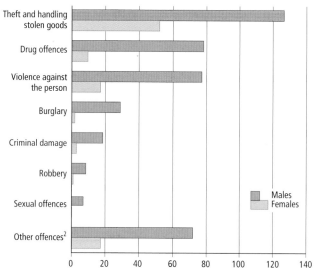

1 See Appendix, Part 9: Types of offence in England and Wales.
2 Includes fraud and forgery and indictable motoring offences.

Source: Office for Criminal Justice Reform, Ministry of Justice

(34 per cent), with around one-half (46 per cent) of offenders sentenced for criminal damage and 43 per cent of those sentenced for burglary receiving this sentence (Table 9.13). Offenders committing indictable drugs offences were most commonly fined along with those convicted of 'other indictable offences' (32 per cent and 31 per cent respectively). More than one-half of those found guilty of sexual offences (56 per cent) and robbery (54 per cent) were sentenced to immediate custody. Motoring offences vary in severity and this is reflected in the variety of sentences given (see also Figure 9.17). Of those found guilty of indictable motoring offences in 2007, 29 per cent were sentenced to immediate custody, 26 per cent were given a community sentence and 23 per cent were fined.

In Northern Ireland 7,600 offenders were sentenced for indictable offences in 2007. A fine was the most common sentence for all offences apart from robbery, sexual offences and burglary, where the most common sentence was immediate custody (85 per cent, 55 per cent and 45 per cent respectively).

One aim of the criminal justice system is to try to prevent offenders from committing further crimes, so the measurement of reoffending is of considerable policy interest. One measure of adult reoffending, on which the Ministry of Justice reoffending target is based, is the frequency of reoffences committed per 100 offenders. This measure is based on the number of offences committed within one year by offenders who were released from prison or had commenced a court order under probation supervision. In 2006 there were 146 offences per 100 offenders, a decrease of 32 per cent since 2002 when the rate was 215 offences per 100 offenders.

Another way to measure adult reoffending is the actual yes/no (binary) reoffending rate. This rate counts the proportion of adult offenders released from custody or commencing a court order under probation supervision who offended at least once during a one-year follow-up period, and where the offence resulted in a conviction at court (see Appendix, Part 9: Reoffenders). This measure is therefore based purely on the number of reoffenders, however many offences they may commit during the follow-up period. Of the offenders leaving prison or starting a community sentence in the first quarter of 2006, 39 per cent reoffended within one year, the lowest reoffending rate since the series began with the 2000 cohort and a decrease from the 42 per cent who reoffended in 2005. There was an overall decline in the reoffending rate by age; 48 per cent of 18 to 20-year-olds in 2006 reoffended within one year, more than double the rate among offenders aged 50 and over (Figure 9.14). However, offenders in this older age

Table 9.13

Offenders sentenced for indictable offences: by type of offence[1] and type of sentence,[2] 2007

England & Wales   Percentages

	Discharge	Fine	Community sentence	Suspended sentence order	Immediate custody	Other	All sentenced (=100%) (thousands)
Theft and handling stolen goods	21	13	38	6	19	3	105.5
Drug offences	18	32	23	6	18	2	44.5
Violence against the person	7	5	38	17	30	4	42.1
Burglary	4	2	43	10	39	2	23.5
Fraud and forgery	17	11	32	12	26	2	19.9
Criminal damage	22	10	46	4	11	9	12.3
Motoring	4	23	26	16	29	2	5.5
Robbery	-	-	39	5	54	1	8.9
Sexual offences	3	3	27	9	56	3	5.1
Other offences	9	31	23	8	20	9	45.0
All indictable offences	14	16	34	9	24	4	312.3

1 See Appendix, Part 9: Types of offence in England and Wales.
2 See Appendix, Part 9: Sentences and orders.

Source: Ministry of Justice

group had the greatest increase in the reoffending rate, increasing from 13 per cent in 2000 to 19 per cent in 2006.

Reoffending among juveniles is measured in a similar way to adults and covers juveniles aged ten to 17 released from

Figure 9.14

One-year reoffending rate:[1] by age

England & Wales

Percentages

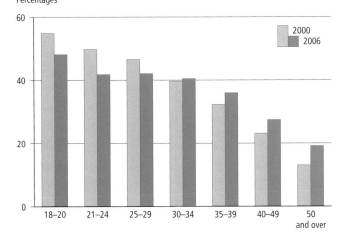

1 Percentage of all offenders reoffending at least once during the one-year follow-up period, where the reoffence resulted in conviction at court. Includes offenders aged 18 and over discharged from prison, or starting a court order supervised by the probation service, in the first quarter (January–March) of the year.

Source: Ministry of Justice

custody, starting a non-custodial court disposal or those given an out-of-court disposal (see Appendix, Part 9: Reoffenders – juveniles). In 2006 the reoffending rate for juveniles was the same as that for adults (39 per cent). Although this was slightly lower than the 40 per cent reoffending rate in 2000, the rate for juveniles has remained between 38 and 39 per cent since 2002. Juveniles committed 123 offences per 100 juvenile offenders in 2006, a 19 per cent decrease from the reoffending rate of 151 per 100 offenders in 2000.

Prisons and sentencing

Prison is the usual destination for offenders given custodial sentences or those who break the terms of their non-custodial sentence. The prison population (those held in prison or police cells, see Appendix, Part 9: Prison population for more details) in Great Britain was relatively stable in the 1980s and early 1990s but in the mid-1990s the population began to increase (Figure 9.15 overleaf). The largest increase, 10 per cent, occurred between 1996 and 1997. Apart from small decreases of less than 1 per cent in 1999 and 2000, the prison population increased every year since 1991 and in 2008 reached 91,000, almost double the population of 1980 and 4 per cent higher than in 2007.

This 4 per cent increase in the average prison population in 2008 was recorded for both sentenced and remand (which includes untried and convicted but unsentenced) prisoners.

9

Figure 9.15

Average prison[1] population

Great Britain

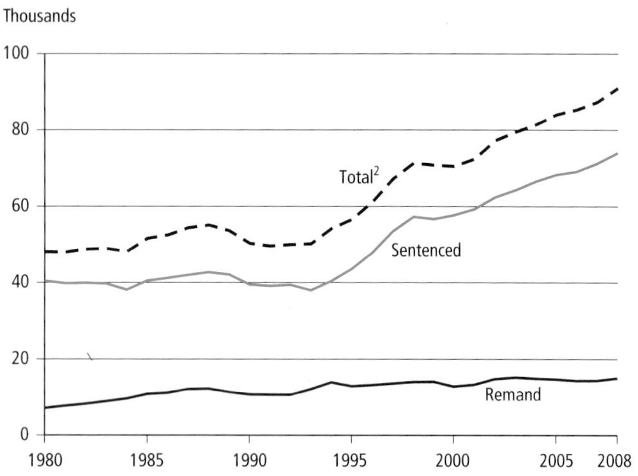

Thousands

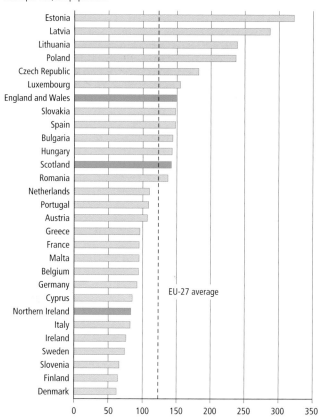

1 Includes prisoners held in police cells.
2 Includes non-criminal prisoners (for example, those held under the *Immigration Act 1971*).

Source: Ministry of Justice; Scottish Government

The annual average number of sentenced prisoners in Great Britain increased by 83 per cent between 1980 and 2008, from around 40,000 to 74,000, while the number of remand prisoners more than doubled, from 7,000 to 15,000.

Northern Ireland's prison population fell during the 1980s and 1990s to a low of 910 in 2001. One reason for the decrease in the late 1990s was the implementation of the *Northern Ireland (Sentences) Act 1998*, arising from the Belfast Agreement (Good Friday Agreement), which resulted in the release of a number of prisoners between 1998 and 2000. However, the prison population in Northern Ireland has increased progressively since that time and the population in 2007, of 1,470 prisoners, was around 61 per cent higher than in 2001.

In 2007 the prison population rate in England and Wales was 149 prisoners per 100,000 population. This was 21 per cent higher than the EU-27 average rate of 123 per 100,000 population, and the seventh highest in the EU-27 (Figure. 9.16). The prison population rate in Scotland was 142 per 100,000 population (15 per cent higher than the EU average) but the population in Northern Ireland, at 83 per 100,000 population, was 32 per cent lower and the seventh lowest in the EU-27. With the exception of Luxembourg, England and Wales had the highest prison population rate of the original EU-15 member states (see Appendix, Part 4: Accession to the European Union (EU)). The highest rate of the EU-27 was in Estonia, at 322 per 100,000 population and the lowest was Denmark, at 62 per 100,000 population. However, comparing prison populations across the EU is difficult because the

Figure 9.16

Prison population:[1] EU comparison,[2] 2007

Rates per 100,000 population

1 As at 1 September. Number of prisoners, including pre-trial detainees/remand prisoners.
2 Data for England and Wales, Scotland and Northern Ireland are presented separately because of the different criminal justice systems in these countries.

Source: Ministry of Justice

number of prisoners in custody at any one time depends on the individual penal systems in operation in each country.

Prison is just one way of dealing with offenders and in recent years there has been an increase in the use of non-criminal proceedings, such as the use of fixed penalties (fines) for a number of different crimes, including motoring offences. Overall in 2006 there were a total of 12.7 million motoring offences in England and Wales, equivalent to a rate of 422 motoring offences per 1,000 licensed vehicles. The total number of offences dealt with increased from 9.5 million in 1996 to 13.7 million in 2004 although the number then decreased in each of the following two years to 2006. Although the number of motoring offences in 2006 was the lowest number dealt with since 2002, the number receiving penalty charge notices was at the highest level in the last decade; from 3.5 million in 1996 to 7.8 million in 2006 (Figure 9.17).

This increase reflects the change in the treatment of summary motor offences, such as parking, from using criminal penalties

Figure 9.17

Motor vehicle offences: by action taken

England & Wales
Millions

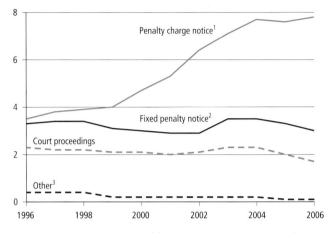

1 Civil notices issued by a council for apparent contraventions to the council's Traffic Regulation Order (bylaw regulations).
2 Notices issued by police officers and police traffic wardens to motorists who commit parking and bus-lane offences governed by criminal law.
3 Includes written warnings and vehicle defect rectification scheme (VDRS) notices.

Source: Ministry of Justice

pursued through the courts to a civil system in which offences are dealt with by the use of fines. This change was reflected in a decrease in the number of offences dealt with using court proceedings, to reach 1.7 million in 2006 and a further fall to 1.4 million in 2007 the lowest number dealt with in this way since the time series began in 1996. In 2007, court proceedings were most often taken for offences within the 'licence, insurance and record-keeping offences' category (including offences of 'driving while disqualified' and 'using motor vehicle uninsured against third party risks') amounting to 724,000, or 51 per cent of offences in 2007, compared with 921,000 in 2006.

Driving while using a hand-held mobile phone became an offence on 1 December 2003 and in 2006 there were 168,500 offences of 'use of hand-held mobile phone while driving' dealt with by the police and parking attendants. Of these, around 98 per cent were dealt with by fixed penalties with the remainder being dealt with by court proceedings or written warnings. In 2007 there were 14,000 court proceedings for 'use of hand-held mobile phone while driving', up from 2,700 in 2006, reflecting the large number of police force areas taking action against drivers using hand-held mobile phones while driving.

As well as dealing with offenders by the use of non-criminal proceedings such as fines, there are a number of measures aimed at reducing and preventing crime and reoffending. In

England and Wales these measures include community orders, intended to move low-level offenders away from custodial sentences, which can be used instead of, or alongside, other sentences or orders. In addition there are a number of interventions aimed specifically at anti-social behaviour and, in particular, a range of measures to help parents and agencies such as youth offending teams to deal with anti-social behaviour by young people. The interventions available range from one-off fines (fixed penalty notices and penalty notices for disorder) to non-legal agreements, contracts and warnings (including acceptable behaviour contracts and parenting contracts) to court orders that prohibit the perpetrator from specific anti-social behaviours – anti-social behaviour orders (ASBOs) and parenting orders.

ASBOs were introduced in 1999 and are aimed at protecting the public rather than punishing the perpetrator (see Appendix, Part 9: Anti-social behaviour orders (ASBOs)). However, while an ASBO is a civil order that will not appear on an individual's criminal record, a breach of an ASBO is a criminal offence punishable by a fine or a custodial sentence. In 2006, 2,706 ASBOs were issued in England and Wales. Of these around three-fifths (1,625) were issued to individuals aged 18 and over, and two-fifths (1,054) were issued to ten to 17-year-olds (Figure 9.18). The number of ASBOs issued increased every year between 2001 and 2005, but between 2005 and 2006 there was a 34 per cent decrease. This decrease does not necessarily indicate a reduction in the offending behaviour but rather a change in the types of intervention used.

Figure 9.18

Number of anti-social behaviour orders (ASBOs) issued:[1] by age

England & Wales
Numbers

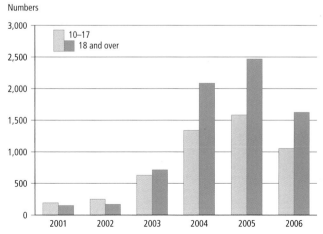

1 Issued at all HM Courts and reported to the Home Office by the Courts Service.

Source: Home Office

As well as ASBOs, acceptable behaviour contracts (ABCs) are written agreements that form a contract between the offender and their local authority, Youth Inclusion Support Panel, landlord or the police. The aim is to engage the individual in recognising the negative effects of their offending behaviour on others and encourage them to stop. Between October 2003 and September 2007 around 30,000 ABCs were issued in England and Wales.

The *Anti-Social Behaviour Act 2003* and the *Criminal Justice Act 2003* introduced measures aimed at involving parents in reducing anti-social and offending behaviour in the form of parenting contracts (PCs) and parenting orders (POs). A PC is a voluntary written agreement between a youth offending team worker and the parents of a child who is, or is likely to become, involved in criminal or anti-social behaviour. A PO is made in similar circumstances by a court (criminal, family or magistrates') and can be applied where parents are unwilling to co-operate (see Appendix, Part 9: Parenting contracts and parenting orders). Between October 2003 and September 2007 around 9,000 PCs and more than 2,000 POs were issued in England and Wales. As with ABCs, a large proportion (around two-fifths) of the total number of PCs and POs were issued between January and September 2007, indicating a rise in the use of these interventions as a form of reducing anti-social behaviour.

Alongside this increase in the range of sentences and orders available for dealing with young offenders (aged ten to 17), a number of measures were also taken to reduce the time taken for them to be dealt with in the criminal justice system. In 1997 the Government set a target to maintain the average time from arrest to sentence specifically for persistent young offenders at or below 71 days (see Appendix, Part 9: Persistent young offenders). This was one-half the average number of days from arrest to sentence in 1996 of 142 days. The target of 71 days was reached in 2002 and has since remained below this level apart from in 2006, when it was 72 days (Figure 9.19). Between 2006 and 2007 there was a reduction of seven days in the time between arrest and sentencing to 65 days. The first half of 2008 showed a provisional decrease of a further seven days to 58 days.

Overall performance against this target is largely determined by timeliness in the magistrates' courts, where at least nine-tenths of all persistent young offender cases are heard. Although the average number of days between arrest and sentence is much longer for cases at Crown courts, and there was an increase in this time between 2005 and 2006 (from 191 to 214 days), this has little impact on overall timeliness because of the small number of cases involved.

Figure 9.19

Average number of days from arrest to sentence for persistent young offenders[1]

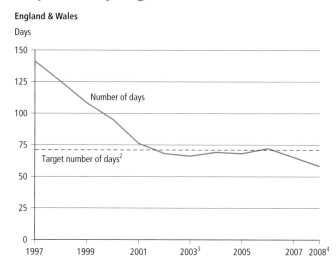

England & Wales

Days

1 Young offenders are those aged 10 to 17. See Appendix, Part 9: Persistent young offenders.
2 Target for average number of days between arrest and sentence, set by the Government in 1997, is 71 days.
3 Figures will differ from those previously published due to re-calculation of time series. See Appendix, Part 9: Average time from arrest to sentence.
4 Data are for January to June 2008.

Source: Ministry of Justice

Police and other resources

There were around 142,000 full-time equivalent police officers in England and Wales in 2008. Around one-quarter (24 per cent) were female and of these 85 per cent were constables, 10 per cent were sergeants and 3 per cent were inspectors. Less than 1 per cent of female police officers were in the senior Association of Chief Police Officers (ACPO) ranks. Overall there has been an increase in the number of police officers in the last ten years, from around 125,000 in 1998, and the proportion of female officers has increased from 16 per cent.

The proportion of police officers who are from an ethnic minority group in England and Wales has also increased over the last decade, from 2 per cent in 1999 to 4 per cent in 2008 (Figure 9.20). In 2008, 4 per cent of constables were from an ethnic minority compared with 2 per cent of chief superintendents. For all other ranks of police officer around 3 per cent were from an ethnic minority.

The proportion of officers who were from an ethnic minority group varied by police force area in England and Wales. In 2008 the London Metropolitan police force area had the highest proportion of ethnic minority officers, at 8 per cent. West Midlands police force had the second highest proportion, at 7 per cent, followed by Leicestershire with 6 per cent. The

Figure 9.20

Ethnic[1] minority officers as a proportion of all police officers[2,3]

England & Wales

Percentages

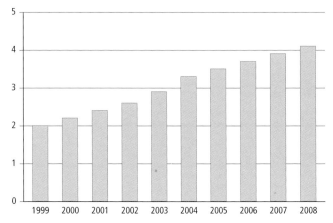

1 See Appendix, Part 1: Classification of ethnic groups.
2 As at 31 March in each year.
3 Proportions for 1999 to 2002 were calculated using the headcount ethnic minority officer strength as a proportion of all full-time equivalent officer strength. The proportions from 2003 were calculated using full-time equivalent ethnic minority strength as a proportion of all full-time equivalent officer strength.

Source: Home Office

police force area with the lowest proportion of ethnic minority officers was North Wales, at less than one-half of 1 per cent. Of the 142,000 police officers in England and Wales in 2008, 2 per cent were Asian or Asian British and 1 per cent each were Black or Black British, or Mixed. In Northern Ireland the proportion of police officers who are from an ethnic minority group has increased every year since 2004, from 0.24 per cent to 0.4 per cent in 2008.

According to the 2007/08 British Crime Survey, almost two-thirds (65 per cent) of people in England and Wales had overall confidence in the police in their local area (Table 9.21), a 1 percentage point increase since 2006/07. More than four-fifths (83 per cent) agreed that the local police would treat them with respect if they had contact with them and almost two-thirds (64 per cent) agreed that their local police would treat everyone fairly regardless of who they are, and that they understand the issues affecting their community (62 per cent). People had the least confidence in relying on their local police to deal with minor crimes (43 per cent).

In Northern Ireland three-fifths (60 per cent) of people had overall confidence in the local police in 2007/08. Four-fifths (81 per cent) agreed that the police would treat them with respect if they had contact with them, around the same proportion as those in England and Wales. The proportions of people agreeing that the police treat everyone fairly regardless

Table 9.21

Perceptions[1] of the local police, 2007/08

England & Wales — Percentages

Would treat you with respect if you had contact with them	83
Treat everyone fairly regardless of who they are	64
Understand the issues that affect this community	62
Are dealing with things that matter to people in the community	51
Can be relied upon to be there when you need them	48
Can be relied on to deal with minor crimes	43
Overall confidence in the local police[2]	65

1 Proportion of respondents who strongly agreed/tended to agree with the statement.
2 Based on question 'Taking everything into account I have confidence in the police in this area'.

Source: British Crime Survey, Home Office

of who they are and that they can be relied on to deal with minor crimes were the same as those for England and Wales (64 per cent and 43 per cent respectively).

The 2007/08 BCS showed that the level of confidence that people in England and Wales had in the criminal justice system (CJS) as a whole had increased compared with 2006/07 in five of the seven areas covered. In particular, the proportion of people who were fairly or very confident that the CJS was effective in bringing people who commit crimes to justice increased by 3 percentage points since 2006/07 to 44 per cent. This is the same increase as the proportion who were either very or fairly confident that the CJS meets the needs of victims of crime (from 33 per cent to 36 per cent between 2006/07 and 2007/08). These increases follow a general decrease in confidence between 2005/06 and 2006/07.

The CJS is one of the major public services in England and Wales. It comprises the Police Service, the Crown Prosecution Service, HM Courts Service, the National Offender Management Service (covering prisons and probation) and the Youth Justice Board. HM Courts Service is responsible for managing the magistrates' courts, the Crown courts, county courts, the High Court and Court of Appeal in England and Wales (see Appendix, Part 9: Courts system in England and Wales).

The judiciary, that is the judges, magistrates and other adjudicators as well as support personnel who keep the courts system running smoothly, account for a large proportion of the courts system resources. In 2008 there were more than 3,800 members of the judiciary serving in England and Wales, of which the largest group (34 per cent) were recorders

9

Table 9.22

Composition of the judiciary:[1] by sex and ethnic group,[2] 2008[3]

England & Wales   Percentages

	Sex		Ethnicity		
	Male	Female	White	Ethnic minority group	All (numbers)
Heads of Division	100.0	0.0	100.0	0.0	5
Lords of Appeal in Ordinary	91.7	8.3	100.0	0.0	12
Lord Justices of Appeal	91.9	8.1	100.0	0.0	37
High Court judges	90.0	10.0	97.3	2.7	110
Circuit judges	86.7	13.3	96.9	3.1	653
Recorders	85.1	14.9	95.3	4.7	1,305
Judge advocates	100.0	0.0	100.0	0.0	9
Deputy judge advocates	91.7	8.3	100.0	0.0	12
District judges (county courts)	77.6	22.4	95.4	4.6	438
District judges (magistrates' courts)	77.2	22.8	97.8	2.2	136
Deputy district judges (county courts)	72.7	27.3	96.0	4.0	773
Deputy district judges (magistrates' courts)	76.0	24.0	92.8	7.2	167
Masters, registrars, costs judges and district judges (Principal Registry of the Family Division)	77.1	22.9	97.9	2.1	48
Deputy masters, deputy registrars, deputy costs judges and deputy district judges (Principal Registry of the Family Division)	66.1	33.9	95.7	4.3	115
All	81.0	19.0	95.9	4.1	3,820

1 See Appendix, Part 9: Judiciary of England and Wales.
2 See Appendix, Part 1: Classification of ethnic groups.
3 As at 1 April 2008.

Source: Judicial Database, Judiciary of England and Wales

(barristers or solicitors who are appointed part-time judges). A further one-quarter (25 per cent) of the judiciary were deputy district judges, 17 per cent were circuit judges and 15 per cent were district judges. Four-fifths (81 per cent) of the total judiciary were men (Table 9.22). Of the women in the judiciary, 35 per cent were deputy district judges and 27 per cent were recorders. The most common position to be held by men was recorder (36 per cent) (see Appendix, Part 9: Judiciary of England and Wales for further information on the separate roles in the judicial system). In 2008, 4 per cent of the judiciary in England and Wales were from an ethnic minority group; 7 per cent of deputy district judges (magistrates' courts), 5 per cent of recorders and district judges (county courts), and smaller proportions, or none, among more senior positions.

Chapter 10

Housing

- There was an increase in the number of owner-occupied dwellings in the UK every year between 1981 and 2006, but between 2006 and 2007 there was a small decrease. (Figure 10.4)

- In 2007, 63 per cent of lone parent households with dependent children in Great Britain lived in rented property compared with 19 per cent of couple households with dependent children. (Table 10.5)

- In 2006/07, 82 per cent of householders in England were satisfied with both their neighbourhood and their accommodation, an increase from 79 per cent in 1996/97. (Page 153)

- In 2006/07, 63 per cent of private renters in England who did not expect to buy their own home felt they were unlikely ever to be able to afford to buy a property. (Table 10.17)

- The number of property transactions per month in the UK halved between January and November 2008, from 104,000 to 52,000. (Figure 10.18)

- There was a 25 per cent increase in the number of property repossessions in the UK between 2006 and 2007, from 20,900 to 26,200, and a further 53 per cent increase to 40,000, between 2007 and 2008. (Page 157)

A range of socio-economic and demographic factors affect where a person lives, the tenure, type and condition of their home, their living conditions, and their satisfaction with the area where they live. In recent years purchasing a home has become expensive. House prices increased by around 240 per cent between 1992 and 2007 and in 2007 the average dwelling price in England was more than seven times average annual earnings. This made it particularly difficult for first-time buyers to get on to the property ladder. The economic downturn in 2008 affected the financial situation of people in the UK and made it difficult to get finance either to move or to purchase a home.

Housing stock and housebuilding

The number of dwellings in Great Britain increased dramatically over the last century, from 7.7 million in 1901 to 25.9 million in 2007 (Figure 10.1). Although the stock of dwellings increased in every decade from 1900, there were smaller increases between 1911 and 1921 and in the 1920s. This was partly because the First World War led to a slow-down in new building and some existing buildings were damaged. Since the early 1950s the number of dwellings in Great Britain has nearly doubled, from 13.8 million in 1951 to 25.9 million in 2007. The rise in housing stock reflects the greater demand for homes caused by the increasing population (see Chapter 1: Population, Table 1.1) and more particularly, a trend towards smaller households that has emerged since the 1970s (see Chapter 2: Households and families, Household composition section).

Figure 10.1

Dwelling stock[1,2]

Great Britain

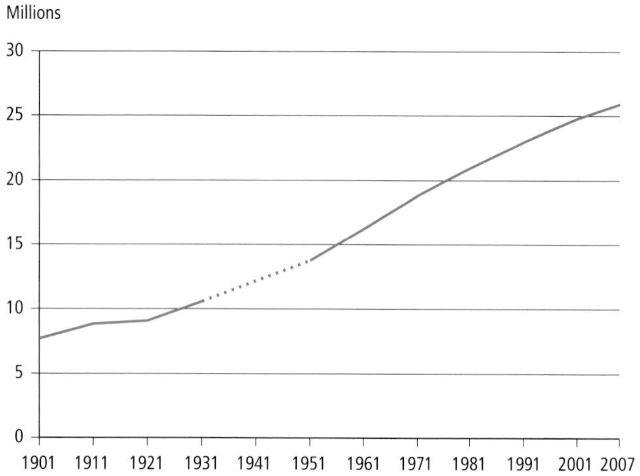

Millions

1 See Appendix, Part 10: Dwelling stock.
2 No census was undertaken in 1941, so data for this year is plotted as the mid-point between 1931 and 1951.

Source: Communities and Local Government

The number of dwellings in Great Britain has increased every year since 1971. However, so have both the population and the number of households. During the period 1971 to 2007 there was a 38 per cent increase in the number of dwellings from 18.8 million in 1971 to 25.9 million, which exceeded the 31 per cent increase in the number of households from 18.6 million to 24.4 million (see Chapter 2: Households and families, Table 2.1). The population of Great Britain increased by 9 per cent over this period, from 54.3 million to 59.2 million. More recently, between 2006 and 2007, the increase in the number of dwellings was just 1 per cent.

In 2006/07 there were almost 22 million dwellings in England, of which more than four-fifths (82 per cent) were houses or bungalows and one in six (16 per cent) were flats or maisonettes (Table 10.2). Almost one-third (32 per cent) were semi-detached (7 million dwellings) and around one-quarter each were terraced (28 per cent) or detached (23 per cent), 6.1 million and 5.0 million dwellings respectively. More than three-quarters (76 per cent) of the 3.6 million flats were purpose-built.

In 2006/07 the South East had the largest proportion of dwellings (16 per cent) of all the regions in England, followed by London and the North West (15 per cent and 14 per cent respectively). There were variations in types of dwelling by region. For example 92 per cent of homes in the East Midlands were houses or bungalows, compared with 55 per cent in London. Semi-detached homes were the most common type of accommodation in all regions with the exception of London, where flats were the most common, and the South East and South West, where detached homes were more common (29 per cent and 33 per cent respectively). The proportion of homes that were flats or maisonettes in London (44 per cent) was on average four times higher than in any other English region. Of these, 31 per cent were purpose-built and 13 per cent were conversions. A further 31 per cent of homes in London were terraced houses.

The existing housing stock in England reflects hundreds of years of housebuilding. One-fifth (20 per cent) of the current stock was built before the end of the First World War. The damage caused to the nation's housing stock during the Second World War led to the provision of new housing being a post-war government priority; 61 per cent of dwellings in England were built after 1945, particularly between 1965 and 1984. Housebuilding has continued and 7 per cent of dwellings were built since 1995. There are notable regional variations in the age of dwelling stock. Homes in London tend to be older than in other areas; around one-quarter (26 per cent) of dwellings in London

Table 10.2

Housing stock: by region and type of dwelling, 2006/07

England

Percentages

	House or bungalow[1]			Flat or maisonette		All dwellings[2] (=100%) (thousands)
	Detached	Semi-detached	Terraced	Purpose-built	Conversion	
North East	15	41	31	12	1	1,137
North West	17	37	33	9	2	3,027
Yorkshire and the Humber	20	38	31	8	2	2,218
East Midlands	35	38	19	6	1	1,880
West Midlands	23	38	28	9	1	2,293
East	30	31	26	9	2	2,414
London	5	19	31	31	13	3,192
South East	29	28	25	12	4	3,536
South West	33	28	24	10	4	2,291
England	23	32	28	13	4	21,989

1 Includes terraced bungalows that have been reclassified from flats to terraced bungalows because the building they are in contains one floor.
2 Includes other types of accommodation such as caravans, mobile homes and houseboats.

Source: Survey of English Housing, Communities and Local Government

were built before the end of the First World War, while 4 per cent were built since 1995. In contrast 16 per cent of dwellings in the East Midlands were built before 1919 and 10 per cent since 1995.

In the early years after the Second World War, local authorities in the UK undertook most of the housing construction. In the mid-1950s private enterprise housebuilding increased dramatically and has been the dominant sector since 1959. In 2007/08, 87 per cent of new homes were built by the private enterprise sector (Figure 10.3).

Housebuilding completions in the UK, which include houses, bungalows and flats (see Appendix, Part 10: Housebuilding completions), peaked in 1968 when 426,000 dwellings were completed. More than one-half (53 per cent) of these were built by private enterprise and 47 per cent were built by the social sector, primarily local authorities but also including registered social landlords (RSLs), see Appendix, Part 10: Private and social sectors. Since the early 1990s RSLs – predominantly housing associations – have dominated building in the social sector, accounting for 99 per cent of social sector completions in 2007/08. In the housebuilding sector as a whole, there was a 2 per cent decrease in the number of completions between 2006/07 and 2007/08. This decrease, from 219,000 to 214,000, was the first since 2001/02.

In 2007/08, 167,000 new homes were completed in England, a slight decrease from the number completed in 2006/07

(168,000). The number of new homes completed in each region of England decreased between 2006/07 and 2007/08 with the exceptions of the North West and the South East, where there were increases of 12 per cent and 10 per cent respectively.

Figure 10.3

Housebuilding completions:[1,2] by sector

United Kingdom

Thousands

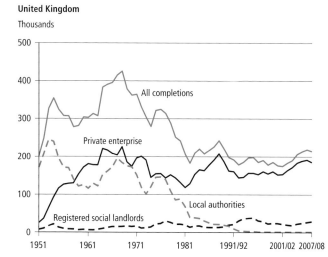

1 See Appendix, Part 10: Dwelling stock, Housebuilding completions, and Private and social sectors.
2 From 1990/91 data are for financial years.

Source: Communities and Local Government; Welsh Assembly Government; Scottish Government; Department for Social Development, Northern Ireland

10

Tenure and accommodation

One of the most notable housing trends in the UK since the early 1980s is the increase in owner occupation (see Appendix, Part 10: Tenure). Every year between 1981 and 2006 there was an increase in the number of owner-occupied dwellings in the UK, an increase of 49 per cent over the period to reach a total of 18.5 million (Figure 10.4). However, between 2006 and 2007 the number of dwellings that were owner-occupied decreased by 1 per cent. There was a 26 per cent increase in the number of dwellings that were privately rented between 1981 and 2006, and a further 10 per cent increase (300,000 dwellings) between 2006 and 2007.

The number of homes rented from local authorities fell by 59 per cent to 2.6 million between 1981 and 2007. This decline is partly explained by the increase in owner occupancy over the period, including the increase in former council tenants buying their homes under 'right-to-buy' schemes and the availability of shared ownership schemes for key workers, social sector tenants and those in priority housing need. In addition, the number of homes rented from private landlords increased in the early 1980s and although the number then decreased it has continued to show a steady increase since the early 1990s. Since 2001, more than 600,000 local authority dwellings have been transferred to registered social landlords (RSLs) under large-scale voluntary transfer (LSVT) arrangements (see Appendix, Part 10: Sales and transfers of local authority dwellings). This explains much of the

change in the proportion renting from RSLs rather than local authorities. The number of homes rented from RSLs increased from 0.5 million in 1981 to 2.2 million in 2005 and has remained at this level since.

Since the early 1980s those renting from local authorities in England, with secure tenancies of at least two years' standing, have been entitled to purchase their home under the 'right-to-buy' scheme. Sales under this scheme peaked at 167,000 properties in 1982/83. They have declined since then with some periods of increase, most notably between 1987/88 and 1988/89 and between 1998/99 and 1999/2000. Between 2004/05 and 2005/06 sales almost halved from 50,000 to 27,000. In 2007/08, there were around 12,000 sales of

Figure 10.4

Stock of dwellings:[1] by tenure[2]

United Kingdom
Millions

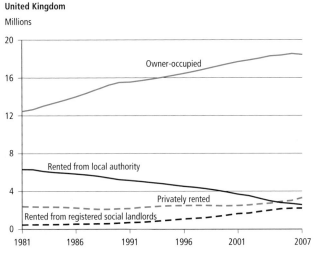

1 See Appendix, Part 10: Dwelling stock. Data for England, Wales and Scotland are at 31 March, and Northern Ireland data are at 31 December the previous year, except for 1991, where census figures are used.
2 See Appendix, Part 10: Private and social sectors, and Tenure.

Source: Communities and Local Government; Welsh Assembly Government; Scottish Government; Department for Social Development, Northern Ireland

Table 10.5

Household composition: by tenure of household reference person,[1] 2007

Great Britain					Percentages
	Owned outright	Owned with mortgage	Privately rented[2]	Rented from social sector	All tenures
One person households					
Under state pension age[3]	18	42	16	24	100
Over state pension age[3]	58	5	6	31	100
One family households					
Couple[4]					
No children	47	36	8	8	100
Dependent children[5]	10	71	7	12	100
Non-dependent children only	37	48	3	12	100
Lone parent[4]					
Dependent children[5]	5	32	15	48	100
Non-dependent children only	34	30	3	33	100
Other households[6]	19	34	30	17	100
All households[7]	31	40	9	19	100

1 See Appendix, Part 10: Tenure, and Appendix, Part 7: Household reference person.
2 Includes tenants in rent-free accommodation and squatters.
3 State pension age is currently 65 for men and 60 for women.
4 Other individuals who were not family members may also be included.
5 See Appendix, Part 2: Families. May also include non-dependent children.
6 Comprising two or more unrelated adults or two or more families.
7 Includes a small number of same-sex couples.

Source: General Household Survey (Longitudinal), Office for National Statistics

10

'right-to-buy' properties, a decrease of 29 per cent on the previous year and the lowest number since the scheme was introduced. There has been a year-on-year decline in right-to-buy sales since 2005, when changes in the eligibility rules under the *Housing Act 2004* meant that new tenants have to be resident in the property for five years before they can buy.

In 2007, two-fifths (40 per cent) of households in Great Britain were buying their homes with a mortgage (Table 10.5). Almost one-third (31 per cent) owned their homes outright and more than one-quarter (28 per cent) rented their homes (19 per cent from the social sector and 9 per cent privately). There was little change in these proportions from 2006.

Tenure varies markedly according to the size and composition of the household. In 2007 lone parent households with dependent children were more likely than any other type of household in Great Britain to rent property rather than own it. Almost two-thirds (63 per cent) of lone parent households with dependent children rented their home, mostly from registered social landlords or local authorities, while more than one-third (37 per cent) lived in owner-occupied accommodation. In

contrast, more than four-fifths (81 per cent) of couple households with dependent children were owner-occupiers, the majority with a mortgage, and around 12 per cent rented from the social sector.

In Northern Ireland in 2007/08 more than seven in ten (72 per cent) households owned their homes (either outright or with a mortgage), a similar proportion to Great Britain (71 per cent). The patterns of tenure in relation to household type were also very similar to those in Great Britain, with almost two-thirds (64 per cent) of lone parent households with dependent children living in rented housing and more than one-third (36 per cent) owning their home, either outright or with a mortgage. Among couple households with dependent children, 70 per cent owned their homes with a mortgage and a further 17 per cent owned their homes outright.

The type of home that people live in may reflect the size and type of their household, where they live and what they are provided with or can afford. In 2007, 82 per cent of households in Great Britain lived in a house or bungalow, whether it was detached, semi-detached or terraced (Table 10.6).

Table 10.6

Household composition: by type of dwelling, 2007

Great Britain   Percentages

	House or bungalow			Flat or maisonette		
	Detached	Semi-detached	Terraced	Purpose-built	Other[1]	All dwellings[2]
One person households						
Under state pension age[3]	11	22	31	28	9	100
Over state pension age[3]	18	28	25	25	3	100
One family households						
Couple[4]						
No children	31	31	24	10	3	100
Dependent children[5]	28	36	28	7	1	100
Non-dependent children only	31	36	28	5	0	100
Lone parent[4]						
Dependent children[5]	8	30	38	20	4	100
Non-dependent children only	13	40	37	8	1	100
Other households[6]	19	27	34	14	6	100
All households[7]	23	31	28	15	3	100

1 Includes converted flats, part of a house and rooms.
2 Includes other types of accommodation, such as mobile homes.
3 State pension age is currently 65 for men and 60 for women.
4 Other individuals who were not family members may also be included.
5 See Appendix, Part 2: Families. May also include non-dependent children.
6 Comprising two or more unrelated adults or two or more families.
7 Includes a small number of same-sex couples.

Source: General Household Survey (Longitudinal), Office for National Statistics

Semi-detached houses and terraced houses were the most common type of dwelling, lived in by 31 per cent and 28 per cent of all households, respectively.

Among households with dependent children, couples were more likely than lone parents to live in a house or bungalow (92 per cent and 76 per cent respectively). The most common type of housing lived in by couples with dependent children were semi-detached houses (36 per cent). More than one-quarter (28 per cent) of couple households with dependent children lived in terraced houses compared with 38 per cent of lone parent households with dependent children. Lone parents with dependent children were more than twice as likely as couples with dependent children to live in a purpose-built flat or maisonette (20 per cent compared with 7 per cent).

One person households were far more likely than family households to live in a flat. In 2007, 32 per cent of one person households lived in a flat compared with 11 per cent of family households. Among those under state pension age (65 for men and 60 for women) 37 per cent lived in either a purpose-built or a converted flat, compared with 28 per cent of those over state pension age.

In Northern Ireland more than nine in ten (92 per cent) households lived in a house or bungalow in 2007/08. The proportion of Northern Ireland households living in a flat or maisonette was 9 per cent, one-half the proportion for Great Britain (18 per cent). Couples in Northern Ireland with dependent children were more likely than lone parents with dependent children to live in a house (99 per cent compared with 95 per cent). One person households were the most likely of all households to live in a flat; 22 per cent of those under state pension age compared with 20 per cent of those over state pension age.

Tenure varies by the age of the household, as measured by the age of the household reference person (see Appendix, Part 7: Household reference person). People aged under 30 were the least likely of all age groups to own their homes, 22 per cent of under 25-year-olds and 51 per cent of 25 to 29-year-olds were owner-occupiers, and the most likely to rent from the private sector, 40 per cent and 27 per cent respectively (Table 10.7). The largest proportion (38 per cent) of social sector tenants were aged under 25, although nearly one-third (31 per cent) of householders aged 80 and over were also in this tenure group, the second most common tenure among this age group after owner-occupiers (64 per cent). Householders aged 45 to 64 were the most likely to own their homes with more than one-quarter (27 per cent) of those aged 45 to 59 and more than one-half

Table 10.7

Tenure: by age of household reference person,[1] 2007

Great Britain
Percentages

	Under 25	25–29	30–44	45–59	60–64	65–69	70–79	80 and over	All ages
Owner-occupied									
Owned outright	1	1	6	27	58	66	72	61	31
Owned with mortgage	21	51	67	50	23	9	4	3	40
All owner-occupied	22	51	73	77	81	75	76	64	72
Privately rented									
Unfurnished[2]	24	17	9	5	3	2	4	5	7
Furnished	16	10	2	1	1	1	1	1	2
All privately rented[3]	40	27	11	6	4	3	4	6	9
Rented from social sector									
Local authority	24	12	9	9	9	14	11	18	11
Housing association[4]	15	9	7	8	6	7	8	12	8
All rented from social sector	38	22	16	17	15	22	19	31	19

1 See Appendix, Part 10: Tenure, and Appendix, Part 7: Household reference person.
2 Includes 'partly furnished'.
3 Includes tenants whose accommodation goes with the job of someone in the household, and squatters.
4 Since 1996 housing associations are more correctly described as registered social landlords (RSLs). See Appendix, Part 10: Private and social sectors.

Source: General Household Survey (Longitudinal), Office for National Statistics

(58 per cent) of those aged 60 to 64 owning their home outright.

The pattern was the same in Northern Ireland in 2007/08, with those aged under 30 being the least likely of all age groups to own their homes, 14 per cent among those under 25 and 49 per cent of 25 to 29-year-olds. Those aged under 30 were also most likely to be private renters (57 per cent). More than seven in ten (72 per cent) households owned their homes, either outright or with a mortgage, 16 per cent rented from the social sector and 12 per cent rented from the private sector.

Tenure also varies by the ethnic group of the household reference person (see Appendix, Part 1: Classification of ethnic groups, and Chapter 2: Households and families, Reference persons text box on page 14). In England in Q2 (April–June) 2007 the Labour Force Survey (LFS) found that more than seven in ten (72 per cent) of white householders owned their homes either outright or with a mortgage, compared with one-half (50 per cent) of ethnic minority respondents (Table 10.8). Almost three-quarters (73 per cent) of Indian householders owned

Table 10.8

Ethnic group:[1] by tenure,[2] 2007[3]

England   Percentages

	Owned outright	Owned with mortgage	Rented from social sector	Privately rented	All tenures (=100%) (thousands)
White	33	39	17	11	18,986
British	33	40	17	10	17,811
Other White	22	30	14	33	1,175
Mixed	9	35	35	22	119
Indian	28	45	8	19	335
Pakistani	20	44	17	18	197
Bangladeshi[4]	10	27	49	14	83
Black Caribbean	15	33	43	9	282
Black African	4	27	41	29	247
Chinese[4]	16	37	7	39	86
Other ethnic group	10	30	24	35	448
All households	31	39	18	12	20,784

1 Ethnic group of household reference person. See Appendix, Part 1: Classification of ethnic groups, and Chapter 2: Households and families, Reference persons text box on page 14.
2 See Appendix, Part 10: Tenure.
3 Data are at Q2 (April–June) and are not seasonally adjusted. See Appendix, Part 4: Labour Force Survey.
4 These estimates have a large sampling error because of their small sample sizes and, for Bangladeshis, the clustering of the Bangladeshi population.

Source: Communities and Local Government from the Labour Force Survey

their home compared with around two-thirds (65 per cent) of Pakistani householders and less than one-third (30 per cent) of Black Africans. Black African householders were the most likely of all ethnic groups in England to rent (70 per cent) with 41 per cent renting from the social sector and 29 per cent from the private sector. Bangladeshi householders were the most likely to rent from the social sector (49 per cent) and Chinese householders the most likely to rent from the private sector (39 per cent). However, ethnic minority respondents comprised 9 per cent of all householders in 2007 and care should therefore be taken when looking at tenure by ethnic group because of the small number of respondents in some ethnic groups.

Homelessness

The homeless are among the poorest and most disadvantaged members of society. The *Housing Act 1996* places a statutory duty on local authorities to provide assistance to people who are homeless or threatened with homelessness and fall within a priority need group. Priority need groups include pregnant women and people with dependent children. The number of households accepted as homeless and in priority need in England peaked in 2003/04, at 135,000 and since then have more than halved with annual reductions.

Just over 63,000 households were accepted as homeless and in priority need in England in 2007/08 and almost one-half (49 per cent) were one parent households; 45 per cent were lone parent households headed by a woman and 4 per cent were lone parent households headed by a man (Figure 10.9 overleaf). One person households made up more than one-quarter (26 per cent) of the total number of households accepted as homeless, with 14 per cent being males living alone and 12 per cent being females living alone.

In 2007/08 more than one-third (34 per cent) of households accepted as homeless in Wales were female lone parents, compared with 3 per cent who were male lone parents. Almost one-quarter (24 per cent) of households accepted as homeless were male one person households and one-fifth (20 per cent) were female one person households.

Homelessness often results from changes in personal circumstances. In 2007/08, 36 per cent of all households in England were in this situation because relatives or friends were no longer able or willing to provide them with accommodation, compared with 26 per cent in 1997/98. Other reasons for being accepted as homeless include the breakdown of a relationship (18 per cent) and because of mortgage arrears (4 per cent).

The Government has a target that by 2010 the number of households living in temporary accommodation in England will

10

Figure 10.9

Homelessness acceptances:[1] by household composition, 2007/08

England

Percentages

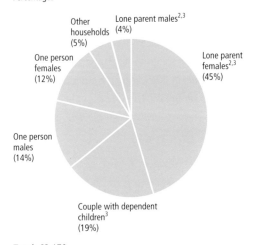

Total: 63,170

1 Households accepted as homeless and in priority need by local authorities.
2 Lone parents with dependent children.
3 See Appendix, Part 2: Families.

Source: Communities and Local Government

Figure 10.10

Homeless households in temporary accommodation[1]

England

Thousands

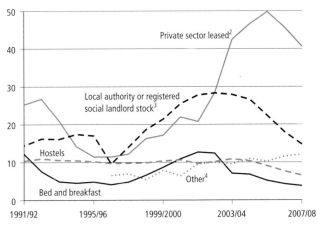

1 Excludes 'homeless at home' cases. See Appendix, Part 10: Homeless at home. Data are at 31 March each year, and include households awaiting the outcome of homeless enquiries.
2 Prior to 1996/97, includes those accommodated directly with a private sector landlord.
3 Prior to 1996/97, includes all 'Other' types of accommodation.
4 From 1996/97 onwards, includes mobile homes (such as caravans and portacabins) or being accommodated directly with a private sector landlord.

Source: Communities and Local Government

be reduced to 50,500. On 31 March 2008 there were 77,500 households living in temporary accommodation. The greatest proportion was the 40,000 (52 per cent of the total) homeless households living in self-contained property leased from the private sector.

Under the *Homelessness (Suitability of Accommodation) (England) Order 2003*, local authorities can no longer place families with children in bed and breakfast (B&B) accommodation except in an emergency, and then for no longer than six weeks. Between March 2003 and March 2008 the total number of homeless households living in B&B accommodation fell by 69 per cent from 12,000 to 4,000. Over the same period, the proportion of homeless households living in hostels showed a slight decline from 11 per cent in March 2003 to 8 per cent in March 2008 (Figure 10.10).

In Wales there were 2,880 homeless households living in temporary accommodation in 2007/08. Of these, 31 per cent (898 households) were living in private sector leased accommodation. This proportion has increased every year since 2003/04 when it was 9 per cent. Over the same period the proportion in B&B accommodation decreased from 24 per cent to 10 per cent.

Housing condition and satisfaction with area

To be considered 'decent' a dwelling must meet the statutory minimum standard for housing, be in a reasonable state of repair, have reasonably modern facilities and have a reasonable level of thermal comfort, that is sufficient heating and insulation. Until April 2006 the statutory minimum for housing was the 'Fitness Standard'. This was replaced by the Housing Health and Safety Rating System (HHSRS), which is used to assess health and safety risks to potential occupants posed by deficiencies in the design or maintenance of the accommodation. Homes with 'Category 1' hazards (the most serious) are deemed to be non-decent (see Appendix, Part 10: Decent home standard).

Under the original definition of decent homes (incorporating the Fitness Standard) the number of non-decent homes in England fell from 9.1 million in 1996 to 5.9 million in 2006. Total dwelling stock increased over the period (see Figure 10.1), the net outcome of new construction, demolition and change of use, and this also contributed to the decrease in the proportion of all dwellings classified as non-decent, from 45 per cent to 27 per cent (Table 10.11). The proportion of social sector homes considered non-decent fell at a faster rate than the proportion in the private sector.

Table 10.11

Non-decent homes:[1,2] by tenure[3]

England   Percentages

	1996	2001	2003	2004	2005	2006 (Fitness definition)	2006 (HHSRS definition)
Private sector[4]							
Owner-occupied	40	29	28	27	25	24	35
Privately rented	62	51	48	43	41	40	47
All private sector	43	32	30	29	27	26	36
Social sector[4]							
Local authority	54	42	40	35	34	33	32
Registered social landlords	48	33	29	26	24	24	25
All rented from social sector	53	39	35	31	29	29	29
All tenures	45	33	31	29	27	27	35

1 See Appendix, Part 10: Decent home standard, for explanation of the different definitions of decent homes.
2 The housing health and safety rating system (HHSRS) came into force in April 2006 and replaced the fitness standard as the statutory element of the decent home standard. The HHSRS will be used in future data on decent homes.
3 See Appendix, Part 10: Tenure.
4 See Appendix, Part 10: Private and social sectors.

Source: English House Condition Survey, Communities and Local Government

The replacement of the Fitness Standard with the HHSRS as the statutory criterion for the decent homes standard in 2006 has led to an increase in the proportion of homes classed as non-decent. Estimates of non-decent homes based on this updated definition of decency are not comparable with those based on the original definition, so trend data using the updated definition are not available. However, 2006 estimates were made for both definitions through the English House Condition Survey. Under the updated definition the proportion of non-decent homes was 35 per cent, 8 percentage points higher than when using the original definition of the standard. While the change in definition led to an overall increase in the proportion of homes considered non-decent, there was no change among social sector homes.

The increased likelihood of having 'Category 1' hazards mainly results from original design and construction features of older homes and the private housing sector accounts for the great majority of these. In consequence, private sector housing is more likely to be non-decent than social sector homes under the updated definition; 36 per cent compared with 29 per cent in 2006.

Not meeting the statutory standard for housing, that is being a 'Category 1' hazard under the HHSRS, was the most common reason for homes to fail the decent home standard in 2006 (62 per cent). However, while this was the most common reason among private sector dwellings (65 per cent), among social sector homes the most common reason for failing was not providing a reasonable level of thermal comfort (49 per cent).

Non-decent homes are just one element of poor living conditions. Another aspect is living in a poor neighbourhood, defined in the English House Condition Survey as being in the 10 per cent of homes in neighbourhoods with the 'worst' problems relating to upkeep and condition of private and public space and buildings in the immediate environment of the home (see Appendix, Part 10: Poor living conditions). Households experiencing poor living conditions are often disadvantaged. There are a number of reasons for this, such as age, long-term illness or disability or having limited resources to make improvements.

Vulnerable households are those that receive at least one of the principal means-tested or disability benefits (see Appendix, Part 10: Vulnerable households). In 2006 more than one-third (34 per cent) of vulnerable households with dependent children aged under 16 in England, lived in non-decent housing, as did a similar proportion (33 per cent) of lone parent households (Table 10.12 overleaf). Around one-fifth of both these vulnerable groups also lived in a poor neighbourhood (22 and 19 per cent respectively).

Least likely to live in non-decent homes were non-vulnerable households with dependent children (30 per cent) and a

Table 10.12

Poor living conditions:[1] by households with dependent children,[2] 2006

England   Percentages

	Non-decent homes[3]	Poor neighbourhood	Excess cold	Homes in serious disrepair
All households with children	31	13	8	8
Vulnerable[4] households with children	34	22	6	12
Non-vulnerable[4] households with children	30	8	9	7
Lone parent households[5]	33	19	7	12
All households	34	10	11	9

1 See Appendix, Part 10: Poor living conditions, for explanation of the different elements of poor living conditions.
2 Dependent children aged under 16 only; does not include young people aged 16 to 18 in full-time education.
3 Using the 2006 updated definition of decent homes. See Appendix, Part 10: Decent home standard.
4 Vulnerable households are those in receipt of at least one of the principal means-tested or disability related benefits/tax credits. Includes lone parent households in receipt of benefits. See Appendix, Part 8: Expenditure on social protection benefits.
5 Does not include lone parent households who are vulnerable.

Source: English House Condition Survey, Communities and Local Government

markedly lower proportion of these households lived in a poor neighbourhood (8 per cent). Overall, 34 per cent of all households lived in non-decent homes in 2006. The proportion of households with dependent children living in non-decent homes was lower than this (31 per cent).

Another indicator of the quality of housing and living conditions is overcrowding. This is commonly measured by the bedroom standard, which measures the number of bedrooms available to a household against the number required, given the household's size and composition (see Appendix, Part 10: Bedroom standard). In 2006/07, 2.4 per cent of households in England were one bedroom below the bedroom standard, and hence defined as overcrowded (Table 10.13). A further 0.3 per cent of properties were two bedrooms or more below the standard, defined as severely overcrowded. The proportion of households either overcrowded or severely overcrowded has remained relatively stable over the period 2001/02 to 2006/07. The proportions of households either at the standard or one bedroom above the standard both decreased by 1 percentage point over the period 2001/02 to 2006/07 (to 25.2 per cent and 35.5 per cent respectively) while the proportion with two or more bedrooms above the standard increased by 2 percentage points, suggesting that people in England were living in less crowded accommodation in 2006/07. While this may indicate that households are living in larger homes it is also likely to be a reflection of the increase in one person households (see Chapter 2: Households and families, Table 2.1).

Overcrowding varies according to the tenure of the household in England. In the three years to 2006/07 it was lowest among owner-occupiers, at 1 per cent. In contrast, 6 per cent of social renters and 5 per cent of private renters lived in accommodation one or more bedrooms below the bedroom standard. There were also differences by the ethnic group (see Appendix, Part 1: Classification of ethnic groups) of the household with 2 per cent of White households living in

Table 10.13

Overcrowding and under-occupation[1,2]

England   Percentages

	2001/02	2002/03	2003/04	2004/05	2005/06	2006/07
Two bedrooms or more below standard[3]	0.2	0.2	0.2	0.2	0.2	0.3
One bedroom below standard[4]	2.2	2.2	2.2	2.2	2.3	2.4
At standard	26.3	25.8	25.4	25.2	25.3	25.2
One bedroom above standard	36.7	36.6	36.6	36.2	35.8	35.5
Two or more bedrooms above standard	34.5	35.2	35.7	36.1	36.4	36.6
All households (=100%) (thousands)	20,505	20,452	20,441	20,604	20,761	20,879

1 Based on the bedroom standard, which compares the number of bedrooms available with the number required, given the household size and composition. See Appendix, Part 10: Bedroom standard.
2 Because of small sample sizes a three-year moving average is used. For example, the 2006/07 figure represents the average for the three-year period 2004/05, 2005/06 and 2006/07.
3 Severely overcrowded.
4 Overcrowded.

Source: Survey of English Housing, Communities and Local Government

overcrowded accommodation compared with 11 per cent of ethnic minority households, although much of this difference could be explained by the differences in tenure between these groups (see Table 10.8).

Overall satisfaction with the area lived in varies by type of household. In England, 87 per cent of all households were very or fairly satisfied with their area in 2006/07, compared with 9 per cent who were very or fairly dissatisfied. Couples with no dependent children were the most satisfied with the area where they lived (88 per cent very or fairly satisfied) while lone parents with dependent children were the least satisfied (78 per cent satisfied and 15 per cent dissatisfied) (Table 10.14). Seven per cent of lone parent households with dependent children were very dissatisfied with their area compared with 2 to 3 per cent among the other household types.

On average, satisfaction with their local area increases with age of the householder, from 80 per cent among 16 to 24-year-olds to 92 per cent among those aged 75 and over. There were also variations by socio-economic group (see Appendix: Part 3, National Statistics Socio-economic Classification (NS-SEC)). The proportion of people in routine or intermediate occupations who were dissatisfied with their area (10 per cent each) was

Table 10.14

Satisfaction with area: by type of household,[1] 2006/07

England				Percentages
	All satisfied	Neither satisfied nor dissatisfied	All dissatisfied	All households
One person households				
Male	86	7	7	100
Female	87	4	9	100
Couple households				
Couple, no dependent children	88	4	8	100
Couple with dependent children	87	5	8	100
Lone parent with dependent children	78	7	15	100
Other multi-person households[2]	85	5	10	100

1 Excludes households where the respondent was not the household reference person nor spouse/partner. See Appendix, Part 7: Household reference person.
2 Includes multi-family households and lone parents with non-dependent children.

Source: Survey of English Housing, Communities and Local Government

double the proportion of those who were higher managers and professionals (5 per cent). In 2006/07, 82 per cent of householders in England were satisfied with both their neighbourhood and their accommodation, an increase from 79 per cent in 1996/97. Households who rented their home were less satisfied with their local area than owner-occupiers; 80 per cent of social sector tenants and 85 per cent of private renters were satisfied compared with 89 per cent of owner-occupiers.

Also important among those living in rented accommodation is satisfaction with their landlord. In 2006/07 those living in privately rented accommodation in England were generally more satisfied with their landlords than were social sector tenants. This applied across all household types with the exception of couples with no dependent children, for which 76 per cent each of private and social sector tenants were satisfied with their landlord. The largest difference in satisfaction between private and social renters was among couples with dependent children; 73 per cent of these private renters were satisfied compared with 61 per cent of those renting from the social sector.

Housing mobility

In 2006/07, around one in ten (11 per cent) of all households in England had moved to their current home within the previous 12 months, a total of 2.3 million households. Just less than 400,000 of these were new households. Of these new households, just less than one-half (48 per cent) were renting from the private sector and 30 per cent were buying their home with a mortgage, including shared ownership (see page 146) (Figure 10.15 overleaf). The proportion of new households renting from the social sector has decreased from 25 per cent in 1999/2000 to 20 per cent in 2006/07.

In 2006/07 the average length of time householders had lived in their current home was nine years. This length of time varied by tenure of the householder; the average time among those who owned their home outright was 22 years, compared with two years among private renters. More than one-half (55 per cent) of private renters had lived in their home for less than two years (Table 10.16 overleaf).

Around one in six (16 per cent) of householders who owned their homes outright had lived there for 40 years or more, compared with 5 per cent of social renters and 3 per cent of private renters. Those buying their homes with a mortgage also tended to stay in their homes for a number of years, with nearly one-quarter each having lived in their current homes for five to nine years or ten to 19 years (23 per cent and 24 per cent respectively). More than one-fifth (21 per cent) of

10

Figure 10.15

New households:[1] by tenure[2]

England

Percentages

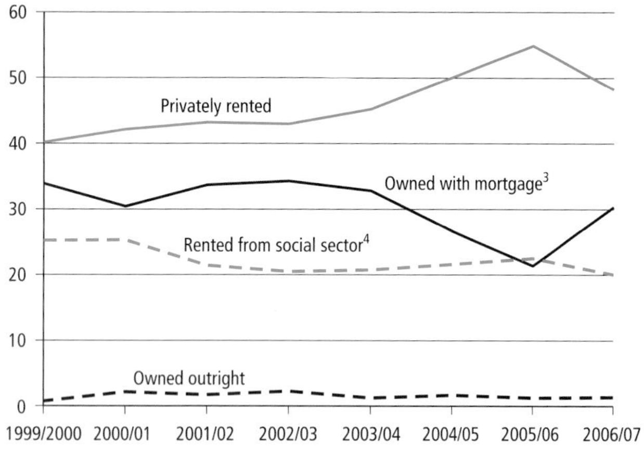

1 New heads of household resident less than one year.
2 See Appendix, Part 10: Tenure.
3 Includes shared ownership.
4 Includes local authority and housing association tenants.

Source: Survey of English Housing, Communities and Local Government

social sector tenants had also lived in their current homes for each of these periods of time.

There has been a gradual increase in the proportion of households living in privately rented accommodation in England and Wales over the last 20 years, from 9 per cent in 1988 to 13 per cent in 2007. Changes in lifestyle may have contributed to this increase. For example, more young people are going to university (see Chapter 3: Education and training, Table 3.9) and some leave home to live in shared accommodation before

setting up their own homes. In recent years increasing house prices (see Figure 10.19) have made it more difficult to purchase a home, meaning that people who may otherwise have purchased their home are increasingly remaining in, or moving back to, their parental homes, or are living in rented accommodation.

The 2006/07 Survey of English Housing asked people aged 25 and over who were still living with their parents their main reason for still being 'at home'. More than one-third (35 per cent) of 25 to 29-year-olds and more than one-quarter (28 per cent) of 30 to 34-year-olds were living with their parents because they could not afford to buy or rent their own homes. A further 10 per cent of 50 to 59-year-olds were living in their parental home because of their financial situation (see also Chapter 2: Households and families, Table 2.9). Among those aged 25 to 29, 400,000 men were still living at home, twice the number of women (almost 200,000) in the same age group.

In England in 2006/07, around six in ten (57 per cent) of private renters expected to buy their own property at some point. The majority (63 per cent) of private renters who did not expect to buy felt that they were unlikely ever to be able to afford to purchase their own home (Table 10.17). Financial concerns were commonly cited among those private renters not expecting to buy a home; 14 per cent felt that their job was not secure enough and 11 per cent did not want to be in debt. However, one-fifth (20 per cent) of private renters were happy with their current living situation and one in ten (9 per cent) did not want the commitment that owning a home involved.

Table 10.16

Length of time in current accommodation: by tenure,[1] 2006/07

England

Percentages

	Less than 1 year	1 year	2 years	3–4 years	5–9 years	10–19 years	20–29 years	30–39 years	40 years or more	Average number of years
All owner-occupiers	6	5	7	10	18	22	15	9	8	11.6
Owned outright	3	2	3	5	12	20	22	17	16	22.4
Owned with a mortgage	9	8	9	14	23	24	10	2	1	7.1
Social renters	10	8	8	12	21	21	10	5	5	7.8
Private renters	38	17	13	11	10	5	2	2	3	1.7
All tenures	11	7	8	11	18	20	12	7	6	8.9

1 See Appendix, Part 10: Tenure.

Source: Survey of English Housing, Communities and Local Government

Table 10.17

Reasons given by private renters for not buying a property,[1] 2006/07

England	Percentages
It is unlikely I will ever be able to afford it	63
I like it where I am	20
I do not have a secure enough job	14
I would not want to be in debt	11
I wouldn't want that sort of commitment	9
I prefer the flexibility of renting	8
Repairs and maintenance would be too costly	6
Other	21

1 Around 40 per cent of private renters said that they do not expect to buy a property. These respondents were then asked to select their reason, or reasons, from a showcard. Percentages do not sum to 100 per cent as respondents could give more than one answer.

Source: Survey of English Housing, Communities and Local Government

Housing market and finance

Housing mobility is linked to the state of the housing market. Over the past 40 years the economy and the housing market have mirrored one another, with booms and slumps in one tending to contribute to the other. The number of property transactions in England and Wales rose during the 1980s, mainly as a result of existing owner-occupiers moving home and an increase in the availability of affordable private stock because of the 'right-to-buy' initiative. Changes to the mortgage lending market in the 1980s may also have been a contributing factor to the 1980s property boom, when new households opted for ownership rather than renting. Following sharp increases in the interest rate in the two years from 1988 (from 7.4 per cent in mid-1988 to around 15 per cent two years later), the annual number of property transactions halved from a peak of 2.2 million to 1.1 million by 1992, after which it fluctuated for several years in a generally upward direction. There was a similar boom in the housing market in the early to mid-2000s. The number of property transactions in England and Wales, including commercial premises, reached 1.8 million in 2007, the highest number since 1988.

In April 2008 the way that property transactions were counted was changed, with data based on the new system backdated to April 2005 to allow a consistent time series. Under the new system, transactions are based on actual completions instead of the number of stamp duty land tax certificates issued, and properties valued at less than £40,000 are excluded. By removing transactions at the very bottom of the market, data are closer to counting the sales of dwellings rather than all

Figure 10.18

Property transactions,[1] 2005 to 2008

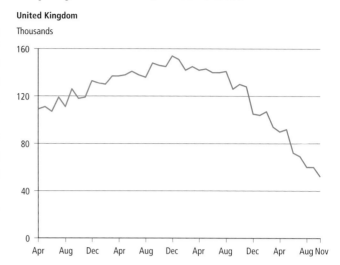

United Kingdom

Thousands

1 Number of residential property transactions with a value of £40,000 or more. Transactions are allocated to the month in which the transaction was completed.

Source: HM Revenue and Customs

transactions because the majority of properties under £40,000 are commercial properties.

There were 1.7 million residential property transactions in the UK in 2006 and although the number of transactions remained high in 2007, at 1.6 million, there were decreases almost every month throughout that year, indicating the beginning of a downturn in the housing market. There was a noticeable decrease at the end of the year, from 142,000 transactions in April to 105,000 transactions in December (Figure 10.18). Between January and November 2008 there were 870,000 residential property transactions, a large decrease from the 1.5 million transactions during the same period in 2007. The number of transactions halved throughout the year in 2008, from 104,000 in January to 52,000 in November. There was a slight increase in the number of transactions between September and October 2008, the first increase since May and only the third in the year.

Directly linked to the number of property transactions are changes in the average dwelling price. Despite some decline in the number of transactions throughout 2007, as noted above, the overall number was similar to 2006 and this was reflected in the average price, which continued to increase. At £223,405, the average dwelling price in the UK in 2007 was 9 per cent higher than the 2006 average of £204,813 based on simple average house prices.

The increase in house prices over the last ten years has made affordability a particular concern for first-time buyers. In 1997 the average house price was around three-and-one-half times

10

Figure 10.19

Average dwelling prices:[1] by type of buyer

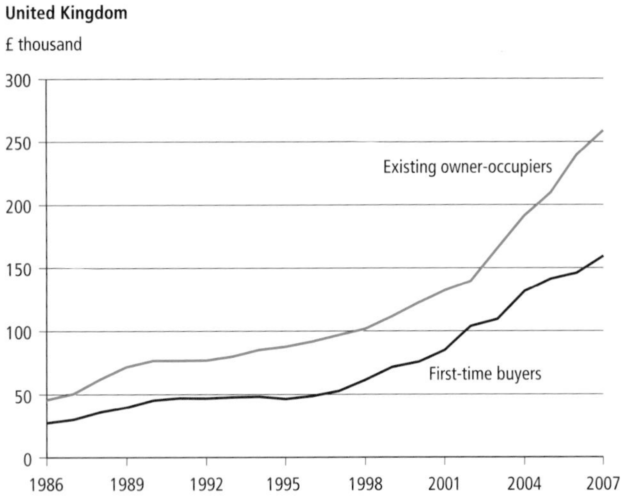

United Kingdom

£ thousand

1 Uses simple average prices. See Appendix, Part 10: Average dwelling prices.

Source: Communities and Local Government

average earnings, and by 2007 this had more than doubled to around seven times average earnings. Over this period the average price paid by first-time buyers in the UK rose by more than 200 per cent (not adjusting for inflation) to £159,500 (Figure 10.19). The average price paid by existing owner-occupiers increased by 168 per cent over the same period, to £258,500. Between 2006 and 2007, the average price increase, using simple average house prices, was 8 per cent for both first-time buyers and existing owner-occupiers.

While the increase between 2006 and 2007 for first-time buyers was larger than the 3 per cent increase between 2005

and 2006, the increase for owner-occupiers over the same period was less than the previous 12 per cent increase. This suggests that the housing market difficulties experienced towards the end of 2007 had more effect on first-time buyers than on those moving from one owned home to another. This is partly because it became difficult for first-time buyers to get a mortgage because lenders started requiring larger deposits. Owner-occupiers, on the other hand, were able to fund their purchase with equity already built up in their homes. In addition, owners could compensate for any decrease in the value of their homes by paying less for their onward purchase.

Average house prices in the UK declined throughout 2008, from £221,130 in January to £199,732 in November, according to monthly data for 2008 based on house prices at mortgage completion stage (see Appendix, Part 10: Average dwelling prices).

Housing costs make up a substantial proportion of household budgets. In England in 2006/07, owner-occupied households spent on average 16 per cent of gross monthly household income on mortgage repayments. This was the largest proportion over the period 1999/2000 to 2006/07 (Table 10.20).

The proportion of income that is spent on mortgage repayments varies by the type of household. Lone parents with dependent children spent almost one-quarter (24 per cent) of their monthly income on mortgage repayments compared with 16 per cent for couples with dependent children. Multi-person households spent more than one-fifth (22 per cent) on mortgage repayments while one person households spent on average 19 per cent. For all household types, the proportion of

Table 10.20

Mortgage repayments as a proportion of household income: by type of household

England

Percentages

	1999/2000	2000/01	2001/02	2002/03	2003/04	2004/05	2005/06	2006/07
One person households	16	17	16	15	16	17	19	19
Couple households								
Couple, no dependent children	11	12	11	11	12	13	14	14
Couple with dependent children	13	14	13	12	13	14	15	16
Lone parent with dependent children	22	23	23	21	21	22	26	24
Other multi-person households[1]	17	22	23	18	16	20	21	22
All households	13	14	13	12	13	14	15	16

1 Includes multi-family households and lone parents with non-dependent children.

Source: Survey of English Housing, Communities and Local Government

Figure 10.21

Proportion of income spent on housing costs:[1] EU comparison, 2005

Percentages

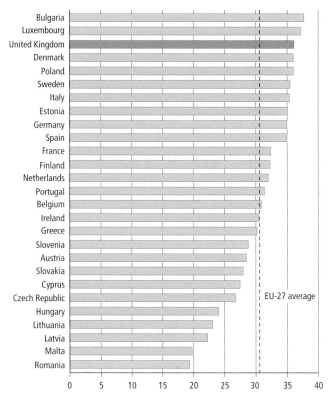

1 Includes mortgage and rent payments, insurances, utilities, and repairs and maintenance.

Source: Eurostat

income spent on mortgages increased between 1999/2000 and 2006/07. Owner-occupier couples with no dependent children spent the smallest proportion of all types of household on mortgage repayments over this period, 14 per cent in 2006/07.

As well as mortgage repayments or rent there are a number of other costs involved in owning or running a home. These include insurance (both buildings and contents), utilities such as gas, electricity and water, and repairs and maintenance. The European Union (EU-27) average proportion of income spent on housing costs was 31 per cent in 2005 (Figure 10.21). The UK had the third highest proportion of income spent on housing costs in the EU-27 in 2005, spending more than one-third (36 per cent) of household income on housing costs. Households in Bulgaria spent the highest proportion of income on housing costs (38 per cent), followed by Luxembourg (37 per cent). People living in Romania spent the smallest proportion on housing costs, 19 per cent in 2005, one-half of the proportion spent by people in Bulgaria.

Base interest rates and mortgage interest rates (and therefore repayments) rose during the early 1980s and early 1990s,

when the UK economy was hit by recession. Repayments became increasingly difficult for some people, particularly those whose financial circumstances changed, and those who had borrowed a high proportion of the value of their properties and had high mortgage repayments.

When people fall behind with their mortgage repayments and are unable to reach an alternative arrangement with their mortgage lender, a county court possession summons may be issued, with the view to obtaining a court order. Not all orders result in repossession; courts often make suspended orders, which provide for arrears to be paid off within a reasonable period. However, when repayments cannot be made the mortgage lender will repossess the property. At its peak in 1992, 205,000 loans were in arrears by six to 12 months in the UK, and 68,500 properties were repossessed (Figure 10.22). However, largely because of lower interest rates, arrears and repossessions fell between 1992 and 2004, when 29,900 loans were in arrears by six to 12 months and 8,200 homes were repossessed. Since 2004 the number of properties in arrears by six to 12 months has generally increased, and was 41,100 in 2007. Over the same period, repossessions increased more than threefold, to 26,200. There was a 25 per cent increase in repossessions between 2006 and 2007.

In 2008 the economic downturn in the UK continued to present challenges to the housing market and in the first nine months of 2008 there were 54,100 mortgages in arrears by

Figure 10.22

Mortgage loans in arrears and property repossessions[1]

United Kingdom

Thousands

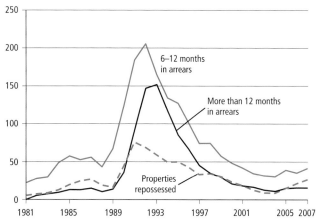

1 Mortgages in arrears and properties repossessed at end of period. Estimates cover only members of the Council of Mortgage Lenders; these account for more than 95 per cent of first charge mortgages. See Appendix, Part 10: Mortgage arrears and repossessions.

Source: Council of Mortgage Lenders

10

six to 12 months and 30,200 repossessions. In February 2009 the Council of Mortgage Lenders (CML) reported that there were a total of 40,000 repossessions in 2008, a 53 per cent increase from 2007. The CML forecasts that there will be 75,000 repossessions in 2009. However, in December 2008 the Government announced proposals for an additional new home guarantee scheme, aimed at limiting repossessions by reducing the pressure on homeowners who have difficulty meeting their mortgage repayments. The scheme will be designed to allow people who fall into arrears because of sickness, redundancy or loss of income to defer a proportion of their interest payments on their loans for two years. This policy aims to reduce the number of homes repossessed during 2009 and 2010.

Chapter 11

Environment

- Nearly six in ten (57 per cent) people aged 15 and over in the EU-27 countries in 2007 said that climate change concerned them. (Table 11.1)

- Renewable energy accounted for around 5 per cent of all electricity generated in the UK in 2007, around three-and-one-half times more than in 1991. (Table 11.4)

- In 2007, nearly two-thirds (64 per cent) of adults aged 16 and over in England stated they never left their television on stand-by overnight. (Table 11.6)

- Of the 28.5 million tonnes of municipal waste produced in England in 2007/08, more than one-half (54 per cent) went to landfill compared with 85 per cent in 1997/98. (Page 164)

- The Environment Agency recorded 827 serious pollution incidents in England and Wales in 2007, a fall of 36 per cent since 2000 and 9 per cent since 2006. (Table 11.11)

- The UK was around 61 per cent self-sufficient in all food in 2007 and 74 per cent self-sufficient in indigenous-type food. (Figure 11.20)

DATA

Download data by clicking the online pdf

www.statistics.gov.uk/ socialtrends39

Environmental problems like pollution, global warming, loss of biodiversity and ozone depletion do not respect national boundaries. As a result, the environment is of concern to the global population. The UK Government has developed environment-related policies and regulations and along with the other European Union member states, has a strategy for sustainable development to try and protect the environment and reduce the negative impacts caused by human activity. With the cost of energy increasing and the debate on climate change becoming more intense, governments, business and individuals are taking measures to conserve energy and cut their energy needs.

Environmental concerns and behaviour

Almost six in ten (57 per cent) people aged 15 and over in the European Union (EU-27) countries stated in 2007 that climate change was an environmental concern common to them – the most common cited (Table 11.1). Around four in ten people across the EU-27 were concerned about water pollution (42 per cent) or air pollution (40 per cent). Around one-quarter were concerned about the depletion of natural resources and the growing amount of waste (26 per cent and 24 per cent respectively). Climate change was the most common concern for adults in 21 of the EU-27 member states with adults in Cyprus and Sweden reporting the greatest proportion of respondents concerned (79 per cent and 71 per cent respectively); this was also the most common concern for UK respondents (53 per cent). In Slovenia, both climate change and water pollution were the most common environmental concerns, reported by over six in ten (61 per cent) people. Water pollution or air pollution were the most common environmental concerns reported by people in Bulgaria, the Czech Republic, Estonia, Latvia, Lithuania and Malta. Three of these countries are Baltic states, where concern about water pollution could be connected to the eutrophication (over-richness of nutrients from pollutants in water, resulting in too many water plants and depleted oxygen levels causing the death of aquatic creatures) of the Baltic Sea. Of the other two environmental issues shown in Table 11.1, the growing problem of waste was most commonly reported as an environmental concern by people in Malta (45 per cent), possibly because Malta has the highest population density of all EU-27 member states, while the depletion of natural resources was most commonly reported as an environmental concern by respondents in the Netherlands (38 per cent).

According to the 2007 Survey of Public Attitudes and Behaviours towards the Environment, 6 per cent of adults aged 16 and over in England 'don't really do anything that is

Table 11.1

Selected environmental issues that concern EU citizens,[1] 2007

Percentages

	Depletion of natural resources	Growing waste	Air pollution	Water pollution	Climate change
Cyprus	22	11	36	57	79
Sweden	31	17	35	52	71
Germany	30	19	36	40	69
Greece	25	13	34	60	67
Denmark	23	25	31	52	65
Luxembourg	24	23	44	47	63
Finland	34	31	37	56	62
Slovenia	19	28	50	61	61
France	37	27	43	46	59
Belgium	31	31	50	42	58
Ireland	22	29	32	40	58
Hungary	23	35	51	49	57
Romania	17	19	46	45	57
Austria	31	18	33	41	57
Spain	25	7	34	38	57
Portugal	25	22	49	46	54
Netherlands	38	26	45	39	53
United Kingdom	27	36	42	35	53
Slovakia	27	39	48	47	51
Malta	7	45	64	32	51
Czech Republic	23	39	44	54	50
Bulgaria	19	24	50	45	48
Poland	15	41	41	45	47
Italy	21	18	39	35	47
Estonia	21	31	38	64	39
Lithuania	15	21	45	58	38
Latvia	14	37	41	55	38
EU-27	26	24	40	42	57

1 Respondents aged 15 and over were shown a list from which they chose the five main environmental issues that worried them. Percentages do not sum to 100 per cent as respondents could give more than one answer.

Source: Eurobarometer, European Commission

environmentally-friendly' with the remainder doing at least one or two things. More than four in ten (41 per cent) stated that they 'do quite a few things that are environmentally-friendly'; one-third (33 per cent) said they 'do one or two things', while around one-fifth (19 per cent) claimed to be environmentally-friendly in 'most things' or 'everything' they do. Patterns of environmental behaviour varied by household composition.

Table 11.2

Attitudes towards current lifestyle and the environment:[1] by type of household, 2007

England   Percentages

	Don't really do anything that is environmentally-friendly	Do one or two things that are environmentally-friendly	Do quite a few things that are environmentally-friendly	Environmentally-friendly in most things I do	Environmentally-friendly in everything I do
One person households					
Under state pension age[2]	10	34	33	21	1
Over state pension age[2]	3	22	39	29	6
Couple households					
No children	4	32	45	17	2
Dependent children	6	40	42	10	1
Non-dependent children	5	35	46	10	2
Over state pension age[2]	3	18	42	34	4
Lone parent households					
Dependent children	13	36	37	13	1
Non-dependent children	9	31	39	17	4
Two or more unrelated adults	4	30	46	13	2
Other households	6	33	39	17	2

1 The question asked was 'Which of these would you say best describes your current lifestyle?' Does not include respondents who answered 'don't know'.
2 State pension age is currently 65 for men and 60 for women.

Source: Department for Environment, Food and Rural Affairs

People over state pension age (65 for men and 60 for women), whether in a one person household or as part of a couple household, were more likely than other types of household to perform environmentally-friendly tasks in 'most things' or 'everything they do', 35 per cent and 38 per cent respectively (Table 11.2). In contrast, lone parents with dependent children were less likely than other household types to carry out environmentally-friendly tasks, 13 per cent stated that they 'don't really do anything that is environmentally-friendly' while 1 per cent were environmentally-friendly in 'everything they do'. Around eight in ten couples in a household with children tended to do 'one or two things' or 'quite a few things that were environmentally-friendly', with 82 per cent of those with dependent children and 81 per cent with non-dependent children doing so.

Use of resources

Renewable energy is seen as environmentally friendly and the Government is committed to increasing the contribution renewable sources make to future electricity generation. However, conventional methods continue to be the main generators of electricity in use. Between 1990 and 2007 the total fuel used for electricity generation rose by around 10 per cent from 76 million tonnes of oil equivalent to 84 million tonnes. In 1990, coal was the main fuel used to generate electricity, as it had been for many decades. But the contribution of coal, and to a lesser extent oil, started to decline during the 1990s, while the use of natural gas increased. This trend generally levelled off after 1999 (Figure 11.3 overleaf). In 2007, coal was still the fuel most used for generating electricity (33 million tonnes of oil equivalent) just above natural gas (30 million tonnes of oil equivalent). The contribution of nuclear power peaked in 1998, at more than 23 million tonnes of oil equivalent and around 29 per cent of the total fuel used. By 2007 this had fallen to levels last seen in the late 1980s, at around 14 million tonnes of oil equivalent and 17 per cent of total fuel used. This was partly because of the closures of the two oldest nuclear stations, Dungeness A and Sizewell A, at the end of 2006. However, levels of nuclear energy generation are set to rise in the long term as the Government announced its support in January 2008 for a new generation of nuclear power stations that are likely to come on-stream later in the next decade. Other fuels used for electricity generation, including renewable sources (although at small levels), increased by more than four times between 1990

11

Figure 11.3

Fuels used for electricity generation

United Kingdom

Million tonnes of oil equivalent

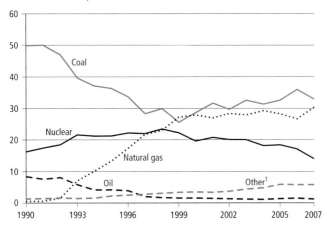

1 Includes coke oven gas, blast furnace gas, waste products from chemical processes, refuse derived fuels and renewable sources.

Source: Department of Energy and Climate Change

and 2007, from more than one million tonnes of oil equivalent to almost six million tonnes of oil equivalent.

Renewable energy accounted for around 5 per cent of all electricity generated in the UK in 2007. This was equivalent to 19,664 gigawatt hours (GWh), more than three-and-one-half times that of 1991 (Table 11.4). Biofuels accounted for the

Table 11.4

Electricity generation: by renewable sources

United Kingdom				GWh[1]
	1991	2001	2006	2007
Wind and wave	9	965	4,225	5,274
Hydro	4,624	4,055	4,593	5,088
Biofuels				
Landfill gas	208	2,507	4,424	4,677
Co-firing with fossil fuels	..	..	2,528	1,956
Municipal solid waste combustion[2]	150	880	1,083	1,177
Sewage sludge digestion	328	363	456	517
Other biomass[3]	1	776	797	964
Solar photo-voltaics	..	2	11	11
Total	5,320	9,549	18,116	19,664

1 Gigawatt hours.
2 Biodegradable part only.
3 Includes electricity from farm waste digestion, poultry litter combustion, meat and bone combustion, straw and short rotation coppice.

Source: Department of Energy and Climate Change

largest proportion of electricity generated from renewable sources (9,291 GWh) followed by wind and wave power (5,274 GWh) and hydroelectricity (5,088 GWh). Wind and wave power has been the fastest growing renewable source, with electricity generation increasing by almost five-and-one-half times since 2001.

The proportion of electricity generated from renewable sources varies across the EU-27. More than one-half (56.6 per cent) of electricity generated in Austria in 2006 and nearly one-half (48.2 per cent) in Sweden came from renewable sources. This compared with an EU-27 average of 14.5 per cent. Along with Cyprus and Malta, which generate no electricity from renewable sources, the lowest proportions were in Estonia and Poland, 1.4 per cent and 2.9 per cent respectively.

In January 2008 the European Commission put forward differentiated targets for each EU member state to source a certain amount of all their energy needs from renewable sources, based on the per capita gross domestic product (GDP) of each country. According to this proposal each member state should increase its share of renewable energies to increase the present EU share of 8.5 per cent to 20.0 per cent by 2020. Agreement was reached in December 2008 on the amount by which each EU member state would increase its share. The UK agreed to increase its share from 1.3 per cent in 2005 to 15.0 per cent in 2020. The target date for adopting this legislation is the first half of 2009.

Domestic energy consumption in the UK increased by 32 per cent between 1970 and 2004, but fell by 9 per cent between 2004 and 2007, so overall consumption was 19 per cent higher in 2007 than in 1970. In 1970 most domestic energy came from coal (39 per cent), but by 2007, gas accounted for more than two-thirds (68 per cent) of domestic energy consumption. Most final domestic energy use in the UK is for the purposes of space heating, which accounted for 58 per cent (26.4 million tonnes of oil equivalent) in 2006 and had generally increased by 19 per cent since 1970 (Figure 11.5). The use of energy for space heating increased at a slower rate than some other energy demands because of improvements in levels of home insulation, double glazing and more efficient home heating. According to a report by the Department for Business, Enterprise and Regulatory Reform (BERR), if insulation levels had stayed at their 1970 levels then domestic energy consumption in 2006 is likely to have been nearly 50 per cent higher. Similarly heating systems are more efficient, but if they had remained at 1970 efficiency levels, consumption in 2006 is likely to have been more than 50 per cent higher. One-quarter (25 per cent) of domestic

Figure 11.5

Household energy consumption: by final use

United Kingdom

Index numbers (1970=100)

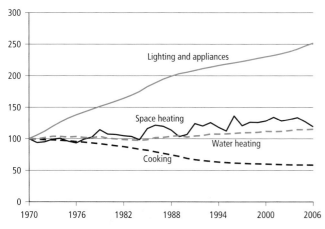

Source: Department of Energy and Climate Change; Building Research Establishment

energy consumption is used for heating water (11.4 million tonnes of oil equivalent). Between 1970 and 2006 energy consumed by lighting and electrical appliances in the UK increased by 152 per cent, reflecting the increasing number of electrical appliances in households. However, this category only accounts for around 15 per cent of all consumption (6.7 million tonnes of oil equivalent). Energy used for cooking in the home accounts for around 3 per cent of household consumption (1.3 million tonnes of oil equivalent) and has fallen by 41 per cent since 1970. This fall is partly explained by changes in technologies and lifestyle, for example, ownership of a microwave oven in more than 85 per cent of households, a greater availability of convenience food and people eating out more frequently in 2006 than in 1970.

In a survey by Populus in September 2008, more than eight in ten (84 per cent) adults aged 18 and over in Great Britain stated that they were concerned about energy prices. Prices for domestic energy continued to rise between 2006 and 2007. According to the retail prices index (see Appendix, Part 6: Retail prices index), the prices paid by domestic customers for all fuel and light rose by 4.1 per cent in real terms between 2006 and 2007. Domestic electricity prices, including VAT, rose by 5.0 per cent in real terms between 2006 and 2007. Domestic gas prices, including VAT, rose by 4.7 per cent and prices for domestic coal and smokeless fuels rose by 4.2 per cent (see also Chapter 6: Expenditure).

Getting people to be more environmentally-friendly in their home is an important way to conserve energy. In 2007 adults aged 16 and over in England were asked about their behaviour related to energy and water efficiency in the home. Nearly

Table 11.6

Behaviour relating to energy and water efficiency in the home,[1,2] 2007

England   Percentages

	Always, very often or quite often	Sometimes or occasionally	Never
Leave TV on stand-by overnight	24	11	64
Leave a mobile charger switched on at the socket when not in use	20	17	63
Leave lights on in rooms that are not being used	13	37	50
Keep the tap running while you brush your teeth	34	19	46
Leave the heating on when you go out for a few hours	23	35	41
Fill the kettle with more water than you are going to use	28	34	37
Have a bath rather than a shower	32	31	37
Put more clothes on when feeling cold rather than putting on, or turning up, the heating	55	30	15

1 Respondents were asked how often they personally performed these actions.
2 Does not include respondents who answered 'don't know'. People who stated 'not applicable' or 'cannot do this' were excluded from the categories 'Leave a mobile charger switched on at the socket when not in use' and 'Have a bath rather than a shower'.

Source: Department for Environment, Food and Rural Affairs

two-thirds (64 per cent) never left their television on stand-by overnight, but nearly one-quarter (24 per cent) left it on stand-by quite often, very often or always (Table 11.6). More than six in ten (63 per cent) never left their mobile charger switched on at the socket when not in use. One-fifth (20 per cent) of adults did this at least quite often, with young people aged 16 to 29 the most likely to leave their charger on. One-half (50 per cent) of all adults never left lights on in rooms that were not being used; this was particularly true of older people aged 65 and over, where more than two-thirds (67 per cent) never did this. Less than four in ten people (37 per cent) sometimes or occasionally left lights on in rooms that were not being used, with 13 per cent stating that they did this at least quite often. While brushing their teeth, around one-third of adults (34 per cent) kept the tap running at least quite often, whereas 46 per cent never did this. Young people were more likely to do this always or very often, particularly young women aged 16 to 29 (34 per cent). The majority (58 per cent) of adults left the heating on at least occasionally when going out for a few hours but more than one-half (55 per cent) of adults would put more clothes on at least quite often when feeling cold instead of putting on, or turning up,

11

the heating. Women were more likely than men to do this, 60 per cent compared with 51 per cent.

Waste management

Each year millions of tonnes of waste are produced from households, commerce and industry. Most of this ends up in landfill, where space is limited and where biodegradable waste generates methane, a powerful greenhouse gas. In addition, energy is used to make new products to replace products that could have been recycled rather than thrown away, which also contributes to climate change. Municipal waste is mainly household waste plus any commercial waste collected by waste collection authorities and waste resulting from the clearance of fly-tipped materials. There are three principal ways of treating municipal waste – landfill, incineration, and recovery and recycling (see Appendix, Part 11: Waste management).

Around 517 kilograms of municipal waste was produced on average per person in the EU-27 member states in 2006 (Table 11.7). Around two-fifths (41 per cent) per person was put in a landfill site and about one-fifth (19 per cent) incinerated. The remainder was assumed to have been recovered and recycled. More than nine-tenths (91 per cent) of both Lithuania's and Poland's municipal waste per person was put in landfill sites, while the UK, Estonia, Ireland and Finland disposed of around six-tenths (60 per cent) of municipal waste per person to landfill, considerably above the EU-27 average of 41 per cent. In contrast, Germany and the Netherlands disposed hardly any municipal waste per person to landfill (1 per cent and 2 per cent respectively), while Belgium, Sweden and Denmark put 5 per cent of municipal waste per person in landfill sites. Germany, the Netherlands, Belgium and Austria were assumed to have recycled and recovered more than 60 per cent of municipal waste per person. In Denmark incineration was the single main method of disposal and more than one-half (55 per cent) of Denmark's municipal waste per person was treated in this way.

The total amount of municipal waste produced in England in 2007/08 was 28.5 million tonnes, a rise of 11 per cent since 1997/98. Households generated 25.3 million tonnes (89 per cent), equivalent to 495 kilograms of household waste per person in 2007/08. More than one-half (54 per cent) of municipal waste in England went to landfill compared with 85 per cent ten years earlier, while more than one-third (34 per cent) was recycled or composted compared with 8 per cent in 1997/98. Waste disposed of by burning and incinerating to produce energy increased from 6 per cent to 11 per cent over the same period. The recycling rate for household waste (total household recycling as a proportion of total household waste) in England

Table 11.7

Municipal waste management: EU comparison, 2006[1,2]

Percentages

	Municipal waste landfilled	Municipal waste incinerated	Municipal waste recovered	Municipal waste generated (=100%) (Kg per capita)
Ireland	59	0	41	804
Cyprus	88	0	12	745
Denmark	5	55	40	737
Luxembourg	19	38	43	702
Malta	86	0	14	652
Netherlands	2	34	64	625
Austria	10	29	61	617
United Kingdom	60	9	31	588
Spain	50	7	43	583
Germany	1	32	68	566
France	35	33	32	553
Italy	52	12	36	548
Sweden	5	47	48	497
Finland	59	9	33	488
Belgium	5	33	62	475
Hungary	80	8	11	468
Estonia	60	0	40	466
Bulgaria	80	0	20	446
Greece	87	0	13	443
Portugal	63	22	15	435
Slovenia	84	1	16	432
Latvia	71	0	28	411
Lithuania	91	0	9	390
Romania	85	0	15	385
Slovakia	78	12	10	301
Czech Republic	79	10	11	296
Poland	91	0	8	259
EU-27	41	19	40	517

1 Data for waste recovery and recycling are not collected from countries but calculated as the difference between municipal waste generation and municipal waste incinerated and landfilled.
2 For definitions see Appendix, Part 11: Waste management.

Source: Eurostat

was around 35 per cent in 2007/08. In Wales, 32 per cent of household waste was recycled or composted, in Scotland 33 per cent was recycled or composted, while in Northern Ireland 32 per cent of household waste was recycled.

Map 11.8

Household waste recycling:[1] by waste disposal authority,[2] 2007/08

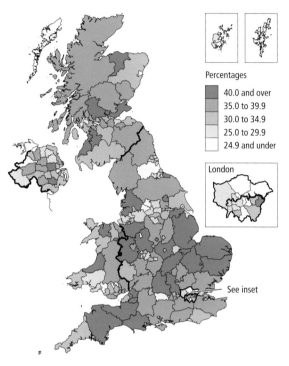

Percentages

- 40.0 and over
- 35.0 to 39.9
- 30.0 to 34.9
- 25.0 to 29.9
- 24.9 and under

London

See inset

1 Includes composting.
2 Mainly counties or unitary authorities. Metropolitan districts in West Yorkshire, South Yorkshire, Tyne and Wear and West Midlands. Data are collected separately for Wigan Metropolitan District and Isles of Scilly Local Authority District. London contains statutory joint waste authorities and London boroughs. Data are collected for Council Areas in Scotland and for District Council Areas in Northern Ireland.

Source: Department for Environment, Food and Rural Affairs; Welsh Assembly Government; Scottish Environment Protection Agency; Department of Environment, Northern Ireland

There continued to be a wide variation in household recycling rates achieved by waste disposal authorities or councils across the UK in 2007/08. The rates varied from 13 per cent in the London Borough of Tower Hamlets and 14 per cent in the Isles of Scilly, to 51 per cent in Somerset County Council and Lincolnshire County Council (Map 11.8). More than 60 per cent of all authorities achieved a recycling rate of 30 per cent or more, while around 11 per cent of authorities had a recycling rate of less than 25 per cent. The waste authority with the highest recycling rate in Wales was Ceredigion, where 45 per cent of all household waste was recycled. In Scotland the highest rate was in South Ayrshire (45 per cent) and in Northern Ireland the highest recycling rate was in Antrim (49 per cent).

Compost followed by paper and card constitute a large proportion of household waste collected for recycling in England, accounting for 36 per cent and 18 per cent respectively of the total amount by weight in 2007/08

Table 11.9

Materials collected from households for recycling[1]

England				Thousand tonnes
	1996/97	2001/02	2006/07	2007/08
Compost[2]	279	954	2,895	3,189
Paper and card	600	981	1,535	1,599
Co-mingled[3]	77	221	1,121	1,563
Glass	311	426	840	902
Scrap metal and white goods	199	369	601	728
Textiles	32	46	103	598
Cans[4]	18	26	80	113
Plastics	6	8	49	83
Other[5]	2	155	751	66
Total	1,678	3,186	7,976	8,841

1 Includes data from different types of recycling schemes collecting waste from household sources, including private/voluntary schemes such as kerbside and 'bring' systems.
2 Includes organic materials (kitchen and garden waste) collected for centralised composting.
3 Co-mingled materials are separated after collection.
4 Includes ferrous and aluminium cans.
5 Includes oils, batteries, aluminium foil, books and shoes.

Source: Department for Environment, Food and Rural Affairs

(Table 11.9). The amount of compost collected from households has increased more rapidly, increasing between 1996/97 and 2007/08 from 0.3 million to almost 3.2 million tonnes. The amount of paper and card collected has grown steadily in recent years, in line with most types of waste. Glass made up 10 per cent, while co-mingled collections – that is collection of a number of recyclable materials in the same box or bin (for example paper, cans and plastics) – together with other materials (such as wood, furniture and oils) made up 18 per cent. According to a report by the Waste and Resources Action Programme (WRAP) around 4.9 million tonnes of food waste were collected in 2007 from households in England through regular and separate food waste collections. This was equivalent to 240 kilograms each year per household or an average 4.6 kilograms per week. (See Appendix, Part 11: Food waste). Throwing away a lot of food waste is avoidable and the most common food types that were thrown away in 2007 were potatoes, sliced bread, apples, and meat or fish mixed meals.

Pollution

Pollution is defined as any chemical or physical agent such as noise in an inappropriate location or concentration that causes

11

instability, disorder, harm or discomfort to the physical systems or living organisms they are in.

Air pollution comes from a variety of sources. Fossil fuel combustion is the main source of air pollution in the UK, with road transport and power stations being the largest contributors. Emissions of air pollutants, other than from fossil fuel combustion are more evenly spread among different sources, although road transport and electricity generation are again important contributors. The *Environment Act 1995*, which covers England, Scotland and Wales, and the *Environment (Northern Ireland) Order 2002*, requires all local authorities in the UK to review and assess air quality in their area.

Emissions of the major air pollutants in the UK have generally been falling since the 1970s, and the rate of decline has accelerated since 1989 (Figure 11.10). Carbon monoxide (CO) is the most prevalent air pollutant. It can affect humans and animals and is harmful because it reduces the capacity of the blood to carry and deliver oxygen around the body. While the largest source of CO is road transport, smaller contributions come from the combustion of organic matter, for example in power stations and waste incineration. Emissions of carbon monoxide fell by 81 per cent between 1970 and 2006 and by around 72 per cent since 1990. The probable reason for this was that exhaust emissions standards were introduced for petrol cars in the early 1990s, which in most cases meant fitting a catalytic converter to reduce pollutants from car exhausts.

Figure 11.10

Emissions of selected air pollutants[1]

United Kingdom
Million tonnes

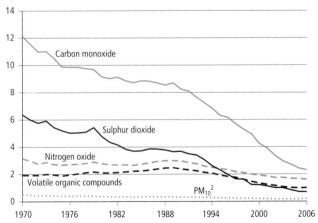

1 See Appendix, Part 11: Air pollutants.
2 Particulate matter that is less than 10 microns in diameter.

Source: Department for Environment, Food and Rural Affairs; AEA Energy and Environment

Sulphur dioxide (SO_2) is an acid gas that can affect both human and animal health, and vegetation. It affects the lining of the nose, throat and lungs, particularly among those with asthma and chronic lung disease, and is one of the pollutants that form 'acid rain' leading to the destruction of crops and forests in the UK and elsewhere. UK emissions are dominated by combustion of fuels such as coal and heavy oils in power stations and refineries. In some parts of the UK, notably Northern Ireland, coal is a significant source of energy for domestic use. SO_2 emissions fell by 81 per cent between 1990 and 2006, largely as a result of the reduction in coal use by power stations. Following this change, the rate of decline slowed after 1999.

Nitrogen oxides (NO_x) are also acid gases that have similar effects to sulphur dioxide. Road transport is the main source of NO_x, followed by the electricity supply industry and other industrial and commercial sectors. Emissions of NO_x pollutants fell by 46 per cent between 1990 and 2006, again mainly as a result of catalytic converters being fitted on petrol cars and reductions in emissions from large combustion plants.

Particulate matter is derived from both human-made and natural sources (such as sea spray and Saharan dust). Particulate matter consists of very small liquid and solid particles floating in the air. Of great concern to public health are the particles small enough to be inhaled into the deepest parts of the lung. In the UK the biggest human-made sources are fuel combustion and transport. Total emissions of particulate matter fell by 50 per cent between 1990 and 2006, partly because of the reduction in emissions from power stations, the installation of abatement equipment and increased efficiency and use of natural gas for electricity generation.

Another major pollutant in the air is ozone, which can cause respiratory problems. Ozone is not emitted directly into the atmosphere but is a secondary pollutant, produced by reactions between nitrogen dioxide, hydrocarbons and sunlight. Ozone levels are usually high in rural areas, particularly in hot, still, sunny weather conditions, giving rise to 'summer smog'. Rural ozone levels in the UK averaged 67 micrograms per cubic metre in 2007, compared with 74 micrograms per cubic metre in 2006 and 68 micrograms per cubic metre in 1993. Urban background ozone levels were 57 micrograms per cubic metre in 2007 compared with 61 micrograms per cubic metre in 2006 and 42 micrograms per cubic metre in 1993. The decreased ozone in 2007 was probably because the summer was cooler than the hot summer of 2006.

Pollution incidents of the air, water and land are monitored by the Environment Agency. There are four categories of pollution

Table 11.11

Serious pollution incidents:[1] by source

England & Wales					Numbers
	2000	2001	2005	2006	2007
Waste management facilities	230	485	151	124	159
Other industry	242	241	115	107	118
Sewage and water industry	156	181	166	141	104
Agriculture	256	226	130	85	72
Domestic	49	81	45	41	33
Transport	101	68	27	24	19
Other[2]	258	572	356	388	322
Total incidents	1,292	1,854	990	910	827

1 Serious pollution incidents that fall within Categories 1 and 2.
  See Appendix, Part 11: Pollution incidents.
2 Includes pollution incidents that cannot easily be categorised in any of
  the above, for example abandoned mines, recreation and sports, and
  catering and accommodation.

Source: Environment Agency

incidents of which two are deemed serious. Category 1 incidents, classified as 'most severe', are defined as those that have a persistent and/or extensive effect on quality of the air, land or water. They may cause major damage to the ecosystem; cause major damage to agriculture and/or commerce; or have a serious impact on the human population. Category 2 incidents, classified as 'severe', have similar but less serious effects (see Appendix, Part 11: Pollution incidents).

In 2007 the Environment Agency recorded 827 Category 1 or Category 2 incidents overall in England and Wales, a fall of 36 per cent since 2000 and 9 per cent since 2006 (Table 11.11). Of these serious incidents, 522 were water pollution, 222 land pollution and 151 air pollution (some of these incidents can be pollution to more than one medium). The main causes of these incidents were failures of containment and control including leaks or spillage of polluting substances. All sectors that can be categorised showed a decrease in the number of serious incidents since 2000, with transport and agriculture incidents showing the largest falls (81 per cent and 72 per cent respectively). The highest number of serious incidents recorded in 2007 was in the waste management facility sector where there were 159 incidents. Although this was nearly one-third (31 per cent) fewer incidents than in 2000, the number of incidents in waste management facilities has fluctuated markedly in the years between 2000 and 2007, with 485 serious incidents in 2001 and 124 in 2006. Specific waste materials, which include asbestos, household rubbish and vehicle parts, were involved in 17 per cent of serious pollution

incidents in 2007. The second most common pollutant was sewage, which was found at 15 per cent of serious incidents.

The quality of water is monitored at recognised bathing areas inland and at the coast. In 2007, almost 21,400 bathing places in the EU-27 countries were monitored under the EC Bathing Water Directive (76/160/EEC) during the bathing season (see Appendix, Part 11: Bathing waters). Of these 14,550 were coastal bathing waters and 6,820 were inland bathing waters. Overall, 95 per cent of coastal bathing waters in the EU-27 complied with the mandatory standards of the directive, and 86 per cent complied with the more stringent guideline standards (Table 11.12 overleaf). Nearly nine in ten (89 per cent) inland bathing waters complied with the mandatory standards of the directive and more than six in ten (63 per cent) complied with the guideline standards. When looking at the compliance rates of individual member states it must be noted that for some countries only a small number of bathing waters were tested, so their rates are not as reliable as for other countries. Compliance with the mandatory standards for coastal waters was highest in Finland, the Netherlands and Latvia (100 per cent). The UK had a mandatory compliance rate of 97 per cent. The lowest rate was in Romania (29 per cent). Cyprus had the highest rate for compliance in coastal waters with the guideline standards of the directive (99 per cent), while 76 per cent of UK coastal bathing places complied. Only 11 inland waters in the UK were monitored as bathing areas: all complied with the mandatory guidelines and five of them (45 per cent) met the more stringent guideline standards.

Global warming and climate change

Climate change is in the news. It refers to the long-term change in the patterns of average weather, temperature and wind and rainfall. Before the industrial revolution, climate was influenced entirely by natural events and processes, for example, large volcanic eruptions, tropical storms and variations in ocean currents. Over the last 100 years, when human activity has added to natural effects, the Earth has warmed by around 0.7 degrees Celsius (°C) and since the 1970s by around 0.4°C.

In 2007 the fourth Intergovernmental Panel on Climate Change (IPCC) Assessment Report stated that the warming of the climate and the role of human activities in this were unequivocal, and that the world would warm further as a result of past emissions alone. The panel also concluded that without effective international efforts, greenhouse gas emissions will continue to grow rapidly. On current projections, this would result in the climate warming by between 1.7°C and 4.0°C by 2100, depending on the continued levels of

Table 11.12

Bathing water quality: EU comparison,[1] 2007

Percentages

	Inland waters			Coastal waters		
	Number of bathing waters tested	Guideline compliance	Mandatory compliance	Number of bathing waters tested	Guideline compliance	Mandatory compliance
Finland	266	78.6	97.4	99	57.6	100.0
Netherlands	555	58.4	97.3	86	90.7	100.0
Latvia	232	78.4	94.8	46	84.8	100.0
Greece	6	50.0	66.7	2,049	95.5	99.5
Spain	174	37.9	87.4	1,901	88.7	99.1
Cyprus	.	.	.	100	99.0	99.0
Belgium	75	44.0	77.3	40	50.0	97.5
Ireland	9	66.7	100.0	122	81.1	96.7
United Kingdom	11	45.5	100.0	573	76.4	96.5
France	1,339	53.7	92.4	1,897	77.7	95.7
Malta	.	.	.	87	89.7	95.4
Sweden	441	68.3	95.5	406	63.1	95.1
Portugal	92	43.5	93.5	427	86.7	94.6
Germany	1,588	76.6	92.1	351	80.3	93.7
Lithuania	70	47.1	98.6	15	60.0	93.3
Denmark	113	84.1	96.5	1,158	80.9	92.9
Italy	777	55.3	65.6	4,929	91.7	92.9
Estonia	38	68.4	97.4	34	41.2	91.2
Bulgaria	3	100.0	100.0	89	76.4	89.9
Poland	257	42.4	79.4	89	33.7	80.9
Slovenia	18	33.3	88.9	19	68.4	68.4
Romania	..	..	..	35	2.9	28.6
Austria	268	72.8	97.8	.	.	.
Slovakia	38	76.3	86.8	.	.	.
Luxembourg	20	45.0	85.0	.	.	.
Hungary	238	53.8	79.0	.	.	.
Czech Republic	188	54.3	72.9	.	.	.
EU-27	6,816	62.6	88.7	14,552	86.1	95.2

1 During the bathing season. Bathing areas insufficiently sampled or not sampled according to the Bathing Water Directive 76/160/EEC are not included. See Appendix, Part 11: Bathing waters.

Source: Eurostat

emissions. Globally this will mean intense heat waves, droughts and flooding, and in some parts of the world this will cause food shortages and disease. For the UK, climate change means warmer, drier summers with many more heat waves. These will be accompanied by milder, wetter winters, higher sea levels and increased risk of flooding to coastal areas.

The main human influence on the global climate is emission of the key greenhouse gases – carbon dioxide (CO_2), methane (CH_4) and nitrous oxide (N_2O). The accumulation of these gases in the Earth's atmosphere strengthens the greenhouse effect, causing heat from the sun to be trapped near the Earth's surface.

Figure 11.13

Source of greenhouse gas emissions:[1] by selected UK sector[2]

United Kingdom

Million tonnes of carbon dioxide equivalent

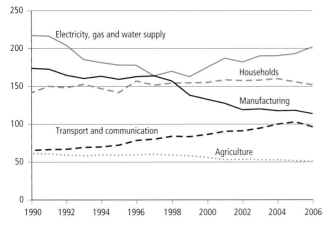

1 Carbon dioxide, methane, nitrous oxide, hydrofluorocarbons, perfluorocarbon and sulphur hexafluoride expressed as million tonnes of carbon dioxide equivalent.
2 Data from Office for National Statistics' Environmental Accounts. See Appendix, Part 11: Environmental Accounts.

Source: Office for National Statistics; AEA Energy and Environment

According to the Office for National Statistics' Environmental Accounts (see Appendix, Part 11: Environmental Accounts), greenhouse gas emissions from households accounted for one-fifth (20.9 per cent) of all emissions in the UK in 2006. All other sectors in the economy accounted for four-fifths (79.1 per cent). The largest source was the electricity, gas and water supply industry, which contributed around 27.8 per cent of all emissions (201 million tonnes of CO_2 equivalent) (Figure 11.13). Emissions from this sector rose by 4.5 per cent between 2005 and 2006, continuing an upward trend since the late 1990s, but were still 7.2 per cent less in 2006 than they had been in 1990. The other main non-household contributors were the manufacturing industry, which emitted 15.7 per cent (114 million tonnes of CO_2 equivalent) of emissions, and the transport and communications industry, which emitted 13.3 per cent (96 million tonnes of CO_2 equivalent). Since 1990, emissions from the manufacturing industry fell 34.6 per cent, from 174 million tonnes. However, greenhouse gas emissions from the transport and communication industry rose by almost one-half (47.0 per cent) since 1990, from around 66 million tonnes of CO_2 equivalent. This rise mainly reflects increases in emissions from the UK-owned air transport industry and sea transport industry. Greenhouse gas emissions from the UK-owned air industry more than doubled from 2.5 per cent in 1990 to 6.0 per cent in 2006. Over the same period the proportion of greenhouse gas emissions from agriculture changed very little, accounting for between 7.0 per cent and

8.0 per cent of emissions. One of the main greenhouse gases emitted from the agriculture sector is methane, mainly from ruminant stock, such as cows. Agriculture accounts for 37 per cent of all methane emissions.

Households were responsible for greenhouse gas emissions totalling 152 million tonnes of CO_2 equivalent in 2006, a fall of 2.5 per cent since 2005 but 7.2 per cent higher than in 1990. Taking all sectors together, most of the reduction in total greenhouse gas emissions occurred between 1990 and 1999, when they fell by 10.1 per cent. However, since 1999 the total has decreased by just 0.4 per cent.

Under the 1997 Kyoto Protocol, the UK has a legally binding target to reduce its emissions of a 'basket' of six greenhouse gases by 12.5 per cent over the period 2008 to 2012. This reduction is against 1990 emission levels for CO_2, CH_4 and N_2O, and 1995 levels for hydrofluorocarbons (HFCs), perfluorocarbons (PFCs) and sulphur hexafluoride (SF_6) – see Appendix, Part 11: Global warming and climate change. Additionally, in October 2008, the Government announced that the UK was committed to cutting the basket of greenhouse gas emissions by 80 per cent on 1990 levels by 2050. The Government also intends to move towards a goal of reducing CO_2 emissions to 20 per cent below 1990 levels by 2010. In 2007 emissions of the basket of six greenhouse gases, weighted by global warming potential were at their lowest compared with the 1990 base year level, at 639 million tonnes of CO_2 equivalent, a fall of around 17 per cent (Figure 11.14). CO_2 is the main greenhouse gas and accounted for around

Figure 11.14

Emissions of greenhouse gases[1]

United Kingdom

Million tonnes of carbon dioxide equivalent

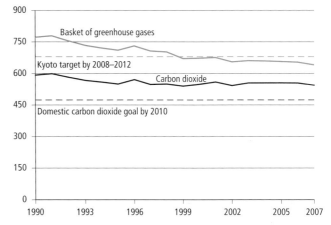

1 See Appendix, Part 11: Global warming and climate change.

Source: Department for Environment, Food and Rural Affairs; AEA Energy and Environment

11

Figure 11.15

Difference in average surface temperature: deviation from 1961–90 average[1]

Global and Central England[2]
Degrees Celsius

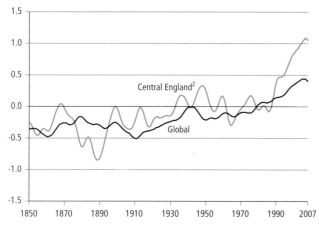

1 Data are smoothed to remove short-term variation from the time series to get a clearer view of the underlying changes. See, Appendix, Part 11: Average temperatures.
2 Central England temperature is representative of a roughly triangular area of the UK enclosed by Bristol, Lancashire and London.

Source: Hadley Centre for Climate Prediction and Research

85 per cent of total emissions in 2006. Estimates for 2007 were net emissions of CO_2 of 543.7 million tonnes, 2 per cent lower than in 2006. This decrease was partly explained by the switch from coal to natural gas in electricity generation, and by a lower use of fossil fuel by both households and industry. However, in 2007 CO_2 emissions were an estimated 70 million tonnes above the 2010 domestic target of 473.7 tonnes.

Both global and local (in 'Central England' a triangular area enclosed by Bristol, Lancashire and London) average surface temperatures have risen since the late 19th century, although there have been fluctuations around this trend (Figure 11.15). During the 20th century the annual mean temperature for Central England warmed by about 1.0°C. The 1990s were exceptionally warm, about 0.6°C warmer than the 1961–90 average temperature (see Appendix, Part 11: Average temperatures). This trend continued into the 21st century and the warmest year ever measured in Central England was 2006, with an annual average temperature of 10.8°C (1.3°C above the average) followed by 1990 (1.2°C above the average); 2007 was the joint tenth warmest year on record along with 1959 and 2004 (1.0°C above the average).

Over the last century, global surface temperatures increased by 0.3°C to 0.6°C, beyond the range of estimated average temperatures experienced on Earth over the last 1,000 years. The last time global temperatures were below the 1961–90 average was in 1986 (0.06°C below the average). Since then

surface temperatures have continued to rise across the world.

Average annual rainfall across the UK varies enormously from around 5,000 millimetres in parts of the western highlands of Scotland to around 500 millimetres in parts of the East of England and the Thames estuary. Overall, the wettest areas are in the western half of the country because they are nearest to the normal track of rain-bearing depressions and contain the most mountainous parts of the UK. On average, rainfall across the UK is distributed fairly evenly through the year, but summer rainfall was greater than winter rainfall for extended periods during the 19th century in England and Wales (Figure 11.16). In contrast, in the 20th century and particularly since the 1960s, there has been a tendency towards wetter winters and drier summers. Between 1995 and 2004, winter rainfall on average exceeded summer rainfall by between 80 and 100 millimetres, the greatest margin in records stretching back to 1766. However, dry winters in 2004/05 and 2005/06 resulted in severe drought conditions. Although the 2006/07 winter rainfall was well within the normal range, the May to July 2007 rainfall total was the highest in the 241-year England and Wales rainfall series and triggered widespread and severe flooding.

The warming temperatures of the 20th century over Central England resulted in the growing season (a period of time each year during which plants can grow) generally becoming longer. The thermal growing season is defined as beginning when the temperature exceeds 5.5°C in spring on five consecutive days

Figure 11.16

Winter and summer rainfall[1,2]

England & Wales
Millimetres

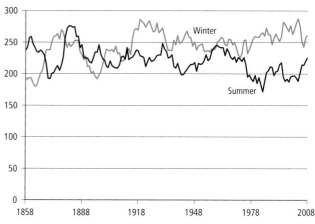

1 Figures are ten-year rolling averages ending in year shown.
2 Winter is December to February, summer is June to August.

Source: Climate Research Unit, University of East Anglia; Hadley Centre for Climate Prediction and Research; Centre for Ecology & Hydrology (Wallingford)

Figure 11.17

Length of the thermal growing season: deviation from the 1961–90 average[1]

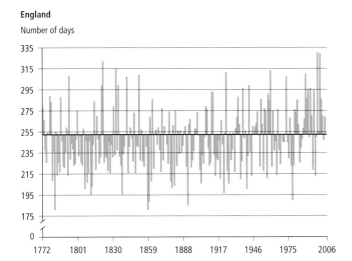

England

Number of days

1 The 1961–90 average was 252 days.

Source: Department for Environment, Food and Rural Affairs

and ending when the temperature is below 5.5°C on five consecutive days in autumn/winter. Figure 11.17 looks at the length of the growing season in England in relation to the 1961–90 average of 252 days. Between 1920 and 1960 the growing season increased by an average 0.7 days per year

because of the early onset of spring and the late onset of winter. Since 1980 the growing season has increased by an average of 1.7 days per year because of the early onset of spring but with no change in the onset of winter. The earliest start of the thermal growing season was in 2002, which began on 13 January, while the longest growing season was in 2000, which consisted of 330 days. In contrast the shortest growing seasons were 181 days in 1782 and 1859.

Countryside, farming and wildlife

Across the UK there is considerable variety in how agricultural land is used (see Appendix, Part 11: Land use). In 2007, the English region with the most land used for agricultural purposes (1.9 million hectares) was the South West, where more than one-half (51 per cent) was permanent grass (Table 11.18). Second was the East (1.4 million hectares) where around 70 per cent of land was either under crops or bare fallow. This region also had the largest proportion of set-aside land in the UK (7 per cent) (see Appendix, Part 11: Set-aside land). After London, the North East had the smallest area of land used for agricultural purposes (0.6 million hectares), 40 per cent of which was permanent grass. Scotland had 6.2 million hectares of agricultural land of which 65 per cent was rough grazing. Wales and Northern Ireland had 1.5 million hectares and

Table 11.18

Agricultural land use:[1] by region, 2007

United Kingdom   Percentages

	Crops and bare fallow	Temporary grass	Permanent grass	Rough grazing	Woodland	Set-aside	All other land	All agricultural land (=100%) (thousand hectares)
England	42	7	36	6	3	4	2	9,291
North East	26	5	40	22	3	3	1	587
North West	12	10	58	16	2	1	1	919
Yorkshire and the Humber	46	5	31	10	2	4	2	1,091
East Midlands	60	5	24	3	2	5	2	1,230
West Midlands	37	9	44	2	3	3	2	959
East	70	2	13	2	4	7	3	1,428
London	34	6	40	4	6	5	5	13
South East	43	7	34	2	6	5	3	1,195
South West	26	11	51	4	4	2	2	1,869
Wales	5	7	69	14	5	-	1	1,460
Scotland	9	5	15	65	5	1	1	6,192
Northern Ireland	5	12	66	14	1	-	1	1,015

1 For definitions of categories, see Appendix, Part 11: Land use.

Source: Department for Environment, Food and Rural Affairs; Scottish Government

11

1.0 million hectares of agricultural land respectively, and around two-thirds was permanent grassland (69 per cent and 66 per cent respectively).

In 2007 the UK produced 19.0 million tonnes of cereals on 2.9 million hectares of land. This was a fall in production of 8.5 per cent from 2006, mainly because of the hot dry spring, followed by lack of sunshine and persistent wet weather between May and July, which caused increased incidences of disease, delays to harvesting and, in a small number of cases, a total loss of crops. Other arable crops such as oil seed rape, sugar beet and hops were grown on 1.2 million hectares. Potatoes and horticulture, including vegetables, fruits, and plants and flowers, were grown on 0.3 million hectares.

Organic farming is a form of agriculture that largely excludes the use of synthetic fertilisers and pesticides, plant growth regulators, and livestock feed additives. As far as possible, organic farmers rely on crop rotation, crop residues, animal manures and mechanical cultivation to maintain soil productivity, supply plant nutrients and control weeds, insects and pests. In January 2007 around 499,000 hectares (almost 3 per cent of total agricultural land) in the UK were fully organic, and a further 121,000 hectares were being converted to organically managed land (Figure 11.19). This was a considerable rise since 1994 when around 28,000 hectares were fully organic, and around 3,000 hectares were in conversion. The total area of organically managed land peaked in 2003 as some farmers sought alternatives to conventional farming in response to falling farm incomes and increases in the payment rates

under organic farming support schemes. Since 2003 organically managed land has declined, although there was very little change between 2006 and 2007. England had the largest area of organically managed land in the UK, which includes land in conversion, with 296,000 hectares (48 per cent of the UK total), followed by Scotland with 235,000 hectares (38 per cent), Wales with 79,000 hectares (13 per cent), and Northern Ireland with 9,000 hectares (1 per cent).

Food self-sufficiency is calculated as the farm-gate value of raw food production divided by the total value of raw food for human consumption. The UK has not been self-sufficient in food for more than 150 years. Before the 1830s the UK was around 90 to 100 per cent self-sufficient in food except at times of poor harvests. By around the 1870s the UK was around 60 per cent self-sufficient and this fell to around 40 per cent by the start of the First World War. In the 1930s self-sufficiency was at a low of around 30 to 40 per cent, before rising again after the Second World War. In 2007 the UK was around 61 per cent self-sufficient in all food and 74 per cent in indigenous-type food (Figure 11.20). This was a slight rise of 1 percentage point and 2 percentage points respectively since 2006, a result of the increased value of home-produced milk, oil seed rape and cereals. However, this was a fall of 11 percentage points and 9 percentage points since 1988. The recent decline in self-sufficiency reflects a lack of export growth after 1994 and a tailing off of agricultural output. There are various factors causing this downward trend. Long-term factors include the changing tastes of the general public towards more exotic and varied food, the low level of

Figure 11.19

Organically managed land[1]

United Kingdom

Thousand hectares

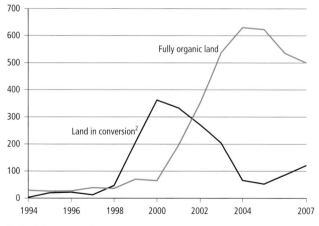

1 As at January each year.
2 Converting land to organic production can take two to three years.

Source: Department for Environment, Food and Rural Affairs

Figure 11.20

Self-sufficiency in food production[1]

United Kingdom

Percentages

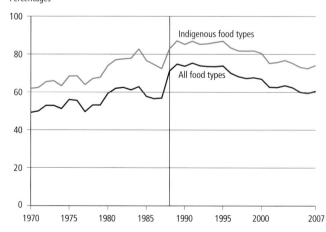

1 In 1998 a new methodology was used that revised data from 1970 to 1988. See Appendix, Part 11: Self-sufficiency in food.

Source: Department for Environment, Food and Rural Affairs

trade restrictions, generally cheap transport and communication and the wide sourcing by large buyers, like supermarkets. Short-term factors include the ban on UK beef in 1996 following an outbreak of bovine spongiform encephalopathy (BSE), which affected home consumption, foot-and-mouth disease in 2001, which further affected both production and consumption, and reforms to the Common Agricultural Policy (CAP) in 1993 and 1999 that ended the expansionist trends of the 1970s and 1980s.

Wild bird populations are good indicators of the general state of the environment, as they have a wide range of habitats and tend to be at, or near to, the top of the food chain. The size of the total population of the UK's breeding bird species has been relatively stable over the last 37 years. However, the trends for different species groups vary. The steepest decline has been in the population of farmland species, of which there are 19 different species. In 2007 they were at their lowest level, at around one-half (52 per cent) of their 1970 level (Figure 11.21). Some farmland species such as the goldfinch and the stock dove have recovered from large declines in the 1980s, and farmland generalists such as the wood pigeon and jackdaw, have maintained their populations. The birds most at risk are those that feed mainly or solely on farmland, such as the tree sparrow, corn bunting, turtle dove and grey partridge, whose populations have declined by more than 50 per cent since 1970.

Figure 11.21

Population of wild birds:[1] by species group

United Kingdom
Index numbers (1970=100)

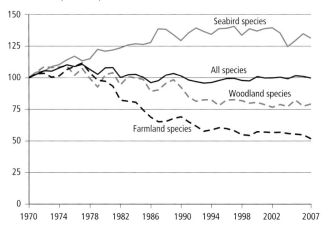

1 It was not possible to complete the Breeding Birds Survey in 2001 because of restrictions imposed during the outbreak of foot-and-mouth disease. Estimates for that year are based on the average for 2000 and 2002 for individual species. See Appendix, Part 11: Wild bird species.

Source: British Trust for Ornithology; Royal Society for the Protection of Birds; Department for Environment, Food and Rural Affairs

The woodland bird population, of which there are 38 species, was around 21 per cent lower in 2007 than in the early 1970s, with the main decrease taking place in the late 1980s and early 1990s. This was probably because of changes in woodland structure, which includes the different kinds of trees, the increase in woodland age and a reduction in active woodland management. Increasing numbers of deer have also affected woodland bird numbers as they browse their way through the forest undergrowth on which the birds depend for food and nest sites. Birds that breed or feed mainly in woodland, such as the lesser redpoll, spotted flycatcher, willow tit and tree pipit, showed the greatest declines in population of all woodland birds. However, populations of other woodland species, such as the great spotted woodpecker, nuthatch, blackcap and green woodpecker have more than doubled since 1970.

Since 1970 seabird populations have increased by around 31 per cent with the great skua, razorbill and northern gannet doubling in number. However, populations of some of the 19 seabird species, such as the herring gull, arctic skua and kittiwake, declined over the period. According to a study by the Centre for Ecology and Hydrology, the population of the Atlantic puffin declined by around 30 per cent on the Isle of May, in the Firth of Forth in Scotland in 2008; this had previously been one of the most successful breeding colonies on the North Sea. According to the report, the most likely explanation was that adult birds were starving to death during the winter and that they could be victims of declining fish stocks in the North Sea.

Fish are a traditional food resource and are a vital element of the ocean's ecosystem. The level of spawning stock (adult fish) biomass is used to determine whether the population of each stock is at a sustainable level. Historic trends in spawning stock biomass vary from species to species and stocks can fluctuate substantially over relatively short periods (Figure 11.22 overleaf). The main factor affecting this is the low number of juvenile fish entering the stock. Pollution of the sea is another factor, but this has a negligible overall impact because concentrations of contaminants in sea water are generally low.

To prevent over-exploitation, there must be a balance between fishing and the natural ability of fish stocks to regenerate. Most stocks have been over-fished at some time in their history. For example, the North Sea herring population was seriously depleted by over-fishing in the 1970s, leading to the closure of the fishery between 1978 and 1982 to allow recovery. The stock subsequently declined again to low levels during the 1990s, following a second period of excessive fishing and, more recently, following a number of years of low numbers of juvenile fish entering the stock. The North Sea cod spawning

11

stock has also been reduced to very low levels as a result of over-fishing. It decreased from 159,000 tonnes in 1964 to 31,000 tonnes in 2006, a decline of 80 per cent. It is currently increasing, following strong management actions, such as restrictions on the number of days boats are allowed to fish and the catches they can take. In 2007, cod spawning stock had increased to 37,000 tonnes, and at the beginning of 2009 spawning biomass is forecast to reach 70,000 tonnes. Overall in 2007, 36 per cent of 25 assessed fish stocks around the UK were categorised as being at full reproductive capacity and harvested in a sustainable way. Less than one-quarter (24 per cent) of the assessed stocks had spawning levels that were insufficient to guarantee stock replenishment and required rebuilding; examples are the Irish Sea and West of Scotland cod stocks. For such stocks that are considered at risk, management plans have been developed with the aim of recovering the spawning biomass to safe levels to ensure future sustainability.

Figure 11.22

North Sea fish stocks[1]

Thousand tonnes

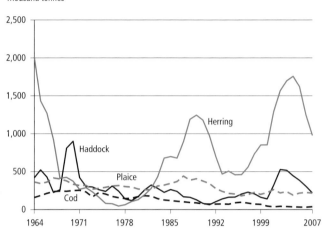

1 Spawning stock biomass (the total weight of all sexually mature fish in a population).

Source: Centre for Environment, Fisheries and Agriculture Science; International Council for the Exploration of the Sea

Chapter 12

Transport

- The total distance travelled by people in Great Britain increased by 95 per cent since 1971, to 817 billion passenger kilometres in 2007. (Table 12.1)

- The proportion of households with two cars in Great Britain increased from 6 per cent in 1971 to 27 per cent in 2007. (Figure 12.4)

- Motoring costs rose by 95 per cent between 1987 and 2008 in the UK, compared with a rise in the 'All items' retail prices index (RPI) of 110 per cent. (Figure 12.12)

- The average prices of premium unleaded petrol and diesel in the UK reached a peak in July 2008, at 119.6 pence per litre and 133.0 pence per litre respectively. (Figure 12.14)

- In Great Britain in 2007, 2,946 people died as a result of road accidents, a 7 per cent decrease from 2006, with deaths among car users decreasing by 11 per cent over the same period. (Page 185)

- There was a 52 per cent increase in the number of domestic passengers at UK airports between 1997 and 2007. (Table 12.20)

Long term trends have continued in many areas of transport and travel over the last ten years. Trends including the increase in the distance each person travels in a year, the rising number of cars on the roads and the ever-increasing reliance on the car as a means of transport. Overseas travel, particularly by air, increased substantially over the decade, though it still accounts for a very small proportion of total distance travelled. However, within these trends there are pronounced variations in people's travel patterns depending, for example, on their age, sex, where they live, their access to public transport or a private motor vehicle, and income.

Travel patterns

People in Great Britain travelled 817 billion passenger kilometres (508 billion passenger miles) in 2007 by road, rail and air (Table 12.1), almost double the 419 billion passenger kilometres travelled in 1971. Car and van travel accounts for the largest share of overall distance travelled, making up 84 per cent of all passenger kilometres travelled in 2007, a rise of 120 per cent from 1971.

There was a rapid increase in the distance travelled by car and van in the 1980s, but this changed to more gradual growth from the 1990s. The total distance travelled by car and van rose by an average of nearly 5 per cent a year in the 1980s compared with an annual average of 1 per cent between 1991 and 2007.

Table 12.1

Passenger transport: by mode

Great Britain					Billion passenger kilometres
	1971	1981	1991	2001	2007
Road[1]					
Car and van[2]	313	394	582	654	689
Bus and coach	60	48	44	47	50
Bicycle	4	5	5	4	4
Motorcycle	4	10	6	5	6
All road	381	458	637	710	749
Rail[3]	35	34	39	47	59
Air[4]	2	3	5	8	10
All modes	419	495	681	765	817

1 Road transport data from 1993 onwards are not directly comparable with earlier years. See Appendix, Part 12: Road traffic.
2 Includes taxis.
3 Data for rail relate to financial years (for example 1970/71).
4 Data for air are domestic flights only and include Northern Ireland, the Channel Islands and the Isle of Man.

Source: Department for Transport

Around one in seven (14 per cent) of all travel in 1971 was by bus and coach, accounting for 60 billion passenger kilometres. This declined to a low of 43 billion passenger kilometres in 1992 but has since risen to around 50 billion passenger kilometres in 2007, accounting for 6 per cent of all travel (see also the section on Public transport later in this chapter).

Although rail travel increased from 35 billion to 59 billion passenger kilometres between 1971 and 2007 it has fallen from 8 per cent to 7 per cent as a proportion of the total distance travelled. Travel by rail reached its lowest point in 1982 when 31 billion passenger kilometres were travelled, but six years later this had risen to 41 billion passenger kilometres. Rail travel declined again during the early to mid-1990s but there has been a steady increase in passenger kilometres throughout the late 1990s and into the new century. From 2000, the distance travelled by rail continued to rise steadily by an average of 3 per cent a year (see also the section on Public transport later in this chapter).

The distance travelled by domestic air flights in 2007 is five times that travelled in 1971, accounting for 10 billion passenger kilometres. Although air travel showed the fastest growth of any means of transport over the period, it represented only 1 per cent of the total domestic distance travelled in Great Britain in 2007 (see also the section on International travel at the end of this chapter).

In Great Britain an average 7,133 miles (11,479 kilometres) were travelled per person in 2006, 2 per cent more than in 1995–97 (Table 12.2). Car travel accounted for four-fifths of the total distance travelled in 2006 and this proportion has remained fairly stable since 1995–97. The second most common mode of transport used was rail, at 8 per cent of the total distance travelled (541 miles per person per year, including London Underground), a 2 per cent increase from 2005 and a 42 per cent increase from 1995–97.

The average distance travelled per person by bus in Great Britain decreased by 3 per cent in 2006 to 453 miles from the 1995–97 total of 468 miles. However, in 2003 the average distance travelled per person by bus rose to 512 miles, making up 7 per cent of the total distance travelled during that year. Walking accounted for almost 3 per cent of the total distance travelled per person per year in 2006, the same proportion as for other modes of transport, which included travel by taxi, motorcycle, air and ferries.

The number of trips made, distance travelled and time spent travelling by all modes of transport varies according to whether a household owns a car. In 2006 people from car owning

Table 12.2

Average distance travelled:[1] by mode

Great Britain   Miles

	1995–97	1998–2000	2003	2005	2006
Car driver[2]	3,623	3,725	3,660	3,682	3,660
Car passenger[2]	2,082	2,086	2,098	2,063	2,033
Walk[3]	200	198	201	197	201
Bus[4]	468	474	512	476	453
Rail[5]	380	467	452	528	541
Bicycle	43	40	37	36	39
Other[6]	184	174	231	225	206
All modes	6,981	7,164	7,192	7,208	7,133

1 Average distance travelled per person per year. See Appendix, Part 12:
  National Travel Survey.
2 Includes van drivers and passengers.
3 Short walks were believed to be under-recorded in 2002 and 2003
  compared with other years.
4 Includes private hire buses, local and non-local buses and London
  buses.
5 Includes London Underground.
6 Includes taxi/minicab, motorcycle/moped, other private vehicles,
  domestic air and ferries, light rail.

Source: National Travel Survey, Department for Transport

Figure 12.3

Distance travelled per person: by household income quintile group[1] and mode of transport, 2006

Great Britain

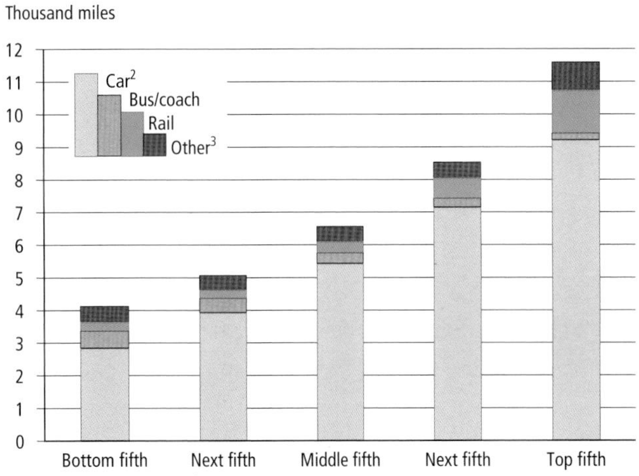

Thousand miles

1 Households are ranked according to their income and then divided into
  five groups of equal size. The bottom fifth, or bottom quintile group,
  is then the 20 per cent of households with the lowest incomes. See
  Chapter 5: Income and wealth, Analysing income distribution text box.
2 Either driver or passenger.
3 Includes walking, cycling, taxi/minicab, motorcycle/moped, other private
  vehicles, domestic air and ferries, light rail.

Source: National Travel Survey, Department for Transport

households in Great Britain made an average of 41 per cent more trips by any mode of transport than those from households without a car. People from car owning households travelled more than two and a half times the distance than those households without a car over the year. However, in 2006 people in households without a car made more than four and one-half times as many trips by bus or coach, three and one-half times as many by taxi, and two-thirds more trips on foot than people in households with a car.

People in car owning households who have a full driving licence, but who are not the main driver of the household, made 18 per cent fewer trips in 2006 than the main driver and travelled around 78 per cent of the distance travelled by the main driver. Non-drivers in car owning households made 18 per cent more trips than people in non-car owning households, they also travelled further, with around two-thirds (62 per cent) more mileage than people in non-car owning households.

Car travel accounts for the greatest proportion of distance travelled in every income quintile group (see Chapter 5: Income and wealth, Analysing income distribution text box on page 66). The total distance travelled per person per year increases as household income increases (Figure 12.3). In Great Britain in 2006 people in the lowest income quintile group (or bottom fifth) travelled an average 2,838 miles (4,566 kilometres) by car, accounting for 69 per cent of the average distance they travelled.

In comparison, people in the highest income quintile group (or top fifth) travelled an average 9,213 miles by car, accounting for 80 per cent of the average distance they travelled.

As income levels increase, distance travelled by bus or coach decreases: 13 per cent of the distance travelled by people in the lowest income quintile group was by bus and coach compared with 2 per cent travelled by those in the highest income group. Conversely, the number of miles travelled per person by rail increased with income. In 2006 individuals in the lowest income quintile group travelled an average 276 miles by rail while those in the highest income quintile group travelled 1,297 miles, representing 7 per cent and 11 per cent of the distance travelled by each group respectively.

Car travel in 2006 also accounted for the greatest proportion of trips made by individuals in each income quintile group in Great Britain, and this proportion rose as income increased. In 2006, 46 per cent of trips made by people in the lowest income quintile group were by car compared with 71 per cent by those in the highest income quintile group. As with distance travelled, individuals in the lowest income quintile group made more trips by bus or coach than those in the highest income quintile group (13 per cent compared with 3 per cent). Trips made by rail increased considerably as income increased: 14 trips per person in the lowest income quintile group were made by rail compared with 61 trips made by those in the highest income quintile group.

Motor vehicles

The proportion of households in Great Britain with one car has remained stable from the early 1970s to 2007, at around 45 per cent over the period (Figure 12.4). However, the proportion of households with no car more than halved, from 48 per cent in 1971 to 23 per cent in 2007, while the proportion of households with two cars increased more than fourfold, from 6 per cent to 27 per cent over the period. The proportion of households with three or more cars also steadily increased to 6 per cent in 2007, an increase of 5 percentage points from 1971. See Appendix, Part 12: Car ownership.

People living in urban areas have better access to more frequent public transport than people living in rural areas, making it easier for them to manage without a car (see Appendix, Part 12: Area type classification). In 2007, 43 per cent of households in London did not own or have access to a car compared with 31 per cent in other built-up metropolitan areas and 10 per cent in rural areas. Around one-half (51 per cent) of households in rural areas had access to two or more cars compared with one-sixth (16 per cent) in London and more than one-quarter (27 per cent) in other metropolitan areas.

The availability of a car is closely related to income. In 2007, 54 per cent of households in Great Britain in the bottom fifth of the income distribution (or lowest income quintile group) did

Figure 12.4

Households with regular use of a car[1]

Great Britain

Percentages

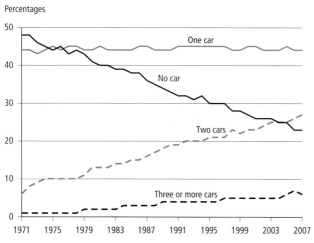

1 See Appendix, Part 12: Car ownership.

Source: General Household Survey (Longitudinal), Office for National Statistics

Figure 12.5

Household car availability: by household income quintile group,[1] 2007

Great Britain

Percentages

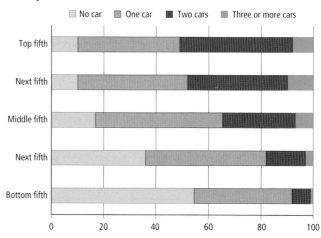

1 Households are ranked according to their income and then divided into five groups of equal size. The bottom fifth, or bottom quintile group, is then the 20 per cent of households with the lowest incomes. See Chapter 5: Income and wealth, Analysing income distribution text box.

Source: National Travel Survey, Department for Transport

not have a car, compared with 10 per cent in the top income quintile group (Figure 12.5). Nearly one-half of households in the second lowest and middle income quintile groups had one car (46 per cent and 49 per cent respectively) compared with nearly two-fifths of households in the lowest and highest income quintile groups (37 per cent and 39 per cent respectively). More than one-half of households in the top income quintile group had two or more cars (51 per cent). This proportion decreases as income decreases to reach 8 per cent among households in the bottom income quintile group.

Nearly one-half (47 per cent) of people aged 17 and over in the bottom income quintile group lived in households without a car compared with less than one in ten (7 per cent) of those in the highest income quintile group. Engine size and the age of household cars also vary by household income. Nearly one-fifth (19 per cent) of cars owned by households in the highest income quintile group in Great Britain in 2007 had engines of over 2000cc compared with nearly one in ten (9 per cent) in the lowest income quintile group. The higher the household income, the greater the likelihood of owning a new vehicle. In 2007, 10 per cent of cars owned by people in the highest income quintile group were less than a year old and 15 per cent were more than 10 years old. This compares with 4 per cent and 31 per cent respectively for cars owned by the lowest income quintile group.

Table 12.6

Average daily flow[1] of motor vehicles: by class of road[2]

Great Britain   Thousands

	1983	1988	1993	1998	2001	2007
Motorways	31.2	49.6	58.2	68.7	71.6	77.4
All 'A' roads	11.3	13.7	11.3	12.4	12.6	13.2
Urban major roads	17.2	19.4	19.2	20.2	20.1	20.0
Rural major roads	8.7	11.3	8.9	10.0	10.3	11.0
All major roads[3]	..	..	14.4	16.3	16.7	17.7
All minor roads	1.1	1.3	1.3	1.3	1.4	1.5
All roads	2.1	2.9	2.9	3.2	3.3	3.6

1 Flow at an average point on each class of road.
2 Motorways include trunk motorways and principal motorways. Urban major roads include roads in built up areas prior to 1993. Rural major roads include roads in non-built up areas prior to 1993. See Appendix, Part 12: Road traffic.
3 Includes all trunk and principal motorways and 'A' roads.

Source: National Road Traffic Survey, Department for Transport

Traffic growth varies according to the general level of activity in the economy. In the period between 1985 and 2007, the greatest growth in traffic was in the period of strong economic growth in the late 1980s, while there was little growth during the recession of the early 1990s. This was followed by a period of stronger growth in the mid to late 1990s. Between 1983 and 2007, average daily traffic flows increased by 71 per cent to 3,600 vehicles per day in Great Britain, averaged over all classes of road (Table 12.6). Motorways had the highest flow of vehicles, at 77,400 vehicles per day in 2007; this was nearly two and one-half times the flow in 1983 (31,200 vehicles). There were also large increases in traffic flow on major roads in rural areas during the same period (26 per cent), while the increase on urban major roads was 16 per cent.

There are certain factors affecting the daily flow of vehicles across Great Britain, such as regional population. In 2007, the average daily flow across all roads in England was 4,000 vehicles per day, twice the average for Scotland (2,000 vehicles per day) which was also lower than Wales (2,300 vehicles per day). The busiest motorways in 2007 were in the London Region, with an average flow of 97,400 vehicles per day. The quietest motorways were in Scotland, with an average daily flow of 44,300 vehicles. Motorways in Wales had an average daily flow of 67,400 vehicles. The busiest section of motorway in Great Britain in 2007 was the M25 western links from the A1(M) to the M23, with an average daily flow of 147,000 vehicles, and the quietest was the M74 between Glasgow and the Scottish border, averaging 35,000 vehicles per day.

More than 1.7 million car driving tests were taken in Great Britain in 2007/08, 49 per cent by men and 51 per cent by women. Although more women took the test the proportion of men who passed was higher, at 47 per cent compared with 41 per cent. For men and women aged 17 to 24 the pass rates were similar, at 49 per cent and 45 per cent respectively, with 594,243 tests being taken by men and 597,929 by women. Although more women take their driving test than men, the pass rates for men are consistently higher than those for women in all age groups, and the pass rates for both sexes fall as age increases (Figure 12.7). In 2007/08, 69 per cent more women than men took a driving test between the age of 50 to 59 (13,252 compared with 7,857) and 111 per cent more women aged between 60 and 69 (3,136 tests taken by women compared with 1,483 taken by men).

In Northern Ireland more than 65,000 people took their driving test in 2007/08, 47 per cent were men and 53 per cent were women. As in Great Britain, men were more likely to pass than women, particularly in the older age groups; 51 per cent of men under the age of 25 passed the test compared with 43 per cent of women while for those aged 45 and over, 49 per cent of men passed compared with 39 per cent of women.

The number of young adults holding full car driving licences in Great Britain has decreased since the early 1990s, although this

Figure 12.7

Car driving test pass and failure rates:[1] by sex and age, 2007/08

Great Britain

Percentages

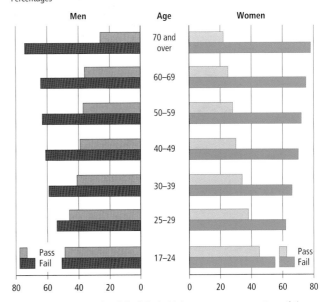

1 People who passed or failed their driving test as a proportion of those in each age group who took a test.

Source: Driving Standards Agency

trend has reversed in recent years. In 2007, 38 per cent of those aged 17 to 20 held a licence, compared with 27 per cent in 2004 and 32 per cent in 2005. There has been a large increase in the proportion of older women holding a driving licence. Between 1995/97 and 2007 the proportion of women aged 60 to 69 holding licences increased from 45 per cent to 63 per cent, while for women aged 70 and over the increase was from 21 per cent to 36 per cent. Corresponding figures for men were 83 per cent to 87 per cent for those aged 60 to 69 and 65 per cent to 75 per cent for men aged 70 and over.

Public transport

In terms of the number of journeys taken, buses and coaches are the most widely used form of public transport. More than 4.9 billion passenger journeys in Great Britain were made by local bus in 2006/07, more than double the number of journeys made by rail. Two-fifths of the journeys on local buses took place in London. In Northern Ireland 68 million passenger journeys were made in 2006/07 (64 per cent on Ulsterbus and 36 per cent on the Metro).

In Great Britain, the trend in local bus use, measured by the number of passenger journeys, was generally downwards from 1976–77 and then started to increase from 1999/2000 (Figure 12.8). In terms of the overall distance travelled by buses on bus routes, the low point was reached nearly 15 years earlier in 1985/86, at 2.1 billion kilometres (1.3 billion miles). It then rose until the mid-1990s, when it stabilised at around 2.6 billion kilometres. However, in 2006/07 distance travelled

Figure 12.8

Bus travel[1]

Great Britain

Index numbers (1981–82=100)

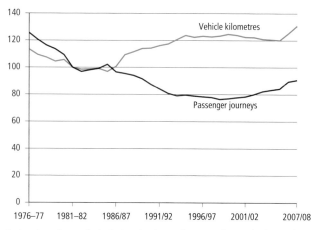

1 Local services only. Includes street-running trams but excludes modern 'supertram' systems. Financial years from 1985/86.

Source: Department for Transport

Table 12.9

Frequency and reliability of local buses[1]

Great Britain   Percentages

	2002	2004	2006
Frequency of local buses			
Frequent[2]	77	75	78
Neither frequent nor infrequent	8	9	8
Infrequent[2]	15	16	14
Reliability of local buses			
Reliable[2]	80	77	80
Neither reliable nor unreliable	6	8	8
Unreliable[2]	14	15	13

1 Respondents were asked 'How would you rate the frequency of local buses' and 'How would you rate the reliability of local buses'. Those who did not use buses, had no local service or no opinion are excluded.
2 Data are for those who responded 'very' or 'fairly' for each statement.

Source: National Travel Survey, Department for Transport

by bus rose to 2.7 billion kilometres in Great Britain. In Northern Ireland 70 million kilometres were travelled by bus in 2006/07, a rise of 3 per cent from 2005/06.

The distance people live from their nearest bus stop affects how much they use buses. In 2007, 86 per cent of households in Great Britain lived within six minutes walk of a bus stop and of those, 29 per cent travelled by bus at least once a week compared with 14 per cent of those living 14 minutes or more away from their nearest bus stop.

People in households in Great Britain were asked to rate the frequency and reliability of their local buses through the National Travel Survey, conducted by the Department for Transport. Findings show that since 2002 the proportion of households rating their local bus service as very/fairly frequent or reliable remained reasonably constant, between three-quarters and four-fifths for both indicators (Table 12.9). However, the proportion of households rating their local bus service as very frequent increased from 22 per cent in 2002 to 28 per cent in 2006. Over the same period the proportion of households rating their local service as very/fairly infrequent or unreliable also remained relatively unchanged, at one in seven.

Travel on local buses is most common among people aged under 30 and those aged 60 and over, partly reflecting the lower proportions of driving licence holders in these age groups compared with those aged 30 to 59. In 2007, more than one-half (51 per cent) of 17 to 20-year-olds reported using a local bus at least once a week, compared with

32 per cent of people aged 21 to 29, 31 per cent of those aged 60 to 69, and 36 per cent of those aged 70 and over.

The *Transport Act 2000* required all local authorities to provide assistance with bus fares to a minimum standard of one-half fare for women aged 60 and over, men aged 65 and over (lowered to aged 60 since April 2003) and disabled persons. From 1 April 2006, free local concessionary bus travel was introduced in England for disabled passengers and those aged 60 and over. In 2007 the take-up rate for the scheme in England was 68 per cent, an increase of 5 percentage points from the previous year. There was variation by area type, with take-up ranging from 49 per cent in rural areas to 85 per cent in London. However, this gap is narrowing as take-up has increased more among rural residents than in other areas.

Since April 2008, residents in England who are aged 60 and over or who are 'eligible disabled' are entitled to a free annual bus pass giving free off-peak travel on local buses anywhere in England. Off-peak travel is between 9.30 am and 11 pm Monday to Friday and all day at weekends and on public holidays. In Wales, residents who are aged 60 and over are entitled to a free bus pass, which can be used at any time of

the day, to travel on all local bus services in Wales. Scotland offers free bus passes as in Wales for residents who are aged 60 and over and for those who qualify on the grounds of disability, which also includes free travel on scheduled long distance coach services within Scotland. In Northern Ireland residents aged 65 and over can travel on buses for free with a Senior SmartPass. In October 2008 this scheme was extended to residents aged 60 to 64.

The number of passenger journeys made on Great Britain's railway network (including underground and metro systems) rose by 300 million between 2005/06 and 2007/08 to 2.5 billion, an increase of 13 per cent (Table 12.10). Between 2006/07 and 2007/08 the increase in journeys was 6 per cent (146 million). In Northern Ireland, passenger journeys increased by 1.8 million (23 per cent) between 2005/06 and 2007/08 and by one million (12 per cent) between 2006/07 and 2007/08.

In Great Britain there were around 1.3 billion rail passenger journeys per year in the early 1980s and, apart from a period in the early 1990s when journey numbers fell, the number of journeys generally increased. In 2007/08 more than 1.2 billion passenger journeys were made on the national rail network,

Table 12.10

Passenger rail journeys:[1] by operator

Great Britain | | | | | | | Millions
	1981	1991/92	1996/97	2001/02	2003/04	2005/06	2007/08
Main line/underground							
National rail	719	792	801	960	1,012	1,082	1,232
London Underground	541	751	772	953	948	970	1,096
Glasgow Underground	11	14	14	14	13	13	14
All national rail and underground	1,271	1,557	1,587	1,927	1,973	2,065	2,342
Light railways and trams							
Docklands Light Railway	.	8	17	41	48	54	67
Tyne and Wear Metro	14	41	35	33	38	36	40
Croydon Tramlink	.	.	.	18	20	23	27
Manchester Metrolink	.	.	13	18	19	20	20
Sheffield Supertram	.	.	8	11	12	13	15
Nottingham Express Transit	.	.	.	.	.	10	10
Midland Metro	.	.	.	5	5	5	5
Blackpool Trams	6	5	5	5	4	4	3
All light railways and trams	20	54	78	132	147	162	187
All journeys by rail	1,291	1,611	1,665	2,059	2,119	2,229	2,529

1 Excludes railways and tramways operated principally as tourist attractions.

Source: Department for Transport

the fourth consecutive year running that passenger journeys on the network have exceeded one billion. Overall, national rail and London Underground accounted for almost all rail journeys in 2007/08, at 49 per cent and 43 per cent respectively.

Light railways and trams accounted for 7 per cent of rail journeys in Great Britain in 2007/08, compared with 1.5 per cent in 1981. Passenger journeys on light railways and trams more than doubled from around 80 million to 187 million between the mid-1990s and 2007/08. Several new light railways and tram lines were built or extended during the last 11 years, such as the Croydon Tramlink in south London and the Metrolink in Manchester. Over the next decade, further extensions to the Docklands Light Railway are proposed as part of the transport system for the Olympic Games and Paralympic Games in 2012, alongside new lines and extensions elsewhere in Great Britain.

Prices and expenditure

The Office of Rail Regulation compiles a rail fare prices index, using data gathered by Atos Origin, which provides a measure of the change in the prices charged by train operating companies (TOCs) to rail passengers. Overall, fares in Great Britain increased by 64 per cent between 1995 and 2008 (Table 12.11). Over the same period the 'All items' retail prices index (RPI) increased by 44 per cent, giving an increase of 14 per cent in real terms. However, prices charged by long distance operators over the period rose by 89 per cent, a 31 per cent increase in real terms.

In spring 2008 rail passengers aged 16 and over in Great Britain were asked about their satisfaction with various aspects of rail travel, from ticket prices to punctuality/reliability of train

Table 12.11

Rail fare prices index[1,2]

Great Britain						Index numbers (1995=100)
	1995	1999	2001	2006	2007	2008
All operators	100	114	120	146	154	164
London and South East operators	100	113	116	136	143	151
Long distance operators	100	116	127	164	175	189
Regional operators	100	112	117	137	143	151
Retail prices index[3] (all items)	100	112	117	133	139	144

1 As at January each year.
2 See Appendix, Part 12: Rail fares index.
3 See Appendix, Part 6: Retail prices index.

Source: Atos Origin from the Office of Rail Regulation

services. The National Passenger Survey (NPS), conducted by Passenger Focus (the independent national rail consumer watchdog) found that eight in ten (80 per cent) of people were satisfied overall with station and train facilities, an increase of 2 percentage points from spring 2007 but at the same level as spring 2006. When asked about value for money for the price of their ticket, 40 per cent of passengers were satisfied and 39 per cent were dissatisfied, virtually the same responses as those given in spring 2007 and spring 2006. The NPS also found that 79 per cent of passengers interviewed in spring 2008 were satisfied with the punctuality/reliability of their service, up from 77 per cent in spring 2007 and from 74 per cent in 1999 when the survey began. However, 13 per cent of passengers were dissatisfied.

For London and the South East operators 79 per cent of passengers were satisfied overall with station and train facilities in spring 2008, compared with 77 per cent in spring 2007. For long distance operators the proportion of passengers who were satisfied overall was 83 per cent in spring 2008, this was down 4 percentage points from spring 2007 and for most service areas passenger satisfaction was lower than in spring 2007. The majority (84 per cent) of passengers using regional operators were satisfied with their journey overall, an increase from spring 2007 (82 per cent satisfied).

Motoring costs in the UK as measured by the 'All motoring expenditure' component of the RPI rose by 95 per cent between January 1987 and January 2008, slightly less than the rise in the 'All items' RPI measure of general inflation of 110 per cent (see Chapter 5: Income and wealth). Between January 2007 and January 2008 motoring costs contributed to the rise in the annual RPI rate, mainly from petrol and oil prices rising in January 2008 after falling in January 2007. There was also a small upward effect from maintenance of motor vehicles where, overall, prices rose by more than January 2007 (Figure 12.12). However, there was a large, partially offsetting, downward effect from the purchase of motor vehicles, with prices rising at a slower rate than in 2007. There was also a small downward effect from car insurance, which also increased by less than last year.

Vehicle tax and insurance rose by 202 per cent during the period January 1987 and January 2008, although costs fell slightly in the mid-1990s, and maintenance costs rose to 220 per cent above the 1987 level. The cost of petrol and oil more than doubled between 1987 and 2000, before rising to a peak in 2008 of 205 per cent above its 1987 level.

Bus, coach and rail fares in the UK rose by considerably more than the rate of general inflation between 1987 and 2008. Bus and coach fares rose by 183 per cent and rail fares rose by

Figure 12.12

Passenger transport prices[1]

United Kingdom

Index numbers (1987=100)

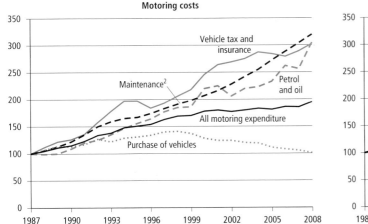

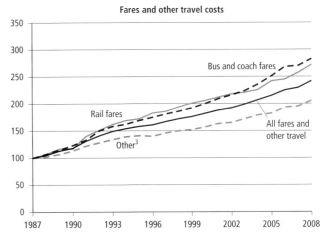

1 At January each year based on the retail prices index (RPI). For comparison, the 'All items' RPI measure of general inflation in January 2008 was 210.
   See Appendix, Part 6: Retail prices index.
2 Includes spare parts and accessories, roadside recovery services, MOT test fee, car service, labour charges and car wash.
3 Includes taxi and minicab fares, self-drive and van hire charges, ferry and sea fares, air fares, road tolls, purchase of bicycles/boats and car park charges.

Source: Office for National Statistics

172 per cent. Overall, the 'All fares and other travel' index rose by 142 per cent.

In 2007, transport and travel costs accounted for 16 per cent of all household expenditure in the UK. Table 12.13 overleaf shows that after taking into account the effects of inflation there was little change overall in expenditure on transport and travel costs between 1997/98 and 2007 (an increase in real terms of 1 per cent over this period). There was however stronger growth (6 per cent in real terms) in total household expenditure over the same period.

Between 1997/98 and 2007 the largest increase in motoring expenditure was on insurance and taxation, at 22 per cent, followed by petrol, diesel and other oils, which increased by 11 per cent. Over the same period, the purchase of cars, vans and motorcycles saw the largest decrease, at 13 per cent.

Expenditure on bus and coach fares decreased by 32 per cent between 1997/98 and 2007, while expenditure on rail and tube fares increased by 30 per cent over the same period. Overall, however, spending on fares and other travel costs increased by 4 per cent during this period.

Of the £61.80 spent on motoring per week in 2007, nearly one-half (47 per cent) was spent on the operation of personal transport (£28.80 per week). Most of this was spent on petrol, diesel and other oils (£18.30 per week), with repairs, servicing, spares and accessories together with other motoring costs making up the remainder. In comparison, in 1997/98

44 per cent of motoring expenditure was spent on the operation of personal transport (£27.00 per week), including £16.60 spent on petrol, diesel and other oils per week.

The average price of premium unleaded petrol and diesel fluctuates, and reached a peak of 119.6 pence per litre for premium unleaded and 133.0 pence per litre for diesel in the UK in July 2008 (Figure 12.14 overleaf). The price then began to fall and in December 2008 the average price was 89.1 pence per litre for premium unleaded petrol and 101.2 pence per litre for diesel.

Over the period January 1999 to December 2008, the largest monthly increase for premium unleaded petrol was in June 2000, at 6 per cent, while for diesel the largest monthly increase was in March 1999, at 8 per cent. This was partially the result of an increase in the duty rate for both premium unleaded petrol and diesel. The largest decrease for premium unleaded petrol was in November 2008, at 12 per cent lower than the previous month, this month saw also the largest decrease for diesel where the percentage change from October 2008 was 8 per cent.

In November 2008 the UK was the 12th most expensive country in the EU-27 in which to buy premium unleaded petrol, at 94.7 pence per litre, while Finland was the most expensive, at 114.4 pence per litre. The cheapest priced unleaded petrol was in Lithuania, at 71.2 pence per litre, around one-quarter less on average than in the UK. For diesel, the UK was the

Table 12.13

Household expenditure on transport in real terms[1]

United Kingdom

£ per week

	1997/98	1999/00	2001/02[2]	2003/04	2005/06	2007[3]
Motoring costs						
Cars, vans and motorcycle purchase	26.10	28.20	30.40	31.90	25.60	22.80
Repairs, servicing, spares and accessories	8.10	7.80	8.20	7.90	8.60	8.10
Motor vehicle insurance and taxation[4]	8.30	9.10	10.80	11.80	12.40	10.10
Petrol, diesel and other oils	16.60	17.80	17.40	16.90	18.70	18.30
Other motoring costs	2.30	2.30	2.10	2.20	2.50	2.40
All motoring expenditure	61.50	65.30	68.90	70.60	67.80	61.80
Fares and other travel costs						
Rail and tube fares	1.90	2.30	2.20	2.10	2.20	2.50
Bus and coach fares	1.80	1.70	1.70	1.60	1.60	1.20
Taxi, air and other travel costs[5]	5.90	5.80	6.00	6.20	6.80	6.30
All fares and other travel costs[6]	9.70	9.80	9.90	9.90	10.60	10.10
Motoring and all fares	71.10	75.10	78.80	80.50	78.40	71.80
Total expenditure	433.20	446.40	468.90	473.50	474.30	459.20

1 At 2007 prices deflated by the 'RPI all items' retail prices index. Expenditure rounded to the nearest 10 pence. See Appendix, Part 6: Household expenditure, and Retail prices index.
2 From 2001/02 onwards data include children's expenditure, and are weighted based on the population figures from the 2001 Census.
3 Figures prior to 2007 are shown based on weighted data using nonresponse weights based on the 1991 Census and population figures from the 1991 and 2001 Censuses. For 2007, figures shown are based on weighted data using updated weights, with nonresponse weights and population figures based on the 2001 Census.
4 Excludes boat insurance.
5 Includes combined fares.
6 Includes expenditure on bicycles and boats – purchases and repairs.

Source: Family Expenditure Survey and Expenditure and Food Survey, Office for National Statistics

Figure 12.14

Premium unleaded petrol[1] and diesel pump prices

United Kingdom

Pence per litre

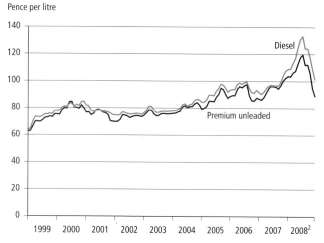

1 Unleaded petrol that is rated at 95 Research Octane Number. Does not include super unleaded petrol.
2 Data for December 2008 are provisional.

Source: Department of Energy and Climate Change

second most expensive country in the EU-27 in November 2008, at 108.6 pence per litre, while Ireland was the most expensive, at 111.8 pence per litre. The cheapest priced diesel was again in Lithuania, at 79.0 pence per litre. These figures have been brought together in a common currency using market exchange rates.

Across the EU-27 taxes and duties form a major component of petrol prices – 60 per cent on average in mid-November 2008 for premium unleaded petrol and 49 per cent on average for diesel. The tax component in the UK on unleaded petrol was the fourth highest in the EU, at 68 per cent. Germany had the highest tax component, at 71 per cent, while Malta had the lowest, at 48 per cent. As with unleaded petrol, the major component of the price of diesel in the UK was tax and duty (61 per cent) and was the highest in the EU.

Transport safety

The Government has targets for substantial improvements in road safety. By 2010, in Great Britain, the aim is to reduce the

Table 12.15

Passenger death rates:[1] by mode of transport[2]

Great Britain   Rate per billion passenger kilometres

	1981	1991	1996	2001	2006
Motorcycle	115.8	94.6	108.4	112.1	106.7
Walk	76.9	69.8	55.9	47.5	35.5
Bicycle	56.9	46.5	49.8	32.6	31.5
Car	6.1	3.7	3.0	2.8	2.5
Van	3.7	2.1	1.0	0.9	0.6
Bus or coach	0.3	0.6	0.2	0.2	0.3
Rail[3]	1.0	0.8	0.4	0.3	0.1
Water	0.4	-	0.8	0.4	0.3
Air	0.2	-	-	-	-

1 See Appendix, Part 12: Passenger death rates.
2 Motorcycle, bicycle, car and van includes driver and passenger
   fatalities. Water includes fatalities on UK registered merchant vessels.
   Air includes fatalities involving UK registered airline aircraft in UK and
   foreign airspace.
3 Financial years up to 1996 (1995/96). Includes train accidents and
   accidents occurring through movement of railway vehicles.

Source: Department for Transport

number of people killed or seriously injured in road accidents
per 100 million vehicle kilometres by 40 per cent compared
with the average in 1994–98. Similar targets exist for Northern
Ireland (see Appendix, Part 12: Road safety). In Great Britain in
2007, 2,946 people died as a result of road accidents, a
7 per cent decrease from 2006, with deaths among car users
decreasing by 11 per cent over the same period. There was a
3 per cent decrease in the number of serious injuries and a
4 per cent decrease in those slightly injured as a result of road
accidents over the same period.

The safety levels of most forms of transport in Great Britain are
much improved compared with the early 1980s, and
improvements in most areas have continued since the early
1990s. Motorcycling, walking and cycling have the highest
fatality rates per kilometre travelled than any other form of
transport in Great Britain (Table 12.15). In 2006 the highest
death rate continued to be for motorcycle users, at 106.7
deaths per billion passenger kilometres travelled. This was over
40 times greater than the death rate for car users.

In 2006, 49 per cent of those killed in road accidents in Great
Britain were travelling in cars, 22 per cent were pedestrians,
20 per cent were riders or passengers of motorcycles and
5 per cent were cyclists. Occupants of buses, coaches and goods
vehicles accounted for the remaining 4 per cent of deaths.

Department for Transport figures show that on weekdays the
highest hourly number of pedestrian fatalities or serious injuries

in Great Britain in 2007 occurred between the hours of 3pm
and 4pm. In 2007 there were 607 people killed or seriously
injured at this time of day, equating to an average of nearly
two people per day. Among car users the highest number of
fatalities or serious injuries occurred between 5pm and 6pm,
at 596 in 2007, again equating to an average of two people
per day.

The UK has a good record for road safety compared with most
other EU countries. Across the EU-27 the UK had one of the
lowest road death rates for all persons, at 5.4 per 100,000
population in 2006, with only Sweden, the Netherlands and
Malta recording lower rates (Table 12.16). Lithuania had the
highest recorded road death rate for all persons, at 22.3 per
100,000 population. The EU-27 average was 10.2 per 100,000
population. The UK rate was also substantially lower than that
in some other industrialised nations such as the United States
(14.3 per 100,000 population), Republic of Korea (13.1) and
Iceland (10.4).

The UK also has a relatively good record in terms of road
fatalities involving children. In 2006 the UK road accident death
rate for children aged under 15 was 1.4 per 100,000

Table 12.16

Road deaths: EU comparison, 2006

Rate per 100,000 population

	All persons	Children[1]		All persons	Children[1]
Lithuania	22.3	..	Portugal	9.2	1.3[2]
Latvia	17.8	..	Austria	8.9	1.8
Estonia	15.2	..	Ireland	8.7	..
Greece	14.9	2.4	Luxembourg	7.8	..
Poland	13.8	2.5	France	7.7	1.2
Bulgaria	13.5	..	Finland	6.4	0.6
Slovenia	13.2	3.2	Germany	6.2	1.2
Hungary	13.0	..	Denmark	5.6	1.3
Romania	11.5	..	United Kingdom	5.4	1.4
Cyprus	11.0	..	Sweden	4.9	1.0
Slovakia	10.8	..	Netherlands	4.5	1.3
Czech Republic	10.4	..	Malta	2.7	..
Belgium	10.2	1.8			
Italy	9.7	..	EU-27 average	10.2	..
Spain	9.4	1.8			

1 Aged under 15.
2 Based on 2005 population data.

Source: International Road Traffic and Accident Database (Organisation
for Economic Co-operation and Development); International Transport
Forum; Eurostat and CARE (EU road accidents database)

Table 12.17

Road casualties: by age and type of road user, 2007

Great Britain   Percentages

	Pedestrians	Pedal cyclists	Motorcycle users	Car users	All road users[1]
Under 16[2]	32	22	1	6	10
16–24	19	17	37	29	26
25–34	12	20	20	20	19
35–44	10	17	21	17	17
45–54	7	11	12	12	11
55–64	6	6	5	8	7
65–74	5	2	1	4	4
75 and over	7	1	-	3	3
All casualties[3] (=100%) (thousands)	30.2	16.2	23.5	161.4	247.8

1 Includes other road users, and cases where road user type was not reported.
2 In some cases age 0 may have been coded where the age of the casualty was not reported.
3 Includes cases where age was not reported.

Source: Department for Transport

population. Slovenia had the highest rate in the EU-27, 3.2 per 100,000 population, of those that reported. The UK rate was again lower than some other industrialised nations, with the Republic of Korea reporting a rate of 3.1 per 100,000 population and the United States, at 3.0 per 100,000 population.

The UK had the fifth lowest recorded rate in the EU-27 for all pedestrian deaths in 2006, at 1.2 per 100,000 population. The lowest in the EU-27 was the Netherlands, at 0.4 per 100,000 population, while Poland had the highest, at 4.7 per 100,000 population. The UK had a similar ranking in the number of child pedestrian deaths, having the sixth lowest rate, at 0.6 per 100,000 population. Finland had the lowest rate possible, at 0.0 per 100,000 population, while Slovenia had the highest rate, at 1.1 per 100,000 population.

In Great Britain in 2007 there were 247,780 road casualties of all severities, a 4 per cent reduction from 2006. Those under 16-years-old formed the highest proportion of pedestrian casualties, at 32 per cent (Table 12.17). People aged 16 to 24 were more likely to be casualties from motorcycle or car use, at 37 per cent (8,615 casualties) and 29 per cent (46,417 casualties) respectively, than from any other mode of transport. For motorcycle users this was an increase of 0.3 per cent from 2006 while for car users it was a decrease of 4 per cent.

According to the Department for Transport report, Road Casualties Great Britain: 2007, young drivers aged under 25

and older drivers aged over 69 are more likely to have a contributory factor recorded than drivers aged between 25 and 69. Contributory factors describe the key actions and failures that led directly to the actual impact to aid investigation of how accidents might be prevented. Young drivers, particularly men, are more likely to have factors related to speed and behaviour recorded, whereas older drivers are more likely to have factors related to vision and judgement recorded. Failing to look properly was the most frequently reported contributory factor and was reported in 35 per cent of all accidents, followed by failure to judge the other person's path/speed (19 per cent) and being careless, reckless or in a hurry (17 per cent). For fatal accidents the most frequently reported contributory factor was loss of control, which was reported in 33 per cent of fatal accidents. Loss of control was also the second largest contributory factor for serious accidents (19 per cent), following failure to look properly, at 30 per cent.

Alcohol is a major contributor to road accidents. The Road Safety Act 1967 established a legal alcohol limit for drivers, set at 80 milligrams of alcohol in 100 millilitres of blood and made it an offence to drive when over this limit. The Act also gave the police the power to carry out breath testing to determine whether an individual's alcohol level is above the limit of 35 micrograms of alcohol in 100 millilitres of breath. For many years the Government has run national publicity campaigns to discourage drink driving. The number of casualties from road accidents involving illegal alcohol levels in the UK fell sharply between the mid-1980s and early 1990s, from 24,900 in 1987 to 15,600 in 1993 (Figure 12.18). Between 1999 and 2002 the

Figure 12.18

Casualties from road accidents involving illegal alcohol levels:[1] by severity

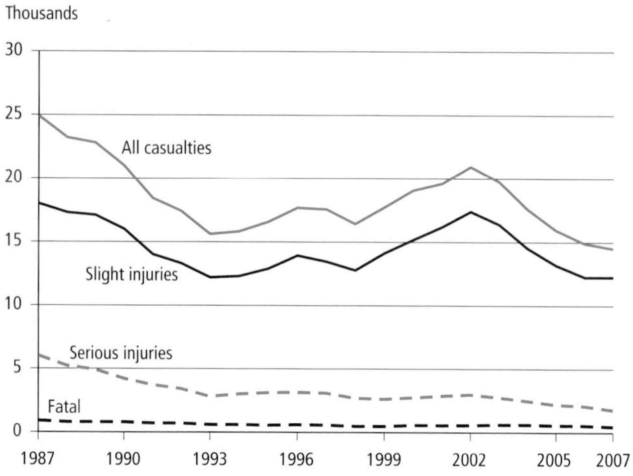

1 See Appendix, Part 12: Road safety.

Source: Department for Transport; Police Service of Northern Ireland

number of casualties rose to 20,900 before falling to less than 14,500 in 2007.

The number of deaths from road accidents involving illegal alcohol levels declined steadily from less than 1,000 in 1987 to approximately 600 a year in the early to mid-1990s. Following a further decline to around 500 deaths in 1998 and 1999, the number of deaths was relatively stable again, at around 600 a year between 2000 and 2007. Serious injuries from road accidents involving illegal alcohol levels decreased by more than one-half during the 1980s and 1990s to around 2,600 in 1999, and in 2007 fell to around 1,800.

According to the British Social Attitudes Survey, 87 per cent of adults in Great Britain in 2007 agreed or agreed strongly that if someone has drunk any alcohol they should not drive, while 75 per cent agreed or agreed strongly that anyone caught drink-driving should be banned for at least five years. However, 75 per cent of adults agreed or agreed strongly that most people don't know how much alcohol they can drink before being over the legal drink-drive limit.

International travel

The number of trips abroad made by UK residents in 2007, at 69.5 million visits, was the same as the record set in 2006 (Table 12.19). This was a 51 per cent increase on the number of trips made in 1997. In 1997 air travel accounted for 66 per cent of all modes of travel abroad by UK residents while in 2007 it accounted for 81 per cent. The proportion of trips made by sea declined over the same period from 25 per cent to 12 per cent, and trips made through the Channel Tunnel also decreased from 9 per cent to 7 per cent. Holidays accounted for almost two-thirds of trips made abroad by UK residents, 63 per cent in 1997 and 65 per cent in 2007.

In 2007 men in the UK made more visits abroad than women, 38 million visits compared with 31 million visits, and were more likely to travel abroad for business (19 per cent of visits) than women (6 per cent). The preferred mode of travel for business trips made by men was air, at 84 per cent (5.9 million visits). Holidays accounted for a high proportion of women's travel abroad (70 per cent of all trips) with air travel accounting for 83 per cent of trips made for that purpose (17.9 million visits).

In 2007, 32.8 million visits were made to the UK by overseas residents, 29 per cent more visits than those made in 1997 when 25.5 million visits were made to the UK. Of the total number of trips made to the UK by overseas residents in 2007, 25.1 million were made by air and the remainder made by sea or through the Channel Tunnel. Holidays accounted for 10.8 million (33 per cent) of all trips to the UK by overseas residents, followed by visiting friends and relatives in the UK (30 per cent) and business trips (27 per cent).

According to the British Social Attitudes Survey, 66 per cent of adults in Great Britain in 2007 agreed or agreed strongly that people should be able to travel by plane as much as they like, while 30 per cent disagreed or disagreed strongly that the price of a plane ticket should reflect the environmental damage that flying causes, even if this makes air travel much more expensive.

Between 1997 and 2007 there has been a continued and substantial rise in the number of air passengers at UK airports. Over the same period there was a 52 per cent increase in the number of domestic passengers at UK airports (Table 12.20 overleaf). All the major airports, except London Heathrow, experienced growth in domestic air passengers between these years. The largest increases in domestic air passengers were at London City airport, seven times the number in 2007

Table 12.19

International travel by UK residents: by mode of travel and purpose of visit

United Kingdom   Percentages

	1997				2007			
	Air	Sea	Channel Tunnel	All modes	Air	Sea	Channel Tunnel	All modes
Holiday	66	61	54	63	65	68	61	65
Visiting friends and relatives	13	14	8	13	18	15	12	18
Business	18	9	14	16	13	7	18	13
Other	2	17	24	8	3	10	9	4
All purposes (=100%) (millions)	30.3	11.5	4.1	46.0	56.3	8.5	4.6	69.5

Source: International Passenger Survey, Office for National Statistics

Table 12.20

Air passengers:[1] by UK civil airport

United Kingdom

Millions

	1997		2001		2007	
	Domestic	International	Domestic	International	Domestic	International
London Heathrow	7.2	50.6	6.6	53.8	5.8	62.1
London Gatwick	2.4	24.4	3.0	28.1	4.0	31.1
London Stansted	1.2	4.2	2.0	11.6	2.6	21.2
Manchester	2.5	13.3	2.8	16.3	3.2	18.7
London Luton	0.7	2.5	1.8	4.8	1.5	8.4
Birmingham	1.1	4.8	1.2	6.5	1.5	7.6
Nottingham East Midlands	0.4	1.5	0.3	2.0	0.7	4.7
Bristol	0.3	1.2	0.5	2.1	1.3	4.6
Liverpool (John Lennon)	0.3	0.4	0.7	1.5	0.8	4.6
Glasgow	3.2	2.8	3.8	3.4	4.6	4.1
Newcastle	0.8	1.8	1.0	2.4	1.7	3.9
Edinburgh	3.2	0.9	4.3	1.8	5.6	3.4
London City	0.1	1.1	0.5	1.2	0.7	2.2
Leeds Bradford	0.5	0.8	0.4	1.1	0.6	2.2
Belfast International	1.8	0.7	2.6	1.0	3.4	1.8
Cardiff	0.1	1.0	0.1	1.4	0.4	1.7
Aberdeen	1.7	0.9	1.7	0.9	1.9	1.5
Belfast City (George Best)	1.3	-	1.2	-	2.1	0.1
Other UK airports	3.3	1.9	3.8	2.9	6.2	8.0
All UK airports	32.1	114.7	38.4	142.8	48.7	192.0

1 Domestic traffic is counted both at the airport of departure and the airport of arrival. International traffic is counted at the airport of arrival.

Source: Civil Aviation Authority

compared with 1997 and Cardiff airport, four times as many over the same period.

There were nearly four times as many passengers on international flights as there were on domestic flights at UK airports in 2007. Between 1997 and 2007 the largest increases in numbers of international passengers were at London Stansted (17.0 million), London Heathrow (11.5 million), London Gatwick (6.7 million), London Luton (5.9 million) and Manchester (5.4 million). These include passengers in transit to other countries who do not stop overnight in the UK. Other airports have also expanded. Liverpool, for example, experienced an elevenfold increase in the number of international passengers between 1997 and 2007.

The Department for Transport forecasts that demand for air travel is set to continue. Mid-range estimates made in January 2009 suggest that between 2010 and 2030 passenger

numbers at UK airports will grow from 270 million to 464 million. Growth in international passengers is forecast to increase by more than two-thirds from 215 million to 363 million passengers, while growth in domestic passengers is set to double from 50 million to 101 million passengers annually.

In 2007, 189 million passengers were carried between the UK and abroad, an increase of 5 per cent on 2006 (Figure 12.21). UK airlines accounted for 106 million passengers carried, around 56 per cent of the total. Between 2006 and 2007 both UK and overseas airlines carried an increasing number of passengers, up by 4 per cent and 6 per cent respectively. However, the biggest change occurred in non-scheduled services by overseas airlines, down by 7 per cent over the year. Between 1997 and 2007 there was a 65 per cent increase in the number of passengers carried between the UK and abroad;

Figure 12.21

Air passengers travelling overseas from UK civil airports:[1] by type of airline

Millions

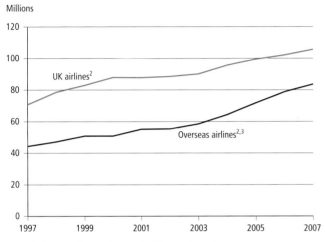

1 Excludes travel to and from the Channel Islands.
2 Includes scheduled and non-scheduled services.
3 Includes airlines of UK Overseas Territories.

Source: Civil Aviation Authority

passengers using scheduled services increased by 92 per cent, while passengers using non-scheduled services decreased by 2 per cent.

In 2007 there were around 1.5 million flights between the UK and abroad, an increase of 3 per cent from 2006 and a 44 per cent increase from 1997, when there were around 1.1 million flights. UK airlines made around 0.8 million flights abroad in 2007, 55 per cent of the total, and of these, 75 per cent were scheduled services. Overseas airlines made a total of around 0.7 million flights between the UK and abroad, 96 per cent of which were scheduled services. Between 1997 and 2007, the number of scheduled services from the UK to abroad increased by 58 per cent while the number of non-scheduled services decreased by 3 per cent.

12

Chapter 13

Lifestyles and social participation

- Nearly nine in ten homes (87 per cent) in the UK had a digital television service at the end of the first quarter in 2008. (Figure 13.2)

- Less than one-half (44 per cent) of people aged 15 and over in Great Britain read a national daily newspaper in the 12 months to June 2008, compared with 72 per cent in the 12 months to June 1978. (Table 13.6)

- UK residents took a record 45.4 million holiday trips abroad in 2007, an increase of 56 per cent since 1997. (Page 199)

- Between 2003 and 2007, holiday trips by UK residents to Latvia increased by 1,164 per cent, from 4,000 holiday trips to around 50,000. (Figure 13.12)

- In 2007/08, 90 per cent of pupils in England took part in at least two hours or more high quality physical education and out-of-hours school sport each week during term time, an increase of 21 per cent since 2004/05. (Page 200)

- Nearly one-half (49 per cent) of all those aged eight to 17 in the UK who use the Internet had a page or profile on a social networking site in 2007. (Figure 13.19)

People's lifestyle are based on individual choices, influenced by personal characteristics, circumstances, interests and social interactions. In some ways how people spend their leisure time has changed significantly over the years. For example, rapid advances in technology have affected many aspects of people's lives, providing greater access to information and increased choice in leisure and entertainment. However, traditional leisure and entertainment activities, such as watching television, reading, listening to music, attending arts events, gambling and going on holiday remain popular. Many individuals also continue to participate in sports, spend time with family and friends, and help other people in their communities.

Leisure and entertainment activities

With digital television services providing more channels and programmes than the analogue equivalent, as well as advanced interactive shows and games, and high definition channels, the television remains a popular medium of entertainment. Watching television was the most common leisure activity for more than eight in ten men and women (84 per cent and

85 per cent respectively) aged 16 and over in England in 2006/07 (Figure 13.1). For both men (75 per cent) and women (82 per cent) spending time with family and friends was the second most common leisure activity. However, there were also differences between the sexes in how they spend their leisure time. Men were more likely than women to participate in physical activities such as sport and exercise (58 per cent compared with 43 per cent) and DIY (46 per cent compared with 26 per cent). Women were more likely than men to spend their free time shopping, with three-quarters (75 per cent) doing so compared with around one-half of men (53 per cent). Similarly, women were more likely than men to take part in cultural activities such as reading (73 per cent compared with 56 per cent) and attending the theatre or music concerts (40 per cent compared with 34 per cent).

The economic downturn that began in 2008 meant that many people either had fewer resources or were worried about having fewer resources in the months ahead. In a survey by Populus, adults aged 18 and over in Great Britain were asked in September 2008 if they expected to do certain leisure or retail activities more or less in the coming 12 months than they had

Figure 13.1

Selected activities performed in free time:[1] by sex, 2006/07

England

Percentages

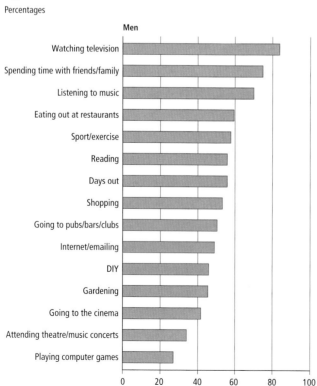

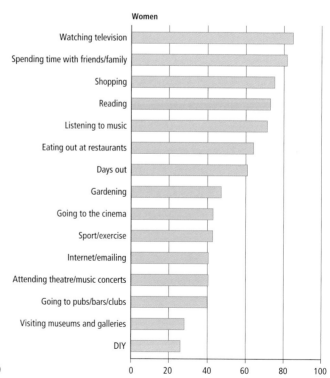

1 Percentages do not sum to 100 per cent as respondents could give more than one answer. Respondents were shown a list of activities and asked to pick the things that they did in their free time. The most popular 15 activities performed by men and women were selected.

Source: Taking Part: The National Survey of Culture, Leisure and Sport, Department for Culture, Media and Sport

done in the past. More than one-half expected to do less shopping for luxury food and major purchases (59 per cent and 56 per cent respectively). Almost one-half (48 per cent) expected to be less likely to take a holiday abroad, while 7 per cent stated that they were more likely to take one. More than one-quarter (27 per cent) expected to be less likely to take a holiday in the UK, while one-fifth (20 per cent) expected to be more likely to do this. More than four in ten (42 per cent) planned to spend more time staying at home relaxing and socialising in the 12 months after interview, while the same proportion (42 per cent) planned to cut down on going out to relax and socialise.

In 2008 the process known as the 'digital switchover' began, whereby the UK's analogue television broadcast signal started being switched off and replaced with a digital signal, television region by television region. Any television set not converted to digital when the switchover takes place will no longer receive television programmes. The process started in the Border television region and will end in London, parts of the Meridian area, Tyne Tees and Ulster Television regions in 2012.

Nearly nine in ten homes (87 per cent) in the UK had a digital television service at the end of the first quarter in 2008 (Figure 13.2), a rise of 71 percentage points since 2000. Much of the recent growth in take-up of digital television services has been driven by the take-up of a digital terrestrial television service. In 2000, 3 per cent of households had this service connected to their main television set. This increased more than twelvefold to 38 per cent of households at the end

Figure 13.2

Household take-up of digital television: by type of service[1]

United Kingdom
Percentages

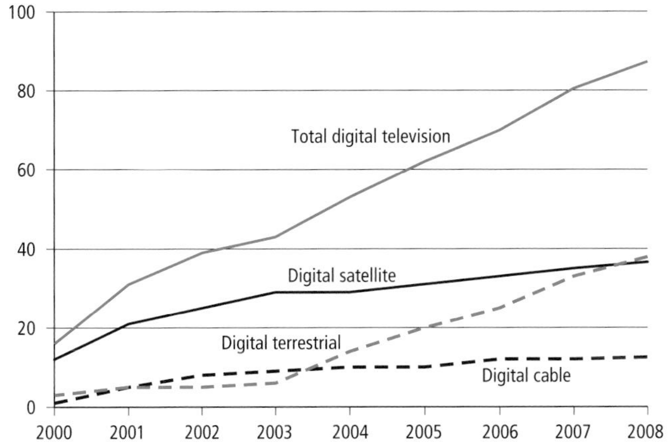

1 Digital service on main television set. Data are at Q1 (January–March) in each year.

Source: Ofcom

of the first quarter in 2008, and digital terrestrial overtook digital satellite as the most common way of receiving a digital television service. More than one-third of homes (37 per cent) received a digital satellite service on their main set, while around 13 per cent of homes received a digital cable service.

National or local news was the most common type of programme viewed on television in England in 2006/07. News programmes were watched by nearly seven in ten (69 per cent) adults aged 16 and over (Table 13.3 overleaf). Films and comedy programmes were the next most common types watched (66 per cent and 58 per cent respectively). People's viewing habits varied by age. Watching news programmes increased with age, with almost one-half (48 per cent) of young people aged 16 to 24 watching news compared with more than four-fifths (81 per cent) of people aged 65 and over. In contrast, around 40 per cent of those aged 16 to 24 watched popular music programmes, reality programmes or observational documentaries compared with around 10 per cent of those aged 65 and over. Programmes covering lifestyle subjects such as food and cookery, home and DIY, and gardening were more likely to have been watched by people aged 25 and over than by younger people. Live sport coverage, however, was watched by a similar proportion of all age groups (around 52 per cent), and was more likely to be viewed by men than women (69 per cent compared with 35 per cent). Women tended to watch 'soaps' more than men (59 per cent compared with 29 per cent) and food and cookery programmes (43 per cent compared with 26 per cent).

Another way to watch television is through the Internet through an Internet Protocol Television (IPTV) service over an asymmetric digital subscriber line (ADSL) connection, see Appendix, Part 13: Digital television, although this technology is still very much in its infancy. According to Ofcom (the independent regulator for the UK communications industries covering television, radio, telecommunications and wireless communication services) around 70,000 (0.3 per cent) of households in the UK claimed to be using an ADSL connection to receive a digital television service on their main television set in the second quarter of 2008.

In 2008, 33.9 million adults aged 16 and over (71 per cent of the UK adult population) accessed the Internet in the three months prior to interview, of these people more than one-third (34 per cent) either listened to the radio or watched television through the Internet (Table 13.4 overleaf). The most common audiovisual activity was downloading and/or listening to music (other than through a web radio station), performed by nearly four in ten (38 per cent) recent Internet users. Nearly one-quarter (24 per cent) uploaded content they had created

Table 13.3

Selected types of television programmes viewed:[1] by age, 2006/07

England

Percentages

	16–24	25–34	35–44	45–64	65 and over	All aged 16 and over
News[2]	48	63	70	74	81	69
Films	76	71	68	64	57	66
Comedy	71	63	60	53	48	58
Live sport coverage	50	49	52	52	53	52
Wildlife	28	40	46	59	67	51
Soaps	55	45	40	40	48	45
Food and cookery	21	35	35	40	38	35
Quiz shows	28	26	26	35	45	33
Current affairs or politics	13	25	29	38	40	31
Home and DIY	19	31	36	34	21	29
Gardening	5	13	22	37	48	28
Reality programmes or observational documentaries	40	35	27	15	8	23
Popular music programmes	42	27	22	15	10	21

1 Respondents were asked 'Thinking about when you watch television, what type of programmes do you watch nowadays?'
2 National or local news.

Source: Taking Part: The National Survey of Culture, Leisure and Sport, Department for Culture, Media and Sport

Table 13.4

Audiovisual uses of the Internet: by sex, 2008[1]

United Kingdom

Percentages

	Men	Women	All
Downloading and/or listening to music[2]	43	33	38
Listening to web radio and/or watching web television	41	27	34
Uploading self-created content to any website to be shared	25	24	24
Downloading and/or watching movies, short films or video files[3]	29	17	23
Downloading computer or video games or their updates	19	7	13
Using browser-based news feeds for reading news content on websites	17	7	12
Using peer-to-peer file sharing for exchanging movies, music or video files	16	9	12
Playing networked games with others	13	7	10
Using podcast services to automatically receive audio or video files of interest	13	5	9

1 Adults who used the Internet in the three months prior to interview. Data were collected in January, February and March for Great Britain and January for Northern Ireland.
2 Other than web radio.
3 Other than web television.

Source: Omnibus Survey, Office for National Statistics

to a website to be shared. Downloading and/or watching movies, short films or video files (other than a web television service), was reported by 23 per cent. In all bar one of the audiovisual categories shown in Table 13.4, men were considerably more likely to use the Internet in this way than women. More than four in ten (41 per cent) men who used the Internet in the three months prior to interview listened to the radio or watched television through the Internet compared with 27 per cent of women. Similarly, nearly three in ten (29 per cent) men who were recent Internet users downloaded and/or watched movies, short films or video files compared with less than one-fifth (17 per cent) of women. Around one-quarter of both men and women (25 per cent and 24 per cent respectively) uploaded content that they had created.

In 2007, Ofcom asked survey respondents which media activity they would miss the most if they were all taken away. Responses varied considerably by age, although watching television would be the most-missed media activity for all age groups except those aged 16 to 19, who would miss the mobile phone the most (Figure 13.5). Missing being able to watch television initially declines with age from nearly two-thirds (64 per cent) of children aged five to seven, to 52 per cent of those aged eight to 11, 29 per cent for those aged 12 to 15 and 20 per cent of young people aged 16 to 19.

Figure 13.5

Selected media activities that would be missed the most: by age,[1] 2007

United Kingdom

Percentages

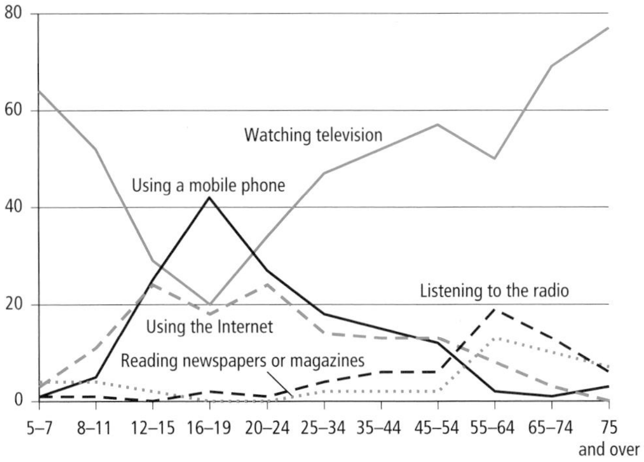

1 Data were drawn from two separate surveys (for those aged 5 to 15 and for those aged 16 and over), therefore comparisons are indicative only. Children aged 5 to 15 were asked 'Of the media activity you do almost every day, which one of these would you miss doing the most if it got taken away?' Data were collected April to September. Adults aged 16 and over were asked 'Which one of these media activities would you miss doing the most?' Data were collected October to December.

Source: Ofcom

Table 13.6

Readership of national daily newspapers[1]

Great Britain   Percentages

	1978	1988	1998	2008
The Sun	29	25	21	16
Daily Mail	13	10	11	11
Daily Mirror	28	20	14	8
The Daily Telegraph	8	6	5	4
The Times	2	2	4	4
Daily Express	16	10	6	3
Daily Star	.	8	4	3
The Guardian	2	3	3	2
The Independent	.	2	2	1
Financial Times	2	2	1	1
Any national daily newspaper[2]	72	67	56	44

1 Adults aged 15 and over. In the 12 months to June each year.
2 Includes the above newspapers and *The Daily Record* in 1978, *The Daily Record* and *Today* in 1988 and *The Daily Record*, *The Sporting Life* and the *Racing Post* in 1998 and 2008.

Source: National Readership Survey

However, the proportion of the 16 to 19 age group that would miss using a mobile phone the most was more than double that for television, at 42 per cent. From the age of 20 the appreciation of watching television increased with age, apart from a dip for those aged 55 to 64. A higher proportion of this age group than other age groups would miss the radio or newspapers and magazines the most. By the age of 75 and over more than three-quarters (77 per cent) would miss the television the most. The Internet would be missed most by those aged 12 to 15 and 20 to 24 (24 per cent for both groups). For those aged 25 and over, appreciation of both the mobile phone and the Internet decreased with age. Men aged 16 and over were more likely to miss the Internet than women (15 per cent compared with 9 per cent), while women were more likely to miss watching television than men (54 per cent compared with 49 per cent).

The proportion of people reading a daily newspaper has been declining for a number of years. On an average day less than one-half (44 per cent) of all people aged 15 and over in Great Britain read a national daily newspaper in the 12 months to June 2008, compared with 72 per cent in the 12 months to June 1978 (Table 13.6). In 2008 men were more likely than women to read a national daily newspaper (48 per cent compared with 41 per cent). *The Sun* was the most popular national daily newspaper over the period but its estimated

readership had virtually halved, with nearly three in ten people (29 per cent) reading it in 1978 compared with 16 per cent by 2008. The *Daily Mirror* was the second most popular newspaper in 1978, with nearly the same proportion of readers (28 per cent) as *The Sun*, but by 2008 the estimated proportion of adults reading the *Daily Mirror* had fallen by more than two-thirds, to 8 per cent. The second most popular newspaper in 2008 was the *Daily Mail,* with a readership totalling 11 per cent of the adult population, having been fourth behind the *Daily Express* in 1978.

A slightly larger proportion of people were estimated to read Sunday national newspapers in 2008 than daily national papers (47 per cent compared with 44 per cent). The *News of the World* remained the most popular Sunday newspaper in 2008 as it has been for the last 30 years, with 16 per cent of adults claiming to read it, though this was less than one-half the proportion in 1978 (31 per cent). The second most widely read Sunday newspaper was *The Mail on Sunday* (12 per cent).

Possible reasons for the decline in national daily newspaper readership could be the advent of free newspapers such as *Metro,* which is distributed in major cities and is estimated to be read by 6 per cent of the adult population in Great Britain, and the availability of national and local news on the television (see Table 13.3) and online. In 2008 almost one-half (48 per cent) of adults aged 16 and over in the UK who used the Internet in the three months prior to interview had read or downloaded online news or magazines. In 2008, six of the top ten most-read general weekly magazines were television guides such as *What's on TV* and the *Radio Times*, the remaining four being *Auto Trader*, *Nuts*, *Zoo* and *The Big Issue,* which is published on behalf of and sold by homeless people. The top weekly women's magazine was *Take a Break*, read by 10 per cent of women, followed by *OK!* and *Hello!* read by 9 per cent and 7 per cent of women respectively.

According to the Taking Part Survey, carried out by the Department of Culture, Media and Sport, the fourth most common leisure activity for adults in England in 2006/07 was reading, with more than six in ten people (65 per cent) doing so. According to the 2007 British Social Attitudes Survey, more than one-quarter (27 per cent) of adults aged 18 and over in Great Britain read books daily, with a further 34 per cent reading books either several times a week or several times a month. Women were more likely than men to read books daily (33 per cent compared with 21 per cent). The National Year of Reading was celebrated in 2008 which aimed to provide new opportunities to read. It also guided people, especially children and young people, on how to get help and support through schools and libraries, and demonstrated the importance of reading in the early years for children's later literacy development.

According to the National Foundation for Educational Research nearly seven in ten (69 per cent) children aged nine and nearly six in ten (59 per cent) aged 11 in England enjoyed reading in 2007 (Figure 13.7). Less than one-fifth of children of both ages thought reading was boring, 14 per cent and 18 per cent respectively. Around one in ten children of both ages found reading difficult (11 per cent of those aged nine and 8 per cent of those aged 11). The largest difference (13 percentage points) between the two ages was for those who enjoyed reading with an adult's help. A high proportion of children of both ages stated that they liked reading comics or magazines (71 per cent of those aged nine and 77 per cent of those aged 11). However, when asked what they read at home, story books were the most popular reading material for those aged nine (78 per cent). They were the second most popular reading material after magazines for those aged 11 (78 per cent liked reading magazines and 73 per cent liked story books).

According to the Public Lending Right, *Harry Potter and the Half-Blood Prince* by J K Rowling was the most borrowed children's fiction book in public libraries in the UK between July 2006 and June 2007 for the second year running, followed by *Candyfloss* by Jacqueline Wilson. The most borrowed children's non-fiction book was *The Woeful Second World War* by Terry

Figure 13.7

Selected attitudes to reading of children aged 9 and 11, 2007

England
Percentages

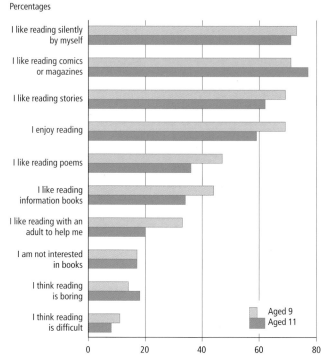

Source: National Foundation for Educational Research

Deary. *At Risk* by Patricia Cornwell was the most borrowed fiction title for adults and *The Meaning of the 21st Century* by James Martin was the most borrowed adult non-fiction book.

Around two-thirds (66 per cent) of adults aged 16 and over in England attended an arts event, excluding going to the cinema, in 2006/07. Attendance is measured as at least one visit in the 12 months prior to interview. More than one-half (52 per cent) attended once or twice, while one-third (33 per cent) attended three or four times. Around seven in ten couples with or without children, and the same proportion of people under state pension age (65 for men and 60 for women) living alone, attended an arts event (70 per cent, 68 per cent and 67 per cent respectively), while a much lower proportion (50 per cent) of single pensioners living alone did so (Table 13.8). The most common type of arts event attended by all types of household, apart from lone parent households, was going to a theatre performance, with around two in five couples with or without children doing so (39 per cent and 40 per cent respectively). The most common arts activity attended by lone parent households was carnival and street art events, with one-third (33 per cent) attending. The likelihood of attending an arts event varied by age, with people aged 25 to 64 more likely to do so than those in the younger and older age groups.

Table 13.8

Top ten arts events attended:[1] by household composition, 2006/07

England

Percentages

	One person households[2]		One family households			
	Under state pension age[3]	Over state pension age[3]	Couple with no children	Couple with children	Lone parent	Other households
Theatre performance[4]	33	30	40	39	31	30
Carnival and street arts[5]	29	15	25	31	33	26
Live music event[6]	30	7	24	25	23	31
Exhibition of art, photography or sculpture	26	16	25	19	14	19
Craft exhibition	12	15	18	14	9	8
Classical music performance	9	11	10	5	2	5
Culturally specific festival	6	2	5	7	5	6
Jazz performance	7	4	7	4	3	6
Event connected with books or writing	5	3	5	5	4	4
Opera or operetta	4	5	5	2	2	2
Any attendance	67	50	68	70	63	65

1 Attendance is at least one visit to an art event, excluding the cinema, in the 12 months prior to interview. Percentages do not sum to 100 per cent as respondents could give more than one answer.
2 People in 'one person' households do not have children living with them.
3 State pension age is currently 65 for men and 60 for women.
4 Includes play/drama and other theatre.
5 Carnival and street arts have been merged.
6 Excluding jazz and classical music performances.

Source: Taking Part: The National Survey of Culture, Leisure and Sport, Department for Culture, Media and Sport

More than seven in ten (71 per cent) of those aged 25 to 64 had attended an arts event in the 12 months prior to interview, compared with 66 per cent of those aged 16 to 24 and 53 per cent of those aged 65 and over. Around one-third (34 per cent) of all adults had not attended an art event in the 12 months prior to interview. The main reasons given were that they were not really interested (33 per cent), had difficulty finding the time (29 per cent) or their health was not good enough (16 per cent).

The arts are one of the causes that benefited from grants made by the National Lottery. In England the arts received £2.17 billion between November 1994 and March 2006 from National Lottery funds. There were more than 25,000 awards, with 292 awards of more than £1 million. Theatre and drama benefited most (£568 million) followed by music and the visual arts (£491 million and £484 million respectively). According to the British Gambling Prevalence Survey, the National Lottery draw was the most popular gambling activity in Great Britain in 2007, with 57 per cent of adults aged 18 and over in Great Britain having purchased at least one ticket in the 12 months prior to interview. However, this proportion has fallen since 1999 when 65 per cent of adults participated. In a study published by the National Lottery Commission, the most

important reason given by both men and women who played the National Lottery draw games at least once a month in the UK was to win the jackpot or the lottery (46 per cent of men and 47 per cent of women) (Figure 13.9 overleaf). More than one-fifth (21 per cent) of men participated in the draw in the hope of changing their lives by becoming a millionaire and being able to retire or to not work again, compared with 13 per cent of women who participated. However, a slightly higher proportion of women than men participated in the hope of winning enough to enhance their current lives by taking a holiday or paying off debts or a mortgage (10 per cent compared with 8 per cent). Very few men and women gave as their reason for playing to help good causes or give to charity (4 per cent of men and 3 per cent of women).

Holidays

In 2007, 76.8 million holiday trips in the UK including at least a one night stay were made by adults aged 16 and over resident in the UK. Holiday trips include pleasure and leisure, and visiting friends or relatives for a holiday. In the UK the most visited region by UK residents taking a holiday was the South West, with nearly 19 per cent (equivalent to 14.5 million trips) of all holidays within the UK lasting one night or more being

Figure 13.9

Reasons for participation in National Lottery draw-based games:[1] by sex, 2006

United Kingdom

Percentages

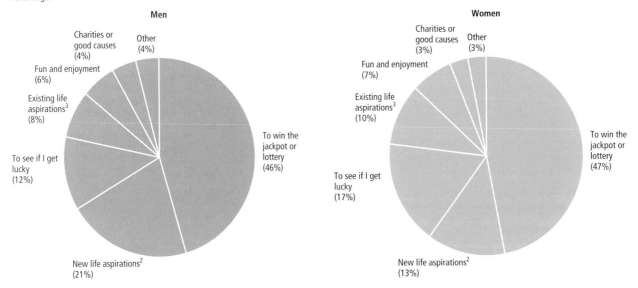

1 As a proportion of all responses from those playing the National Lottery draws at least monthly. The question asked was 'Why do you play the National Lottery draws?'
2 Includes to become a millionaire, life change, to retire and not to work again.
3 Includes to go on holiday, to pay off debts or a mortgage, instant money, and habit.

Source: National Lottery Commission

spent there (Map 13.10). The second most popular destination was the South East (13 per cent), followed by the North West and Scotland (both 11 per cent). Around six in ten (61 per cent) holidays, not including visits to friends and family, were of one to three nights duration, 32 per cent were of four to seven nights duration and the remainder were eight nights or more.

Many holiday trips as well as days out involve a visit to the UK's many visitor attractions such as country parks and farms, historic properties, theme parks, zoos, gardens, museums and galleries, and places of worship. The most visited attractions with free admission in England in 2007 were Xscape Milton Keynes (an attraction that combines extreme sports such as ice and rock climbing with other leisure activities such as cinemas and restaurants) and Blackpool Pleasure Beach, with around 6.9 million and 5.5 million visitors respectively. The most visited attractions that charged admission were the Tower of London and St Paul's Cathedral in London, with around 2.1 and 1.6 million visitors respectively. The most visited attractions with free admission in Scotland in 2007 were Kelvingrove Art Gallery and Museum in Glasgow and the National Gallery of Scotland complex in Edinburgh, with around 2.2 million and 1.4 million visitors respectively. Edinburgh Castle and Edinburgh Zoo were the most popular attractions charging admission, with around 1.3 and 0.6 million visitors respectively. In Wales

Map 13.10

UK residents' holidays within the UK:[1] by region of destination, 2007

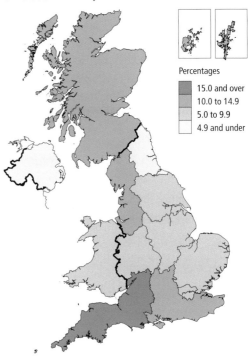

Percentages

- 15.0 and over
- 10.0 to 14.9
- 5.0 to 9.9
- 4.9 and under

1 Trips for 'holiday/pleasure/leisure' and 'visiting friends and relatives – mainly holiday' lasting one night or more taken by UK residents aged 16 and over.

Source: United Kingdom Tourism Survey, VisitBritain

the most popular free attractions were the Wales Millennium Centre and St Fagans: National History Museum in Cardiff (0.9 and 0.6 million visitors respectively). Pembrey Country Park and Oakwood Theme Park were the most popular paid attractions, with 0.4 and 0.3 million visitors. In Northern Ireland, the most popular free attractions were the Giant's Causeway Visitor Centre and Crawfordsburn Country Park with around 0.7 million visitors each in 2007. Belfast Zoological Gardens and W5, an interactive science discovery centre, were the most popular paid attractions with 0.3 and 0.2 million visitors.

UK residents made a record 45.4 million holiday trips abroad in 2007 (see also International travel in Chapter 12: Transport). The number of holiday trips abroad has increased by 56 per cent since 1997 and is a continuation of the trend of the rise in overseas holidays over nearly four decades, from 6.7 million in 1971. The package holiday (see Appendix, Part 13: Package holiday) is still very common among UK residents when they holiday abroad. In 2007, 18.7 million holiday trips abroad were package holidays. However, package holidays as a proportion of all holidays abroad have decreased over time. In 2002 package holidays peaked at 20.6 million, which was more than one-half (52 per cent) of all overseas holidays compared with 41 per cent in 2007. The fall in package holidays has mainly occurred for holiday trips taken in Europe. In 2007 almost four in ten (39 per cent) holidays to Europe were package-based compared with 56 per cent in 2000 (Figure 13.11). Package holidays to North America and other countries outside Europe have remained stable as a proportion

of the total in the past few years. In 2007 more than one-half (56 per cent) of all holidays to countries (other than North America and Europe) and around one-third (32 per cent) of holidays to North America were package-based.

Despite some broadening of the tourist season the times of the year when holidays are taken have remained broadly unchanged. In 2007, 17 per cent of holidays abroad were taken in January to March, 26 per cent in April to June, 37 per cent in July to September, coinciding with the main school holidays and 20 per cent in October to December. Around eight in ten holidays abroad by UK residents in 2007 were taken in Europe. Spain was the most popular destination, accounting for nearly three in ten holidays (27 per cent). France was the second most popular destination (17 per cent of all holidays). Eight of the ten most popular destinations in 2007 were in the EU-27. The exceptions were North America (2.7 million visits) and Turkey (1.3 million visits). Six of the top ten destinations that have shown the largest proportional growth in holiday trips between 2003 and 2007 were states that joined the EU in 2004 (Latvia, Slovakia, Poland, Estonia, Lithuania and Slovenia) (Figure 13.12). Holiday trips to Latvia had the highest proportional growth (1,164 per cent) increasing from 4,000 holiday trips in 2003 to around 50,000 in 2007, followed by Slovakia (957 per cent) and Poland (719 per cent). Holiday trips to parts of North Africa, such as Algeria, Libya, Morocco and Sudan, increased nearly four times (297 per cent). Trips to

Figure 13.11

UK residents' package holiday visits abroad[1]

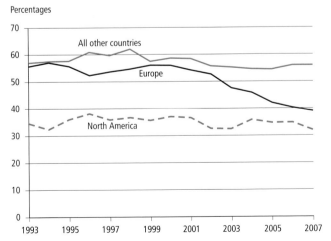

1 As a proportion of all holidays to the destination. See Appendix, Part 13: International Passenger Survey (IPS).

Source: International Passenger Survey, Office for National Statistics

Figure 13.12

Holiday destinations that have shown the largest percentage growth,[1] 2003 to 2007

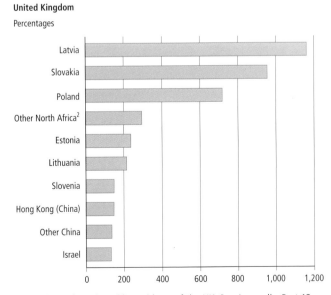

1 Holidays taken abroad by residents of the UK. See Appendix, Part 13: International Passenger Survey (IPS).
2 Includes Algeria, Libya, Morocco and Sudan.

Source: International Passenger Survey, Office for National Statistics

Hong Kong (China) and the rest of China increased by 148 per cent and 136 per cent respectively.

Sporting activities

Beijing in China was the venue for the 2008 Olympic and Paralympic Games. These were the most watched games in history having been broadcast to more people in more regions around the world than any other Olympic Games. People in the UK mainly watched the games on television or through the Internet. The next Olympic Games will be held in London in 2012, making it easier for British people to attend live Olympic events. According to the 2007 British Social Attitudes Survey, nearly one-half (49 per cent) of all adults aged 18 and over in Great Britain had attended a sports event at least once a year as a spectator. More than one-third (36 per cent) attended an event several times a year but less than several times a month, and 12 per cent attended several times a week or several times a month. Men were more likely than women to be a spectator, with six in ten (60 per cent) men attending an event at least once a year compared with four in ten (40 per cent) women.

A rather lower proportion of adults take an active part in sport compared with the proportion who attend sports events as spectators. In 2006/07, 40 per cent of all adults in England had participated in a moderate intensity sport for at least 30 minutes in the week prior to interview, and 22 per cent had participated for at least 30 minutes on at least three separate days in the week prior to interview. The most popular active sports participated in during the four weeks prior to interview were indoor swimming or diving (15 per cent), health, fitness, gym or body-conditioning activities (14 per cent), and recreational cycling (10 per cent). Of the 19 per cent of adults who had not participated in an active sport during the 12 months prior to interview nearly one-half (47 per cent) stated that this was because their health was not good enough (Table 13.13). The age group with the highest proportion of people stating this reason (71 per cent) were aged 65 and over. Averaged across all ages, less than one-fifth of all adults found it either difficult to find the time (18 per cent) or were not really interested in participating (17 per cent). More than four in ten (42 per cent) of those aged 25 to 44 found it difficult to find the time to participate in sport, which may have been because of employment restraints or child care responsibilities. Time was also one of the main factors deterring young people aged 16 to 24 from participating in sport, along with not being really interested (33 per cent and 30 per cent respectively). Health was a factor for 10 per cent of young people, while 5 per cent stated that sport participation costs too much and a further 5 per cent stated that they would not enjoy it. People who were encouraged to participate in sports as children were more

Table 13.13

Main reason for non-participation in an active sport:[1] by age, 2006/07

England
Percentages

	16–24	25–44	45–64	65 and over	All aged 16 and over
Health not good enough	10	16	35	71	47
Difficult to find the time	33	42	24	2	18
Not really interested	30	21	21	12	17
Too old	0	0	2	6	3
Would not enjoy it	5	3	3	2	3
Costs too much	5	4	3	0	2
Never occurred to me	4	1	2	1	2
No one to do it with	5	1	1	1	1
Too lazy	1	2	2	0	1
Other reasons[2]	8	9	7	4	6

1 Respondents who had not done any sport or recreational physical activity in the 12 months prior to interview.
2 Other reasons include 'don't know', 'fear of injury', 'exercise enough already' and 'changing facilities are not good enough'.

Source: Taking Part: The National Survey of Culture, Leisure and Sport, Department for Culture, Media and Sport

likely to participate in a sport as an adult. In 2006/07, one-quarter (25 per cent) of all adults who had been encouraged as a child had participated in a moderate intensity sport in the 12 months prior to interview, compared with 15 per cent who had not had the encouragement.

Getting children of school age participating in sport and keeping them involved is generally considered to help reduce obesity and improve fitness levels, team spirit, concentration and self-esteem. School sport partnerships (SSPs) are 'families' of schools working together to develop physical education and sport opportunities for all young people. They are made up of secondary, primary (infant and junior schools) and special schools and usually have a Specialist Sports College acting as the hub of the family. By the end of 2007 all of the 21,727 maintained schools in England were arranged into 450 different partnerships.

According to the 2007/08 School Sport Survey, 90 per cent of pupils in SSP schools in England participated in at least two hours or more high quality physical education (PE) and out-of-hours school sport each week, an increase of 21 percentage points since 2004/05. Over nine in ten primary and special school pupils participated in at least two hours of PE and sport (96 per cent and 93 per cent respectively), compared with over eight in ten (83 per cent) secondary school pupils. The proportion of primary school pupils participating in at least two hours or more of high quality PE and sports rose by 32 percentage points

Figure 13.14

Pupils who participate in physical education and out-of-hours sport[1] at school:[2] by year group[3]

England

Percentages

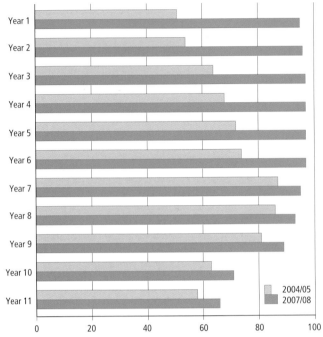

1 For at least two hours of high quality physical education (PE) and out-of-hours sport in a typical week during term time.
2 Schools that are part of a School Sport Partnership (SSP), which are groups of schools working together to develop PE and sport opportunities.
3 See Appendix, Part 3: Stages of education.

Source: Department for Children, Schools and Families

since 2004/05 (Figure 13.14). The largest increases were for Years 1 and 2 (44 percentage points and 42 percentage points respectively). Secondary schools saw the least improvement since 2004/05 with a rise of 8 percentage points overall, with Years 10 and 11 still at a relatively low level (71 per cent and 66 per cent respectively) compared with other school years. The proportion of special school pupils participating in at least two hours or more of high quality PE and sports rose by 24 percentage points over the period. Across all types of schools and school years, pupils spend on average 1 hour 58 minutes each week on curriculum PE. More than nine in ten schools offered football, dance, gymnastics, athletics and cricket during the academic year 2007/08 and more than eight in ten schools offered rounders, swimming and netball.

Social participation and networking

One of the ways individuals contribute to their community is through volunteering. According to the Citizenship Survey, informal volunteering, which is giving unpaid help as an individual to people who are not relatives, was carried out by

64 per cent of adults at least once in the 12 months prior to interview and by 36 per cent in the month prior to interview in April to June 2008 in England. Formal volunteering, which is giving unpaid help through groups, clubs and organisations to benefit other people or the environment, was carried out by 41 per cent of people at least once in the 12 months prior to interview, and by 26 per cent in the month prior to interview. According to the 2006/07 Taking Part Survey carried out by the Department for Culture, Media and Sport, the most common types of voluntary work undertaken by respondents in the 12 months prior to interview in England were raising or handling money or taking part in sponsored events – these activities were undertaken by more than one-third (34 per cent) of volunteers (Figure 13.15). More than three in ten (31 per cent) of those volunteering organised or helped to run an event, and almost one-quarter (23 per cent) were members of a committee. Coaching or tuition was undertaken by 15 per cent of volunteers, with more men than women doing this kind of voluntary work, 19 per cent compared with 10 per cent. However, most types of voluntary work were done by a similar proportion of male and female volunteers.

The benefits that volunteering brings for individuals and communities are well recognised, but it can have a beneficial impact to the volunteer as well, ranging from satisfaction and

Figure 13.15

Types of voluntary work undertaken, 2006/07[1]

England

Percentages

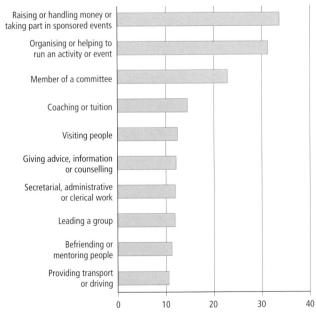

1 As a proportion of all who had done voluntary work in the 12 months prior to interview.

Source: Taking Part: The National Survey of Culture, Leisure and Sport, Department for Culture, Media and Sport

Table 13.16

Selected benefits from formal volunteering: by age,[1] 2006/07

England

Percentages

	16–34	35–44	45–54	55–64	65 and over	All aged 16 and over
I get satisfaction from seeing the results	98	99	100	95	95	97
I really enjoy it	98	96	95	96	94	96
I meet people and make friends	87	80	84	84	91	86
It gets me out of myself	68	66	63	57	82	69
It makes me feel needed	63	70	61	63	76	67
It gives me more confidence	75	57	65	55	68	65
It gives me the chance to learn new skills	80	60	60	55	47	61
It gives me a position in the community	49	38	35	25	40	38
It gives me the chance to improve my employment prospects	53	26	18	8	3	23
It gives me the chance to get a recognised qualification	25	13	15	6	5	13

1 All formal volunteers who volunteered regularly with their main organisation and stated that the reasons were very or fairly important to them. Percentages do not sum to 100 per cent as respondents could give more than one answer. Those who said 'don't know' or refused to respond are excluded.

Source: Helping Out: A national survey of volunteering and charitable giving, Cabinet Office

enjoyment through to personal and professional development. In 2006/07, the most important benefits identified by regular formal volunteers in England were the sense of satisfaction seeing the results of volunteering or the enjoyment of being involved (97 per cent and 96 per cent respectively) (Table 13.16). Social interaction through meeting people and making friends and by getting people out of themselves were also common benefits identified by 86 per cent and 69 per cent of volunteers respectively, as were feelings of self worth, such as feeling needed or gaining confidence (67 per cent and 65 per cent respectively). Although volunteers of all age groups gave satisfaction from seeing the results and overall enjoyment as the most important personal benefits, the importance of other benefits varied by age. Young people aged 16 to 34 were most likely of all age groups to feel that volunteering gave them a chance to gain new skills, enhance their employment prospects, gain a position in the community and get a recognised qualification. Older people aged 65 and over were most likely of all groups to see volunteering as something that gave them the chance to meet people and make friends, got them out of themselves or made them feel needed. Both young people 16 to 34 and older people aged 65 and over were more likely than other age groups to feel that volunteering would give them more confidence (75 per cent and 68 per cent respectively).

Giving gifts of money to charities is another important way in which people can care for others and support organisations

whose aims they share. According to the Charities Aid Foundation and the National Council of Voluntary Organisations, the average donation per adult in the UK in 2007/08 was £18 (£33 per donor) and the total amount donated was an estimated £10.6 billion. More than one-half (56 per cent) of adults gave at least once a month. Religious causes accounted for the largest share of the total donated (18 per cent), closely followed by medical research (15 per cent). In 2006/07 more than one-half (52 per cent) of adults in England who had donated to charity in the four weeks prior to interview did so because they felt the work of the particular charity was important (Figure 13.17). More than four in ten (41 per cent) felt it was the right thing to do, and more than three in ten (31 per cent) just felt like giving. Some adults donated because of a self-interest, for example because of something that had happened to them or a relative (25 per cent) or because they felt they might benefit from the charity in the future (22 per cent) or because it made them feel good (17 per cent). The most common reason for adults not donating to charity in the 12 months prior to interview was that they did not have enough money to spare; this reason was given by nearly six in ten (58 per cent) adults who did not donate. A feeling that charities wasted too much money on administration was also a reason why people did not donate, given by 16 per cent of non-givers.

Cultivating and developing relationships and friendships is an important part of life, and becomes all the more important

Figure 13.17

Most common reasons for donating to charity, 2006/07[1]

England

Percentages

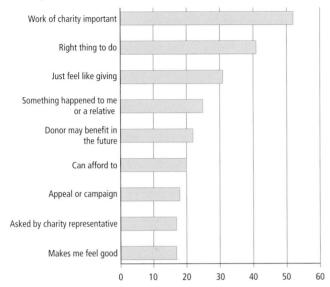

1 All respondents donating in the four weeks prior to interview were shown a list of possible reasons for donating and asked to select their main reason for doing so. Those who said 'don't know' or refused to respond are excluded. Percentages do not sum to 100 per cent as respondents could give more than one answer.

Source: Helping Out: A national survey of volunteering and charitable giving, Cabinet Office

when people are worried or stressed. According to the 2007 British Social Attitudes Survey more than one-half (51 per cent) of adults aged 18 and over in Great Britain stated that the most likely person they would talk to if they were feeling especially worried, stressed or down would be their spouse or partner with whom they lived. This was particularly true for men; six in ten (60 per cent) men compared with more than four in ten (42 per cent) women preferred to talk to their spouse or partner they lived with. Talking to a close female friend was preferred by 15 per cent of women while a further 10 per cent talked to their mother or stepmother. For men, their mother or stepmother or a close male friend were the next preferred people to talk to (8 per cent and 7 per cent respectively).

When people need emotional support or want to catch up with friends and family, they use a variety of ways of communicating. These vary from personal interaction, such as a face to face conversation, to interacting through the use of new technology such as the Internet. The most popular ways of communicating with close friends and family (not including a spouse or partner) was either face-to-face or by a telephone conversation. Almost all adults aged 18 and over in Great

Britain used these methods of communication in 2007 (98 per cent and 97 per cent respectively). The least favoured way of communicating was through an Internet service (excluding email) such as chat rooms and instant messaging, although this method was still reported by 21 per cent of adults. While both men and women preferred to use face-to-face conversation or the telephone to communicate with family and friends, the regularity of communicating varied between the sexes. More than one-half (51 per cent) of women had a face-to-face conversation to catch up with close friends or relatives every day or almost every day compared with 37 per cent of men, although around 35 per cent of both men and women had a face-to-face conversation at least once or twice a week but less than every day or almost every day (Table 13.18 overleaf). Nearly one-half (47 per cent) of women use the telephone every day or almost every day to catch up with close friends or relatives compared with 27 per cent of men, while around 38 per cent of both men and women used it at least once or twice a week but less than every day or almost every day. Around two-thirds of both men and women caught up with family and friends by text through a mobile phone (65 per cent and 66 per cent respectively) and again a greater proportion of women than men communicated this way every day or almost every day (35 per cent compared with 27 per cent). Around three in ten men and women used email to communicate to close friends and family at least once or twice a week, or every day or almost every day (29 per cent and 28 per cent respectively). Before email became popular, sending a letter or note was a common way of catching up or lending emotional support. This method of communication is still used; in 2007 more than six in ten (62 per cent) women reported that they had sent letters or notes compared with 44 per cent of men, with the largest proportion of both men and women sending one less than once or twice a month (34 per cent and 42 per cent of women).

Another way of communicating socially can be through the Internet or mobile phone. Users of social networking websites can create their own online pages or profile and are able to construct and display online a network of contacts (often referred to as 'friends'). Through these sites users can then communicate with their 'friends' or people outside their list of contacts via email or in a more public way such as posting comments or photos for all to see. These sites are very popular with young people. According to Ofcom nearly one-half (49 per cent) of all those aged eight to 17 in the UK who use the Internet had a page or profile on a social networking site in 2007. Of these, more than one-quarter (27 per cent) aged eight to 11, more than five in ten (55 per cent) aged 12 to 15, and nearly seven in ten

Table 13.18

Regularity of emotional support or 'catching up' with close friends or relatives:[1] by sex and mode of contact, 2007

Great Britain   Percentages

	Face-to-face conversation	Telephone conversation	Text message	Letter or note	email	Internet services[2]
Men						
Every day or almost every day	37	27	27	1	12	7
At least once or twice a week	35	38	17	1	17	5
At least once or twice a fortnight	12	13	6	1	9	2
At least once or twice a month	7	9	7	7	11	4
Less than once or twice a month	5	7	9	34	11	6
Never	4	4	35	56	40	76
Women						
Every day or almost every day	51	47	35	1	10	5
At least once or twice a week	34	38	16	4	18	5
At least once or twice a fortnight	6	6	6	4	7	2
At least once or twice a month	6	4	5	12	12	2
Less than once or twice a month	3	2	4	42	8	4
Never	1	2	34	38	45	82

1 The question asked of adults aged 18 and over was 'How often (using ways in the table) do you contact a close friend, relative or someone else close to you (apart from your spouse or partner) about how you're feeling or just to catch up'.
2 Includes instant messaging, chat rooms and other Internet services. Excludes email.

Source: British Social Attitudes Survey, National Centre for Social Research

(67 per cent) aged 16 to 17 had a page or a profile on a site (Figure 13.19). In contrast, 15 per cent of parents who were aware of social networking sites and who had young people aged eight to 17 who used the Internet had a profile themselves. For more than nine in ten (92 per cent) young people aged eight to 17 who had a page or profile on a social networking site, the main reasons for using social networking sites were staying in touch with family and friends they see regularly or looking at other people's pages or profiles. Nearly eight in ten (79 per cent) used the sites for staying in touch with family and friends that they saw rarely and six in ten (59 per cent) used the sites to make new friends. Around two-thirds (65 per cent) of parents of those aged eight to 17 with profiles on a social networking site laid down rules or placed restrictions on their child's use of social networking sites. Three out of ten parents insisted on rules or restrictions about meeting new people online (30 per cent), and giving out personal details (27 per cent of parents). Around 17 per cent of parents had a rule or restriction about meeting in person new people befriended online.

Figure 13.19

Proportion of parents and children who have a profile on a social networking site:[1] by age, 2007

United Kingdom
Percentages

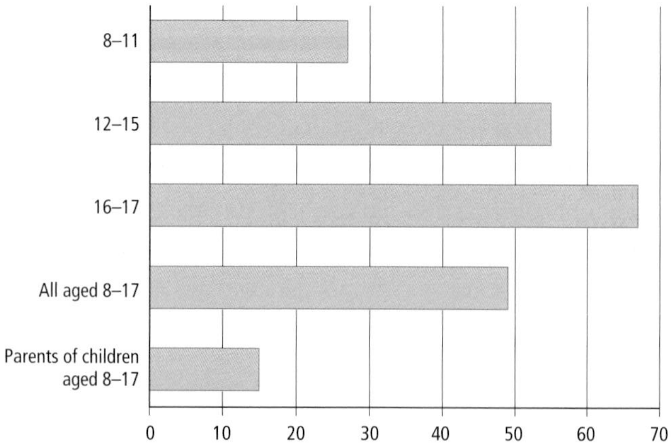

1 All those aged 8 to 17 who were aware of social networking sites and parents of children aged 8 to 17 who use the Internet were asked the question 'Do you have a page or profile on a social network site?'

Source: Ofcom

References, further reading and websites

Chapter 1: Population

References and further reading

Ageing and Mortality Statistics in the UK, National Statistician's Annual Article on the Population, available at:
http://www.statistics.gov.uk/cci/article.asp?ID=2079

Annual Report of the Registrar General for Northern Ireland, Northern Ireland Statistics and Research Agency, available at:
http://www.nisra.gov.uk/demography/default.asp22.htm

Annual Report of the Registrar General for Scotland, General Register Office for Scotland, available at:
http://www.gro-scotland.gov.uk/statistics/annrep/index.html

Asylum Statistics United Kingdom, 2007, Home Office, available at:
http://www.homeoffice.gov.uk/rds/pdfs08/hosb1108.pdf

Birth Statistics, England and Wales (Series FM1), ONS, Internet only publication, available at:
www.statistics.gov.uk/statbase/Product.asp?vlnk=5768

Bradford B (2006), *Who are the 'Mixed' ethnic group?* Internet only publication, ONS, available at:
www.statistics.gov.uk/CCI/article.asp?ID=1580

Census 2001: First results on population for England and Wales, (ONS), TSO, available at:
www.statistics.gov.uk/census2001/downloads/pop2001ew.pdf

Control of Immigration: Statistics, United Kingdom, 2006, TSO, available at:
http://www.homeoffice.gov.uk/rds/pdfs08/hosb1008.pdf

Europe in Figures – Population, Eurostat, available at:
http://epp.eurostat.ec.europa.eu/cache/ITY_OFFPUB/KS-CD-06-001-01/EN/KS-CD-06-001-01-EN.PDF

Health Statistics Quarterly, ONS, Palgrave Macmillan, available at:
http://www.statistics.gov.uk/statbase/Product.asp?vlnk=6725

International Migration Statistics (Series MN), ONS, Internet only publication, available at:
www.statistics.gov.uk/statbase/Product.asp?vlnk=507

Key Population and Vital Statistics (Series VS/PP1), ONS/TSO, available at:
http://www.statistics.gov.uk/statbase/Product.asp?vlnk=539

Kramer S, *The Fragile Male*, British Medical Journal, available at:
http://www.bmj.com/cgi/content/full/321/7276/1609

Mid-year Population Estimates, Northern Ireland, Northern Ireland Statistics and Research Agency, available at:
http://www.nisra.gov.uk/demography/default.asp17.htm

Mid-2007 Population Estimates Scotland, General Register Office for Scotland, Internet only publication, available at:
http://www.gro-scotland.gov.uk/statistics/publications-and-data/population-estimates/mid-2007-population-estimates-scotland/index.html

Mid-year Population Estimates, United Kingdom, ONS, available at:
http://www.statistics.gov.uk/statbase/Product.asp?vlnk=15106

Mortality Statistics for England and Wales (Series DH2), ONS, Internet only publications, available at:
http://www.statistics.gov.uk/statbase/Product.asp?vlnk=618

National Population Projections, UK (Series PP2), ONS, available at:
http://www.statistics.gov.uk/StatBase/Product.asp?vlnk=8519

Persons Granted British Citizenship, United Kingdom, 2007, Home Office, available at:
www.homeoffice.gov.uk/rds/pdfs08/hosb0508.pdf

Population in Europe 2007: first results, Eurostat, available at:
http://epp.eurostat.ec.europa.eu/cache/ITY_OFFPUB/KS-SF-08-081/EN/KS-SF-08-081-EN.PDF

Population Projections, Northern Ireland, Northern Ireland Statistics and Research Agency, available at:
http://www.nisra.gov.uk/demography/default.asp20.htm

Population Projections, Scotland, General Register Office for Scotland, available at:
http://www.gro-scotland.gov.uk/statistics/publications-and-data/popproj/projected-population-of-scotland-(2006-based)/index.html

Population Projections for Wales (sub-national), Welsh Assembly Government / Welsh Office Statistical Directorate, available at:
http://new.wales.gov.uk/docrepos/40382/40382313/statistics/population/pop-2007/sb49-2007?lang=en

Population Trends, ONS, Palgrave Macmillan, available at:
http://www.statistics.gov.uk/STATBASE/Product.asp?vlnk=6303

World Population Prospects: The 2006 Revision, United Nations, available at:
http://www.un.org/esa/population/publications/wpp2006/wpp2006.htm

Other useful websites

National Statistics
www.statistics.gov.uk

Eurostat
www.europa.eu.int/comm/eurostat

General Register Office for Scotland
www.gro-scotland.gov.uk

Government Actuary's Department
www.gad.gov.uk

Home Office Immigration and Asylum Statistics
www.homeoffice.gov.uk/rds/immigration-assylum-stats.html

Northern Ireland Statistics and Research Agency
www.nisra.gov.uk

Scottish Government
www.scotland.gov.uk

United Nations Population Division
www.un.org/esa/population/unpop.htm

Welsh Assembly Government
www.wales.gov.uk

Chapter 2: Households and families

References and further reading

Abortion Statistics, England and Wales: 2007, Department of Health, available at:
http://www.dh.gov.uk/en/Publicationsandstatistics/Publications/PublicationsStatistics/DH_085508

Abortion Statistics, 2007, ISD Scotland, available at:
http://www.isdscotland.org/isd/1918.html

Adoption Statistics (Series FM2), Office for National Statistics, available at:
http://www.statistics.gov.uk/statbase/Product.asp?vlnk=581

Annual Report of the Registrar General for Northern Ireland, Northern Ireland Statistics and Research Agency, available at:
http://www.nisra.gov.uk/demography/default.asp22.htm

Annual Report of the Registrar General for Scotland, General Register Office for Scotland, available at:
http://www.gro-scotland.gov.uk/statistics/index.html

Barlow A, Burgoyne C, Clery E and Smithson J, *Cohabitation and the law: myths, money and the media*, in *British Social Attitudes: the 24th Report*

Birth Statistics, England and Wales (Series FM1), Office for National Statistics, available at:
http://www.statistics.gov.uk/statbase/Product.asp?vlnk=5768

Continuous Household Survey, Northern Ireland Statistics and Research Agency, available at:
http://www.csu.nisra.gov.uk/survey.asp134.htm

Duncan S and Phillips M, *New families for partners, but traditional families for parents?* in *British Social Attitudes: the 24th Report*

Focus on Families, Office for National Statistics, available at:
http://www.statistics.gov.uk/focuson/families

Focus on People & Migration, Office for National Statistics, available at:
http://www.statistics.gov.uk/focuson/Migration

General Household Survey, Office for National Statistics, available at:
http://www.statistics.gov.uk/ghs

Health Statistics Quarterly, Office for National Statistics, available at:
http://www.statistics.gov.uk/statbase/Product.asp?vlnk=6725

HFEA Guide to infertility, Human Fertilisation and Embryology Authority, available at:
http://www.hfea.gov.uk/en/406.html

Marriages Abroad, Government Actuary's Department, available at:
http://www.gad.gov.uk/Demography_Data/Marital_status_projections/2003/marriages_abroad.asp

Population Trends, Office for National Statistics, available at:
http://www.statistics.gov.uk/statbase/Product.asp?vlnk=6303

Rise in ageing population and people living alone drives household growth, Communities and Local Government, available at:
http://www.communities.gov.uk/news/corporate/riseageing

Summary statistics on children in care and children adopted from care, British Association for Adoption & Fostering, available at:
http://www.baaf.org.uk/info/stats/index.shtml

Other useful websites

National Statistics
www.statistics.gov.uk

British Association for Adoption & Fostering
www.baaf.org.uk

Communities and Local Government
www.communities.gov.uk

Department of Health
www.dh.gov.uk

Eurostat
www.europa.eu.int/comm/eurostat

General Register Office for Scotland
www.gro-scotland.gov.uk

Government Actuary's Department
www.gad.gov.uk

Human Fertilisation and Embryology Authority
www.hfea.gov.uk

Northern Ireland Statistics and Research Agency
www.nisra.gov.uk

Scottish Government
www.scotland.gov.uk

Welsh Assembly Government
www.wales.gov.uk

National Employer Skills Survey 2007, Learning and Skills Council, available at:
http://readingroom.lsc.gov.uk/lsc/National/nat-nessurvey2007mainreport-may08.pdf

Research Report: Childcare and Early Years Survey 2007 Parents' Use, Views and Experiences, National Centre for Social Research for the Department for Children, Schools and Families, available at:
http://www.dcsf.gov.uk/research/data/uploadfiles/DCSF-RR025(1).pdf

Research Report: Parental Involvement in Children's Education 2007, BMRB Social Research for the Department of Children, Schools and Families, available at:
http://www.dcsf.gov.uk/research/data/uploadfiles/DCSF-RR034.pdf

Research Report: Skills in Scotland 2006, Futureskills Scotland for the Scottish Government, available at:
http://www.scotland.gov.uk/Resource/Doc/919/0065315.pdf

Statistical Volume: Education and Training Statistics for the United Kingdom 2008, (Internet only), Department for Children, Schools and Families, available at:
http://www.dcsf.gov.uk/rsgateway/DB/VOL/v000823/index.shtml

Workforce Training in England 2006, IFF Research Ltd for the Department for Education and Skills, available at:
http://www.dfes.gov.uk/research/data/uploadfiles/RR848.pdf

Youth Cohort Study & Longitudinal Study of Young People in England: The Activities and Experiences of 16 year olds: England 2007, Department for Children, Schools and Families, available at:
http://www.dcsf.gov.uk/rsgateway/DB/SBU/b000795/YCS_LSYPE_Bulletin_final.pdf

Other useful websites

National Statistics
www.statistics.gov.uk

Department for Children, Schools and Families
Homepage/Trends/Research and Statistics gateway
www.dcsf.gov.uk
www.dcsf.gov.uk/trends
www.dcsf.gov.uk/rsgateway

Department for Innovation, Universities and Skills
www.dius.gov.uk

Higher Education Statistics Agency
www.hesa.ac.uk

Learning and Skills Council
www.lsc.gov.uk

National Centre for Social Research
www.natcen.ac.uk

National Foundation for Educational Research
www.nfer.ac.uk

Northern Ireland Department for Employment and Learning
www.delni.gov.uk

Northern Ireland Department of Education
www.deni.gov.uk

Organisation for Economic Co-operation and Development
www.oecd.org

Office for Standards in Education
www.ofsted.gov.uk

Scottish Government
www.scotland.gov.uk

Welsh Assembly Government
www.wales.gov.uk

Chapter 3: Education and training

References and further reading

British Social Attitudes, Hard copy, National Centre for Social Research, available at:
http://www.natcen.ac.uk/natcen/pages/op_socialattitudes.htm#bsa

Chapter 4: Labour market

References and further reading

Employment of foreign workers in the United Kingdom: 1997 to 2008, Office for National Statistics, available at:

http://www.statistics.gov.uk/elmr/07_08/downloads/ELMR_Jul08_Clancy.pdf

Labour disputes in 2007, Office for National Statistics, available at:
http://www.statistics.gov.uk/elmr/06_08/downloads/ELMR_Jun08_Hale.pdf

Labour Market Guide, Office for National Statistics, available at:
http://www.statistics.gov.uk/about/data/guides/LabourMarket/

Local area labour markets: Statistical indicators July 2008, Office for National Statistics, available at:
http://www.statistics.gov.uk/downloads/theme_labour/LALM_statistical_indicators_Jul08.pdf

Public sector employment, Office for National Statistics, available at:
http://www.statistics.gov.uk/pdfdir/pse0908.pdf

The third work-life balance employee survey: Main findings, Department of Business, Enterprise and Regulatory Reform, available at:
http://www.berr.gov.uk/files/file42645.pdf

Trade union membership 2007, Department of Business, Enterprise and Regulatory Reform, available at:
http://stats.berr.gov.uk/UKSA/tu/tum2008.pdf

Work and worklessness among households, Office for National Statistics, available at:
http://www.statistics.gov.uk/pdfdir/work0808.pdf

Other useful websites

National Statistics
www.statistics.gov.uk

Department for Business, Enterprise and Regulatory Reform
www.berr.gov.uk

Department for Enterprise, Trade and Investment
Northern Ireland
www.detini.gov.uk

Department for Work and Pensions
www.dwp.gov.uk

Eurostat
www.europa.eu.int/comm/eurostat

Jobcentre Plus
www.jobcentreplus.gov.uk

Learning and Skills Council
www.lsc.gov.uk

National Centre for Social Research
www.natcen.ac.uk

Scottish Government
www.scotland.gov.uk

Welsh Assembly Government
www.wales.gov.uk

Chapter 5: Income and wealth

References and further reading

Annual Survey of Hours and Earnings, Internet only publication, ONS, available at:
www.statistics.gov.uk/StatBase/Product.asp?vlnk=13101

Brewer M, Goodman A, Myck M, Shaw J and Shephard A (2004) *Poverty and Inequality in Britain: 2004*, Commentary no. 96, Institute for Fiscal Studies

Changing Households: The British Household Panel Survey, Institute for Social and Economic Research

Clark T and Leicester A (2004) *Inequality and two decades of British tax and benefit reforms* Fiscal Studies, vol. 25, pp 129–58

Economic and Labour Market Trends, ONS, Palgrave Macmillan, available at:
www.statistics.gov.uk/StatBase/Product.asp?vlnk=308

Eurostat National Accounts ESA, Eurostat

Family Resources Survey, Department for Work and Pensions

Fiscal Studies, Institute for Fiscal Studies

Households Below Average Income, 1994/95–2005/06 (revised), Department for Work and Pensions

Income and Wealth. The Latest Evidence, Joseph Rowntree Foundation

Opportunity for All Annual Report, Department for Work and Pensions

Pension Trends, ONS, Palgrave Macmillan, available at:
www.statistics.gov.uk/StatBase/Product.asp?vlnk=14173

The Pensioners' Incomes Series, Department for Work and Pensions, available at:
www.dwp.gov.uk/asd/pensioners_income.asp

United Kingdom National Accounts (The Blue Book), ONS, Palgrave Macmillan, available at:
www.statistics.gov.uk/StatBase/Product.asp?vlnk=1143

Other useful websites

National Statistics
www.statistics.gov.uk

Centre for Economic Performance
http://cep.lse.ac.uk/

Department for Children, Schools and Families
www.dcsf.gov.uk

Department for Work and Pensions
www.dwp.gov.uk

Eurostat
www.europa.eu.int/comm/eurostat

HM Revenue and Customs
www.hmrc.gov.uk

HM Treasury
www.hm-treasury.gov.uk

Institute for Fiscal Studies
www.ifs.org.uk

Institute for Social and Economic Research
www.iser.essex.ac.uk

National Centre for Social Research
www.natcen.ac.uk

National Savings and Investments
www.nsandi.com

Chapter 6: Expenditure

References and further reading

Consumer Trends, Internet only publication, ONS, available at:
www.statistics.gov.uk/consumertrends

Family Spending, ONS, Palgrave Macmillan, available at:
www.statistics.gov.uk/StatBase/Product.asp?vlnk=361

Financial Risk Outlook Report, 2008, Financial Services Authority
http://www.fsa.gov.uk/pubs/plan/financial_risk_outlook_2008.pdf

Focus on Consumer Price Indices, ONS, Palgrave Macmillan, available at:
www.statistics.gov.uk/StatBase/Product.asp?vlnk=867

Households Below Average Income, 1994/95–2005/06, Department for Work and Pensions
http://www.dwp.gov.uk/mediacentre/pressreleases/2007/apr/drc027-230407.asp

Other useful websites

APACS – The UK Payments Association
www.apacs.org.uk

Bank of England
www.bankofengland.co.uk

Department for Work and Pensions
www.dwp.gov.uk/

Financial Services Authority
www.fsa.gov.uk/

Insolvency Service
www.insolvency.gov.uk

Chapter 7: Health

References and further reading

Alcohol-related deaths 1991–2007, ONS, available at:
www.statistics.gov.uk/CCI/nugget.asp?ID=1091&Pos=1&ColRank=28
&Rank=1000

Alcohol-related deaths by occupation, England and Wales, 2001–2005, available at: Health Statistics Quarterly, No.35:
www.statistics.gov.uk/cci/article.asp?ID=1851&POS=2&ColRank=1&
Rank=1

Annual Report of the Registrar General for Northern Ireland, Northern Ireland Statistics and Research Agency, available at:
http://www.nisra.gov.uk/archive/demography/publications/
annual_reports/2007/RG2007.pdf

Annual Report of the Registrar General for Scotland, General Register Office for Scotland, available at:
www.gro-scotland.gov.uk/statistics/publications-and-data/
annual-report-publications/rgs-annual-review-2007/index.html

At Least Five a Week – Evidence on the Impact of Physical Activity and its Relationship to Health, A Report from the Chief Medical Officer, Department of Health, available at:
www.dh.gov.uk/PublicationsAndStatistics/Publications/
PublicationsPolicyAndGuidance/
PublicationsPolicyAndGuidanceArticle/fs/en?CONTENT_
ID=4080994&chk=1Ft1Of

Choosing Health – Making Healthy Choices Easier, Cm6374, TSO, available at:
www.dh.gov.uk/PublicationsAndStatistics/Publications/
PublicationsPolicyAndGuidance/
PublicationsPolicyAndGuidanceArticle/fs/en?CONTENT_
ID=4094550&chk=aN5Cor

Contraception and Sexual Health, 2007/08, ONS, Palgrave Macmillan, available at:
www.statistics.gov.uk/downloads/theme_health/contra2007-8.pdf

Family Food – Report on the Expenditure and Food Survey, Department for Environment, Food and Rural Affairs, available at:
https://statistics.defra.gov.uk/esg/publications/efs/default.asp

Focus on Health 2006, ONS, available at:
www.statistics.gov.uk/focuson/health

General Household Survey (Longitudinal) 2006, Internet only publication, ONS, available at:
www.statistics.gov.uk/ghs

Geographic variations in deaths related to drug misuse in England and Wales between 1993 and 2006, available in Health Statistics Quarterly, 2008, Vol. 39, page 14:
http://nswebcopy/statbase/Product.asp?vlnk=6725

Health Expectancies in the United Kingdom 2003, Health Statistics Quarterly, no 33, pp 69–70, ONS, available at:
www.statistics.gov.uk/downloads/theme_health/hsq33web.pdf

Health in Scotland. The Annual Report of the Chief Medical Officer on the State of Scotland's Health, Scottish Executive, available at:
www.scotland.gov.uk/Publications/2007/11/15135302/0

Health Statistics Quarterly, available on the ONS website:
http://nswebcopy/statbase/Product.asp?vlnk=6725

Health Statistics Wales, Welsh Assembly Government, available at:
www.wales.gov.uk/topics/statistics/theme/health/?lang=en

Health Survey for England, Information Centre for health and social care, available at:

www.ic.nhs.uk/statistics-and-data-collections/health-and-lifestyles-
related-surveys/health-survey-for-England

HIV in the UK, 2008 report; Health Protection Agency, available at:
http://www.hpa.org.uk/webw/
HPAweb&Page&HPAwebAutoListName/Page/1203439654589?p=120
3439654589

Inequalities in young people's health: HBSC international report from the 2005/2006 survey, World Health Organisation Regional Office for Europe, available at:
www.euro.who.int/datapublications/Publications/
Catalogue/20080616_1

Mortality Statistics for England and Wales (Series DH1, 2, 3, 4), Internet only publications ONS, available at:
www.statistics.gov.uk/statbase/Product.asp?vlnk=620
www.statistics.gov.uk/statbase/Product.asp?vlnk=618
www.statistics.gov.uk/statbase/Product.asp?vlnk=6305
www.statistics.gov.uk/statbase/Product.asp?vlnk=621

ONS drug-related deaths database: first results for England and Wales, 1993–1997, available in Health Statistics Quarterly, 2000, Vol. 5, page 35.
http://nswebcopy/statbase/Product.asp?vlnk=6725

On the State of the Public Health – The Annual Report of the Chief Medical Officer of the Department of Health, Department of Health, available at:
www.dh.gov.uk/en/Publicationsandstatistics/Publications/
AnnualReports/DH_076817

Opinions (Omnibus) Survey, Office for National Statistics, available at:
www.ons.gov.uk/about/who-we-are/our-services/omnibus-survey/
index.html

Population Trends, ONS, Palgrave Macmillan, available at:
www.statistics.gov.uk/statbase/Product.asp?vlnk=6303

Quinn M, Wood H, Cooper N and Rowan S (2005) *Cancer Atlas of the United Kingdom and Ireland 1991–2000*, ONS, Palgrave Macmillan, available at:
www.statistics.gov.uk/statbase/Product.asp?vlnk=14059

Registrations of cancer diagnosed in 2006, England, Office for National Statistics, available at:
www.statistics.gov.uk/downloads/theme_health/MB1-37/
MB1_37_2006.pdf

Report of the Chief Medical Officer, Department of Health, Social Services and Public Safety, Northern Ireland, available at:
www.dhsspsni.gov.uk/index/phealth/cmoannualreport.htm

Results of the ICD-10 bridge coding study, England and Wales, 1999, Health Statistics Quarterly, no 14, pp 75–83, available at:
www.statistics.gov.uk/downloads/theme_health/HSQ14_v4.pdf

Sexually transmitted infections and Men who have sex with Men in the UK: 2008 report; Health Protection Agency, available at:
http://www.hpa.org.uk/webw/
HPAweb&Page&HPAwebAutoListName/Page/1203439654589?p=120
3439654589

Sexually transmitted Infections and Young People in the UK: 2008 report, Health Protection Agency Centre for Infections, available at:
http://www.hpa.org.uk/web/HPAweb&HPAwebStandard/
HPAweb_C/1216022460726

Sexually transmitted infections in black African and black Caribbean communities in the UK: 2008 report. Health Protection Agency, available at:
http://www.hpa.org.uk/webw/
HPAweb&Page&HPAwebAutoListName/Page/1203439654589?p=120
3439654589

Smoking-related Behaviour and Attitudes 2006, Internet only publications ONS, available at:
www.statistics.gov.uk/downloads/theme_health/smoking2006.pdf

Tackling Health Inequalities: Status Report on the Programme for Action, Department of Health, available at:
www.dh.gov.uk/en/Publicationsandstatistics/Publications/
PublicationsPolicyAndGuidance/DH_062903

The NHS Cancer Plan 2000, NHS, available at:
www.dh.gov.uk/prod_consum_dh/groups/dh_digitalassets/@dh/@
en/documents/digitalasset/dh_4014513.pdf

*Trends and geographical variations in alcohol-related death in the UK,
1991–2004*, Health Statistics Quarterly, 2007, no 33, pp 9–10, available at:
www.statistics.gov.uk/downloads/theme_health/hsq33web.pdf

United Kingdom Health Statistics 2006, ONS, Palgrave Macmillan,
available at:
www.statistics.gov.uk/downloads/theme_health/ukhs2/ukhs2_rel1_
superseded.pdf

Welsh Health: Annual Report of the Chief Medical Officer, Welsh Assembly
Government, available at:
http://wales.gov.uk/topics/health/ocmo/communications/
annualreport/2007/?lang=en

World Health Statistics, World Health Organisation, available at:
www.who.int/whosis/en/

Other useful websites

Department for Environment, Food and Rural Affairs
www.defra.gov.uk

Department of Health
www.dh.gov.uk

Department of Health, Social Services and Public Safety, Northern Ireland
www.dhsspsni.gov.uk/stats&research/index.asp

General Register Office for Scotland
www.gro-scotland.gov.uk

Government Actuary's Department
www.gad.gov.uk

Health Protection Agency
www.hpa.org.uk

Health Behaviour in School-aged Children
www.hbsc.org/

The NHS Information Centre for health and social care
www.ic.nhs.uk

Information Services Division Scotland
www.isdscotland.org

Northern Ireland Cancer Registry
www.qub.ac.uk/nicr

Northern Ireland Statistics and Research Agency
www.nisra.gov.uk

Scottish Government
www.scotland.gov.uk

Welsh Assembly Government
www.wales.gov.uk

Welsh Cancer Intelligence and Surveillance Unit
www.velindre-tr.wales.nhs.uk/wcisu

Chapter 8: Social protection

References and further reading

Annual Statistical Publication Notices, Scottish Government, available at:
http://www.scotland.gov.uk/Topics/Statistics/

Benefit expenditure and caseload information, Department for Work and
Pensions, available at:
www.dwp.gov.uk/asd/asd4/expenditure.asp

British Social Attitudes – The 25th Report, National Centre for Social
Research, Sage publications, available at:
www.natcen.ac.uk/natcen/pages/nm_pressreleases.htm

The Carers, Employment and Services Report 4, Carers UK, available at:
http://www.carersuk.org/Policyandpractice/Research/
CarersEmploymentandServices/1201172496

Children looked after statistics in Scotland, available at:
www.scotland.gov.uk/Topics/Statistics/Browse/Children/
PubChildrenLookedAfter

*Community Care Statistics 2007: Home Help/Care Services for Adults,
England* – NHS, available at:
http://www.ic.nhs.uk/statistics-and-data-collections/social-care/
adult-social-care-information/community-care-statistics-2007-08:-
grant-funded-services-for-adults-england

Conolly and Kerr (2008), *Families with children in Britain: Findings from the
2006 Families and Children Study (FACS)*, Department for Work and
Pensions, Corporate Document Services, available at:
www.dwp.gov.uk/asd/asd5/report_abstracts/rr_abstracts/rra_486.asp

ESSPROS Manual 1996, Eurostat

Family Resources Survey, Department for Work and Pensions, available at:
www.dwp.gov.uk/asd/frs

General Household Survey 2007, Internet only publication, ONS,
available at:
www.statistics.gov.uk/ghs

Health Statistics Wales, Children and young people, Welsh assembly
Government, available at:
http://new.wales.gov.uk/topics/?lang=en

Hospital Statistics for Northern Ireland, Department of Health, Social
Services and Public Safety, Northern Ireland, available at
www.dhsspsni.gov.uk/index/stats_research/stats-activity_stats-2.htm

Mooney E, Fitzpatrick M, and Hewitt R (2007) *Children Order Statistical
Bulletin*, Department of Health, Social Services and Public Safety, Northern
Ireland, available at:
www.dhsspsni.gov.uk/stats-cib-children_order_bulletin

*Referrals, assessments and children and young people on child protection
registers, England (First Release)*, Department for children, schools and
families, available at:
www.dcsf.gov.uk/rsgateway/whatsnew.shtml

Social Services Statistics Wales, Local Government Data Unit, available at:
www.dataunitwales.gov.uk

Other useful websites

National Statistics
www.statistics.gov.uk

Carers UK
www.carersuk.org

Charities Aid Foundation
www.cafonline.org

Department for Children, Schools and Families
www.dcsf.gov.uk

Department of Health, Social Services and Public Safety, Northern Ireland
www.dhsspsni.gov.uk

Department for Social Development, Northern Ireland
www.dsdni.gov.uk

Department for Work and Pensions
www.dwp.gov.uk

Department of Health
www.dh.gov.uk

Eurostat
www.europa.eu.int/comm/eurostat

Local Government Data Unit
www.dataunitwales.gov.uk
www.unedddatacymru.gov.uk

National Society for the Prevention of Cruelty to Children
www.nspcc.org.uk

The NHS Information Centre for health and social care
www.ic.nhs.uk

The Organisation for Economic Co-operation and Development
www.oecd.org

Scottish Government
www.scotland.gov.uk

Welsh Assembly Government
www.wales.gov.uk

Chapter 9: Crime and justice

References and further reading

Circumstances of crime, Neighbourhood Watch membership and perceptions of policing: Supplementary volume 3 to Crime in England and Wales 2006/07, Home Office, available at:
http://www.homeoffice.gov.uk/rds/pdfs08/hosb0608.pdf

Crime in England and Wales 2007/08, Home Office, available at:
http://www.homeoffice.gov.uk/rds/pdfs08/hosb0708.pdf

Crime in England and Wales 2006/07, Home Office, available at:
http://www.homeoffice.gov.uk/rds/pdfs07/hosb1107.pdf

Criminal Justice System Strategic plan 2008–2011, Office for Criminal Justice Reform (OCJR), available at:
http://www.cjsonline.gov.uk/downloads/application/pdf/1_Strategic_Plan_ALL.pdf

Criminal Statistics England and Wales 2007, available at:
http://www.justice.gov.uk/publications/criminalannual.htm

A Guide to anti-social behaviour orders and acceptable behaviour contracts (2007), Home Office, available at:
www.crimereduction.homeoffice.gov.uk/asbos/asbos9.pdf

Home Office Research Findings, Home Office, available at:
www.homeoffice.gov.uk/rds/pubsintro1.html

Home Office Statistical Bulletins, Home Office, available at:
www.homeoffice.gov.uk/rds/hosbpubs1.html

Homicides, Firearm offences and Intimate Violence 2006/07: Supplementary Volume 2 to Crime in England and Wales 2006/07, Home Office, available at:
http://www.homeoffice.gov.uk/rds/pdfs08/hosb0308.pdf

Hough M, Hunter G, Jacobson J, and Cossalter S, Research Report 04, *The impact of the Licensing Act 2003 on levels of crime and disorder: an evaluation,* Institute of Public Policy Research, Kings College London

Northern Ireland Crime Survey Bulletins, Northern Ireland Office, available at:
http://www.nio.gov.uk/statistics-research/publications.htm

Northern Ireland Judicial Statistics, Northern Ireland Court Service, available at:
http://www.courtsni.gov.uk/en-GB/Publications/Targets_and_Performance/

Offender Management Caseload Statistics, Ministry of Justice, available at:
http://www.justice.gov.uk/publications/prisonandprobation.htm

Offending, Crime and Justice Survey, 2006, Home Office, available at:
http://www.homeoffice.gov.uk/rds/pdfs08/hosb0908.pdf

Police Service of Northern Ireland Annual Statistics, 2007/08, Police Service of Northern Ireland, available at:
http://www.psni.police.uk/index/updates/updates_statistics/update_crime_statistics.htm

Population in Custody: Monthly tables, Ministry of Justice, available at:
http://www.justice.gov.uk/publications/populationincustody.htm

Recorded Crime in Scotland 2007/08, Scottish Government, available at:
http://www.scotland.gov.uk/Publications/2008/09/29155946/0

Scotland crime and justice statistics, Scottish Government, available at:
http://www.scotland.gov.uk/Topics/Statistics/Browse/Crime-Justice

Scottish Crime and Victimisation Survey 2006, Scottish Government, available at:
http://www.scotland.gov.uk/Publications/2007/10/12094216/13

Sentencing Statistics, 2007 England and Wales (annual)
http://www.justice.gov.uk/publications/prisonandprobation.htm

Other useful websites

Court Service
www.hmcourts-service.gov.uk

Criminal Justice System
www.cjsonline.org

Crown Prosecution Service
www.cps.gov.uk

Department of Constitutional Affairs
www.dca.gov.uk

Home Office
www.homeoffice.gov.uk

Judiciary of England and Wales
www.judiciary.gov.uk

Ministry of Justice
www.justice.gov.uk

Northern Ireland Court Service
www.courtsni.gov.uk

Northern Ireland Office
www.nio.gov.uk

Northern Ireland Prison Service
www.niprisonservice.gov.uk

Police Service of Northern Ireland
www.psni.police.uk

Prison Service for England and Wales
www.hmprisonservice.gov.uk

Scottish Government
www.scotland.gov.uk

Scottish Prison Service
www.sps.gov.uk

Welsh Assembly Government
www.wales.gov.uk

Chapter 10: Housing

References and further reading

Continuous Household Survey, Northern Ireland Statistics and Research Agency, available at:
http://www.csu.nisra.gov.uk/survey.asp29.htm

e-digest Statistics about: Land Use and Land Cover – Urbanisation in England, Department for Environment, Food and Rural Affairs (DEFRA), available at:
www.defra.gov.uk/environment/statistics/land/lduse.htm

English House Condition Survey 2006, Communities and Local Government, TSO, available at:
http://www.communities.gov.uk/publications/corporate/statistics/ehcs2006annualreport

General Household Survey (Longitudinal) 2007, Internet only publication, ONS, available at:
www.statistics.gov.uk/ghs

Housing in England: Survey of English Housing, Communities and Local Government, TSO, available at:
http://www.communities.gov.uk/publications/corporate/statistics/housingengland2006-07

Housing Statistics 2008, Communities and Local Government, TSO, available at:
http://www.communities.gov.uk/publications/corporate/statistics/housingstatistics2008

Lifetime Homes, Lifetime Neighbourhoods: A National Strategy for Housing in an Ageing Society, Communities and Local Government, available at:
http://www.communities.gov.uk/publications/housing/lifetimehomesneighbourhoods

New Projections of households for England and the Regions to 2029 (2007), Communities and Local Government, TSO, available at: www.communities.gov.uk/news/corporate/new-projection-households

Scottish House Condition Survey, Scottish Government, available at: www.scotland.gov.uk/Topics/Statistics/SHCS

Statistical Bulletins on Housing, Scottish Executive, available at: www.scotland.gov.uk/Topics/Housing

Other useful websites

National Statistics
www.statistics.gov.uk

Communities and Local Government
www.communities.gov.uk

Council of Mortgage Lenders
www.cml.org.uk

Department for Social Development, Northern Ireland
www.dsdni.gov.uk

HM Revenue and Customs
www.hmrc.gov.uk

Land Registry
www.landregistry.gov.uk

Neighbourhood Renewal Unit
www.neighbourhood.gov.uk

Northern Ireland Statistics and Research Agency
www.nisra.gov.uk

Scottish Government
www.scotland.gov.uk

Welsh Assembly Government
www.wales.gov.uk

Chapter 11: Environment

References and further reading

Agriculture in the United Kingdom, Department for Environment, Food and Rural Affairs, TSO, available at: http://statistics.defra.gov.uk/esg/publications/auk/default.asp

Air Quality Strategy for England, Scotland, Wales and Northern Ireland, Department for Environment, Food and Rural Affairs, TSO, available at: www.defra.gov.uk/environment/airquality/index.htm

Attitudes of European citizens towards the environment, European Commission, available at: http://ec.europa.eu/public_opinion/archives/ebs/ebs_295_en.pdf

Bathing water quality, 2007 bathing season, Eurostat, available at: http://ec.europa.eu/environment/water/water-bathing/summary_report_2008.html

Digest of United Kingdom Energy Statistics 2008, Department for Business, Enterprise and Regulatory Reform, TSO, available at: http://www.berr.gov.uk/whatwedo/energy/statistics/publications/dukes/page45537.html

e-Digest of Environmental Statistics, Department for Environment, Food and Rural Affairs, available at: www.defra.gov.uk/environment/statistics/index.htm

Energy consumption in the UK, Department for Business, Enterprise and Regulatory Reform, available at: www.berr.gov.uk/whatwedo/energy/statistics/publications/ecuk/page17658.html

Energy Trends, Department for Business, Enterprise and Regulatory Reform, available at: www.berr.gov.uk/energy/statistics/publications/trends/index.html

Ensuring the UK's Food Security in a Changing World, Department for Environment, Food and Rural Affairs, available at:

http://www.defra.gov.uk/foodrin/policy/pdf/Ensuring-UK-Food-Security-in-a-changing-world-170708.pdf

Europe in figures – Eurostat yearbook 2008, Eurostat, available at: http://epp.eurostat.ec.europa.eu/pls/portal/url/page/PGP_MISCELLANEOUS/PGE_DOC_DETAIL?p_product_code=KS-CD-07-001

Hydrological Summaries for the United Kingdom, Centre for Ecology and Hydrology Wallingford and British Geological Survey, available at: www.ceh.ac.uk/data/nrfa/water_watch.html

Municipal Waste Management, Welsh Assembly Government, available at: http://new.wales.gov.uk/topics/environmentcountryside/epq/waste_recycling/municipalwastemanagement/;jsessionid=9WkSJvKD2YyvlldLQdXLQTJB2jgzxMwTtV8Cr3Tw8Pf284S60rh3!-1130397166?lang=en

Municipal Waste Statistics, Department for Environment, Food and Rural Affairs, available at: www.defra.gov.uk/environment/statistics/wastats/

Organic Statistics UK, Department for Environment, Food and Rural Affairs, available at: http://statistics.defra.gov.uk/esg/statnot/orguk.pdf

Quarterly Energy Prices, Department for Business, Enterprise and Regulatory Reform, available at: http://www.berr.gov.uk/whatwedo/energy/statistics/publications/prices/index.html

Pollution incidents, Environment Agency, available at: http://www.environment-agency.gov.uk/research/library/data/34363.aspx

Survey of Public Attitudes to Quality of Life and to the Environment – 2007, Department for Environment, Food and Rural Affairs, available at: www.defra.gov.uk/environment/statistics/pubatt/index.htm

Sustainable Development Indicators in your Pocket 2008, Department for Environment, Food and Rural Affairs, available at: http://www.defra.gov.uk/sustainable/government/progress/data-resources/sdiyp.htm

The Environment in your Pocket 2008, Department for Environment, Food and Rural Affairs, available at: www.defra.gov.uk/environment/statistics/eiyp/index.htm

The food we waste, Waste & Resources Action Programme, available at: http://www.wrap.org.uk/applications/publications/publication_details.rm?id=698&publication=5635&programme=wrap

Wild bird populations 2007, Department for Environment, Food and Rural Affairs, available at: http://www.defra.gov.uk/Environment/statistics/wildlife/download/pdf/NSBirds20081031.pdf

Other useful websites

Centre for Ecology and Hydrology
www.ceh-nerc.ac.uk

Centre for Environment, Fisheries & Aquaculture Science
www.cefas.co.uk/

Department of Energy and Climate Change
www.decc.gov.uk

Department for Environment, Food and Rural Affairs
www.defra.gov.uk

Department of the Environment Northern Ireland
www.doeni.gov.uk

Environment Agency
www.environment-agency.gov.uk

Eurostat
www.europa.eu.int/comm/eurostat

Northern Ireland Statistics and Research Agency
www.nisra.gov.uk

Populus
www.populuslimited.com/

Scottish Environment Protection Agency
www.sepa.org.uk

Scottish Government
www.scotland.gov.uk

Waste & Resources Action Programme
www.wrap.org.uk/

Welsh Assembly Government
www.wales.gov.uk

Chapter 12: Transport

References and further reading

British Social Attitudes – The 25th Report, National Centre for Social Research, Sage publications, available at:
www.natcen.ac.uk/natcen/pages/nm_pressreleases.htm

Driving Standards Agency Annual Report and Accounts 2007/08, Driving Standards Agency, TSO, available at:
http://www.official-documents.gov.uk/document/hc0708/hc07/0738/0738.asp

European Union Energy and Transport in Figures, 2007, European Commission, available at:
http://ec.europa.eu/dgs/energy_transport/figures/pocketbook/2007_en.htm

Focus on Personal Travel: 2005 edition, Department for Transport, TSO, available at:
www.dft.gov.uk/pgr/statistics/datatablespublications/personal/focuspt/2005/focusonpersonaltravel2005edi5238

General Household Survey (Longitudinal) 2007, Internet only publication, ONS, available at:
www.statistics.gov.uk/ghs

Injury Road Traffic Collision Statistics Annual Report 2007/08, Police Service of Northern Ireland, available at:
http://www.psni.police.uk/injury_road_traffic_stats_financial_year_2007-08.pdf

National Passenger Survey Spring 2008, Passenger Focus, available at:
www.passengerfocus.org.uk/your-experiences/content.asp?dsid=496

National Rail Trends 2006–07 Yearbook, Office of Rail Regulator, available at:
www.rail-reg.gov.uk/server/show/ConWebDoc.8802

National Travel Survey Bulletins, Department for Transport, available at:
http://www.dft.gov.uk/pgr/statistics/recentpubs/recentpublications

A New Deal for Transport: Better for Everyone (2005), Department for Transport, TSO, available at:
www.dft.gov.uk/about/strategy/whitepapers/previous/anewdealfortransportbetterfo5695

Northern Ireland Transport Statistics Annual 2007–2008, Department for Regional Development Northern Ireland, available at:
http://www.drdni.gov.uk/transport_statistics_annual_2007-08.pdf

Office of Rail Regulation Annual report 2007–08, Office of Rail Regulation, available at:
http://www.rail-reg.gov.uk/server/show/nav.1240

Road Accidents Scotland 2007, Scottish Government, available at:
http://www.scotland.gov.uk/Topics/Statistics/Browse/Transport-Travel/PubRoadAcc

Road Casualties Great Britain 2007 – Annual Report, Department for Transport, TSO, available at:
http://www.dft.gov.uk/pgr/statistics/datatablespublications/accidents/casualtiesgbar/roadcasualtiesgreatbritain20071

Road Casualties: Wales 2006, Welsh Assembly Government, available at:
http://new.wales.gov.uk/topics/statistics/publications/rcw2006/?lang=en

Scottish Government Transport publications and bulleting pages, available at:

http://www.scotland.gov.uk/Topics/Statistics/Browse/Transport-Travel/Publications

Scottish Household Survey 2007, available at:
http://www.scotland.gov.uk/Topics/Statistics/16002/PublicationAnnual

Scottish Transport Statistics: No 26, 2007 Edition, Scottish Executive, available at:
http://www.scotland.gov.uk/Publications/2007/12/14120610/9

Securing the Future – UK Government sustainable development strategy (2005), Department for Environment, Food and Rural Affairs, TSO, available at:
http://www.defra.gov.uk/sustainable/government/progress/index.htm

Traffic Speeds and Congestion 2006, Department for Transport, available at:
http://www.dft.gov.uk/pgr/statistics/datatablespublications/roadstraffic/speedscongestion/roadstatstsc/roadstats07tsc

Transport Statistics Bulletins and Reports, Department for Transport, available at:
http://www.dft.gov.uk/pgr/statistics/recentpubs/recentpublications

Transport Statistics for Great Britain 2008, Department for Transport, TSO, available at:
http://www.dft.gov.uk/pgr/statistics/datatablespublications/tsgb/2008edition/

Transport Trends 2008, Department for Transport, TSO, available at:
http://www.dft.gov.uk/pgr/statistics/datatablespublications/trends/current/

Travel Trends, ONS, Palgrave Macmillan, available at:
www.statistics.gov.uk/statbase/Product.asp?vlnk=1391

Vehicle Licensing Statistics 2007, Department for Transport, available at:
http://www.dft.gov.uk/pgr/statistics/datatablespublications/vehicles/licensing/vehiclelicensingstatistics2007

Vehicle Speeds in Great Britain 2007, Department for Transport, available at:
http://www.dft.gov.uk/pgr/statistics/datatablespublications/roadstraffic/speedscongestion/roadstatstsc/roadstats07tsc

Welsh Transport Statistics, Welsh Assembly Government, available at:
http://new.wales.gov.uk/topics/statistics/theme/transport/?lang=en

Other useful websites

National Statistics
www.statistics.gov.uk

Civil Aviation Authority, Economic Regulation Group
www.caa.co.uk/homepage.aspx

Department of Energy and Climate Change
www.decc.gov.uk

Department of the Environment Northern Ireland
www.doeni.gov.uk

Department for Regional Development Northern Ireland
www.drdni.gov.uk

Department for Transport
www.dft.gov.uk

European Commission Directorate-General Energy and Transport
www.ec.europa.eu/dgs/energy_transport/index_en.html

National Centre for Social Research
www.natcen.ac.uk

Office of Rail Regulation
www.rail-reg.gov.uk

Passenger Focus
www.passengerfocus.org.uk

Police Service of Northern Ireland
www.psni.police.uk

Scottish Government
www.scotland.gov.uk

Welsh Assembly Government
www.wales.gov.uk

Chapter 13: Lifestyles and social participation

References and further reading

Citizenship Survey: April–June 2008, England, Communities and Local Government, available at:
http://www.communities.gov.uk/publications/corporate/statistics/citizenshipsurveyq12008-09

Helping Out, a national survey of volunteering and charitable giving, 2006/07, Cabinet Office, available at:
www.cabinetoffice.gov.uk/third_sector/Research_and_statistics/third_sector_research/helping_out.aspx

Internet Access 2008, First Release, Office for National Statistics, available at:
http://www.statistics.gov.uk/pdfdir/iahi0808.pdf

Media Literacy Audit: Report on UK children's media literacy, Ofcom, available at:
http://www.ofcom.org.uk/advice/media_literacy/medlitpub/medlitpubrss/ml_childrens08/ml_childrens08.pdf

Media Literacy Audit: Report on UK adults' media literacy, Ofcom, available at:
http://www.ofcom.org.uk/advice/media_literacy/medlitpub/medlitpubrss/ml_adult08/ml_adults08.pdf

Quick S, *2007/08 School Sport Survey*, Department for Children, Schools and Families, available at:
http://www.dcsf.gov.uk/research/programmeofresearch/projectinformation.cfm?projectid=15567&resultspage=1

Sainsbury M and Clarkson R, *Reading at Ages Nine and Eleven, Full Report (2008)*, available at:
http://www.nfer.ac.uk/publications/pdfs/downloadable/RAQ.pdf

Social Networking, a quantitative and qualitative report into attitudes, behaviours and use, Ofcom, available at:
http://www.ofcom.org.uk/advice/media_literacy/medlitpub/medlitpubrss/socialnetworking/report.pdf

Taking Part: The National Survey of Culture, Leisure and Sport, Department of Culture, Media and Sport, available at:
http://www.culture.gov.uk/reference_library/research_and_statistics/4828.aspx

Travel Trends: Data tables on the 2007 International Passenger Survey, available at:
http://www.statistics.gov.uk/statbase/Product.asp?vlnk=1391

UK Giving 2008, Charities Aid Foundation and National Council of Voluntary Organisations, available at:
www.cafonline.org/ukgiving

Wardle H, Sproston K, Orford J, Erens B, Griffiths M, Constantine R, and Pigott S, *British Gambling Prevalence Survey 2007*, available at:
http://www.gamblingcommission.gov.uk/Client/detail.asp?ContentId=311

Other useful websites

Cabinet Office
www.cabinetoffice.gov.uk

Charities Aid Foundation
www.cafonline.org

Communities and Local Government
www.communities.gov.uk

Department for Children, Schools and Families
www.dcsf.gov.uk

Department for Culture, Media and Sport
www.culture.gov.uk

Gambling Commission
www.gamblingcommission.gov.uk

National Centre for Social Research
www.natcen.ac.uk

National Foundation for Educational Research
www.nfer.ac.uk

National Lottery Commission
www.natlotcomm.gov.uk

National Readership Survey
www.nrs.co.uk/

Ofcom
www.ofcom.org.uk/research

Populus
www.populus.co.uk

Public Lending Right
www.plr.uk.com

VisitBritain
www.visitbritain.co.uk/

Geographical areas

The European Union, 1 January 2007

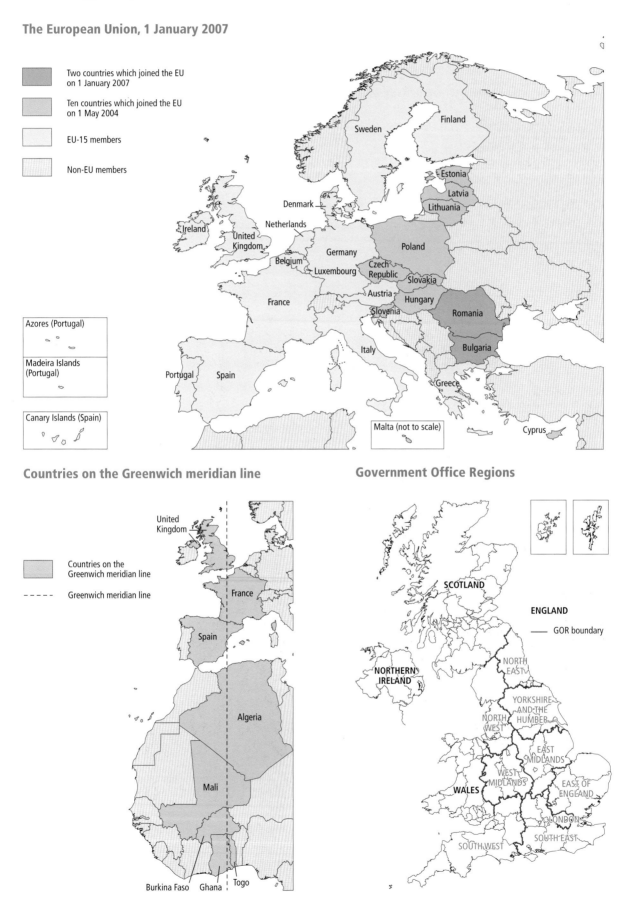

Two countries which joined the EU on 1 January 2007

Ten countries which joined the EU on 1 May 2004

EU-15 members

Non-EU members

Sweden
Finland
Estonia
Latvia
Lithuania
Denmark
Ireland
Netherlands
United Kingdom
Belgium
Germany
Poland
Luxembourg
Czech Republic
Slovakia
Austria
Hungary
France
Slovenia
Romania
Italy
Bulgaria
Portugal
Spain
Greece
Malta (not to scale)
Cyprus

Azores (Portugal)

Madeira Islands (Portugal)

Canary Islands (Spain)

Countries on the Greenwich meridian line

Countries on the Greenwich meridian line

Greenwich meridian line

United Kingdom
France
Spain
Algeria
Mali
Burkina Faso   Ghana   Togo

Government Office Regions

SCOTLAND
ENGLAND
GOR boundary
NORTHERN IRELAND
NORTH EAST
YORKSHIRE AND THE HUMBER
NORTH WEST
EAST MIDLANDS
WEST MIDLANDS
EAST OF ENGLAND
WALES
LONDON
SOUTH EAST
SOUTH WEST

Waste Disposal Authorities

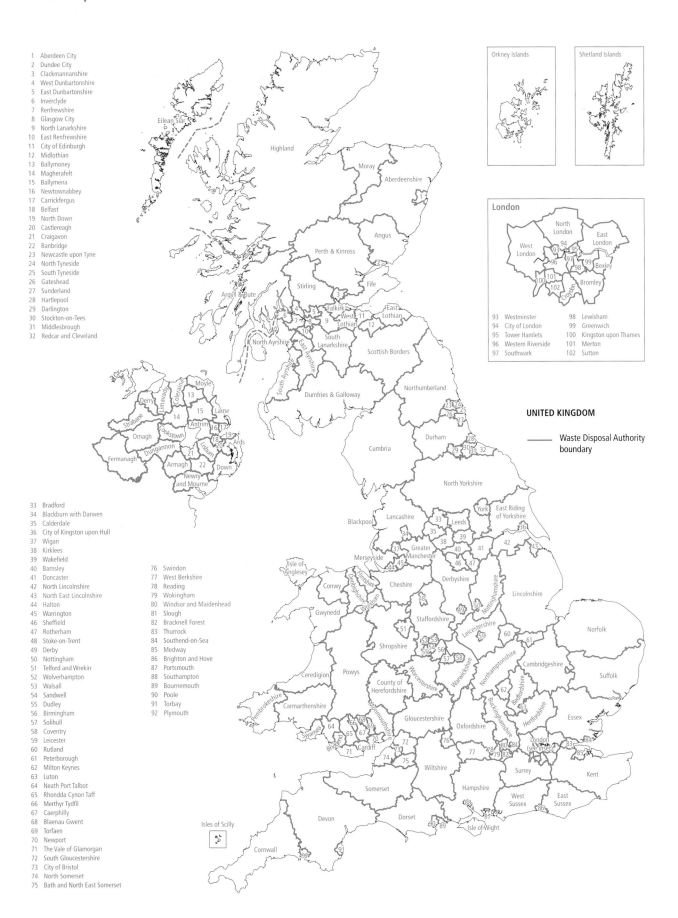

1 Aberdeen City
2 Dundee City
3 Clackmannanshire
4 West Dunbartonshire
5 East Dunbartonshire
6 Inverclyde
7 Renfrewshire
8 Glasgow City
9 North Lanarkshire
10 East Renfrewshire
11 City of Edinburgh
12 Midlothian
13 Ballymoney
14 Magherafelt
15 Ballymena
16 Newtownabbey
17 Carrickfergus
18 Belfast
19 North Down
20 Castlereagh
21 Craigavon
22 Banbridge
23 Newcastle upon Tyne
24 North Tyneside
25 South Tyneside
26 Gateshead
27 Sunderland
28 Hartlepool
29 Darlington
30 Stockton-on-Tees
31 Middlesbrough
32 Redcar and Cleveland

33 Bradford
34 Blackburn with Darwen
35 Calderdale
36 City of Kingston upon Hull
37 Wigan
38 Kirklees
39 Wakefield
40 Barnsley
41 Doncaster
42 North Lincolnshire
43 North East Lincolnshire
44 Halton
45 Warrington
46 Sheffield
47 Rotherham
48 Stoke-on-Trent
49 Derby
50 Nottingham
51 Telford and Wrekin
52 Wolverhampton
53 Walsall
54 Sandwell
55 Dudley
56 Birmingham
57 Solihull
58 Coventry
59 Leicester
60 Rutland
61 Peterborough
62 Milton Keynes
63 Luton
64 Neath Port Talbot
65 Rhondda Cynon Taff
66 Merthyr Tydfil
67 Caerphilly
68 Blaenau Gwent
69 Torfaen
70 Newport
71 The Vale of Glamorgan
72 South Gloucestershire
73 City of Bristol
74 North Somerset
75 Bath and North East Somerset

76 Swindon
77 West Berkshire
78 Reading
79 Wokingham
80 Windsor and Maidenhead
81 Slough
82 Bracknell Forest
83 Thurrock
84 Southend-on-Sea
85 Medway
86 Brighton and Hove
87 Portsmouth
88 Southampton
89 Bournemouth
90 Poole
91 Torbay
92 Plymouth

London

93 Westminster
94 City of London
95 Tower Hamlets
96 Western Riverside
97 Southwark
98 Lewisham
99 Greenwich
100 Kingston upon Thames
101 Merton
102 Sutton

UNITED KINGDOM

—— Waste Disposal Authority boundary

Local or Unitary Authorities[1]

England

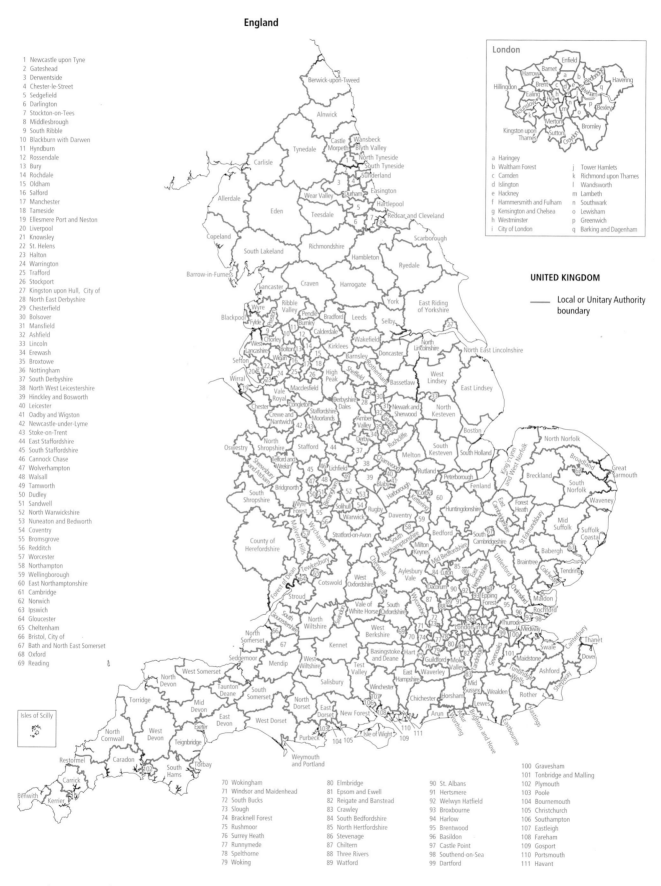

1 Newcastle upon Tyne
2 Gateshead
3 Derwentside
4 Chester-le-Street
5 Sedgefield
6 Darlington
7 Stockton-on-Tees
8 Middlesbrough
9 South Ribble
10 Blackburn with Darwen
11 Hyndburn
12 Rossendale
13 Bury
14 Rochdale
15 Oldham
16 Salford
17 Manchester
18 Tameside
19 Ellesmere Port and Neston
20 Liverpool
21 Knowsley
22 St. Helens
23 Halton
24 Warrington
25 Trafford
26 Stockport
27 Kingston upon Hull, City of
28 North East Derbyshire
29 Chesterfield
30 Bolsover
31 Mansfield
32 Ashfield
33 Lincoln
34 Erewash
35 Broxtowe
36 Nottingham
37 South Derbyshire
38 North West Leicestershire
39 Hinckley and Bosworth
40 Leicester
41 Oadby and Wigston
42 Newcastle-under-Lyme
43 Stoke-on-Trent
44 East Staffordshire
45 South Staffordshire
46 Cannock Chase
47 Wolverhampton
48 Walsall
49 Tamworth
50 Dudley
51 Sandwell
52 North Warwickshire
53 Nuneaton and Bedworth
54 Coventry
55 Bromsgrove
56 Redditch
57 Worcester
58 Northampton
59 Wellingborough
60 East Northamptonshire
61 Cambridge
62 Norwich
63 Ipswich
64 Gloucester
65 Cheltenham
66 Bristol, City of
67 Bath and North East Somerset
68 Oxford
69 Reading

70 Wokingham
71 Windsor and Maidenhead
72 South Bucks
73 Slough
74 Bracknell Forest
75 Rushmoor
76 Surrey Heath
77 Runnymede
78 Spelthorne
79 Woking

80 Elmbridge
81 Epsom and Ewell
82 Reigate and Banstead
83 Crawley
84 South Bedfordshire
85 North Hertfordshire
86 Stevenage
87 Chiltern
88 Three Rivers
89 Watford

90 St. Albans
91 Hertsmere
92 Welwyn Hatfield
93 Broxbourne
94 Harlow
95 Brentwood
96 Basildon
97 Castle Point
98 Southend-on-Sea
99 Dartford

100 Gravesham
101 Tonbridge and Malling
102 Plymouth
103 Poole
104 Bournemouth
105 Christchurch
106 Southampton
107 Eastleigh
108 Fareham
109 Gosport
110 Portsmouth
111 Havant

London

a Haringey
b Waltham Forest
c Camden
d Islington
e Hackney
f Hammersmith and Fulham
g Kensington and Chelsea
h Westminster
i City of London
j Tower Hamlets
k Richmond upon Thames
l Wandsworth
m Lambeth
n Southwark
o Lewisham
p Greenwich
q Barking and Dagenham

UNITED KINGDOM

——— Local or Unitary Authority boundary

1 Local or unitary authorities in England, unitary authorities in Wales, council areas in Scotland and district council areas in Northern Ireland.

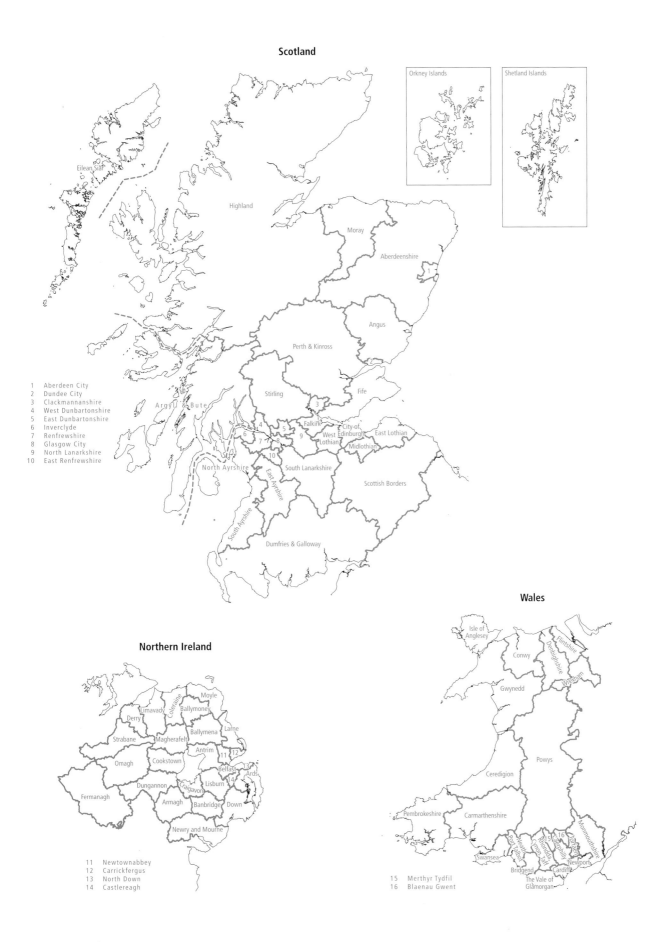

Scotland

Orkney Islands

Shetland Islands

Eilean Siar

Highland

Moray

Aberdeenshire

Angus

Perth & Kinross

Fife

Argyll & Bute

Stirling

3

Falkirk

City of Edinburgh

East Lothian

West Lothian

Midlothian

6 4 5

7 8

9

10

North Ayrshire

South Lanarkshire

Scottish Borders

East Ayrshire

South Ayrshire

Dumfries & Galloway

1   Aberdeen City
2   Dundee City
3   Clackmannanshire
4   West Dunbartonshire
5   East Dunbartonshire
6   Inverclyde
7   Renfrewshire
8   Glasgow City
9   North Lanarkshire
10 East Renfrewshire

Northern Ireland

Moyle
Coleraine
Limavady
Ballymoney
Derry
Ballymena
Larne
Strabane
Magherafelt
Antrim
11 12
Omagh
Cookstown
Belfast
13
Dungannon
Craigavon
Lisburn
14
Ards
Fermanagh
Armagh
Banbridge
Down
Newry and Mourne

11 Newtownabbey
12 Carrickfergus
13 North Down
14 Castlereagh

Wales

Isle of Anglesey
Conwy
Denbighshire
Flintshire
Wrexham
Gwynedd
Powys
Ceredigion
Pembrokeshire
Carmarthenshire
15 16
Neath Port Talbot
Rhondda Cynon Taf
Caerphilly
Torfaen
Monmouthshire
Swansea
Bridgend
Cardiff
Newport
The Vale of Glamorgan

15 Merthyr Tydfil
16 Blaenau Gwent

Major surveys

	Frequency	Sampling frame	Type of respondent	Coverage	Effective sample size[1] (most recent survey included in *Social Trends*)	Response rate (percentages)
Annual Population Survey	Continuous	Postcode Address File	All adults in household	UK	360,000 individuals	[2]
Annual Survey of Hours and Earnings	Annual	HM Revenue & Customs PAYE records	Employee	UK	141,000 employees	83
British Crime Survey	Annual	Postcode Address File	Adult in household	E&W	46,983 addresses	76
British Social Attitudes Survey	Annual	Postcode Address File	One adult aged 18 and over per household	GB	3,347 adults aged 18 and over	52–53[3]
Census of Population	Decennial	Detailed local	Adult in household	UK	Full count	98
Citizenship Survey	Continuous	Postcode Address File	One adult per household	E&W	2,403 core and 1,437 boost	58
Continuous Household Survey	Continuous	Valuation and Lands Agency Property	All adults in household	NI	3,980 addresses	65
English House Condition Survey	Continuous[4]	Postcode Address File	Any one householder	E	31,917 addresses	51[4]
English Longitudinal Study of Ageing	Ad-hoc	Health Survey for England Study	People aged over 50 who responded to the Health Survey for England study	E	12,000	70.4
Expenditure and Food Survey	Continuous	Postcode Address File in GB, Valuation and Lands Agency list in NI	All adults in households aged 16 or over[5]	UK	10,929 addresses[5]	57[5]
Families and Children Study	Annual	Child benefit records[6]	Recipients of child benefit (usually mothers)	GB	8,939 households[6]	84[6]
Family Resources Survey	Continuous	Postcode Address File	All members in household	UK	43,166 households	60
General Household Survey	Continuous	Postcode Address File	All adults in household	GB	12,203 households	73[7]
Health Survey for England, 2006	Continuous	Postcode Address File	All adults aged 16 and over in household and up to a maximum of 2 children	E	12,652 households	71[8]
Health Survey for England, 2007	Continuous	Postcode Address File	All adults aged 16 and over in household and up to a maximum of 2 children	E	6,369 households	71[9]
International Passenger Survey	Continuous	International passengers	Individual traveller	UK[10]	259,000 individuals	80
Labour Force Survey	Continuous	Postcode Address File	All adults in household	UK	60,000 households	67.7[11]
Longitudinal Study of Young People in England	Annual	School records	Young person and his/her parents/guardians	E	11,393 households	90[12]
National Employers Skills Survey	Annual	Experian	Employer	E	79,018 employers	35
National Passenger Survey	Twice yearly	Passengers at 650 stations	Railway passengers	GB	50,000 individuals	37
National Travel Survey	Continuous	Postcode Address File	All household members	GB	13,687 households per year	61[13]

	Frequency	Sampling frame	Type of respondent	Coverage	Effective sample size[1] (most recent survey included in *Social Trends*)	Response rate (percentages)
Northern Ireland Crime Survey	Continuous	Land and Property Services Agency (LPSA) list of domestic addresses	One person aged 16 and over from each household	NI	6,051 addresses	65
Offending, Crime and Justice Survey	Annual	Postcode Address File	Young people in private households aged 10 to 25	E&W	5,353	[14]
Omnibus Survey	Continuous	Postcode Address File	Adults aged 16 and over living in private households	GB	Approximately 12,000[15]	66
Omnibus Survey (e-society)	Continuous	Postcode Address File	Adults aged 16 and over living in private households	UK	6,000 adults aged 16 and over	61
Retail Sales Inquiry	Continuous	Inter Departmental Business Register[16]	Retailers	GB	Approximately 5,000	63[16]
Survey of English Housing	Continuous	Postcode Address File	Household	E	27,395 households	64
Scottish Crime and Victimisation Survey	Continuous	Postcode Address File	One adult in household	S	4,988	71
Scottish Household Survey	Continuous	Postcode Address File	Highest earning householder or spouse/partner and one adult aged 16 or over	S	10,000 households per year	66
Survey of Personal Incomes	Annual	HM Revenue & Customs PAYE, Claims and Self-assessment records	Individuals/taxpayers	UK	540,000 individuals	[17]
Taking Part Survey	Continuous	Postcode Address File	One adult aged 16 and over in private households and, where appropriate, one child aged between 11 and 15	E	24,174 adults aged 16 and over	55
Wealth and Assets Survey	Continuous	Postcode Address File	All adults in household	GB[18]	15,360	55[18]
Work and Pensions Longitudinal Study	Quarterly	Benefit claimants	Benefit claimants/beneficiaries	GB	All benefit claimants	[19]
Youth Cohort Study	Annual	School records	Young person	E	7,525 young people	69

1 Effective sample size includes nonrespondents but excludes ineligible households.
2 The Annual Population Survey includes the English Local Labour Force Survey, Welsh Local Labour Force Survey, Scottish Labour Force Survey, Annual Population Survey 'Boost' and waves 1 and 5 of the Quarterly Labour Force Survey.
3 Response rate refers to 2007 survey.
4 Although the EHCS runs on a continuous basis, its reporting is based on a rolling two year sample. The EHCS response combines successful outcomes from two linked surveys where information is separately gathered about the household and the dwelling for each address.
5 There is an optional diary for children aged 7 to 15 in Great Britain. Basic sample for Great Britain only. Response rate refers to Great Britain.
6 The overall response rate is given, which is the number of interviews as a proportion of the total initial sample.
7 Response rate for fully and partially responding households.
8 There were an additional 3,383 households in the boost sample (which was an additional sample of 2 to 15-year-olds) with a response rate of 73 per cent.
9 There were an additional 5,121 households in the boost sample with a response rate of 75 per cent.
10 Includes UK and overseas residents.
11 Response rate to first wave interviews of the quarterly LFS over the period April–June 2008.
12 Response rate quoted refers to waves 2 to 4, which were conducted in 2008.
13 Sixty one per cent of eligible households were recorded as being 'fully productive'. However, a further 7 per cent co-operated partially with the survey, and the data from these households can be used on a limited basis.
14 Eighty five per cent for the panel sample and 67 per cent for the fresh sample.
15 Achieved sample size per Omnibus cycle. The Omnibus interviews at one household per sampled address and one adult per household. Data are weighted to account for the fact that respondents living in smaller households would have a greater chance of selection.
16 Average response rate for 2006.
17 Response rate not applicable as data are drawn from administrative records.
18 Excludes Scotland North of Caledonian Canal, Scottish Highlands and Isles of Scilly. Response rate refers to fully or partially responding households between July 2006 and June 2007.
19 Response rate not applicable as data are drawn from administrative records.

Symbols and conventions

Reference years	Where, because of space constraints, a choice of years has to be made, the most recent year or a run of recent years is shown together with the past population census years (2001, 1991, 1981, etc) and sometimes the mid-points between census years (1996, 1986, etc). Other years may be added if they represent a peak or trough in the series.
Financial year	For example, 1 April 2006 to 31 March 2007 would be shown as 2006/07.
Academic year	For example, September 2006 to July 2007 would be shown as 2006/07.
Combined years	For example, 2004–07 shows data for more than one year that have been combined.
Geography	Where possible Social Trends uses data for the UK as a whole. When UK data are not available, or data from the constituent countries of the UK are not comparable, data for Great Britain or the constituent countries are used. Constituent countries can advise where data are available that are equivalent but not directly comparable with those of other constituent countries.
Units on tables	Where one unit predominates it is shown at the top of the table. All other units are shown against the relevant row or column. Figures are shown in italics when they represent percentages.
Rounding of figures	In tables where figures have been rounded to the nearest final digit, there may be an apparent discrepancy between the sum of the constituent items and the total as shown.
Provisional and estimated data	Some data for the latest year (and occasionally for earlier years) are provisional or estimated. To keep footnotes to a minimum, these have not been indicated; source departments will be able to advise if revised data are available.
Billion	This term is used to represent one thousand million.
Household reference person	Sometimes it is necessary to select one person in a household to indicate the general characteristics of the household. For this purpose the household reference person has replaced the head of household in all government-sponsored household surveys after 2000–01. The household reference person is identified during the interview and is:

    a. the householder (in whose name the accommodation is owned or rented); or

    b. in households with joint householders, the person with the highest income or, if both householders have the same income, the oldest householder.

Seasonal adjustment	Unless otherwise stated, unadjusted data have been used.
Dependent children	Those aged under 16, or single people aged 16 to 18 who have not married and are in full-time education unless otherwise indicated.
State pension age (SPA)	The age at which pensions are normally payable by the state pension scheme, currently 65 for men and 60 for women.
EU	Unless otherwise stated, data relate to the enlarged European Union of 27 countries (EU-27) as constituted since 1 January 2007. EU-25 refers to the 25 members of the EU before enlargement in May 2004 from the 15 original members (EU-15).
Ireland	Refers to the Republic of Ireland and does not include Northern Ireland.

Sources   Sources are usually listed as the name by which the source is currently known. In some instances, requests have been made to show the source name at the time the data were compiled. Specific instances have been recorded in relevant appendix entries.

Symbols   The following symbols have been used throughout *Social Trends*:

    .. not available

    .   not applicable

    *   data have been suppressed to protect confidentiality

    -   negligible (less than one-half the final digit shown)

    0   nil

Appendix

Part 1: Population

Population estimates and projections

The estimated and projected populations are of the resident population of an area, that is all those usually resident there, whatever their nationality. Members of HM Forces stationed outside the UK are excluded; members of foreign forces stationed in the UK are included. Students are taken to be resident at their term-time addresses. Figures for the UK do not include the population of the Channel Islands or the Isle of Man.

The population estimates for mid-2001 to mid-2007 are based on results from the 2001 Census and have been updated to reflect subsequent births, deaths, net migration and other changes. The estimates used in this publication were released on 21 August 2008 and are available at: www.statistics.gov.uk/statbase/Product.asp?vlnk=15106.

The most recent set of national population projections published for the UK are based on the populations of England, Wales, Scotland and Northern Ireland at mid-2006. These were released on 23 October 2007 and further details are available at: www.statistics.gov.uk/CCI/nscl.asp?id=7595

Classification of ethnic groups

The recommended classification of ethnic groups for National Statistics data sources was changed in 2001 to bring it broadly in line with the 2001 Census.

There are two levels to this classification. Level 1 is a classification into five main ethnic groups. Level 2 provides a finer, more detailed classification of Level 1. The preference is for the Level 2 categories to be adopted wherever possible. The two levels and the categories are in the box below.

Direct comparisons should not be made between the figures produced using this new classification and those based on the previous classification.

Further details can be found on the National Statistics website: www.statistics.gov.uk/about/classifications/downloads/ns_ethnicity_statement.doc

Internal migration estimates

The estimates of internal migration presented in this volume are based on data provided by the National Health Service Central Register (NHSCR), which records movements of patients between former health authority (HA) areas in England and Wales. Using this data source, the definition of an internal migrant is someone who moves from one former HA to another and registers with a different doctor. Historically, internal migration estimates were only available at the former HA level; these were equivalent to shire counties, metropolitan districts and groupings of London boroughs. HA-level migration estimates are available from 1975 on a quarterly rolling year basis.

Internal migration estimates by age and sex became available for all local authority areas in 1999. By obtaining a download from each patient register and by combining all the patient register extracts together, the Office for National Statistics creates a total register for the whole of England and Wales. Comparing records in one year with those of the previous year enables identification of people who have changed their postcode. Estimates at local authority level are made by constraining the migration estimates from the patient registers with the NHSCR estimates at the former HA level.

It has been established that internal migration data under-report the migration of men aged between 16 and 36. Currently, however, there are no suitable sources of data available to enable adjustments or revisions to be made to the estimates. Further research is planned on this topic and new data sources may become available in the future.

International migration estimates

An international migrant is defined as someone who changes his or her country of usual residence for a period of at least a year, so that the country of destination becomes the country of usual residence. The richest source of information on international migrants comes from the International Passenger Survey (IPS), which is a sample survey of passengers arriving at, and departing from, the main UK air and sea ports and the Channel Tunnel. This survey provides migration estimates based on respondents' intended length of stay in the UK or abroad.

Adjustments are made to account for people who do not realise their intended length of stay. An estimate is made for the number of people who initially come to or leave the UK for a short period but subsequently stay for a year or longer ('visitor switchers'). The number of people who intend to be migrants, but who in reality stay in the UK or abroad for less than a year ('migrant switchers') are also estimated.

Data from other sources are used to supplement the IPS migration estimates. Home Office asylum seeker data are used to estimate the number of asylum seekers and their dependants who enter

Classification of ethnic groups

Level 1	Level 2
White	White
	British
	Irish
	Other White background
	All White groups
Mixed	White and Black Caribbean
	White and Black African
	White and Asian
	Other Mixed background
	All Mixed groups
Asian or Asian British	Indian
	Pakistani
	Bangladeshi
	Other Asian background
	All Asian groups
Black or Black British	Caribbean
	African
	Other Black background
	All Black groups
Chinese or other ethnic Group	Chinese
	Other ethnic group
	All Chinese or Other groups
All ethnic groups	All ethnic groups
Not stated	Not stated

or leave the country without being counted in the IPS. Estimates of migration between the UK and Ireland are made using information from the Irish Central Statistics Office.

Part 2: Households and families

Households

Although definitions differ slightly across surveys and the census, they are broadly similar.

A household is a person living alone or a group of people who have the address as their only or main residence and who either share one meal a day or share the living accommodation.

Students: those living in halls of residence are recorded under their parents' household and included in the parents' family type in the Labour Force Survey (LFS), although some surveys/projections include such students in the institutional population.

In the General Household Survey (GHS) (Longitudinal) (see below), young people aged 16 and over who live away from home for purposes of either work or study and come home only for holidays are not included at the parental address.

Families

Children: Never-married people of any age who live with one or both parent(s). They include stepchildren and adopted children (but not foster children) and also grandchildren, where the parent(s) are absent.

Dependent children: In the 1971 and 1981 Censuses, dependent children were defined as never-married children in families who were either under 15 years of age, or aged 15 to 24 and in full-time education. In the 1991 Census, the Labour Force Survey (LFS) and the General Household Survey (GHS) (Longitudinal), dependent children are childless never-married children in families who are aged under 16, or aged 16 to 18 and in full-time education and living in the household and, in the 1991 Census, economically inactive (see Glossary in Chapter 4: Labour Market page 61). In the 2001 Census a dependent child is a person aged under 16 in a household (whether or not in a family) or aged 16 to 18, in full-time education and living in a family with their parent(s).

A family: A married or cohabiting couple, either with or without their never-married child or children (of any age), including couples with no children or a lone parent together with his or her never-married child or children, provided they have no children of their own. A family could also consist of a grandparent(s) with their grandchild or grandchildren if the parents of the grandchild or grandchildren are not usually resident in the household. In the LFS, a family unit can also comprise a single person. LFS family units include non-dependent children (who can in fact be adult) those aged 16 and over and not in full-time education, provided they have never married and have no children of their own in the household.

One family and no others: A household comprises one family and no others if there is only one family in the household and there are no non-family people.

Multi-family household: A household containing two or more people who cannot be allocated to a single family as defined in 'a family' above. This includes households with two or more unrelated adults and can also include a grandparent(s) with their child or children and grandchild or grandchildren in one household.

A lone parent family: In the census is a father or mother together with his or her never-married child or children. A lone parent family in the LFS consists of a lone parent, living with his or her never-married child or children, provided these children have no children of their own living with them. A lone parent family in the GHS consists of a lone parent, living with his or her never-married dependent child or children, provided these children have no children of their own. Married lone mothers whose husbands are not defined as resident in the household are not classified as lone parents. Evidence suggests the majority are separated from their husband either because he usually works away from home or for some other reason that does not imply the breakdown of the marriage.

Multi-sourced tables

Tables 2.1, 2.2 and 2.3 have multiple sources. To create long time series it is necessary to combine these sources even though they are not always directly comparable. Most of the multi-sourced tables include a combination of the General Household Survey (GHS) (Longitudinal), the Labour Force Survey (LFS) and the Census. For further information about the GHS see below and for the LFS see Appendix, Part 4: Labour Force Survey.

General Household Survey

The General Household Survey (GHS) (Longitudinal) is an interdepartmental multi-purpose continuous survey carried out by the Office for National Statistics (ONS) collecting information from people living in private households in Great Britain. The survey has run continuously since 1971, except for breaks in 1997/78 (when the survey was reviewed) and 1999/2000 when the survey was redeveloped.

In 2005 the GHS adopted a new sample design in line with European requirements, changing from a cross-sectional to a longitudinal design. The purpose of this change was to help monitor European social policy by comparing poverty indicators and changes over time across the European Community. The GHS design changed to a four-yearly rotation where respondents are followed up and re-interviewed up to four times. Around 75 per cent of the people surveyed in 2006 had also completed an interview in 2005.

Between April 1994 and April 2005, the GHS was conducted on a financial year basis, with fieldwork spread evenly across the year April–March. However, in 2005 the survey period reverted to the calendar year. The 2006 survey ran from January to December.

Further details of the methodological changes made during 2005 can be found in the appendices to the GHS at:
www.statistics.gov.uk/ghs

The GHS collects information on a range of topics. These are:

- smoking
- drinking
- households, families and people
- housing and consumer durables
- marriage and cohabitation
- occupational and personal pension schemes

The GHS provides authoritative estimates in the topics of smoking and drinking. A detailed summary and a longer report on these topics can be found at:
www.statistics.gov.uk/ghs

Civil partnership

The *Civil Partnership Act 2004* came into force on 5 December 2005 and enables same-sex couples aged 16 and over to obtain legal recognition of their relationship. Couples who form a civil partnership have a new legal status, that of 'civil partner'.

Civil partners have equal treatment to married couples in a range of legal matters, including:

- tax, including inheritance tax
- employment benefits
- most state and occupational pension benefits
- income-related benefits, tax credits and child support
- duty to provide reasonable maintenance for your civil partner and any children of the family
- ability to apply for parental responsibility for your civil partner's child
- inheritance of a tenancy agreement
- recognition under intestacy rules
- access to fatal accidents compensation
- protection from domestic violence
- recognition for immigration and nationality purposes

True birth order

At birth registration, the number of previous births is only collected for births within marriage; therefore information on birth order is not complete. The partial information on birth order from registration data is supplemented with data from the General Household Survey (Longitudinal) to give an estimate of true birth order. True birth order estimates for England and Wales have recently been updated to incorporate the latest information from the General Household Survey for 2004–06. For more detail on the General Household Survey, see above.

Conceptions

Conception statistics used in Table 2.19 include pregnancies that result in either a maternity at which one or more live births or stillbirths occur, or a legal abortion under the *Abortion Act 1967.* Conception statistics do not include miscarriages or illegal abortions. Dates of conception are estimated using recorded gestation for abortions and stillbirths, and assuming 38 weeks gestation for live births.

Part 3: Education and training

Stages of education

Education takes place in several stages: early years, primary, secondary, further and higher education, and is compulsory for all children in the UK between the ages of 5 (4 in Northern Ireland) and 16. The non-compulsory fourth stage, further education, covers non-advanced education, which can be taken at both further (including tertiary) education colleges, higher education institutions and increasingly in secondary schools. The fifth stage, higher education, is study beyond GCE A levels and their equivalent, which, for most full-time students, takes place in universities and other higher education institutions.

Organisation of compulsory school years

	Pupil ages	Year group
England and Wales		
Key Stage 1	5–7	1–2
Key Stage 2	7–11	3–6
Key Stage 3	11–14	7–9
Key Stage 4	14–16	10–11
Northern Ireland		
Key Stage 1	4–8	1–4
Key Stage 2	8–11	5–7
Key Stage 3	11–14	8–10
Key Stage 4	14–16	11–12
Scotland		
(Curriculum	4/5–6/7	P1–P3
following	6/7–6/8	P3–P4
national	7/8–9/10	P4–P6
guidelines from	9/10–/1011	P6–P7
ages 5 to 14)	10/11–12/13	P7–S2
NQ[1]	13/14–14/15	S3–S4

1 Standard Grades are part of the National Qualifications (NQ) framework in Scotland. They are broadly equivalent to GCSEs.

Early years education

In recent years there has been a major expansion of early years education. Many children under five attend state nursery schools or nursery classes within primary schools. Others may attend playgroups in the voluntary sector or in privately run nurseries. In England and Wales many primary schools also operate an early admissions policy where they admit children under five into what are called 'reception classes'. The *Education Act 2002* extended the National Curriculum (see below) for England to include the foundation stage. The foundation stage was introduced in September 2000 and covers children's education from the age of three to the end of the reception year, when most are just five and some almost six years old. The Early Years Foundation Stage (EYFS) came into force in September 2008. It is a play-based early learning framework for care, learning and development for children in all registered early years settings from birth to five. The EYFS builds on and replaces the *Birth to three matters* framework, as well as the *Curriculum Guidance for the Foundation Stage*, and the *National Standards for Under 8s Day Care and Childminding*.

Figure 3.1 covers children in early years education in maintained nursery and primary schools, independent and special schools. Other provision also takes place in non-school education settings in the private and voluntary sector, such as nurseries (which usually provide care, education and play for children up to the age of five), playgroups and pre-schools (which provide childcare, play and early years education, usually for children aged between two and five), children's centres (for children under five), and through accredited childminders. In Scotland data are based on children who are registered for ante-pre-school and pre-school education in local authority centres at the time of the annual Pre-school Education and Daycare Census, as a proportion of all those who are eligible for early years education. Census dates differed over the years for pre-school education in Scotland as follows: from 1970/71 to 1973/74 and 2000/01 to present day this was January registrations, for 1998/99 this was February registrations and for all other years it was September registrations. For more information on data for Scotland see: **www.scotland.gov.uk/Topics/Statistics/Browse/Children/PubPreSchoolEdChildcare**

Primary education

The primary stage covers three age ranges: nursery (under 5), infant (5 to 7 or 8) and junior (8 or 9 to 11 or 12). In Scotland and Northern Ireland, there is generally no distinction between infant and junior schools. Most public sector primary schools take both boys and girls in mixed classes. It is usual to transfer straight to secondary school at age 11 (in England, Wales and Northern Ireland) but in England some children make the transition through middle schools catering for various age ranges between 8 and 14. Depending on their individual age ranges, middle schools are classified as either primary or secondary. In Scotland, pupils start school based on their age as at the end of February rather than at the start of the academic year, and so generally start secondary school at age 11 or 12.

Secondary education

Public provision of secondary education in an area may consist of a combination of different types of school, the pattern reflecting historical circumstances and the policy adopted by the local authority. Comprehensive schools largely admit pupils without reference to ability or aptitude and cater for all the children in a neighbourhood. In some areas they co-exist with grammar, secondary modern or technical schools. In Northern Ireland, post-primary education is provided by grammar schools and non-selective secondary schools. In England, the Specialist Schools Programme helps schools, in partnership with private sector sponsors and supported by additional government funding, to establish distinctive identities through their chosen specialisms. Specialist schools have a focus on their chosen subject area but must meet the National Curriculum requirements and deliver a broad and balanced education to all pupils. Any maintained secondary school in England can apply to be designated as a specialist school in one of ten specialist areas: arts, business and enterprise, engineering, humanities, languages, mathematics and computing, music, science, sports, and technology. Schools can also combine any two specialisms. Academies, operating in England, are all-ability state-funded schools that provide free education. They have sponsors from a wide range of backgrounds, including universities and colleges, educational trusts, charities, the business sector and faith communities. Sponsors establish a charitable trust, which appoints the majority of governors to the academy governing body. The Department for Children, Schools and Families (DCSF) Secretary of State announced in July 2007 that future academies (that is not including those with a signed agreement, although they could if they wished) would be required to follow the National Curriculum programmes of study in English, mathematics, and information and communication technology (ICT). This is different to the previous model whereby academies had to teach English, mathematics, ICT and science to all pupils.

Special schools

Special schools (day or boarding) provide education for children who require specialist support to complete their education, for example, because they have physical or other difficulties. Many pupils with special educational needs are educated in mainstream schools. All children attending special schools are offered a curriculum designed to overcome their learning difficulties and to enable them to become self-reliant. Since December 2005 special schools in England have also been able to apply for the special educational needs (SEN) specialism, under the Specialist Schools Programme (see Secondary education above). They can apply for a curriculum specialism, but not for both the SEN and a curriculum specialism.

Pupil referral units

Pupil referral units (PRUs) are legally a type of school established and maintained by a local authority to provide education for children of compulsory school age who may otherwise not receive suitable education. The aim of such units is to provide suitable alternative education on a temporary basis for pupils who may not be able to attend a mainstream school. The focus of the units should be to get pupils back into a mainstream school. Pupils in the units may include: teenage mothers, pupils excluded from school, school-phobics and pupils in the assessment phase of a statement of special educational needs (SEN).

Further education

The term further education may be used in a general sense to cover all non-advanced courses taken after the period of compulsory education, but more commonly it excludes those staying on at secondary school and those in higher education, that is doing courses in universities and colleges leading to qualifications above GCE A level, Higher Grade (in Scotland), General National Vocational Qualifications/National Vocational Qualifications (GNVQ/NVQ) level 3, and their equivalents. Since 1 April 1993, sixth-form colleges in England and Wales have been included in the further education sector.

Further education figures for 2006/07 shown in Table 3.9 are whole year counts. However, over the period covered in the table, there is a mixture of whole year and annual snapshot counts, as well as a combination of enrolment and headcounts. There are also other factors, such as mode of study, the inclusion/exclusion of students funded by specific bodies or at certain types of institutions, which have not been constant over time.

Higher education
Higher education (HE) is defined as courses that are of a standard that is higher than GCE A level, the Higher Grade of the Scottish Certificate of Education/National Qualification, GNVQ/NVQ level 3 or the Edexcel (formerly BTEC) or Scottish Qualifications Authority (SQA) National Certificate/Diploma. There are three main levels of HE courses:

- undergraduate courses, which include first degrees, first degrees with qualified teacher status, enhanced first degrees, first degrees obtained concurrently with a diploma, and intercalated first degrees (where first degree students, usually in medicine, dentistry or veterinary medicine, interrupt their studies to complete a one-year course of advanced studies in a related topic)

- other undergraduate courses, which include all other HE courses, for example Higher National Diplomas and Diplomas in HE

- postgraduate courses leading to higher degrees, diplomas and certificates, including postgraduate certificates of education (PGCE) and professional qualifications that usually require a first degree as entry qualification

As a result of the *1992 Further and Higher Education Act*, former polytechnics and some other HE institutions were designated as universities in 1992/93. Students normally attend HE courses at HE institutions, but some attend at further education colleges. In Scotland, around one-fifth of HE students study at a college. Some also attend institutions that do not receive public grants (such as the University of Buckingham) and these numbers are excluded from the tables.

Up to 2000/01 figures for HE students in Table 3.9 are annual snapshots taken around November or December each year, depending on the type of institution, except for further education colleges in Scotland from 1998/99, for which counts are based on the whole year. From 2001/02 figures for HE institutions are based on the Higher Education Statistics Agency (HESA) 'standard registration' count, and are not directly comparable with previous years. The Open University is included in these estimates.

The National Curriculum

England and Wales
Under the *Education Reform Act 1988*, a National Curriculum has been progressively introduced into primary and secondary schools in England and Wales. This consists of English (or the option of Welsh as a first language in Wales), mathematics and science. The second

level of curriculum additionally comprises the so-called 'foundation' subjects, such as history, geography, art, music, information technology, design and technology, and physical education (and Welsh as a second language in Wales). The *Education Act 2002* extended the National Curriculum for England to include the foundation stage (see Stages of education above). It has six areas of learning:

- personal

- social and emotional development

- communication, language and literacy

- mathematical development

- knowledge and understanding of the world

- physical development and

- creative development

Measurable targets have been defined for the four Key Stages, corresponding to ages 7, 11, 14 and 16 (see above). Pupils are assessed formally at the ages of 7, 11 and 14 by a mixture of teacher assessments and by national tests (statutory testing at Key Stages 1 to 3 has been abolished in Wales with the last tests taking place in 2005 at Key Stage 3) in the core subjects of English, mathematics and science (and in Welsh speaking schools in Wales, Welsh as a first language), though the method varies between subjects and countries. Sixteen-year-olds are assessed by the GCSE examination. Statutory authorities have been set up for England and for Wales to advise the Government on the National Curriculum and promote curriculum development generally.

Expected attainment levels in England

	Attainment expected
Key Stage 1	Level 2 or above
Key Stage 2	Level 4 or above
Key Stage 3	Level 5 or above
Key Stage 4	GCSE

Northern Ireland
Northern Ireland has its own common curriculum that is similar, but not identical, to the National Curriculum in England and Wales. Assessment arrangements in Northern Ireland became statutory from September 1996 and Key Stage 1 pupils are assessed at age eight.

Scotland
In Scotland there is no statutory national curriculum. Responsibility for the management and delivery of the curriculum belongs to education authorities and head teachers. Pupils aged 5 to 14 study a broad curriculum based on national guidelines, which set out the aims of study, the ground to be covered and the way the pupils' learning should be assessed and reported. Progress is measured by attainment of six levels based on the expectation of the performance of the majority of pupils on completion of certain stages between the ages of 5 and 14: Primary 3 (age 7/8), Primary 4 (age 8/9), Primary 7 (age 11/12) and Secondary 2 (age 13/14). It is recognised that pupils learn at different rates and some will reach the various levels before others.

The 5 to 14 curriculum areas in Scotland are:

- language

- mathematics

- environmental studies

- expressive arts

- religious and moral education with personal and social development and

- health education

In Secondary 3 and 4, it is recommended that the core curriculum of all pupils should include study within the following eight modes:

- language and communication

- mathematical studies and applications

- scientific studies and applications

- social and environmental studies

- technological activities and applications

- creative and aesthetic activities

- physical education and

- religious and moral education

For Secondary 5 and 6, these eight modes are important in structuring the curriculum, although each pupil is not expected to study under each mode but rather the curriculum will be negotiated. The Scottish curriculum 3 to 18 is being reviewed under *A Curriculum for Excellence*.

Main categories of educational establishments

Educational establishments in the UK are administered and financed in several ways. Most schools are controlled by local authorities (LAs), which are part of the structure of local government, but some are 'assisted', receiving grants direct from central government sources and being controlled by governing bodies that have a substantial degree of autonomy. Completely outside the public sector are non-maintained schools run by individuals, companies or charitable institutions.

Up to March 2001 further education (FE) courses in FE sector colleges in England and Wales were largely funded through grants from the respective Further Education Funding Councils (FEFCs). In April 2001, however, the Learning and Skills Council (LSC) took over the responsibility for funding the FE sector in England, and the National Council for Education and Training for Wales (part of Education and Learning Wales – ELWa) did so for Wales. The LSC in England is also responsible for funding provision for FE and some non-prescribed higher education in FE sector colleges; in addition, it funds some FE provided by LA maintained and other institutions referred to as 'external institutions'. From April 2006 FE funding in Wales became the responsibility of the Welsh Assembly Government. The Scottish Further and Higher Education Funding Council (SFC) funds FE colleges in Scotland, while the Department for Employment and Learning funds FE colleges in Northern Ireland.

Higher education (HE) courses in HE establishments are largely publicly funded through block grants from the HE funding councils in England and Scotland, the Higher

Education Funding Council in Wales, and the Department for Employment and Learning in Northern Ireland. In addition, some designated HE, mainly Higher National Diplomas (HND)/ Higher National Certificates (HNC) is funded by these sources. The FE sources mentioned above fund the remainder.

School admissions policy

The School Admissions Code (the code) came into force in February 2007 with the aim of ensuring equal and fair access to schools. The code requires admission authorities, local authorities and governing bodies to ensure clear, objective and fair admission arrangements that do not disadvantage one child compared to another. For more information on the code see: www.dcsf.gov.uk/consultations/ downloadableDocs/6757-SchoolAdmissionsCode.pdf

Special educational needs (SEN) data

Information for England presented in Figure 3.4 is mainly drawn from two sources: the Schools' Census (SC) and the SEN2 Survey. Figures sourced from SC and the SEN2 Survey are not directly comparable.

The SC has collected information on pupils with special educational needs (SEN) on the census date in January from schools since 1985. It is completed by schools and records those pupils with and without statements who are educated at the school, regardless of which local authority (LA) is responsible. Figures for pupils with SEN without statements were collected from maintained primary and secondary schools for the first time in 1995.

The SEN2 Survey has collected information on children with statements on the census date in January and new statements made in the previous calendar year from LAs since 1984. SEN2 is completed by LAs and records those children for whom the LA is responsible (regardless of whether they are educated in the LA's own maintained schools, in schools in other LAs, in the non-maintained or independent sectors or educated other than at school).

In January 2002, the SC introduced a major change in that primary, secondary and special schools reported data at an individual pupil level for the first time. While the overall collection of pupil level data for these schools was successful, it is possible that some discontinuity in the time series data has resulted from this underlying change in data collection. For instance, the national trend in SEN pupils with statements between 2001 and 2002 in SC is different from that shown in the SEN2 survey. While there are valid reasons as to why the figures will be different between these surveys, it is unusual for the trends to differ to this degree.

Qualifications

England, Wales and Northern Ireland
In England, Wales and Northern Ireland, the main examination for school pupils at the minimum school leaving age is the General Certificate of Secondary Education (GCSE), which can be taken in a wide range of subjects. This replaced the GCE O Level and Certificate of Secondary Education (CSE) examinations in 1987 (1988 in Northern Ireland). In England, Wales

and Northern Ireland, the GCSE is awarded in eight grades, A* to G, the highest four (A* to C) being regarded as equivalent to O level grades A to C or CSE grade 1. Data on GCSE attainment by ethnic group presented in Figure 3.15 are taken from the Longitudinal Study of Young People in England and the Youth Cohort Study. Although similar administrative data for England are available from the National Pupil Database, these data are not available as far back as 1999. For more information on the National Pupil Database see the Department for Children, Schools and Families (DCSF) website: www.dcsf.gov.uk

GCE A level is usually taken after a further two years of study in a sixth form or equivalent, passes being graded from A (the highest) to E (the lowest).

In September 2000 following the Qualifying for Success consultations in 1997, a number of reforms were introduced to the qualifications structure for young people aged 16 to 19. Under these reforms, students were encouraged to follow a wide range of subjects in their first year of post-16 study, with students expected to study four Advanced Subsidiaries (AS) before progressing three of them on to full A levels in their second year. New specifications introduced in 2001 are in place and A levels now comprise units, normally six for a full A level and three for the AS level, which is one-half a full A level. The full A level is normally taken either over two years (modular) or as a set of exams at the end of the two years (linear). In addition, students are encouraged to study a combination of both general and vocational advanced level examinations.

The AS qualification equates to the first year of study of a traditional A level, while the programmes of study in the second year of the full A level are called 'A2' and represent the harder elements of the traditional A level. The AS is a qualification in its own right, whereas A2 modules do not make up a qualification in their own right, but when taken together with the AS units they comprise a full A level.

Scotland
In Scotland, National Qualifications (NQs) are offered to students. These include Standard Grades, National Courses and National Units. The Standard Grade is awarded in seven grades, through three levels of study: Credit (1 or 2), General (3 or 4) and Foundation (5 or 6). Students who do not achieve grade 1 to 6, but do complete the course, are awarded a grade 7. Standard Grade courses are made up of different parts called 'elements', with an exam at the end. National Courses are available at Intermediate, Higher and Advanced Higher, and consist of National Units that are assessed by the school/college, plus an external assessment. Grades are awarded on the basis of how well a student does in the external assessment, having passed all the National Units. Pass grades are awarded at A, B and C. Grade D is awarded to a student who just fails to get a grade C. Standard Grades 1 to 3 and Intermediate 2 grades A to C are equivalent to GCSE grades A* to C. Standard Grades 4 to 6, Intermediate 1 grades B to C or Access 3 (pass) are equivalent to grades D to G at GCSE level. Intermediate courses can be taken as an alternative to Standard Grade or as a

stepping stone to Highers. Access units are assessed by the school/college, with no exam. Groups of units in a particular subject area can be built up at Access 2 and 3 to lead to 'cluster awards'. In Scotland, pupils generally sit Highers one year earlier than pupils in the rest of the UK sit A levels.

Vocational qualifications
After leaving school, people can study towards higher academic qualifications such as degrees. However, a large number of people choose to study towards qualifications aimed at a particular occupation or group of occupations – these qualifications are called vocational qualifications.

Vocational qualifications were initially split into three groups: National Vocational Qualifications (NVQs), General National Vocational Qualifications (GNVQs) and Vocationally Related Qualifications (VRQs), however GNVQs were phased out between 2005 and 2007.

- NVQs are based on an explicit statement of competence derived from an analysis of employment requirements. They are awarded at five levels. Scottish Vocational Qualifications (SVQs) are the Scottish equivalent

- GNVQs were a vocational alternative to GCSEs and GCE A levels. General Scottish Vocational Qualifications (GSVQs) were the Scottish equivalent. They were awarded at three levels: Foundation, Intermediate and Advanced, although Advanced GNVQs were subsequently redesigned and relaunched as Vocational A levels or, more formally, Advanced Vocational Certificates of Education (VCEs)

- there are a large number of other vocational qualifications, which are not NVQs, SVQs, (or former GNVQs or GSVQs). For example, a Business and Technology Education Council (BTEC) Higher National Diploma (HND) or a City & Guilds craft award

Other qualifications (including academic qualifications) are often expressed as being equivalent to a particular NVQ level so that comparisons can be easily made:

- an NVQ level 1 is equivalent to one or more GCSEs at grade G (but is lower than five GCSE grades A* to C), a BTEC general certificate, a Youth Training certificate, and to other Royal Society of Arts (RSA) and City & Guilds craft qualifications

- an NVQ level 2 is equivalent to five GCSEs at grades A* to C, a former Intermediate GNVQ, an RSA diploma, a City & Guilds craft or a BTEC first or general diploma

- an NVQ level 3 is equivalent to two A levels, a former Advanced GNVQ, an International Baccalaureate, an RSA advanced diploma, a City & Guilds advanced craft, an Ordinary National Diploma (OND) or Ordinary National Certificate (ONC) or a BTEC National Diploma

- an NVQ level 4 is equivalent to a first degree, an HND or HNC, a BTEC Higher Diploma, an RSA Higher Diploma, a nursing qualification or other higher education qualification below a higher degree

- an NVQ level 5 is equivalent to a higher degree

National Statistics Socio-economic Classification (NS-SEC)

From 2001 the National Statistics Socio-economic Classification (NS-SEC) was adopted for all official surveys, in place of social class based on occupation and socio-economic group. NS-SEC is itself based on the Standard Occupational Classification 2000 (SOC2000, see Appendix, Part 4) and details of employment status (whether as employer, self employed or employee).

The NS-SEC is an occupationally based classification designed to provide coverage of the whole adult population. The version of the classification, which will be used for most analyses, has eight classes, the first of which can be subdivided. These are:

National Statistics Socio-economic Classification (NS-SEC)

1 Higher managerial and professional occupations, subdivided into:
    1.1 Large employers and higher managerial occupations
    1.2 Higher professional occupations
2 Lower managerial and professional occupations
3 Intermediate occupations
4 Small employers and own account workers
5 Lower supervisory and technical operations
6 Semi-routine occupations
7 Routine occupations
8 Never worked and long-term unemployed

The classes can be further grouped into:

i   Managerial and professional occupations   1,2
ii   Intermediate occupations   3,4
iii Routine and manual occupations   5,6,7
iv   Never worked and long term unemployed   8

Users have the option to include these classes in the overall analysis or keep them separate. The long-term unemployed are defined as those unemployed and seeking work for 12 months or more. Members of HM Forces, who were shown separately in tables of social class, are included within the NS-SEC. Residual groups that remain unclassified include students and those with inadequately described occupations.

Further details can be found on the National Statistics website: www.statistics.gov.uk/methods_quality/ns_sec/default.asp

Joint Academic Coding System

The Joint Academic Coding System (JACS) was introduced into the Higher Education Statistics Agency (HESA) data collection in 2002/03 and forms the basis of the data presented in Table 3.10. This subject-based classification measures subjects studied at UK higher education institutions and looks similar to that previously used by HESA (HESACODE), although it has been devised in a different way (therefore subject data between the two classifications are

not comparable). The JACS system defines the principal subjects studied at UK higher education institutions and aggregates them into 19 headline subject areas, as shown in Table 3.10. The subject areas do not overlap and cover the entire range of principal subjects.

For more information on JACS, see the HESA website: www.hesa.ac.uk/index.php?option=com_content&task=view&id=158&Itemid=233

National Employers Skills Survey

The National Employers Skills Survey (NESS) is an annual series of employer surveys to investigate skills deficiencies and the role of workforce development among employers in England. The aim of the NESS study is to provide the Learning and Skills Council (LSC) and its partners with information on the current and future skill needs of employers in England, and how these needs vary by size of industry, occupation, region and local LSC areas.

In Figure 3.13 employers who had experienced skills gaps were asked to define what skills they felt needed improving for an occupation where staff were considered not fully proficient (if an establishment had at least two occupations with skills gaps then the occupation was chosen at random).

Classification of the Functions of Government (COFOG)

In 2007 Her Majesty's Treasury (HMT) changed the presentation of public expenditure statistical analysis (PESA) categories to bring analysis in closer alignment to the UN Classification of the Functions of Government (COFOG). COFOG describes the functions of government in ten categories (general public services; defence; public order and safety; economic affairs; environment protection; housing and community amenities; health; recreation, culture and religion; education; and social protection) and within these categories there is a further breakdown of the functions into sub-sets. Departmental expenditure is allocated to these sub-sets, which create the overall function categories.

For further details on the classification see: www.hm-treasury.gov.uk/pes_function.htm

Part 4: Labour market

Labour market statistics

For more information on labour market statistics, sources and analysis, including information about all aspects of the Office for National Statistics' labour market outputs, see the Labour Market Review 2006 www.statistics.gov.uk/labourmarketreview/ and the online Guide to Labour Market Statistics www.statistics.gov.uk/about/data/guides/LabourMarket/

Labour Force Survey

The Labour Force Survey (LFS) is the largest regular household survey in the UK and much of the labour market data published are measured by the LFS. The concepts and definitions used in

the LFS are agreed by the International Labour Organisation (ILO), an agency of the United Nations. The definitions are used by European Union (EU) member states and members of the Organisation for Economic Co-operation and Development.

The LFS results refer to people resident in private households and some non-private accommodation in the UK. For most people residence at an address is unambiguous. People with more than one address are counted as resident at the sample address if they regard that as their main residence. The following are also counted as being resident at an address:

- people who normally live there, but are on holiday, away on business, or in hospital, unless they have been living away from the address for six months or more

- children aged 16 and under, even if they are at boarding or other schools

- students aged 16 and over are counted as resident at their normal term-time address even if it is vacation time and they may be away from it

People resident in two categories of non-private accommodation are also included in the LFS sample, namely those in NHS accommodation, and students in halls of residence. Students are included through the parental home.

On 22 August 2007 the Office for National Statistics (ONS) published the 2006-based mid-year population estimates for the UK and on 13 September 2007 ONS published the 2006 quarter 2 (Q2) experimental population estimates for England and Wales. These revised population estimates have been incorporated into LFS sourced tables and figures in the chapter. For more information see: www.statistics.gov.uk/pdfdir/lmsuk0808.pdf

An EU requirement exists whereby all member states must have a labour force survey based on calendar quarters. The UK LFS complied with this from May 2006. The survey previously used seasonal quarters where, for example, the March–May months covered the spring quarter, June–August was summer and so forth. This has now changed to calendar quarters where microdata are available for January–March (Q1), April–June (Q2), July–September (Q3) and October–December (Q4).

ONS has produced a set of historical estimates covering the monthly periods between 1971 and 1991, which are fully consistent with post-1992 LFS data. The data cover headline measures of employment, unemployment, economic activity, economic inactivity and hours worked. These estimates were published on an experimental basis in 2003 and following further user consultation and quality assurance, these estimates were made National Statistics. As such, they represent ONS's best estimate of the headline labour market series over this period. The labour market chapter uses data from these estimates only where headline data are reported since the historical estimates are not yet available for subgroups of the population, other than by sex and for key age groups.

Annual Population Survey

The Annual Population Survey (APS) was introduced in 2004. The APS included all the data of the annual local area Labour Force Survey (LFS) in the UK, as well as a further sample boost aimed at achieving a minimum number of economically active respondents in the sample in each local authority district in England. This sample boost was withdrawn after 2005. The first APS covered the calendar year 2004, rather than the annual local area LFS period of March to February. Also, the annual local area LFS data are published only once a year, whereas the APS data are published quarterly, with each publication including a year's data. Like the local area LFS data set, the APS data are published by local authority area. However, the APS data contain an enhanced range of variables providing a greater level of detail than the LFS about the resident household population of an area, in particular on ethnic group, health and sex.

For more information on local area labour market statistics, see: 'Local area labour markets: statistical indicators July 2007', www.statistics.gov.uk/StatBase/Product. asp?vlnk=14160

Accession to the European Union (EU)

Until 2004 the EU consisted of 15 member states (EU-15): Austria, Belgium, Denmark, Finland, France, Germany, Greece, Ireland, Italy, Luxembourg, Netherlands, Portugal, Spain, Sweden and the UK. In May 2004, a further ten states joined the EU to create an EU-25: Cyprus, the Czech Republic, Estonia, Hungary, Latvia, Lithuania, Malta, Poland, Slovakia, and Slovenia. Cyprus and Malta already had close links with the UK, having only gained independence from the UK in 1960 and 1964 respectively and so for the purpose of analysis the remaining eight countries are grouped together as the A8. Finally, in January 2007, Bulgaria and Romania joined the EU (EU-27).

Employment status by country of birth

From May 2008, the Office for National Statistics (ONS) has presented information on migrant workers that is consistent with the definitions used in wider labour market publications. For employment levels this means that the population aged 16 and over is used, rather than the population of working age (defined as 16 to 64 for men, and 16 to 59 for women). For employment rates, the population of working age will continue to be used. ONS will continue to use country of birth to determine a person's status as a migrant worker. Since 1997 employment levels and rates have risen for both UK and non-UK born people irrespective of the definition used. However, under the 'aged 16 and over' definition, the difference between the increases in UK born and non-UK born employment levels is smaller than under the 'working age' definition. This is because the new definition shows a greater increase in UK born employment levels. This is attributed to large numbers of UK born people working past state pension age (65 for men and 60 for women) who are included under the new definition, but not the old.

The migrant population of the UK can be described in a number of ways. For example, migrant status can be determined on the basis of a person's country of birth, nationality (according to citizenship) or how recently they arrived. This can be complex. For example, a person born in France could hold a British passport (through family) and therefore, depending on the definition used, may be categorised as a UK or non-UK employee. In addition, their current stay may be their first or one of many. ONS has preferred to define migrant workers to the UK by country of birth because this cannot change, whereas citizenship can change over time. In addition, the country of birth definition allows investigation using the 'year of arrival' question in the LFS. This question can be used to investigate the length of time a migrant worker has been in the UK, although the LFS cannot be used to distinguish accurately between short and long-term migrants.

The country of birth rule is not without problems because a number of people classified as foreign born were either British at birth, or have subsequently acquired citizenship. Others may consider themselves British, irrespective of their citizenship, or hold dual nationality. However, the country of birth gives an indication of the country of origin and the background of the worker.

For more information see: www.statistics.gov. uk/elmr/07_08/downloads/ELMR_Jul08_ Clancy.pdf

Standard Occupational Classification 2000 (SOC2000)

The Standard Occupational Classification (SOC2000) was first published in 1990 (SOC90) to replace both the Classification of Occupations 1980, and the Classification of Occupations and Dictionary of Occupational Titles. SOC90 was revised and updated in 2000 to produce SOC2000. There is no exact correspondence between SOC90 and SOC2000 at any level.

The two main concepts that SOC2000 is used to investigate are:

- kind of work performed and

- the competent performance of the tasks and duties

The structure of SOC2000 is four-tier covering:

- major groups/numbers

- sub-major groups/numbers

- minor groups/numbers and

- unit groups/numbers (occupations)

For example, the group/number breakdown for the occupation of a chemist is as follows:

major group	2	Professional occupations
sub-major group	21	Science and technology professionals
minor group	211	Science professionals
unit group	2111	Chemists

SOC2000 comprises 9 major groups, 25 sub-major groups, 81 minor groups and 353 unit groups (occupations). The major groups are:

- managers and senior officials

- professional occupations

- associate professional and technical occupations

- administrative and secretarial occupations

- skilled trades occupations

- personal service occupations

- sales and customer service occupations

- process, plant and machine operatives

- elementary occupations

For more information on SOC2000 see: www.statistics.gov.uk/methods_quality/ ns_sec/soc2000.asp

Standard Industrial Classification 2003

A Standard Industrial Classification (SIC) was first introduced into the UK in 1948 for use in classifying business establishments and other statistical units by the type of economic activity in which they are engaged. The classification provides a framework for the collection, tabulation, presentation and analysis of data and its use promotes uniformity. In addition, it can be used for administrative purposes and by non-government bodies as a convenient way of classifying industrial activities into a common structure.

Since 1948 the classification has been revised in 1958, 1968, 1980, 1992 and 2003. Figure 4.11 uses the SIC 2003. Revision is necessary because over time new products and the new industries to produce them emerge, and shifts of emphasis occur in existing industries. It is not always possible for the system to accommodate such developments and so the classification is updated.

For further information about SIC see: www.statistics.gov.uk/methods_quality/sic/ downloads/UK_SIC_Vol1(2003).pdf

Labour disputes

Statistics of stoppages of work caused by labour disputes in the UK relate to disputes connected with terms and conditions of employment. Small stoppages involving fewer than ten workers or lasting less than one day are excluded from the statistics unless the aggregate number of working days lost in the dispute is 100 or more. Disputes not resulting in a stoppage of work are not included in the statistics.

Workers involved and working days lost relate to persons both directly and indirectly involved (unable to work although not party to the dispute) at the establishments where the disputes occurred. People laid off and working days lost at establishments not in dispute, for example because of resulting shortages of supplies, are excluded.

There are difficulties in ensuring complete recording of stoppages, in particular for short disputes lasting only a day or so, or involving only a few workers. Any under-recording would affect the total number of stoppages much more than the number of working days lost.

For more information, see 'Labour disputes in 2007'. www.statistic.gov.uk/elmr/06_08/downloads/ELMR_Jun08_Hale.pdf

Part 5: Income and wealth

Household income data sources

The data for the household sector as derived from the National Accounts have been compiled according to the definitions and conventions set out in the European System of Accounts 1995 (ESA95). Estimates for the household sector cannot be separated from the sector for non-profit institutions serving households and so the data in *Social Trends* cover both sectors. The most obvious example of a non-profit institution is a charity. This sector also includes many other organisations of which universities, trade unions, and clubs and societies are the most important. Non-profit making bodies receive income mainly in the form of property income (that is, investment income) and of other current receipts. The household sector differs from the personal sector, as defined in the National Accounts prior to the introduction of ESA95, in that it excludes unincorporated private businesses apart from sole traders. The household sector also includes people living in institutions such as nursing homes, as well as people living in private households. More information is given in *United Kingdom National Accounts Concepts, Sources and Methods* published by The Stationery Office and is available on the Office for National Statistics (ONS) website: **www.statistics.gov.uk/downloads/theme_economy/Concepts_Sources_&_Methods.pdf**

In ESA95, household income includes the value of national insurance contributions and pension contributions made by employers on behalf of their employees. It also shows property income (that is, income from investments) net of payments of interest on loans. In both these respects, national accounts' conventions diverge from those normally used when collecting data on household income from household surveys. Employees are usually unaware of the value of the national insurance contributions and pension contributions made on their behalf by their employer, and so such data are rarely collected. Payments of interest are usually regarded as items of expenditure rather than reductions of income. In Figure 5.6, household income excludes employers' national insurance and pension contributions and includes property income gross of payment of interest on loans, to correspond more closely with the definition generally used in household surveys.

Survey sources differ from the National Accounts in a number of other important respects. They cover the population living in households and some cover certain parts of the population living in institutions such as nursing homes, but all exclude non-profit making institutions. Survey sources are also subject to under-reporting and non-response bias. In the case of household income surveys, investment income is commonly underestimated, as is income from self-employment. All these factors mean that the survey data on income used in most of this

chapter are not entirely consistent with the National Accounts household sector data.

Purchasing power parities

The international spending power of sterling depends both on market exchange rates and on the ratios of prices between the UK and other countries. Purchasing power parities (PPPs) are the rates of currency conversion that equalise the purchasing power of different currencies (or, in the case of countries in the euro zone, the purchasing power of the euro in different countries) by eliminating the differences in price levels between countries. PPPs indicate the number of units of a common currency needed to buy the same volume of goods and services in each country.

The purchasing power standard (PPS) is the name given by Eurostat to the artificial currency unit in which a range of economic indicators are expressed, for example, gross domestic product, earnings, and household expenditure. These units are calculated based on PPPs, and so reflect differences in national price levels that are not taken into account by market exchange rates. Thus they enable meaningful volume comparisons of economic indicators between countries.

Households Below Average Income (HBAI)

Information on the distribution of income based on the Family Resources Survey is provided in the Department for Work and Pensions (DWP) publication *Households Below Average Income: 1994/95–2006/07*, available both in hard copy and on the DWP website: **www.dwp.gov.uk/asd/hbai.asp**. This publication provides estimates of patterns of personal disposable income in the UK, and of changes in income over time. It attempts to measure people's potential living standards as determined by disposable income. Although as the title would suggest, HBAI concentrates on the lower part of the income distribution, it also provides estimates covering the whole of the income distribution.

In 2002/03, the Family Resources Survey was extended to cover Northern Ireland. Data presented from 2002/03 cover the UK rather than Great Britain. NI data have been imputed back to 1998/99, and for aggregate time series estimates are shown for Great Britain up to 1997/98 and for the UK since 1998/99. Estimates for the UK are very similar to those for Great Britain.

Disposable household income includes all flows of income into the household, principally

earnings, benefits, occupational and private pensions, and investments. It is net of tax, employees' national insurance contributions, council tax, contributions to occupational pension schemes (including additional voluntary contributions), maintenance and child support payments, and parental contributions to students living away from home.

Two different measures of disposable income are used in HBAI: before and after housing costs are deducted. This is principally to take into account variations in housing costs that do not correspond to comparable variations in the quality of housing. Housing costs consist of rent, water rates, community charges, mortgage interest payments, structural insurance, ground rent and service charges.

HBAI estimates for 1979 to 1993/94 inclusive have been derived from the Family Expenditure Survey. This survey was conducted on a calendar year basis from 1979 to 1993, and on a financial year basis from 1993/94 onwards. Because of the relatively small sample size of this survey, from 1988 onwards data from two survey years have been pooled to produce HBAI estimates. From 1994/95 onwards, the data source is the Family Resources Survey, which is conducted on a financial year basis.

Equivalisation scales

In the analysis of income distribution it is customary to adjust household income using an equivalence scale to take into account variations in the size and composition of households. This reflects the common sense notion that a household of five adults will need a higher income than will a single person living alone to enjoy a comparable standard of living. An overall equivalence value is calculated for each household by summing the appropriate scale values for each household member. Equivalised household income is then calculated by dividing household income by the household's equivalence value. The scales conventionally take a couple as the reference point with an equivalence value of one; equivalisation therefore tends to increase relatively the incomes of single person households (since their incomes are divided by a value of less than one) and to reduce incomes of households with three or more persons.

From 2007 the Department for Work and Pensions (DWP) changed from using the McClements equivalence scales to the OECD equivalence scales in their analysis of the income distribution. For further information see *Households Below Average Income 1994/95–2005/06 (revised)* available on the DWP website:

OECD equivalence scales:

Household member	Before housing costs	After housing costs
First adult	0.67	0.58
Spouse	0.33	0.42
Other second adult	0.33	0.42
Third adult	0.33	0.42
Subsequent adults	0.33	0.42
Children aged under 14 years	0.20	0.20
Children aged 14 years and over	0.33	0.42

McClements equivalence scales:

Household member	Before housing costs	After housing costs
First adult (head)	0.61	0.55
Spouse of head	0.39	0.45
Other second adult	0.46	0.45
Third adult	0.42	0.45
Subsequent adults	0.36	0.40
Each dependant aged:		
0–1	0.09	0.07
2–4	0.18	0.18
5–7	0.21	0.21
8–10	0.23	0.23
11–12	0.25	0.26
13–15	0.27	0.28
16 years and over	0.36	0.38

www.dwp.gov.uk/asd/hbai.asp. The McClements equivalence scales are still used by DWP to produce the persistent poverty estimates from the British Household Panel Survey (BHPS). The BHPS raw data are supplied by the Institute for Social and Economic Research (ISER). Both the OECD and McClements scales exist in two versions, one for adjusting incomes before housing costs and one for adjusting income after housing costs.

The change from the McClements to the OECD equivalence scale has meant that it is no longer possible to present as long a time series in Social Trends as has been presented in previous editions. A full time series is available from 1987 onwards, and estimates are also available for 1979 and 1981.

The McClements scale continues to be used to adjust income in Figure 5.13 and Table 5.19.

Gini coefficient

The Gini coefficient is the most widely used summary measure of the degree of inequality in an income distribution. The first step is to rank the distribution in ascending order. The coefficient can then best be understood by considering a graph of the cumulative income share against the cumulative share of households – the Lorenz curve. This would take the form of a diagonal line for complete equality where all households had the same income, while complete inequality, where one household received all the income and the remainder received none, would be represented by a curve comprising the horizontal axis and the right-hand vertical axis. The area between the Lorenz curve and the diagonal line of complete equality and inequality gives the value of the Gini coefficient. As inequality increases (and the Lorenz curve bellies out) so does the Gini coefficient until it reaches its maximum value of 1 with complete inequality.

Pensioners' income

Information on the income of pensioners based on the Family Resources Survey is provided in the Department for Work and Pensions (DWP) publication Pensioners' Income Series, the latest year of which is 2006/07 and is available on the DWP website: www.dwp.gov.uk/asd/asd6/pensioners_income.asp. It contains estimates

and interpretation of trends in the levels and sources of pensioners' incomes over time.

Single pensioners are people over state pension age (65 for men and 60 for women). Pensioner couples are married or cohabiting couples where one or more are over state pension age.

In 2002/03, the Family Resources Survey was extended to cover Northern Ireland. Data presented for pensioners' income from 2002/03 cover the UK rather than Great Britain. Estimates for the UK are very similar to those for Great Britain.

Earnings surveys

The Annual Survey of Hours and Earnings (ASHE) replaced the New Earnings Survey (NES) from October 2004. ASHE improves on NES by extending the coverage of the survey sample, introducing weighting and publishing estimates of quality for all survey outputs. The new survey methodology produces weighted estimates, using weights calculated by calibrating the survey responses to totals from the Labour Force Survey by occupation, sex, region and age. It also focuses on median levels of pay rather than the mean. The ASHE survey sample design was improved to include employees who have either changed or started new jobs between the survey sample identification and the survey reference date. Full details of the methodology of ASHE can be found on the ONS website at: www.statistics.gov.uk/articles/nojournal/ASHEMethod_article.pdf

Back series using ASHE methodology applied to NES data sets are available for 1997 to 2003 at: www.statistics.gov.uk/statbase/Product.asp?vlnk=13101. Because it was not possible to impute for the supplementary information collected in ASHE in the NES data sets, data for 2004 are available on two bases: estimates excluding supplementary information, which are comparable with the 1997 to 2003 back series, and estimates including supplementary information, which are comparable with 2005 onwards.

A small number of methodological changes were also introduced in 2007 to improve the quality of the ASHE results. These include changes to the sample design as well as the introduction of an automatic occupation coding

tool. These changes were also taken back to 2006 so that data for 2006 are available on two bases: estimates for 2006 comparable with 2004 and 2005, and estimates for 2006 comparable with 2007 onwards.

Net wealth of the household sector

Revised balance sheet estimates of the net wealth of the household (and non-profit institutions) sector were published in an article in Economic Trends November 1999 www.statistics.gov.uk/cci/article.asp?ID=41&Pos=1&ColRank=1&Rank=1. These figures are based on the new international system of national accounting and incorporate data from new sources. Quarterly estimates of net financial wealth (excluding tangible and intangible assets) are published in Financial Statistics.

Part 6: Expenditure

Household expenditure

The estimates of household final consumption expenditure that appear in the National Accounts measure expenditure on goods and services by UK residents. This includes:

- the value of income in kind
- imputed rent for owner-occupied dwellings
- the purchase of second-hand goods less the proceeds of sales of used goods

Excluded are:

- interest and other transfer payments
- all business expenditure
- the purchase of land and buildings (and associated costs)

Expenditure is classified according to the internationally recognised Classification of Individual Consumption by Purpose (COICOP), which has 12 categories of household expenditure:

- food and non-alcoholic drinks
- alcoholic drinks and tobacco
- clothing and footwear
- housing, water and fuel
- household goods and services
- health
- transport
- communication
- recreation and culture
- education
- restaurants and hotels
- miscellaneous goods and services

In addition, household final consumption expenditure includes expenditure by UK resident households that takes place abroad, and excludes expenditure by non-residents in the UK.

Estimates of household final consumption expenditure are produced using a range of data sources. Both value and volume estimates are available, which provide reliable information about how expenditure has changed over time.

Until September 2003 UK economic growth was calculated using 'fixed base aggregation'. Under this method the detailed estimates for growth for different parts of the economy were summed to a total by weighting each component according to its share of total expenditure in 1995. The year from which this information was drawn was updated at five-yearly intervals. Since September 2003 UK economic growth has been calculated by 'annual chain-linking'. This uses information updated every year to give each component the most relevant weight that can be estimated. This method has been used for estimating change in household expenditure since 1971.

For further details see *Consumer Trends* at: **www.statistics.gov.uk/consumertrends**

Expenditure and Food Survey

Estimates of household expenditure are also available directly from the Expenditure and Food Survey (EFS) and are published in *Family Spending*. The EFS covers all private households (that is, not people living in institutions such as prisons, retirement homes or in student accommodation) and provides information about how expenditure patterns differ across different types of households. However, unlike the National Accounts estimates (see Household expenditure above), only estimates of the value of expenditure are available (that is, current price estimates) and the survey results are not intended to be used to measure change over time.

The EFS was created in April 2001 by merging the Family Expenditure Survey (FES) with the National Food Survey (NFS). The EFS continues to produce the information previously provided by the FES. From January 2006 survey results are published for calendar years (rather than financial years), in anticipation of the EFS being integrated in the Continuous Population Survey (CPS).

The EFS also uses the Classification of Individual Consumption by Purpose (COICOP, see above), although the definition of household expenditure is not exactly the same as that used in the National Accounts. For example, there are some differences in the treatment of housing-related expenditure. Within the National Accounts, an estimate of imputed rent for owner-occupied dwellings is included in the category 'Housing, water and fuel'. Results from the EFS do not include imputed rent for owner occupiers but mortgage interest payments are included in an additional category 'Other expenditure items'.

For further details see *Family Spending* at: **www.statistics.gov.uk/familyspending**

Retail prices index

The retail prices index (RPI) is the most long-standing measure of inflation in the UK. It measures the average change from month to month in the prices of goods and services purchased by most households in the UK. The spending pattern on which the index is based is revised each year, mainly using information from the Expenditure and Food Survey (EFS, see above). It covers the goods and services purchased by private households, excluding:

- high income households, defined as those households with a total income within the top 4 per cent of all households, as measured by each quarter's EFS

- 'pensioner' households, which derive at least three-quarters of their total income from state pensions and benefits

It is considered that such households are likely to spend their money on atypical things and including them in the scope of the RPI would distort the overall average. Expenditure patterns of one person and two person 'pensioner' households differ from those of the households that the RPI is based on. Separate indices have been compiled for such pensioner households since 1969, and quarterly averages are published in *Focus on Consumer Price Indices*, available on the National Statistics website. They are chained indices constructed in the same way as the RPI. It should, however, be noted that the pensioner indices exclude housing costs.

A guide to the RPI can be found on the National Statistics website: **www.statistics.gov.uk/rpi**

Retail sales index

The retail sales index (RSI) is a measurement of monthly movements in the average weekly retail turnover of retailers in Great Britain. All retailers selected for the Retail Sales Inquiry are asked to provide estimates of total retail turnover, including sales from stores, e-commerce (including over the Internet), mail order, stalls and markets, and door-to-door sales. Retail turnover is defined as the value of sales of goods to the general public for personal and household use.

The sample is addressed to approximately 5,000 retailers of all sizes every month. All of the largest 900 retailers are included in the sample together with a random sample of smaller retailers. Estimates are produced for each type of store by size-band. These detailed estimates are aggregated to produce estimates of weekly sales for 17 retail sectors, the main industry aggregates and retailing as a whole.

Headline data are presented in constant prices (volume) seasonally adjusted and at current prices (value) non-seasonally adjusted. For further details see retail sales at: **www.statistics.gov.uk/rsi**

Consumer prices index

The consumer prices index (CPI) is the main measure of inflation used within the Government's monetary policy framework. Prior to 10 December 2003, this index was published as the harmonised index of consumer prices.

The methodology of the CPI is similar to that of the RPI (see above) but differs in the following ways:

- in the CPI, the geometric mean is used to aggregate the prices at the most basic level, whereas the RPI uses arithmetic means

- a number of RPI series are excluded from the CPI, most particularly, those mainly relating to owner occupiers' housing costs (for example, mortgage interest payments, house depreciation, council tax and buildings insurance)

- the coverage of the CPI indices is based on the Classification of Individual Consumption by Purpose (COICOP, see above), whereas the RPI uses its own bespoke classification

- the CPI includes series for university accommodation fees, foreign students' university tuition fees, unit trust and stockbrokers charges, none of which are included in the RPI

- the index for new car prices in the RPI is imputed from movements in second-hand car prices, whereas the CPI uses a quality adjusted index based on published prices of new cars

- the CPI weights are based on expenditure by all private households, foreign visitors to the UK and residents of institutional households. In the RPI, weights are based on expenditure by private households only, excluding the highest income households, and pensioner households mainly dependent on state benefits

- in the construction of the RPI weights, expenditure on insurance is assigned to the relevant insurance heading. For the CPI weights, the amount paid out in insurance claims is distributed among the COICOP headings according to the nature of the claims expenditure with the residual (that is, the service charge) being allocated to the relevant insurance heading

A guide to the CPI can be found on the National Statistics website: **www.statistics.gov.uk/cpi**

Internationally, the CPI is known as the harmonised index of consumer prices (HICP). HICPs are calculated in each member state of the European Union (EU-27), according to rules specified in a series of European regulations developed by Eurostat in conjunction with the EU member states. HICPs are used to compare inflation rates across the EU-27. Since January 1999 the European Central Bank (ECB) has used HICPs as the measure of price stability across the euro area.

Further details can be found on the ECB website: **www.ecb.int/mopo/html/index.en.html**

CPI estimates for years prior to 1996 had to be estimated using available data sources. For 1988 to 1995 the CPI was estimated from archived RPI price quotes and historical weights data, and aggregated up to the published COICOP weights. Therefore, the estimated CPI is based on the RPI household population and not all private households, and it does not account for all items included in the official CPI.

For more information about how these historical estimates were produced see the 'Harmonised Index of Consumer Prices: Historical Estimates' paper in *Economic Trends*, no.541.

Part 7: Health

Expectation of life

The expectation of life is the average total number of years that a person of that age could be expected to live, if the rates of mortality at each age were those experienced in that year. The mortality rates that underlie the expectation of life figures are based, up to 2006, on total deaths occurring in each year for England and Wales, and total deaths registered in each year for Scotland and Northern Ireland.

Healthy life expectancy and disability-free life expectancy

Healthy life expectancy (HLE) and disability-free life expectancy are summary measures of population health that combine mortality and ill health. In contrast to life expectancy, these two indicators measure both the quality and quantity of life. Essentially they partition life expectancy into the following two components:

- years lived free from ill health or disability

- years lived in ill health or with disability

Life expectancy indicators are independent of the age structure of the population and represent the average health expectation of a synthetic birth cohort experiencing current rates of mortality and ill health over their lifetime.

HLE at birth is defined as the number of years that a newly born baby can expect to live in good or fairly good health if he or she experienced current mortality rates and 'good' or 'fairly good' health rates, based on self-assessed general health for different age groups during their lifespan. The calculation of HLE uses Office for National Statistics (ONS) data on life expectancy, and the General Household Survey (GHS) (Longitudinal), Continuous Household Survey (CHS), and census data on self-assessed health, specifically responses to the question 'Over the last 12 months would you say your health has on the whole been good, fairly good, or not good?' 'Good' and 'fairly good' responses are taken as a positive measure of health. The GHS was not conducted in either 1997 or 1999. The resulting modifications to the annual series of HLE data are:

- no data points were calculated for the years 1996, 1998 and 2000

- the data points for 1997 and 1999 were each calculated using two years of GHS health data: 1997 on 1996 and 1998 data, and 1999 on 1998 and 2000 data

Furthermore, HLE estimates for 2001 were calculated using the revised methodology to incorporate improved population estimates from the 2001 Census and changes in weighting methodology in the GHS. They are therefore not directly comparable with previous years. However, the level of change was small and the new series can be used to monitor trends over the longer term.

Disability-free life expectancy, defined as expected years lived without a limiting long standing illness, is calculated in the same way as HLE, except that it uses the GHS/CHS age-sex rates of 'without limiting long-standing illness' instead of the rates of 'good/fairly good health'.

Standardised rates

Directly age-standardised incidence rates enable comparisons to be made between geographical areas over time, and between the sexes, which are independent of changes in the age structure of the population. In each year the crude rates in each five-year age group are multiplied by the European standard population (see table below) for that age group. These are then summed and

divided by the total standard population for these age groups to give an overall standardised rate.

International Classification of Diseases

The International Classification of Diseases (ICD) is a coding scheme for diseases and cause of death. The Tenth Revision of the ICD (ICD10) was introduced for coding the underlying cause of death in Scotland from 2000 and in the rest of the UK from 2001. The causes of death included in Figure 7.3 correspond to the following ICD10 codes: circulatory diseases I00–I99: cancer C00–D48: and respiratory diseases J00–J99. Rates for 2000 are for England and Wales only.

The data presented in Figure 7.3 cover three different revisions of the ICD. Although they have been selected according to the codes that are comparable, there may still be differences between years that are the result of changes in the rules used to select the underlying cause of death. This can be seen in deaths from respiratory diseases where different interpretation of these rules were used to code the underlying cause of death from 1983 to 1992, and from 2001 onwards in England and Wales, and 2000 onwards in Scotland.

The cancer trends data presented in Figure 7.7 and Figure 7.8 correspond to the following two sets of cancer specific ICD9 and ICD10 codes. ICD9 codes correspond to the period up to 1994, ICD10 codes correspond to the period from 1995 when the coding for cancer incidence was changed.

European standard population

The age distribution of the European standard population is presented in the table below. See also Standardised rates (above).

Household income group

The standard breakdown in the Health Survey for England looks at equivalised household income. Household income was established by means of a show-card on which banded incomes were presented. There has been increasing interest recently in using the measures of equivalised income that adjust income to take account of the number of persons in the household. To derive this, each household member is given a score depending, for adults, on the number of adults apart from the household reference person (see below), and for

International Classification of Diseases for cancers, Ninth and Tenth Revisions

ICD 9		ICD 10	
Code 151	Stomach	C16	Stomach
Code 153	Colon	C18	Colon
Code 154	Rectum	C19–C20	Rectum
Code 153,154	Colorectal	C18–C21	Colorectal
Code 162	Lung	C33-C34	Lung
Code 174	Breast	C50	Breast
Code 179	Uterus	C54	Uterus
Code 183	Ovary	C56–C57	Ovary
Code 185	Prostate	C61	Prostate
Code 188	Bladder	C67	Bladder
C00–C97	excluding C44	All malignant cancers excluding non-melanoma skin cancer	

European standard population

Age	Population
Under 1	1,600
1–4	6,400
5–9	7,000
10–14	7,000
15–19	7,000
20–24	7,000
25–29	7,000
30–34	7,000
35–39	7,000
40–44	7,000
45–49	7,000
50–54	7,000
55–59	6,000
60–64	5,000
65–69	4,000
70–74	3,000
75–79	2,000
80–84	1,000
85 and over	1,000
Total	100,000

dependent children, on their age. The total household income is divided by the sum of the scores to provide the measure of equivalised household income. All individuals in each household were allotted to the equivalised household income quintile group to which their household had been allocated. (See also Appendix, Part 5: Equivalisation scales).

Breast cancer and cervical cancer screening programmes

Figures for the two cancer screening programmes are snapshots of the coverage of the target population for each programme, at 31 March, for each year presented. The target population for breast screening services is women aged between 50 and 64, but the target population for cervical screening is different in each country.

In England, the target population for cervical screening is women aged 25 to 64, in Wales and Northern Ireland it is 20 to 64, and in Scotland it is 20 to 60.

Data for women who do not require screening, for example as a result of surgery, are not included. Northern Ireland data refer to the proportion of women aged between 20 and 64 who received at least one adequate cervical smear test in the previous five years. As such, they may include a small number of women who have been counted more than once because of an early recall for screening.

Figures for breast screening are provided for the target population of 50 to 64-year-olds, except in Wales where the target population is women aged 53 to 64. Figures for England and Wales are based on software that provides the eligibility and screening status of the current registered population, woman by woman. Breast screening figures for Northern Ireland are based on the proportion of invited women screened, while those for Scotland are estimates based on numbers screened and mid-year population estimates. Figures for England and Wales are therefore not directly comparable with those for Scotland and Northern Ireland.

Alcohol consumption

Estimates of alcohol consumption in surveys are given in standard units derived from assumptions about the alcohol content of different types of drink, combined with information from the respondent about the volume drunk. Following recent changes to the type of alcoholic drinks available, the alcohol content of drinks, and variable quantities, it became necessary to reconsider the assumptions made in obtaining estimates of alcohol consumption.

The changes in conversion factor are discussed in detail in a paper in the National Statistics Methodology series, which also includes a table giving the original and updated factors for converting alcohol volume to units. See Goddard E (2007) *Estimating alcohol consumption from survey data: updated method of converting volumes to units*, National Statistics Methodology Series NSM 37 (Office for National Statistics 2007), also available at: **www.statistics.gov. uk/statbase/product.asp?vlnk=15067**

It was clear from the research undertaken that all surveys, including the General Household Survey (GHS) (Longitudinal), have been undercounting the number of units in some types of drink – predominantly wine, but also to a lesser degree beer, lager and cider. For example, using the latest method one-half pint of strong beer, lager or cider has 2 units, the number of units in a glass of wine depends on the size of glass and is counted as 2 units if the glass size is unspecified and a bottle of alcopop has 1.5 units.

Household reference person

From April 2000 the General Household Survey (see Appendix, Part 2) adopted the term 'household reference person' in place of 'head of household'. As of April 2001 the Survey of English Housing (SHE) also adopted the term.

The household reference person (HRP) for both surveys is identified during the interview and is defined as the member of the household who:

- owns the household or accommodation or
- is legally responsible for the rent of the accommodation or
- has the household accommodation as an emolument or perquisite or
- has the household accommodation by virtue of some relationship to the owner who is not a member of the household

The household reference person must always be a householder, whereas the head of the household was always the husband for a couple household, who might not be a householder. For joint householders, the HRP will be the householder with the highest income. If two or more householders have exactly the same income the HRP is the eldest.

The definition of HRP used in survey data differs from that defined in the Reference persons text box in Chapter 2: Households and families, which is based on economic activity and is used for vital statistics.

Alcohol-related causes of death

The Office for National Statistics (ONS) definition of alcohol-related deaths includes only those causes regarded as being most directly a result of alcohol consumption. Apart from deaths from accidental poisoning with alcohol, the definition excludes other external causes of deaths, such as road traffic deaths and other accidents.

For the years 1980–2000 the cause of death was defined using the International Classification of Diseases, Ninth Revision (ICD9) (see above). The codes used by ONS to define alcohol-related deaths are listed below:

International Classification of Diseases for alcohol-related illness, Ninth Revision

Code 291	Alcoholic psychoses
Code 303	Alcohol dependence syndrome
Code 305.0	Non-dependent abuse of alcohol
Code 425.5	Alcoholic cardiomyopathy
Code 571	Chronic liver disease and cirrhosis (Excluding 571.6 – Biliary cirrhosis)
Code E860	Accidental poisoning by alcohol

For the years 2001–07 the International Classification of Diseases, Tenth Revision (ICD10) was used. To maintain comparability with earlier years the following codes were used:

International Classification of Diseases for alcohol-related illness, Tenth Revision

F10	Mental and behavioural disorders due to use of alcohol
G31.2	Degeneration of nervous system due to alcohol
G62.1	Alcoholic polyneuropathy
I42.6	Alcoholic cardiomyopathy
K29.2	Alcoholic gastritis
K70	Alcoholic liver disease
K73	Chronic hepatitis, not elsewhere classified
K74	Fibrosis and cirrhosis of liver (Excluding K74.3-K74.5 – Biliary cirrhosis)
K86.0	Alcohol induced chronic pancreatitis
X45	Accidental poisoning by and exposure to alcohol
X65	Intentional self-poisoning by and exposure to alcohol
Y15	Poisoning by and exposure to alcohol, undetermined intent

Death related to drug misuse

These figures represent the number of deaths where the underlying cause of death is regarded as poisoning, drug abuse or drug dependence and where any substances controlled under the *Misuse of Drug Act (1971)* was mentioned on the death certificate. The data on drug misuse deaths do not include deaths from other causes that may have been related to drug taking (for example, road traffic accidents or HIV/AIDS).

ONS monitors deaths from drug-related poisoning using a special database, developed to enable the analysis of deaths by the specific substances involved. Substances involved in deaths from drug-related poisoning include over-the-counter, prescription and illegal drugs. The deaths included are certified by coroners following post-mortem and inquest. Details of this database were published in 'ONS drug-related deaths database: first results for England and Wales, 1993–1997' in *Health Statistics Quarterly No. 5*. The latest report on deaths from drug-related poisoning was published in *Health Statistics Quarterly No. 39* on 28 August 2008.

Prescription Cost Analysis System

Data from the Prescription Cost Analysis System cover all prescriptions dispensed by community pharmacists and dispensing doctors in England. The system covers prescriptions originating from general practices and also those written by nurses, dentists and hospital doctors provided they are dispensed in the community. Also included are prescriptions written in Wales, Scotland, Northern Ireland and the Isle of Man but dispensed in England. Information on items dispensed in hospitals is not available.

Body mass index

The body mass index (BMI) shown in Figure 7.16 is the most widely used index of obesity among adults aged 16 and over. The BMI standardises weight for height and is calculated as weight (kg)/height (m)^2. Underweight is defined as a BMI of less than 18.5; desirable 18.5 to less than 25; overweight 25 to less than 30; and obese 30 and over.

There is ongoing debate on the definition of overweight and obesity in children. For children, BMI changes substantially with age, rising steeply in infancy, falling during the pre-school years and then rising again into adulthood. For this reason, child BMI needs to be assessed against standards that make allowance for age. Because of differences in growth rates, it is not possible to apply a universal formula in calculating obesity and overweight in children. The 1990 UK national BMI percentile classification is therefore used, which gives a BMI threshold for each age above which a child is considered overweight or obese. Those children within the 85th to 95th percentile are classified as overweight and those above the 95th percentile are classified as obese, compared with the 1990 BMI UK reference data. The percentiles are given for each sex and age. According to this method, 15 per cent of children had a BMI within the 85th to 95th percentile in 1990, and 5 per cent of children were above the 95th percentile, and were thus classified as overweight or obese respectively. Increases over 15 per cent and 5 per cent in the proportion of children who exceed the reference 85th and 95th percentiles, over time, indicate an upward trend in prevalence of those overweight and obese.

New HIV diagnoses database

The HIV and Aids new diagnoses database at the national Centre for Infections of the Health Protection Agency collects information on new HIV diagnoses, first AIDS diagnoses and deaths in HIV-infected individuals.

Numbers of new HIV diagnoses are presented by year of diagnoses. Numbers will include individuals who have an existing infection as well as those who have a newly acquired infection. Therefore, the number of new HIV diagnoses cannot be used to estimate incidence.

As reporting of new HIV diagnoses is voluntary a reporting delay needs to be considered. Data for a given year will increase substantially for a period of at least one year after the end of that calendar year. For example, 2007 data will substantially increase from the end of 2007 until the end of 2008 as more diagnoses are input onto the database. Taking this into consideration it is worth noting the archive date of the data presented. For example, data presented for 2006 from an end-June 2007 archive will be more complete than data taken from an end-December 2006 archive.

The Survey of Prevalent HIV Infections Diagnosed (SOPHID) is carried out by the National Centre for Infections of the Heath Protection Agency on behalf of the Department of Health and aims to collect data on all individuals seen for HIV care at an NHS site in England, Wales and Northern Ireland within a calendar year. Scottish data are collected by Health Protection Scotland and combined with the final dataset to create a UK dataset.

SOPHID aims to provide national regional and local epidemiological profiles of persons accessing HIV care in the UK to inform the commissioning of better HIV services and the monitoring of prevention activities.

The survey is run twice a year in London and annually outside London. The London survey includes Brighton, Hastings and Eastbourne and covers attendances from January to June and from July to December, whereas the survey outside London covers attendances for the whole calendar year. Annual national results are based on data from the two London surveys, the survey run outside London and paediatric data (children under 15 years of age) from the Institute of Child Health. Duplicates are removed from the final amalgamated dataset.

Part 8: Social protection

Expenditure on social protection benefits

Cash benefits
Income support: Periodic payments to people with insufficient resources. Conditions for entitlement may be related to personal resources and to nationality, residence, age, availability for work and family status. The benefit may be paid for a limited or an unlimited period. It may be paid to the individual or to the family, and be provided by central or local government.

Other cash benefits: Support for destitute or vulnerable people to help alleviate poverty or assist in difficult situations. These benefits may be paid by private non-profit organisations.

Benefits in kind
Accommodation: Shelter and board provided to destitute or vulnerable people, where these services cannot be classified under another function. This may be short term in reception centres, shelters and others, or on a more regular basis in special institutions, boarding houses, reception families, and others.

Rehabilitation of alcohol and drug abusers: Treatment of alcohol and drug dependency aimed at reconstructing the social life of the abusers, making them able to live an independent life. The treatment is usually provided in reception centres or special institutions.

Other benefits in kind: Basic services and goods to help vulnerable people, such as counselling, day shelter, help with carrying out daily tasks, food, clothing and fuel. Means-tested legal aid is also included.

General practitioners

General practitioner (GP) retainers are practitioners who provide service sessions in general practice. They are employed by GP partnerships to undertake sessions and are allowed to work a maximum of four sessions of approximately one-half a day each week. GP registrars are fully registered practitioners who are being trained for general practice under an arrangement approved by the Secretary of State for Health.

The Personal Medical Services (PMS) contract with GPs was introduced in 1998 as a local alternative to the national General Medical Services (GMS) contract. PMS contracts are locally negotiated contracts between the primary care trust (PCT) and the PMS provider enabling, for example, flexible provision of services in accordance with specific local circumstances.

In-patient activity

In Table 8.11 in-patient data for England are based on finished consultant episodes (FCEs). Data for Wales, Scotland and Northern Ireland are based on deaths and discharges and transfers between specialities (between hospitals in Northern Ireland).

An FCE is a completed period of care of a patient using a bed, under one consultant, in a particular National Health Service (NHS) Trust or directly managed unit. If a patient is transferred

from one consultant to another within the same hospital, this counts as an FCE but not a hospital discharge. If a patient is transferred from one hospital to another provider, this counts as an FCE and a hospital discharge. Data for England, Wales and Northern Ireland exclude NHS beds and activity in joint-user and contractual hospitals. For Scotland, data for joint-user and contractual hospitals are included.

Length of stay

A standard measure used in hospitals, indicating the number of days that a patient occupied a bed in the hospital prior to discharge.

Length of stay is calculated as the difference in days between the admission date and the discharge date, where both are given. Length of stay is based on hospital spells and only applies to ordinary admissions.

- 0 day stay – patients who are admitted and discharged on the same calendar date

- 1 day stay – patients who are admitted and discharged on consecutive days, this will include some patients whose stay is less than 24 hours

- 2 or more days stay – all other lengths of stay admissions

Dentists

In 2007/08 England and Wales introduced a new measure to record the number of dentists following a consultation exercise. The new definition is 'the number of dental performers who have any NHS activity recorded against them via FP17 claim forms at any time in the year that met the criteria for inclusion within the annual reconciliation process'.

Benefit units

A benefit unit is a single adult or couple living as married and any dependent children, where the head is below state pension age (60 for women and 65 for men) and where one or both are in receipt of a benefit. A pensioner benefit unit is a single person over state pension age or a couple where one or both adults are over state pension age.

Pension schemes

A pension scheme is a plan offering benefits to members upon retirement. Schemes are provided by the state, employers and insurance firms, and are differentiated by a wide range of rules governing membership eligibility, contributions, benefits and taxation.

Occupational pension scheme: An arrangement (other than accident or permanent health insurance) organised by an employer (or on behalf of a group of employers) to provide benefits for employees on their retirement and for their dependants on their death.

Personal pension scheme: A scheme where the contract to pay contributions in return for retirement benefits is between an individual and a pension provider, usually an insurance firm. Individuals may choose to join such schemes, for example, to provide a primary source of retirement income for the self-employed, or to provide a secondary income to employees who are members of occupational schemes. These schemes may be facilitated (but not provided) by an employer.

Stakeholder pension scheme: Available since 2001, a flexible, portable, personal pension arrangement (provided by insurance companies with capped management charges) that must meet the conditions set out in the *Welfare Reform and Pensions Act 1999* and be registered with the Pensions Regulator. They can be facilitated by an employer. Where an employer of five or more staff offers no occupational pension and an employee earns more than the lower earnings limit (the entrance level for paying tax), the provision of access to a stakeholder scheme with contributions deducted from payroll is compulsory.

Children looked after by local authorities

Scotland has a different definition of children looked after, so data are not directly comparable with the rest of the UK. Children under a supervision requirement in Scotland are considered to be in the care of their local authority, while in the rest of the UK, they are not.

In Great Britain children looked after under an agreed series of short-term placements are excluded.

In England and Wales children's homes include homes, hostels and secure units. In Northern Ireland this category includes homes and secure units but excludes hostels, which are included in the 'other accommodation' category. In Scotland, children's homes include homes and hostels (including those for children with learning and physical disabilities) and secure units.

Data for the 'placement with parents' category used in Great Britain are collected as 'placed with family' in Northern Ireland, which refers to children for whom a care order exists and who are placed with their parents, a person who is not a parent but who has parental responsibility for the child or, where a child was in care and there was a residence order in force with respect to him/her immediately before the care order was made, a person in whose favour the residence order was made.

Data for the 'placed for adoption' category is not collected for Northern Ireland. In Scotland this category includes children placed with prospective adopters.

In Scotland the 'other' category includes children staying in the community with friends/relatives and 'other community' (for example, supported accommodation) and those children staying in residential schools and 'other residential' (for example, women's refuge, local authority (LA) or voluntary hostels for offenders or for drug/alcohol abusers).

Part 9: Crime and justice

Prevalence rates and incidence rates

Prevalence rates show the proportion of the British Crime Survey (BCS) sample who were victims of an offence once or more during the year. Unlike the BCS incidence rates, they only take account of whether a household or person was a victim of a specific crime once or more in the recall period, but not of the number of times victimised. Prevalence rates are taken as equivalent to 'risk'.

Incidence rates describe the number of crimes experienced per household or adult in the BCS or police-recorded crime statistics.

Types of offence in England and Wales

The figures are compiled from police returns to the Home Office or directly from court computer systems.

Indictable offences in England and Wales cover those offences that can only be tried at the Crown Court and include the more serious offences.

Summary offences are those for which a defendant would normally be tried at a magistrates' court and are generally less serious – the majority of motoring offences fall into this category.

Triable-either-way offences are triable either on indictment or summarily.

Recorded crime statistics broadly cover the more serious offences. Up to March 1998 most indictable and triable-either-way offences were included, as well as some summary offences; from April 1998, all indictable and triable-either-way offences were included, plus a few closely related summary offences.

Recorded offences are the most readily available measures of the incidence of crime, but do not necessarily indicate the true level of crime. Many less serious offences are not reported to the police and cannot, therefore, be recorded. Moreover, the propensity of the public to report offences to the police is influenced by a number of factors and may change over time.

From 2000 some police forces have changed their systems to record the allegations of victims unless there is credible evidence that a crime has *not* taken place. In April 2002 the National Crime Recording Standard (NCRS, see below) formalised these changes across England and Wales. There have been changes to the methodology of the British Crime Survey (BCS). Between 1982 and 2001 the survey was carried out every two years, and reported on victimisation in the previous calendar year. From 2001/02 onwards the surveys cover the financial year of interviews and report on victimisation in the 12 months prior to interview on an annual basis.

This change makes the BCS estimates more comparable with figures collected by the police. Because of the significant changes taking place in both these measures of crime, direct comparisons with figures for previous years cannot be made.

Types of offence in Scotland

In Scotland the term 'crime' is reserved for the more serious offences (broadly equivalent to 'indictable' and 'triable-either-way' offences in England and Wales) while less serious crimes are called 'offences'. The seriousness of an act is *generally* based on the maximum sentence that can be imposed.

Police-recorded crime data included in this report are based on a count of the numbers of crimes and offences recorded and cleared up by the police. Amendments (such as the deletion of incidents found on investigation not to be criminal) that arise after the end of the financial year are not generally incorporated. Offences recorded by the British Transport Police, the Ministry of Defence and the Civil Nuclear Constabulary (previously known as the UK Atomic Energy Authority) are also not included.

In one criminal incident, several crimes or offences may occur, for example, a house may be broken into and vandalised and the occupants assaulted. In multiple offence incidents, all the offences are counted rather than one for the incident as a whole; that is, the counting system is offence-based rather than incident-based. Statistics are therefore not directly comparable with statistics on action taken against offenders, as one offence may lead to several persons being charged. Equally, an offender may be charged with several offences.

Motor vehicle offences do not include *stationary* motor vehicle offences dealt with by the issue of a fixed penalty ticket. However, offences dealt with under the vehicle defect rectification scheme and offences for which the procurator fiscal offers a fixed penalty are included in the figures. In addition to this, *moving* traffic offences that are the subject of a police conditional offer of a fixed penalty are also included, for example, speeding, traffic directions offences.

The Scottish Crime and Victimisation Survey (SCVS) 2006 was the eighth in a series of crime surveys in Scotland. In 1982 and 1988, Scotland participated in sweeps of the British Crime Survey (BCS) co-ordinated by the Home Office. In 1993, the Scottish Office commissioned the first independent Scottish Crime Survey (SCS), which extended coverage to the whole of mainland Scotland, together with the larger islands, and this survey was repeated in 1996, 2000 and 2003. In 2004 the survey was re-launched as the Scottish Crime and Victimisation Survey (SCVS) and was telephone-based. It was decided that a SCVS would be conducted face-to-face in 2006 with a sample size of 5,000, as an interim measure prior to the re-launch of the survey on a larger sample size in 2007. Fieldwork for the new Scottish Crime and Justice Survey began in April 2008 and the first results will be available in late 2009.

Types of offence in Northern Ireland

In recording crime, the Police Service of Northern Ireland (PSNI) broadly follows the Home Office rules for counting crime. As from 1 April 1998 notifiable offences are recorded on the same basis as those in England and Wales. Before the revision of the rules, criminal damage offences in Northern Ireland excluded those where the value of the property damaged was less than £200. The National Crime Recording Standard (NCRS, see below) was introduced within PSNI in April 2002.

See 'Availability and comparability of data from constituent countries' entry below for information on the differences in the legal system in Scotland compared with England and Wales, and Northern Ireland.

National Crime Recording Standard

Changes in the counting rules for recorded crime on 1 April 1998 affected both the methods of counting and the coverage for recorded crime and had the effect of inflating the number of crimes recorded. For some offence groups – more serious violence against the person and burglary – there was little effect on the number recorded. However, the changes have had more effect on figures for minor violence and criminal damage.

In April 2002 the National Crime Recording Standard (NCRS) was introduced in England and Wales, and in Northern Ireland, with the aim of taking a more victim-centred approach and providing more consistency between forces. Before 2002 police forces in England and Wales did not necessarily record a crime that was reported if there was no evidence to support the claim of the victim. Therefore crimes recorded from 1 April 2002 are not comparable with earlier years.

It is not possible to assess the effect of NCRS on recorded firearm crimes. NCRS inflated the overall number of violence against the person and criminal damage offences, but has less effect on the number of robberies. Many firearm offences are among the less serious categories, and these types of offences are among those most affected by NCRS.

The introduction of the NCRS may have had an effect on the recorded crime detection rate, but this is difficult to quantify.

Scottish Crime Recording Standard
In April 2004 the Association of Chief Police Officers in Scotland (ACPOS) implemented the Scottish Crime Recording Standard (SCRS) following recommendations from Her Majesty's Inspectorate of Constabulary (HMIC), which means that no corroborative evidence is required initially to record a crime-related incident as a crime if so perceived by the victim. In consequence of this more victim-oriented approach, the HMIC expected the SCRS to increase the numbers of minor crimes recorded by the police, such as minor crimes of vandalism and minor thefts. However, the HMIC also expected that the SCRS would not have much impact on the figures for the more serious crimes, such as serious assault, sexual assault, robbery or housebreaking.

Unfortunately it was not possible to estimate the exact impact of SCRS on the recorded crime figures. Around the time that the standard was implemented police also introduced centralised call centres, which encouraged the reporting of incidents to the police. The Scottish Government had hoped that the underlying trends in crime would be monitored through a new, much larger, Scottish Crime and Victimisation Survey (SCVS), but this has not proved possible.

Availability and comparability of data from constituent countries

There are a number of reasons why recorded crime statistics in England and Wales, Northern Ireland and Scotland cannot be directly compared:

Different legal systems: The legal system operating in Scotland differs from that in England and Wales, and Northern Ireland. For example, in Scotland children aged under 16 accused of offending are normally dealt with by the Children's Hearings system rather than the courts.

Differences in classification: There are significant differences in the offences included within the recorded crime categories used in Scotland and the categories of notifiable offences used in England, Wales, and Northern Ireland. Scottish figures are divided into 'offences' (less serious criminal acts) and 'crimes' (the more serious criminal acts). The seriousness of an act is generally based on the maximum sentence that can be imposed. Scottish figures of 'crime' have therefore been grouped in an attempt to approximate to the classification of notifiable offences in England, Wales and Northern Ireland.

Counting rules: In all parts of the UK, only the main offence occurring within an incident is counted.

Burglary: This term is not applicable to Scotland where the term used is 'housebreaking' and includes domestic as well as commercial premises.

Theft from vehicles: In Scotland data have only been separately identified from January 1992. The figures include theft by opening lock-fast places from a motor vehicle and other theft from a motor vehicle.

Comparable crimes

Comparable crimes are a set of offences that are covered by both the British Crime Survey (BCS) and police-recorded crime. Various adjustments are made to the recorded crime categories to maximise comparability with the BCS. Comparable crime is used to compare trends in police and BCS figures, and to identify the amount of crime that is not reported to the police and not recorded by them. The comparable subset includes common assaults (and assaults on a constable), and vehicle interference and tampering. Four-fifths (80 per cent) of BCS offences reported through interviews in the 2007/08 interview sample fall into categories that can be compared with crimes recorded under the new police coverage of offences adopted from 1 April 1998. With the introduction of new police counting rules in 1998/99, the 'old' comparable subset that was used, up to and including the 1998 BCS, was updated as it excluded common assaults, other household theft and other theft of personal property.

Homicides

The term 'homicide' covers the offences of murder, manslaughter and infanticide. Murder and manslaughter are common law offences that have never been defined by statute, although they have been modified by statute. The offence of 'infanticide' was created by the *Infanticide Act 1922* and refined by the *Infanticide Act 1938 (s1)*.

Homicide offences included in this report are shown according to the year in which the police initially recorded the offence as homicide. This is

not necessarily the year in which the incident took place or the year in which any court decision was made. The 2007/08 data refer to the position as at 4 November 2008, when recording closed down for the purpose of analysis, and will change as subsequent court hearings take place or other information is received. Because of differences in recording practice with respect to 'no crimes', data from the homicide index do not necessarily agree with the recorded crime data.

Perceived likelihood of being a victim of crime

The perceived likelihood of burglary is based on those who say they are very or fairly likely to have their home burgled in the next year. Perceived likelihood of violent crime is a composite measure of anyone who thinks they are very or fairly likely to be *either* mugged/robbed, *or* physically attacked by a stranger in the next year, or both. Perceived likelihood of vehicle crime is a composite measure of vehicle owners who think they are very or fairly likely to either have a car/van stolen, *or* have something stolen from a car/van in the next year, or both. All the perceived likelihood questions in the British Crime Survey are asked of respondents, irrespective of whether they have been a victim of crime in the previous 12 months.

Sentences and orders

The following are the main sentences and orders that can be imposed upon people found guilty. Some types of sentence or order can only be given to offenders in England and Wales in certain age groups. Under the framework for sentencing contained in the *Criminal Justice Acts 1991, 1993* and the *Powers of Criminal Courts (Sentencing) Act 2000* the sentence must reflect the seriousness of the offence. The sentences explained below are available for adults aged 18 and over but a similar range of sentences is available for juveniles aged 10 to 17 and these have been identified where relevant:

Absolute and conditional discharge
A court may make an order discharging a person absolutely or (except in Scotland) conditionally where it is inexpedient to inflict punishment and, before 1 October 1992, where a probation order was not appropriate. An order for conditional discharge runs for a period of not more than three years as the court specifies, the condition being that the offender does not commit another offence within the period so specified. In Scotland a court may also discharge a person with an admonition.

Community sentences
The term 'community sentence' refers to attendance centre orders, reparation orders, action plan orders, drug treatment and testing orders, community orders, community rehabilitation orders, community punishment orders, community punishment and rehabilitation orders, supervision orders, curfew orders and referral orders. Under the *Criminal Justice and Courts Services Act 2000*, certain community orders current at 1 April 2001 were renamed. Probation orders were renamed community rehabilitation orders, community service orders were renamed community punishment orders and combination orders were

renamed community punishment and rehabilitation orders.

Attendance centre order: Available in England, Wales and Northern Ireland for young offenders and involves deprivation of free time.

Reparation order: Introduced under the *Powers of Criminal Courts (Sentencing) Act 2000*. This requires the offender to make an apology to the victim or to apologise in person. Maximum duration of the order is 24 hours and is only available to juveniles aged 10 to 18 in England and Wales.

Action plan order: An order imposed for a maximum of three months in England, Wales and Northern Ireland to address certain behavioural problems. This is again available for the younger age groups and is considered as early intervention to stop serious offending.

Drug treatment and testing order: This is imposed as a treatment order to reduce the person's dependence on drugs and to test if the offender is complying with treatment. The length of order can run from six months to three years in England, Wales and Northern Ireland. This was introduced under the *Powers of Criminal Courts (Sentencing) Act 2000* for persons aged 16 and over. In Scotland, drug treatment and testing orders were introduced in phases on a court by court basis from 1999 onwards. They are now available in almost every Sheriff and High Court in Scotland.

Court orders: The term 'court orders' used in the text includes all the above 'orders'. It does not include any pre- or post-release supervision.

Community sentences: This term refers to all court orders except for suspended sentence orders and deferred sentences, which may have a custodial component to the sentence.

Community order: For offences committed on or after 4 April 2005 the new community order, introduced under the *Criminal Justice Act 2003*, replaced all existing community sentences for adults. Under this order, one or more of 12 possible requirements must be added, such as supervision, unpaid work and drug treatment. The Act also introduced a new suspended sentence order for offences that pass the custody threshold. One or more of the same set of 12 possible requirements must be added to this order. Unless considered dangerous those sentenced to 12 months or more in custody, who will be released on licence at the halfway point of the sentence, will remain on licence, and subject to recall if they breach the conditions of their licence, for the entire remaining period of their sentence, instead of to the three-quarter point.

Community rehabilitation order: An offender sentenced to a community rehabilitation order is under the supervision of a probation officer (social worker in Scotland) whose duty it is (in England and Wales, and Northern Ireland) to advise, assist and befriend him or her, but the court has the power to include any other requirement it considers appropriate. A cardinal feature of the order is that it relies on the co-operation of the offender. Community rehabilitation orders may be given for any period between six months and three years inclusive.

Punishment order: An offender who is convicted of an offence punishable with imprisonment may be sentenced to perform unpaid work for not more than 240 hours (300 hours in Scotland), and not less than 40 hours. Sentences of a minimum of 20 hours community service are given for persistent petty offending or fine default. In Scotland the *Law Reform (Miscellaneous Provisions) (Scotland) Act 1990* requires that community service can only be ordered where the court would otherwise have imposed imprisonment or detention. Probation and community service may be combined in a single order in Scotland. Community punishment orders came into effect under the *Powers of Criminal Courts (Sentencing) Act 2000* when they replaced supervision orders.

Community punishment and rehabilitation order: The *Criminal Justice Act 1991* introduced the combination order in England and Wales only, which combines elements of both probation supervision and community service. Meanwhile, Article 15 of the Criminal Justice (NI) Order 1996 introduced the combination order to Northern Ireland. The *Powers of Criminal Courts (Sentencing) Act 2000* brought into effect the community punishment and rehabilitation order, known as the combination order, which requires an offender to be under a probation officer and to take on unpaid work.

Detention and imprisonment
Detention and training order: This was introduced for juveniles aged 10 to 18 under the *Powers of Criminal Courts (Sentencing) Act 2000*. It is for juveniles who have committed a serious crime. They can serve the sentence at a young offender institution, at a local authority establishment, or at a local authority secure training centre. The sentence given is from four to 24 months, but sentences can run consecutively.

Imprisonment: Is the custodial sentence for adult offenders. Home Office or Scottish Government consent is needed for release or transfer. In the case of mentally disordered offenders, hospital orders, which may include a restriction order, may be considered appropriate.

A new disposal, the 'hospital direction', was introduced in 1997. The court, when imposing a period of imprisonment, can direct that the offender be sent directly to hospital. On recovering from the mental disorder, the offender is returned to prison to serve the balance of their sentence.

The *Criminal Justice Act 1991* abolished remission and substantially changed the parole scheme in England and Wales. Those serving sentences of less than four years, imposed on or after 1 October 1992, are subject to automatic conditional release and are released, subject to certain criteria, halfway through their sentence. Home detention curfews result in selected prisoners being released up to two months early with a tag that monitors their presence during curfew hours. Those serving sentences of four years or longer are considered for discretionary conditional release after having served half their sentence, but are automatically released at the two-thirds point of sentence.

The *Crime (Sentences) Act 1997*, implemented on 1 October 1997, included, for persons aged

18 or over, an automatic life sentence for a second serious violent or sexual offence unless there are exceptional circumstances. All offenders serving a sentence of 12 months or more are supervised in the community until the three-quarters point of sentence. A life sentence prisoner may be released on licence subject to supervision and is always liable to recall.

In Scotland the *Prisoners and Criminal Proceedings (Scotland) Act 1993* changed the system of remission and parole for prisoners sentenced on or after 1 October 1993. Those serving sentences of less than four years are released unconditionally after having served half of their sentence, unless the court specifically imposes a supervised release order that subjects them to social work supervision after release. Those serving sentences of four years or more are eligible for parole at half sentence. If parole is not granted then they will automatically be released on licence at the two-thirds point of sentence subject to days added for breaches of prison rules. All such prisoners are liable to be 'recalled on conviction' or for breach of conditions of licence, if between the date of release and the date on which the full sentence ends he/she commits another offence that is punishable by imprisonment, or breaches his/her licence conditions. The offender may be returned to prison for the remainder of that sentence whether or not a sentence of imprisonment is also imposed for the new offence.

Management of Offenders etc. (Scotland) Act 2005 introduced home detention curfew in Scotland. From 3 July 2006, certain prisoners serving less than four years and assessed as presenting a low risk of re-offending, can be released on licence between two weeks and four months early. They are subject to electronically monitored restrictions on their movements for up to 12 hours per day for the remainder of their sentence.

Custody probation order: An order unique to Northern Ireland, reflecting the different regime there that applies in respect of remission and the general absence of release on licence. The custodial sentence is followed by a period of supervision for a period of between one and three years.

Fully suspended sentences
These may only be passed in exceptional circumstances. In England, Wales and Northern Ireland, sentences of imprisonment of two years or less may be fully suspended. A court should not pass a suspended sentence unless a sentence of imprisonment would be appropriate in the absence of a power to suspend. The result of suspending a sentence is that it will not take effect unless during the period specified the offender is convicted of another offence punishable with imprisonment. Suspended sentences are not available in Scotland.

Fines
The *Criminal Justice Act 1993* introduced new arrangements from 20 September 1993, whereby courts are required to fit an amount for the fine that reflects the seriousness of the offence and that takes account of an offender's means. This system replaced the more formal unit fines scheme included in the *Criminal Justice Act*

237

1991. The 1993 Act also introduced the power for courts to arrange deduction of fines from income benefit for those offenders receiving such benefits. The *Law Reform (Miscellaneous Provision) (Scotland) Act 1990* as amended by the *Criminal Procedure (Scotland) Act 1995* provides for the use of supervised attendance orders by selected courts in Scotland. The *Criminal Procedure (Scotland) Act 1995* also makes it easier for courts to impose a supervised attendance order in the event of a default and enables the court to impose a supervised attendance order in the first instance for 16 and 17-year-olds.

Reoffenders

The measurement of reoffending has undergone a change from *Social Trends 38*, as amendments to the existing measure of reoffending, as well as the development of two new measures, were introduced in 2008. All the reoffending measures cover adults (aged 18 and over) released from custody or commencing a court order (sentences under probation supervision, excluding fines) in the first quarters of the cohorts (2000, 2002, 2003, 2004, 2005 and 2006) whose reoffence resulted in a conviction at court. The use of first quarter data (1 January to 31 March) arises from the administrative effort required to match criminal records and enables results to be more timely without compromising reliability and comparability.

The actual (or 'yes/no') reoffending rate presented in Figure 9.14 allows the assessment of whether or not an offender has reoffended during a one-year follow-up period and is subsequently convicted. This is a change from the measure presented in *Social Trends 38*, which assessed reoffending within a two-year period, and makes the data more timely as well as bringing it in line with the measurement period for juvenile reoffending (see below).

The two new measures of reoffending are the frequency and the severity rate.

The *frequency* of reoffending shows the number of reoffences being committed, enabling a better understanding of the impacts of programmes and interventions, which do not just lead to complete desistance by offenders but may also reduce the volume of reoffences offenders commit.

The *severity rate* (or rate of the most serious reoffences committed) enables the monitoring of reoffences classified as most serious. These are the reoffences that cause the most harm to society, despite being a small subset of the overall volume of reoffences committed.

Reoffenders – juveniles

The measures of reoffending among juveniles (aged 10 to 17) follow the same format as those among adults (see above). They cover juveniles released from custody (either from prison, secure training centres or secure children's homes) or those given a pre-court disposal or commencing a non-custodial court disposal in the first quarter of the cohort years (2000 to 2006), whose reoffences resulted in a conviction at court or a pre-court disposal.

Prison population

Population in custody includes those held in prison or police cells. They include prisoners on remand (both untried and those who have been convicted but remain unsentenced), prisoners under sentence and non-criminal prisoners (for example those held under the *Immigration Act 1971*). They also include those held in police cells.

The new indeterminate sentence of imprisonment (or detention) for public protection came into effect on 4 April 2005 and applies to offenders who are convicted of a serious offence (that is a specified sexual or violent offence carrying a maximum penalty of ten years' imprisonment or more) and who are considered by the court to pose a 'significant risk to members of the public of serious harm'.

Anti-social behaviour orders (ASBOs)

Anti-social behaviour orders (ASBOs) are court orders that aim to protect the public rather than punish the perpetrator. However, they prohibit the perpetrator from specific anti-social behaviours, for example by banning them from continuing the offending behaviour, from visiting certain areas or from spending time with a particular group of friends.

An ASBO is a civil order, not a criminal penalty, which means it won't appear on an individual's criminal record. However, a breach of an ASBO is a criminal offence punishable by a fine or up to five years in prison. ASBOs are issued for a minimum of two years.

ASBOs are community-based interventions designed to encourage local communities to become actively involved in reporting crime and anti-social behaviour, helping to build and protect the community.

Parenting contracts and parenting orders

Parenting contract
A voluntary written agreement between a youth offending team (YOT) worker and the parents of a child who is, or is likely to become, involved in criminal or anti-social behaviour. A contract consists of two elements:

- a statement by the parents or guardians that they agree to comply for a specified period with requirements specified in the contract and

- a statement by the YOT worker agreeing to provide support to the parents or guardians for the purpose of complying with the contract

The requirements specified in the contract may include, in particular, a requirement to attend a parenting programme (see 'Parenting orders' below).

Parenting order
A parenting order is made in similar circumstances to a parenting contract by a criminal court, family court or magistrates' court acting under civil jurisdiction, and can be applied where parents are unwilling to co-operate. The core requirement of a parenting order is that the parent attends a parenting programme to help them address their child's misbehaviour. Parenting programmes can include counselling or guidance sessions to help them to provide appropriate care, protection, support and control for the young person and focus on ways to help prevent further offending.

The court may also include in the order specific requirements for the parent, for example, ways in which they should exercise control over the child's behaviour. These can include ensuring that the child is home during certain hours, attends school, avoids other disruptive people, attends any relevant programmes or courses (such as for anger management or drug or alcohol misuse) or avoids unsupervised visits to certain areas such as shopping centres.

Failing, without reasonable excuse, to comply with the parenting order is a criminal offence.

Persistent young offenders

The definition of a persistent young offender is a person aged 10 to 17 who has been sentenced by any criminal court in the UK on three or more separate occasions, for one or more recordable offence, and within three years of the last sentencing occasion is subsequently arrested or has information laid against them for a further recordable offence.

The figures presented in Figure 9.19 come from separate monitoring exercises covering offenders sentenced in each of the calendar years from 1996 to 2007, and for 2008 from January to June.

Convictions for offences that met the following criteria were counted in determining whether an offender had three qualifying sentencing occasions:

- offences committed in the UK (including Channel Islands and Isle of Man) by youths aged 10 to 17 but not over 17 at the date of charge, summons, reporting or (in a few instances) arrest

- the offender was 18 years of age or under at the start of the year in which they were sentenced for the offence

- where an offender was sentenced for more than one offence at a time only one offence was counted

- offences against which there was no conviction, for example, acquittals, were excluded

- offences for breaches of previous sentence orders (for example, probation) are not normally counted

Once offenders with three or more previous sentencing occasions had been identified, further sentencing occasions were examined to see if the date of the offence fell within three years of the previous sentencing occasion. If so, offences were then checked against the criteria below to determine whether to include them in the monitoring:

- offences proceeded against in courts outside England and Wales were excluded

- offences handled by a police force outside England and Wales were excluded

Average time from arrest to sentence

The Ministry of Justice produces monthly figures on the time taken between arrest and sentence for persistent young offenders (see above), to monitor their pledge to halve the 1996 figure from 142 days to 71 days.

The calculation of the target figure of 71 days, and performance against that target, uses data from the police national computer and police forces. The data cover those individuals who fell within the definition of persistent young offender at the date of arrest, and also those who were brought within the definition by further convictions before the time of sentence.

The data in Figure 9.19 and those produced thereafter are calculated using an amended methodology to that used in publications prior to May 2006. The new methodology has been applied to remove the double counting of arrest to process times for those offences processed at arrest. Full application required the re-calculating of time-series figures and this has resulted in substantive changes on the previously published numbers.

Courts system in England and Wales

The courts system consists of civil courts (including the High Court and county courts, see below), the magistrates' courts and Crown courts, each of which preside over different types of crimes and complaints.

Civil courts
The main civil courts are the High Court and the county courts. The High Court is divided into three divisions:

- the *Queen's Bench Division* deals with disputes relating to contracts, general commercial matters and breaches of duty – known as 'liability in tort' – covering claims of negligence, nuisance or defamation

- the *Chancery Division* deals with disputes relating to land, wills, companies and insolvency

- the *Family Division* deals with matrimonial matters, including divorce, and the welfare of children

Magistrates' courts also have some civil jurisdiction, mainly in family proceedings. Most appeals in civil cases go to the Court of Appeal (Civil Division) and may go from there to the House of Lords. Since July 1991, county courts have been able to deal with all contract and tort cases and actions for recovery of land, regardless of value. Cases are presided over by a judge who almost always sits without a jury. Jury trials are limited to specified cases, for example, actions for libel.

Magistrates' courts
Virtually all criminal cases start in a magistrates' court and more than 95 per cent of cases are also completed here. In addition, magistrates' courts deal with many civil cases, mostly family matters plus liquor licensing and betting and gaming work. Cases in the magistrates' courts are usually heard by panels of three magistrates (Justices of the Peace). The youth court is a specialised form of magistrates' court where almost all 10 to 17-year-olds will have their case dealt with. As in the magistrates' court, the case will be heard by magistrates or by a district judge (magistrates' courts).

Crown Court
The Crown Court deals with more serious criminal cases transferred from the magistrates' court, such as murder, rape and robbery. It also hears appeals against decisions made in the magistrates' courts and deals with cases sent from magistrates' courts for sentence.

Judiciary of England and Wales

The judiciary includes the judges, magistrates and other adjudicators, as well as support personnel who keep the courts system in England and Wales running smoothly and includes the civil, family and criminal jurisdictions.

Civil justice
Judicial roles in the civil jurisdiction include the following:

Court of appeal – Civil division
The Civil Division of the Court of Appeal hears appeals from all divisions of the High Court and, in some instances from the county courts and certain tribunals. High Court judges are assigned to one of the three divisions of the High Court – the Chancery Division, the Queen's Bench and the Family Division.

High Court – Queen's Bench (Civil)
Judges who sit in the Queen's Bench Division of the High Court deal with 'common law' business, that is actions relating to contract except those specifically allocated to the Chancery Division, and civil wrongs (known as tort). High Court judges who sit in these courts hear cases involving prolonged examination of technical issues, for example, construction disputes. Judges of the Queen's Bench Division also sit in the employment appeals tribunal.

High Court – Chancery Division (Civil)
The principal business of judges who sit in the Chancery Division is corporate and personal insolvency disputes, business, trade and industry disputes, the enforcement of mortgages, intellectual property matters, copyright and patents, disputes relating to trust property and contentious probate actions.

Circuit judges – civil
Circuit judges may deal solely with civil, family or criminal work, or divide their time between the three. Circuit judges deal with a variety of civil and family cases and may specialise in particular areas of law, for example, commercial. Circuit judges generally hear claims worth over £15,000 or those involving greater complexity or importance.

Recorders – civil
Recorders civil sit as fee-paid judges in county courts. Some recorders civil may also be authorised to deputise for specialist civil circuit judges, for example, in the Chancery Division, the Mercantile Court and the Technology and Construction Court. The statutory jurisdiction of a recorder is in general identical to that of a circuit judge, although the usual practice is that recorders do not hear appeals from district judges. The jurisdiction covers almost the whole field of civil law and is mostly concurrent with that of the High Court.

District judges
District judges are full-time judges who deal with the majority of cases in the county courts of England and Wales. Their work involves:

- dealing with civil disputes such as personal injury cases

- claims for damages and injunctions

- possession proceedings against mortgage borrowers and property tenants

- claims for reasonable provision out of the estates of deceased persons

Deputy district judges
A deputy district judge is appointed to sit in the county court or in a High Court District Registry to case manage and try civil, family, costs, enforcement and insolvency cases. They try small claims and fast track cases, family ancillary relief hearings, hear interim applications and make procedural directions preparing cases for trial. Their jurisdiction is broadly similar to that of a full-time district judge although they have limited authority to deal with family cases involving children.

Magistrates
Magistrates, also known as Justices of the Peace, are unpaid trained members of their local community. Although most magistrates deal with criminal work, they also decide many civil matters, particularly in relation to family work. Magistrates' civil roles include dealing with cases such as non-payment of council tax. Magistrates deal with more than 95 per cent of all criminal cases, either in the adult court, or in the youth court.

Criminal justice
Judicial roles in the criminal jurisdiction include the following:

Court of Appeal – Criminal Division
The judges of the Court of Appeal are the 'Heads of Division' (the Lord Chief Justice of England and Wales, the Master of the Rolls, the President of the Queen's Bench Division, the President of the Family Division and the Chancellor of the High Court) and the Lords Justices of Appeal. The Criminal Division hears appeals from the Crown court.

High Court – Criminal jurisdiction
High Court judges can hear the most serious and sensitive cases in the Crown court (for example, murder) and some sit with Appeal Court judges in the Criminal Division of the Court of Appeal. Most High Court judges sit in the Queen's Bench Division. They will also deal at first instance with the more serious criminal cases heard in the Crown court.

Circuit judge
Circuit judges are appointed to one of six regions of England and Wales and sit in the Crown and county courts within their particular region. Some circuit judges deal specifically with criminal or civil cases, while some are authorised to hear public and/or private law family cases.

Recorders
Recorders are fee-paid, part-time, judges. For many it is the first step on the judicial ladder to appointment to the circuit bench. Recorders' jurisdiction is broadly similar to that of a circuit judge, but they generally handle less complex or serious matters coming before the court.

District judge (magistrates' courts)
The role of a district judge (magistrates' courts) is to complement the work of the magistracy. They are legally qualified, salaried judges and they usually deal with complex matters that come before magistrates' courts. District judges (magistrates' courts) also have jurisdiction to hear cases under the *Extradition Acts* and the *Fugitive Offender Acts*.

Magistrates
For a single criminal offence committed by an adult, a magistrate's sentencing powers include the imposition of fines, community service orders, probation orders or a period of not more than six months in custody (see 'Sentences and orders' above). Magistrates may also sit in the Crown court with a judge to hear appeals from magistrates' courts against conviction or sentence and proceedings on committal to the Crown court for sentence.

Magistrates – youth courts
Magistrates are specially trained to sit in youth courts where procedures are slightly more informal than in adult criminal courts. To engage with young defendants, magistrates deliberately talk directly to them rather than always through their legal representative. In criminal cases the youth court has jurisdiction to deal with all offences committed by a juvenile except homicide, which has to be dealt with in a higher court. Sentences are quite different in that they specifically address the needs of young offenders.

Family justice
The family justice system exists to help families avoid disputes as far as possible but also, if disputes or problems should arise, to enable them to resolve those problems quickly and with the minimum of pain caused to those involved. If at all possible the parties are encouraged to resolve their disputes out of court, for example, through mediation, on the grounds that they are more likely to stick to any agreement if they themselves have had a role in formulating it.

When disputes do come to the courts, the cases are dealt with by magistrates and judges specially trained to deal with issues affecting families. These disputes often involve very difficult circumstances, for example, relationship breakdown or child contact. Judges and magistrates work to make the circumstances of family disputes less adversarial and hearings can often be quite informal with, for example, all parties sitting around a table.

Part 10: Housing

Dwelling stock

The definition of a dwelling follows the census definition applicable at that time. Currently the 2001 Census definition is used, which defines a dwelling as 'structurally separate accommodation'. This was determined primarily by considering the type of accommodation, as well as separate and shared access to multi-occupied properties.

In all stock figures vacant dwellings are included but non-permanent dwellings are generally excluded. For housebuilding statistics, only data on permanent dwellings are collected.

Estimates of the total dwelling stock, stock changes and the tenure distribution in the UK are made by Communities and Local Government for England, the Scottish Government, the Welsh Assembly Government, and the Northern Ireland Department for Social Development. These are primarily based on census output data for the number of dwellings (or households converted to dwellings) from the censuses of population for the UK.

Adjustments are carried out if there are specific reasons to do so. Census year figures are based on outputs from the censuses. For years between censuses, the total figures are obtained by projecting the base census year's figure forward annually. The increment is based on the annual total number of completions plus the annual total net gain from other housing statistics, that is, conversions, demolitions and changes of use.

Estimates of dwelling stock by tenure category are based on other sources where it is considered that for some specific tenure information, these are more accurate than census output data. In this situation it is assumed that the other data sources also contain vacant dwellings, but it is not certain and it is not expected that these data are very precise. Thus the allocation of vacant dwellings to tenure categories may not be completely accurate and the margin of error for tenure categories is wider than for estimates of total stock.

For local authority stock, figures supplied by local authorities are more reliable than those in the 2001 Census. Similarly, it was found that the Housing Corporation's own data are more accurate than census output data for the registered social landlord (RSL) stock. Hence only the privately rented or with a job or business tenure data were taken directly from the Census. The owner-occupied data were taken as the residual of the total from the Census. For non-census years, the same approach was adopted except for the privately rented or with a job or business, for which Labour Force Survey results were used (see Appendix, Part 4: Labour Force Survey).

In the Survey of English Housing, data for privately rented unfurnished accommodation include accommodation that is partly furnished.

For further information on the methodology used to calculate stock by tenure and tenure definitions for the UK, see Appendix B Notes and Definitions in the Communities and Local Government annual volume *Housing Statistics* or the housing statistics page of the Communities and Local Government website at: **www.communities.gov.uk/housing/ housingresearch/housingstatistics/**

Housebuilding completions

Housebuilding statistics cover building of all permanent dwellings, including houses, bungalows and flats. In principle a dwelling is regarded as completed when it becomes ready for occupation, whether it is occupied or not. In practice there are instances where the timing could be delayed and some completions are missed, for example, because no completion certificates were requested by the owner.

Tenure definition for housebuilding is only slightly different from that used for dwelling stock figures (see above).

Private and social sectors

'Social sector' housing includes all local authority (or public) housing as well as registered social landlord (RSL) and housing association (HA) housing. For housing data, RSLs and HAs are generally separated to identify the extent of social housing.

Where the term 'private sector' is used in housing policy and housing statistics, it generally means the 'private housing' sector or non-social housing sector, that is owner-occupied dwellings and those rented privately, including those that go with a job or business and not those owned by RSLs or HAs.

For housebuilding starts and completions data, especially the former, there is a small possibility that some dwellings built for RSLs and HAs could have been counted as 'private enterprise' and vice versa. This is because sometimes the builders themselves are not sure of the precise ownership or the ownership may keep evolving and it is not final until it is sold.

Tenure

There are four tenure categories available for dwelling stock and household figures. These are:

- owner-occupied (or private enterprise in the case of housebuilding statistics, that is dwellings financed and built by private developers for owner-occupiers or private landlords, whether persons or companies). This includes accommodation that is owned outright or is being bought with a mortgage

- rented privately, defined as all non-owner-occupied property other than that rented from local authorities and registered social landlords (RSLs) plus that rented from private or public bodies by virtue of employment. This includes property occupied rent-free by someone other than the owner. New build privately rented dwellings will be included in the housebuilding private enterprise figures

- rented from RSLs, but for stock figures non-registered housing associations are excluded and subsumed within owner-occupied as are RSL shared ownership and shared equity dwellings; for housebuilding figures the RSL tenure includes social rent, intermediate rent and low-cost home ownership RSL new build dwellings

- rented from local authorities. In Scotland dwellings rented from local authorities include those rented from Scottish Homes, formerly the Scottish Special Housing Association

Sales and transfers of local authority dwellings

Right to buy was established by the *Housing Act 1980* and was introduced across Great Britain in October 1980. In England large scale voluntary transfers (LSVTs) of stock have been principally to housing associations and registered social landlords (RSLs). Figures include transfers supported by estate renewal challenge funding (ERCF). The figures for 1993 include 949 dwellings transferred under Tenants' Choice. In Scotland LSVTs to RSLs and the small number of transfers to housing associations are included.

Homeless at home

These are households who have been accepted by the local authority as being owed a main homelessness duty and for whom arrangements have been made for them, with consent, to remain in their existing accommodation for the immediate future.

Decent home standard

The definition of a decent home is one that meets **all** of the following criteria:

- meets the statutory minimum for housing. This was the Fitness Standard up to April 2006 when it was replaced by the Housing Health and Safety Rating System (see below)

- is in a reasonable state of repair

- has reasonably modern facilities and services

- provides a reasonable degree of thermal comfort, that is it has efficient heating and effective insulation

Housing Health and Safety Rating System (HHSRS)

The HHSRS is the statutory tool used to assess the risks posed by a home to occupants in residential properties in England and Wales. It replaced the Fitness Standard in April 2006.

The purpose of the HHSRS assessment is not to set a standard but to generate objective information to determine and inform enforcement decisions. There are 29 types of hazard, each separately rated, based on risk to the potential occupant who is most vulnerable to that hazard. The individual hazard scores are grouped into ten bands where the highest bands A–C (representing scores of 1,000 or more) are considered to pose Category 1 hazards. Local authorities have a duty to act where Category 1 hazards are present. Local authorities may take into account the vulnerability of the actual occupant in determining the best course of action.

For the purposes of the decent homes standard (see above), homes posing a Category 1 hazard are 'non-decent' on the criterion that to be 'decent' a home must meet the statutory minimum requirements.

The English House Condition Survey (EHCS) is not able to replicate the HHSRS assessment in full as part of a large scale survey. Its assessment employs a mix of hazards that are directly assessed by surveyors in the field and others that are indirectly assessed from detailed related information collected.

Not all hazards are covered by the EHCS but it is expected that those included account for more than 95 per cent of all Category 1 hazards. See *2006 English House Condition Survey Technical Report* for the full list of hazards and details of how the EHCS collects and models information on the HHSRS, available at: **www.communities.gov.uk/housing/ housingresearch/housingsurveys/ englishhousecondition/ehcsreports/**

Poor living conditions

Vulnerable households
For the purposes of private sector housing support related to decent homes (see above), these are households in receipt of at least one of the principal means tested or disability-related benefits and tax credits.

Poor neighbourhood
This is the 10 per cent of households living in neighbourhoods with 'worst' problems related to the upkeep and condition of private and public space and buildings in the immediate environment of the home. It is a summary

indicator based on a factor score developed from surveyors' visual assessments of 16 problems in the immediate neighbourhood. For more details see the *2006 English House Condition Survey Technical Report* (see link in HHSRS section above).

Excess cold (HHSRS Category 1 hazard)
Households living in homes with Category 1 hazard relating to excess cold under the Housing Health and Safety Rating System. The English House Condition Survey uses a proxy indicator of homes with an energy efficiency rating of less than 35 under the 2001 Standard Assessment Procedure (SAP) to indicate homes with excess cold. The SAP is an index based on calculated annual space and water heating costs for a standard heating regime for a home, and is expressed on a scale of 1 (highly energy inefficient) to 100 (highly energy efficient, with 100 representing zero energy cost).

The detailed methodology for calculating the SAP to monitor energy efficiency was comprehensively updated in 2005 to reflect developments in the energy efficiency technologies and knowledge of dwelling performance. The rating scale was revised to run between 1 and 100 under the 2005 methodology. Under the 2001 methodology the scale ran between 1 and 120. Therefore, a SAP rating under the 2001 methodology is not comparable with the one calculated under the 2005 methodology.

Homes in serious disrepair
Based on the 10 per cent of dwellings (whether occupied or vacant) with highest repair costs per square metre of floor area. See the *2006 English House Condition Survey Annual Report* for a more detailed definition, available at: **www.communities.gov.uk/publications/ corporate/statistics/ehcs2006annualreport**

Bedroom standard

The bedroom standard concept is used to estimate occupation density by allocating a standard number of bedrooms to each household in accordance with its age/sex/marital status composition and the relationship of the members to one another. A separate bedroom is allocated to each married or cohabiting couple, and any other person aged 21 and over, each pair of adolescents aged 10 to 20 of the same sex and each pair of children aged under 10. Any unpaired person aged 10 to 20 is paired, if possible with a child under 10 of the same sex, or, if that is not possible, is given a separate bedroom, as is any unpaired child under 10. This standard is then compared with the actual number of bedrooms (including bedsitters) available for the sole use of the household, and deficiences or excesses are tabulated. Bedrooms converted to other uses are not counted as available unless they have been denoted as bedrooms by the informants; bedrooms not actually in use are counted unless uninhabitable. If a household has fewer bedrooms than implied by the standard then it is deemed to be overcrowded. As a bed-sitter will meet the bedroom standard for a single-person household or for a married/cohabiting couple, single-person and couple households without children cannot be overcrowded according to the bedroom standard.

Average dwelling prices

Information on dwelling prices at national and regional levels are collected and published by Communities and Local Government on a monthly basis. Until August 2005 data came from a sample survey of mortgage completions, the Survey of Mortgage Lenders (SML). The SML covered around 50 banks and building societies that are members of the Council of Mortgage Lenders (CML). From September 2005 data come from the Regulated Mortgage Survey (RMS), which is conducted by BankSearch and the CML.

There are two main methods of calculating house prices; simple average prices and mix-adjusted prices. Simple average prices are more volatile as they will be influenced by changes in the mix of properties bought in each period. This effect is removed by applying fixed weights to the process at the start of each year to create mix-adjusted house prices, based on the average mix of properties purchased during the previous three years, and these weights are applied to prices during the year.

The RMS collects 100 per cent of completions data from those mortgage lenders who take part (and as a result the sample size increased to around 50,000 from September 2005). Annual figures have been derived as an average of the monthly prices. The annual change in price is shown as the average percentage change over the year and is calculated from the house price index. The mix-adjusted average price excludes sitting tenant (right to buy) purchases, cash purchases, remortgages and further loans.

Mortgage arrears and repossessions

Figures are estimates of arrears on all first charge loans held by Council of Mortgage Lenders (CML) members, both regulated and unregulated, and include buy-to-let. First charge loans are the first mortgage on a property. Any additional loans secured against the property on top of this are not first charge loans. The lender with the first charge has the first call on the property if the borrower defaults on the loan. Figures presented here do not include arrears relating to other secured lending, or to firms that are not CML members. These estimates are based on reporting by a sample of CML members, which are then grossed up to represent the lending undertaken by CML members as a whole. In the first half of 2008 these accounted for about 97 per cent of first charge mortgages.

Figures are revised as better information about rates of growth and performance in different parts of the market becomes available so care should be taken when looking at changes over time as lenders newly reporting figures may distort comparisons. Trends in the number of months' arrears data may also be distorted by changes in mortgage rates. When rates change this may alter the contractual mortgage repayments due and so affect the number of months that a given arrears amount represents. In the case of variable rate products, with lower mortgage rates a given amount of arrears represents a higher number of monthly payments. Properties in possession are not counted as arrears. Buy-to-let mortgages, where a receiver of rent has been appointed, are also not counted as arrears.

Part 11: Environment

Waste management

Treatment of municipal waste can be classified into three principal categories:

- *landfill*, which is defined as depositing waste into or on land, including specially engineered landfill, and temporary storage of more than one year on permanent sites

- *incineration*, which refers to the thermal treatment of waste in a specifically designed plant

- *recycling and recovery*, which refers to any waste management operation that diverts a waste material from the waste stream resulting in a certain product with a potential economic or ecological result

Food waste

Definition of 'meat or fish mixed meal' is a collection of waste that was classified as being clearly from one meal where meat or fish was the main ingredient of the remains; this includes ready meals and home-cooked meals.

To calculate total food waste and average food waste per household, data were weighted according to the proportion of the following four household types in the UK: single occupancy; unrelated adults; family of adults; family with children.

Air pollutants

Volatile organic compounds (VOCs) are ozone precursors and comprise a wide range of chemical compounds including hydrocarbons, oxygenates and halogen containing species. Methane (CH_4) is an important component of VOCs but its environmental impact derives principally from its contribution to global warming. The major environmental impact of non-methane VOCs lies in their involvement in the formation of ground level ozone. Most VOCs are non-toxic or are present at levels well below guideline values. Others, such as benzene and 1, 3-butadiene, are of concern because of their potential impact on human health.

PM_{10} is airborne particulate matter. Specifically, it is that fraction of 'black smoke' that is thought most likely to be deposited in the lungs. It can be defined as the fraction resulting from a collection from black smoke by a size selective sampler that collects smaller particles preferentially, capturing 50 per cent of 10 micron aerodynamic diameter particles, more than 95 per cent of 5 micron particles, and less than 5 per cent of 20 micron particles.

Pollution incidents

The Environment Agency defines four categories of pollution incidents:

Category 1: The most severe incidents, which involve one or more of the following:

- potential or actual persistent effect on water quality or aquatic life

- closure of potable water, industrial or agricultural abstraction necessary

- major damage to aquatic ecosystems

- major damage to agriculture and/or commerce

- serious impact on man, or

- major effect on amenity value

Category 2: Severe incidents, which involve one or more of the following:

- notification to abstractors necessary

- significant damage to aquatic ecosystems

- significant effect on water quality

- damage to agriculture and/or commerce

- impact on man, or

- impact on amenity value to public, owners or users

Category 3: Minor incidents, involving one or more of the following:

- a minimal effect on water quality

- minor damage to aquatic ecosystems

- amenity value only marginally affected, or

- minimal impact on agriculture and/or commerce

Category 4: Incidents where no impact on the environment occurred.

Bathing waters

Bathing water can be any running or still freshwater and sea water (except for water intended for therapeutic purposes and water used in swimming pools) where bathing is explicitly authorised by national authorities, where bathing is not banned and where bathing is traditionally practised by a large number of bathers. Sampling begins two weeks before the start of the bathing season and is carried out every other week at places where the daily average of bathers is highest throughout the season. The period during which bathers can be expected in bathing areas depends largely on local bathing rules and weather conditions. A bathing season can also vary within a member state. In the European Union it usually runs from the end of May until the end of September.

Coliforms are microorganisms found in the intestinal tract of animals and human beings. When found in water it indicates fecal pollution and potentially hazardous bacterial contamination. Faecal streptococci are also natural inhabitants of the gut of humans and other warm-blooded animals. However, as they have a greater ability to survive outside of the gut, they could be used as an indicator of less recent contamination by sewage.

Directive 76/160/EEC concerning the quality of bathing waters sets the following mandatory standards for the coliform parameters:

- 10,000 per 100 millilitres for total coliforms

- 2,000 per 100 millilitres for faecal coliforms

The directive requires that at least 95 per cent of samples taken for each of these parameters over the bathing season must meet the mandatory values. In practice this has been interpreted in the following manner: where 20 samples are taken only one sample for each parameter may exceed the mandatory values for the water to pass the coliform standards; where less than 20 samples are taken none may exceed the mandatory values for the water to pass the coliform standards.

The Bathing Water Directive also sets more stringent guideline microbiological standards. To comply with the guideline standards, bathing waters must not exceed values of 500 total coliforms per 100 millilitres and 100 faecal coliforms per 100 millilitres in 80 per cent of water quality samples, and 100 faecal streptococci per 100 millilitres in 90 per cent of samples taken.

Environmental accounts

Environmental Accounts are satellite accounts to the National Accounts. As such they use similar concepts and classifications of industry to those employed in the National Accounts. They reflect the frameworks recommended by the European Union and United Nations for developing such accounts. For more information, please refer to the UK Environmental Accounts website.

Office for National Statistics (ONS) Environmental Accounts measure air emissions on an UK residents basis. This means that all emissions generated from transport at home and abroad by UK resident households and businesses are included. Emissions related to non-resident households and businesses travel and transport within the UK are excluded. Producing statistics on this basis allows for a more consistent comparison with key National Accounts indicators such as gross domestic product and Gross Value Added.

Global warming and climate change

Emissions estimates for the UK are updated annually to reflect revisions in methodology and the availability of new information. These adjustments are applied retrospectively to earlier years and hence there are differences from the data published in previous editions of *Social Trends*.

In Figure 11.14, the Kyoto reduction targets cover a basket of six gases: carbon dioxide (CO_2), methane (CH_4), nitrous oxide (N_2O), hydrofluorocarbons (HFCs), perfluorocarbons (PFCs) and sulphur hexafluoride (SF_6). For the latter three gases signatories to the Kyoto Protocol may choose to use 1995, rather than 1990, as the base year from which to calculate targets, since data for 1995 for these gases tend to be more widely available and more reliable than for 1990. The UK announced in its Climate Change Programme that it would use 1995 as the base year for the fluorinated gases – therefore the 'base year' emissions for the UK target differ slightly from UK emissions in 1990.

Emissions of the six greenhouse gases are presented based on their relative contribution to global warming. Limited allowance is given in the Protocol for the absorption of CO_2 by forests, which act as so-called carbon sinks. Carbon dioxide emissions in Figure 11.14 are reported as total emissions minus removals from the atmosphere by carbon sinks.

Average temperatures

The World Meteorological Organisation (WMO) requires the calculation of average temperatures for consecutive periods of 30 years, with the latest covering the 1961–90 period. Thirty years was chosen as a period long enough to eliminate year-to-year variations.

Land use

Land use refers to the main activity taking place on an area of land, for example, farming, forestry or housing. Land cover refers specifically to the make up of the land surface, for example, whether it comprises arable crops, trees or buildings.

In Table 11.18 the figures for agricultural land use are derived from the Agricultural and Horticultural surveys carried out by the Department for Environment, Food and Rural Affairs (DEFRA) and the other UK Agricultural Departments in June each year.

Data for 'Grasses and rough grazing' include sole right and common rough grazing and Other agricultural land contains set aside and other land on agricultural holdings, for example farm roads, yards, buildings, gardens, ponds. Data exclude woodland on agricultural holdings, which is included in 'Forest and woodland'.

Information on the area of forest and woodland in Great Britain is compiled by the Forestry Commission and covers both private and state-owned land. Estimates are based on the provisional results of the National Inventory of Woodland and Trees for 1995–99 and extrapolated forward using information about new planting and other changes. Data for Northern Ireland are compiled separately by the Forest Service, an agency of the Northern Ireland Department of Agriculture and Rural Development (DARD) and also cover both private and state-owned land.

There is no comparable source of information on the amount of urban land in the UK, and the figures for the 'Urban land and land not otherwise specified' category are derived by subtracting land used for agricultural and forestry purposes from the land area. Figures include land used for urban and other purposes, for example, transport and recreation, and non-agricultural, semi-natural environments, for example, sand dunes, grouse moors and non-agricultural grasslands, and inland waters.

Set-aside land

Set-aside land is a proportion of farmland that is taken out of production to reduce surpluses or to maintain or increase prices of a specific crop.

Self-sufficiency in food

The significant revision upwards is the result of changes introduced to improve the estimation by seeking a higher level of internal consistency and recognising the higher proportion of processed products as opposed to unprocessed commodities imported in recent years. The biggest effect has been the introduction of factors to devalue processed imports to the value of their unprocessed food content. This has significantly reduced the estimated value of food consumption. In 2000 this methodology incorporated a more accurate estimate of production for human consumption. These changes have reduced the overall estimates of self-sufficiency by about 2 percentage points.

Wild bird species

Species in italics are specialists, while the remainder are generalists. A generalist species is able to thrive in a wide variety of environmental conditions and can make use of a variety of different resources. Specialist species can only thrive in a narrow range of environmental conditions and/or have a limited diet.

Woodland species (38)
Blackbird, *Blackcap*, Blue Tit, Bullfinch, Capercaillie, Chaffinch, *Chiffchaff*, *Coal Tit*, *Crossbill*, Dunnock, *Garden Warbler*, *Goldcrest*, *Great Spotted Woodpecker*, Great Tit, *Green Woodpecker*, *Hawfinch*, *Jay*, *Lesser Redpoll*, *Lesser Spotted Woodpecker*, Lesser Whitethroat, Long-tailed Tit, *Marsh Tit*, *Nightingale*, *Nuthatch*, *Pied flycatcher*, *Redstart*, Robin, *Siskin*, Song Thrush, *Sparrowhawk*, *Spotted Flycatcher*, *Tawny Owl*, *Tree Pipit*, *Treecreeper*, *Willow Tit*, *Willow Warbler*, *Wood Warbler*, Wren.

Farmland species (19)
Corn Bunting, *Goldfinch*, Greenfinch, *Grey Partridge*, Jackdaw, Kestrel, *Lapwing*, Linnet, Reed Bunting, Rook, *Skylark*, Starling, *Stock Dove*, Tree Sparrow, *Turtle Dove*, *Whitethroat*, Woodpigeon, *Yellowhammer*, Yellow Wagtail.

Seabird species (19)
Arctic Skua, Arctic Tern, Black-backed Gull, Black-headed Gull, Common Guillemot, Common Gull, Common Tern, Cormorant, Fulmar, Great Black-backed Gull, Great Skua, Herring Gull, Kittiwake, Little Tern, Northern Gannet, Puffin, Razorbill, Sandwich Tern, Shag.

Part 12: Transport

Road traffic

Road traffic is estimated from a network of manual traffic counts, which count traffic for a single 12-hour period, and automatic traffic counters, which count traffic 24 hours a day throughout the whole year. There are around 22,000 manual count points that are counted between every one to eight years, with around 9,000 counts carried out each year. There are around 190 automatic traffic counters.

Improvements were made to the methodology used to estimate minor road traffic in 2004. From 2000 to 2003 trends in traffic flow, derived from a relatively small number of automatic traffic counters, were used to update 1999 base-year estimates. For the annual estimates made from and including 2004, the trends were derived from a set of some 4,200 manual traffic counts instead.

For more details, see *How the National Road Traffic Estimates are made* available on the Department for Transport website, **www.dft.gov.uk/matrix/forms/estimates. aspx**

National Travel Survey

The National Travel Survey (NTS) is designed to provide a databank of personal travel information for Great Britain. It has been conducted as a continuous survey since July 1988, following ad hoc surveys since the mid-1960s. The NTS is designed to identify long-term trends and is not suitable for monitoring short-term trends.

In 2006 a weighting strategy was introduced to the NTS and applied retrospectively to data for 1995 onwards. The weighting methodology adjusts for non-response bias and also adjusts for the drop-off in the number of trips recorded by respondents during the course of the travel week. All results now published for 1995 onwards are based on weighted data, and direct comparisons cannot be made to previously published unweighted data.

During 2006 nearly 8,300 households provided details of their personal travel by filling in travel diaries over the course of a week. The drawn sample size from 2002 has nearly trebled compared with previous years following recommendations in a National Statistics Review of the NTS. This enables most results to be presented on a single year basis from 2002. Previously data was shown for a three-year period because of the smaller sample size.

In 2007 slightly more than 8,400 households participated fully in the survey providing information by interview and completing a seven-day travel diary. An additional 800 households participated in the household interviews but did not all complete a diary; although these cases cannot be used for trip-level analysis, their data are included in all analysis at household, individual and vehicle level. Analysis presented for 2007 within this publication is therefore based on data from nearly 9,300 responding households, covering slightly less than 22,000 individuals.

NTS data are collected from two main sources. Firstly face to face interviews are carried out to collect information on the households, all individual members within the household and all vehicles that they have access to. Each household member is then asked to record details of their trips over a seven-day period in a travel diary, allowing travel patterns to be linked with individual and household characteristics. The 2007 NTS only presents data collected from interviews and does not cover data from travel diaries.

Travel included in the NTS covers all trips by British residents within Great Britain for personal reasons, including travel in the course of work.

A trip is defined as a one-way course of travel having a single main purpose. It is the basic unit of personal travel defined in the survey. A round trip is split into two trips, with the first ending at a convenient point about halfway round as a notional stopping point for the outward destination and return origin. A stage is that portion of a trip defined by the use of a specific method of transport or of a specific ticket (a new stage being defined if either the mode or the ticket changes).

Households consist of one or more people who have the sampled address as their only or main residence and who either share at least one main meal a day or share the living accommodation (see also Appendix, Part 2: Households).

Household income is the total gross income of all members of the household, from whatever source, before deduction of income tax, national insurance or pension contributions.

Cars are regarded as household cars if they are either owned by a member of the household, or available for the private use of household members. Company cars provided by an employer for the use of a particular employee (or director) are included, but cars borrowed temporarily from a company pool are not.

The main driver of a household car is the household member who drives the furthest in that car in the course of a year.

The purpose of a trip is normally taken to be the activity at the destination, unless that destination is 'home', in which case the purpose is defined by the origin of the trip. The classification of trips to 'work' is also dependent on the origin of the trip. The following purposes of trips are distinguished:

Commuting: Trips to a usual place of work from home, or from work to home.

Business: Personal trips in the course of work, including a trip in the course of work back to work. This includes all work trips by people with no usual place of work (for example, site workers) and those who work at or from home.

Education: Trips to school or college, etc, by full-time students, students on day-release and part-time students following vocational courses.

Escort: Used when the traveller has no purpose of his or her own, other than to escort or accompany another person; for example, taking a child to school.

Escort commuting is escorting or accompanying someone from home to work or from work to home.

Shopping: All trips to shops or from shops to home, even if there was no intention to buy.

Personal business: Visits to services, for example, hairdressers, launderettes, dry-cleaners, betting shops, solicitors, banks, estate agents, libraries, churches; or for medical consultations or treatment, or for eating and drinking, unless the main purpose was social or entertainment.

Social or entertainment: Visits to meet friends, relatives, or acquaintances, both at someone's home or at a pub, restaurant, etc; all types of entertainment or sport, clubs, and voluntary work, non-vocational evening classes, political meetings, etc.

Holidays or day trips: Trips (within Great Britain) to or from any holiday (including stays of four nights or more with friends or relatives) or trips for pleasure (not otherwise classified as social or entertainment) within a single day.

Just walk: Walking for pleasure trips along public highways, including taking the dog for a walk and jogging.

Scotland NTS data are based on a small annual sample size (1,000 households) so results are not possible at local authority or regional transport partnership level. For results at this level the Scottish Household Survey is an alternative source.

Car ownership

The figures for household ownership include four-wheeled and three-wheeled cars, off-road vehicles, minibuses, motorcaravans, dormobiles, and light vans. Company cars normally available for household use are also included.

Area type classification

In the National Travel Survey (see above),

households in Great Britain are classified according to whether they are within an urban area of at least 3,000 population or in a rural area. Urban areas are subdivided for the purpose of this publication as follows:

- London boroughs – the whole of the Greater London Authority

- Metropolitan built-up areas – the built-up areas of the former metropolitan counties of Greater Manchester, Merseyside, West Midlands, West Yorkshire, Tyne and Wear and Strathclyde (excludes South Yorkshire)

- Large urban – self-contained urban areas with more than 250,000 population

- Medium urban – self-contained urban areas more than 25,000 but not more than 250,000 population

- Small/medium urban – self-contained urban areas with more than 10,000 but not more than 25,000 population

- Small urban – self-contained urban areas with more than 3,000 but not more than 10,000 population

- Rural – all other areas, including urban areas, with less than 3,000 population

Prior to 1996, 'small urban' and 'small/medium urban' were combined into one category covering self-contained urban areas with more than 3,000 but not more than 25,000 population.

England and Wales
The classification specifies urban areas based on the extent of urban development indicated on Ordnance Survey maps. An urban area is a tract of continuously built-up urban land extending 20 hectares or more. Urban areas thus defined but less than 200 metres apart are combined into a single urban area.

Scotland
In Scotland postcodes were classified as urban or rural using population density. Urban postcodes were then aggregated together to form localities using a minimum population of 500 together with other rules.

Rail fares index

Methodology
The rail fares price index provides a measure of the change in the prices charged by train operating companies (TOCs) to rail passengers. This index takes into account the range of price changes and presents the average change in prices taken from the millions of transactions that take place each year. Essentially, the index gives an indication of what a person would need to spend to purchase the same set of tickets that they chose to buy in the previous year. Some passengers will have experienced greater or lesser fare changes than shown by the average changes calculated.

The Office of Rail Regulation (ORR) aims to represent all rail travel in England, Scotland and Wales in the index. ORR has therefore sought, as far as is practically possible, to construct the index so that it covers the cost of travel only. This is done by excluding fares that include

'extras' so as not to distort the index. Where the purchase of a 'rail' ticket includes additional services such as multi-modal ticket for urban areas, bus tickets, entrance fees to attractions, etc, it is excluded from the index. An exception to this is the London Travelcard. ORR has included this in the index because such tickets are so important in the earnings of train operators and purchases by rail passengers. In addition, TOCs influence price changes associated with these tickets.

As the index is based on millions of transactions covering more than 90 per cent of the total earnings from fares, the omissions are considered to have a negligible impact on the aggregate indices.

The other exclusions are listed below:

- newly introduced tickets are not properly accounted for in their first year as the index's price information is based on snapshots from January Year 1 and Year 2

- the index does not include short-term temporary fares/promotions

- newly introduced tickets are not properly accounted for in their first year as the index's price information is based on snapshots from January Year 1 and Year 2

- the index does not include short-term temporary fares/promotions

- the index does not take immediate account of passenger 'switching' ticket types following the introduction/deletion of certain tickets

- coverage is limited to transactions recorded in the ticketing system LENNON the index excludes flows whose total annual earnings are below certain thresholds. This is to reduce the volume of data and excludes only those flows that generate minimal earnings (typically a maximum of £50 per annum)

- the index excludes flows for which ONS were unable to find price information for either of the two reference years, for example a ticket type that is introduced after the first reference date

Other comments
Fare levels are compared against the previous January (the reference period) to ensure that the rail fares price index is in line with standard ONS practice for the construction of consumer price indices. Changes in fares are weighted together according to the pattern of expenditure in the calendar year preceding the reference period. This means that the weights used in the calculation of the January 2007 rail fares price index, referenced on January 2006, are based on expenditure patterns for the calendar year 2006

Passenger death rates

Passenger fatality rates given in Table 12.15 can be interpreted as the risk a traveller runs of being killed, per billion kilometres travelled. The coverage varies for each mode of travel and care should be exercised in drawing comparisons between the rates for different modes.

The table provides information on passenger fatalities. Where possible travel by drivers and other crew in the course of their work has been excluded. Exceptions are for private journeys and those in company-owned cars and vans, where drivers are included.

Figures for all modes of transport exclude confirmed suicides and deaths through natural causes. Figures for air, rail and water exclude trespassers and rail excludes attempted suicides. Accidents occurring in airports, seaports and railway stations that do not directly involve the mode of transport concerned are also excluded, for example, deaths sustained on escalators or falling over packages on platforms.

The figures are compiled by the Department for Transport. Further information is available in the annual publications *Road Casualties Great Britain: Annual Report and Transport Statistics Great Britain*. Both are published by The Stationery Office and are available at: **www.dft. gov.uk/transtat**

The following definitions are used:

Air: Accidents involving UK registered airline aircraft in UK and foreign airspace. Fixed wing and rotary wing aircraft are included but air taxis are excluded. Accidents cover UK airline aircraft around the world, not just in the UK.

Rail: Train accidents and accidents occurring through movement of railway vehicles in Great Britain. As well as national rail the figures include accidents on underground and tram systems, Eurotunnel and minor railways.

Water: Figures for travel by water include both domestic and international passenger carrying services of UK registered merchant vessels.

Road: Figures refer to Great Britain and include accidents occurring on the public highway (including footways) in which at least one road vehicle or a vehicle in collision with a pedestrian is involved and which becomes known to the police within 30 days of its occurrence. Figures include both public and private transport.

Bus or coach: Figures for work buses are included. From 1 January 1994, the casualty definition was revised to include only those vehicles equipped to carry 17 or more passengers regardless of use. Prior to 1994 these vehicles were coded according to construction, whether or not they were being used for carrying passengers. Vehicles constructed as buses that were privately licensed were included under 'Bus and coach' but public service vehicles (PSV) licensed minibuses were included under cars.

Car: Includes taxis, invalid tricycles, three-wheeled and four-wheeled cars and minibuses. Prior to 1999 motorcaravans were also included.

Van: Vans mainly include vehicles of the van type constructed on a car chassis. From 1 January 1994 these are defined as those vehicles not 3.5 tonnes maximum permissible gross vehicle weight. Prior to 1994 the weight definition was not more than 1.524 tonnes unladen.

Two-wheeled motor vehicle: Mopeds, motor scooters and motorcycles (including motorcycle combinations).

Pedal cycle: Includes tandems, tricycles and toy cycles ridden on the carriageway.

Pedestrian: Includes persons riding toy cycles on the footway, persons pushing bicycles, pushing or pulling other vehicles or operating pedestrian controlled vehicles, those leading or herding animals, occupants of prams or wheelchairs, and people who alight safely from vehicles and are subsequently injured.

Road safety

The Government targets for Great Britain are that by 2010, compared with the average for a number of indicators between 1994–98, the proportion of people killed or seriously injured in road accidents per 100 million vehicle kilometres will be reduced by 40 per cent; the proportion of children killed or seriously injured, by 50 per cent, and the proportion of people slightly injured, by 10 per cent.

The Northern Ireland Road Safety Strategy 2002–2012 aims to reduce the proportion of people killed or seriously injured on Northern Ireland's roads each year by one-third, compared with the average for the period 1996–2000, and to reduce the proportion of children killed or seriously injured on Northern Ireland's roads each year by one-half.

The *Road Safety Act 1967* established a legal alcohol limit for drivers, set at 80 milligrams of alcohol in 100 millilitres of blood and made it an offence to drive when over this limit. The Act also gave the police the power to carry out breath testing to determine whether an individual's alcohol level was above the limit of 35 micrograms of alcohol in 100 millilitres of breath.

Data for Great Britain in Figure 12.18 are provisional for 2007 and are derived from three sources. Two sources of data are used to assess the extent and characteristics of drink-drive accidents in Great Britain; the third source provides information on compliance with drink-drive restrictions. These sources are:

- coroners' data. Coroners in England and Wales and procurators fiscal in Scotland provide information about the level of alcohol in the blood of road accident fatalities aged 16 and over who die within 12 hours of a road accident

- STATS19 breath test data. The personal injury road accident reporting system (STATS19) provides data on injury accidents in which the driver or rider survived and was also breath-tested at the roadside. If the driver or rider refused to provide a breath test specimen they are considered to have failed the test unless they are deemed unable to take the test for medical reasons

- police force screening breath-test data. In England and Wales the Ministry of Justice provides information from breath tests carried out at the roadside following a moving traffic offence, road accident or suspicion of alcohol use

Once the drink-drive accidents have been identified using coroners' and STATS19 data,

then the resulting casualties in these accidents are identified from STATS19 data.

Completeness of data and reliability of estimates
Both sources of data from the police and coroners on drink-drive accidents are incomplete. In recognition of the uncertainty associated with the estimates produced from this data the numbers of accidents and casualties are rounded to the nearest ten.

Provisional and final estimates
As coroners' data are available for analysis a year later than the main road accident data, final estimates can only be made 18 months in arrears. Around 58 per cent of data expected to be available were available for inclusion in the provisional estimates. The provisional estimates for serious and slight accidents depend on breath-test data and do not change in the final estimates. The coroners' data affect only the numbers of casualties from fatal accidents and these form a small proportion of serious and slight casualties. The estimates for fatalities depend mainly on coroners' data and are particularly susceptible to revision between the provisional and final figures.

Part 13: Lifestyles and social participation

Digital television

An asymmetric digital subscriber line (ADSL) is a digital technology that allows the use of a standard telephone line to provide high-speed data communications such as a television service.

Package holiday

A package holiday must be sold or offered for sale, be sold at an inclusive price, be pre-arranged and include a minimum of two of the following three elements:

- transport

- accommodation

- other tourist services (not ancillary to transport or accommodation) accounting for a significant proportion of the package, such as a tour guide

International Passenger Survey (IPS)

Holidays to North America include: Canada (including Greenland and St Pierre et Miquelon) and the USA (including Puerto Rico and US Virgin Islands).

Holidays to Europe include: All countries in the EU-27 plus other central and eastern Europe, North Cyprus, Faroe Islands, Gibraltar, Iceland, Norway, Switzerland (including Lichtenstein), Turkey, the former USSR and the states of former Yugoslavia.

Holidays to 'Other North Africa' include Algeria, Libya, Morocco and Sudan.

The IPS collects information on whether tourists travel independently or on some form of package trip. Figure 13.11 shows package holidays as a proportion of all holidays.

Index